*5th Editi*

# *Lond*
# *Bus Hand*

# *British Bus Publishing*

## Body codes used in the Bus Handbook series:

### Type:
| | |
|---|---|
| A | Articulated vehicle |
| B | Bus, either single-deck or double-deck |
| BC | Interurban - high-back seated bus |
| C | Coach |
| M | Minibus with design capacity of 16 seats or less |
| N | Low-floor bus (*Niederflur*), either single-deck or double-deck |
| O | Open-top bus (CO = convertible - PO = partial open-top) |

### Seating capacity is then shown. For double-decks the upper deck quantity is followed by the lower deck.
Please note that seating capacities shown are generally those provided by the operator. It is common practice, however, for some vehicles to operate at different capacities when on certain duties.

### Door position:
| | |
|---|---|
| C | Centre entrance/exit |
| D | Dual doorway. |
| F | Front entrance/exit |
| R | Rear entrance/exit (no distinction between doored and open) |
| T | Three or more access points |

### Equipment:-
| | | | |
|---|---|---|---|
| T | Toilet | TV | Training vehicle. |
| M | Mail compartment | RV | Used as tow bus or engineers' vehicle. |
| L | Lift for wheelchair (post 2005 express coaches are fitted with lifts as standard) | | |

### Allocation:
| | |
|---|---|
| s | Ancillary vehicle |
| t | Training bus |
| u | out of service or strategic reserve; refurbishment or seasonal requirement |
| w | Vehicle is withdrawn and awaiting disposal. |

e.g. - B32/28F is a double-deck bus with thirty-two seats upstairs, twenty-eight down and a front entrance/exit.
N43D is a low-floor bus with two or more doorways.

### Re-registrations:
Where a vehicle has gained new index marks the details are listed at the end of each fleet showing the current mark, followed in sequence by those previously carried starting with the original mark.

### Annual books are produced for the major groups:
The Stagecoach Bus Handbook
The First Bus Handbook
The Arriva Bus Handbook
The Go-Ahead Bus Handbook
The National Express Coach Handbook
*Some editions for earlier years are available. Please contact the publisher.*

### Regional books in the series:
The Scottish Bus Handbook
The Welsh Bus Handbook
The Ireland & Islands Bus Handbook
English Bus Handbook: Smaller Groups
English Bus Handbook: Notable Independents
English Bus Handbook: Coaches

### Associated series:
The Hong Kong Bus Handbook
The Malta Bus Handbook
The Leyland Lynx Handbook
The Postbus Handbook
The Mailvan Handbook
The Fire Brigade Handbook (fleet list of each local authority fire brigade)
The Police Range Rover Handbook

*Some earlier editions of these books are still available. Please contact the publisher on 01952 255669.*

# The London Bus Handbook

This fifth edition of the *London Bus Handbook* is dedicated to those operators that are contracted to Transport for London (TfL) for the provision of normal passenger services, rail replacement duties and other minor contracts. Also included are the providers of the major sightseeing tours. A list of current editions of the series is shown on page 2.

Quality digital photographs for inclusion in the series are welcome, for which a fee is payable for these selected. Unfortunately, the publishers cannot accept responsibility for any loss and request you show your name on the CD/DVD disc submitted.

To keep the fleet information up to date we recommend the Ian Allan publication, *Buses*, published monthly, or for more detailed information, the PSV Circle monthly news sheets or the LOTS monthly news letter, *The London Bus*.

The writer and publisher would be glad to hear from readers should any information be available which corrects or enhances that given in this publication.

Editor - Colin Lloyd
Series Editor - Bill Potter

Acknowledgments:
We are grateful to Tom Johnson, Stuart Martin, friends of Colin Lloyd, the PSV Circle and the management of the operating companies for their kind assistance and co-operation in the compilation of this book.

*The front cover photograph is by Mark Lyons; Page 1 picture by Dave Heath and the rear cover views are by Richard Godfrey.*

*Earlier editions of the London Bus Handbook, most of which are available from our website:*

ISBN: 9781904875550
Published by *British Bus Publishing Ltd*, 16 St Margaret's Drive, Wellington, Telford, TF1 3PH

*Telephone: 01952 255669 - Web: www.britishbuspublishing.co.uk*
© British Bus Publishing Ltd, June 2011

# Contents

**The traditional Routemaster is now confined to tourist routes and special events. Seen in Kensington Grove on route 9, ALD913B was new to London Transport as RM1913 and is now numbered 39813 within the First fleet, although this new number is not displayed.** *Mark Lyons*

# ABELLIO

Abellio Group Ltd, 301 Camberwell New Road, London SE5 0TF

## 2001-2013  ADL Trident E400H Hybrid  ADL Enviro 400 4.4m  N37/26D  On order

| | | | | | | | | | | | |
|---|---|---|---|---|---|---|---|---|---|---|---|
| 2001 | WL | - | 2005 | WL | - | 2008 | WL | - | 2011 | WL | - |
| 2002 | WL | - | 2006 | WL | - | 2009 | WL | - | 2012 | WL | - |
| 2003 | WL | - | 2007 | WL | - | 2010 | WL | - | 2013 | WL | - |
| 2004 | WL | - | | | | | | | | | |

## 8001-8004  ADL Dart 8.8m  ADL Mini Pointer  N29F  2006

| | | | | | | | | | | | |
|---|---|---|---|---|---|---|---|---|---|---|---|
| 8001 | BF | LJ56ONH | 8002 | BF | LJ56ONK | 8003 | BF | LJ56ONL | 8004 | BF | LJ56ONM |

| | | | | | | |
|---|---|---|---|---|---|---|
| 8006 | BC | Y116HWB | Dennis Dart SLF 8.9m | Alexander ALX200 | N28F | 2001 |
| 8008 | BC | Y118HWB | Dennis Dart SLF 8.9m | Alexander ALX200 | N28F | 2001 |

## 8013-8020  ADL Dart 8.8m  ADL Mini Pointer  N29F  2004

| | | | | | | | | | | | |
|---|---|---|---|---|---|---|---|---|---|---|---|
| 8013 | BC | BX54DLZ | 8015 | BC | BX54DMF | 8017 | BC | BX54DMU | 8019 | BC | BX54DMY |
| 8014 | BC | BX54DME | 8016 | BC | BX54DMO | 8018 | BC | BX54DMV | 8020 | BC | BX54DMZ |

## 8024-8037  ADL Dart 8.8m  ADL Mini Pointer  N29F  2005

| | | | | | | | | | | | |
|---|---|---|---|---|---|---|---|---|---|---|---|
| 8024 | BC | BU05HDY | 8027 | BC | BU05HFB | 8031 | BC | BU05HFK | 8036 | BC | BU05HFW |
| 8025 | BC | BU05HEJ | 8028 | BC | BU05HFC | 8035 | BC | BU05HFV | 8037 | BC | BU05HFX |
| 8026 | BC | BU05HFA | 8029 | BC | BU05HFD | | | | | | |

## 8041-8062  Dennis Dart SLF 8.8m  Plaxton Pointer MPD  N24F*  2000-01  *seating varies

| | | | | | | | | | | | |
|---|---|---|---|---|---|---|---|---|---|---|---|
| 8041 | TF | V301MDP | 8046 | BF | V306MDP | 8052 | WS | X312KRX | 8058 | TF | Y864KTF |
| 8042 | TF | V302MDP | 8047 | BF | V307MDP | 8053 | WS | X313KRX | 8059 | WS | X319KRX |
| 8043 | TF | V303MDP | 8048 | BF | V308MDP | 8054 | WS | X314KRX | 8061 | WS | X322KRX |
| 8044 | TF | V304MDP | 8049 | BF | V309MDP | 8055 | WS | X315KRX | 8062 | WS | Y38YVV |
| 8045 | TF | V305MDP | 8051 | WS | X311KRX | 8057 | WS | X317KRX | | | |

| | | | | | | |
|---|---|---|---|---|---|---|
| 8064 | BF | RA51KVS | Dennis Dart SLF 8.8m | Plaxton Pointer MPD | N29F | 2002 |

## 8065-8074  TransBus Dart 8.8m  TransBus Mini Pointer  N26F  2002  Wings Buses, 2004

| | | | | | | | | | | | |
|---|---|---|---|---|---|---|---|---|---|---|---|
| 8065 | BC | SK02TZN | 8068 | BF | SK02TZR | 8071 | BF | SK02TZU | 8073 | BF | SK02TZW |
| 8066 | BF | SK02TZO | 8069 | BF | SK02TZS | 8072 | BF | SK02TZV | 8074 | BF | SK02TZX |
| 8067 | BF | SK02TZP | 8070 | BF | SK02TZT | | | | | | |

## 8086-8095  TransBus Dart 8.8m  TransBus Mini Pointer  N24F  2003

| | | | | | | | | | | | |
|---|---|---|---|---|---|---|---|---|---|---|---|
| 8086 | BF | KV03ZFM | 8089 | BF | KV03ZFR | 8092 | BF | KV03ZFU | 8094 | BF | KV03ZFX |
| 8087 | BF | KV03ZFN | 8090 | BF | KV03ZFS | 8093 | BF | KV03ZFW | 8095 | BF | KV03ZFY |
| 8088 | BF | KV03ZFP | 8091 | BF | KV03ZFT | | | | | | |

## 8101-8109  ADL Dart 4 8.9m  ADL Enviro 200  N26F  2006-08

| | | | | | | | | | | | |
|---|---|---|---|---|---|---|---|---|---|---|---|
| 8101 | TF | LJ56VSP | 8104 | TF | LJ56VSV | 8106 | TF | LJ56VSY | 8108 | BC | YX58DTY |
| 8102 | TF | LJ56VST | 8105 | TF | LJ56VSX | 8107 | BC | YX58DTV | 8109 | BC | YX58DTZ |
| 8103 | TF | LJ56VSU | | | | | | | | | |

## 8110-8118  ADL Dart  -  N26F  On order

| | | | | | | | | | | | |
|---|---|---|---|---|---|---|---|---|---|---|---|
| 8110 | - | - | 8113 | - | - | 8115 | - | - | 8117 | - | - |
| 8111 | - | - | 8114 | - | - | 8116 | - | - | 8118 | - | - |
| 8112 | - | - | | | | | | | | | |

## 8301-8318  ADL Dart 9.3m  ADL Pointer  N23D  2004

| | | | | | | | | | | | |
|---|---|---|---|---|---|---|---|---|---|---|---|
| 8301 | WL | BX54DKA | 8304 | WL | BX54DKF | 8307 | WL | BX54DKL | 8310 | WL | BX54DKV |
| 8302 | WL | BX54DKD | 8305 | WL | BX54DKJ | 8308 | WL | BX54DKO | 8318 | WL | BX54DLU |
| 8303 | WL | BX54DKE | 8306 | WL | BX54DKK | 8309 | WL | BX54DKU | | | |

## 8321-8329  ADL Dart 4 9.3m  ADL Enviro 200  N23D  2010

| | | | | | | | | | | | |
|---|---|---|---|---|---|---|---|---|---|---|---|
| 8321 | WL | YX10EBA | 8324 | WL | YX10EBF | 8326 | WL | YX10EBJ | 8328 | WL | YX10EBL |
| 8322 | WL | YX10EBC | 8325 | WL | YX10EBG | 8327 | WL | YX10EBK | 8329 | WL | YX10EBM |
| 8323 | WL | YX10EBD | | | | | | | | | |

Abellio is a division of Nederlands Railways established to operate public transport contracts outside the Netherlands and currently has bases in several European countries, notably in the UK, Germany and the Czech Republic. The London and Surrey operations were acquired from National Express. Pictured in North Greenwich is 8473, LF06YRJ, with one of the last Pointer bodies to be built. *Dave Heath*

### 8330-8342

| | | | | | | | | | | | ADL Dart 4 9.3m | | ADL Enviro 200 | | N23D | 2011 |

| 8330 | WL | YX11AHA | 8334 | WL | YX11AHF | 8337 | WL | YX11AHK | 8340 | WL | YX11AHO |
|---|---|---|---|---|---|---|---|---|---|---|---|
| 8331 | WL | YX11AHC | 8335 | WL | YX11AHG | 8338 | WL | YX11AHL | 8341 | WL | YX11AHP |
| 8332 | WL | YX11AHD | 8336 | WL | YX11AHJ | 8339 | WL | YX11AHN | 8342 | WL | YX11AHU |
| 8333 | WL | YX11AHE | | | | | | | | | |

### 8417-8420

Dennis Dart SLF 10.1m — East Lancs EL2000 — N30D — 2000 — Wings Buses, 2004

| 8417 | WS | W435CRN | 8418 | WS | W436CRN | 8419 | WS | W437CRN | 8420 | BF | W438CRN |
|---|---|---|---|---|---|---|---|---|---|---|---|

### 8434-8440

Dennis Dart SLF 10.1m — Plaxton Pointer 2 — N30D — 2001

| 8434 | BC | RX51FGG | 8436 | BC | RX51FGK | 8438 | BC | RX51FGN | 8440 | BC | RX51FGP |
|---|---|---|---|---|---|---|---|---|---|---|---|
| 8435 | BC | RX51FGJ | 8437 | BC | RX51FGM | 8439 | BC | RX51FGO | | | |

### 8441-8452

TransBus Dart 10.1m — TransBus Pointer — N30D* — 2002 — *8452 is N29D

| 8441 | TF | KM02HFP | 8444 | TF | KM02HFT | 8447 | TF | RD02BJK | 8450 | TF | RD02BJV |
|---|---|---|---|---|---|---|---|---|---|---|---|
| 8442 | TF | KM02HFR | 8445 | TF | KM02HFU | 8448 | TF | RD02BJO | 8451 | TF | RD02BJX |
| 8443 | TF | KM02HFS | 8446 | TF | KM02HFV | 8449 | TF | RD02BJU | 8452 | BC | RD02BJZ |

### 8453-8465

Dennis Dart SLF 10.2m — Caetano Nimbus — N25D — 2001-02

| 8453 | TF | RA51KGE | 8457 | TF | RA51KKG | 8460 | TF | RL02FOT | 8463 | TF | RL02FVN |
|---|---|---|---|---|---|---|---|---|---|---|---|
| 8454 | TF | RA51KKD | 8458 | TF | RA51KKH | 8461 | WS | RL02FOU | 8464 | WS | RL02ZTB |
| 8455 | TF | RA51KKE | 8459 | TF | RA51KLE | 8462 | TF | RL02FVM | 8465 | WS | RL02ZTC |
| 8456 | TF | RA51KKF | | | | | | | | | |

| 8466 | TF | GM03TGM | | TransBus Dart SLF 10.2m | | Caetano Nimbus | | N29D | 2003 | | |
|---|---|---|---|---|---|---|---|---|---|---|---|

### 8467-8472

TransBus Dart SLF 10.2m — Caetano Nimbus — N29D — 2004

| 8467 | WS | HX04HTP | 8469 | WS | HX04HTU | 8471 | WS | HX04HTY | 8472 | WS | HX04HTZ |
|---|---|---|---|---|---|---|---|---|---|---|---|
| 8468 | WS | HX04HTT | 8470 | WS | HX04HTV | | | | | | |

### 8473-8477

ADL Dart 10.1m — ADL Pointer — N29D — 2006

| 8473 | WL | LF06YRJ | 8475 | WL | LF06YRL | 8476 | WL | LF06YRM | 8477 | WL | LF06YRN |
|---|---|---|---|---|---|---|---|---|---|---|---|
| 8474 | WL | LF06YRK | | | | | | | | | |

The Dart 4 is Alexander Dennis' chassis for the Enviro 200, the successor to the Pointer. From the 2011 delivery, 8556, YX11AEE, is seen passing the Elephant and Castle while heading for Victoria. *Dave Heath*

### 8478-8487

| | | | | | | | | |
|---|---|---|---|---|---|---|---|---|
| | Dennis Dart SLF 10.2m | | | Plaxton Pointer | | N30D | 2002 | Armchair, Brentford |

| 8478 | TF | KP02PWV | 8481 | TF | KP02PVU | 8484 | TF | KM02HGE | 8486 | TF | KU52YKR |
|---|---|---|---|---|---|---|---|---|---|---|---|
| 8479 | TF | KP02PVE | 8482 | TF | KM02HGF | 8485 | TF | KU52YKO | 8487 | TF | KU52YKS |
| 8480 | TF | KP02PUK | 8483 | TF | KP02PUJ | | | | | | |

### 8501-8506

| | | | | | | | |
|---|---|---|---|---|---|---|---|
| ADL Dart 4 10.2m | | | ADL Enviro 200 | | N29D | 2006 | |

| 8501 | BC | LJ56ONN | 8503 | BC | LJ56ONP | 8505 | BC | LJ56ONS | 8506 | BC | LJ56ONT |
|---|---|---|---|---|---|---|---|---|---|---|---|
| 8502 | BC | LJ56ONO | 8504 | BC | LJ56ONR | | | | | | |

### 8507-8515

| | | | | | | | |
|---|---|---|---|---|---|---|---|
| ADL Dart 4 10.2m | | | ADL Enviro 200 | | N29D | 2008 | |

| 8507 | WS | LJ08CZP | 8510 | WS | LJ08CZT | 8512 | WS | LJ08CZV | 8514 | WS | LJ08CZY |
|---|---|---|---|---|---|---|---|---|---|---|---|
| 8508 | WS | LJ08CZR | 8511 | WS | LJ08CZU | 8513 | WS | LJ08CZX | 8515 | WS | LJ08CZZ |
| 8509 | WS | LJ08CZS | | | | | | | | | |

### 8516-8528

| | | | | | | | |
|---|---|---|---|---|---|---|---|
| ADL Dart 4 10.2m | | | ADL Enviro 200 | | N29D | 2009 | |

| 8516 | BC | YX59BYJ | 8520 | BC | YX59BYN | 8523 | BC | YX59BYR | 8526 | BC | YX59BYU |
|---|---|---|---|---|---|---|---|---|---|---|---|
| 8517 | BC | YX59BYK | 8521 | BC | YX59BYO | 8524 | BC | YX59BYS | 8527 | BC | YX59BYV |
| 8518 | BC | YX59BYL | 8522 | BC | YX59BYP | 8525 | BC | YX59BYT | 8528 | BC | YX59BYW |
| 8519 | BC | YX59BYM | | | | | | | | | |

### 8529-8566

| | | | | | | | |
|---|---|---|---|---|---|---|---|
| ADL Dart 4 10.2m | | | ADL Enviro 200 | | N29D | 2010-11 | |

| 8529 | TF | YX10FEF | 8539 | TF | YX10FEV | 8549 | TF | YX10FFL | 8558 | QB | YX11AEG |
|---|---|---|---|---|---|---|---|---|---|---|---|
| 8530 | TF | YX10FEG | 8540 | TF | YX10FFA | 8550 | TF | YX10FFM | 8559 | QB | YX11AEJ |
| 8531 | TF | YX10FEH | 8541 | TF | YX10FFB | 8551 | TF | YX10FFN | 8560 | QB | YX11AEK |
| 8532 | TF | YX10FEJ | 8542 | TF | YX10FFC | 8552 | QB | YX11AEA | 8561 | QB | YX11AEL |
| 8533 | TF | YX10FEK | 8543 | TF | YX10FFD | 8553 | QB | YX11AEB | 8562 | QB | YX11AEM |
| 8534 | TF | YX10FEM | 8544 | TF | YX10FFE | 8554 | QB | YX11AEC | 8563 | QB | YX11AEN |
| 8535 | TF | YX10FEO | 8545 | TF | YX10FFG | 8555 | QB | YX11AED | 8564 | QB | YX11AEO |
| 8536 | TF | YX10FEP | 8546 | TF | YX10FFH | 8556 | QB | YX11AEE | 8565 | QB | YX11AEP |
| 8537 | TF | YX10FET | 8547 | TF | YX10FFJ | 8557 | QB | YX11AEF | 8566 | QB | YX11AET |
| 8538 | TF | YX10FEU | 8548 | TF | YX10FFK | | | | | | |

Outside the Transport for London (TfL) area the livery applied is mostly white as shown by 8766, LK56JKE, at Hampton Court. This East Lancs Spryte-bodied Dart operates a tendered service for Surrey County Council. The batch was latterly operated for Surrey by First. *Richard Godfrey*

### 8567-8575 — ADL Dart 4 10.2m — ADL Enviro 200 — N29D — On order

| | | | | | | | | |
|---|---|---|---|---|---|---|---|---|
| 8567 | - | - | 8570 | - | - | 8572 | - | - | 8574 | - | - |
| 8568 | - | - | 8571 | - | - | 8573 | - | - | 8575 | - | - |
| 8569 | - | - | | | | | | | | | |

### 8576-8604 — ADL Dart 4 10.2m — ADL Enviro 200 — N29D — On order

| | | | | | | | | |
|---|---|---|---|---|---|---|---|---|
| 8576 | - | - | 8584 | - | - | 8591 | - | - | 8598 | - | - |
| 8577 | - | - | 8585 | - | - | 8592 | - | - | 8599 | - | - |
| 8578 | - | - | 8586 | - | - | 8593 | - | - | 8600 | - | - |
| 8579 | - | - | 8587 | - | - | 8594 | - | - | 8601 | - | - |
| 8580 | - | - | 8588 | - | - | 8595 | - | - | 8602 | - | - |
| 8581 | - | - | 8589 | - | - | 8596 | - | - | 8603 | - | - |
| 8582 | - | - | 8590 | - | - | 8597 | - | - | 8604 | - | - |
| 8583 | - | - | | | | | | | | | |

| 8708 | BF | R508SJM | Dennis Dart SLF 10.6m | Plaxton Pointer | N39F | 1998 |
|---|---|---|---|---|---|---|
| 8718 | BF | S518TCF | Dennis Dart SLF 10.7m | Plaxton Pointer 2 | N39F | 1998 |
| 8719 | BF | S519TCF | Dennis Dart SLF 10.7m | Plaxton Pointer 2 | N39F | 1998 |

### 8737-8753 — Dennis Dart SLF 11m — Caetano Nimbus — N33D — 2003

| | | | | | | | | |
|---|---|---|---|---|---|---|---|---|
| 8737 | TF | RN52EOV | 8745 | TF | RN52FPA | 8748 | TF | RN52FRF | 8751 | TF | RN52FXD |
| 8743 | TF | RN52EYK | 8746 | TF | RN52FPC | 8749 | TF | RN52FVR | 8752 | TF | RN52FYO |
| 8744 | TF | RN52EYL | 8747 | TF | RN52FRD | 8750 | TF | RN52FVS | 8753 | TF | RN52FZA |

### 8761-8774 — ADL Dart 11.4m — East Lancs Myllennium — N39F — 2006-07 — *Operated for Surrey CC*

| | | | | | | | | |
|---|---|---|---|---|---|---|---|---|
| 8761 | BF | LK55ACX | 8765 | BF | LK06BWD | 8769 | BF | LK56JKN | 8772 | BF | LK07CBF |
| 8762 | BF | LK55ADU | 8766 | BF | LK56JKE | 8770 | BF | LK56JKO | 8773 | BF | LK07CBV |
| 8763 | BF | LK55ADV | 8767 | BF | LK56JKF | 8771 | BF | LK56JKV | 8774 | BF | LK07CBX |
| 8764 | BF | LK06BWC | 8768 | BF | LK56JKJ | | | | | | |

### 8801-8805 — VDL Bus SB180 LF 10.3m — Wrightbus Electrocity — N26D — 2007

| | | | | | | | | |
|---|---|---|---|---|---|---|---|---|
| 8801 | WL | LJ57YAY | 8803 | WL | LJ57YBA | 8804 | WL | LJ57YAW | 8805 | WL | LJ57YBB |
| 8802 | WL | LJ57YAX | | | | | | | | | |

**Abellio's double-deck fleet comprises Wrightbus Eclipse Gemini-bodied Volvos and Enviro 400s. Reaching the end of Waterloo Bridge while working route 188 in central London is 9029, BX55XMB.** *Richard Godfery*

### 8842-8852

Optare Solo M850 — Optare — N28F — 2001-02

| | | | | | | | | | | |
|---|---|---|---|---|---|---|---|---|---|---|
| 8842 | BF | YT51EAX | 8848 | BF | YT51EBG | 8850 | BF | YP02LCC | 8852 | BF | YP02LCF |
| 8844 | BF | YT51EBA | | | | | | | | | |

### 9001-9020

Volvo B7TL 10.6m — Wrightbus Eclipse Gemini — N45/24D — 2004

| | | | | | | | | | | | |
|---|---|---|---|---|---|---|---|---|---|---|---|
| 9001 | WL | BX54DHJ | 9006 | WL | BX54DHO | 9011 | WL | BX54DJD | 9016 | WL | BX54DJO |
| 9002 | WL | BX54DHK | 9007 | WL | BX54DHP | 9012 | WL | BX54DJE | 9017 | WL | BX54DJU |
| 9003 | WL | BX54DHL | 9008 | WL | BX54DHV | 9013 | WL | BX54DJF | 9018 | WL | BX54DJV |
| 9004 | WL | BX54DHM | 9009 | WL | BX54DHY | 9014 | WL | BX54DJJ | 9019 | WL | BX54DJY |
| 9005 | WL | BX54DHN | 9010 | WL | BX54DHZ | 9015 | WL | BX54DJK | 9020 | WL | BX54DJZ |

### 9021-9065

Volvo B7TL 10.6m — Wrightbus Eclipse Gemini — N45/24D — 2005

| | | | | | | | | | | | |
|---|---|---|---|---|---|---|---|---|---|---|---|
| 9021 | WL | BX55XLS | 9033 | WL | BX55XMG | 9044 | WL | BX55XMV | 9055 | WL | BX55XNJ |
| 9022 | WL | BX55XLT | 9034 | WL | BX55XMH | 9045 | WL | LF55CZA | 9056 | WL | BX55XNK |
| 9023 | WL | BX55XLU | 9035 | WL | BX55XMJ | 9046 | WL | BX55XMW | 9057 | WL | BX55XNL |
| 9024 | WL | BX55XLV | 9036 | WL | BX55XMK | 9047 | WL | BX55XMZ | 9058 | WL | BX55XNM |
| 9025 | WL | BX55XLW | 9037 | WL | BX55XML | 9048 | WL | LF55CYZ | 9059 | WL | BX55XNN |
| 9026 | WL | BX55XLY | 9038 | WL | BX55XMM | 9049 | WL | LF55CYY | 9060 | WL | BX55XNO |
| 9027 | WL | BX55XLZ | 9039 | WL | BX55XMP | 9050 | WL | LF55CYX | 9061 | WL | BX55XNP |
| 9028 | WL | BX55XMA | 9040 | WL | BX55XMR | 9051 | WL | LF55CYW | 9062 | WL | BX55XNR |
| 9029 | WL | BX55XMB | 9041 | WL | BX55XMS | 9052 | WL | LF55CYV | 9063 | WL | BX55XNS |
| 9030 | WL | BX55XMC | 9042 | WL | BX55XMT | 9053 | WL | LF55CZB | 9064 | WL | BX55XNT |
| 9031 | WL | BX55XMD | 9043 | WL | BX55XMU | 9054 | WL | BX55XNG | 9065 | WL | BX55XNU |
| 9032 | WL | BX55XME | | | | | | | | | |

### 9066-9073

Volvo B7TL 10.6m — Wrightbus Eclipse Gemini — N45/23D — 2006

| | | | | | | | | | | | |
|---|---|---|---|---|---|---|---|---|---|---|---|
| 9066 | WS | BX55XNV | 9068 | BC | BX55XNY | 9070 | WL | LF06YRC | 9072 | WL | LF06YRE |
| 9067 | BC | BX55XNW | 9069 | WL | BX55XNZ | 9071 | BC | LF06YRD | 9073 | BC | LF06YRG |

### 9401-9427 — ADL Trident 2 10.2m / ADL Enviro400 / N41/26D / 2007

| | | | | | | | | |
|---|---|---|---|---|---|---|---|---|
| 9401 | QB | LJ56VSZ | 9408 | QB | LJ56VTK | 9415 | QB | LJ56VTU |
| 9402 | QB | LJ56VTA | 9409 | QB | LJ56VTL | 9416 | QB | LJ56VTV |
| 9403 | QB | LJ56VTC | 9410 | QB | LJ56VTM | 9417 | QB | LJ56VTW |
| 9404 | QB | LJ56VTD | 9411 | QB | LJ56VTN | 9418 | QB | LJ56VTX |
| 9405 | QB | LJ56VTE | 9412 | QB | LJ56VTO | 9419 | QB | LJ56VTY |
| 9406 | QB | LJ56VTF | 9413 | QB | LJ56VTP | 9420 | QB | LJ56VTZ |
| 9407 | QB | LJ56VTG | 9414 | QB | LJ56VTT | 9421 | QB | LJ56VUA |

| | | | | | |
|---|---|---|---|---|---|
| 9422 | QB | LJ56VUB |
| 9423 | QB | LJ56VUC |
| 9424 | QB | LJ56VUD |
| 9425 | QB | LJ56VUE |
| 9426 | QB | LJ56VUF |
| 9427 | QB | LJ56VUG |

### 9428-9466 — ADL Trident 2 10.2m / ADL Enviro400 / N41/26D / 2009

| | | | | | | | | | | | |
|---|---|---|---|---|---|---|---|---|---|---|---|
| 9428 | WL | LJ09CAA | 9438 | WL | LJ09CBX | 9448 | QB | LJ09CCX | 9458 | QB | LJ09CDX |
| 9429 | WL | LJ09CAE | 9439 | WL | LJ09CBY | 9449 | QB | LJ09CCY | 9459 | QB | LJ09CDY |
| 9430 | WL | LJ09CAO | 9440 | WL | LJ09CCA | 9450 | QB | LJ09CCZ | 9460 | QB | LJ09CDZ |
| 9431 | WL | LJ09CAU | 9441 | WL | LJ09CCD | 9451 | QB | LJ09CDE | 9461 | QB | LJ09CEA |
| 9432 | WL | LJ09CAV | 9442 | WL | LJ09CCE | 9452 | QB | LJ09CDF | 9462 | QB | LJ09CEF |
| 9433 | WL | LJ09CAX | 9443 | WL | LJ09CCF | 9453 | QB | LJ09CDK | 9463 | QB | LJ09CEK |
| 9434 | WL | LJ09CBF | 9444 | WL | LJ09CCK | 9454 | QB | LJ09CDN | 9464 | QB | LJ09CEN |
| 9435 | WL | LJ09CBO | 9445 | WL | LJ09CCN | 9455 | QB | LJ09CDO | 9465 | QB | LJ09CEO |
| 9436 | WL | LJ09CBU | 9446 | QB | LJ09CCO | 9456 | QB | LJ09CDU | 9466 | QB | LJ09CEU |
| 9437 | WL | LJ09CBV | 9447 | QB | LJ09CCU | 9457 | QB | LJ09CDV | | | |

### 9467-9504 — ADL Trident 2 10.2m / ADL Enviro400 / N41/26D / 2009

| | | | | | | | | | | | |
|---|---|---|---|---|---|---|---|---|---|---|---|
| 9467 | QB | LJ09OJZ | 9477 | QB | LJ09OKL | 9487 | QB | LJ09OKW | 9496 | QB | LJ09OLK |
| 9468 | QB | LJ09OKA | 9478 | QB | LJ09OKM | 9488 | QB | LJ09OKX | 9497 | QB | LJ09OLM |
| 9469 | QB | LJ09OKB | 9479 | QB | LJ09OKN | 9489 | QB | LJ09OKZ | 9498 | QB | LJ09OLN |
| 9470 | QB | LJ09OKC | 9480 | QB | LJ09OKO | 9490 | QB | LJ09OLA | 9499 | QB | LJ09OLO |
| 9471 | QB | LJ09OKD | 9481 | QB | LJ09OKP | 9491 | QB | LJ09OLB | 9500 | QB | LJ09OLP |
| 9472 | QB | LJ09OKE | 9482 | QB | LJ09OKR | 9492 | QB | LJ09OLC | 9501 | QB | LJ09OLR |
| 9473 | QB | LJ09OKF | 9483 | QB | LJ09OKS | 9493 | QB | LJ09OLE | 9502 | QB | LJ09OLT |
| 9474 | QB | LJ09OKG | 9484 | QB | LJ09OKT | 9494 | QB | LJ09OLG | 9503 | QB | LJ09OLU |
| 9475 | QB | LJ09OKH | 9485 | QB | LJ09OKU | 9495 | QB | LJ09OLH | 9504 | QB | LF59XDZ |
| 9476 | QB | LJ09OKK | 9486 | QB | LJ09OKV | | | | | | |

### 9505-9523 — ADL Trident 2 10.2m / ADL Enviro400 / N41/26D / 2009

| | | | | | | | | | | | |
|---|---|---|---|---|---|---|---|---|---|---|---|
| 9505 | QB | SN59AVR | 9510 | QB | SN59AVX | 9515 | QB | SN59AWF | 9520 | QB | SN59AWO |
| 9506 | QB | SN59AVT | 9511 | QB | SN59AVY | 9516 | QB | SN59AWG | 9521 | QB | SN59AWP |
| 9507 | QB | SN59AVU | 9512 | QB | SN59AVZ | 9517 | QB | SN59AWH | 9522 | QB | SN59AWR |
| 9508 | QB | SN59AVV | 9513 | QB | SN59AWA | 9518 | QB | SN59AWJ | 9523 | QB | SN59AWU |
| 9509 | QB | SN59AVW | 9514 | QB | SN59AWC | 9519 | QB | SN59AWM | | | |

### 9715-9730 — Dennis Trident 9.9m / Alexander ALX400 4.4m / N45/20D / 2000

| | | | | | | | | | | | |
|---|---|---|---|---|---|---|---|---|---|---|---|
| 9715 | TF | V315KGW | 9718 | QB | V318KGW | 9725 | TF | V325KGW | 9729 | BC | V329KGW |
| 9716 | WL | V316KGW | 9722 | WL | V322KGW | 9727 | BC | V327KGW | 9730 | BC | V330KGW |
| 9717 | WL | V317KGW | 9723 | TF | V323KGW | 9728 | BC | V328KGW | | | |

The Enviro 400 body mounted on the Alexander Dennis Trident 2 chassis has been selected by Abellio for recent deliveries. Park Lane is the location for this view of 9518, SN59AWJ, as it works service 414.
*Colin Lloyd*

## 9732-9772    Dennis Trident 9.9m    Alexander ALX400 4.4m    N43/20D    2001

| | | | | | | | | | | |
|---|---|---|---|---|---|---|---|---|---|---|
| 9732 | u | Y32HWB | 9743 | BC | YN51KUY | 9754 | BC | YN51KVL | 9764 | BC | YN51KVX |
| 9733 | u | Y133HWB | 9744 | BC | YN51KVA | 9755 | BC | YN51KVM | 9765 | BC | YN51KVZ |
| 9734 | u | Y134HWB | 9746 | BC | YN51KVC | 9756 | BC | YN51KVO | 9766 | BC | YN51KWA |
| 9735 | TFt | Y235HWB | 9747 | BC | YN51KVD | 9757 | BC | YN51KVP | 9767 | BC | YN51KWB |
| 9737 | BC | Y37HWB | 9748 | BC | YN51KVE | 9758 | BC | YN51KVR | 9768 | BC | YN51KWC |
| 9738 | QBt | Y38HWB | 9749 | BC | YN51KVF | 9759 | BC | YN51KVS | 9769 | BC | YN51KWD |
| 9739 | WL | YN51KUU | 9750 | BC | YN51KVG | 9760 | BC | YN51KVT | 9770 | BC | YN51KWE |
| 9740 | BC | YN51KUV | 9751 | BC | YN51KVH | 9761 | BC | YN51KVU | 9771 | BC | YN51KWF |
| 9741 | BC | YN51KUW | 9752 | BC | YN51KVJ | 9762 | BC | YN51KVV | 9772 | BC | YN51KWG |
| 9742 | BC | YN51KUX | 9753 | BC | YN51KVK | 9763 | BC | YN51KVW | | | |

## 9773-9829    TransBus Trident 9.9m    TransBus ALX400 4.4m    N43/19D    2002

| | | | | | | | | | | |
|---|---|---|---|---|---|---|---|---|---|---|
| 9773 | BC | KU02YBH | 9783 | QB | KV02URX | 9793 | QB | KV02USJ | 9821 | QB | LG52XYY |
| 9774 | BC | KU02YBJ | 9784 | QB | KV02URY | 9794 | QB | KV02USL | 9822 | QB | LG52XYZ |
| 9775 | BC | KU02YBK | 9785 | QB | KV02URZ | 9813 | QB | LG52XZB | 9823 | QB | LG52XZA |
| 9776 | QB | KU02YBL | 9786 | QB | KV02USB | 9814 | QB | LB52URZ | 9824 | QB | LG52XZS |
| 9777 | QB | KU02YBM | 9787 | QB | KV02USC | 9815 | QB | LG52XWE | 9825 | QB | LG52XZR |
| 9778 | QB | KU02YBN | 9788 | QB | KV02USD | 9816 | QB | LG52XYK | 9826 | QB | LG52XYL |
| 9779 | QB | KU02YBO | 9789 | QB | KV02USE | 9817 | QB | LG52XYM | 9827 | QB | LG52XZT |
| 9780 | QB | KU02YBP | 9790 | QB | KV02USF | 9818 | QB | LG52XYP | 9828 | QB | LG52XYJ |
| 9781 | QB | KU02YBR | 9791 | QB | KV02USG | 9819 | QB | LG52XYO | 9829 | WL | LG52XWD |
| 9782 | QB | KU02YBS | 9792 | QB | KV02USH | 9820 | QB | LG52XYN | | | |

## 9830-9843    TransBus Trident 9.9m    TransBus ALX400    N43/20D    2003    Metroline, 2011

| | | | | | | | | | | |
|---|---|---|---|---|---|---|---|---|---|---|
| 9830 | WL | KN52NCE | 9834 | WL | KN52NDF | 9838 | WL | KN52NDZ | 9841 | WL | KN52NEU |
| 9831 | WL | KN52NDC | 9835 | WL | KN52NDG | 9839 | WL | KN52NEJ | 9842 | WL | KN52NEY |
| 9832 | WL | KN52NDD | 9836 | WL | KN52NDJ | 9840 | WL | KN52NEO | 9843 | WL | KN52NFA |
| 9833 | WL | KN52NDE | 9837 | WL | KN52NDY | | | | | | |

Ancillary vehicles:

| | | | | | | | |
|---|---|---|---|---|---|---|---|
| 8901 | QBt | SN51SXK | Dennis Dart SLF 10.1m | Plaxton Pointer 2 | N29D | 2001 | London United, 2010 |
| 8902 | THt | SN51SZF | Dennis Dart SLF 10.1m | Plaxton Pointer 2 | N29D | 2001 | London United, 2010 |

## Depots and allocations:

### Battersea (Silverthorne Road) - QB

| | | | | | | | | |
|---|---|---|---|---|---|---|---|---|
| Dart 4 | 8552 | 8553 | 8554 | 8555 | 8556 | 8557 | 8558 | 8559 |
| | 8560 | 8561 | 8562 | 8563 | 8564 | 8565 | 8566 | |
| Trident | 9717 | 9776 | 9777 | 9778 | 9779 | 9780 | 9781 | 9782 |
| | 9783 | 9784 | 9785 | 9786 | 9787 | 9788 | 9789 | 9790 |
| | 9791 | 9792 | 9793 | 9794 | 9812 | 9813 | 9814 | 9815 |
| | 9816 | 9817 | 9818 | 9819 | 9820 | 9821 | 9822 | 9823 |
| | 9824 | 9825 | 9826 | 9827 | 9828 | | | |
| Trident 2 | 9401 | 9402 | 9403 | 9404 | 9405 | 9406 | 9407 | 9408 |
| | 9409 | 9410 | 9411 | 9412 | 9413 | 9414 | 9415 | 9416 |
| | 9417 | 9418 | 9419 | 9420 | 9421 | 9422 | 9423 | 9424 |
| | 9425 | 9426 | 9427 | 9446 | 9447 | 9448 | 9449 | 9450 |
| | 9451 | 9452 | 9453 | 9454 | 9455 | 9456 | 9457 | 9458 |
| | 9459 | 9460 | 9461 | 9462 | 9463 | 9464 | 9465 | 9466 |
| | 9467 | 9468 | 9469 | 9470 | 9471 | 9472 | 9473 | 9474 |
| | 9475 | 9476 | 9477 | 9478 | 9479 | 9480 | 9481 | 9482 |
| | 9483 | 9484 | 9485 | 9486 | 9487 | 9488 | 9489 | 9490 |
| | 9491 | 9492 | 9493 | 9494 | 9495 | 9496 | 9497 | 9498 |
| | 9499 | 9500 | 9501 | 9502 | 9503 | 9504 | 9505 | 9506 |
| | 9507 | 9508 | 9509 | 9510 | 9511 | 9512 | 9513 | 9514 |
| | 9515 | 9516 | 9517 | 9518 | 9519 | 9520 | 9521 | 9522 |
| | 9523 | | | | | | | |

### Beddington Cross (Beddington Lane) - BC

| | | | | | | | | |
|---|---|---|---|---|---|---|---|---|
| Dart | 8006 | 8008 | 8013 | 8014 | 8015 | 8016 | 8017 | 8018 |
| | 8019 | 8020 | 8024 | 8025 | 8026 | 8027 | 8028 | 8029 |
| | 8031 | 8035 | 8036 | 8037 | 8038 | 8065 | 8434 | 8435 |
| | 8436 | 8437 | 8438 | 8439 | 8440 | 8452 | | |
| Dart 4 | 8107 | 8108 | 8109 | 8501 | 8502 | 8503 | 8504 | 8505 |
| | 8506 | 8516 | 8517 | 8518 | 8519 | 8520 | 8521 | 8522 |

| | | | | | | | |
|---|---|---|---|---|---|---|---|
| | 8523 | 8524 | 8525 | 8526 | 8527 | 8528 | |
| Volvo B7TL | 9067 | 9068 | 9071 | 9072 | 9073 | | |
| Trident | 9727 | 9729 | 9730 | 9737 | 9740 | 9741 | 9742 | 9743 |
| | 9744 | 9746 | 9747 | 9748 | 9749 | 9750 | 9751 | 9752 |
| | 9753 | 9754 | 9755 | 9756 | 9757 | 9758 | 9759 | 9760 |
| | 9761 | 9762 | 9763 | 9764 | 9765 | 9766 | 9767 | 9768 |
| | 9769 | 9770 | 9771 | 9772 | 9773 | 9774 | 9775 | |

## Byfleet (Wintersells Road)  - BF

| | | | | | | | |
|---|---|---|---|---|---|---|---|
| Solo | 8842 | 8844 | 8848 | 8850 | 8852 | | |
| Dart | 8001 | 8002 | 8003 | 8004 | 8046 | 8047 | 8048 | 8049 |
| | 8064 | 8066 | 8067 | 8068 | 8069 | 8070 | 8071 | 8072 |
| | 8073 | 8074 | 8086 | 8087 | 8088 | 8089 | 8090 | 8091 |
| | 8092 | 8093 | 8094 | 8095 | 8420 | 8708 | 8718 | 8719 |
| | 8761 | 8762 | 8763 | 8764 | 8765 | 8766 | 8767 | 8768 |
| | 8769 | 8770 | 8771 | 8772 | 8773 | 8774 | 8842 | 8844 |
| | 8850 | 8852 | | | | | | |

## Hayes (North Hyde Gardens) - WS

| | | | | | | | |
|---|---|---|---|---|---|---|---|
| Dart | 8051 | 8052 | 8053 | 8054 | 8055 | 8057 | 8059 | 8061 |
| | 8062 | 8417 | 8418 | 8419 | 8461 | 8464 | 8465 | 8467 |
| | 8468 | 8469 | 8470 | 8471 | 8472 | | | |
| Dart 4 | 8507 | 8508 | 8509 | 8510 | 8511 | 8512 | 8513 | 8514 |
| | 8515 | | | | | | | |
| Volvo B7TL | 9066 | | | | | | | |

## Twickenham (Stanley Road)  - TF

| | | | | | | | |
|---|---|---|---|---|---|---|---|
| Dart | 8041 | 8042 | 8043 | 8044 | 8045 | 8058 | 8441 | 8442 |
| | 8443 | 8444 | 8445 | 8446 | 8447 | 8448 | 8449 | 8450 |
| | 8451 | 8452 | 8453 | 8454 | 8455 | 8456 | 8457 | 8458 |
| | 8459 | 8460 | 8462 | 8463 | 8466 | 8478 | 8479 | 8480 |
| | 8482 | 8483 | 8484 | 8485 | 8486 | 8487 | 8737 | 8743 |
| | 8744 | 8745 | 8746 | 8747 | 8748 | 8749 | 8750 | 8751 |
| | 8752 | 8753 | | | | | | |
| Dart 4 | 8101 | 8101 | 8102 | 8103 | 8104 | 8105 | 8106 | 8529 |
| | 8530 | 8531 | 8532 | 8533 | 8534 | 8535 | 8536 | 8537 |
| | 8538 | 8539 | 8540 | 8541 | 8542 | 8543 | 8544 | 8545 |
| | 8546 | 8547 | 8548 | 8549 | 8550 | 8551 | | |
| Trident | 9715 | 9723 | 9725 | | | | | |

## Walworth (Camberwell New Road) - WL

| | | | | | | | |
|---|---|---|---|---|---|---|---|
| Dart | 8301 | 8302 | 8303 | 8304 | 8305 | 8306 | 8307 | 8308 |
| | 8309 | 8310 | 8318 | 8473 | 8474 | 8475 | 8476 | 8477 |
| Dart4 | 8321 | 8322 | 8323 | 8324 | 8325 | 8326 | 8327 | 8328 |
| | 8329 | 8330 | 8331 | 8332 | 8333 | 8334 | 8335 | 8336 |
| | 8337 | 8338 | 8339 | 8340 | 8341 | 8342 | | |
| VDL SB180 Hybrid | 8801 | 8802 | 8803 | 8804 | 8805 | | | |
| Volvo B7TL | 9001 | 9002 | 9003 | 9004 | 9005 | 9006 | 9007 | 9008 |
| | 9009 | 9010 | 9011 | 9012 | 9013 | 9014 | 9016 | 9017 |
| | 9018 | 9019 | 9020 | 9021 | 9022 | 9023 | 9024 | 9025 |
| | 9026 | 9027 | 9028 | 9029 | 9030 | 9031 | 9032 | 9033 |
| | 9034 | 9035 | 9036 | 9037 | 9038 | 9039 | 9040 | 9041 |
| | 9042 | 9043 | 9044 | 9045 | 9046 | 9047 | 9048 | 9049 |
| | 9050 | 9051 | 9052 | 9054 | 9055 | 9056 | 9057 | 9058 |
| | 9059 | 9060 | 9061 | 9062 | 9063 | 9064 | 9065 | 9069 |
| | 9070 | | | | | | | |
| Trident | 9716 | 9717 | 9722 | 9739 | 9829 | 9830 | 9831 | 9832 |
| | 9833 | 9834 | 9835 | 9836 | 9837 | 9838 | 9839 | 9840 |
| | 9841 | 9842 | 9843 | | | | | |
| Trident 2 | 9428 | 9429 | 9430 | 9431 | 9432 | 9433 | 9434 | 9435 |
| | 9436 | 9437 | 9438 | 9439 | 9440 | 9441 | 9442 | 9443 |
| | 9444 | 9445 | | | | | | |

# ARRIVA LONDON

Arriva London North Ltd, 16 Watsons Road, Wood Green, London, N22 7TZ
Arriva London South Ltd, Croydon Bus Garage, Brighton Road, South Croydon, CR2 6EL

## ADL61-81

Dennis Dart SLF 9.4m — Alexander ALX200 — N23D — 2000 — Arriva The Shires, 2005

| | | | | | | | | | | | |
|---|---|---|---|---|---|---|---|---|---|---|---|
| 61 | CN | W461XKX | 66 | EC | W466XKX | 72 | EC | W472XKX | 77 | EC | W477XKX |
| 62 | CN | W462XKX | 67 | EC | W467XKX | 73 | EC | W473XKX | 78 | EC | W478XKX |
| 63 | CN | W463XKX | 68 | EC | W468XKX | 74 | EC | W474XKX | 79 | EC | W479XKX |
| 64 | CN | W464XKX | 69 | EC | W469XKX | 75 | EC | W475XKX | 81 | EC | W481XKX |
| 65 | CN | W465XKX | 71 | EC | W471XKX | 76 | EC | W476XKX | | | |

## ADL969-983

Dennis Dart SLF 10.2m — Alexander ALX200 — N27D — 1998

| | | | | | | | | | | | |
|---|---|---|---|---|---|---|---|---|---|---|---|
| 969 | EC | S169JUA | 973 | AE | S173JUA | 977 | EC | S177JUA | 981 | AE | S181JUA |
| 970 | EC | S170JUA | 974 | EC | S174JUA | 978 | EC | S178JUA | 982 | AE | S182JUA |
| 971 | EC | S171JUA | 975 | EC | S175JUA | 979 | EC | S179JUA | 983 | AE | S183JUA |
| 972 | EC | S172JUA | 976 | EC | S176JUA | 980 | EC | S180JUA | | | |

| | | | | | | |
|---|---|---|---|---|---|---|
| DLA1 | Et | R101GNW | DAF DB250 10.6m | Alexander ALX400 | N45/19D | 1998 |

## DLA11-64

DAF DB250 10.6m — Alexander ALX400 — N45/19D — 1998-99

| | | | | | | | | | | | |
|---|---|---|---|---|---|---|---|---|---|---|---|
| 11 | WN | S211JUA | 21 | Et | S221JUA | 30 | CNt | S230JUA | 47 | EC | S247JUA |
| 12 | WN | S212JUA | 22 | CNt | S322JUA | 31 | CNt | S231JUA | 54 | TH | S254JUA |
| 13 | WN | S213JUA | 23 | Et | S223JUA | 32 | Et | S232JUA | 55 | EC | S255JUA |
| 14 | WN | S214JUA | 24 | CNt | S224JUA | 33 | Et | S233JUA | 56 | CNt | S256JUA |
| 15 | WN | S215JUA | 25 | Et | S225JUA | 34 | CNt | S234JUA | 57 | EC | S257JUA |
| 16 | WN | S216JUA | 26 | CNt | S226JUA | 35 | Et | S235JUA | 58 | EC | S258JUA |
| 17 | WN | S217JUA | 27 | CNt | S227JUA | 37 | Et | S237JUA | 62 | TH | S262JUA |
| 18 | WN | S218JUA | 28 | CNt | S228JUA | 39 | EC | S239JUA | 63 | TH | S263JUA |
| 19 | WN | S219JUA | 29 | CNt | S229JUA | 45 | CNt | S245JUA | 64 | TH | S264JUA |
| 20 | WN | S220JUA | | | | | | | | | |

**Arriva plc was acquired by Deutsche Bahn on 27 August 2010, though its expanding European operations are still managed from the Sunderland headquarters. Dennis Dart ADL76, W476XKX, features the Alexander ALX200 body that has recently been refurbished. It is seen at Chingford rail station.** *Dave Heath*

Complementing the ALX200 single-deck is the ALX400 double-deck model, seen here on a Dutch-built DAF DB250 chassis. Arriva Bus and Coach is the importer of the DAF, now VDL, products. DLA296, Y496UGC, is seen passing through Grants Hill on Route 123. *Richard Godfrey*

### DLA94-125

| | | | | | | | | | | | | |
|---|---|---|---|---|---|---|---|---|---|---|---|---|
| | | DAF DB250 10.6m | | | Alexander ALX400 | | | N45/17D* | 1999 | *seating varies | | |
| 94 | w | T294FGN | 110 | E | T310FGN | 116 | E | T316FGN | 121 | E | T421GGO |
| 95 | w | T295FGN | 111 | E | T311FGN | 117 | E | T317FGN | 122 | E | T322FGN |
| 106 | w | T306FGN | 112 | E | T312FGN | 118 | E | T318FGN | 123 | E | T323FGN |
| 107 | w | T307FGN | 113 | E | T313FGN | 119 | E | T319FGN | 124 | E | T324FGN |
| 108 | E | T308FGN | 114 | E | T314FGN | 120 | E | T320FGN | 125 | E | T325FGN |
| 109 | E | T309FGN | 115 | E | T315FGN | | | | | | |

### DLA126-189

| | | | | | | | | | | | | |
|---|---|---|---|---|---|---|---|---|---|---|---|---|
| | | DAF DB250 10.2m | | | Alexander ALX400 | | | N43/18D* | 1999-2000 | *seating varies | | |
| 126 | E | V326DGT | 142 | N | V342DGT | 158 | N | V358DGT | 174 | N | W374VGJ |
| 127 | E | V327DGT | 143 | N | V343DGT | 159 | E | V359DGT | 175 | TC | W432WGJ |
| 128 | E | V628LGC | 144 | N | V344DGT | 160 | E | V660LGC | 176 | TC | W376VGJ |
| 129 | E | V329DGT | 145 | N | V345DGT | 161 | E | V361DGT | 177 | TC | W377VGJ |
| 130 | E | V330DGT | 146 | N | V346DGT | 162 | E | V362DGT | 178 | TC | W378VGJ |
| 131 | E | V331DGT | 147 | N | V347DGT | 163 | E | V363DGT | 179 | TC | W379VGJ |
| 132 | EC | V332DGT | 148 | N | V348DGT | 164 | E | V364DGT | 180 | TC | W433WGJ |
| 133 | TC | V633LGC | 149 | N | V349DGT | 165 | E | V365DGT | 181 | TC | W381VGJ |
| 134 | w | V334DGT | 150 | E | V650LGC | 166 | N | W366VGJ | 182 | TC | W382VGJ |
| 135 | TC | V335DGT | 151 | E | V351DGT | 167 | N | W367VGJ | 183 | TC | W383VGJ |
| 136 | N | V336DGT | 152 | E | V352DGT | 168 | N | W368VGJ | 184 | TC | W384VGJ |
| 137 | N | V337DGT | 153 | E | V353DGT | 169 | N | W369VGJ | 185 | TC | W385VGJ |
| 138 | E | V338DGT | 154 | N | V354DGT | 170 | N | W431WGJ | 186 | TC | W386VGJ |
| 139 | E | V339DGT | 155 | N | V355DGT | 171 | N | W371VGJ | 187 | TC | W387VGJ |
| 140 | E | V640LGC | 156 | N | V356DGT | 172 | N | W372VGJ | 188 | TC | W388VGJ |
| 141 | E | V341DGT | 157 | N | V357DGT | 173 | N | W373VGJ | 189 | TC | W389VGJ |

### DLA190-223

| | | | | | | | | | | | | |
|---|---|---|---|---|---|---|---|---|---|---|---|---|
| | | DAF DB250 10.2m | | | Alexander ALX400 | | | N43/18D* | 2000 | *seating varies | | |
| 190 | WN | W434WGJ | 199 | WN | W399VGJ | 208 | BN | W408VGJ | 216 | TC | X416FGP |
| 191 | WN | W391VGJ | 200 | WN | W435WGJ | 209 | BN | W409VGJ | 217 | TC | X417FGP |
| 192 | WN | W392VGJ | 201 | WN | W401VGJ | 210 | BN | W438WGJ | 218 | TC | X418FGP |
| 193 | WN | W393VGJ | 202 | WN | W402VGJ | 211 | BN | W411VGJ | 219 | TC | X419FGP |
| 194 | WN | W394VGJ | 203 | WN | W403VGJ | 212 | BN | W412VGJ | 220 | TC | X501GGO |
| 195 | WN | W395VGJ | 204 | AR | W404VGJ | 213 | BN | W413VGJ | 221 | TC | X421FGP |
| 196 | WN | W396VGJ | 205 | BN | W436WGJ | 214 | TC | W414VGJ | 222 | TC | X422FGP |
| 197 | WN | W397VGJ | 206 | BN | W437WGJ | 215 | TC | X415FGP | 223 | TC | X423FGP |
| 198 | WN | W398VGJ | 207 | BN | W407VGJ | | | | | | |

*The London Bus Handbook*

The DLA class has been the mainstay of Arriva's London fleet since 1998 though earlier vehicles are now being replaced. DLA275, Y475UGC illustrates the latest all-over red livery now speciafied by TfL. *Mark Lyons*

### DLA224-256

DAF DB250 10.2m — Alexander ALX400 — N43/19D* — 2000-01 — *seating varies

| 224 | TC | X424FGP | 233 | AR | X433FGP | 241 | AR | X441FGP | 249 | AR | X449FGP |
|-----|----|---------|-----|----|---------|-----|----|---------|-----|----|---------|
| 225 | AR | X425FGP | 234 | AR | X434FGP | 242 | AR | X442FGP | 250 | TC | X506GGO |
| 226 | AR | X426FGP | 235 | AR | X435FGP | 243 | AR | X443FGP | 251 | TC | X451FGP |
| 227 | AR | X427FGP | 236 | BN | X436FGP | 244 | AR | X504GGO | 252 | TC | X452FGP |
| 228 | AR | X428FGP | 237 | AR | X437FGP | 245 | AR | X445FGP | 253 | TC | X453FGP |
| 229 | AR | X429FGP | 238 | AR | X438FGP | 246 | AR | X446FGP | 254 | TC | X454FGP |
| 230 | AR | X502GGO | 239 | AR | X439FGP | 247 | AR | X447FGP | 255 | TC | X507GGO |
| 231 | AR | X431FGP | 240 | AR | X503GGO | 248 | AR | X448FGP | 256 | TC | X508GGO |
| 232 | AR | X432FGP | | | | | | | | | |

### DLA270-319

DAF DB250 10.2m — Alexander ALX400 — N43/19D* — 2000-01 — *seating varies

| 270 | BN | Y452UGC | 283 | AR | Y483UGC | 296 | AR | Y496UGC | 308 | EC | Y508UGC |
|-----|----|---------|-----|----|---------|-----|----|---------|-----|----|---------|
| 271 | BN | Y471UGC | 284 | AR | Y484UGC | 297 | AR | Y497UGC | 309 | EC | Y509UGC |
| | | | 285 | AR | Y485UGC | 298 | AR | Y498UGC | 310 | EC | Y527UGC |
| 273 | AR | Y473UGC | 286 | AR | Y486UGC | 299 | EC | Y499UGC | 311 | BN | Y511UGC |
| 274 | AR | Y474UGC | 287 | AR | Y487UGC | 300 | EC | Y524UGC | 312 | BN | Y512UGC |
| 275 | AR | Y475UGC | 288 | AR | Y488UGC | 301 | EC | Y501UGC | 313 | BN | Y513UGC |
| 276 | AR | Y476UGC | 289 | AR | Y489UGC | 302 | EC | Y502UGC | 314 | BN | Y514UGC |
| 277 | AR | Y477UGC | 290 | AR | Y523UGC | 303 | EC | Y503UGC | 315 | BN | Y529UGC |
| 278 | AR | Y478UGC | 291 | AR | Y491UGC | 304 | EC | Y504UGC | 316 | BN | Y516UGC |
| 279 | AR | Y479UGC | 292 | AR | Y492UGC | 305 | EC | Y526UGC | 317 | BN | Y517UGC |
| 280 | AR | Y522UGC | 293 | AR | Y493UGC | 306 | EC | Y506UGC | 318 | BN | Y518UGC |
| 281 | AR | Y481UGC | 294 | AR | Y494UGC | 307 | EC | Y507UGC | 319 | BN | Y519UGC |
| 282 | AR | Y482UGC | 295 | AR | Y495UGC | | | | | | |

### DLA322-336

DAF DB250 10.2m — TransBus ALX400 — N45/20D* — 2003 — *seating varies

| 322 | TH | LG52DAO | 326 | TH | LG52DBV | 330 | TH | LG52DCF | 334 | TH | LG52DCX |
|-----|----|---------|-----|----|---------|-----|----|---------|-----|----|---------|
| 323 | TH | LG52DAU | 327 | TH | LG52DBY | 331 | TH | LG52DCO | 335 | TH | LG52DCY |
| 324 | TH | LG52DBO | 328 | TH | LG52DBZ | 332 | TH | LG52DCU | 336 | TH | LG52DCZ |
| 325 | TH | LG52DBU | 329 | TH | LG52DCE | 333 | TH | LG52DCV | | | |

Wrightbus bodywork has also been offered on the DAF DB250 chassis, the results shown here in DW60, LJ04LFF. Allocated to Brixton depot it is seen operating route 137 in Park Lane. *Terry Longhurst*

### DLA337-389

DAF DB250 10.2m    TransBus ALX400    N45/20D*    2003    *seating varies

| 337 | TH | LJ03MFX | 351 | EC | LJ03MKZ | 364 | EC | LJ03MKL | 377 | TH | LJ03MTK |
|-----|----|---------|-----|----|---------|-----|----|---------|-----|----|---------|
| 338 | TH | LJ03MFY | 352 | EC | LJ03MLE | 365 | EC | LJ03MWE | 378 | TH | LJ03MTU |
| 339 | TH | LJ03MFZ | 353 | EC | LJ03MLF | 366 | EC | LJ03MWF | 379 | TH | LJ03MTV |
| 340 | TH | LJ03MGE | 354 | EC | LJ03MLK | 367 | EC | LJ03MWG | 380 | TH | LJ03MTY |
| 341 | TH | LJ03MGU | 355 | EC | LJ03MJX | 368 | EC | LJ03MWK | 381 | TH | LJ03MTZ |
| 342 | TH | LJ03MGV | 356 | EC | LJ03MJY | 369 | EC | LJ03MWL | 382 | TH | LJ03MUA |
| 343 | TH | LJ03MDV | 357 | EC | LJ03MKA | 370 | EC | LJ03MUY | 383 | TH | LJ03MUB |
| 344 | TH | LJ03MDX | 358 | EC | LJ03MKC | 371 | TH | LJ03MVC | 384 | TH | LJ03MYU |
| 345 | TH | LJ03MDY | 359 | EC | LJ03MKD | 372 | TH | LJ03MVD | 385 | TH | LJ03MYV |
| 346 | TH | LJ03MDZ | 360 | EC | LJ03MKE | 373 | TH | LJ03MVE | 386 | TH | LJ03MYX |
| 347 | TH | LJ03MEU | 361 | EC | LJ03MKF | 374 | TH | LJ03MSY | 387 | TH | LJ03MYY |
| 348 | EC | LJ03MKU | 362 | EC | LJ03MKG | 375 | TH | LJ03MTE | 388 | TH | LJ03MYZ |
| 349 | EC | LJ03MKV | 363 | EC | LJ03MKK | 376 | TH | LJ03MTF | 389 | TH | LJ03MZD |
| 350 | EC | LJ03MKX | | | | | | | | | |

### DLP15-20

DAF DB250 10.6m    Plaxton President    N45/19D    1999

| 15 | E | T215XBV | 17 | E | T217XBV | 19 | E | T219XBV | 20 | E | T220XBV |
|----|---|---------|----|---|---------|----|---|---------|----|---|---------|
| 16 | E | T216XBV | 18 | E | T218XBV | | | | | | |

### DLP40-75

DAF DB250 10.6m    Plaxton President    N45/21D    2001

| 40 | AD | Y532UGC | 49 | AD | Y549UGC | 58 | AD | LJ51DKF | 67 | AD | LJ51DLD |
|----|----|---------|----|----|---------|----|----|---------|----|----|---------|
| 41 | AD | Y541UGC | 50 | AD | LJ51DJU | 59 | AD | LJ51DKK | 68 | AD | LJ51DLF |
| 42 | AD | Y542UGC | 51 | AD | LJ51DJV | 60 | AD | LJ51DKL | 69 | AD | LJ51DLK |
| 43 | AD | Y543UGC | 52 | AD | LJ51DJX | 61 | AD | LJ51DKN | 70 | WN | LJ51DLN |
| 44 | AD | Y544UGC | 53 | AD | LJ51DJY | 62 | AD | LJ51DKO | 71 | AD | LJ51DLU |
| 45 | AD | Y533UGC | 54 | AD | LJ51DJZ | 63 | AD | LJ51DKU | 72 | AD | LJ51DLV |
| 46 | AD | Y546UGC | 55 | AD | LJ51DKA | 64 | AD | LJ51DKV | 73 | AD | LJ51DLX |
| 47 | AD | Y547UGC | 56 | AD | LJ51DKD | 65 | AD | LJ51DKX | 74 | AD | LJ51DLY |
| 48 | AD | Y548UGC | 57 | AD | LJ51DKE | 66 | AD | LJ51DKY | 75 | AD | LJ51DLZ |

### DLP76-90

DAF DB250 10.2m    TransBus President    N43/19D*    2002    *seating varies

| 76 | E | LJ51OSX | 80 | E | LJ51ORC | 84 | E | LJ51ORK | 88 | E | LF02PKD |
|----|---|---------|----|---|---------|----|---|---------|----|---|---------|
| 77 | E | LJ51OSY | 81 | E | LJ51ORF | 85 | E | LJ51ORL | 89 | E | LF02PKE |
| 78 | E | LJ51OSZ | 82 | E | LJ51ORG | 86 | E | LF02PKA | 90 | E | LF02PKJ |
| 79 | E | LJ51ORA | 83 | E | LJ51ORH | 87 | E | LF02PKC | | | |

*The London Bus Handbook*

## DLP91-110
DAF DB250 10.6m — TransBus President — N45/19D* — 2002 — *seating varies

| | | | | | | | | | | | |
|---|---|---|---|---|---|---|---|---|---|---|---|
| 91 | E | LF52URS | 96 | E | LF52URX | 101 | E | LF52URG | 106 | E | LF52URM |
| 92 | E | LF52URT | 97 | E | LF52URB | 102 | E | LF52URH | 107 | E | LF52UPP |
| 93 | E | LF52URU | 98 | E | LF52URC | 103 | E | LF52URJ | 108 | E | LF52UPR |
| 94 | E | LF52URV | 99 | E | LF52URD | 104 | E | LF52URK | 109 | E | LF52UPS |
| 95 | E | LF52URW | 100 | E | LF52URE | 105 | E | LF52URL | 110 | E | LF52UPT |

## DW1-50
DAF DB250 10.3m — Wrightbus Pulsar Gemini — N43/21D — 2003

| | | | | | | | | | | | |
|---|---|---|---|---|---|---|---|---|---|---|---|
| 1 | TC | 801DYE | 14 | TC | LJ03MWC | 27 | TC | LJ53BGK | 39 | CN | LJ53NHF |
| 2 | TC | LJ03MWN | 15 | TC | LJ03MWD | 28 | TC | LJ53BGO | 40 | CN | LJ53NHG |
| 3 | TC | LJ03MWP | 16 | TC | LJ03MVF | 29 | TC | LJ53BGU | 41 | CN | LJ53NHH |
| 4 | TC | LJ03MWU | 17 | TC | LJ03MVG | 30 | TC | LJ53NHV | 42 | CN | LJ53NHK |
| 5 | TC | LJ03MWV | 18 | TC | LJ53NHT | 31 | TC | LJ53NHX | 43 | CN | LJ53NHL |
| 6 | TC | LJ03MVT | 19 | TC | WLT719 | 32 | TC | LJ53NHY | 44 | CN | VLT244 |
| 7 | TC | WLT807 | 20 | TC | LJ53BFP | 33 | TC | LJ53NHZ | 45 | CN | LJ53NHN |
| 8 | TC | LJ03MVV | 21 | TC | LJ53BFU | 34 | TC | 734DYE | 46 | CN | LJ53NHO |
| 9 | TC | LJ03MVW | 22 | TC | 822DYE | 35 | TC | LJ53NJF | 47 | CN | LJ53NHP |
| 10 | TC | LJ03MVX | 23 | TC | LJ53BFX | 36 | TC | LJ53NJK | 48 | CN | WLT348 |
| 11 | TC | LJ03MVY | 24 | TC | LJ53BFY | 37 | CN | LJ53NJN | 49 | CN | LJ53NGU |
| 12 | TC | LJ03MVZ | 25 | TC | 725DYE | 38 | CN | LJ53NHE | 50 | CN | LJ53NGV |
| 13 | TC | LJ03MWA | 26 | TC | LJ53BGF | | | | | | |

## DW51-93
VDL Bus DB250 10.3m — Wrightbus Pulsar Gemini — N43/22D — 2004

| | | | | | | | | | | | |
|---|---|---|---|---|---|---|---|---|---|---|---|
| 51 | CN | LJ04LDX | 62 | BN | LJ04LDC | 73 | BN | LJ04LDC | 84 | BN | LJ04LFX |
| 52 | CN | LJ04LDY | 63 | BN | LJ04LDD | 74 | BN | LJ04LGL | 85 | BN | WLT385 |
| 53 | CN | LJ04LDZ | 64 | BN | WLT664 | 75 | BN | LJ04LGN | 86 | BN | LJ04LFZ |
| 54 | CN | LJ04LEF | 65 | BN | LJ04LDF | 76 | BN | WLT676 | 87 | BN | LJ04LGA |
| 55 | BN | LJ04LEU | 66 | BN | LJ04LDK | 77 | BN | LJ04LGV | 88 | BN | LJ04LGC |
| 56 | BN | 656DYE | 67 | BN | LJ04LDL | 78 | BN | LJ04LGW | 89 | BN | LJ04LGD |
| 57 | BN | LJ04LFB | 68 | BN | LJ04LDN | 79 | BN | LJ04LGX | 90 | BN | LJ04LGE |
| 58 | BN | LJ04LFD | 69 | BN | LJ04LDU | 80 | BN | LJ04LGY | 91 | BN | LJ04LFG |
| 59 | BN | LJ04LFE | 70 | BN | WLT970 | 81 | BN | LJ04LFU | 92 | BN | LJ04LFH |
| 60 | BN | LJ04LFF | 71 | BN | LJ04LGF | 82 | BN | LJ04LFV | 93 | BN | LJ04LFK |
| 61 | BN | LJ04LDA | 72 | BN | LJ04LGG | 83 | BN | LJ04LFW | | | |

## DW94-102
VDL Bus DB250 10.3m — Wrightbus Pulsar Gemini — N43/22D — 2004

| | | | | | | | | | | | |
|---|---|---|---|---|---|---|---|---|---|---|---|
| 94 | CN | LJ54BFP | 97 | CN | WLT997 | 99 | CN | LJ54BFZ | 101 | CN | LJ54BGF |
| 95 | CN | VLT295 | 98 | CN | LJ54BFY | 100 | CN | LJ54BGE | 102 | BN | LJ54BGK |
| 96 | CN | LJ54BFV | | | | | | | | | |

## DW103-133
VDL Bus DB250 10.3m — Wrightbus Pulsar Gemini — N43/22D — 2005

| | | | | | | | | | | | |
|---|---|---|---|---|---|---|---|---|---|---|---|
| 103 | BN | LJ05BJV | 111 | BN | LJ05BHP | 119 | BN | 319CLT | 127 | BN | LJ05BNL |
| 104 | BN | LJ05BJX | 112 | BN | LJ05BHU | 120 | BN | LJ05BMZ | 128 | BN | LJ05GKX |
| 105 | BN | LJ05BJY | 113 | BN | LJ05BHV | 121 | BN | LJ05BNA | 129 | BN | LJ05GKY |
| 106 | BN | LJ05BJZ | 114 | BN | LJ05BHW | 122 | BN | LJ05BNB | 130 | BN | LJ05GKZ |
| 107 | BN | LJ05BKA | 115 | BN | LJ05BHX | 123 | BN | LJ05BND | 131 | BN | LJ05GLF |
| 108 | BN | LJ05BHL | 116 | BN | LJ05BHY | 124 | BN | LJ05BNE | 132 | BN | LJ05GLK |
| 109 | BN | LJ05BHN | 117 | BN | LJ05BHZ | 125 | BN | LJ05BNF | 133 | BN | LJ05GLV |
| 110 | BN | LJ05BHO | 118 | BN | LJ05BMV | 126 | BN | LJ05BNK | | | |

## DW201-262
VDL Bus DB300 10.4m — Wrightbus Pulsar Gemini 2 — N41/24D — 2009

| | | | | | | | | | | | |
|---|---|---|---|---|---|---|---|---|---|---|---|
| 201 | CT | LJ09KRO | 217 | CT | LJ09STX | 233 | CT | LJ59AEC | 248 | CT | LJ59AAO |
| 202 | CT | LJ09SUO | 218 | CT | LJ09STZ | 234 | CT | LJ59AED | 249 | CT | LJ59AAU |
| 203 | CT | LJ09SUU | 219 | CT | LJ09SUA | 235 | CT | LJ59AEE | 250 | CT | LJ59AAV |
| 204 | CT | LJ09SUV | 220 | CT | LJ09SUF | 236 | CT | LJ59AEF | 251 | CT | LJ59AAX |
| 205 | CT | LJ09SUX | 221 | CT | LJ09SUH | 237 | CT | LJ59AEG | 252 | CT | LJ59AAY |
| 206 | CT | LJ09SUY | 222 | CT | LJ59AAO | 238 | CT | LJ59AEK | 253 | CT | LJ59AAZ |
| 207 | CT | LJ09SVA | 223 | CT | LJ59AAU | 239 | CT | LJ59AEL | 254 | CT | LJ59GVC |
| 208 | CT | LJ09SVC | 224 | CT | LJ59AET | 240 | CT | LJ59AEM | 255 | CT | LJ59GVE |
| 209 | CT | LJ09SVD | 225 | CT | LJ59AEU | 241 | CT | LJ59AEN | 256 | CT | LJ59GVF |
| 210 | CT | LJ09SVE | 226 | CT | LJ59AEV | 242 | CT | LJ59ACU | 257 | CT | LJ59GVG |
| 211 | CT | LJ09SVF | 227 | CT | LJ59AEW | 243 | CT | LJ59ACV | 258 | CT | LJ59GVK |
| 212 | CT | LJ09SSO | 228 | CT | LJ59AEX | 244 | CT | LJ59ACX | 259 | CT | LJ59GTF |
| 213 | CT | LJ09SSU | 229 | CT | LJ59AEY | 245 | CT | LJ59AAF | 260 | CT | LJ59GTU |
| 214 | CT | LJ09SSV | 230 | CT | LJ59AEZ | 246 | CT | LJ59AAK | 261 | CT | 361CLT |
| 215 | CT | LJ09SSX | 231 | CT | LJ59AEA | 247 | CT | LJ59AAN | 262 | CT | LJ59GUA |
| 216 | CT | LJ09SSZ | 232 | CT | LJ59AEB | | | | | | |

## DW263-295

VDL Bus DB300 10.4m  Wrightbus Pulsar Gemini 2  N41/24D  2009-10

| | | | | | | | | | |
|---|---|---|---|---|---|---|---|---|---|
| 263 | CT | LJ59LXU | 272 | CT | LJ59LWV | 280 | BN | LJ59LWG | 288 | BN | LJ59LWR |
| 264 | CT | LJ59LXV | 273 | CT | LJ59LWW | 281 | BN | LJ59LWH | 289 | BN | LJ59LVH |
| 265 | CT | LJ59LXW | 274 | CT | LJ59LWX | 282 | BN | LJ59LWK | 290 | BN | LJ59LVV |
| 266 | CT | LJ59LXX | 275 | CT | LJ59LWY | 283 | BN | LJ59LWL | 291 | BN | LJ59LVW |
| 267 | CT | LJ59LXY | 276 | CT | LJ59LWZ | 284 | BN | LJ59LWM | 292 | BN | LJ59LVX |
| 268 | CT | LJ59LXZ | 277 | CT | LJ59LXA | 285 | BN | LJ59LWN | 293 | BN | LJ59LVY |
| 269 | CT | LJ59LWS | 278 | CT | LJ59LXB | 286 | BN | LJ59LWO | 294 | BN | LJ59LVZ |
| 270 | CT | LJ59LWT | 279 | CT | LJ59LWF | 287 | BN | LJ59LWP | 295 | BN | LJ59LWA |
| 271 | CT | LJ59LWU | | | | | | | | | |

## DW296-336

VDL Bus DB300 10.4m  Wrightbus Pulsar Gemini 2  N41/24D  2010-11

| | | | | | | | | | |
|---|---|---|---|---|---|---|---|---|---|
| 296 | BN | LJ10CUH | 307 | AR | LJ10CVP | 317 | AR | LJ10CVD | 327 | AR | LJ60AYK |
| 297 | BN | LJ10CUK | 308 | AR | LJ10CUO | 318 | AR | LJ60AXX | 328 | AR | LJ60AYM |
| 298 | AR | LJ10CVE | 309 | AR | LJ10CUU | 319 | AR | LJ60AXY | 329 | AR | LJ60AYN |
| 299 | AR | LJ10CVF | 310 | AR | LJ10CUV | 320 | AR | LJ60AXZ | 330 | AR | LJ60AYO |
| 300 | AR | LJ10CVG | 311 | AR | LJ10CUW | 321 | AR | LJ60AYA | 331 | AR | LJ60AYP |
| 301 | AR | LJ10CVH | 312 | AR | LJ10CUX | 322 | AR | LJ60AYB | 332 | AR | LJ60AYR |
| 302 | AR | LJ10CVK | 313 | AR | LJ10CUY | 323 | AR | LJ60AYC | 333 | AR | LJ60AYS |
| 303 | AR | LJ10CVL | 314 | AR | LJ10CVA | 324 | AR | LJ60AYD | 334 | AR | LJ60AYT |
| 304 | AR | LJ10CVM | 315 | AR | LJ10CVB | 325 | AR | LJ60AYE | 335 | AR | LJ60AYU |
| 305 | AR | LJ10CVN | 316 | AR | LJ10CVC | 326 | AR | LJ60AYH | 336 | AR | LJ60AWW |
| 306 | AR | LJ10CVO | | | | | | | | | |

## DW401-464

VDL Bus DB300 10.4m  Wrightbus Pulsar Gemini 2  N41/24D  2011

| | | | | | | | | | |
|---|---|---|---|---|---|---|---|---|---|
| 401 | CT | LJ11AEO | 417 | CT | LJ11AEK | 433 | SF | LJ11AEA | 449 | SF | LJ11AAU |
| 402 | CT | LJ11AEP | 418 | CT | LJ11AEL | 434 | SF | LJ11ABK | 450 | SF | LJ11AAX |
| 403 | CT | LJ11AET | 419 | CT | LJ11AEM | 435 | SF | LJ11ABN | 451 | SF | LJ11AAY |
| 404 | CT | LJ11AEU | 420 | CT | LJ11AEN | 436 | SF | LJ11ABO | 452 | SF | LJ11AAZ |
| 405 | CT | LJ11AEV | 421 | CT | LJ11ACV | 437 | SF | LJ11ABU | 453 | SF | LJ11ABF |
| 406 | CT | LJ11AEW | 422 | CT | LJ11ACX | 438 | SF | LJ11ABV | 454 | SF | LJ11EGE |
| 407 | CT | LJ11AEX | 423 | CT | LJ11ACY | 439 | SF | LJ11ABX | 455 | SF | LJ11EGF |
| 408 | CT | LJ11AEY | 424 | CT | LJ11ACZ | 440 | SF | LJ11ABZ | 456 | SF | LJ11EGK |
| 409 | CT | LJ11AEZ | 425 | - | - | 441 | SF | LJ11ACF | 457 | SF | LJ11EGU |
| 410 | CT | LJ11AFA | 426 | - | - | 442 | SF | LJ11ACO | 458 | SF | LJ11EGV |
| 411 | CT | LJ11AEB | 427 | - | - | 443 | SF | LJ11ACU | 459 | SF | LJ11EGX |
| 412 | CT | LJ11AEC | 428 | SF | LJ11ADO | 444 | SF | LJ11AAE | 460 | SF | LJ11EGY |
| 413 | CT | LJ11AED | 429 | SF | LJ11ADU | 445 | SF | LJ11AAF | 461 | SF | LJ11EGZ |
| 414 | CT | LJ11AEE | 430 | SF | LJ11ADV | 446 | SF | LJ11AAK | 462 | SF | LJ11EHB |
| 415 | CT | LJ11AEF | 431 | SF | LJ11ADX | 447 | SF | LJ11AAN | 463 | SF | LJ11EHC |
| 416 | CT | LJ11AEG | 432 | SF | LJ11ADZ | 448 | SF | LJ11AAO | 464 | SF | LJ11EFS |

## DW465-498

VDL Bus DB300 10.4m  Wrightbus Pulsar Gemini 2  N41/24D  On order

| | | | | | | | | | |
|---|---|---|---|---|---|---|---|---|---|
| 465 | - | - | 474 | - | - | 483 | - | - | 491 | - | - |
| 466 | - | - | 475 | - | - | 484 | - | - | 492 | - | - |
| 467 | - | - | 476 | - | - | 485 | - | - | 493 | - | - |
| 468 | - | - | 477 | - | - | 486 | - | - | 494 | - | - |
| 469 | - | - | 478 | - | - | 487 | - | - | 495 | - | - |
| 470 | - | - | 479 | - | - | 488 | - | - | 496 | - | - |
| 471 | - | - | 480 | - | - | 489 | - | - | 497 | - | - |
| 472 | - | - | 481 | - | - | 490 | - | - | 498 | - | - |
| 473 | - | - | 482 | - | - | | | | | | |

## DWL1-22

DAF SB120 10.2mAEC  Wrightbus Cadet  N27D*  2001  *seating varies

| | | | | | | | | | |
|---|---|---|---|---|---|---|---|---|---|
| 1 | TH | Y801DGT | 7 | TH | LJ51DDK | 13 | E | LJ51DDX | 18 | EC | LJ51DFC |
| 2 | TH | Y802DGT | 8 | TH | LJ51DDL | 14 | E | LJ51DDY | 19 | EC | LJ51DFD |
| 3 | TH | Y803DGT | 9 | TH | LJ51DDN | 15 | TH | LJ51DDZ | 20 | EC | LJ51DFE |
| 4 | TH | Y804DGT | 10 | EC | LJ51DDO | 16 | TH | LJ51DEU | 21 | EC | LJ51DFF |
| 5 | TH | Y805DGT | 11 | TH | LJ51DDU | 17 | EC | LJ51DFA | 22 | EC | LJ51DFG |
| 6 | TH | Y806DGT | 12 | TH | LJ51DDV | | | | | | |

## DWL23-29

DAF SB120 10.8m  Wrightbus Cadet  N30D  2002

| | | | | | | | | | |
|---|---|---|---|---|---|---|---|---|---|
| 23 | E | LF02PLU | 25 | E | LF02PLX | 27 | E | LF02PMO | 29 | E | LF02PMV |
| 24 | E | LF02PLV | 26 | E | LF02PLZ | | | | | | |

**Wrightbus Cadet bodywork is fitted to the DAF SB120s in the Arriva London fleet. The type is represented by DWS10, LJ53NFY, one of six based at Croydon.** *Terry Longhurst*

### DWL30-55

| | | | DAF SB120 10.2m | | | Wrightbus Cadet | | | N26D* | | 2002 | *seating varies |
|---|---|---|---|---|---|---|---|---|---|---|---|---|

| 30 | CNt | LF02PMX | 37 | Et | LF02PNO | 44 | Et | LF52UTB | 50 | Et | LF52UOB |
|---|---|---|---|---|---|---|---|---|---|---|---|
| 31 | CNt | LF02PMY | 38 | Et | LF02PNU | 45 | EC | LF52UNW | 51 | EC | LF52UOC |
| 32 | CNt | LF02PNE | 39 | Et | LF02PNV | 46 | EC | LF52UNX | 52 | WN | LF52UOD |
| 33 | CNt | LF02PNJ | 40 | Et | LF02PNX | 47 | EC | LF52UNY | 53 | WN | LF52UOE |
| 34 | CNt | LF02PNK | 41 | Et | LF02PNY | 48 | EC | LF52UNZ | 54 | WN | LF52USZ |
| 35 | Et | LF02PNL | 42 | EC | LF02POA | 49 | EC | LF52UOA | 55 | WN | LF52UTA |
| 36 | Et | LF02PNN | 43 | EC | LF02POH | | | | | | |

### DWL56-67

| | | | DAF SB120 10.2m | | | Wrightbus Cadet | | | N26D* | | 2003 | *seating varies |
|---|---|---|---|---|---|---|---|---|---|---|---|---|

| 56 | WN | LJ03MUW | 59 | CN | LJ03MZG | 62 | CN | LJ03MYH | 65 | CN | LJ03MYM |
|---|---|---|---|---|---|---|---|---|---|---|---|
| 57 | WN | LJ03MZE | 60 | CN | LJ03MZL | 63 | CN | LJ03MYK | 66 | CN | LJ53NGX |
| 58 | CN | LJ03MZF | 61 | CN | LJ03MYG | 64 | CN | LJ03MYL | 67 | CN | LJ53NGY |

### DWS1-18

| | | | DAF SB120 9.4m | | | Wrightbus Cadet2 | | | N26D | | 2003 | |
|---|---|---|---|---|---|---|---|---|---|---|---|---|

| 1 | CN | LJ53NGZ | 6 | CN | LJ53NFT | 11 | CN | LJ53NFZ | 15 | CN | LJ53NGN |
|---|---|---|---|---|---|---|---|---|---|---|---|
| 2 | CN | LJ53NHA | 7 | CN | LJ53NFU | 12 | CN | LJ53NGE | 16 | CN | LJ53NFE |
| 3 | CN | LJ53NHB | 8 | CN | LJ53NFV | 13 | CN | LJ53NGF | 17 | CN | LJ53NFF |
| 4 | CN | LJ53NHC | 9 | CN | LJ53NFX | 14 | CN | LJ53NGG | 18 | CN | LJ53NFG |
| 5 | CN | LJ53NHD | 10 | CN | LJ53NFY | | | | | | |

### EN1-13

| | | | ADL Dart 4 8.9m | | | ADL Enviro200 | | | N26F | | 2008 | |
|---|---|---|---|---|---|---|---|---|---|---|---|---|

| 1 | LV | LJ57USS | 5 | LV | LJ57USW | 8 | LV | LJ57USZ | 11 | LV | LJ57UTC |
|---|---|---|---|---|---|---|---|---|---|---|---|
| 2 | LV | LJ57UST | 6 | LV | LJ57USX | 9 | LV | LJ57UTA | 12 | LV | LJ57UTE |
| 3 | LV | LJ57USU | 7 | LV | LJ57USY | 10 | LV | LJ57UTB | 13 | LV | LJ57UTF |
| 4 | LV | LJ57USV | | | | | | | | | |

### ENL1-9

| | | | ADL Dart 4 10.2m | | | ADL Enviro200 | | | N29D | | 2007 | |
|---|---|---|---|---|---|---|---|---|---|---|---|---|

| 1 | TC | LJ07ECW | 4 | TC | LJ07ECZ | 6 | TC | LJ07EDF | 8 | TC | LJ07EBP |
|---|---|---|---|---|---|---|---|---|---|---|---|
| 2 | TC | LJ07ECX | 5 | TC | LJ07EDC | 7 | TC | LJ07EBO | 9 | TC | LJ07EBU |
| 3 | TC | LJ07ECY | | | | | | | | | |

Alexander Dennis' Enviro 200 Dart is the most popular of the midibuses. Most are built at the Plaxton facility in Scarborough with a small number at Falkirk. Seen in Enfield, ENL12, LJ58AVV, is from the 2008 intake and is seen here heading for Potters Bar rail station. *Dave Heath*

### ENL10-48

ADL Dart 4 10.2m    ADL Enviro200    N29D    2008-09

| | | | | | | | | | | | |
|---|---|---|---|---|---|---|---|---|---|---|---|
| 10 | E | LJ58AVT | 20 | E | LJ58AVE | 30 | WN | LJ09KPR | 40 | WN | LJ09KOX |
| 11 | E | LJ58AVU | 21 | TC | LJ58AUV | 31 | WN | LJ09KPT | 41 | WN | LJ09KPA |
| 12 | E | LJ58AVV | 22 | TC | LJ58AUW | 32 | WN | LJ09KPU | 42 | WN | LJ09KPE |
| 13 | E | LJ58AVX | 23 | TC | LJ58AUX | 33 | WN | LJ09KPV | 43 | WN | LJ09KPF |
| 14 | E | LJ58AVY | 24 | TC | LJ58AUY | 34 | WN | LJ09KPX | 44 | WN | LJ09KPG |
| 15 | E | LJ58AVZ | 25 | TC | LJ58AVB | 35 | WN | LJ09KPY | 45 | WN | LJ09KPK |
| 16 | E | LJ58AWA | 26 | TC | LJ58AVC | 36 | WN | LJ09KPZ | 46 | WN | LJ09KPL |
| 17 | E | LJ58AWC | 27 | TC | LJ58AVD | 37 | WN | LJ09KRD | 47 | WN | LJ09KPN |
| 18 | E | LJ58AWF | 28 | TC | LJ58AUC | 38 | WN | LJ09KRE | 48 | WN | LJ09KPO |
| 19 | E | LJ58AWG | 29 | TC | LJ58AUE | 39 | WN | LJ09KRF | | | |

### ENL49-74

ADL Dart 4 10.2m    ADL Enviro200    N29D    2010

| | | | | | | | | | | | |
|---|---|---|---|---|---|---|---|---|---|---|---|
| 49 | DX | LJ10CSF | 56 | DX | LJ10CSX | 63 | DX | LJ60AYF | 69 | DX | LJ60AYN |
| 50 | DX | LJ10CSO | 57 | DX | LJ10CSY | 64 | DX | LJ60AYG | 70 | DX | LJ60AYO |
| 51 | DX | LJ10CSU | 58 | DX | LJ10CSZ | 65 | DX | LJ60AYH | 71 | DX | LJ60AYP |
| 52 | DX | LJ59LVL | 59 | DX | LJ10CTE | 66 | DX | LJ60AYK | 72 | DX | LJ60AYS |
| 53 | DX | LJ59LVM | 60 | DX | LJ10CTF | 67 | DX | LJ60AYL | 73 | DX | LJ60AXV |
| 54 | DX | LJ59LVN | 61 | DX | LJ10CTK | 68 | DX | LJ60AYM | 74 | DX | LJ60AXW |
| 55 | DX | LJ10CSV | 62 | DX | LJ60ATY | | | | | | |

### ENS1-14

ADL Dart 4 9.3m    ADL Enviro200    N24D    2007

| | | | | | | | | | | | |
|---|---|---|---|---|---|---|---|---|---|---|---|
| 1 | CT | LJ07EDK | 4 | CT | LJ07EDR | 9 | CT | LJ07EEA | 12 | CT | LJ07ECN |
| 2 | CT | LJ07EDL | 5 | CT | LJ07EDU | 10 | CT | LJ07EEB | 13 | CT | LJ07ECT |
| 3 | CT | LJ07EDO | 6 | CT | LJ07EDV | 11 | CT | LJ07ECF | 14 | CT | LJ07ECU |
| 4 | CT | LJ07EDP | 7 | CT | LJ07EDX | | | | | | |

### ENX1-8

ADL Dart 4 10.8m    ADL Enviro200    N    On order

| | | | | | | | | | | | |
|---|---|---|---|---|---|---|---|---|---|---|---|
| 1 | E | - | 3 | E | - | 5 | E | - | 7 | E | - |
| 2 | E | - | 4 | E | - | 6 | E | - | 8 | E | - |

### HV1-6

Volvo B5L Hybrid 10.4m    Wrightbus Gemini 2    N39/21D    2009

| | | | | | | | | | | | |
|---|---|---|---|---|---|---|---|---|---|---|---|
| 1 | AR | LJ09KRU | 3 | AR | LJ09KOH | 5 | AR | LJ09KOV | 6 | AR | LJ09KOW |
| 2 | AR | LJ09KOE | 4 | AR | LJ09KOU | | | | | | |

*The London Bus Handbook*

Development of hybrid buses continues apace. Showing the latest TfL branding for the type, and the re-introduced *bull's eye* logo is HV25, LJ60JGY allocated to Tottenham. This batch uses the Wrightbus Gemini 2 model built on Volvo's B5L chassis that was introduced in 2010. *Mark Lyons*

### HV7-26

| | | | | | | | | | | | |
|---|---|---|---|---|---|---|---|---|---|---|---|
| | | Volvo B5L Hybrid 10.4m | | | Wrightbus Gemini 2 | | N39/21D | 2010 | | | |
| 7 | AR | LJ60AWY | 12 | AR | LJ60AXD | 17 | AR | LJ60AWH | 22 | AR | LJ60AWR |
| 8 | AR | LJ60AWZ | 13 | AR | LJ60AXF | 18 | AR | LJ60AWM | 23 | AR | LJ60AWU |
| 9 | AR | LJ60AXA | 14 | AR | LJ60AXG | 19 | AR | LJ60AWN | 24 | AR | LJ60AWV |
| 10 | AR | LJ60AXB | 15 | AR | LJ60AWF | 20 | AR | LJ60AWO | 25 | AR | LJ60JGY |
| 11 | AR | LJ60AXC | 16 | AR | LJ60AWG | 21 | AR | LJ60AWP | 26 | AR | LJ60JGZ |

### HV27-46

| | | | | | | | | | | | |
|---|---|---|---|---|---|---|---|---|---|---|---|
| | | Volvo B5L Hybrid 10.4m | | | Wrightbus Gemini 2 | | N39/21D | 2011 | | | |
| 27 | SF | LJ11EFT | 32 | SF | LJ11EFY | 37 | SF | LJ11EFF | 42 | SF | LJ11EFN |
| 28 | SF | LJ11EFU | 33 | SF | LJ11EFZ | 38 | SF | LJ11EFG | 43 | SF | LJ11EFO |
| 29 | SF | LJ11EFV | 34 | SF | LJ11EGC | 39 | SF | LJ11EFK | 44 | SF | LJ11EFP |
| 30 | SF | LJ11EFW | 35 | SF | LJ11EGD | 40 | SF | LJ11EFL | 45 | SF | LJ11EFR |
| 31 | SF | LJ11EFX | 36 | SF | LJ11EFE | 41 | SF | LJ11EFM | 46 | SF | LJ11EEU |

### HW1-5

| | | | | | | | | | | | |
|---|---|---|---|---|---|---|---|---|---|---|---|
| | | Wrightbus Gemini DB250 | | | Wrightbus | | N41/24D | 2009 | | | |
| 1 | WN | LJ09KRG | 3 | WN | LJ58AVK | 4 | WN | LJ09KRK | 5 | WN | LJ09KRN |
| 2 | WN | LJ58AVG | | | | | | | | | |

### MA1-20

| | | | | | | | | | | | |
|---|---|---|---|---|---|---|---|---|---|---|---|
| | | Mercedes-Benz Citaro O530G | | | | | AB49T | 2004 | | | |
| 1 | u | BX04MWW | 4 | EC | BX04MXA | 11 | EC | BX04MXJ | 17 | EC | BX04MXR |
| 2 | EC | BX04MWY | 7 | EC | BX04MXD | 15 | EC | BX04MXN | 18 | EC | BX04MXS |
| 3 | EC | BX04MWZ | 8 | EC | BX04MXE | 16 | EC | BX04MXP | 20 | LV | BX04MXU |

### MA22-76

| | | | | | | | | | | | |
|---|---|---|---|---|---|---|---|---|---|---|---|
| | | Mercedes-Benz Citaro O530G | | | | | AB49T | 2004 | | | |
| 22 | EC | BX04MXW | 39 | EC | BX04NEJ | 53 | LV | BX04MYZ | 66 | LV | BX04NCV |
| 26 | EC | BX04MYB | 42 | LV | BX04MYJ | 55 | LV | BX04MZE | 67 | LV | BX04NCY |
| 27 | EC | BX04MYC | 43 | LV | BX04MYK | 56 | LV | BX04MZG | 68 | LV | BX04NCZ |
| 28 | EC | BX04MYD | 44 | EC | BX04MYL | 57 | LV | BX04MZJ | 69 | LV | BX04NDC |
| 29 | EC | BX04MYF | 45 | LV | BX04MYM | 58 | LV | BX04MZL | 70 | LV | BX04NDE |
| 30 | EC | BX04MYY | 46 | LV | BX04MYN | 59 | LV | BX04MZN | 71 | LV | BX04NDF |
| 31 | EC | BX04MYZ | 47 | LV | BX04MYR | 60 | LV | BX04NBK | 72 | LV | BX04NDJ |
| 34 | EC | BX04NDU | 48 | LV | BX04MYS | 61 | LV | BX04NBL | 73 | LV | BX04NDK |
| 35 | EC | BX04NDV | 49 | LV | BX04MYT | 62 | LV | BX04NCF | 74 | LV | BX04NDL |
| 36 | EC | BX04NDY | 50 | LV | BX04MYU | 63 | LV | BX04NCJ | 75 | LV | BX04NDN |
| 37 | EC | BX04NDZ | 51 | LV | BX04MYV | 64 | LV | BX04NCN | 76 | LV | BX04NEN |
| 38 | EC | BX04NEF | 52 | LV | BX04MYW | 65 | LV | BX04NCU | | | |

The number of articulated buses in London continues to decline. Many of those previously operated by Arriva have been reallocated across the group with some now based in Leicester, Runcorn and Malta where Arriva has been awarded the contract for the whole bus network. MA81, BU05VFE, is seen on route 73, and is alloacted to Lea Valley though shown carrying CT garage code. *Terry Longhurst*

### MA77-157

| | | | | | | | | | | | |
|---|---|---|---|---|---|---|---|---|---|---|---|
| | | | Mercedes-Benz Citaro O530G | | | | | AB49T | 2005 | | |
| 77 | LV | BX05UWV | 84 | LV | BU05VFG | 91 | EC | BX55FUH | 98 | EC | BX55FUV |
| 78 | LV | BX05UWW | 85 | LV | BU05VFD | 92 | EC | BX55FUJ | 99 | EC | BX55FUW |
| 79 | LV | BX05UWY | 86 | LV | BU05VFH | 93 | LV | BX55FUM | 144 | w | BX55FXH |
| 80 | LV | BX05UWZ | 87 | LV | BU05VFJ | 94 | EC | BX55FUO | 153 | w | BX55FXT |
| 81 | LV | BU05VFE | 88 | LV | BX05UXD | 95 | EC | BX55FUP | 155 | w | BX55FXV |
| 82 | LV | BU05VFF | 89 | LV | BX55FWA | 96 | EC | BX55FUT | 156 | w | BX55FXW |
| 83 | LV | BX05UXC | 90 | LV | BX55FWB | 97 | EC | BX55FUU | 157 | w | BX55FXY |

### PDL19-38

| | | | | | | | | | | | |
|---|---|---|---|---|---|---|---|---|---|---|---|
| | | | Dennis Dart SLF 10.7m | | | Plaxton Pointer 2 | | N31D | 2000 | | |
| 19 | TH | X519GGO | 24 | AE | X524GGO | 29 | AE | X529GGO | 34 | AE | X534GGO |
| 20 | TH | X471GGO | 25 | AE | X475GGO | 30 | AE | X481GGO | 35 | AE | X485GGO |
| 21 | TH | X521GGO | 26 | AE | X526GGO | 31 | AE | X531GGO | 36 | AE | X536GGO |
| 22 | TH | X522GGO | 27 | AE | X527GGO | 32 | AE | X532GGO | 37 | AE | X537GGO |
| 23 | AE | X523GGO | 28 | AE | X478GGO | 33 | AE | X533GGO | 38 | AE | X538GGO |

### PDL45-49

| | | | | | | | | | | | |
|---|---|---|---|---|---|---|---|---|---|---|---|
| | | | Dennis Dart SLF 8.8m | | | Plaxton Pointer MPD | | N23F* | 2001 | *seating varies | |
| 45 | AR | X546GGO | 47 | AR | X247PGT | 48 | AR | X248PGT | 49 | AR | X249PGT |
| 46 | AR | X246PGT | | | | | | | | | |

### PDL50-69

| | | | | | | | | | | | |
|---|---|---|---|---|---|---|---|---|---|---|---|
| | | | Dennis Dart SLF 8.8m | | | Plaxton Pointer MPD | | N23F* | 2001 | *seating varies | |
| 50 | AR | LJ51DAA | 55 | DX | LJ51DBV | 60 | DX | LJ51DCF | 65 | u | LJ51DCY |
| 51 | AR | LJ51DAO | 56 | DX | LJ51DBX | 61 | DX | LJ51DCO | 66 | u | LJ51DCZ |
| 52 | DX | LJ51DAU | 57 | DX | LJ51DBY | 62 | u | LJ51DCU | 67 | u | LJ51DDA |
| 53 | DX | LJ51DBO | 58 | DX | LJ51DBZ | 63 | u | LJ51DCV | 68 | u | LJ51DDE |
| 54 | DX | LJ51DBU | 59 | DX | LJ51DCE | 64 | u | LJ51DCX | 69 | LV | LJ51DDF |

### PDL70-94

| | | | | | | | | | | | |
|---|---|---|---|---|---|---|---|---|---|---|---|
| | | | TransBus Dart 8.8m | | | TransBus Mini Pointer | | N29F* | 2002 | *seating varies | |
| 70 | EC | LF02PTZ | 77 | EC | LF52UON | 83 | EC | LF52URZ | 89 | EC | LF52USJ |
| 71 | EC | LF52UOG | 78 | EC | LF52UOO | 84 | EC | LF52USB | 90 | EC | LF52USL |
| 72 | EC | LF52UOH | 79 | EC | LF52UOP | 85 | EC | LF52USC | 91 | EC | LF52URN |
| 73 | EC | LF52UOJ | 80 | EC | LF52UOR | 86 | EC | LF52USD | 92 | EC | LF52URO |
| 74 | EC | LF52UOK | 81 | EC | LF52UNV | 87 | EC | LF52USG | 93 | EC | LF52URP |
| 75 | EC | LF52UOL | 82 | EC | LF52URY | 88 | EC | LF52USH | 94 | EC | LF52URR |
| 76 | EC | LF52UOM | | | | | | | | | |

Arriva London retains a few Routemaster buses in its heritage fleet. April 2011 in Norbury and RM2217, CUV217C, was working a special anniversary event. *Dave Heath*

### PDL95-116      ADL Dart 9.3m      ADL Pointer      N27D      2005

| | | | | | | | | | | |
|---|---|---|---|---|---|---|---|---|---|---|
| 95 | EC | LJ54BCX | 101 | LV | LJ54BBF | 107 | LV | LJ54LHG | 112 | EC | LJ54LHN |
| 96 | EC | LJ54BAA | 102 | LV | LJ54BBK | 108 | LV | LJ54LHH | 113 | EC | LJ54LHO |
| 97 | EC | LJ54BAO | 103 | LV | LJ54BBN | 109 | LV | LJ54LHK | 114 | EC | LJ54LHP |
| 98 | CN | LJ54BAU | 104 | LV | LJ54BBO | 110 | EC | LJ54LHL | 115 | CT | LJ54LHR |
| 99 | EC | LJ54BAV | 105 | LV | LJ54BBU | 111 | EC | LJ54LHM | 116 | CT | LJ54LGV |
| 100 | EC | LJ54BBE | 106 | LV | LJ54LHF | | | | | |

### PDL117-123      ADL Dart 10.1m      ADL Pointer      N29D      2005

| | | | | | | | | | | |
|---|---|---|---|---|---|---|---|---|---|---|
| 117 | TC | LJ05GOP | 119 | TC | LJ05GOX | 121 | TC | LJ05GPK | 123 | TC | LJ05GPU |
| 118 | TC | LJ05GOU | 120 | TC | LJ05GPF | 122 | TC | LJ05GPO | | | |

### PDL124-136      ADL Dart 9.3m      ADL Pointer      N24D      2006

| | | | | | | | | | | |
|---|---|---|---|---|---|---|---|---|---|---|
| 124 | CN | LJ56APZ | 128 | CN | LJ56ARX | 131 | CN | LJ56ASU | 134 | CN | LJ56AOW |
| 125 | CN | LJ56ARF | 129 | CN | LJ56ARZ | 132 | CN | LJ56ASV | 135 | CN | LJ56AOX |
| 126 | CN | LJ56ARO | 130 | CN | LJ56ASO | 133 | CN | LJ56ASX | 136 | CN | LJ56AOY |
| 127 | CN | LJ56ARU | | | | | | | | |

### PDL137-145      ADL Dart 8.8m      ADL Mini Pointer      N23F      2006-07      Arriva Southern Counties, '11

| | | | | | | | | | | |
|---|---|---|---|---|---|---|---|---|---|---|
| 137 | LV | SN06BPE | 140 | E | SN06BPU | 142 | E | SN06BPX | 144 | E | SN06BPZ |
| 138 | LV | SN06BPF | 141 | E | SN06BPV | 143 | E | SN06BPY | 145 | E | SN06BRF |
| 139 | LV | SN06BPK | | | | | | | | |

| | | | | | | |
|---|---|---|---|---|---|---|
| RM5 | N | VLT5 | AEC Routemaster R2RH | Park Royal | B36/28R | 1959 |
| RM6 | N | VLT6 | AEC Routemaster R2RH | Park Royal | B36/28R | 1959 |
| RML901 | u | WLT901 | AEC Routemaster R2RH/1 | Park Royal | B40/32R | 1963 |
| RM1124 | u | VYJ806 | AEC Routemaster R2RH | Park Royal | B36/28R | 1965 |
| RMC1453 | N | 453CLT | AEC Routemaster R2RH | Park Royal | B36/28R | 1962 |
| RMC1464 | N | 464CLT | AEC Routemaster R2RH | Park Royal | O36/28R | 1962 |
| RM2217 | N | CUV217C | AEC Routemaster R2RH | Park Royal | B36/28R | 1965 |
| RML2355 | N | CUV335C | AEC Routemaster R2RH/1 | Park Royal | B40/32R | 1965 |

Arriva London uses the prefix T for Alexander Dennis Enviro 400-bodied Trident 2s of which almost two hundred are now in service. Recent arrival T113, LJ59LYS, is seen in Brixton. *Dave Heath*

### T1-65

| | | ADL Trident 2 10.1m | | | ADL Enviro 400 | | | N41/26D | | 2008 |
|---|---|---|---|---|---|---|---|---|---|---|
| 1 | AD | LJ08CVS | 18 | DX | LJ08CVO | 34 | AD | LJ08CTZ | 50 | TC | LJ08CTO |
| 2 | AD | LJ08CVT | 19 | DX | 519CLT | 35 | AD | LJ08CUA | 51 | TC | LJ08CYC |
| 3 | AD | LJ08CVU | 20 | DX | LJ08CVR | 36 | AD | LJ08CUE | 52 | TC | LJ08CYE |
| 4 | AD | LJ08CVV | 21 | DX | LJ08CUU | 37 | AD | LJ08CUG | 53 | TC | LJ08CYF |
| 5 | AD | 205CLT | 22 | DX | LJ08CUV | 38 | AD | LJ08CUH | 54 | TC | LJ08CYG |
| 6 | AD | LJ08CVX | 23 | DX | LJ08CUW | 39 | AD | LJ08CUK | 55 | TC | LJ08CYH |
| 7 | AD | LJ08CVY | 24 | DX | 324CLT | 40 | AD | LJ08CUO | 56 | TC | LJ08CYK |
| 8 | AD | LJ08CVZ | 25 | DX | LJ08CUY | 41 | AD | LJ08CSO | 57 | TC | LJ08CYL |
| 9 | AD | LJ08CWA | 26 | DX | LJ08CVA | 42 | AD | LJ08CSU | 58 | TC | LJ08CYO |
| 10 | AD | LJ08CWC | 27 | AD | LJ08CVB | 43 | AD | LJ08CSV | 59 | TC | LJ08CYP |
| 11 | AD | LJ08CVF | 28 | AD | LJ08CVC | 44 | AD | LJ08CSX | 60 | TC | LJ08CYS |
| 12 | DX | LJ08CVG | 29 | AD | LJ08CVD | 45 | TC | LJ08CSY | 61 | TC | LJ08CXR |
| 13 | DX | LJ08CVH | 30 | AD | 330CLT | 46 | TC | LJ08CSZ | 62 | TC | LJ08CXS |
| 14 | DX | LJ08CVK | 31 | AD | LJ08CTV | 47 | TC | LJ08CTE | 63 | TC | LJ08CXT |
| 15 | DX | LJ08CVL | 32 | AD | LJ08CTX | 48 | TC | LJ08CTF | 64 | TC | LJ08CXU |
| 16 | DX | LJ08CVM | 33 | AD | LJ08CTY | 49 | TC | LJ08CTK | 65 | TC | LJ08CXV |
| 17 | DX | 217CLT | | | | | | | | |

### T66-83

| | | ADL Trident 2 10.1m | | | ADL Enviro 400 | | | N41/26D | | 2009 |
|---|---|---|---|---|---|---|---|---|---|---|
| 66 | AE | LJ59ACY | 71 | AE | LJ59ADZ | 76 | AE | LJ59ABO | 80 | AE | LJ59ABZ |
| 67 | AE | LJ59ACZ | 72 | AE | LJ59AEA | 77 | AE | LJ59ABU | 81 | AE | LJ59ACF |
| 68 | AE | LJ59ADO | 73 | AE | LJ59ABF | 78 | AE | LJ59ABV | 82 | AE | LJ59ACO |
| 69 | AE | LJ59ADV | 74 | AE | LJ59ABK | 79 | AE | LJ59ABX | 83 | AE | LJ59AAE |
| 70 | AE | 70CLT | 75 | AE | LJ59ABN | | | | | |

### T84-117

| | | ADL Trident 2 10.1m | | | ADL Enviro 400 | | | N41/26D | | 2009-10 |
|---|---|---|---|---|---|---|---|---|---|---|
| 84 | N | LJ59LZD | 93 | N | 593CLT | 102 | N | LJ59LZB | 110 | N | LJ59LYK |
| 85 | N | 185CLT | 94 | N | LJ59LYT | 103 | N | LJ59LZC | 111 | N | LJ59LYO |
| 86 | N | LJ59LZF | 95 | N | LJ59LYU | 104 | N | LJ59LYA | 112 | N | LJ59LYP |
| 87 | N | LJ59LZG | 96 | N | LJ59LYV | 105 | N | LJ59LYC | 113 | N | LJ59LYS |
| 88 | N | LJ59LZH | 97 | N | LJ59LYW | 106 | N | LJ59LYD | 114 | N | LJ59LXP |
| 89 | N | LJ59LZK | 98 | N | 398CLT | 107 | N | LJ59LYF | 115 | N | LJ59LXR |
| 90 | N | LJ59LZL | 99 | N | LJ59LYY | 108 | N | LJ59LYG | 116 | N | LJ59LXS |
| 91 | N | LJ59LZM | 100 | N | LJ59LYZ | 109 | N | LJ59LYH | 117 | N | LJ59LXT |
| 92 | N | LJ59LZN | 101 | N | LJ59LZA | | | | | |

### T118-144

ADL Trident 2 10.1m — ADL Enviro 400 — N41/26D — 2010

| 118 | TC | LJ10HVO | 125 | TH | LJ10HVE | 132 | TH | LJ10HUA | 139 | TH | LJ10HUY |
|---|---|---|---|---|---|---|---|---|---|---|---|
| 119 | TC | LJ10HVP | 126 | TH | LJ10HVF | 133 | TH | LJ10HUB | 140 | TH | LJ10HUZ |
| 120 | TC | LJ10HVR | 127 | TH | LJ10HVG | 134 | TH | LJ10HUK | 141 | TH | LJ10HTT |
| 121 | TC | LJ10HVA | 128 | TH | LJ10HVH | 135 | TH | LJ10HUO | 142 | TH | LJ10HTU |
| 122 | TH | LJ10HVB | 129 | TH | LJ10HVK | 136 | TH | LJ10HUP | 143 | TH | LJ10HTV |
| 123 | TH | LJ10HVC | 130 | TH | LJ10HVL | 137 | TH | LJ10HUU | 144 | TH | LJ10HTX |
| 124 | TH | LJ10HVD | 131 | TH | LJ10HTZ | 138 | TH | LJ10HUV | | | |

### T145-193

ADL Trident 2 10.1m — ADL Enviro 400 — N41/26D — 2010

| 145 | LV | LJ60AVR | 158 | LV | LJ60AWF | 170 | AE | LJ60AUV | 182 | DX | LJ60AUL |
|---|---|---|---|---|---|---|---|---|---|---|---|
| 146 | LV | LJ60AVT | 159 | LV | LJ60AWG | 171 | AE | LJ60AUW | 183 | DX | LJ60AUM |
| 147 | LV | LJ60AVU | 160 | LV | LJ60AWK | 172 | AE | LJ60AUX | 184 | DX | LJ60AUN |
| 148 | LV | LJ60AVV | 161 | LV | LJ60AWL | 173 | AE | LJ60AUY | 185 | DX | LJ60ASX |
| 149 | LV | LJ60AVW | 162 | LV | LJ60AWN | 174 | AE | LJ60AVB | 186 | DX | LJ60ASZ |
| 150 | LV | LJ60AVX | 163 | LV | LJ60AWO | 175 | AE | LJ60ATZ | 187 | DX | LJ60ATF |
| 151 | LV | LJ60AVY | 164 | LV | LJ60AWP | 176 | AE | LJ60AUA | 188 | DX | LJ60ATK |
| 152 | LV | LJ60AVZ | 165 | LV | LJ60AUO | 177 | AE | LJ60AUC | 189 | DX | LJ60ATN |
| 153 | LV | LJ60AWA | 166 | LV | LJ60AUP | 178 | AE | LJ60AUE | 190 | DX | LJ60ATO |
| 154 | LV | LJ60AWB | 167 | LV | LJ60AUR | 179 | AE | LJ60AUF | 191 | DX | LJ60ATU |
| 155 | LV | LJ60AWC | 168 | LV | LJ60AUT | 180 | DX | LJ60AUH | 192 | DX | LJ60ATV |
| 156 | LV | LJ60AWD | 169 | AE | LJ60AUU | 181 | DX | LJ60AUK | 193 | DX | LJ60ATX |
| 157 | LV | LJ60AWE | | | | | | | | | |

### VLA1-55

Volvo B7TL 10.6m — TransBus ALX400 4.4m — N49/21D — 2003

| 1 | N | LJ03MYP | 15 | N | LJ03MXH | 29 | N | LJ53BDO | 43 | N | LJ53BCV |
|---|---|---|---|---|---|---|---|---|---|---|---|
| 2 | N | LJ03MYR | 16 | N | LJ03MXK | 30 | N | LJ53BDU | 44 | N | LJ53BCX |
| 3 | N | LJ03MYS | 17 | N | LJ03MXL | 31 | N | LJ53BDV | 45 | N | LJ53BCY |
| 4 | N | LJ03MYT | 18 | N | LJ03MXM | 32 | N | LJ53BDX | 46 | N | LJ53BAA |
| 5 | N | LJ03MXV | 19 | N | LJ03MXN | 33 | N | LJ53BDY | 47 | N | LJ53BAO |
| 6 | N | LJ03MXW | 20 | N | LJ03MXP | 34 | N | LJ53BDZ | 48 | N | LJ53BAU |
| 7 | N | LJ03MXX | 21 | N | LJ53BFK | 35 | N | LJ53BEO | 49 | N | LJ53BAV |
| 8 | N | LJ03MXY | 22 | N | LJ53BFL | 36 | N | LJ53BBV | 50 | N | LJ53BBE |
| 9 | N | LJ03MXZ | 23 | N | LJ53BFM | 37 | N | LJ53BBX | 51 | N | LJ53BBF |
| 10 | N | LJ03MYA | 24 | N | LJ53BFN | 38 | N | LJ53BBZ | 52 | N | LJ53BBK |
| 11 | N | LJ03MYB | 25 | N | LJ53BFO | 39 | N | LJ53BCF | 53 | N | LJ53BBN |
| 12 | N | LJ03MYC | 26 | N | LJ53BCZ | 40 | N | LJ53BCK | 54 | N | LJ53BBO |
| 13 | N | LJ03MYD | 27 | N | LJ53BDE | 41 | N | LJ53BCO | 55 | N | LJ53BBU |
| 14 | N | LJ03MYF | 28 | N | LJ53BDF | 42 | N | LJ53BCU | | | |

**Allocated to Barking depot, T192, LJ60ATV, is seen in Ilford while heading for Becontree Heath on route 150. A further seventy-sight Enviro 400s are on order for January 2012.** *Mark Lyons*

### VLA56-69

| | | | Volvo B7TL 10.6m | | TransBus ALX400 4.4m | N49/22D | 2004 |
|---|---|---|---|---|---|---|---|

| 56 | N | LJ04LFL | 60 | N | LJ04LFR | 64 | N | LJ04YWT | 67 | N | LJ04YWW |
|---|---|---|---|---|---|---|---|---|---|---|---|
| 57 | N | LJ04LFM | 61 | N | LJ04LFS | 65 | N | LJ04YWU | 68 | N | LJ04YWX |
| 58 | N | LJ04LFN | 62 | N | LJ04LFT | 66 | N | LJ04YWV | 69 | N | LJ04YWY |
| 59 | N | LJ04LFP | 63 | N | LJ04YWS | | | | | | |

### VLA70-73

| | | | Volvo B7TL 10.6m | | TransBus ALX400 4.4m | N49/22D | 2004 |
|---|---|---|---|---|---|---|---|

| 70 | N | LJ04YWZ | 71 | N | LJ04YXA | 72 | N | LJ04YXB | 73 | N | LJ04YWE |
|---|---|---|---|---|---|---|---|---|---|---|---|

### VLA74-128

| | | | Volvo B7TL 10.1m | | ADL ALX400 | N45/19D | 2004-05 |
|---|---|---|---|---|---|---|---|

| 74 | AR | LJ54BGO | 88 | AR | LJ54BDF | 102 | AR | LJ54BCU | 116 | N | LJ54BKG |
|---|---|---|---|---|---|---|---|---|---|---|---|
| 75 | AR | LJ54BEO | 89 | AR | LJ54BDO | 103 | AR | LJ54BCV | 117 | N | LJ54BKK |
| 76 | AR | LJ54BEU | 90 | AR | LJ54BDU | 104 | N | LJ05BKY | 118 | N | LJ54BKL |
| 77 | AR | LJ54BFA | 91 | AR | LJ54BDV | 105 | N | LJ05BKZ | 119 | N | LJ54BKN |
| 78 | AR | LJ54BFE | 92 | AR | LJ54BDX | 106 | N | LJ05BLF | 120 | N | LJ54BKO |
| 79 | AR | LJ54BFF | 93 | AR | LJ54BDY | 107 | N | LJ05BLK | 121 | N | LJ54BKU |
| 80 | AR | LJ54BFK | 94 | AR | LJ54BDZ | 108 | N | LJ05BLN | 122 | BN | LJ54BKV |
| 81 | AR | LJ54BFL | 95 | AR | LJ54BBV | 109 | N | LJ05BLV | 123 | BN | LJ54BKX |
| 82 | AR | LJ54BFM | 96 | AR | LJ54BBX | 110 | N | LJ05BLX | 124 | BN | LJ54BJE |
| 83 | AR | LJ54BFN | 97 | AR | LJ54BBZ | 111 | N | LJ05BLY | 125 | BN | LJ54BJF |
| 84 | AR | LJ54BFO | 98 | AR | LJ54BCE | 112 | N | LJ05BMO | 126 | BN | LJ54BJK |
| 85 | AR | LJ54BCY | 99 | AR | LJ54BCF | 113 | N | LJ05BMU | 127 | BN | LJ54BJO |
| 86 | AR | LJ54BCZ | 100 | AR | LJ54BCK | 114 | N | LJ05BKD | 128 | BN | LJ54BJU |
| 87 | AR | LJ54BDE | 101 | AR | LJ54BCO | 115 | N | LJ05BKF | | | |

### VLA129-143

| | | | Volvo B7TL 10.1m | | ADL ALX400 | N45/19D | 2005 |
|---|---|---|---|---|---|---|---|

| 129 | DX | LJ05GLZ | 133 | DX | LJ05GPY | 137 | DX | LJ05GRU | 141 | DX | LJ05GSU |
|---|---|---|---|---|---|---|---|---|---|---|---|
| 130 | DX | LJ05GME | 134 | DX | LJ05GPZ | 138 | DX | LJ05GRX | 142 | DX | LJ55BTE |
| 131 | DX | LJ05GMF | 135 | DX | LJ05GRF | 139 | DX | LJ05GRZ | 143 | DX | LJ55BTF |
| 132 | DX | LJ05GPX | 136 | DX | LJ05GRK | 140 | DX | LJ05GSO | | | |

### VLA144-179

| | | | Volvo B7TL 10.1m | | ADL ALX400 | N45/19D | 2005 |
|---|---|---|---|---|---|---|---|

| 144 | BN | LJ55BTO | 153 | BN | LJ55BRV | 162 | BN | LJ55BUP | 171 | BN | LJ55BUZ |
|---|---|---|---|---|---|---|---|---|---|---|---|
| 145 | BN | LJ55BTU | 154 | BN | LJ55BRX | 163 | BN | LJ55BUR | 172 | BN | LJ55BVD |
| 146 | BN | LJ55BTV | 155 | BN | LJ55BRZ | 164 | BN | LJ55BUS | 173 | BN | LJ55BVE |
| 147 | BN | LJ55BTX | 156 | BN | LJ55BSO | 165 | BN | LJ55BUT | 174 | BN | LJ55BVF |
| 148 | BN | LJ55BTY | 157 | BN | LJ55BSU | 166 | BN | LJ55BUU | 175 | BN | LJ55BVG |
| 149 | BN | LJ55BTZ | 158 | BN | LJ55BSV | 167 | BN | LJ55BUV | 176 | BN | LJ55BVH |
| 150 | BN | LJ55BUA | 159 | BN | LJ55BSX | 168 | BN | LJ55BUW | 177 | BN | LJ55BVK |
| 151 | BN | LJ55BUE | 160 | BN | LJ55BSY | 169 | BN | LJ55BUX | 178 | BN | LJ55BVL |
| 152 | BN | LJ55BPZ | 161 | BN | LJ55BSZ | 170 | BN | LJ55BUY | 179 | BN | LJ55BVM |

**VLA88, LJ54BDF, was seen on Route 168 which is normally worked by twenty T or VLW types from Ash Grove garage. This near-side view shows the dual-door arrangement that is mostly confined to London operations in Britain.**
*Terry Longhurst*

Wrightbus Eclipse Gemini bodied Volvo buses were supplied to Arriva London between 2001 and 2003. Illustrating the model is VLW58, LF02PTU, seen on route 141 at Manor House. *Dave Heath*

## VLW7-41     Volvo B7TL 10.1m     Wrightbus Eclipse Gemini    N41/21D*    2001-02    *seating varies

| | | | | | | | | | | | |
|---|---|---|---|---|---|---|---|---|---|---|---|
| 7 | WN | LJ51DFL | 16 | WN | LJ51DGE | 25 | WN | LJ51DHC | 34 | WN | LJ51DHP |
| 8 | WN | LJ51DFN | 17 | WN | LJ51DGF | 26 | WN | LJ51DHD | 35 | WN | LJ51DHV |
| 9 | WN | LJ51DFO | 18 | WN | LJ51DGO | 27 | WN | VLT27 | 36 | WN | LJ51DHX |
| 10 | WN | LJ51DFP | 19 | WN | LJ51DGU | 28 | WN | LJ51DHF | 37 | WN | LJ51DHY |
| 11 | WN | LJ51DFU | 20 | WN | LJ51DGV | 29 | WN | LJ51DHG | 38 | WN | LJ51DHZ |
| 12 | WN | VLT12 | 21 | WN | LJ51DGX | 30 | WN | LJ51DHK | 39 | WN | LJ51DJD |
| 13 | WN | LJ51DFX | 22 | WN | LJ51DGY | 31 | WN | LJ51DHL | 40 | WN | LJ51DJE |
| 14 | WN | LJ51DFY | 23 | WN | LJ51DGZ | 32 | WN | VLT32 | 41 | WN | LJ51OSK |
| 15 | WN | LJ51DFZ | 24 | WN | LJ51DHA | 33 | WN | LJ51DHO | | | |

## VLW42-104     Volvo B7TL 10.1m     Wrightbus Eclipse Gemini    N41/21D*    2002-03    *seating varies

| | | | | | | | | | | | |
|---|---|---|---|---|---|---|---|---|---|---|---|
| 42 | WN | LF02PKO | 58 | WN | LF02PTU | 74 | WN | LF52UTM | 90 | CT | LF52URA |
| 43 | WN | LF02PKU | 59 | WN | LF02PTX | 75 | WN | LF52USM | 91 | CT | LF52UPD |
| 44 | WN | LF02PKV | 60 | WN | LF02PTY | 76 | WN | LF52USN | 92 | CT | WLT892 |
| 45 | WN | LF02PKX | 61 | WN | LF02PVE | 77 | WN | LF52USO | 93 | CT | LF52UPG |
| 46 | WN | LF02PKY | 62 | WN | LF02PVJ | 78 | WN | LF52USS | 94 | CT | LF52UPH |
| 47 | WN | VLT47 | 63 | WN | LF02PVK | 79 | WN | LF52UST | 95 | CT | WLT895 |
| 48 | WN | LF02PLJ | 64 | WN | LF02PVL | 80 | WN | LF52USU | 96 | CT | LF52UPK |
| 49 | WN | LF02PLN | 65 | WN | LF02PVN | 81 | WN | LF52USV | 97 | E | WLT897 |
| 50 | WN | LF02PLO | 66 | WN | LF02PVO | 82 | WN | LF52USW | 98 | E | LF52UPM |
| 51 | WN | WLT751 | 67 | WN | LF52UTC | 83 | WN | LF52USX | 99 | E | LG52DDA |
| 52 | WN | LF02PSO | 68 | WN | LF52UTE | 84 | WN | LF52USY | 100 | E | LG52DDE |
| 53 | WN | LF02PSU | 69 | WN | LF52USE | 85 | WN | LF52UPV | 101 | E | LG52DDF |
| 54 | WN | WLT554 | 70 | WN | LF52UTG | 86 | CT | LF52UPW | 102 | E | LG52DDJ |
| 55 | WN | LF02PSY | 71 | WN | LF52UTH | 87 | CT | LF52UPX | 103 | E | LG52DDK |
| 56 | WN | LF02PSZ | 72 | WN | WLT372 | 88 | CT | WLT888 | 104 | DX | LG52DDL |
| 57 | WN | LF02PTO | 73 | WN | LF52UTL | 89 | CT | LF52UPZ | | | |

## VLW105-179    Volvo B7TL 10.1m    Wrightbus Eclipse Gemini    N41/21D*    2002-03    *seating varies

| | | | | | | | | | | | | | | |
|---|---|---|---|---|---|---|---|---|---|---|---|---|---|---|
| 105 | DX | LJ03MHU | 124 | E | LF52UOX | 143 | SF | LJ03MFA | 162 | SF | LJ03MRX |
| 106 | DX | LJ03MHV | 125 | E | LF52UOY | 144 | SF | LJ03MFE | 163 | SF | LJ03MRY |
| 107 | DX | LJ03MHX | 126 | AE | LF52UPA | 145 | SF | LJ03MFF | 164 | SF | LJ03MSU |
| 108 | DX | LJ03MHY | 127 | AE | LF52UPB | 146 | SF | LJ03MFK | 165 | SF | LJ03MSV |
| 109 | DX | LJ03MHZ | 128 | AE | LF52UPC | 147 | SF | LJ03MBF | 166 | SF | LJ03MSX |
| 110 | DX | LJ03MJE | 129 | AE | LG52DAA | 148 | SF | LJ03MBU | 167 | SF | LJ03MMU |
| 111 | DX | LJ03MJF | 130 | AE | LJ03MGZ | 149 | SF | LJ03MBV | 168 | SF | LJ03MMV |
| 112 | DX | LJ03MJK | 131 | AE | LJ03MHA | 150 | SF | LJ03MBX | 169 | SF | LJ03MMX |
| 113 | DX | LJ03MJU | 132 | AE | LJ03MHE | 151 | SF | LJ03MBY | 170 | SF | LJ03MOA |
| 114 | DX | LJ03MJV | 133 | AE | LJ03MHF | 152 | SF | LJ03MDE | 171 | SF | LJ03MOF |
| 115 | DX | LJ03MGX | 134 | AE | LJ03MHK | 153 | SF | LJ03MDF | 172 | SF | LJ03MOV |
| 116 | DX | LJ03MGY | 135 | AE | LJ03MHL | 154 | SF | LJ03MDK | 173 | SF | VLT173 |
| 117 | E | LF52UPN | 136 | AE | LJ03MHM | 155 | SF | LJ03MDN | 174 | SF | LJ03MPF |
| 118 | E | LF52UPO | 137 | AE | LJ03MHN | 156 | SF | LJ03MDU | 175 | SF | LJ03MPU |
| 119 | E | LF52UOS | 138 | SF | LJ03MFN | 157 | SF | LJ03MPX | 176 | SF | LJ03MPV |
| 120 | E | LF52UOT | 139 | SF | LJ03MFP | 158 | SF | LJ03MPY | 177 | SF | LJ03MLL |
| 121 | E | LF52UOU | 140 | SF | LJ03MFU | 159 | SF | LJ03MPZ | 178 | SF | LJ03MLN |
| 122 | E | LF52UOV | 141 | SF | LJ03MFV | 160 | SF | LJ03MRU | 179 | SF | LJ03MLV |
| 123 | E | LF52UOW | 142 | SF | LJ03MEV | 161 | SF | LJ03MRV | | | |

## VLW180-199    Volvo B7TL 10.6m    Wrightbus Eclipse Gemini    N45/24D    2003

| | | | | | | | | | | | |
|---|---|---|---|---|---|---|---|---|---|---|---|
| 180 | SF | LJ03MLX | 185 | SF | LJ03MMF | 190 | SF | LJ03MXR | 195 | SF | LJ53BEU |
| 181 | SF | LJ03MLY | 186 | SF | LJ03MMK | 191 | SF | LJ03MXS | 196 | SF | LJ53BEY |
| 182 | SF | LJ03MLZ | 187 | AE | LJ03MKM | 192 | SF | LJ03MXT | 197 | SF | LJ53BFA |
| 183 | SF | LJ03MMA | 188 | SF | LJ03MKN | 193 | SF | LJ03MXU | 198 | SF | LJ53BFE |
| 184 | SF | LJ03MME | 189 | SF | LJ03MYN | 194 | SF | LJ03MWX | 199 | SF | LJ53BFF |

Special event vehicles:

Previous registrations:

| | | | |
|---|---|---|---|
| 70CLT | LJ59ADX | LJ53MHX | LJ53MHX, WLT531 |
| 124CLT | 124CLT, VYJ806 | T324FGN | T324FGN, 99D53451 |
| 185CLT | LJ59LZE | T325FGN | T325FGN, 99D53440 |
| 205CLT | LJ08CVW | V423DGT | V435DGT |
| 217CLT | LJ08CVN | V435DGT | V423DGT |
| 319CLT | LJ05BMY | VLT12 | LJ51DFV |
| 324CLT | LJ08CUX | VLT27 | LJ51DHE |
| 330CLT | LJ08CVE | VLT32 | LJ51DHN |
| 361CLT | LJ59GTZ | VLT47 | LF02PKZ |
| 398CLT | LJ59LYX | VLT173 | LJ03MPE |
| 519CLT | LJ08CVP | VLT244 | LJ53NHM |
| 593CLT | LJ59LZO | VLT295 | LJ54BFU |
| 656DYE | LJ04LFA | WLT348 | LJ53NGO |
| 725DYE | LJ53BGE | WLT372 | LF52UTJ |
| 734DYE | LJ53NJE | WLT385 | LJ04LFY |
| 801DYE | LJ03MWM | WLT531 | -- |
| 822DYE | LJ53BFV | WLT554 | LF02PSX |
| BU05VFD | BU05VFD, 185CLT | WLT664 | LJ04LDE |
| BX04MXB | BX04MXB, 205CLT | WLT676 | from new |
| BX04MXR | BX04MXR, 217CLT | WLT719 | LJ53NHU |
| BX04NBL | BX04NBL, 361CLT | WLT751 | LF02PRZ |
| BX04NDE | BX04NDE, 70CLT | WLT807 | LJ03MVU |
| BX05UWZ | BX05UWZ, 430CLT | WLT888 | LF52VPY |
| BX55FUM | BX55FUM, 593CLT | WLT892 | LF52UPE |
| BX55FUV | BX55FUV, 398CLT | WLT895 | LF52UPJ |
| LF52USE | LF52USE, VLT25 | WLT897 | LF52UPL |
| LJ03MMX | LJ03MMX, VLT25 | WLT970 | LJ04LDV |
| LJ08CVY | LJ08CVY, 7CLT | WLT997 | LJ54BFX |

## Depots and allocations:

### Barking (Ripple Road, IG11 0ST) - DX

| Dart | PDL52 | PDL53 | PDL54 | PDL55 | PDL56 | PDL57 | PDL58 | PDL59 |
|---|---|---|---|---|---|---|---|---|
| | PDL60 | PDL61 | | | | | | |
| Dart 4 | ENL49 | ENL50 | ENL51 | ENL52 | ENL53 | ENL54 | ENL55 | ENL56 |
| | ENL57 | ENL58 | ENL59 | ENL60 | ENL61 | ENL62 | ENL63 | ENL64 |
| | ENL65 | ENL66 | ENL67 | ENL68 | ENL69 | ENL70 | ENL71 | ENL72 |
| | ENL73 | ENL74 | | | | | | |
| Volvo B7TL | VLA129 | VLA130 | VLA131 | VLA132 | VLA133 | VLA134 | VLA135 | VLA136 |
| | VLA137 | VLA138 | VLA139 | VLA140 | VLA141 | VLA142 | VLA143 | VLW105 |
| | VLW106 | VLW107 | VLW108 | VLW109 | VLW110 | VLW111 | VLW112 | VLW113 |
| | VLW114 | VLW115 | VLW116 | | | | | |
| Trident 2 | T12 | T13 | T14 | T15 | T16 | T17 | T18 | T19 |
| | T20 | T21 | T22 | T23 | T24 | T25 | T26 | T180 |
| | T181 | T182 | T183 | T184 | T185 | T186 | T187 | T188 |
| | T189 | T190 | T191 | T192 | T193 | | | |

### Brixton (Streatham Hill, SW2 4TB) - BN

*Outstation: Battersea*

| DB250 | DLA205 | DLA206 | DLA207 | DLA208 | DLA209 | DLA212 | DLA213 | DLA236 |
|---|---|---|---|---|---|---|---|---|
| | DAL270 | DLA271 | DLA290 | DLA311 | DLA312 | DLA313 | DLA314 | DLA315 |
| | DLA316 | DLA317 | DLA318 | DLA319 | DW55 | DW56 | DW57 | DW58 |
| | DW59 | DW60 | DW61 | DW62 | DW63 | DW64 | DW65 | DW66 |
| | DW67 | DW68 | DW69 | DW70 | DW71 | DW72 | DW73 | DW74 |
| | DW75 | DW76 | DW77 | DW78 | DW79 | DW80 | DW81 | DW82 |
| | DW83 | DW84 | DW85 | DW86 | DW87 | DW88 | DW89 | DW90 |
| | DW91 | DW92 | DW93 | DW102 | DW103 | DW104 | DW105 | DW106 |
| | DW107 | DW108 | DW109 | DW110 | DW111 | DW112 | DW113 | DW114 |
| | DW115 | DW116 | DW117 | DW118 | DW119 | DW120 | DW121 | DW122 |
| | DW123 | DW124 | DW125 | DW126 | DW127 | DW128 | DW129 | DW130 |
| | DW131 | DW132 | DW133 | | | | | |
| DB300 | DW280 | DW281 | DW282 | DW283 | DW284 | DW285 | DW286 | DW287 |
| | DW288 | DW289 | DW290 | DW291 | DW292 | DW293 | DW294 | DW295 |
| | DW296 | DW297 | | | | | | |
| Volvo B7TL | VLA122 | VLA123 | VLA124 | VLA125 | VLA126 | VLA127 | VLA128 | VLA144 |
| | VLA145 | VLA146 | VLA147 | VLA148 | VLA149 | VLA150 | VLA151 | VLA152 |
| | VLA153 | VLA154 | VLA155 | VLA156 | VLA157 | VLA158 | VLA159 | VLA160 |
| | VLA161 | VLA162 | VLA163 | VLA164 | VLA165 | VLA166 | VLA167 | VLA168 |
| | VLA169 | VLA170 | VLA171 | VLA172 | VLA173 | VLA174 | VLA175 | VLA176 |
| | VLA177 | VLA178 | VLA179 | | | | | |

### Cambridge Heath (Ash Grove, E8 4RH) - AE

| Dart | PDL23 | PDL24 | PDL25 | PDL26 | PDL27 | PDL28 | PDL29 | PDL30 |
|---|---|---|---|---|---|---|---|---|
| | PDL31 | PDL32 | PDL33 | PDL34 | PDL35 | PDL36 | PDL37 | PDL38 |
| Trident 2 | T66 | T67 | T68 | T69 | T70 | T71 | T72 | T73 |
| | T74 | T75 | T76 | T77 | T78 | T79 | T80 | T81 |
| | T82 | T83 | T169 | T170 | T171 | T172 | T173 | T174 |
| | T175 | T176 | T177 | T178 | T179 | | | |
| Volvo B7TL | VLA126 | VLA127 | VLA128 | VLA129 | VLA130 | VLA131 | VLA132 | VLA133 |
| | VLA134 | VLA135 | VLA136 | VLA137 | | | | |

### Clapton (Bohemia Place, Mare Street, E8 1DU) - CT

| Dart | PDL115 | PDL116 | | | | | | |
|---|---|---|---|---|---|---|---|---|
| Dart 4 | ENS1 | ENS2 | ENS3 | ENS4 | ENS5 | ENS6 | ENS7 | ENS8 |
| | ENS9 | ENS10 | ENS11 | ENS12 | ENS13 | ENS14 | | |
| DB300 | DW201 | DW202 | DW203 | DW204 | DW205 | DW206 | DW207 | DW208 |
| | DW209 | DW210 | DW211 | DW212 | DW213 | DW214 | DW215 | DW216 |
| | DW217 | DW218 | DW219 | DW220 | DW221 | DW222 | DW223 | DW224 |
| | DW225 | DW226 | DW227 | DW228 | DW229 | DW230 | DW231 | DW232 |

|  |  |  |  |  |  |  |  |  |
|---|---|---|---|---|---|---|---|---|
|  | DW233 | DW234 | DW235 | DW236 | DW237 | DW238 | DW239 | DW240 |
|  | DW241 | DW242 | DW243 | DW244 | DW245 | DW246 | DW247 | DW248 |
|  | DW249 | DW250 | DW251 | DW252 | DW253 | DW254 | DW255 | DW256 |
|  | DW257 | DW258 | DW259 | DW260 | DW261 | DW262 | DW263 | DW264 |
|  | DW265 | DW266 | DW267 | DW268 | DW269 | DW270 | DW271 | DW272 |
|  | DW273 | DW274 | DW275 | DW276 | DW277 | DW278 | DW279 |  |
|  | DW401 | DW402 | DW403 | DW404 | DW405 | DW406 | DW407 | DW408 |
|  | DW409 | DW410 | DW411 | DW412 | DW413 | DW414 | DW415 | DW416 |
|  | DW417 | DW418 | DW419 | DW420 | DW421 | DW422 | DW423 | DW424 |
| Volvo B7TL | VLW86 | VLW87 | VLW88 | VLW89 | VLW90 | VLW91 | VLW92 | VLW93 |
|  | VLW94 | VLW95 | VLW96 |  |  |  |  |  |

## Croydon (Beddington Farm Road, CR40 4XB) - CN

|  |  |  |  |  |  |  |  |  |
|---|---|---|---|---|---|---|---|---|
| Dart | ADL61 | ADL62 | ADL63 | ADL64 | ADL65 | PDL98 | PDL124 | PDL125 |
|  | PDL126 | PDL127 | PDL128 | PDL129 | PDL130 | PDL131 | PDL132 | PDL133 |
|  | PDL134 | PDL135 | PDL136 |  |  |  |  |  |
| SB120 | DWL58 | DWL59 | DWL60 | DWL61 | DWL62 | DWL63 | DWL64 | DWL65 |
|  | DWL66 | DWL67 | DWS1 | DWS2 | DWS3 | DWS4 | DWS5 | DWS6 |
|  | DWS7 | DWS8 | DWS9 | DWS10 | DWS11 | DWS12 | DWS13 | DWS14 |
|  | DWS15 | DWS16 | DWS17 | DWS18 |  |  |  |  |
| DB250 | DW38 | DW39 | DW40 | DW41 | DW42 | DW43 | DW44 | DW45 |
|  | DW46 | DW47 | DW48 | DW49 | DW50 | DW51 | DW52 | DW53 |
|  | DW54 | DW94 | DW95 | DW96 | DW97 | DW98 | DW99 | DW100 |
|  | DW101 |  |  |  |  |  |  |  |
| *Ancillary* | *DLA22* | *DLA24* | *DLA26* | *DLA27* | *DLA28* | *DLA29* | *DLA30* | *DLA31* |
|  | *DLA34* | *DLA45* | *DLA56* | *DWL30* | *DWL31* | *DWL32* | *DWL33* | *DWL34* |

## Croydon (Brighton Road, South Croydon) - TC

|  |  |  |  |  |  |  |  |  |
|---|---|---|---|---|---|---|---|---|
| Dart | PDL117 | PDL118 | PDL119 | PDL120 | PDL121 | PDL122 | PDL123 |  |
| Dart 4 | ENL1 | ENL2 | ENL3 | ENL4 | ENL5 | ENL6 | ENL7 | ENL8 |
|  | ENL9 | ENL21 | ENL22 | ENL23 | ENL24 | ENL25 | ENL26 | ENL27 |
|  | ENL28 | ENL29 |  |  |  |  |  |  |
| DB250 | DLA132 | DLA133 | DLA135 | DLA175 | DLA176 | DLA177 | DLA178 | DLA179 |
|  | DLA180 | DLA181 | DLA182 | DLA183 | DLA184 | DLA185 | DLA186 | DLA187 |
|  | DLA188 | DLA189 | DLA215 | DLA216 | DLA217 | DLA218 | DLA219 | DLA220 |
|  | DLA221 | DLA222 | DLA223 | DLA224 | DLA250 | DLA251 | DLA252 | DLA253 |
|  | DLA254 | DLA255 | DLA256 | DW1 | DW2 | DW3 | DW4 | DW5 |
|  | DW6 | DW7 | DW8 | DW9 | DW10 | DW11 | DW12 | DW13 |
|  | DW14 | DW15 | DW16 | DW17 | DW18 | DW19 | DW20 | DW21 |
|  | DW22 | DW23 | DW24 | DW25 | DW26 | DW27 | DW28 | DW29 |
|  | DW30 | DW31 | DW32 | DW33 | DW34 | DW35 | DW36 | DW37 |
| Trident 2 | T45 | T46 | T47 | T48 | T49 | T50 | T51 | T52 |
|  | T53 | T54 | T55 | T56 | T57 | T58 | T59 | T60 |
|  | T61 | T62 | T63 | T64 | T65 | T118 | T119 | T120 |
|  | T121 |  |  |  |  |  |  |  |

## Edmonton (Towpath Road, Stonehill Business Park, N18 3QX) - EC

|  |  |  |  |  |  |  |  |  |
|---|---|---|---|---|---|---|---|---|
| Dart | ADL66 | ADL67 | ADL68 | ADL69 | ADL71 | ADL72 | ADL73 | ADL74 |
|  | ADL75 | ADL76 | ADL77 | ADL78 | ADL79 | ADL81 | ADL969 | ADL970 |
|  | ADL971 | ADL972 | ADL973 | ADL974 | ADL975 | ADL976 | ADL977 | ADL978 |
|  | ADL979 | ADL980 | PDL70 | PDL71 | PDL72 | PDL73 | PDL74 | PDL75 |
|  | PDL76 | PDL77 | PDL78 | PDL79 | PDL80 | PDL81 | PDL82 | PDL83 |
|  | PDL84 | PDL85 | PDL86 | PDL87 | PDL88 | PDL89 | PDL90 | PDL91 |
|  | PDL92 | PDL93 | PDL94 | PDL95 | PDL96 | PDL97 | PDL99 | PDL100 |
|  | PDL109 | PDL110 | PDL111 | PDL112 | PDL113 | PDL114 |  |  |
| SB120 | DWL10 | DWL18 | DWL20 | DWL21 | DWL22 | DWL42 | DWL43 | DWL45 |
|  | DWL46 | DWL47 | DWL48 | DWL49 | DWL51 |  |  |  |
| Citaro G | MA1 | MA2 | MA3 | MA4 | MA7 | MA8 | MA11 | MA15 |
|  | MA16 | MA17 | MA18 | MA19 | MA20 | MA22 | MA26 | MA27 |
|  | MA28 | MA29 | MA30 | MA31 | MA34 | MA35 | MA36 | MA37 |
|  | MA38 | MA39 | MA44 | MA92 | MA94 | MA95 | MA96 | MA97 |

*The London Bus Handbook*

| DB250 | MA98 | MA99 | MA144 | MA153 | MA156 | MA157 | | |
|---|---|---|---|---|---|---|---|---|
| | DLA57 | DLA58 | DLA106 | DLA299 | DLA300 | DLA301 | DLA302 | DLA303 |
| | DLA304 | DLA305 | DLA306 | DLA307 | DLA308 | DLA309 | DLA310 | DLA348 |
| | DLA349 | DLA350 | DLA351 | DLA352 | DLA353 | DLA354 | DLA355 | DLA356 |
| | DLA357 | DLA358 | DLA359 | DLA360 | DLA361 | DLA362 | DLA363 | DLA364 |
| | DLA365 | DLA366 | DLA367 | DLA368 | DLA369 | DLA370 | | |

## Enfield (Southbury Road, Ponders End, EN3 4HX) - E

| Dart | PDL62 | PDL64 | PDL65 | PDL66 | PDL67 | PDL68 | PDL140 | PDL141 |
|---|---|---|---|---|---|---|---|---|
| | PDL142 | PDL143 | PDL144 | PDL145 | | | | |
| SB120 | DWL13 | DWL14 | DWL23 | DWL24 | DWL25 | DWL26 | DWL27 | DWL29 |
| Dart 4 | ENL10 | ENL11 | ENL12 | ENL13 | ENL14 | ENL15 | ENL16 | ENL17 |
| | ENL18 | ENL19 | ENL20 | | | | | |
| DB250 | DLA107 | DLA108 | DLA109 | DLA110 | DLA111 | DLA112 | DLA113 | DLA114 |
| | DLA115 | DLA116 | DLA117 | DLA118 | DLA119 | DLA120 | DLA121 | DLA122 |
| | DLA123 | DLA124 | DLA125 | DLA126 | DLA127 | DLA128 | DLA129 | DLA130 |
| | DLA131 | DLA140 | DLA141 | DLA150 | DLA151 | DLA152 | DLA153 | DLA159 |
| | DLA160 | DLA161 | DLA162 | DLA163 | DLA164 | DLA165 | DLP15 | DLP16 |
| | DLP17 | DLP18 | DLP20 | DLP76 | DLP77 | DLP78 | DLP79 | DLP80 |
| | DLP81 | DLP82 | DLP83 | DLP84 | DLP85 | DLP86 | DLP87 | DLP88 |
| | DLP89 | DLP90 | DLP91 | DLP92 | DLP93 | DLP94 | DLP95 | DLP96 |
| | DLP97 | DLP98 | DLP99 | DLP100 | DLP101 | DLP102 | DLP103 | DLP104 |
| | DLP105 | DLP106 | DLP107 | DLP108 | DLP109 | DLP110 | | |
| Volvo B7TL | VLW97 | VLW98 | VLW99 | VLW100 | VLW101 | VLW102 | VLW103 | VLW117 |
| | VLW117 | VLW118 | VLW119 | VLW120 | VLW121 | VLW122 | VLW123 | VLW124 |
| | VLW125 | | | | | | | |

| *Ancillary* | *DLA21* | *DLA23* | *DLA25* | *DLA32* | *DLA33* | *DLA35* | *DLA37* | *DWL35* |
|---|---|---|---|---|---|---|---|---|
| | *DWL36* | *DWL37* | *DWL38* | *DWL39* | *DWL40* | *DWL41* | *DWL44* | *DWL50* |

## Lea Valley (Leeside Road, Edmonton, N17 0SH) - LV

| Dart | PDL63 | PDL69 | | | | | | |
|---|---|---|---|---|---|---|---|---|
| Dart 4/Enviro 200 | EN1 | EN2 | EN3 | EN4 | EN5 | EN6 | EN7 | EN8 |
| | EN9 | EN10 | EN11 | EN12 | EN13 | | | |
| Citaro G | MA42 | MA43 | MA45 | MA46 | MA47 | MA48 | MA49 | MA50 |
| | MA51 | MA52 | MA53 | MA55 | MA56 | MA57 | MA58 | MA59 |
| | MA60 | MA61 | MA62 | MA63 | MA64 | MA65 | MA66 | MA67 |
| | MA68 | MA69 | MA70 | MA71 | MA72 | MA74 | MA75 | MA76 |
| | MA77 | MA78 | MA79 | MA80 | MA81 | MA82 | MA83 | MA84 |
| | MA85 | MA86 | MA87 | MA88 | MA89 | MA90 | MA93 | |
| Trident 2 | T145 | T146 | T147 | T148 | T149 | T150 | T151 | T152 |
| | T153 | T154 | T155 | T156 | T157 | T158 | T159 | T160 |
| | T161 | T162 | T163 | T164 | T165 | T166 | T167 | T168 |

## Norwood (Ernest Avenue, West Norwood, SE27 0HN) - N

| Routemaster | RM5 | RM6 | RMC1463 | RMC1464 | RML2217 | RML2355 | | |
|---|---|---|---|---|---|---|---|---|
| DB250 | DLA136 | DLA137 | DLA138 | DLA139 | DAL142 | DLA143 | DLA144 | DLA145 |
| | DLA146 | DLA147 | DLA148 | DLA149 | DLA154 | DLA155 | DLA156 | DLA157 |
| | DAL158 | DLA166 | DLA167 | DLA168 | DLA169 | DLA170 | DLA171 | DLA172 |
| | DLA173 | DLA174 | | | | | | |
| Volvo B7TL | VLA1 | VLA2 | VLA3 | VLA4 | VLA5 | VLA6 | VLA7 | VLA8 |
| | VLA9 | VLA10 | VLA11 | VLA12 | VLA13 | VLA14 | VLA15 | VLA16 |
| | VLA17 | VLA18 | VLA19 | VLA20 | VLA21 | VLA22 | VLA23 | VLA24 |
| | VLA25 | VLA26 | VLA27 | VLA28 | VLA29 | VLA30 | VLA31 | VLA32 |
| | VLA33 | VLA34 | VLA35 | VLA36 | VLA37 | VLA38 | VLA39 | VLA40 |
| | VLA41 | VLA42 | VLA43 | VLA44 | VLA45 | VLA46 | VLA47 | VLA48 |
| | VLA49 | VLA50 | VLA51 | VLA52 | VLA53 | VLA54 | VLA55 | VLA56 |
| | VLA57 | VLA58 | VLA59 | VLA60 | VLA61 | VLA62 | VLA63 | VLA64 |
| | VLA65 | VLA66 | VLA67 | VLA68 | VLA69 | VLA70 | VLA71 | VLA72 |
| | VLA73 | VLA104 | VLA105 | VLA106 | VLA107 | VLA108 | VLA109 | VLA110 |
| | VLA111 | VLA112 | VLA113 | VLA114 | VLA115 | VLA116 | VLA117 | VLA118 |
| | VLA119 | VLA120 | VLA121 | | | | | |

| Trident 2 | T84 | T85 | T86 | T87 | T88 | T89 | T90 | T91 |
|---|---|---|---|---|---|---|---|---|
| | T92 | T93 | T94 | T95 | T96 | T97 | T98 | T99 |
| | T100 | T101 | T102 | T103 | T104 | T105 | T106 | T107 |
| | T108 | T109 | T110 | T111 | T112 | T113 | T114 | T115 |
| | T116 | T117 | | | | | | |

## Palmers Green (Regents Avenue, N13 5UR) - AD

| DB250 | DLP40 | DLP41 | DLP42 | DLP43 | DLP44 | DLP45 | DLP46 | DLP47 |
|---|---|---|---|---|---|---|---|---|
| | DLP48 | DLP49 | DLP50 | DLP51 | DLP52 | DLP53 | DLP54 | DLP55 |
| | DLP56 | DLP57 | DLP58 | DLP59 | DLP60 | DLP61 | DLP62 | DLP63 |
| | DLP65 | DLP66 | DLP68 | DLP71 | DLP73 | DLP74 | DLP75 | |
| Trident 2 | T1 | T2 | T3 | T4 | T5 | T6 | T7 | T8 |
| | T9 | T10 | T11 | T27 | T28 | T29 | T30 | T31 |
| | T32 | T33 | T34 | T35 | T36 | T37 | T38 | T39 |
| | T40 | T41 | T42 | T43 | T44 | | | |

## Stamford Hill (Rookwood Road, N16 6SS) - SF

| DB250 | DLA39 | DLA51 | DLA54 | DLA55 | DLA62 | DLA72 | | |
|---|---|---|---|---|---|---|---|---|
| Volvo B7TL | VLW138 | VLW139 | VLW140 | VLW141 | VLW142 | VLW143 | VLW144 | VLW145 |
| | VLW146 | VLW147 | VLW148 | VLW149 | VLW150 | VLW151 | VLW152 | VLW153 |
| | VLW154 | VLW155 | VLW156 | VLW157 | VLW158 | VLW159 | VLW160 | VLW161 |
| | VLW162 | VLW163 | VLW164 | VLW165 | VLW166 | VLW167 | VLW168 | VLW170 |
| | VLW171 | VLW174 | VLW176 | VLW177 | VLW178 | VLW179 | VLW180 | VLW181 |
| | VLW183 | VLW184 | VLW185 | VLW188 | VLW189 | VLW190 | VLW191 | VLW192 |
| | VLW193 | VLW194 | VLW195 | VLW196 | VLW197 | VLW199 | | |
| Volvo B5L | HV27 | HV28 | HV29 | HV30 | HV31 | HV32 | HV33 | HV34 |
| | HV35 | HV36 | HV37 | HV38 | HV39 | HV40 | HV41 | HV42 |
| | HV43 | HV44 | HV45 | HV46 | | | | |
| VDL DB300 | DW429 | DW430 | DW431 | DW432 | DW433 | DW434 | DW435 | DW436 |
| | DW437 | DW438 | DW439 | DW440 | DW441 | DW442 | DW443 | DW444 |
| | DW445 | DW446 | DW447 | DW448 | DW449 | DW450 | DW451 | DW452 |
| | DW453 | DW454 | DW455 | DW456 | DW457 | DW458 | DW459 | DW460 |
| | DW461 | DW462 | DW463 | DW464 | | | | |

## Thornton Heath (London Road, CR7 6AU) - TH

| Dart | PDL19 | PDL20 | PDL21 | PDL22 | | | | |
|---|---|---|---|---|---|---|---|---|
| SB120 | DWL1 | DWL2 | DWL3 | DWL4 | DWL5 | DWL6 | DWL7 | DWL8 |
| | DWL9 | DWL11 | DWL12 | DWL15 | DWL16 | DWL17 | DWL19 | |
| DB250 | DLA63 | DLA64 | DLA322 | DLA323 | DLA324 | DLA325 | DLA326 | DLA327 |
| | DLA328 | DLA329 | DLA330 | DLA331 | DLA332 | DLA333 | DLA334 | DLA335 |
| | DLA336 | DLA337 | DLA338 | DLA339 | DLA340 | DLA341 | DLA342 | DLA343 |
| | DLA344 | DLA345 | DLA246 | DLA347 | DLA371 | DLA371 | DLA372 | DLA373 |
| | DLA374 | DLA375 | DLA376 | DLA377 | DLA378 | DLA379 | DLA380 | DLA381 |
| | DLA382 | DLA383 | DLA384 | DLA385 | DLA386 | DLA387 | DLA388 | DLA389 |
| Trident 2 | T122 | T123 | T124 | T125 | T126 | T127 | T128 | T129 |
| | T130 | T131 | T132 | T133 | T134 | T135 | T136 | T137 |
| | T138 | T139 | T140 | T141 | T142 | T143 | T144 | |

## Tottenham (Philip Lane, N17 0XR) - AR

| Dart | PDL45 | PDL46 | PDL47 | PDL48 | PDL49 | PDL50 | PDL51 | |
|---|---|---|---|---|---|---|---|---|
| DB250 | DLA225 | DLA226 | DLA227 | DLA228 | DLA229 | DLA230 | DLA231 | DLA232 |
| | DLA233 | DLA234 | DLA235 | DLA237 | DLA238 | DLA239 | DLA240 | DLA241 |
| DLA242 | DLA243 | DLA244 | DLA245 | DLA246 | DLA247 | DLA248 | DLA249 | DLA273 |
| | DLA274 | DLA275 | DLA277 | DLA278 | DLA279 | DLA280 | DLA281 | DLA282 |
| | DLA283 | DLA284 | DLA285 | DLA286 | DLA287 | DLA288 | DLA289 | DLA291 |
| | DLA292 | DLA293 | DLA294 | DLA295 | DLA296 | DLA297 | DLA298 | DW298 |
| | DW299 | DW300 | DW301 | DW302 | DW303 | DW304 | DW305 | DW306 |
| | DW307 | DW308 | DW309 | DW310 | DW311 | DW312 | DW313 | DW314 |
| | DW315 | DW316 | DW317 | DW318 | DW319 | DW320 | DW321 | DW322 |
| | DW323 | DW324 | DW325 | DW326 | DW327 | DW328 | DW329 | DW330 |
| | DW331 | DW332 | DW333 | DW334 | DW335 | DW336 | | |
| Volvo hybrid | HV1 | HV2 | HV3 | HV4 | HV5 | HV6 | HV7 | HV8 |
| | HV9 | HV10 | HV11 | HV12 | HV13 | HV14 | HV15 | HV16 |
| | HV17 | HV18 | HV19 | HV20 | HV21 | HV22 | HV23 | HV24 |
| | HV25 | HV26 | | | | | | |

Early hybrid buses carried a livery featuring green leaves. The scheme is illustrated by HV14, L60AXG, seen here at Mansion House. This features the Volvo chassis while Arriva also operates class HW, the Wrightbus product that uses VDL components. *Terry Longhurst*

| Volvo B7TL | VLA74 | VLA75 | VLA76 | VLA77 | VLA78 | VLA79 | VLA80 | VLA81 |
|---|---|---|---|---|---|---|---|---|
| | VLA82 | VLA83 | VLA84 | VLA85 | VLA86 | VLA87 | VLA88 | VLA89 |
| | VLA90 | VLA91 | VLA92 | VLA93 | VLA94 | VLA95 | VLA96 | VLA97 |
| | VLA98 | VLA99 | VLA100 | VLA101 | VLA102 | VLA103 | | |

## Wood Green (High Road) - WN

| SB120 | DWL52 | DWL53 | DWL54 | DWL55 | DWL56 | DWL57 | | |
|---|---|---|---|---|---|---|---|---|
| Dart 4 / Enviro 200 | ENL30 | ENL31 | ENL32 | ENL33 | ENL34 | ENL35 | ENL36 | ENL37 |
| | ENL38 | ENL39 | ENL40 | ENL41 | ENL42 | ENL43 | ENL44 | ENL45 |
| | ENL46 | ENL47 | ENL48 | | | | | |
| DB250 | DLA11 | DLA12 | DLA13 | DLA14 | DLA15 | DLA16 | DLA17 | DLA18 |
| | DLA19 | DLA20 | DLA190 | DLA191 | DLA192 | DLA193 | DLA194 | DLA195 |
| | DLA196 | DLA197 | DLA198 | DLA199 | DLA200 | DLA201 | DLA203 | DLP70 |
| Wrightbus Hybrid | HW1 | HW2 | HW3 | HW4 | HW5 | | | |
| Volvo B7TL | VLW7 | VLW8 | VLW9 | VLW10 | VLW11 | VLW12 | VLW13 | VLW14 |
| | VLW15 | VLW16 | VLW17 | VLW18 | VLW19 | VLW20 | VLW21 | VLW22 |
| | VLW23 | VLW24 | VLW25 | VLW26 | VLW27 | VLW28 | VLW29 | VLW30 |
| | VLW31 | VLW32 | VLW33 | VLW34 | VLW35 | VLW36 | VLW37 | VLW38 |
| | VLW39 | VLW40 | VLW41 | VLW42 | VLW43 | VLW44 | VLW45 | VLW46 |
| | VLW47 | VLW48 | VLW49 | VLW50 | VLW51 | VLW52 | VLW53 | VLW54 |
| | VLW55 | VLW56 | VLW57 | VLW58 | VLW59 | VLW60 | VLW61 | VLW62 |
| | VLW63 | VLW64 | VLW65 | VLW66 | VLW67 | VLW68 | VLW69 | VLW70 |
| | VLW71 | VLW72 | VLW73 | VLW74 | VLW75 | VLW76 | VLW77 | VLW78 |
| | VLW79 | VLW80 | VLW81 | VLW82 | VLW83 | VLW84 | VLW85 | |

## Unallocated - u/w

remainder

# ARRIVA - THE ORIGINAL TOUR

The Original Tour Ltd, Jews Road, Wandsworth, SW18 1TB

| | | | | | |
|---|---|---|---|---|---|
| **EMB763** D553YNO | MCW Metrobus DR115/4 | MCW | PO65/31D | 1987 | New World FirstBus, 2001 |
| **EMB764** E964JAR | MCW Metrobus DR115/4 | MCW | PO65/31D | 1987 | New World FirstBus, 2001 |
| **EMB765** E965JAR | MCW Metrobus DR115/4 | MCW | PO65/31D | 1987 | New World FirstBus, 2001 |
| **EMB767** E767JAR | MCW Metrobus DR115/4 | MCW | PO65/31D | 1987 | New World FirstBus, 2001 |
| **EMB769** E769JAR | MCW Metrobus DR115/4 | MCW | PO65/31D | 1987 | New World FirstBus, 2001 |
| **EMB770** E770JAR | MCW Metrobus DR115/4 | MCW | PO65/31D | 1987 | New World FirstBus, 2001 |
| **EMB771** E771JAR | MCW Metrobus DR115/4 | MCW | PO65/31D | 1987 | New World FirstBus, 2001 |
| **EMB773** E773JAR | MCW Metrobus DR115/4 | MCW | PO65/31D | 1987 | New World FirstBus, 2001 |
| **EMB775** D675YNO | MCW Metrobus DR115/4 | MCW | PO65/31D | 1987 | New World FirstBus, 2001 |
| **EMB776** UAR776Y | MCW Metrobus DR115/3 | MCW | O59/33D | 1984 | City Sightseeing, Aus., 04 |
| **EMB777** A735WEV | MCW Metrobus DR115/3 | MCW | O59/33D | 1984 | City Sightseeing, Aus., 04 |
| **EMB778** A737WEV | MCW Metrobus DR115/3 | MCW | O59/33D | 1984 | City Sightseeing, Aus., 04 |
| **EMB779** MXT179 | MCW Metrobus DR115/3 | MCW | O59/33D | 1984 | City Sightseeing, Aus., 04 |
| **EMB780** A755WEV | MCW Metrobus DR115/3 | MCW | O59/33D | 1983 | New World FirstBus, 2004 |
| **EMB781** A750WEV | MCW Metrobus DR115/3 | MCW | O59/33D | 1983 | New World FirstBus, 2004 |
| **EMB782** A749WEV | MCW Metrobus DR115/3 | MCW | O59/33D | 1983 | New World FirstBus, 2004 |
| **EMB783** UAR247Y | MCW Metrobus DR115/3 | MCW | O59/33D | 1987 | New World FirstBus, 2004 |
| **EMB784** UAR250Y | MCW Metrobus DR115/3 | MCW | O59/33D | 1987 | New World FirstBus, 2004 |
| **EMB785** NKJ785 | MCW Metrobus DR115/3 | MCW | O59/33D | 1987 | New World FirstBus, 2004 |

| | | | | | |
|---|---|---|---|---|---|
| **DLP201-214** | DAF DB250 10.6m | Plaxton President | PO45/21F | 1999 | Arriva London, 2006 |

| | | | | | | | | | | | |
|---|---|---|---|---|---|---|---|---|---|---|---|
| **201** | JR | 201KYD | **205** | JR | T205XBV | **209** | JR | T209XBV | **212** | JR | T212XBV |
| **202** | JR | T202XBV | **206** | JR | T206XBV | **210** | JR | T210XBV | **213** | JR | T213XBV |
| **203** | JR | T203XBV | **207** | JR | T207XBV | **211** | JR | T211XBV | **214** | JR | T214XBV |
| **204** | JR | T204XBV | **208** | JR | T208XBV | | | | | | |

**London Original open-top tour service is provided by Arriva. Early examples for this operation include tri-axle Metrobuses re-imported from Hong Kong, while more recent buses have been transferred from the main London fleet. One of the latter, OA343, J343BSH, shows the partial open-top conversion.** *Mark Lyons*

Looking very smart as it shows off the delights of London, DLA204, T204XBV, is one of the fourteen Plaxton President-bodied DAF buses now used on the service. Westminster Bridge with Portcullis House in the background provides the setting for this picture. *Dave Heath*

### OA315-352

| | | | Leyland Olympian | | | Alexander RH | | | P043/25D* 1992 | | Arriva London, 2003-05 |
|---|---|---|---|---|---|---|---|---|---|---|---|
| | | | | | | | | | 321-32/8-40 are CO43/25D; 350-2 are B43/25D | | |

| 315 | JR | J315BSH | 325 | JR | J325BSH | 335 | JR | J335BSH | 344 | JR | J344BSH |
|---|---|---|---|---|---|---|---|---|---|---|---|
| 316 | JR | J316BSH | 326 | JR | J326BSH | 336 | JR | J336BSH | 345 | JR | J345BSH |
| 317 | JR | J317BSH | 327 | JR | J327BSH | 337 | JR | J337BSH | 346 | JR | J346BSH |
| 318 | JR | J318BSH | 328 | JR | J328BSH | 338 | JR | J338BSH | 347 | JR | J347BSH |
| 319 | JR | J319BSH | 329 | JR | J329BSH | 339 | JR | J339BSH | 348 | JR | J348BSH |
| 320 | JR | J320BSH | 330 | JR | J330BSH | 340 | JR | J340BSH | 349 | JR | J349BSH |
| 321 | JR | J321BSH | 331 | JR | J331BSH | 341 | JR | J341BSH | 350 | JR | J350BSH |
| 322 | JR | J322BSH | 332 | JR | J332BSH | 342 | JR | J342BSH | 351 | JR | J351BSH |
| 323 | JR | J323BSH | 333 | JR | J433BSH | 343 | JR | J343BSH | 352 | JR | J352BSH |
| 324 | JR | J324BSH | 334 | JR | J334BSH | | | | | | |

### VLY601-610

| | | | Volvo B7L 10.6m | | | Ayats Bravo City | | | O51/24F | 2005 | |
|---|---|---|---|---|---|---|---|---|---|---|---|
| 601 | JR | LX05GDV | 604 | JR | LX05GEJ | 607 | JR | LX05KNZ | 609 | JR | EU05DVW |
| 602 | JR | LX05GDY | 605 | JR | LX05HRO | 608 | JR | LX05KOA | 610 | JR | EU05DVX |
| 603 | JR | LX05GDZ | 606 | JR | LX05HSC | | | | | | |

### VLE611-620

| | | | Volvo B9TL 10.9m | | | East Lancs Visionaire | | | PO49/31F | 2007 | |
|---|---|---|---|---|---|---|---|---|---|---|---|
| 611 | JR | LJ07XEN | 614 | JR | LJ07XER | 617 | JR | LJ07XEU | 619 | JR | LJ07XEW |
| 612 | JR | LJ07XEO | 615 | JR | LJ07XES | 618 | JR | LJ07XEV | 620 | JR | LJ07UDD |
| 613 | JR | LJ07XEP | 616 | JR | LJ07XET | | | | | | |

Previous registrations:

| | | | | |
|---|---|---|---|---|
| 201KYD | V601LGC | | E770JAR | DU8506 (HK) |
| A735WEV | CZ9920(HK) | | E771JAR | DT9187 (HK) |
| A737WEV | DA2952(HK) | | E773JAR | DU3481 (HK) |
| A749WEV | - | | E964JAR | DT4549 (HK) |
| A750WEV | - | | E965JAR | DV4883 (HK) |
| A755WEV | - | | MXT179 | - (HK), UAR773Y |
| D553YNO | DV471 (HK) | | NKJ785 | - (HK), UAR772Y |
| D675YNO | DV3433(HK) | | UAR247Y | CZ2554(HK) |
| E767JAR | DU3460 (HK) | | UAR250Y | CZ664(HK) |
| E769JAR | DT7256 (HK) | | UAR776Y | |

**Depot:** Jews Road, Wandsworth (WD)
On order are 16 Volvo B9TL with Optare Visionaire partial open-top bodywork.

# ARRIVA THE SHIRES

Arriva The Shires Ltd, 487 Dunstable Road, Luton, LU4 8DS

### 2468-2472 — Optare Solo M780SL — Optare — N25F — 2006

| | | | | | | | | | | |
|---|---|---|---|---|---|---|---|---|---|---|
| **2468** | WD | YJ06YRP | **2470** | WD | YJ06YRS | **2471** | WD | YJ06YRT | **2472** | WD YJ06YRU |
| **2469** | WD | YJ06YRR | | | | | | | | |

### 3704-3710 — VDL Bus SB120 10.8m — Wrightbus Cadet 2 — N28D — 2006

| | | | | | | | | | | |
|---|---|---|---|---|---|---|---|---|---|---|
| **3704** | WD | YJ06LFE | **3706** | WD | YJ06LFG | **3708** | WD | YJ06LFK | **3710** | WD YJ06LDK |
| **3705** | WD | YJ06LFF | **3707** | WD | YJ06LFH | **3709** | WD | YJ06LFL | | |

### 3711-3728 — VDL Bus SB120 10.8m — Wrightbus Cadet 2 — N39F — 2006

| | | | | | | | | | | |
|---|---|---|---|---|---|---|---|---|---|---|
| **3711** | WD | YE06HRA | **3716** | WD | YE06HRJ | **3721** | WD | YE06HPK | **3725** | WD YE06HPP |
| **3712** | WD | YE06HRC | **3717** | WD | YE06HPA | **3722** | WD | YE06HPL | **3726** | WD YE06HPU |
| **3713** | WD | YE06HRD | **3718** | WD | YE06HPC | **3723** | WD | YE06HPN | **3727** | WD YE06HNT |
| **3714** | WD | YE06HRF | **3719** | WD | YE06HPF | **3724** | WD | YE06HPO | **3728** | WD YE06HNU |
| **3715** | WD | YE06HRG | **3720** | WD | YE06HPJ | | | | | |

### 6000-6024 — DAF DB250 — Alexander ALX400 — N45/20D — 2002-03

| | | | | | | | | | | |
|---|---|---|---|---|---|---|---|---|---|---|
| **6000** | WD | KL52CWN | **6007** | WD | KL52CWW | **6013** | WD | KL52CXE | **6019** | WD KL52CXM |
| **6001** | WD | KL52CWO | **6008** | WD | KL52CWZ | **6014** | WD | KL52CXF | **6020** | WD KL52CXN |
| **6002** | WD | KL52CWP | **6009** | WD | KL52CXA | **6015** | WD | KL52CXG | **6021** | WD KL52CXO |
| **6003** | WD | KL52CWR | **6010** | WD | KL52CXB | **6016** | WD | KL52CXH | **6022** | WD KL52CXP |
| **6004** | WD | KL52CWT | **6011** | WD | KL52CXC | **6017** | WD | KL52CXJ | **6023** | WD KL52CXR |
| **6005** | WD | KL52CWU | **6012** | WD | KL52CXD | **6018** | WD | KL52CXK | **6024** | WD KL52CXS |
| **6006** | WD | KL52CWV | | | | | | | | |

### 6025 — WD YJ54CFG — VDL Bus DB250 — Alexander ALX400 — N45/20D — 2005

**Arriva operations that border the TfL network have gained London contracts. Watford depot provides the vehicle requirements that The Shires provides for TfL routes. Optare Solo 2468, YJ06YRP, is seen operating route H2.** *Mark Lyons*

Two of the hybrid buses ordered with the London batch operate for Arriva The Shires. Pictured at Edgware Underground station is 6100, KX59AEE. *Richard Godfrey*

### 6026-6036       VDL Bus DB250 10.2m       Wrightbus Pulsar Gemini       N43/21D       2006

| 6026 | WD | YJ55WPO | 6029 | WD | YJ55WOC | 6032 | WD | YJ55WOM | 6035 | WD | YJ55WOV |
|------|----|---------|------|----|---------|------|----|---------|------|----|---------|
| 6027 | WD | YJ55WOA | 6030 | WD | YJ55WOD | 6033 | WD | YJ55WOR | 6036 | WD | YJ55WOX |
| 6028 | WD | YJ55WOB | 6031 | WD | YJ55WOH | 6034 | WD | YJ55WOU | | | |

| | | | | | | | |
|------|----|---------|------------------------|-------------------------|---------|------|---------------------|
| 6037 | WD | Y521UGC | DAF DB250 10.2m | Alexander ALX400 | N43/20D | 2001 | Arriva London, 2006 |
| 6039 | WD | Y531UGC | DAF DB250 10.2m | Alexander ALX400 | N43/20D | 2001 | Arriva London, 2008 |
| 6040 | WD | S236JUA | DAF DB250 10.2m | Alexander ALX400 | N43/20D | 1999 | Arriva London, 2011 |
| 6041 | WD | LJ05GLY | VDL Bus DB250 10.3m | Wrightbus Pulsar Gemini | N43/22D | 2005 | Arriva London, 2011 |
| 6042 | w  | S284JUA | DAF DB250 10.2m | Alexander ALX400 | N43/20D | 1999 | Arriva London, 2011 |
| 6043 | w  | S285JUA | DAF DB250 10.2m | Alexander ALX400 | N43/20D | 1999 | Arriva London, 2011 |
| 6044 | w  | S291JUA | DAF DB250 10.2m | Alexander ALX400 | N43/20D | 1999 | Arriva London, 2011 |
| 6100 | WD | KX59AEE | VDL Bus DB300 Hybrid | Wrightbus Gemini 2 | N41/24D | 2009 | |
| 6101 | WD | KX59AEF | VDL Bus DB300 Hybrid | Wrightbus Gemini 2 | N41/24D | 2009 | |

*Full details of the all the Arriva fleets can be found in the main Arriva Bus Handbook - see www.britishbuspublishing.co.uk*

## Depots and allocations:

### Watford (St Albans Road, Garston) - WD

| | | | | | | | | |
|---------------|------|------|------|------|------|------|------|------|
| Optare Solo   | 2468 | 2469 | 2470 | 2471 | 2472 | | | |
| DAF/VDL SB120 | 3704 | 3705 | 3706 | 3707 | 3708 | 3709 | 3710 | 3711 |
|               | 3712 | 3713 | 3714 | 3715 | 3716 | 3717 | 3718 | 3719 |
|               | 3720 | 3721 | 3722 | 3723 | 3724 | 3725 | 3726 | 3727 |
|               | 3728 | | | | | | | |
| DB250         | 6000 | 6001 | 6002 | 6003 | 6004 | 6005 | 6006 | 6007 |
|               | 6008 | 6009 | 6010 | 6011 | 6012 | 6013 | 6014 | 6015 |
|               | 6016 | 6017 | 6018 | 6019 | 6020 | 6021 | 6022 | 6023 |
|               | 6024 | 6025 | 6026 | 6027 | 6028 | 6029 | 6030 | 6031 |
|               | 6032 | 6033 | 6034 | 6035 | 6036 | 6037 | 6039 | 6040 |
|               | 6041 | 6042 | 6043 | 6044 | | | | |
| DB300         | 6100 | 6101 | | | | | | |

# ARRIVA SOUTHERN COUNTIES

Arriva Southern Counties Ltd, Invicta House, Armstrong Road, Maidstone, Kent, ME15 6TX

### 1643-1649

| | | | | | | | | | | |
|---|---|---|---|---|---|---|---|---|---|---|
| ADL Dart 4 8.9m | | | ADL Enviro 200 | | | N26F | 2007 | | | |
| 1643 | DA | GN57BPF | 1645 | DA | GN57BPO | 1647 | DA | GN57BPV | 1649 | DA | GN57BPY |
| 1644 | DA | GN57BPK | 1646 | DA | GN57BPU | 1648 | DA | GN57BPX | | | |

### 3291-3303

| | | | | | | | | | | |
|---|---|---|---|---|---|---|---|---|---|---|
| Dennis Dart SLF 10.7m | | | Plaxton Pointer 2 | | | N31D | 2001 | | | |
| 3291 | DA | Y291TKJ | 3294 | DA | Y294TKJ | 3297 | DA | Y297TKJ | 3301 | DA | Y301TKJ |
| 3292 | DA | Y292TKJ | 3295 | DA | Y295TKJ | 3298 | DA | Y298TKJ | 3302 | DA | Y302TKJ |
| 3293 | DA | Y293TKJ | 3296 | DA | Y296TKJ | 3299 | DA | Y299TKJ | 3303 | DA | Y303TKJ |

### 3500-3510

| | | | | | | | | | | |
|---|---|---|---|---|---|---|---|---|---|---|
| DAF SB120 10.2m | | | Wrightbus Cadet | | | N27D | 2002 | | | |
| 3500 | GY | KE51PTY | 3503 | GY | KE51PUF | 3506 | GY | KE51PUK | 3509 | GY | KE51PUV |
| 3501 | GY | KE51PTZ | 3504 | GY | KE51PUH | 3507 | GY | KE51PUO | 3510 | GY | KC51NFO |
| 3502 | GY | KE51PUA | 3505 | GY | KE51PUJ | 3508 | GY | KE51PUU | | | |

| | | | | | | |
|---|---|---|---|---|---|---|
| 3511 | GY | KE51PUY | DAF SB120 9.4m | Wrightbus Cadet | N23D | 2002 |
| 3512 | GY | KC51PUX | DAF SB120 9.4m | Wrightbus Cadet | N23D | 2002 |
| 3513 | GY | KE51PVD | DAF SB120 9.4m | Wrightbus Cadet | N23D | 2002 |

### 3945-3957

| | | | | | | | | | | |
|---|---|---|---|---|---|---|---|---|---|---|
| VDL Bus SB120 9.4m | | | Wrightbus Cadet 2 | | | N24F | 2004 | | | |
| 3945 | DA | GK53AOH | 3948 | DA | GK53AON | 3951 | DA | GK53AOR | 3955 | DA | GK53AOW |
| 3946 | DA | GK53AOJ | 3949 | DA | GK53AOO | 3952 | DA | GK53AOT | 3956 | DA | GK53AOX |
| 3947 | DA | GK53AOL | 3950 | DA | GK53AOP | 3954 | DA | GK53AOV | 3957 | DA | GK53AOY |

**Arriva Southern Counties operates services for TfL in the Dartford area. Swanley is the location for this view of Alexander Dennis Enviro 200 number 1649, GN57BPY.** *Richard Godfrey*

Arriva imports the new VDL SB180 midibus and is currently running a demonstrator with Egyptian-built MCV bodywork. As we go to press it is on long-term loan with Southern Counties where it is numbered 3980, YJ60GGE. It is seen in Swanley in March 2011. *Richard Godfrey*

| 3971 | GY | YE06HPX | DAF SB120 10.8m | | | Wrightbus Cadet 2 | N28D | 2006 | |
| 3972 | GY | YE06HPY | DAF SB120 10.8m | | | Wrightbus Cadet 2 | N28D | 2006 | |
| 3973 | GY | YE06HPZ | DAF SB120 10.8m | | | Wrightbus Cadet 2 | N28D | 2006 | |
| 3980 | DA | YJ60GGE | VDL SB180 10.3m | | | MCV Evolution | N29D | 2010 | *On loan from Arriva B&C* |

### 3982-3996
ADL Dart 4 10.7m — ADL Enviro 200 — N32D — 2007

| 3982 | DA | GN07DLE | 3986 | DA | GN07DLO | 3990 | DA | GN07DLY | 3994 | DA | GN07DMO |
| 3983 | DA | GN07DLF | 3987 | DA | GN07DLU | 3991 | DA | GN07DLZ | 3995 | DA | GN07DMU |
| 3984 | DA | GN07DLJ | 3988 | DA | GN07DLV | 3992 | DA | GN07DME | 3996 | DA | GN07DMV |
| 3985 | DA | GN07DLK | 3989 | DA | GN07DLX | 3993 | DA | GN07DMF | | | |

### 3997-4010
ADL Dart 4 10.8m — ADL Enviro 200 — N29D

| 3997 | GY | GN57BOU | 4001 | GY | GN08CGU | 4005 | GY | GN08CGZ | 4008 | GY | GN08CHF |
| 3998 | GY | GN57BOV | 4002 | GY | GN08CGV | 4006 | GY | GN08CHC | 4009 | GY | GN08CHG |
| 3999 | GY | GN57BPE | 4003 | GY | GN08CGX | 4007 | GY | GN08CHD | 4010 | GY | GN08CHH |
| 4000 | GY | GN08CGO | 4004 | GY | GN08CGY | | | | | | |

### 4023-4027
ADL Dart 4 10.2m — ADL Enviro 200 — N29D — 2009

| 4023 | DA | GN58BUP | 4025 | DA | GN58BUV | 4026 | DA | GN58LVA | 4027 | DA | GN58LVB |
| 4024 | DA | GN58BUU | | | | | | | | | |

### 4028-4035
ADL Dart 4 10.8m — ADL Enviro 200 — N32D — 2009

| 4028 | DA | GN09AVV | 4030 | DA | GN09AVX | 4032 | DA | GN09AVZ | 4034 | DA | GN09AWB |
| 4029 | DA | GN09AVW | 4031 | DA | GN09AVY | 4033 | DA | GN09AWA | 4035 | DA | GN09AWC |

### 4068-4079
ADL Dart 4 10.8m — ADL Enviro 200 — N38F — 2010

| 4068 | GY | GN10KWE | 4071 | GY | GN10KWH | 4074 | GY | VX10EBN | 4077 | GY | VX10EBU |
| 4069 | GY | GN10KWF | 4072 | GY | GN10KWJ | 4075 | GY | VX10EBO | 4078 | GY | VX10EBV |
| 4070 | GY | GN10KWG | 4073 | GY | GN10KWK | 4076 | GY | VX10EBP | 4079 | GY | VX10EBX |

### 6213-6219
DAF DB250 — Wrightbus Pulsar Gemini — N41/24D — 2003

| 6213 | DA | GK53AOA | 6215 | DA | GK53AOC | 6217 | DA | GK53AOE | 6219 | DA | GK53AOG |
| 6214 | DA | GK53AOB | 6216 | DA | GK53AOD | 6218 | DA | GK53AOF | | | |

## 6224-6236

| | | | | | | | | | | | DAF DB250 10.2m | | Alexander ALX400 | | N43/20D | 2000-01 | Arriva London, 2006 |

| | | | | | | |
|---|---|---|---|---|---|---|
| **6224** | DA | X457FGP | **6228** | DA | Y461UGC | **6231** | DA | Y464UGC | **6234** | DA | Y467UGC |
| **6225** | GY | X458FGP | **6229** | DA | Y462UGC | **6232** | DA | Y465UGC | **6235** | DA | Y468UGC |
| **6226** | DA | X459FGP | **6230** | DA | Y463UGC | **6233** | DA | Y466UGC | **6236** | DA | Y469UGC |
| **6227** | DA | Y451UGC | | | | | | | | | |

## 6241-6244

DAF DB250 10.6m — Alexander ALX400 — N45/17F — 2000-01 — Arriva London, 2011

| **6241** | u | S284JUA | **6242** | u | S285JUA | **6243** | u | S291JUA | **6244** | u | S272JUA |
|---|---|---|---|---|---|---|---|---|---|---|---|

**On order**: Thirteen ADL Trident 2s with Enviro 400 bodies for route 160.

*Full details of the all the Arriva fleets can be found in the main Arriva Bus Handbook - see www.britishbuspublishing.co.uk*

## Depots and allocations:

### Dartford (Central Road) - DA

| Dart SLF | 3291 | 3292 | 3293 | 3294 | 3295 | 3296 | 3297 | 3298 |
|---|---|---|---|---|---|---|---|---|
| | 3299 | 3301 | 3302 | 3303 | | | | |
| Dart 4 | 1643 | 1644 | 1645 | 1646 | 1647 | 1648 | 1649 | 3982 |
| | 3983 | 3984 | 3985 | 3986 | 3987 | 3988 | 3989 | 3990 |
| | 3991 | 3992 | 3993 | 3994 | 3995 | 3996 | 4023 | 4024 |
| | 4025 | 4026 | 4027 | 4028 | 4029 | 4030 | 4031 | 4032 |
| | 4033 | 4034 | 4035 | | | | | |
| DAF/VDL SB120 | 3945 | 3946 | 3947 | 3948 | 3949 | 3950 | 3951 | 3952 |
| | 3953 | 3954 | 3955 | 3956 | 3957 | | | |
| VDL SB180 | 3980 | | | | | | | |
| DAF/VDL DB250 | 6213 | 6214 | 6215 | 6216 | 6217 | 6218 | 6219 | 6224 |
| | 6226 | 6227 | 6228 | 6229 | 6230 | 6231 | 6232 | 6233 |
| | 6234 | 6235 | 6236 | | | | | |

### Grays (Europa Park, London Road) - GY

| SB120 Cadet | 3500 | 3501 | 3502 | 3503 | 3504 | 3505 | 3506 | 3507 |
|---|---|---|---|---|---|---|---|---|
| | 3508 | 3509 | 3510 | 3511 | 3512 | 3513 | 3971 | 3972 |
| | 3973 | | | | | | | |
| Dart 4 | 3997 | 3999 | 4000 | 4001 | 4002 | 4003 | 4004 | 4005 |
| | 4006 | 4007 | 4008 | 4009 | 4010 | 4068 | 4069 | 4070 |
| | 4071 | 4072 | 4073 | 4074 | 4075 | 4076 | 4077 | 4078 |
| | 4079 | | | | | | | |
| DAF/VDL DB250 | 6225 | | | | | | | |

**Dual-doored Enviro 200 4025, GN58BUV, from Dartford depot was pictured in Erith in February 2011.**
*Dave Heath*

# THE BIG BUS COMPANY LTD

The Big Bus Company Ltd, 48 Buckingham Palace Road, London, SW1W 0RN

| | | | | | | | |
|---|---|---|---|---|---|---|---|
| **T739** | OHV739Y | Leyland Titan TNLXB2RR | | Leyland | O44/26D | 1983 | |
| **T928** | A928SYE | Leyland Titan TNLXB2RR | | Leyland | O44/26D | 1983 | |
| **T1038** | A638THV | Leyland Titan TNLXB2RR | | Leyland | O44/26D | 1983 | |

### *DA1-12*

Dennis Trident 10m · East Lancs Lolyne · PO45/23D · 2001 · Metrobus, Orpington, 2007-9

| | | | | | | | |
|---|---|---|---|---|---|---|---|
| **DA1** | LV51YCD | **DA4** | LV51YCK | **DA7** | LV51YCO | **DA19** | LV51YCF |
| **DA2** | LV51YCE | **DA5** | LV51YCJ | **DA8** | LV51YCC | **DA11** | LV51YCG |
| **DA3** | LV51YCM | **DA6** | LV51YCH | **DA9** | LV51YCL | **DA12** | LV51YCN |

### *DA201-210*

Volvo B9TL 10.9m · East Lancs Visionaire · PO51/31F · 2008

| | | | | | | | |
|---|---|---|---|---|---|---|---|
| **DA201** | PF08URP | **DA204** | PF08URU | **DA207** | PF08URX | **DA209** | PF08USB |
| **DA202** | PF08URR | **DA205** | PF08URV | **DA208** | PF08URZ | **DA210** | PF08USC |
| **DA203** | PF08URS | **DA206** | PF08URW | | | | |

### *DA211-220*

Volvo B9TL 10.9m · Optare Visionaire · PO51/31F · 2009

| | | | | | | | |
|---|---|---|---|---|---|---|---|
| **DA211** | PN09ENY | **DA214** | PN09EOC | **DA217** | PN09EOF | **DA219** | PN09EOJ |
| **DA212** | PN09EOA | **DA215** | PN09EOD | **DA218** | PN09EOH | **DA220** | PN09EOK |
| **DA213** | PN09EOB | **DA216** | PN09EOE | | | | |

### *DA321-326*

Volvo B9TL 12.35m · Optare Visionaire · PO63/38F · 2010

| | | | | | | | |
|---|---|---|---|---|---|---|---|
| **DA321** | PN10FOC | **DA323** | PN10FOF | **DA325** | PN10FOJ | **DA326** | PN10FOK |
| **DA322** | PN10FOD | **DA324** | PN10FOH | | | | |

| | | | | | | |
|---|---|---|---|---|---|---|
| **DHL14** | B14BUS | Dennis Condor DDA1702 | Duple Metsec | PO62/40D | 1989 | New World First Bus, 2003 |
| **D32** | G32FWC | Dennis Condor DDA1702 | Duple Metsec | O62/40D | 1989 | New World First Bus, 2003 |
| **HD34** | G34FWC | Dennis Condor DDA1702 | Duple Metsec | PO62/40D | 1989 | New World First Bus, 2003 |
| **HD42** | G42FWC | Dennis Condor DDA1702 | Duple Metsec | O62/40D | 1989 | New World First Bus, 2003 |
| **D59** | G59SYE | Dennis Condor DDA1702 | Duple Metsec | O62/40D | 1989 | New World First Bus, 2003 |

**The Big Bus Company is one of the two principal operators of open-top tourist services. Recent deliveries have started to displace the tri-axle buses new to Hong Kong that still dominate the service. The latest arrivals are six 12.35 metre Volvo B9TLs with Optare Visionaire bodywork. DA326, PN10FOK, is seen passing the former County Hall.** *Richard Godfrey*

New to China Motor Bus in Hong King, a batch of Duple Metsec-bodied Dennis Condor buses is used by The Big Bus Company on its services. Several are fully open-top but most are partially so, as shown by HD34, G34FWC, seen in Whitehall. *Richard Godfrey*

| | | | | | | | |
|---|---|---|---|---|---|---|---|
| **MBD67** | G67SYE | Dennis Condor DDA1702 | Duple Metsec | O62/40D | 1989 | New World First Bus, 2003 |
| **D96** | G96SGO | Dennis Condor DDA1702 | Duple Metsec | O62/40D | 1989 | New World First Bus, 2003 |
| **D159** | G159FWC | Dennis Condor DDA1702 | Duple Metsec | O62/40D | 1989 | New World First Bus, 2003 |
| **D418** | F418UJN | Dennis Condor DDA1702 | Duple Metsec | O62/40D | 1989 | New World First Bus, 2003 |
| **HD938** | G938FVX | Dennis Condor DDA1702 | Duple Metsec | PO62/40D | 1989 | New World First Bus, 2003 |
| **HD939** | G939FVX | Dennis Condor DDA1702 | Duple Metsec | PO62/40D | 1989 | New World First Bus, 2003 |
| **D943** | G943FVX | Dennis Condor DDA1702 | Duple Metsec | O62/40D | 1989 | New World First Bus, 2003 |
| **D952** | G952FVX | Dennis Condor DDA1702 | Duple Metsec | O62/40D | 1989 | New World First Bus, 2003 |
| **HD953** | G953FVX | Dennis Condor DDA1702 | Duple Metsec | PO62/40D | 1989 | New World First Bus, 2003 |
| **HD954** | G954FVX | Dennis Condor DDA1702 | Duple Metsec | PO62/40D | 1989 | New World First Bus, 2003 |
| **D956** | G956FVX | Dennis Condor DDA1702 | Duple Metsec | O62/40D | 1989 | New World First Bus, 2003 |
| **HD964** | G963FVX | Dennis Condor DDA1702 | Duple Metsec | PO62/40D | 1989 | New World First Bus, 2003 |
| **D969** | G969FVX | Dennis Condor DDA1702 | Duple Metsec | O62/40D | 1989 | New World First Bus, 2003 |
| **D991** | G991FVX | Dennis Condor DDA1702 | Duple Metsec | O62/40D | 1989 | New World First Bus, 2003 |
| **MBO90** | F90SYE | MCW Metrobus DR115/5 | MCW | O59/34D | 1988 | New World First Bus, '01 |
| **MBO336** | E336NUV | Leyland Olympian ONLXCT/5RV | Alexander RH | O59/34D | 1988 | Kowloon Motor Bus, 2005 |
| **MBO337** | E337NUV | Leyland Olympian ONLXCT/5RV | Alexander RH | O59/34D | 1988 | Kowloon Motor Bus, 2005 |
| **MBO338** | E338NUV | Leyland Olympian ONLXCT/5RV | Alexander RH | O59/34D | 1988 | Kowloon Motor Bus, 2005 |
| **MBHO340** | E340NUV | Leyland Olympian ONLXCT/5RV | Alexander RH | PO59/34D | 1988 | Kowloon Motor Bus, 2005 |
| **MBO351** | E351NUV | Leyland Olympian ONLXCT/5RV | Alexander RH | O59/34D | 1988 | Kowloon Motor Bus, 2006 |
| **MBO352** | E352NUV | Leyland Olympian ONLXCT/5RV | Alexander RH | O59/34D | 1988 | Kowloon Motor Bus, 2006 |
| **MBO353** | E353NUV | Leyland Olympian ONLXCT/5RV | Alexander RH | O59/34D | 1988 | Kowloon Motor Bus, 2006 |
| **MBO354** | E354NUV | Leyland Olympian ONLXCT/5RV | Alexander RH | O59/34D | 1988 | Kowloon Motor Bus, 2006 |
| **MBHO355** | E355NUV | Leyland Olympian ONLXCT/5RV | Alexander RH | PO59/34D | 1988 | Kowloon Motor Bus, 2006 |
| **MBO356** | E356NUV | Leyland Olympian ONLXCT/5RV | Alexander RH | O59/34D | 1988 | Kowloon Motor Bus, 2006 |
| **MBHO357** | E357NUV | Leyland Olympian ONLXCT/5RV | Alexander RH | PO59/34D | 1988 | Kowloon Motor Bus, 2006 |
| **MBO358** | E358NUV | Leyland Olympian ONLXCT/5RV | Alexander RH | PO59/34D | 1988 | Kowloon Motor Bus, 2006 |
| **MBO359** | E359NUV | Leyland Olympian ONLXCT/5RV | Alexander RH | PO59/34D | 1988 | Kowloon Motor Bus, 2006 |
| **MBO360** | E360NUV | Leyland Olympian ONLXCT/5RV | Alexander RH | PO59/34D | 1988 | Kowloon Motor Bus, 2006 |
| **MBO512** | D512UGT | Leyland Olympian ONLXCT/5RV | Alexander RH | O59/34D | 1986 | Kowloon Motor Bus, 2005 |
| **MBO514** | D514UGT | Leyland Olympian ONLXCT/5RV | Alexander RH | O59/34D | 1986 | Kowloon Motor Bus, 2005 |
| **MBOH6519** | D519UGT | Leyland Olympian ONLXCT/5RV | Alexander RH | PO59/34D | 1987 | Kowloon Motor Bus, 2006 |
| **MBO525** | D525UGT | Leyland Olympian ONLXCT/5RV | Alexander RH | O59/34D | 1987 | Kowloon Motor Bus, 2006 |
| **MBO6527** | D527UGT | Leyland Olympian ONLXCT/5RV | Alexander RH | O59/34D | 1987 | Kowloon Motor Bus, 2007 |
| **MBO690** | D690UGT | Leyland Olympian ONLXCT/5RV | Alexander RH | O59/34D | 1986 | Kowloon Motor Bus, 2005 |

**Many of the early tri-axle Olympians supplied to Hong Kong were brought back into Britain. Following refurbishment, MBO356, E356NUV, seen on a sunny day in Oxford Street, is fully open-top.** *Dave Heath*

| MBO692 | D692UGT | Leyland Olympian ONLXCT/5RV | Alexander RH | O59/34D | 1986 | Kowloon Motor Bus, 2005 |
|--------|---------|------------------------------|--------------|---------|------|-------------------------|
| ML15 | B15BUS | MCW Metrobus DR115/1 | MCW | PO61/39D | 1989 | |
| ML16 | B16BUS | MCW Metrobus DR115/1 | MCW | PO61/39D | 1989 | |
| ML20 | B20DMS | MCW Metrobus DR115/5 | MCW | O61/39D | 1988 | New World First Bus, '01 |
| ML69 | F69SYE | MCW Metrobus DR115/5 | MCW | O61/39D | 1988 | New World First Bus, '01 |
| ML153 | F153UJN | MCW Metrobus DR115/1 | MCW | O61/39D | 1989 | |
| ML326 | F326UJN | MCW Metrobus DR115/1 | MCW | O61/39D | 1989 | |
| ML764 | E764JAR | MCW Metrobus DR115/1 | MCW | PO61/39D | 1988 | |
| ML869 | E869JAR | MCW Metrobus DR115/1 | MCW | PO61/39D | 1988 | |
| ML881 | E881JAR | MCW Metrobus DR115/1 | MCW | PO61/39D | 1988 | |
| ML901 | E901JAR | MCW Metrobus DR115/1 | MCW | PO61/39D | 1988 | |
| ML949 | E949JAR | MCW Metrobus DR115/1 | MCW | PO61/39D | 1988 | |

Previous registrations:

| | | | |
|--------|--------------------------|---------|---------------|
| B14BUS | - | E357NUV | EC625 (HK) |
| B15BUS | DZ3401 (HK), F355UJN | E358NUV | EC8251 (HK) |
| B16BUS | - | E359NUV | EC1106 (HK) |
| B20DMS | - | E360NUV | EC1588 (HK) |
| D512UGT | DW7274 (HK) | F59SYE | EF4079 (HK) |
| D514UGT | DY9362 (HK) | F67SYE | EF750 (HK) |
| D519UGT | DY9758 (HK) | F69SYE | - |
| D525UGT | DY9259 (HK) | F90SYE | - |
| D527YGT | DZ110 (HK) | F153UJN | - |
| D690UGT | DT8317 (HK) | F326UJN | - |
| D692UGT | DW3065 (HK) | F418UJN | EF3349 (HK) |
| E764JAR | - | G32FWC | EJ2225 (HK) |
| E869JAR | - | G34FWC | EG2166 (HK) |
| E881JAR | - | G42FWC | EH6321 (HK) |
| E901JAR | - | G96SGO | EF5328 (HK) |
| E949JAR | - | G159FWC | - |
| E336NUV | DW4358 (HK) | G938FVX | EG9356 (HK) |
| E337NUV | DW3683 (HK) | G939FVX | EG857 (HK) |
| E338NUV | DW7793 (HK) | G943FVX | EH7098 (HK) |
| E340NUV | DW8912 (HK) | G952FVX | EH9876 (HK) |
| E351NUV | EC880 (HK) | G953FVX | EG9386 (HK) |
| E352NUV | EC8476 (HK) | G954FVX | EH6884 (HK) |
| E353NUV | EC8262 (HK) | G956FVX | EH4324 (HK) |
| E354NUV | EC8571 (HK) | G964FVX | EG6964 (HK) |
| E355NUV | EC1647 (HK) | G969FVX | EJ3811 (HK) |
| E356NUV | EC7483 (HK) | G991FVX | EG4627 (HK) |

**Marble Arch is the location for this view of DA9, LV51YCL, one of twelve Tridents with East Lancs Lolyne that were new to Metrobus of Orpington and converted to partial open-top in mid-life.** *Dave Heath*

## Depots and allocations:

### EARLSFIELD

| | | | | | | | | |
|---|---|---|---|---|---|---|---|---|
| Titan | T739 | T929 | T1038 | | | | | |
| Trident | DA1 | DA2 | DA3 | DA4 | DA5 | DA6 | DA7 | DA8 |
| | DA9 | DA10 | DA11 | DA12 | | | | |
| Volvo B9TL | DA201 | DA202 | DA203 | DA204 | DA205 | DA206 | DA207 | DA208 |
| | DA209 | DA210 | DA211 | DA212 | DA213 | DA214 | DA215 | DA216 |
| | DA217 | DA218 | DA219 | DA220 | DA321 | DA322 | DA323 | DA324 |
| | DA325 | DA326 | | | | | | |
| Denis Condor | D32 | D59 | D96 | D159 | D418 | D943 | D952 | D956 |
| | D969 | D991 | DHL14 | HD34 | HD42 | HD938 | HD939 | HD953 |
| | HD954 | HD964 | MBD67 | | | | | |
| Metrobus | MBO90 | ML15 | ML16 | ML20 | ML69 | ML153 | ML326 | ML764 |
| | ML869 | ML881 | ML901 | ML949 | | | | |
| Olympian | MBO336 | MBO337 | MBO338 | MBHO340 | MBO351 | MBO352 | MBO353 | MBO354 |
| | MBHO355 | MBO356 | MBHO357 | MBO358 | MBO359 | MBO360 | MBO512 | MBO514 |
| | MBOHB519 | | MBO525 | MBO6527 | MBO690 | MBO692 | | |

*The London Bus Handbook*

# FIRST

First Capital East Ltd, First Capital North Ltd,
Centrewest London Buses Ltd,
Macmillan House, Paddington Station, London, W2 1TY

| 11000 | WJ | BX54EBC | Mercedes-Benz Citaro O530G | | | AN49T | 2004 | Evobus demonstrator, 2006 |
|---|---|---|---|---|---|---|---|---|
| 11005 | WJ | LK53FAO | Mercedes-Benz Citaro O530G | | | AN49T | 2004 | Evobus demonstrator, 2006 |
| 11009 | WJ | LK53FBC | Mercedes-Benz Citaro O530G | | | AN49T | 2004 | Evobus demonstrator, 2006 |

### 11039-11065

Mercedes-Benz Citaro O530G · AN49T · 2005

| 11039 | HY | LK54FKX | 11046 | HY | LK05FDG | 11053 | HY | LK05FCO | 11060 | HY | LK05FCZ |
|---|---|---|---|---|---|---|---|---|---|---|---|
| 11040 | HY | LK54FKW | 11047 | HY | LK05FDL | 11054 | HY | LK05FCP | 11061 | HY | LK05FDA |
| 11041 | HY | LK05FDC | 11048 | HY | LK05EZW | 11055 | HY | LK05FCU | 11062 | HY | LK05FBZ |
| 11042 | HY | LK05FDD | 11049 | HY | LK05EZX | 11056 | HY | LK05FCV | 11063 | HY | LK05FCA |
| 11043 | HY | LK05FDE | 11050 | HY | LK05EZZ | 11057 | HY | LK05FBY | 11064 | HY | LK05FCB |
| 11044 | HY | LK05FDF | 11051 | HY | LK05FCM | 11058 | HY | LK05FCX | 11065 | HY | LK05FCC |
| 11045 | HY | LK05FDJ | 11052 | HY | LK05FCN | 11059 | HY | LK05FCY | | | |

| 11084 | HY | LX03HDH | Mercedes-Benz Citaro O530G | | AN49T | 2003 | East London, 2009 |
|---|---|---|---|---|---|---|---|
| 20201 | DG | T701JLD | Volvo B12T | Plaxton Excalibur | C51F | 1999 | |
| 20202 | DG | T702JLD | Volvo B12T | Plaxton Excalibur | C51F | 1999 | |
| 20203 | DG | T703JLD | Volvo B12T | Plaxton Excalibur | C51F | 1999 | |

### 32306-32327

Volvo B7TL 10.6m · TransBus President 4.4m · N42/23D · 2003

| 32306 | NP | LK03NHF | 32316 | NP | LK03NHX | 32320 | NP | LK03NJF | 32324 | NP | LK03NJX |
|---|---|---|---|---|---|---|---|---|---|---|---|
| 32307 | NP | LK03NHG | 32317 | NP | LK03NHY | 32321 | NP | LK03NJJ | 32325 | NP | LK03NJY |
| 32313 | NP | LK03NHP | 32318 | NP | LK03NHZ | 32322 | NP | LK03NJN | 32326 | NP | LK03NJZ |
| 32314 | NP | LK03NHT | 32319 | NP | LK03NJE | 32323 | NP | LK03NJV | 32327 | NP | LK03NKA |
| 32315 | NP | LK03NHV | | | | | | | | | |

**The number of articulated Mercedes-Benz Citaro buses remaining with First has recently reduced. One that remains is 11061, LK05FDA, seen here on route 18 that is now double-deck. The EA local prefix used to identify the vehicle type.** *Terry Longhurst*

First's Wrightbus-bodies Volvo B7TLs are represented by 32365, LK04HYX, seen passing through the picturesque parts of north-west London. *Mark Lyons*

### 32328-32347

Volvo B7TL 10.6m  Wrightbus Eclipse Gemini  N41/24D  2003

| | | | | | | | | | | | |
|---|---|---|---|---|---|---|---|---|---|---|---|
| 32328 | G | LK53LYH | 32333 | G | LK53LYT | 32338 | G | LK53LYY | 32343 | G | LK53LZD |
| 32329 | G | LK53LYJ | 32334 | G | LK53LYU | 32339 | G | LK53LYZ | 32344 | G | LK53LZE |
| 32330 | G | LK53LYO | 32335 | G | LK53LYV | 32340 | G | LK53LZA | 32345 | G | LK53LZF |
| 32331 | G | LK53LYP | 32336 | G | LK53LYW | 32341 | G | LK53LZB | 32346 | G | LK53LZG |
| 32332 | G | LK53LYR | 32337 | G | LK53LYX | 32342 | G | LK53LZC | 32347 | G | LK53LZH |

### 32349-32370

Volvo B7TL 10.1m  Wrightbus Eclipse Gemini  N41/21D  2004

| | | | | | | | | | | | |
|---|---|---|---|---|---|---|---|---|---|---|---|
| 32349 | ON | LK53LZM | 32355 | ON | LK53LZU | 32361 | X | LK04HYN | 32366 | X | LK04HYY |
| 32350 | ON | LK53LZN | 32356 | ON | LK53LZV | 32362 | X | LK04HYM | 32367 | X | LK04HYA |
| 32351 | ON | LK53LZO | 32357 | ON | LK53LZW | 32363 | X | LK04HYW | 32368 | X | LK04HYS |
| 32352 | ON | LK53LZP | 32358 | ON | LK53LZX | 32364 | X | LK04HYT | 32369 | X | LK04HYU |
| 32353 | ON | LK53LZR | 32359 | ON | LK53MBF | 32365 | X | LK04HYX | 32370 | X | LK04HYV |
| 32354 | ON | LK53LZT | 32360 | ON | LK04HYP | | | | | | |

### 32371-32430

Volvo B7TL 10.1m  Wrightbus Eclipse Gemini  N41/21D  2004

| | | | | | | | | | | | |
|---|---|---|---|---|---|---|---|---|---|---|---|
| 32371 | X | LK04HZA | 32386 | X | LK04HZU | 32401 | X | LK04HXL | 32416 | X | LK04JBY |
| 32372 | X | LK04HZB | 32387 | X | LK04HZV | 32402 | X | LK04HXM | 32417 | X | LK04JBZ |
| 32373 | X | LK04HZC | 32388 | X | LK04HZW | 32403 | X | LK04HXN | 32418 | X | LK04JCJ |
| 32374 | X | LK04HZD | 32389 | X | LK04HZX | 32404 | X | LK04HXP | 32419 | X | LK04JCU |
| 32375 | X | LK04HZE | 32390 | X | LK04HZY | 32405 | X | LK04HXR | 32420 | X | LK04JCV |
| 32376 | X | LK04HZF | 32391 | X | LK04HZZ | 32406 | X | LK04HXS | 32421 | X | LK04JCX |
| 32377 | X | LK04HZG | 32392 | X | LK04HXA | 32407 | X | LK04HXT | 32422 | X | LK04HYZ |
| 32378 | X | LK04HZH | 32393 | X | LK04HXB | 32408 | X | LK04HXU | 32423 | X | LK04JCZ |
| 32379 | X | LK04HZJ | 32394 | X | LK04HXC | 32409 | X | LK04HXV | 32424 | X | LK04HYB |
| 32380 | X | LK04HZL | 32395 | X | LK04HXD | 32410 | X | LK04HXW | 32425 | X | LK04HYC |
| 32381 | X | LK04HZM | 32396 | X | LK04HXE | 32411 | X | LK04HXX | 32426 | X | LK04HYF |
| 32382 | X | LK04HZN | 32397 | X | LK54FNO | 32412 | X | LK04JBE | 32427 | X | LK04HYG |
| 32383 | X | LK04JBU | 32398 | X | LK54FNP | 32413 | X | LK04HZP | 32428 | X | LK04HYH |
| 32384 | X | LK04HZS | 32399 | X | LK04HXH | 32414 | X | LK04JBV | 32429 | X | LK04HYJ |
| 32385 | X | LK04HZT | 32400 | X | LK04HXJ | 32415 | X | LK04JBX | 32430 | X | LK04HYL |

*The London Bus Handbook*

Plaxton's President body was assembled at the Wigan facility latterly known as Northern Counties. Seen opposite Liverpool Street rail station is 33049, LN51GKE. The Trident 1s carry the TN class prefix. *Dave Heath*

### 32495-32502

Volvo B7TL 10.6m    Wrightbus Eclipse Gemini    N41/24D    2004

| | | | | | | | | |
|---|---|---|---|---|---|---|---|
| **32495** | X | LK54FLA | **32497** | X | LK54FLC | **32499** | X | LK54FLE | **32501** | X | LK54FLG |
| **32496** | X | LK54FLB | **32498** | X | LK54FLD | **32500** | X | LK54FLF | **32502** | X | LK54FLH |

### 32658-32668

Volvo B7TL 10.1m    Wrightbus Eclipse Gemini    N41/21D    2005

| | | | | | | | | |
|---|---|---|---|---|---|---|---|
| **32658** | DGu | LK55ACU | **32661** | DGu | LK55AAJ | **32664** | DGu | LK55AAV | **32667** | DGu | LK55AAZ |
| **32659** | DGu | LK55AAE | **32662** | DGu | LK55AAN | **32665** | DGu | LK55AAX | **32668** | DGu | LK55ABF |
| **32660** | DGu | LK55AAF | **32663** | DGu | LK55AAU | **32666** | DGu | LK55AAY | | | |

| | | | | | |
|---|---|---|---|---|---|
| **32806** | DGt | T806LLC | Dennis Trident 9.9m | Plaxton President 4.4m | N39/20D | 1999 |
| **32807** | ONt | T807LLC | Dennis Trident 9.9m | Plaxton President 4.4m | N39/20D | 1999 |
| **32822** | ONt | T822LLC | Dennis Trident 9.9m | Plaxton President 4.4m | N39/20D | 1999 |

### 32893-32968

Dennis Trident 9.9m    Plaxton President 4.4m    N43/24D*    2000-01    *seating varies

| | | | | | | | | |
|---|---|---|---|---|---|---|---|
| **32893** | UX | V893HLH | **32896** | G | V896HLH | **32929** | DG | W929VLN | **32968** | DG | X968HLT |
| **32895** | G | V895HLH | **32907** | UX | W907VLN | **32967** | DG | X967HLT | | | |

### 33020-33036

Dennis Trident 10.5m    Plaxton President 4.4m    N42/23D    2001

| | | | | | | | | |
|---|---|---|---|---|---|---|---|
| **33020** | L | LK51UYX | **33024** | L | LK51UZB | **33027** | L | LK51UYH | **33034** | L | LK51UYR |
| **33021** | L | LK51UYY | **33025** | L | LK51UYF | **33028** | L | LK51UYJ | **33035** | L | LK51UYD |
| **33022** | L | LK51UYZ | **33026** | L | LK51UYG | **33033** | L | LK51UYP | **33036** | DG | LK51UYE |
| **33023** | L | LK51UZA | | | | | | | | | |

### 33037-33071

Dennis Trident 9.9m    Plaxton President 4.4m    N39/20D    2001

| | | | | | | | | |
|---|---|---|---|---|---|---|---|
| **33037** | UX | LN51DWA | **33047** | NP | LN51DVM | **33059** | UX | LN51GJO | **33066** | G | LN51GLF |
| **33039** | NP | LN51DWD | **33048** | NP | LN51GKD | **33061** | G | LN51GKU | **33067** | G | LN51GLJ |
| **33042** | NP | LN51DWG | **33049** | NP | LN51GKE | **33062** | G | LN51GKV | **33068** | G | LN51GLK |
| **33043** | NP | LN51DVG | **33050** | UX | LN51GKF | **33063** | G | LN51GKX | **33069** | G | LN51GLV |
| **33044** | NP | LN51DVH | **33051** | NP | LN51GKG | **33064** | G | LN51GKY | **33070** | G | LN51GLY |
| **33045** | NP | LN51DVK | **33052** | G | LN51GKJ | **33065** | G | LN51GKZ | **33071** | G | LN51GKA |

## 33072-33098 — Dennis Trident 10.5m — Plaxton President 4.4m — N42/23D — 2001-02

| | | | | | | | | | | | |
|---|---|---|---|---|---|---|---|---|---|---|---|
| 33072 | UX | LN51GOC | 33078 | DG | LN51GNJ | 33088 | DG | LN51GMU | 33094 | DG | LN51NRK |
| 33073 | UX | LN51GOE | 33080 | UX | LN51GNP | 33090 | UX | LN51GMX | 33095 | UX | LN51NRL |
| 33074 | UX | LN51GOH | 33081 | UX | LN51GNU | 33091 | DG | LN51GMY | 33096 | DG | LN51GNY |
| 33075 | NP | LN51GOJ | 33085 | DG | LN51GMF | 33092 | DG | LN51GMZ | 33097 | DG | LN51GNZ |
| 33076 | NP | LN51GOK | 33086 | DG | LN51GMG | 33093 | UX | LN51NRJ | 33098 | UXP | LN51GOA |
| 33077 | NP | LN51GNF | 33087 | DG | LN51GMO | | | | | | |

## 33123-33129 — Dennis Trident 9.9m — Plaxton President 4.4m — N39/20D — 2002

| | | | | | | | | | | | |
|---|---|---|---|---|---|---|---|---|---|---|---|
| 33123 | G | LT02NVK | 33125 | G | LT02NVN | 33127 | G | LT02NVP | 33129 | G | LT02NVS |
| 33124 | G | LT02NVM | 33126 | G | LT02NVO | 33128 | G | LT02NVR | | | |

## 33131-33140 — TransBus Trident 10.5m — TransBus President 4.4m — N42/23D — 2002

| | | | | | | | | | | | |
|---|---|---|---|---|---|---|---|---|---|---|---|
| 33131 | UX | LT02ZBX | 33134 | UX | LT02ZCA | 33137 | UX | LT02ZFJ | 33139 | UX | LT02ZFL |
| 33132 | UX | LT02ZBY | 33135 | UX | LT02ZCE | 33138 | UX | LT02ZFK | 33140 | UX | LT02ZFM |
| 33133 | UX | LT02ZBZ | 33136 | UX | LT02ZCF | | | | | | |

## 33178-33199 — TransBus Trident 9.9m — TransBus President 4.4m — N39/20D — 2002

| | | | | | | | | | | | |
|---|---|---|---|---|---|---|---|---|---|---|---|
| 33178 | X | LR02LYX | 33184 | X | LR02LZD | 33190 | X | LT52XAA | 33195 | X | LT52XAF |
| 33179 | X | LR02LYY | 33185 | X | LR02LZE | 33191 | X | LT52XAB | 33196 | X | LT52XAG |
| 33180 | X | LR02LYZ | 33186 | X | LT52WVB | 33192 | X | LT52XAC | 33197 | X | LT52XAH |
| 33181 | X | LR02LZA | 33187 | X | LT52WVC | 33193 | U | LT52XAD | 33198 | X | LT52XAJ |
| 33182 | X | LR02LZB | 33188 | X | LT52WVD | 33194 | X | LT52XAE | 33199 | X | LT52XAK |
| 33183 | X | LR02LZC | 33189 | X | LT52WVE | | | | | | |

## 33229-33232 — TransBus Trident 9.9m — TransBus President 4.4m — N39/20D — 2002

| | | | | | | | | |
|---|---|---|---|---|---|---|---|---|
| 33229 | NP | LT52WXG | 33231 | NP | LT52WXJ | 33232 | DG | LT52WXK |

## 33277-33293 — TransBus Trident 9.9m — TransBus President 4.4m — N39/20D — 2003

| | | | | | | | | | | | |
|---|---|---|---|---|---|---|---|---|---|---|---|
| 33277 | G | LK03NKC | 33282 | G | LK03NKP | 33286 | G | LK03NKU | 33290 | G | LK03NLA |
| 33278 | G | LK03NKD | 33283 | G | LK03NKR | 33287 | G | LK03NKW | 33291 | G | LK03NLC |
| 33279 | G | LK03NKE | 33284 | G | LK03NKS | 33288 | G | LK03NKX | 33292 | G | LK03NLP |
| 33280 | G | LK03NKF | 33285 | G | LK03NKT | 33289 | G | LK03NKZ | 33293 | G | LK03NLR |
| 33281 | G | LK03NKG | | | | | | | | | |

## 33328-33342 — TransBus Trident 9.9m — TransBus President 4.4m — N39/20D — 2003

| | | | | | | | | | | | |
|---|---|---|---|---|---|---|---|---|---|---|---|
| 33328 | UX | LK03UFD | 33332 | UX | LK03UFL | 33336 | UX | LK03UFR | 33340 | UX | LK03UFV |
| 33329 | UX | LK03UFE | 33333 | UX | LK03UFM | 33337 | UX | LK03UFS | 33341 | UX | LK03UFW |
| 33330 | UX | LK03UFG | 33334 | UX | LK03UFN | 33338 | UX | LK03UFT | 33342 | UX | LK03UFX |
| 33331 | UX | LK03UFJ | 33335 | UX | LK03UFP | 33339 | UX | LK03UFU | | | |

## 33343-33386 — TransBus Trident 10.5m — TransBus ALX400 4.4m — N42/21D — 2003

| | | | | | | | | | | | |
|---|---|---|---|---|---|---|---|---|---|---|---|
| 33343 | X | LK53EZV | 33354 | X | LK53FDA | 33365 | X | LK53EYF | 33376 | X | LK53EYV |
| 33344 | X | LK53EZW | 33355 | X | LK53EXT | 33366 | X | LK53EYG | 33377 | X | LK53EYW |
| 33345 | X | LK53EZX | 33356 | X | LK53EXU | 33367 | X | LK53EYH | 33378 | X | LK53EYX |
| 33346 | X | LK53EZZ | 33357 | X | LK53EXV | 33368 | X | LK53EYJ | 33379 | X | LK53EYY |
| 33347 | X | LK53FCF | 33358 | X | LK53EXW | 33369 | X | LK53EYL | 33380 | X | LK53EYZ |
| 33348 | X | LK53FCG | 33359 | X | LK53EXX | 33370 | X | LK53EYM | 33381 | X | LK53EZA |
| 33349 | X | LK53FCJ | 33360 | X | LK53EXZ | 33371 | X | LK53EYO | 33382 | X | LK53EZB |
| 33350 | X | LK53FCL | 33361 | X | LK53EYA | 33372 | X | LK53EYP | 33383 | X | LK53EZC |
| 33351 | X | LK53FCX | 33362 | X | LK53EYB | 33373 | X | LK53EYR | 33384 | X | LK53EZD |
| 33352 | X | LK53FCY | 33363 | X | LK53EYC | 33374 | X | LK53EYT | 33385 | X | LK53EZE |
| 33353 | X | LK53FCZ | 33364 | X | LK53EYD | 33375 | X | LK53EYU | 33386 | X | LK53EZF |

## 33501-33543 — ADL Trident 2 10.1m — ADL Enviro 400 — N41/26D — 2008

| | | | | | | | | | | | |
|---|---|---|---|---|---|---|---|---|---|---|---|
| 33501 | DG | LK57EJN | 33512 | X | LK08LMU | 33523 | NP | LK08FLM | 33534 | NP | SN58CEU |
| 33502 | DG | LK57EJO | 33513 | X | LK08LMV | 33524 | NP | LK08FLN | 33535 | NP | SN58CEV |
| 33503 | DG | LK08FNE | 33514 | X | LK08LMX | 33525 | NP | LK08FLP | 33536 | NP | SN58CEX |
| 33504 | DG | LK08FLX | 33515 | X | LK08LMY | 33526 | NP | LK08FLR | 33537 | NP | SN58CEY |
| 33505 | DG | LK08FKX | 33516 | X | LK08LMZ | 33527 | NP | SN58CDY | 33538 | NP | SN58CFA |
| 33506 | DG | LK08FKY | 33517 | X | LK08FNA | 33528 | NP | SN58CDZ | 33539 | NP | SN58CFD |
| 33507 | DG | LK08FKZ | 33518 | X | LK08FNC | 33529 | NP | SN58CEA | 33540 | NP | SN58CFE |
| 33508 | DG | LK08FLA | 33519 | X | LK08FND | 33530 | NP | SN58CEF | 33541 | NP | SN58CFF |
| 33509 | X | LK08LMA | 33520 | NP | LK08FLH | 33531 | NP | SN58CEJ | 33542 | NP | SN58CFG |
| 33510 | X | LK08LMO | 33521 | NP | LK08FLJ | 33532 | NP | SN58CEK | 33543 | G | SN58CFJ |
| 33511 | X | LK08LMP | 33522 | NP | LK08FLL | 33533 | NP | SN58CEO | | | |

Fleet numbers for the Trident 2s with First commence at 33501 and carry class prefix of DN. Haven Green in Ealing provides the background for this view of 33610, SN09CGU, from the 2009 delivery. *Dave Heath*

### 33544-33574     ADL Trident 2   10.1m     ADL Enviro 400     N41/26D     2008

| | | | | | | | | | | | |
|---|---|---|---|---|---|---|---|---|---|---|---|
| 33544 | DG | SN58CFK | 33552 | DG | SN58CFY | 33560 | DG | SN58CGV | 33568 | DG | SN58CHH |
| 33545 | DG | SN58CFL | 33553 | DG | SN58CFZ | 33561 | DG | SN58CGX | 33569 | DG | SN58CHJ |
| 33546 | DG | SN58CFM | 33554 | DG | SN58CGE | 33562 | DG | SN58CGY | 33570 | DG | SN58CHK |
| 33547 | DG | SN58CFO | 33555 | DG | SN58CGF | 33563 | DG | SN58CGZ | 33571 | DG | SN58CHL |
| 33548 | DG | SN58CFP | 33556 | DG | SN58CGG | 33564 | DG | SN58CHC | 33572 | DG | SN58CHO |
| 33549 | DG | SN58CFU | 33557 | DG | SN58CGK | 33565 | DG | SN58CHD | 33573 | DG | SN58CHR |
| 33550 | DG | SN58CFV | 33558 | DG | SN58CGO | 33566 | DG | SN58CHF | 33574 | DG | SN58CHT |
| 33551 | DG | SN58CFX | 33559 | DG | SN58CGU | 33567 | DG | SN58CHG | | | |

### 33575-33611     ADL Trident 2     ADL Enviro 400     N41/26D     2009

| | | | | | | | | | | | |
|---|---|---|---|---|---|---|---|---|---|---|---|
| 33575 | G | SN09CDU | 33585 | G | SN09CEU | 33594 | G | SN09CFJ | 33603 | G | SN09CFY |
| 33576 | G | SN09CDV | 33586 | G | SN09CEV | 33595 | G | SN09CFK | 33604 | G | SN09CFZ |
| 33577 | G | SN09CDX | 33587 | G | SN09CEX | 33596 | G | SN09CFL | 33605 | G | SN09CGE |
| 33578 | G | SN09CDY | 33588 | G | SN09CEY | 33597 | G | SN09CFM | 33606 | G | SN09CGF |
| 33579 | G | SN09CDZ | 33589 | G | SN09CFA | 33598 | G | SN09CFO | 33607 | G | SN09CGG |
| 33580 | G | SN09CEA | 33590 | G | SN09CFD | 33599 | G | SN09CFP | 33608 | G | SN09CGK |
| 33581 | G | SN09CEF | 33591 | G | SN09CFE | 33600 | G | SN09CFU | 33609 | G | SN09CGO |
| 33582 | G | SN09CEJ | 33592 | G | SN09CFF | 33601 | G | SN09CFV | 33610 | G | SN09CGU |
| 33583 | G | SN09CEK | 33593 | G | SN09CFG | 33602 | G | SN09CFX | 33611 | G | SN09CGV |
| 33584 | G | SN09CEO | | | | | | | | | |

### 33612-33655     ADL Trident 2     ADL Enviro 400     N41/26D     2011

| | | | | | | | | | | | |
|---|---|---|---|---|---|---|---|---|---|---|---|
| 33612 | L | SN11BMU | 33623 | L | SN11BNL | 33634 | L | SN11BOV | 33645 | L | SN11BRV |
| 33613 | L | SN11BMV | 33624 | L | SN11BNO | 33635 | L | SN11BPE | 33646 | L | SN11BRZ |
| 33614 | L | SN11BMY | 33625 | L | SN11BNU | 33636 | L | SN11BPF | 33647 | L | SN11BSO |
| 33615 | L | SN11BMZ | 33626 | L | SN11BNV | 33637 | L | SN11BPK | 33648 | L | SN11BSU |
| 33616 | L | SN11BNA | 33627 | L | SN11BNX | 33638 | L | SN11BPO | 33649 | L | SN11BSV |
| 33617 | L | SN11BNB | 33628 | L | SN11BNY | 33639 | L | SN11BPU | 33650 | L | SN11BSX |
| 33618 | L | SN11BND | 33629 | L | SN11BNZ | 33640 | L | SN11BPV | 33651 | L | SN11BSY |
| 33619 | L | SN11BNE | 33630 | L | SN11BOF | 33641 | L | SN11BPX | 33652 | L | SN11BSZ |
| 33620 | L | SN11BNF | 33631 | L | SN11BOH | 33642 | L | SN11BPY | 33653 | L | SN11BTE |
| 33621 | L | SN11BNJ | 33632 | L | SN11BOJ | 33643 | L | SN11BPZ | 33654 | L | SN11BTO |
| 33622 | L | SN11BNK | 33633 | L | SN11BOU | 33644 | L | SN11BRF | 33655 | L | SN11BTU |

### 34215-34218     Volvo Olympian     Northern Counties Palatine     B47/27D     1998

| | | | | | | | | |
|---|---|---|---|---|---|---|---|---|
| 34215 | DG | S215LLO | 34216 | DG | S216LLO | 34218 | DG | S218LLO |

First operates four examples of the integral **Wrightbus Pulsar Gemini 2 DL** model that uses VDL mechanical components. All four are allocated to Westbourne Park depot from where 35002, LK58EDP, was working route 23 when pictured at Marble Arch. *Terry Longhurst*

### 35001-35004

Wrightbus Pulsar Gemini 2 DL 10.4m　　　　　　　　　　　N41/25D　2009

| 35001 | X | LK58EDO | 35002 | X | LK58EDP | 35003 | X | LK58EDR | 35004 | X | LK58CZS |
|-------|---|---------|-------|---|---------|-------|---|---------|-------|---|---------|

### 36101-36165

Volvo B9TL　　　　　　　　　Wrightbus Eclipse Gemini 2　N41/29D　2011

| 36101 | L | BJ11DSE | 36118 | L | BJ11DVC | 36134 | L | BJ11DTZ | 36150 | L | BJ11EBD |
|-------|---|---------|-------|---|---------|-------|---|---------|-------|---|---------|
| 36102 | L | BJ11DSZ | 36119 | L | BJ11DSY | 36135 | L | BJ11DUH | 36151 | L | BJ11EBC |
| 36103 | L | BJ11DSU | 36120 | L | BJ11DRZ | 36136 | L | BJ11DVV | 36152 | L | BJ11EAE |
| 36104 | L | BJ11DTF | 36121 | L | BJ11DSO | 36137 | L | BJ11DVW | 36153 | L | BJ11DVX |
| 36105 | L | BJ11DSV | 36122 | L | BJ11DTK | 36138 | L | BJ11DVT | 36154 | L | BJ11EAA |
| 36106 | L | BJ11DTV | 36123 | L | BJ11DTX | 36139 | L | BJ11DVU | 36155 | L | BJ11DZZ |
| 36107 | L | BJ11DTY | 36124 | L | BJ11DTU | 36140 | L | BJ11DZX | 36156 | L | BJ11DZY |
| 36108 | L | BJ11DTO | 36125 | L | BJ11DVG | 36141 | L | BJ11EBP | 36157 | L | BJ11EAC |
| 36109 | L | BJ11DUV | 36126 | L | BJ11DUY | 36142 | L | BJ11EAM | 36158 | L | BJ11EAG |
| 36110 | L | BJ11DUA | 36127 | L | BJ11DVA | 36143 | L | BJ11EAF | 36159 | L | BJ11EAP |
| 36111 | L | BJ11DVH | 36128 | L | BJ11DVB | 36144 | L | BJ11EAX | 36160 | L | BJ11EAY |
| 36112 | L | BJ11DVF | 36129 | L | BJ11DVO | 36145 | L | BJ11EBG | 36161 | L | BJ11EBA |
| 36113 | L | BJ11DVP | 36130 | L | BJ11DVN | 36146 | L | BJ11EBL | 36162 | L | BJ11EBK |
| 36114 | L | BJ11DVM | 36131 | L | BJ11DVR | 36147 | L | BJ11EAK | 36163 | L | BJ11EBM |
| 36115 | L | BJ11DVL | 36132 | L | BJ11DSX | 36148 | L | BJ11EAW | 36164 | L | BJ11EBO |
| 36116 | L | BJ11DUU | 36133 | L | BJ11DTN | 36149 | L | BJ11EAO | 36165 | L | BJ11EBN |
| 36117 | L | BJ11DVK | | | | | | | | | |

### 37773-37842

Volvo B9TL　　　　　　　　　Wrightbus Eclipse Gemini 2　N41/29D　2009-10

| 37773 | ON | LK59CWN | 37791 | ON | LK59CXH | 37809 | NP | LK59FDY | 37826 | NP | LK59FDU |
|-------|----|---------|-------|----|---------|-------|----|---------|-------|----|---------|
| 37774 | ON | LK59CWO | 37792 | ON | LK59CXJ | 37810 | NP | LK59FDZ | 37827 | L | BG59FXA |
| 37775 | ON | LK59CWP | 37793 | ON | LK59CXL | 37811 | NP | LK59FEF | 37828 | L | BG59FXB |
| 37776 | ON | LK59CWR | 37794 | ON | LK59CXM | 37812 | NP | LK59FEG | 37829 | L | BG59FXC |
| 37777 | ON | LK59CWT | 37795 | ON | LK59CXN | 37813 | NP | LK59FEH | 37830 | L | BG59FXD |
| 37778 | ON | LK59CWU | 37796 | ON | LK59CXO | 37814 | NP | LK59FEJ | 37831 | L | BG59FXE |
| 37779 | ON | LK59CWV | 37797 | ON | LK59CXP | 37815 | NP | LK59FEM | 37832 | L | BG59FXF |
| 37780 | ON | LK59CWW | 37798 | ON | LK59FCO | 37816 | NP | LK59FEO | 37833 | L | BG59FXH |
| 37781 | ON | LK59CWX | 37799 | ON | LK59FCP | 37817 | NP | LK59FDE | 37834 | L | BV10WVD |
| 37782 | ON | LK59CWY | 37800 | ON | LK59FCU | 37818 | NP | LK59FDF | 37835 | L | BV10WVE |
| 37783 | ON | LK59CWZ | 37801 | ON | LK59FCV | 37819 | NP | LK59FDG | 37836 | L | BV10WVF |
| 37784 | ON | LK59CXA | 37802 | ON | LK59FCX | 37820 | NP | LK59FDJ | 37837 | L | BV10WVG |
| 37785 | ON | LK59CXB | 37803 | ON | LK59FCY | 37821 | NP | LK59FDL | 37838 | L | BV10WVH |
| 37786 | ON | LK59CXC | 37804 | NP | LK59FEP | 37822 | NP | LK59FDM | 37839 | L | BV10WVJ |
| 37787 | ON | LK59CXD | 37805 | NP | LK59FET | 37823 | NP | LK59FDN | 37840 | L | BV10WVK |
| 37788 | ON | LK59CXE | 37806 | NP | LK59FEU | 37824 | NP | LK59FDO | 37841 | L | BV10WVL |
| 37789 | ON | LK59CXF | 37807 | NP | LK59FDV | 37825 | NP | LK59FDP | 37842 | L | BV10WVM |
| 37790 | ON | LK59CXG | 37808 | NP | LK59FDX | | | | | | |

The successor to the Volvo B7TL is the B9TL, a product that, with Wrightbus bodywork, First have sourced for many of their operations. Illustrating the type complete with the latest Gemini 2 front is 37923, BF60VJK, one of the large intake for 2010 allocated to Willesden Junction for the conversion of route 18 from articulated Mercedes-Benz Citaro buses. *Mark Lyons*

### 37843-37889   Volvo B9TL        Wrightbus Eclipse Gemini 2   N39/23D   2010

| | | | | | | | | | | |
|---|---|---|---|---|---|---|---|---|---|---|
| 37843 | NP | BV10WWA | 37855 | NP | BV10WWN | 37867 | HY | BK10WVP | 37879 | HY | BF10LSV |
| 37844 | NP | BV10WWT | 37856 | NP | BV10WWO | 37868 | HY | BK10WVR | 37880 | HY | BF10LSX |
| 37845 | NP | BV10WWC | 37857 | NP | BV10WWP | 37869 | HY | BK10WVS | 37881 | HY | BF10LSY |
| 37846 | NP | BV10WWD | 37858 | NP | BV10WWR | 37870 | HY | BK10WVT | 37882 | HY | BF10LTE |
| 37847 | NP | BV10WWE | 37859 | NP | BV10WWS | 37871 | HY | BK10MEV | 37883 | HY | BF10LTJ |
| 37848 | NP | BV10WWF | 37860 | NP | BV10WWB | 37872 | HY | BK10MFA | 37884 | HY | BV10WVN |
| 37849 | NP | BV10WWG | 37861 | NP | BV10WWU | 37873 | HY | BK10MFE | 37885 | HY | BV10WVO |
| 37850 | NP | BV10WWH | 37862 | NP | BV10WWX | 37874 | HY | BK10MFN | 37886 | HY | BV10WVU |
| 37851 | NP | BV10WWJ | 37863 | NP | BV10WWY | 37875 | HY | BK10MFF | 37887 | HY | BV10WVW |
| 37852 | NP | BV10WWK | 37864 | NP | BV10WWZ | 37876 | HY | BK10MFJ | 37888 | HY | BV10WVX |
| 37853 | NP | BV10WWL | 37865 | HY | BF10LSZ | 37877 | HY | BF10LSO | 37889 | NP | BK10MFO |
| 37854 | NP | BV10WWM | 37866 | HY | BF10LTA | 37878 | HY | BF10LSU | | | |

### 37890-37942   Volvo B9TL        Wrightbus Eclipse Gemini 2   N39/23D   2010

| | | | | | | | | | | |
|---|---|---|---|---|---|---|---|---|---|---|
| 37890 | WJ | BF60UUA | 37904 | WJ | BF60UUR | 37917 | WJ | BF60UUW | 37930 | WJ | BF60VJU |
| 37891 | WJ | BF60UUB | 37905 | WJ | BF60UUP | 37918 | WJ | BF60VHT | 37931 | WJ | BF60VJV |
| 37892 | WJ | BF60UTZ | 37906 | WJ | BF60UUT | 37919 | WJ | BF60VHX | 37932 | WJ | BF60UVB |
| 37893 | WJ | BF60UUD | 37907 | WJ | BF60UUS | 37920 | WJ | BF60VJA | 37933 | WJ | BF60UVA |
| 37894 | WJ | BF60UUC | 37908 | WJ | BF60UUX | 37921 | WJ | BF60VHY | 37934 | WJ | BF60UVD |
| 37895 | WJ | BF60UUE | 37909 | WJ | BF60UUY | 37922 | WJ | BF60VJC | 37935 | WJ | BF60UVG |
| 37896 | WJ | BF60UUJ | 37910 | WJ | BF60UUV | 37923 | WJ | BF60VJK | 37936 | WJ | BF60UVH |
| 37897 | WJ | BF60UUG | 37911 | WJ | BF60UUZ | 37924 | WJ | BF60VJJ | 37937 | WJ | BF60UVO |
| 37898 | WJ | BF60UUK | 37912 | WJ | BF60VHP | 37925 | WJ | BF60VJE | 37938 | WJ | BF60UVE |
| 37899 | WJ | BF60UUH | 37913 | WJ | BF60VHR | 37926 | WJ | BF60VHZ | 37939 | WJ | BF60VJN |
| 37900 | WJ | BF60UUL | 37914 | WJ | BF60VHV | 37927 | WJ | BF60VJG | 37940 | WJ | BF60VJM |
| 37901 | WJ | BF60UUN | 37915 | WJ | BF60VHU | 37928 | WJ | BF60VJD | 37941 | WJ | BF60VJO |
| 37902 | WJ | BF60UUM | 37916 | WJ | BF60VHW | 37929 | WJ | BF60VJL | 37942 | WJ | BF60VJP |
| 37903 | WJ | BF60UUO | | | | | | | | | |

| | | | | | | | |
|---|---|---|---|---|---|---|---|
| 37943 | ON | BK10MFZ | Volvo B5TL | | Wrightbus Eclipse Gemini 2 | N39/23D | 2010 |

The four Wrightbus integrals shown on page 50 followed five Wrightbus Pulsar Gemini 2 Hybrid integral buses supplied to First in 2008. These, too, are allocated to Westbourne Park depot. Pictured operating on heir usual haunt, route 328 is 39003, LK58ECX. *Mark Lyons*

### 39001-39005

| | | | | | | | | |
|---|---|---|---|---|---|---|---|---|
| | | | Wrightbus Pulsar Gemini 2 Hybrid | | | N41/24D | 2008 | |
| 39001 | X | LK58ECV | **39003** | X | LK58ECX | **39004** | X | LK58ECY | **39005** | X | LK58ECZ |
| 39002 | X | LK58ECW | | | | | | |

| | | | | | | | |
|---|---|---|---|---|---|---|---|
| 39735 | X | SMK735F | AEC Routemaster R2RH1 | Park Royal | B40/32R | 1967 | |
| 39804 | X | 204CLT | AEC Routemaster R2RH | Park Royal/Marshall | B36/28R | 1962 | LBL, 2005 |
| 39810 | Xs | 510CLT | AEC Routemaster R2RH | Park Royal | O32/25R | 1962 | London Buses, 2004 |
| 39813 | X | ALD913B | AEC Routemaster R2RH | Park Royal/Marshall | B36/28R | 1964 | LBL, 2005 |
| 39818 | X | 218CLT | AEC Routemaster R2RH | Park Royal/Marshall | B36/28R | 1962 | LBL, 2005 |
| 39827 | X | 627DYE | AEC Routemaster R2RH | Park Royal/Marshall | B36/28R | 1963 | LBL, 2005 |
| 39835 | X | 735DYE | AEC Routemaster R2RH | Park Royal/Marshall | B36/28R | 1963 | LBL, 2005 |
| 39840 | X | 640DYE | AEC Routemaster R2RH | Park Royal/Marshall | B36/28R | 1963 | LBL, 2005 |
| 39862 | X | 562CLT | AEC Routemaster R2RH | Park Royal/Marshall | B36/28R | 1963 | LBL, 2005 |
| 39876 | X | 776DYE | AEC Routemaster R2RH | Park Royal/Marshall | B36/28R | 1963 | LBL, 2005 |
| 39880 | u | 280CLT | AEC Routemaster R2RH | Park Royal/Marshall | B36/28R | 1962 | LBL, 2005 |
| 39950 | Xs | 650DYE | AEC Routemaster R2RH | Park Royal/Marshall | B36/28R | 1963 | Reading Buses, 2000 |

| | | | | | | | |
|---|---|---|---|---|---|---|---|
| 41259 | G | T259JLD | Dennis Dart SLF 8.9m | Marshall Capital | N25F | 1999 | |

### 41291-41298

| | | | | | | | | |
|---|---|---|---|---|---|---|---|---|
| | | | Dennis Dart SLF 9.3m | | | Marshall Capital | N22D | 1999 | |
| 41291 | ON | T291JLD | **41293** | ON | T293JLD | **41295** | ON | T295JLD | **41298** | ON | T298JLD |
| 41292 | ON | T292JLD | **41294** | ON | T294JLD | **41297** | ON | T297JLD | | | |

### 41324-41327

| | | | | | | | | |
|---|---|---|---|---|---|---|---|---|
| | | | Dennis Dart SLF 10.2m | | | Marshall Capital | N28D | 1999 | |
| 41324 | ON | V324GBY | **41325** | ON | V325GBY | **41326** | ON | V326GBY | **41327** | ON | V327GBY |

| | | | | | | | |
|---|---|---|---|---|---|---|---|
| 41356 | DG | V356DLH | Dennis Dart SLF 8.9m | Marshall Capital | N25F | 1999 | |

### 41362-41401

| | | | | | | | | |
|---|---|---|---|---|---|---|---|---|
| | | | Dennis Dart SLF 10.2m | | | Marshall Capital | N28D | 2000 | |
| 41362 | G | W362VLN | **41369** | G | W369VLN | **41377** | ON | W377VLN | **41379** | ON | W379VLN |
| 41368 | G | W368VLN | **41376** | ON | W376VLN | **41378** | ON | W378VLN | **41401** | ON | X401HLR |

## 41403-41431 — Dennis Dart SLF 10.2m — Marshall Capital — N28D — 2001

| | | | | | | | | |
|---|---|---|---|---|---|---|---|---|
| 41403 | ONt | RG51FWX | 41410 | L | RG51FXH | 41420 | ONt | LN51DXD |
| 41404 | ONt | RG51FXA | 41414 | L | LK51JYO | 41421 | ONt | LN51DXE |
| 41405 | L | RG51FXB | 41415 | L | LN51DWY | 41422 | L | LN51DXF |
| 41406 | L | RG51FXC | 41416 | L | LN51DWZ | 41423 | ONt | LN51DXG |
| 41407 | L | RG51FXD | 41417 | L | LN51DXA | 41424 | ONt | LN51DXH |
| 41408 | L | RG51FXE | 41418 | L | LN51DXB | 41425 | ONt | LN51DWJ |
| 41409 | L | RG51FXF | 41419 | WJ | LN51DXC | | | |

| | | | | | |
|---|---|---|---|---|---|
| 41426 | L | LN51DWK | | | |
| 41427 | L | LN51DWL | | | |
| 41428 | L | LN51DWM | | | |
| 41429 | L | LN51DWO | | | |
| 41430 | DG | LN51DWP | | | |
| 41431 | DG | LN51DWU | | | |

## 41433-41449 — Dennis Dart SLF 9.3m — Marshall Capital — N24D — 2001-02

| | | | | | | | | |
|---|---|---|---|---|---|---|---|---|
| 41433 | L | LN51DWW | 41438 | L | LN51DVZ | 41442 | L | LN51DVT |
| 41434 | L | LN51DWX | 41439 | L | LN51DVO | 41443 | L | LN51DVV |
| 41435 | L | LN51DVW | 41440 | L | LN51DVP | 41444 | WJ | LN51DUA |
| 41436 | L | LN51DVX | 41441 | L | LN51DVR | 41445 | WJ | LN51DUH |
| 41437 | L | LN51DVY | | | | | | |

| | | |
|---|---|---|
| 41446 | WJ | LN51DUJ |
| 41447 | WJ | LN51DUU |
| 41448 | WJ | LN51DUV |
| 41449 | WJ | LN51DUY |

## 41474-41486 — TransBus Dart 8.9m — Marshall Capital — N25F — 2002

| | | | | | | | | |
|---|---|---|---|---|---|---|---|---|
| 41474 | DG | LT02NUK | 41478 | DG | LT02NUU | 41481 | DG | LT52WUP |
| 41475 | DG | LT02NUM | 41479 | DG | LT02NUV | 41482 | DG | LT52WUO |
| 41476 | DG | LT02NUO | 41480 | DG | LT02NVE | 41483 | DG | LT02NVH |
| 41477 | DG | LT02NUP | | | | | | |

| | | |
|---|---|---|
| 41484 | DG | LT02NVJ |
| 41485 | DG | LT52WUM |
| 41486 | DG | LT52WUR |

## 41492-41514 — TransBus Dart 10.5m — Caetano Nimbus — N29D — 2003

| | | | | | | | | |
|---|---|---|---|---|---|---|---|---|
| 41492 | L | LK03LMJ | 41498 | L | LK03NLN | 41504 | UX | LK03NLF |
| 41493 | L | LK03LLX | 41499 | L | LK03LNV | 41505 | UX | LK03NLG |
| 41494 | L | LK03LLZ | 41500 | L | LK03LNW | 41506 | UX | LK03NLJ |
| 41495 | L | LK03LME | 41501 | L | LK03LNX | 41507 | UX | LK03NLL |
| 41496 | L | LK03LMF | 41502 | L | LK03NLD | 41508 | UX | LK03NLM |
| 41497 | L | LK03LNU | 41503 | UX | LK03NLE | 41509 | UX | LK03NLT |

| | | |
|---|---|---|
| 41510 | UX | LK03NFY |
| 41511 | UX | LK03NFZ |
| 41512 | L | LK03NGE |
| 41513 | L | LK03NGF |
| 41514 | L | LK03NGG |

## 41520-41544 — TransBus Dart 10.5m — Caetano Nimbus — N28D* — 2003 — *seating varies

| | | | | | | | | |
|---|---|---|---|---|---|---|---|---|
| 41520 | L | LK03UEX | 41527 | L | LK53FDD | 41533 | UX | LK53FDN |
| 41521 | L | LK03UEY | 41528 | UX | LK53FDE | 41534 | UX | LK53FDO |
| 41522 | L | LK03UEZ | 41529 | UX | LK53FDF | 41535 | UX | LK53FDP |
| 41523 | DG | LK03UFA | 41530 | UX | LK53FDG | 41536 | UX | LK53FDU |
| 41524 | L | LK03UFB | 41531 | UX | LK53FDJ | 41537 | UX | LK53FDV |
| 41525 | UX | LK03UFC | 41532 | UX | LK53FDM | 41538 | UX | LK53FDX |
| 41526 | UX | LK53FDC | | | | | | |

| | | |
|---|---|---|
| 41539 | UX | LK53FDY |
| 41540 | UX | LK53FDZ |
| 41541 | UX | LK53FEF |
| 41542 | UX | LK53FEG |
| 41543 | UX | LK53FEH |
| 41544 | UX | LK53FEJ |

| | | | | | | | |
|---|---|---|---|---|---|---|---|
| 41649 | ONt | R649TLM | Dennis Dart SLF 10.2m | Marshall Capital | N33F | 1998 | |

## 41688-41700 — Dennis Dart SLF 9.3m — Marshall Capital — N24D — 2000

| | | | | | | | | |
|---|---|---|---|---|---|---|---|---|
| 41688 | L | X688HLF | 41690 | L | X501JLO | 41698 | L | X698HLF |
| 41689 | L | X689HLF | 41697 | L | X697HLF | 41699 | L | X699HLF |

| | | |
|---|---|---|
| 41700 | L | X502JLO |

## 41731-41745 — Dennis Dart SLF 10.2m — Marshall Capital — N28D — 2000

| | | | | | | | | |
|---|---|---|---|---|---|---|---|---|
| 41731 | L | X731HLF | 41738 | L | X738HLF | 41742 | L | X742HLF |
| 41733 | L | X733HLF | 41740 | L | X504JLO | 41743 | L | X743HLF |
| 41734 | L | X734HLF | | | | | | |

| | | |
|---|---|---|
| 41744 | L | X744HLF |
| 41745 | L | X745HLF |

| | | | | | | | |
|---|---|---|---|---|---|---|---|
| 41746 | L | X746JLO | Dennis Dart SLF 9.3m | Marshall Capital | N24D | 2000 | |
| 41747 | L | X747JLO | Dennis Dart SLF 9.3m | Marshall Capital | N24D | 2000 | |
| 41748 | u | X748JLO | Dennis Dart SLF 9.3m | Marshall Capital | N24D | 2000 | |

## 41763-41772 — Dennis Dart SLF 10.2m — Marshall Capital — N28D — 2000-01

| | | | | | | | | |
|---|---|---|---|---|---|---|---|---|
| 41763 | G | X763HLR | 41766 | L | X766HLR | 41768 | ON | X768HLR |
| 41764 | WJ | X764HLR | 41767 | G | X767HLR | 41769 | ON | X769HLR |
| 41765 | L | X508HLR | | | | | | |

| | | |
|---|---|---|
| 41771 | ONt | X771HLR |
| 41772 | DG | X772HLR |

## 41773-41785 — Dennis Dart SLF 9.3m — Marshall Capital — N27F — 2001

| | | | | | | | | |
|---|---|---|---|---|---|---|---|---|
| 41773 | NP | X773HLR | 41776 | NP | X776HLR | 41778 | NP | X778HLR |
| 41774 | NP | X774HLR | 41777 | NP | X512HLR | 41779 | NP | X779HLR |
| 41775 | NP | X511HLR | | | | | | |

| | | |
|---|---|---|
| 41780 | NP | X513HLR |
| 41785 | NP | X785HLR |

## 41790-41795 — Dennis Dart SLF 9.3m — Marshall Capital — N24D — 2001

| | | | | | | | | |
|---|---|---|---|---|---|---|---|---|
| 41790 | L | LN51GJV | 41792 | L | LN51GJY | 41794 | L | LN51GOP |
| 41791 | L | LN51GJX | 41793 | L | LN51GJZ | | | |

| | | |
|---|---|---|
| 41795 | L | LN51GOU |

## 42515-42519 — TransBus Dart 10.5m — Caetano Nimbus — N29D — 2003

| | | | | | | | | | | |
|---|---|---|---|---|---|---|---|---|---|---|
| 42515 | L | LK03NKH | 42517 | UX | LK03NKL | 42518 | L | LK03NKM | 42519 | L | LK03NKN |
| 42516 | L | LK03NKJ | | | | | | | | |

## 44001-44006 — ADL Dart 4 10.2m — ADL Enviro 200 — N29D — 2008

| | | | | | | | | | | |
|---|---|---|---|---|---|---|---|---|---|---|
| 44001 | DG | LK57EJD | 44003 | DG | LK57EJF | 44005 | DG | LK57EJJ | 44006 | DG | LK57EJL |
| 44002 | DG | LK57EJE | 44004 | DG | LK57EJG | | | | | |

## 44007-44021 — ADL Dart 4 10.2m — ADL Enviro 200 — N29D — 2008

| | | | | | | | | | | |
|---|---|---|---|---|---|---|---|---|---|---|
| 44007 | UX | LK08FNF | 44011 | UX | LK08FKU | 44015 | UX | LK08FLD | 44019 | UX | LK08FLV |
| 44008 | UX | LK08FNG | 44012 | UX | LK08FKV | 44016 | UX | LK08FLE | 44020 | UX | LK08FLW |
| 44009 | UX | LK08FNH | 44013 | UX | LK08FKW | 44017 | UX | LK08FLF | 44021 | UX | LK08FLZ |
| 44010 | UX | LK08FKT | 44014 | UX | LK08FLC | 44018 | UX | LK08FLG | | | |

## 44022-44043 — ADL Dart 4 10.2m — ADL Enviro 200 — N29D — 2008

| | | | | | | | | | | |
|---|---|---|---|---|---|---|---|---|---|---|
| 44022 | ON | YX58DUA | 44028 | ON | YX58DWA | 44034 | ON | YX58DWJ | 44039 | ON | YX58DWP |
| 44023 | ON | YX58DUH | 44029 | ON | YX58DWC | 44035 | ON | YX58DWL | 44040 | ON | YX58DWU |
| 44024 | ON | YX58DUJ | 44030 | ON | YX58DWD | 44036 | ON | YX58DWM | 44041 | ON | YX58DWV |
| 44025 | ON | YX58DUU | 44031 | ON | YX58DWE | 44037 | ON | YX58DWN | 44042 | ON | YX58DWY |
| 44026 | ON | YX58DVY | 44032 | ON | YX58DWF | 44038 | ON | YX58DWO | 44043 | ON | YX58DWZ |
| 44027 | ON | YX58DVZ | 44033 | ON | YX58DWG | | | | | | |

## 44044-44058 — ADL Dart 4 10.2m — ADL Enviro 200 — N29D — 2008

| | | | | | | | | | | |
|---|---|---|---|---|---|---|---|---|---|---|
| 44044 | WJ | YX58FPA | 44048 | WJ | YX58FPF | 44052 | WJ | YX58FPL | 44056 | WJ | YX58FPU |
| 44045 | WJ | YX58FPC | 44049 | WJ | YX58FPG | 44053 | WJ | YX58FPN | 44057 | WJ | YX58FPV |
| 44046 | WJ | YX58FPD | 44050 | WJ | YX58FPJ | 44054 | WJ | YX58FPO | 44058 | WJ | YX58FPY |
| 44047 | WJ | YX58FPE | 44051 | WJ | YX58FPK | 44055 | WJ | YX58FPT | | | |

## 44059-44070 — ADL Dart 4 10.2m — ADL Enviro 200 — N29D — 2009

| | | | | | | | | | | |
|---|---|---|---|---|---|---|---|---|---|---|
| 44059 | WJ | YX58FOF | 44062 | WJ | YX58FOK | 44065 | WJ | YX58FOP | 44068 | WJ | YX58FOV |
| 44060 | WJ | YX58FOH | 44063 | WJ | YX58FOM | 44066 | WJ | YX58FOT | 44069 | WJ | YX58FRC |
| 44061 | WJ | YX58FOJ | 44064 | WJ | YX58FON | 44067 | WJ | YX58FOU | 44070 | WJ | YX58FRD |

## 44071-44082 — ADL Dart 4 10.2m — ADL Enviro 200 — N29D — 2009

| | | | | | | | | | | |
|---|---|---|---|---|---|---|---|---|---|---|
| 44071 | ON | YX58HVA | 44074 | DG | YX58HVD | 44077 | DG | YX58HVG | 44080 | DG | YX58HVK |
| 44072 | DG | YX58HVB | 44075 | DG | YX58HVE | 44078 | DG | YX58HVH | 44081 | DG | YX58HVL |
| 44073 | DG | YX58HVC | 44076 | DG | YX58HVF | 44079 | DG | YX58HVJ | 44082 | WJ | YX58HVM |

## 44083-44098 — ADL Dart 4 10.2m — ADL Enviro 200 — N29D — 2009

| | | | | | | | | | | |
|---|---|---|---|---|---|---|---|---|---|---|
| 44083 | DG | YX09AEA | 44087 | WJ | YX09AEE | 44091 | WJ | YX09AEK | 44096 | WJ | YX09AEP |
| 44084 | DG | YX09AEB | 44088 | WJ | YX09AEF | 44092 | WJ | YX09AEL | 44097 | WJ | YX09AET |
| 44085 | WJ | YX09AEC | 44089 | WJ | YX09AEG | 44093 | WJ | YX09AEM | 44098 | WJ | YX09AEU |
| 44086 | WJ | YX09AED | 44090 | WJ | YX09AEJ | 44095 | WJ | YX09AEO | | | |

**DML44073, YX58HVC, is seen on route 498 at Romford.**
*Colin Lloyd*

A recent intake of Enviro 200-bodied Darts for First includes 44173, YX11AFO, seen on London Road in Barking while operating route 368. *Richard Godfrey*

### 44099-44108
ADL Dart 4 10.2m — ADL Enviro 200 — N29D — 2009

| | | | | | | | | | | |
|---|---|---|---|---|---|---|---|---|---|---|
| 44099 | WJ | YX09AEU | 44102 | WJ | YX09AEY | 44105 | WJ | YX09AFE | 44107 | WJ | YX09AFJ |
| 44100 | WJ | YX09AEV | 44103 | WJ | YX09AEZ | 44106 | WJ | YX09AFF | 44108 | WJ | YX09AFK |
| 44101 | WJ | YX09AEW | 44104 | WJ | YX09AFA | | | | | | |

### 44109-44128
ADL Dart 4 10.2m — ADL Enviro 200 — N29D — 2009

| | | | | | | | | | | |
|---|---|---|---|---|---|---|---|---|---|---|
| 44109 | G | YX09FLA | 44114 | G | YX09FLF | 44119 | G | YX09FLL | 44124 | G | YX09FKU |
| 44110 | G | YX09FLB | 44115 | G | YX09FLG | 44120 | G | YX09FNJ | 44125 | G | YX09FKV |
| 44111 | G | YX09FLC | 44116 | G | YX09FLH | 44121 | G | YX09FNK | 44126 | G | YX09FKW |
| 44112 | G | YX09FLD | 44117 | G | YX09FLJ | 44122 | G | YX09FKS | 44127 | G | YX09FKY |
| 44113 | G | YX09FLE | 44118 | G | YX09FLK | 44123 | G | YX09FKT | 44128 | G | YX09FLM |

### 44129-44166
ADL Dart 4 10.2m — ADL Enviro 200 — N29D — 2010

| | | | | | | | | | | |
|---|---|---|---|---|---|---|---|---|---|---|
| 44129 | HY | YX10BCU | 44139 | HY | YX10BDZ | 44149 | UX | YX10BFK | 44158 | UX | YX10BGE |
| 44130 | HY | YX10BCV | 44140 | HY | YX10BEJ | 44150 | UX | YX10BFM | 44159 | UX | YX10BGF |
| 44131 | HY | YX10BCY | 44141 | HY | YX10BEO | 44151 | UX | YX10BFN | 44160 | L | YX10BGK |
| 44132 | HY | YX10BCZ | 44142 | HY | YX10BEU | 44152 | UX | YX10BFO | 44161 | L | YX10BGO |
| 44133 | HY | YX10BDE | 44143 | HY | YX10BEY | 44153 | UX | YX10BFP | 44162 | L | YX10BGU |
| 44134 | HY | YX10BDF | 44144 | UX | YX10BFA | 44154 | UX | YX10BFU | 44163 | L | YX10BGV |
| 44135 | HY | YX10BDO | 44145 | UX | YX10BFE | 44155 | UX | YX10BFV | 44164 | L | YX10BGY |
| 44136 | HY | YX10BDU | 44146 | UX | YX10BFF | 44156 | UX | YX10BFY | 44165 | UX | YX60BZN |
| 44137 | HY | YX10BDV | 44147 | UX | YX10BFJ | 44157 | UX | YX10BFZ | 44166 | UX | YX60BZO |
| 44138 | HY | YX10BDY | 44148 | UX | YX10BFK | | | | | | |

### 44167-44170
ADL Dart 4 9.3m — ADL Enviro 200 — N24D — 2010

| | | | | | | | | | | |
|---|---|---|---|---|---|---|---|---|---|---|
| 44167 | L | YX60DXL | 44168 | L | YX60DXM | 44169 | L | YX60DXO | 44170 | L | YX60DXP |

### 44171-44193
ADL Dart 4 10.2m — ADL Enviro 200 — N29D — 2011

| | | | | | | | | | | |
|---|---|---|---|---|---|---|---|---|---|---|
| 44171 | DG | YX11AFK | 44177 | DG | YX11AFZ | 44183 | G | YX11AEZ | 44189 | G | YX11CNN |
| 44172 | DG | YX11AFN | 44178 | DG | YX11AGO | 44184 | G | YX11AFA | 44190 | G | YX11CNO |
| 44173 | DG | YX11AFO | 44179 | G | YX11AEU | 44185 | G | YX11AFE | 44191 | G | YX11CNU |
| 44174 | DG | YX11AFU | 44180 | G | YX11AEV | 44186 | G | YX11AFF | 44192 | G | YX11CNV |
| 44175 | DG | YX11AFV | 44181 | G | YX11AEW | 44187 | G | YX11AFJ | 44193 | G | YX11CNY |
| 44176 | DG | YX11AFY | 44182 | G | YX11AEY | 44188 | G | YX11CNK | | | |

First operates several of the shorter, 8.9 metre Dart in single door format. Pictured at Tottenham Hale station is 44424, YX60FUE with the DMS prefix. *Terry Longhurst*

### 44401-44420 ADL Dart 4 8.9m ADL Enviro 200 N26F 2009

| | | | | | | | | | | | |
|---|---|---|---|---|---|---|---|---|---|---|---|
| 44401 | G | YX09FMA | 44406 | G | YX09FMG | 44411 | G | YX09FMO | 44416 | G | YX09FLV |
| 44402 | G | YX09FMC | 44407 | G | YX09FMJ | 44412 | G | YX09FMP | 44417 | G | YX09FLW |
| 44403 | G | YX09FMD | 44408 | G | YX09FMK | 44413 | G | YX09FLN | 44418 | G | YX09FLZ |
| 44404 | G | YX09FME | 44409 | G | YX09FML | 44414 | G | YX09FLP | 44419 | G | YX09FMU |
| 44405 | G | YX09FMF | 44410 | G | YX09FMM | 44415 | G | YX09FLR | 44420 | G | YX09FMV |

### 44421-44432 ADL Dart 4 8.9m ADL Enviro 200 N26F 2011

| | | | | | | | | | | | |
|---|---|---|---|---|---|---|---|---|---|---|---|
| 44421 | NP | YX60FUA | 44424 | NP | YX60FUE | 44427 | NP | YX60FUH | 44430 | NP | YX60FUO |
| 44422 | NP | YX60FUB | 44425 | NP | YX60FUF | 44428 | NP | YX60FUJ | 44431 | NP | YX60FUP |
| 44423 | NP | YX60FUD | 44426 | NP | YX60FUG | 44429 | NP | YX60FUM | 44432 | NP | YX60FUT |

| | | | | | | | |
|---|---|---|---|---|---|---|---|
| 45315 | Us | JDZ2315 | Dennis Dart 8.5m | | Wright Handybus | B30F | 1991 |

### 62991-62998 VDL Bus SB200 LF Fuelcell Wrightbus Pulsar 2 N34D 2010

| | | | | | | | | | |
|---|---|---|---|---|---|---|---|---|---|
| 62991 | L | LK60HPE | 62993 | L | LK60HPJ | 62995 | L | LK60HPN | 62997 | L | - |
| 62992 | L | LK60HPF | 62994 | L | LK60HPL | 62996 | L | - | 62998 | L | - |

| | | | | | | | |
|---|---|---|---|---|---|---|---|
| 90178 | s | F601XMS | Mercedes-Benz 811D | | Alexander Sprint | B26F | 1988 |

# Depots and allocations:

## Alperton (Ealing Road) - ON

| Volvo B7TL | 32349 | 32350 | 32351 | 32352 | 32353 | 32354 | 32355 | 32356 |
|---|---|---|---|---|---|---|---|---|
| | 32357 | 32358 | 32359 | 32360 | | | | |
| Volvo B9TL | 37773 | 37774 | 37775 | 37776 | 37777 | 37778 | 37779 | 37780 |
| | 37781 | 37782 | 37783 | 37784 | 37785 | 37786 | 37787 | 37788 |
| | 37789 | 37790 | 37791 | 37792 | 37793 | 37794 | 37795 | 37796 |
| | 37797 | 37798 | 37799 | 37800 | 37801 | 37802 | 37803 | |
| Dart | 41291 | 41292 | 41293 | 41294 | 41295 | 41297 | 41298 | 41324 |
| | 41325 | 41326 | 41327 | 41376 | 41377 | 41378 | 41379 | 41401 |
| | 41768 | 41769 | | | | | | |
| Dart 4 - Enviro 200 | 44022 | 44023 | 44024 | 44025 | 44026 | 44027 | 44028 | 44029 |
| | 44030 | 44031 | 44032 | 44033 | 44034 | 44035 | 44036 | 44037 |
| | 44038 | 44039 | 44040 | 44041 | 44042 | 44043 | 44071 | |
| *Ancillary* | *32807* | *32822* | *41403* | *41404* | *41420* | *41421* | *41423* | *41424* |
| | *41425* | *41649* | *41771* | | | | | |

## Dagenham (Chequers Lane) - DG

| Volvo B12T | 20101 | 20102 | 20103 | | | | | |
|---|---|---|---|---|---|---|---|---|
| Olympian | 34215 | 34216 | 34218 | | | | | |
| Volvo B7TL | 32657 | 32658 | 32659 | 32660 | 32661 | 32662 | 32663 | 32664 |
| | 32665 | 32666 | 32667 | 32668 | | | | |
| Trident | 32929 | 32967 | 32968 | 33036 | 33078 | 33085 | 33086 | 33087 |
| | 33088 | 33091 | 33092 | 33094 | 33096 | 33097 | 33232 | |
| Trident 2 | 33501 | 33502 | 33503 | 33504 | 33505 | 33506 | 33507 | 33508 |
| | 33544 | 33545 | 33546 | 33547 | 33548 | 33549 | 33550 | 33551 |
| | 33552 | 33553 | 33554 | 33555 | 33556 | 33557 | 33558 | 33559 |
| | 33560 | 33561 | 33562 | 33563 | 33564 | 33565 | 33566 | 33567 |
| | 33568 | 33569 | 33570 | 33571 | 33572 | 33573 | 33574 | |
| Dart | 41356 | 41416 | 41417 | 41418 | 41419 | 41422 | 41430 | 41431 |
| | 41443 | 41474 | 41475 | 41476 | 41477 | 41478 | 41479 | 41480 |
| | 41481 | 41482 | 41483 | 41484 | 41485 | 41486 | 41523 | 41772 |
| Dart 4 | 44001 | 44002 | 44003 | 44004 | 44005 | 44006 | 44072 | 44073 |
| | 44074 | 44075 | 44076 | 44077 | 44078 | 44079 | 44080 | 44081 |
| | 44083 | 44084 | 44171 | 44172 | 44173 | 44174 | 44175 | 44176 |
| | 44177 | 44178 | | | | | | |
| *Ancillary* | *32806* | *41649* | | | | | | |

## Greenford (Greenford Road) - G

| Volvo B7TL | 32328 | 32329 | 32330 | 32331 | 32332 | 32333 | 32334 | 32335 |
|---|---|---|---|---|---|---|---|---|
| | 32336 | 32337 | 32338 | 32339 | 32340 | 32341 | 32342 | 32343 |
| | 32344 | 32345 | 32346 | 32347 | | | | |
| Trident | 32895 | 32896 | 33277 | 33278 | 33279 | 33280 | 33281 | 33282 |
| | 33283 | 33284 | 33285 | 33286 | 33287 | 33288 | 33289 | 33290 |
| | 33291 | 33292 | 33293 | | | | | |
| Trident 2 | 33575 | 33576 | 33577 | 33578 | 33579 | 33580 | 33581 | 33582 |
| | 33583 | 33584 | 33585 | 33586 | 33587 | 33588 | 33589 | 33590 |
| | 33591 | 33592 | 33593 | 33594 | 33595 | 33596 | 33597 | 33598 |
| | 33599 | 33600 | 33601 | 33602 | 33603 | 33604 | 33605 | 33606 |
| | 33607 | 33608 | 33609 | 33610 | 33611 | | | |
| Dart | 41259 | 41362 | 41363 | 41369 | 41763 | 41767 | | |
| Dart 4 | 44109 | 44110 | 44111 | 44112 | 44113 | 44114 | 44115 | 44116 |
| | 44117 | 44118 | 44119 | 44120 | 44121 | 44122 | 44123 | 44124 |
| | 44125 | 44126 | 44127 | 44128 | 44179 | 44180 | 44181 | 44182 |
| | 44183 | 44184 | 44185 | 44186 | 44187 | 44188 | 44189 | 44190 |
| | 44191 | 44192 | 44193 | 44401 | 44402 | 44403 | 44404 | 44405 |
| | 44406 | 44407 | 44408 | 44409 | 44410 | 44411 | 44412 | 44413 |
| | 44414 | 44415 | 44416 | 44417 | 44418 | 44419 | 44420 | |

## Hayes (Rigby Lane) - HY

| | | | | | | | | |
|---|---|---|---|---|---|---|---|---|
| Citaro G | 11039 | 11040 | 11041 | 11042 | 11043 | 11044 | 11045 | 11046 |
| | 11047 | 11048 | 11049 | 11050 | 11051 | 11052 | 11053 | 11054 |
| | 11055 | 11056 | 11057 | 11058 | 11059 | 11060 | 11061 | 11062 |
| | 11063 | 11064 | 11065 | 11084 | | | | |
| Volvo B9TL | 37865 | 37866 | 37867 | 37868 | 37869 | 37870 | 37871 | 37872 |
| | 37873 | 37874 | 37875 | 37876 | 37877 | 37878 | 37879 | 37880 |
| | 37881 | 37882 | 37883 | 37884 | 37885 | 37886 | 37887 | 37888 |
| | 37889 | | | | | | | |
| Dart 4 | 44129 | 44130 | 44131 | 44132 | 44133 | 44134 | 44135 | 44136 |
| | 44137 | 44138 | 44139 | 44140 | 44141 | 44142 | 44143 | |

## Leyton (Lea Interchange) - L

| | | | | | | | | |
|---|---|---|---|---|---|---|---|---|
| Trident | 33020 | 33021 | 33022 | 33023 | 33024 | 33025 | 33026 | 33027 |
| | 33028 | 33033 | 33034 | 33035 | | | | |
| Trident 2 | 33612 | 33613 | 33614 | 33615 | 33616 | 33617 | 33618 | 33619 |
| | 33620 | 33621 | 33622 | 33623 | 33624 | 33625 | 33626 | 33627 |
| | 33628 | 33629 | 33630 | 33631 | 33632 | 33633 | 33634 | 33635 |
| | 33636 | 33637 | 33638 | 33639 | 33640 | 33641 | 33642 | 33643 |
| | 33644 | 33645 | 33646 | 33647 | 33648 | 33649 | 33650 | 33651 |
| | 33652 | 33653 | 33654 | 33655 | | | | |
| Volvo B9TL | 36101 | 36102 | 36103 | 36104 | 36105 | 36106 | 36107 | 36108 |
| | 36109 | 36110 | 36111 | 36112 | 36113 | 36114 | 36115 | 36116 |
| | 36117 | 36118 | 36119 | 36120 | 36121 | 36122 | 36123 | 36124 |
| | 36125 | 36126 | 36127 | 36128 | 36129 | 36130 | 36131 | 36132 |
| | 36133 | 36134 | 36135 | 36136 | 36137 | 36138 | 36139 | 36140 |
| | 36141 | 36142 | 36143 | 36144 | 36145 | 36146 | 36147 | 36148 |
| | 36149 | 36150 | 36151 | 36152 | 36153 | 36154 | 36155 | 36156 |
| | 36157 | 36158 | 36159 | 36160 | 36161 | 36162 | 36163 | 36164 |
| | 36165 | 37827 | 37828 | 37829 | 37830 | 37831 | 37832 | 37833 |
| | 37834 | 37835 | 37836 | 37837 | 37838 | 37839 | 37840 | 37841 |
| | 37842 | | | | | | | |
| Dart | 41405 | 41406 | 41407 | 41408 | 41409 | 41410 | 41414 | 41415 |
| | 41416 | 41417 | 41418 | 41422 | 41426 | 41427 | 41428 | 41429 |
| | 41433 | 41434 | 41435 | 41436 | 41438 | 41439 | 41440 | 41441 |
| | 41442 | 41443 | 41492 | 41493 | 41494 | 41495 | 41496 | 41497 |
| | 41498 | 41499 | 41500 | 41501 | 41502 | 41512 | 41513 | 41514 |
| | 41520 | 41521 | 41522 | 41524 | 41527 | 41688 | 41689 | 41690 |
| | 41697 | 41698 | 41699 | 41700 | 41731 | 41733 | 41734 | 41738 |
| | 41740 | 41742 | 41743 | 41744 | 41745 | 41746 | 41747 | 41748 |
| | 41765 | 41766 | 41790 | 41791 | 41792 | 41793 | 41794 | 41795 |
| | 42516 | 42518 | 42519 | | | | | |
| Dart 4 | 44167 | 44168 | 44169 | 44170 | | | | |
| VDL Fuelcell | 62991 | 62992 | 62993 | 62994 | 62995 | 62996 | 62997 | 62998 |

## Tottenham (Marsh Lane, Northumberland Park) - NP

| | | | | | | | | |
|---|---|---|---|---|---|---|---|---|
| Volvo B7TL | 32306 | 32307 | 32308 | 32309 | 32310 | 32311 | 32312 | 32313 |
| | 32314 | 32315 | 32316 | 32317 | 32318 | 32319 | 32320 | 32321 |
| | 32322 | 32323 | 32324 | 32325 | 32326 | 32327 | | |
| Trident | 33039 | 33042 | 33043 | 33044 | 33045 | 33047 | 33048 | 33049 |
| | 33051 | 33075 | 33076 | 33077 | 33229 | 33231 | 22232 | |
| Trident 2 | 33520 | 33521 | 33522 | 33523 | 33524 | 33525 | 33526 | 33527 |
| | 33528 | 33529 | 33530 | 33531 | 33532 | 33533 | 33534 | 33535 |
| | 33536 | 33537 | 33538 | 33539 | 33540 | 33541 | 33542 | 33543 |
| Volvo B9TL | 37804 | 37805 | 37806 | 37807 | 37808 | 37809 | 37810 | 37811 |
| | 37812 | 37813 | 37814 | 37815 | 37816 | 37817 | 37818 | 37819 |
| | 37820 | 37821 | 37822 | 37823 | 37824 | 37825 | 37826 | 37843 |
| | 37844 | 37845 | 37846 | 37847 | 37848 | 37849 | 37850 | 37851 |
| | 37852 | 37853 | 37854 | 37855 | 37856 | 37857 | 37858 | 37859 |
| | 37860 | 37861 | 37862 | 37863 | 37864 | | | |
| Dart 4 | 44421 | 44422 | 44423 | 44424 | 44425 | 44426 | 44427 | 44428 |
| | 44429 | 44430 | 44431 | 44432 | | | | |

## Uxbridge (Bakers Road) - UX

| Type | | | | | | | | |
|---|---|---|---|---|---|---|---|---|
| Trident | 32893 | 32907 | 33037 | 33050 | 33059 | 33072 | 33073 | 33074 |
| | 33080 | 33082 | 33090 | 33093 | 33095 | 33098 | 33131 | 33132 |
| | 33133 | 33134 | 33135 | 33136 | 33137 | 33138 | 33139 | 33140 |
| | 33328 | 33329 | 33330 | 33331 | 33332 | 33333 | 33334 | 33335 |
| | 33336 | 33337 | 33338 | 33339 | 33340 | 33341 | 33342 | |
| Dart | 41503 | 41504 | 41505 | 41506 | 41507 | 41508 | 41509 | 41510 |
| | 41511 | 41525 | 41526 | 41528 | 41529 | 41530 | 41531 | 41532 |
| | 41533 | 41534 | 41535 | 41536 | 41537 | 41538 | 41539 | 41540 |
| | 41541 | 41542 | 41543 | 41544 | 42515 | 42517 | 42518 | |
| Dart 4 | 44007 | 44008 | 44009 | 44010 | 44011 | 44012 | 44013 | 44014 |
| | 44015 | 44016 | 44017 | 44018 | 44019 | 44020 | 44021 | |

## Westbourne Park (Great Western Road) - X

| Type | | | | | | | | |
|---|---|---|---|---|---|---|---|---|
| Volvo B7TL | 32361 | 32362 | 32363 | 32364 | 32365 | 32366 | 32367 | 32368 |
| | 32369 | 32370 | 32371 | 32372 | 32373 | 32374 | 32375 | 32376 |
| | 32377 | 32378 | 32379 | 32380 | 32381 | 32382 | 32383 | 32384 |
| | 32385 | 32386 | 32387 | 32388 | 32389 | 32390 | 32391 | 32392 |
| | 32393 | 32394 | 32395 | 32396 | 32397 | 32398 | 32399 | 32400 |
| | 32401 | 32402 | 32403 | 32404 | 32405 | 32406 | 32407 | 32408 |
| | 32409 | 32410 | 32411 | 32412 | 32413 | 32414 | 32415 | 32416 |
| | 32417 | 32418 | 32419 | 32420 | 32421 | 32422 | 32423 | 32424 |
| | 32425 | 32426 | 32427 | 32428 | 32429 | 32430 | 32495 | 32496 |
| | 32497 | 32498 | 32499 | 32500 | 32501 | 32502 | | |
| Trident | 33178 | 33179 | 33180 | 33181 | 33182 | 33183 | 33184 | 33185 |
| | 33186 | 33187 | 33188 | 33189 | 33190 | 33192 | 33194 | 33195 |
| | 33196 | 33197 | 33198 | 33199 | 33343 | 33344 | 33345 | 33346 |
| | 33347 | 33348 | 33349 | 33350 | 33351 | 33352 | 33353 | 33354 |
| | 33355 | 33356 | 33357 | 33358 | 33359 | 33360 | 33361 | 33362 |
| | 33363 | 33364 | 33365 | 33366 | 33367 | 33368 | 33369 | 33370 |
| | 33371 | 33372 | 33373 | 33374 | 33375 | 33376 | 33377 | 33378 |
| | 33379 | 33380 | 33381 | 33382 | 33383 | 33384 | 33385 | 33386 |
| Trident 2 | 33509 | 33510 | 33511 | 33512 | 33513 | 33514 | 33515 | 33516 |
| | 33517 | 33518 | 33519 | | | | | |
| Wrightbus Hybrid | 35001 | 35002 | 35003 | 35004 | | | | |
| VDL Hybrid | 39001 | 39002 | 39003 | 39004 | 39005 | | | |
| Routemaster | 39735 | 39804 | 39810 | 39813 | 39818 | 39827 | 39835 | 39840 |
| | 39862 | 39876 | 39950 | | | | | |

## Willesden Junction (Station Road) - WJ

| Type | | | | | | | | |
|---|---|---|---|---|---|---|---|---|
| Citaro G | 11000 | 11005 | 11009 | | | | | |
| Volvo B9TL | 37890 | 37891 | 37892 | 37893 | 37894 | 37895 | 37896 | 37897 |
| | 37897 | 37898 | 37900 | 37901 | 37902 | 37903 | 37904 | 37905 |
| | 37906 | 37907 | 37908 | 37909 | 37910 | 37911 | 37912 | 37913 |
| | 37914 | 37915 | 37916 | 37917 | 37918 | 37919 | 37920 | 37921 |
| | 37922 | 37923 | 37924 | 37925 | 37926 | 37927 | 37928 | 37929 |
| | 37930 | 37931 | 37932 | 37933 | 37934 | 37935 | 37936 | 37937 |
| | 37938 | 37939 | 37940 | 37941 | 37942 | | | |
| Dart | 41415 | 41444 | 41445 | 41446 | 41447 | 41448 | 41449 | |
| Dart 4/Enviro 200 | 44044 | 44045 | 44046 | 44047 | 44048 | 44049 | 44050 | 44051 |
| | 44052 | 44053 | 44054 | 44055 | 44056 | 44057 | 44058 | 44059 |
| | 44060 | 44061 | 44062 | 44063 | 44064 | 44065 | 44066 | 44067 |
| | 44068 | 44069 | 44070 | 44085 | 44086 | 44087 | 44088 | 44089 |
| | 44090 | 44091 | 44092 | 44093 | 44094 | 44095 | 44096 | 44097 |
| | 44098 | 44099 | 44100 | 44101 | 44102 | 44103 | 44104 | 44105 |
| | 44106 | 44107 | 44108 | | | | | |

# GO-AHEAD LONDON

## London Central - London General - Blue Triangle - Docklands Buses

London Central Bus Co Ltd; London General Transport Services Ltd
25 Raleigh Gardens, Mitcham, CR4 3NS

### DOE1-54 — ADL Trident 2 10.3m | Optare Olympus | N43/21D | 2008-09

| | | | | | | | | | | |
|---|---|---|---|---|---|---|---|---|---|---|
| 1 | A | LX58CWN | 15 | A | LX58CXE | 29 | A | LX58CXV | 42 | A | LX09BXL |
| 2 | A | LX58CWO | 16 | A | LX58CXF | 30 | A | LX58CXW | 43 | A | LX09BXM |
| 3 | A | LX58CWP | 17 | A | LX58CXG | 31 | A | LX58CXY | 44 | A | LX09BXO |
| 4 | A | LX58CWR | 18 | A | LX58CXH | 32 | A | LX58CXZ | 45 | A | LX09AXU |
| 5 | A | LX58CWT | 19 | A | LX58CXJ | 33 | A | LX58CYA | 46 | A | LX09AXV |
| 6 | A | LX58CWU | 20 | A | LX58CXK | 34 | A | LX58CYC | 47 | A | LX09AXW |
| 7 | A | LX58CWV | 21 | A | LX58CXL | 35 | A | LX58CYE | 48 | A | LX09AXY |
| 8 | A | LX58CWW | 22 | A | LX58CXN | 36 | A | LX58CYF | 49 | A | LX09AXZ |
| 9 | A | LX58CWY | 23 | A | LX58CXO | 37 | A | LX58CYG | 50 | A | LX09AYA |
| 10 | A | LX58CWZ | 24 | A | LX58CXP | 38 | A | LX09BXG | 51 | A | LX09AYB |
| 11 | A | LX58CXA | 25 | A | LX58CXR | 39 | A | LX09BXH | 52 | A | LX09AYC |
| 12 | A | LX58CXB | 26 | A | LX58CXS | 40 | A | LX09BXJ | 53 | A | LX09AYD |
| 13 | A | LX58CXC | 27 | A | LX58CXT | 41 | A | LX09BXK | 54 | AL | LX09AYE |
| 14 | A | LX58CXD | 28 | A | LX58CXU | | | | | | |

| DP192 | NX | EJ52WXF | Dennis Dart SLF 10.7m | Plaxton Pointer 2 | N36D | 2003 |
|---|---|---|---|---|---|---|

### DP193-205 — TransBus Dart 10.7m | TransBus Pointer | N33D | 2003-04 | Blue Triangle, 2007

| | | | | | | | | | | |
|---|---|---|---|---|---|---|---|---|---|---|
| 193 | SW | EU53PXY | 197 | SW | EU53PYD | 200 | SW | EU53PYH | 203 | SW | EU53PYO |
| 194 | SW | EU53PXZ | 198 | SW | EU53PYF | 201 | SW | EU53PYJ | 204 | SW | EU53PYP |
| 195 | SW | EU53PYA | 199 | SW | EU53PYG | 202 | SW | EU53PYL | 205 | SW | BT04BUS |
| 196 | SW | EU53PYB | | | | | | | | | |

| DP206 | BE | EU04BVD | TransBus Dart 10.7m | TransBus Pointer | N37F | 2004 | Blue Triangle, 2007 |
|---|---|---|---|---|---|---|---|
| DP207 | BE | EU04BVF | TransBus Dart 10.7m | TransBus Pointer | N37F | 2004 | Blue Triangle, 2007 |
| DP208 | BE | SN56AYC | ADL Dart 10.7m | ADL Pointer | N33D | 2006 | Blue Triangle, 2007 |
| DP209 | SI | SN56AYD | ADL Dart 10.7m | ADL Pointer | N33D | 2006 | Blue Triangle, 2007 |

### DW1-12 — DAF SB120 9.4m | Wrightbus Cadet 2 | N23D | 2003 | East Thames, 2009

| | | | | | | | | | | |
|---|---|---|---|---|---|---|---|---|---|---|
| 1 | AL | LF52TKJ | 4 | AL | LF52TJY | 7 | AL | LF52TKO | 10 | AL | LF52TKE |
| 2 | AL | LF52TKC | 5 | AL | LF52TJV | 8 | AL | LF52TKN | 11 | AL | LF52TKN |
| 3 | AL | LF52TKD | 6 | AL | LF52TJX | 9 | AL | LF52TKT | 12 | BX | LF52TKA |

### DW13-37 — VDL Bus SB120 10.8m | Wrightbus Cadet 2 | N30D | 2004 | East Thames, 2009

| | | | | | | | | | | |
|---|---|---|---|---|---|---|---|---|---|---|
| 13 | BX | BX04BXL | 20 | BX | FJ54ZDU | 26 | NX | FJ54ZFA | 32 | NX | FJ54ZUA |
| 14 | BX | BX04BXP | 21 | BX | FJ54ZDV | 27 | NX | FJ54ZTV | 33 | NX | FJ54ZUC |
| 15 | BX | BX04BXN | 22 | BX | FJ54ZDW | 28 | NX | FJ54ZTW | 34 | NX | FJ54ZUD |
| 16 | BX | BX04BXM | 23 | BX | FJ54ZDX | 29 | NX | FJ54ZTX | 35 | NX | FJ54ZVA |
| 17 | BX | FJ54ZDR | 24 | BX | FJ54ZDY | 30 | NX | FJ54ZTY | 36 | NX | FJ54ZVB |
| 18 | BX | FJ54ZDP | 25 | NX | FJ54ZDZ | 31 | NX | FJ54ZTZ | 37 | NX | FJ54ZDC |
| 19 | BX | FJ54ZDT | | | | | | | | | |

### E1-39 — ADL Trident 2 10.1m | ADL Enviro 400 | N41/26D | 2006

| | | | | | | | | | | |
|---|---|---|---|---|---|---|---|---|---|---|
| 1 | SW | SN06BNA | 11 | SW | SN06BNV | 21 | PM | LX06EZR | 31 | PM | LX06EZF |
| 2 | SW | SN06BNB | 12 | SW | SN06BNX | 22 | PM | LX06EZS | 32 | PM | LX06EZG |
| 3 | SW | SN06BND | 13 | SW | SN06BNY | 23 | PM | LX06EZT | 33 | PM | LX06EZH |
| 4 | SW | SN06BNE | 14 | SW | SN06BNZ | 24 | PM | LX06EYY | 34 | PM | LX06ECT |
| 5 | SW | SN06BNF | 15 | SW | SN06BOF | 25 | PM | LX06EYZ | 35 | PM | LX06ECV |
| 6 | SW | SN06BNJ | 16 | PM | LX06EZL | 26 | PM | LX06EZA | 36 | PM | LX06FKL |
| 7 | SW | SN06BNK | 17 | PM | LX06EZM | 27 | PM | LX06EZB | 37 | PM | LX06FKM |
| 8 | SW | SN06BNL | 18 | PM | LX06EZN | 28 | PM | LX06EZC | 38 | SW | LX06FKN |
| 9 | SW | SN06BNO | 19 | PM | LX06EZO | 29 | PM | LX06EZD | 39 | SW | LX06FKO |
| 10 | SW | SN06BNU | 20 | PM | LX06EZP | 30 | PM | LX06EZE | | | |

Go-Ahead operates its main London operation from thirteen depots across the capital as well as its Metrobus operation. The first of over two hundred Enviro 400-bodied Trident 2 buses is E1, SN06BNA, seen in Whitehall while working route 24. *Richard Godfrey*

### E40-56

ADL Trident 2 10.1m    ADL Enviro 400    N41/26D    2006-07

| | | | | | | | | | |
|---|---|---|---|---|---|---|---|---|---|
| **40** | BX | LX56ETD | **45** | BX | LX56ETL | **50** | BX | LX56ETV | **54** | BX | LX56EUB |
| **41** | BX | LX56ETE | **46** | BX | LX56ETO | **51** | BX | LX56ETY | **55** | BX | LX56EUC |
| **42** | BX | LX56ETF | **47** | BX | LX56ETR | **52** | BX | LX56ETZ | **56** | BX | LX56EUD |
| **43** | BX | LX56ETJ | **48** | BX | LX56ETT | **53** | BX | LX56EUA | | | |
| **44** | BX | LX56ETK | **49** | BX | LX56ETU | | | | | | |

### E57-99

ADL Trident 2 10.1M    ADL Enviro 400    N39/25D    2007-08

| | | | | | | | | | |
|---|---|---|---|---|---|---|---|---|---|
| **57** | SW | LX07BYH | **68** | SW | LX57CJO | **79** | SW | LX57CKJ | **90** | SW | LX57CLN |
| **58** | A | LX07BYC | **69** | SW | LX57CJU | **80** | SW | LX57CKK | **91** | SW | LX57CLO |
| **59** | A | LX07BYD | **70** | SW | LX57CJV | **81** | SW | LX57CKL | **92** | SW | LX57CLV |
| **60** | A | LX07BYF | **71** | SW | LX57CJY | **82** | SW | LX57CKN | **93** | SW | LX57CLY |
| **61** | A | LX07BYG | **72** | SW | LX57CJZ | **83** | SW | LX57CKO | **94** | NX | LX08EBP |
| **62** | SW | LX57CHV | **73** | SW | LX57CKA | **84** | SW | LX57CKP | **95** | NX | LX08EBU |
| **63** | SW | LX57CHY | **74** | SW | LX57CKC | **85** | SW | LX57CKU | **96** | NX | LX08EBV |
| **64** | SW | LX57CHZ | **75** | SW | LX57CKD | **86** | SW | LX57CKV | **97** | NX | LX08EBZ |
| **65** | SW | LX57CJE | **76** | SW | LX57CKE | **87** | SW | LX57CKY | **98** | NX | LX08ECA |
| **66** | SW | LX57CJF | **77** | SW | LX57CKF | **88** | SW | LX57CLF | **99** | NX | LX08ECC |
| **67** | SW | LX57CJJ | **78** | SW | LX57CKG | **89** | SW | LX57CLJ | | | |

### E100-128

ADL Trident 2 10.1M    ADL Enviro 400    N39/26D    2009

| | | | | | | | | | |
|---|---|---|---|---|---|---|---|---|---|
| **100** | SW | LX09EZU | **108** | SW | LX09FAO | **115** | SW | LX09FBF | **122** | SW | LX09FBV |
| **101** | SW | LX09EZV | **109** | SW | LX09FAU | **116** | SW | LX09FBG | **123** | SW | LX09FBY |
| **102** | SW | LX09EZW | **110** | SW | LX09FBA | **117** | SW | LX09FBJ | **124** | SW | LX09FBZ |
| **103** | SW | LX09EZZ | **111** | SW | LX09FBB | **118** | SW | LX09FBK | **125** | SW | LX09FCA |
| **104** | SW | LX09FAF | **112** | SW | LX09FBC | **119** | SW | LX09FBN | **126** | SW | LX09FCC |
| **105** | SW | LX09FAJ | **113** | SW | LX09FBD | **120** | SW | LX09FBO | **127** | SW | LX09FCD |
| **106** | SW | LX09FAK | **114** | SW | LX09FBE | **121** | SW | LX09FBU | **128** | SW | LX09FCE |
| **107** | SW | LX09FAM | | | | | | | | | |

The MCV coach building business was founded in late 2002 after buying the assets from the Marshalls of Cambridge operation. The Evolution followed in 2004 and is seen here on an Alexander Dennis Dart chassis. ED6, AE06HCH, is one of that is based at the former Blue Triangle premises in Rainham. *Mark Doggett*

### E129-150

ADL Trident 2 10.1M ADL Enviro 400 N39/26D 2010

| 129 | SW | SN60BZA | 135 | SW | SN60BZG | 141 | AL | SN60BZO | 146 | AL | SN60BZU |
|-----|----|---------|-----|----|---------|-----|----|---------|-----|----|---------|
| 130 | SW | SN60BZB | 136 | SW | SN60BZH | 142 | AL | SN60BZP | 147 | AL | SN60BZV |
| 131 | SW | SN60BZC | 137 | SW | SN60BZJ | 143 | AL | SN60BZR | 148 | AL | SN60BZW |
| 132 | SW | SN60BZD | 138 | AL | SN60BZK | 144 | AL | SN60BZS | 149 | AL | SN60BZX |
| 133 | SW | SN60BZE | 139 | AL | SN60BZL | 145 | AL | SN60BZT | 150 | AL | SN60BZY |
| 134 | SW | SN60BZF | 140 | AL | SN60BZM |     |    |         |     |    |         |

### E151-204

ADL Trident 2 10.1M ADL Enviro 400 N39/26D 2011

| 151 | SW | SN11BTY | 165 | - | - | 179 | - | - | 192 | - | - |
|-----|----|---------|-----|---|---|-----|---|---|-----|---|---|
| 152 | SW | SN11BTZ | 166 | - | - | 180 | - | - | 193 | - | - |
| 153 | SW | SN11BVA | 167 | - | - | 181 | - | - | 194 | - | - |
| 154 | SW | SN11BVE | 168 | - | - | 182 | - | - | 195 | - | - |
| 155 | SW | SN11BVF | 169 | - | - | 183 | - | - | 196 | - | - |
| 156 | SW | SN11BVH | 170 | - | - | 184 | - | - | 197 | - | - |
| 157 | SW | SN11BVJ | 171 | - | - | 185 | - | - | 198 | - | - |
| 158 | SW | SN11BVO | 172 | - | - | 186 | - | - | 199 | - | - |
| 159 | SW | SN11BVP | 173 | - | - | 187 | - | - | 200 | - | - |
| 160 | SW | SN11BVU | 174 | - | - | 188 | - | - | 201 | - | - |
| 161 | SW | SN11BVV | 175 | - | - | 189 | - | - | 202 | - | - |
| 162 | SW | SN11BVW | 176 | - | - | 190 | - | - | 203 | - | - |
| 163 | -  | -       | 177 | - | - | 191 | - | - | 204 | - | - |
| 164 | -  | -       | 178 | - | - |     |   |   |     |   |   |

### ED1-8

ADL Dart 4 10.8m MCV Evolution N29D 2006

| 1 | u | AE06HCJA | 3 | u | AE06HCD | 5 | SI | AE06HCG | 7 | NX | AE06HCJ |
|---|---|----------|---|---|---------|---|----|---------|---|----|---------|
| 2 | u | AE06HCKC | 4 | u | AE06HCF | 6 | SI | AE06HCH | 8 | NX | AE06HCK |

### ED9-17

ADL Dart 4 9.2m MCV Evolution N23D 2006

| 9  | BE | AE56OUH | 12 | BE  | AE56OUL | 14 | BE | AE56OUN | 16 | BE  | AE56OUP |
|----|----|---------|----|-----|---------|----|----|---------|----|-----|---------|
| 10 | BE | AE56OUJ | 13 | BEI | AE56OUM | 15 | BE | AE56OUO | 17 | BEI | AE56OUS |
| 11 | BE | AE56OUK |    |     |         |    |    |         |    |     |         |

Like other operators in London, Go-Ahead is looking at the hybrid options. Five ADL Trident E400H buses are currently working from Stockwell depot with EH4, LX58DDN, seen working route 24 along Whitehall. *Richard Godfrey*

### ED18-28

ADL Dart 4 10.4m     MCV Evolution     N29D     2007

| | | | | | | | | | | | |
|---|---|---|---|---|---|---|---|---|---|---|---|
| 18 | SI | LX07BYJ | 21 | SI | LX07BYM | 24 | SI | LX07BYP | 27 | SI | LX07BYT |
| 19 | SI | LX07BYK | 22 | SI | LX07BYN | 25 | SI | LX07BYR | 28 | SI | LX07BYU |
| 20 | SI | LX07BYL | 23 | SI | LX07BYO | 26 | SI | LX07BYS | | | |

### EH1-5

ADL Trident E400H 10.1m     ADL Enviro 400H     N37/25D     2008-09

| | | | | | | | | | | | |
|---|---|---|---|---|---|---|---|---|---|---|---|
| 1 | SW | LX58DDJ | 3 | SW | LX58DDL | 4 | SW | LX58DDN | 5 | SW | LX58DDO |
| 2 | SW | LX58DDK | | | | | | | | | |

### EH6-20

ADL Trident E400H 10.1m     ADL Enviro 400H     N37/25D     On order

| | | | | | | | | | | | |
|---|---|---|---|---|---|---|---|---|---|---|---|
| 6 | - | - | 10 | - | - | 14 | - | - | 18 | - | - |
| 7 | - | - | 11 | - | - | 15 | - | - | 19 | - | - |
| 8 | - | - | 12 | - | - | 16 | - | - | 20 | - | - |
| 9 | - | - | 13 | - | - | 17 | - | - | | | |

### ELS1-14

Scania N94UB 10.6m     East Lancashire Myllennium     N32D     2002     East Thames, 2009

| | | | | | | | | | | | |
|---|---|---|---|---|---|---|---|---|---|---|---|
| 1 | Q | YU02GHG | 5 | Q | YU02GHD | 9 | Q | YR52VFJ | 12 | Q | YR52VFL |
| 2 | Q | YU02GHH | 6 | Q | YU02GHA | 10 | Q | YR52VFH | 13 | Q | YR52VFM |
| 3 | Q | YU02GHJ | 7 | Q | YU02GHN | 11 | Q | YR52VFK | 14 | Q | YR52VFN |
| 4 | Q | YU02GHK | 8 | Q | YU02GHO | | | | | | |

| | | | | | | |
|---|---|---|---|---|---|---|
| EVL5 | SW | PL51LGF | Volvo B7TL 10.4m | East Lancs Vyking | N45/20D | 2002 |
| EVL15 | SW | PN02XCB | Volvo B7TL 10.4m | East Lancs Vyking | N45/20D | 2002 |
| EVL17 | SW | PN02XCD | Volvo B7TL 10.4m | East Lancs Vyking | N45/20D | 2002 |

### LDP2-14

Dennis Dart SLF 9.2m     Plaxton Pointer     N32F*     1996     *seating varies

| | | | | | | | | | | | |
|---|---|---|---|---|---|---|---|---|---|---|---|
| 2 | SW | P502RYM | 4 | w | P504RYM | 7 | BE | P507RYM | 14 | PL | P514RYM |
| 3 | w | P503RYM | | | | | | | | | |

| | | | | | | |
|---|---|---|---|---|---|---|
| LDP37 | A | P737RYL | Dennis Dart SLF 10m | Plaxton Pointer | N35F | 1996 |

## LDP47-87

Dennis Dart SLF 10m  Plaxton Pointer  N33F  1997

| 47 | AL | R447LGH | 56 | PL | R456LGH | 64 | PL | R464LGH | 87 | w | R487LGH |
|----|----|---------|----|----|---------|----|----|---------|----|----|---------|

## LDP90-117

Dennis Dart SLF 10.1m  Plaxton Pointer 2  N29D  1998-99

| 90 | u | S638JGP | 104 | Q | S104EGK | 109 | w | S109EGK | 114 | w | S114EGK |
|----|----|---------|-----|----|---------|-----|----|---------|-----|----|---------|
| 91 | w | S91EGK | 105 | w | S105EGK | 110 | w | S110EGK | 115 | AL | S115EGK |
| 101 | Q | S101EGK | 106 | w | S106EGK | 111 | w | S954JGX | 116 | AL | S116EGK |
| 102 | NX | S102EGK | 107 | BX | S107EGK | 112 | w | S112EGK | 117 | NX | S117EGK |
| 103 | Q | S103EGK | 108 | w | S108EGK | 113 | BX | S113EGK | | | |

## LDP129-133

Dennis Dart SLF 8.8m  Plaxton Pointer MPD  N28F  2001

| 129 | w | Y829TGH | 131 | w | Y831TGH | 132 | w | Y832TGH | 133 | w | Y833TGH |
|-----|----|---------|-----|----|---------|-----|----|---------|-----|----|---------|
| 130 | w | Y803TGH | | | | | | | | | |

## LDP142-151

Dennis Dart SLF 8.8m  Plaxton Pointer MPD  N28F  2001

| 142 | w | Y842TGH | 145 | w | Y845TGH | 148 | w | Y848TGH | 150 | u | Y805TGH |
|-----|----|---------|-----|----|---------|-----|----|---------|-----|----|---------|
| 143 | w | Y843TGH | 146 | w | Y846TGH | 149 | w | Y849TGH | 151 | PL | Y851TGH |
| 144 | w | Y844TGH | 147 | w | Y847TGH | | | | | | |

## LDP167-190

Dennis Dart SLF 9.3m  Plaxton Pointer 2  N28F  2001

| 167 | PM | Y967TGH | 173 | PM | Y973TGH | 180 | PM | Y908TGH | 186 | PL | Y986TGH |
|-----|----|---------|-----|----|---------|-----|----|---------|-----|----|---------|
| 168 | PM | Y968TGH | 174 | PM | Y974TGH | 181 | PM | Y981TGH | 187 | SI | Y987TGH |
| 169 | PM | Y969TGH | 175 | PM | Y975TGH | 182 | NX | Y982TGH | 188 | Q | Y988TGH |
| 170 | PM | Y907TGH | 176 | PM | Y976TGH | 183 | Q | Y983TGH | 189 | NX | Y989TGH |
| 171 | PM | Y971TGH | 178 | PM | Y978TGH | 184 | Q | Y984TGH | 190 | Q | Y909TGH |
| 172 | PM | Y972TGH | 179 | PM | Y979TGH | 185 | Q | Y985TGH | | | |

## LDP191-227

Dennis Dart SLF 10.1m  Plaxton Pointer 2  N30D*  2002-03  *seating varies

| 191 | AL | SN51UAD | 201 | AL | SN51UAP | 210 | NX | SN51UAZ | 219 | PL | SK52MPF |
|-----|----|---------|-----|----|---------|-----|----|---------|-----|----|---------|
| 192 | AL | SN51UAE | 202 | BX | SN51UAR | 211 | NX | SK52MMU | 220 | PL | SK52MPO |
| 193 | AL | SN51UAF | 203 | A | SN51UAS | 212 | PL | SK52MMV | 221 | PL | SK52MLU |
| 194 | AL | SN51UAG | 204 | A | SN51UAT | 213 | PL | SK52MMX | 222 | PL | SK52MLV |
| 195 | AL | SN51UAH | 205 | A | SN51UAU | 214 | PL | SK52MOA | 223 | PL | SK52MLX |
| 196 | AL | SN51UAJ | 206 | A | SN51UAV | 215 | PL | SK52MOF | 224 | PL | SK52MLY |
| 197 | AL | SN51UAK | 207 | A | SN51UAW | 216 | PL | SK52MOU | 225 | PL | SK52MLZ |
| 198 | AL | SN51UAL | 208 | A | SN51UAX | 217 | PL | SK52MOV | 226 | PL | SK52MMA |
| 199 | AL | SN51UAM | 209 | A | SN51UAY | 218 | PL | SK52MPE | 227 | PL | SK52MME |
| 200 | AL | SN51UAO | | | | | | | | | |

## LDP249-262

TransBus Dart 10.1m  TransBus Pointer  N27D  2003

| 249 | AL | SN53KKF | 253 | AL | SN53KKL | 257 | AL | SN53KKR | 260 | AL | SN53KKV |
|-----|----|---------|-----|----|---------|-----|----|---------|-----|----|---------|
| 250 | AL | SN53KKG | 254 | AL | SN53KKM | 258 | AL | SN53KKT | 261 | AL | SN53KKW |
| 251 | AL | SN53KKH | 255 | AL | SN53KKO | 259 | AL | SN53KKU | 262 | AL | SN53KKX |
| 252 | AL | SN53KKJ | 256 | AL | SN53KKP | | | | | | |

## LDP263-272

ADL Dart 8.8m  ADL Pointer  N23F  2005

| 263 | PL | LX05EYP | 266 | PL | LX05EYT | 269 | PL | LX05EYW | 271 | PL | LX05EXZ |
|-----|----|---------|-----|----|---------|-----|----|---------|-----|----|---------|
| 264 | PL | LX05EYR | 267 | PL | LX05EYU | 270 | PL | LX05EYY | 272 | PL | LX05EYA |
| 265 | PL | LX05EYS | 268 | PL | LX05EYV | | | | | | |

## LDP273-280

ADL Dart 10.1m  ADL Pointer  N28D  2006

| 273 | NX | LX06EYT | 275 | NX | LX06EYV | 277 | NX | LX06FBD | 279 | NX | LX06FAA |
|-----|----|---------|-----|----|---------|-----|----|---------|-----|----|---------|
| 274 | NX | LX06EYU | 276 | NX | LX06EYW | 278 | NX | LX06FBE | 280 | NX | LX06FAF |

## LDP281-291

ADL Dart 8.8m  ADL Pointer  N23F  2006

| 281 | AF | LX06FAJ | 284 | AF | LX06FAO | 287 | SW | LX06FBB | 290 | SW | LX06EZV |
|-----|----|---------|-----|----|---------|-----|----|---------|-----|----|---------|
| 282 | AF | LX06FAK | 285 | AF | LX06FAU | 288 | SW | LX06FBC | 291 | SW | LX06EZW |
| 283 | AF | LX06FAM | 286 | AF | LX06FBA | 289 | SW | LX06EZU | | | |

| LDP292 | PL | LX06EZZ | ADL Dart 10.1m | ADL Pointer | N28D | 2006 |
|--------|----|---------|----------------|-------------|------|------|
| LDP293 | PL | LX06EZJ | ADL Dart 10.1m | ADL Pointer | N28D | 2006 |
| LDP294 | PL | LX06EZK | ADL Dart 10.1m | ADL Pointer | N28D | 2006 |

## LDP295-302

Dennis Dart 10.1m  Plaxton Pointer 2  N30D  1997  Metroline, Harrow, 2010

| 295 | SI | R151RLY | 297 | SI | R146RLY | 299 | SI | R147RLY | 301 | SI | R142RLY |
|-----|----|---------|-----|----|---------|-----|----|---------|-----|----|---------|
| 296 | SI | R124RLY | 298 | SI | R140RLY | 300 | SI | R125RLY | 302 | SI | R153RLY |

Politics has a lot to answer for as London's articulated buses are being withdrawn prematurely. Still allocated to route 12, MAL94, BX54EFB, was seen in Trafalgar Square in July 2010. *Richard Godfrey*

### MAL1-61

Mercedes-Benz Citaro O530G

AN49T 2002-04

| | | | | | | | | | |
|---|---|---|---|---|---|---|---|---|---|
| 1 | Q | BX02YZE | 38 | NX | BD52LNP | 46 | NX | BD52LNA | 54 | NX | BL52ODM |
| 12 | Q | BX02YYT | 39 | NX | BD52LNR | 47 | NX | BD52LNC | 55 | NX | BL52ODN |
| 32 | NX | BN52GWC | 40 | NX | BD52LNT | 48 | NX | BD52LNE | 56 | NX | BL52ODP |
| 33 | NX | BN52GWD | 41 | NX | BD52LNU | 49 | NX | BD52LNF | 57 | NX | BL52ODR |
| 34 | NX | BN52GWE | 42 | NX | BD52LMU | 50 | NX | BD52LNG | 58 | NX | BU04UTM |
| 35 | NX | BN52GVU | 43 | NX | BD52LMV | 51 | NX | BU04EZK | 59 | NX | BL52ODT |
| 36 | NX | BX04NBD | 44 | NX | BD52LMX | 52 | NX | BD52LMO | 60 | NX | BL52ODU |
| 37 | NX | BD52LNO | 45 | NX | BD52LMY | 53 | NX | BL52ODK | 61 | NX | BL52ODV |

### MAL62-94

Mercedes-Benz Citaro O530G

AN49T 2004

| | | | | | | | | | |
|---|---|---|---|---|---|---|---|---|---|
| 62 | Q | BX54EFC | 71 | Q | BX54UCV | 79 | Q | BX54UDJ | 87 | Q | BX54UDU |
| 63 | Q | BX54EFD | 72 | Q | BX54UCW | 80 | Q | BX54UDK | 88 | Q | BX54UDV |
| 64 | Q | BX54UCM | 73 | Q | BX54UCZ | 81 | Q | BX54UDL | 89 | Q | BX54UDW |
| 65 | Q | BX54UCN | 74 | Q | BX54UDB | 82 | Q | BX54UDM | 90 | Q | BX54UDY |
| 66 | Q | BX54UCO | 75 | Q | BX54UDD | 83 | Q | BX54UDN | 91 | Q | BX54UDZ |
| 67 | Q | BX54UCP | 76 | Q | BX54UDE | 84 | Q | BX54UDO | 92 | Q | BX54UEA |
| 68 | Q | BX54UCR | 77 | Q | BX54UDG | 85 | Q | BX54UDP | 93 | Q | BX54UEB |
| 69 | Q | BX54UCT | 78 | Q | BX54UDH | 86 | Q | BX54UDT | 94 | Q | BX54EFB |
| 70 | Q | BX54UCU | | | | | | | | | |

### MAL95-119

Mercedes-Benz Citaro O530G

AN47T 2008

| | | | | | | | | | |
|---|---|---|---|---|---|---|---|---|---|
| 95 | MW | BD57WCY | 102 | MW | BD57WDM | 108 | MW | BD57OXJ | 114 | MW | BD57UYF |
| 96 | MW | BD57WCZ | 103 | MW | BD57WDN | 109 | MW | BD57OXK | 115 | MW | BD57UYG |
| 97 | MW | BD57WDA | 104 | MW | BD57WDP | 110 | MW | BD57OXM | 116 | MW | BD57UYH |
| 98 | MW | BD57WDC | 105 | MW | BD57WDR | 111 | MW | BD57OXN | 117 | MW | BD57UYJ |
| 99 | MW | BD57WDE | 106 | MW | BD57WDS | 112 | MW | BD57OXP | 118 | MW | BD57UYK |
| 100 | MW | BD57WDK | 107 | MW | BD57WDT | 113 | MW | BD57UYE | 119 | MW | BD57UYL |
| 101 | MW | BD57WDL | | | | | | | | | |

| | | | | | | |
|---|---|---|---|---|---|---|
| **MAL120** | Q | LX03HDV | Mercedes-Benz Citaro O530G | AN47T | 2003 | East London, 2009 |

Replacements for the articulated buses on the former Red Arrow services are an increased number of rigid Mercedes-Benz Citaro buses that in total consume more road space. MEC25, BD09ZRJ, is seen passing Lambeth Palace on route 507. *Mark Lyons*

### MEC1-50 — Mercedes-Benz Citaro O530 — N21D — 2009

| | | | | | | | | | |
|---|---|---|---|---|---|---|---|---|---|
| 1 | RA | BG09JJK | 14 | RA | BD09ZPU | 27 | RA | BD09ZVS | 39 | RA | BD09ZWF |
| 2 | RA | BG09JJL | 15 | RA | BD09ZPV | 28 | RA | BD09ZVT | 40 | RA | BD09ZWG |
| 3 | RA | BG09JJU | 16 | RA | BD09ZPW | 29 | RA | BD09ZVU | 41 | RA | BD09ZWH |
| 4 | RA | BG09JJV | 17 | RA | BD09ZPX | 30 | RA | BD09ZVV | 42 | RA | BT09GOH |
| 5 | RA | BG09JJX | 18 | RA | BD09ZPY | 31 | RA | BD09ZVW | 43 | RA | BT09GOJ |
| 6 | RA | BG09JJY | 19 | RA | BD09ZPZ | 32 | RA | BD09ZVX | 44 | RA | BT09GOK |
| 7 | RA | BG09JJZ | 20 | RA | BD09ZRA | 33 | RA | BD09ZVY | 45 | RA | BT09GOP |
| 8 | RA | BG09JKE | 21 | RA | BD09ZRC | 34 | RA | BD09ZVZ | 46 | RA | BT09GOU |
| 9 | RA | BG09JKF | 22 | RA | BD09ZRE | 35 | RA | BD09ZWA | 47 | RA | BT09GOX |
| 10 | RA | BG09JKJ | 23 | RA | BD09ZRF | 36 | RA | BD09ZWB | 48 | RA | BT09GPE |
| 11 | RA | BD09ZPR | 24 | RA | BD09ZRG | 37 | RA | BD09ZWC | 49 | RA | BT09GPF |
| 12 | RA | BD09ZPS | 25 | RA | BD09ZRJ | 38 | RA | BD09ZWE | 50 | RA | BT09GPJ |
| 13 | RA | BD09ZPT | 26 | RA | BD09ZRK | | | | | | |

| | | | | | | | |
|---|---|---|---|---|---|---|---|
| NV170 | AL | R370LGH | Volvo Olympian | Northern Counties Palatine II | CO47/24D | 1997-98 | |
| NV171 | AL | R371LGH | Volvo Olympian | Northern Counties Palatine II | CO47/24D | 1997-98 | |
| NV176 | PL | R376LGH | Volvo Olympian | Northern Counties Palatine II | CO47/24D | 1997-98 | |
| OS1 | SI | MX09HHW | Optare Solo M880SL | Optare | N28F | 2009 | Docklands Buses, 2009 |

*The London Bus Handbook*

## PVL56-143
Volvo B7TL 10m — Plaxton President — N41/19D* — 2000 — *seating varies

| | | | | | | | | | | | | | | |
|---|---|---|---|---|---|---|---|---|---|---|---|---|---|---|
| 56 | BX | W956WGH | 80 | Q | W408WGH | 104 | u | W504WGH | 124 | AL | W524WGH |
| 57 | BX | W457WGH | 82 | Q | W482WGH | 105 | u | W905WGH | 125 | AL | W425WGH |
| 58 | BX | W458WGH | 83 | NX | W483WGH | 106 | AL | W506WGH | 126 | AL | W526WGH |
| 59 | Qt | W459WGH | 84 | AL | W484WGH | 107 | u | W507WGH | 127 | AL | W527WGH |
| 60 | Qt | W996WGH | 85 | SW | W485WGH | 108 | u | W508WGH | 128 | AL | W428WGH |
| 61 | SW | W461WGH | 86 | Q | W486WGH | 109 | NX | W509WGH | 129 | Q | W529WGH |
| 62 | Qt | W462WGH | 87 | AL | W487WGH | 110 | BE | W401WGH | 130 | Qt | W403WGH |
| 63 | NX | W463WGH | 88 | BX | W488WGH | 111 | NX | W511WGH | 131 | Q | W531WGH |
| 64 | BE | W464WGH | 89 | BX | W489WGH | 112 | BX | W512WGH | 132 | Qt | W532WGH |
| 65 | BX | W465WGH | 90 | BX | W409WGH | 113 | SW | W513WGH | 133 | Qt | W533WGH |
| 66 | BE | W466WGH | 91 | BX | W491WGH | 114 | AL | W514WGH | 134 | Qt | W534WGH |
| 67 | BE | W467WGH | 92 | Q | W492WGH | 115 | AL | W415WGH | 135 | Qt | W435WGH |
| 68 | BE | W468WGH | 93 | SW | W493WGH | 116 | AL | W516WGH | 136 | Qt | W536WGH |
| 69 | BE | W469WGH | 94 | NX | W494WGH | 117 | AL | W517WGH | 137 | Qt | W537WGH |
| 70 | BE | W578DGU | 95 | BE | W495WGH | 118 | AL | W518WGH | 138 | Qt | W538WGH |
| 71 | BX | W471WGH | 96 | BE | W496WGH | 119 | AL | W519WGH | 139 | Qt | W539WGH |
| 72 | BX | W472WGH | 97 | BE | W497WGH | 120 | Qt | W402WGH | 140 | Qt | W404WGH |
| 73 | BX | W473WGH | 100 | u | W997WGH | 121 | AL | W521WGH | 141 | Qt | W541WGH |
| 75 | Qt | W475WGH | 101 | u | W501WGH | 122 | AL | W522WGH | 142 | Qt | W542WGH |
| 76 | Qt | W476WGH | 102 | u | W502WGH | 123 | Qt | W523WGH | 143 | Qt | W543WGH |
| 79 | Q | W479WGH | 103 | u | W503WGH | | | | | | |

## PVL144-207
Volvo B7TL 10m — Plaxton President — N41/20D — 2000

| | | | | | | | | | | | | | | |
|---|---|---|---|---|---|---|---|---|---|---|---|---|---|---|
| 144 | AL | X544EGK | 159 | NX | X559EGK | 178 | BX | X578EGK | 193 | SW | X593EGK |
| 145 | AL | X745EGK | 160 | AL | X616EGK | 179 | SI | X579EGK | 194 | SW | X594EGK |
| 146 | AL | X546EGK | 161 | AL | X561EGK | 180 | BE | X508EGK | 195 | AL | X595EGK |
| 147 | AL | X547EGK | 162 | AL | X562EGK | 181 | SI | X581EGK | 196 | AL | X596EGK |
| 148 | AL | X548EGK | 163 | AL | X563EGK | 182 | BE | X582EGK | 197 | AL | X597EGK |
| 149 | AL | X549EGK | 164 | AL | X564EGK | 183 | BE | X583EGK | 198 | SW | X598EGK |
| 150 | Q | X599EGK | 165 | AL | X656EGK | 184 | SI | X584EGK | 199 | SW | X699EGK |
| 151 | SW | X551EGK | 166 | AL | X566EGK | 185 | BE | X585EGK | 200 | SW | X502EGK |
| 152 | AL | X552EGK | 167 | AL | X567EGK | 186 | BE | X586EGK | 201 | SW | X501EGK |
| 153 | AL | X553EGK | 168 | SW | X568EGK | 187 | SI | X587EGK | 202 | SW | X702EGK |
| 154 | AL | X554EGK | 169 | Q | X569EGK | 188 | SW | X588EGK | 203 | SW | X503EGK |
| 155 | AL | X615EGK | 170 | SW | X707EGK | 189 | SW | X589EGK | 204 | SW | X504EGK |
| 156 | NX | X556EGK | 171 | BX | X571EGK | 190 | SW | X509EGK | 205 | SW | X705EGK |
| 157 | NX | X557EGK | 175 | BX | X575EGK | 191 | SW | X591EGK | 206 | SW | X506EGK |
| 158 | NX | X558EGK | 176 | BX | X576EGK | 192 | SW | X592EGK | 207 | SW | X507EGK |

PVL152, X552EGK, is one of the batch of Volvo B7TLs with Plaxton President bodywork supplied in 2000. It is seen complete with London General titles in a style that is being replaced with more prominent Go-Ahead names.
*Terry Longhurst*

## PVL208-272    Volvo B7TL 10m    Plaxton President    N41/20D*    2000    *251-3/62-4 are BC41/20D
*221/2 are N41/25F, 224 is O41/20D

| | | | | | | | | | | | |
|---|---|---|---|---|---|---|---|---|---|---|---|
| 208 | u | Y808TGH | 224 | A | Y824TGH | 239 | u | Y739TGH | 254 | BE | PL51LDU |
| 209 | BE | Y809TGH | 225 | NX | Y825TGH | 240 | u | Y704TGH | 257 | w | PL51LDY |
| 210 | BX | Y801TGH | 226 | A | Y826TGH | 241 | u | Y741TGH | 258 | BE | PL51LDZ |
| 211 | BX | Y811TGH | 227 | u | Y827TGH | 242 | u | Y742TGH | 259 | BE | PL51LEF |
| 212 | u | Y812TGH | 228 | u | Y828TGH | 243 | u | Y743TGH | 260 | BE | PN02XBH |
| 213 | u | Y813TGH | 229 | A | Y729TGH | 244 | PL | Y744TGH | 261 | w | PN02XBJ |
| 214 | SW | Y814TGH | 230 | SW | Y703TGH | 245 | A | Y745TGH | 262 | w | PN02XBK |
| 215 | NX | Y815TGH | 231 | A | Y731TGH | 246 | PL | Y746TGH | 263 | A | PN02XBL |
| 216 | NX | Y816TGH | 232 | SW | Y732TGH | 247 | A | Y747TGH | 264 | NX | PN02XBM |
| 217 | BX | Y817TGH | 233 | SW | Y733TGH | 248 | NX | Y748TGH | 265 | A | PN02XBO |
| 218 | A | Y818TGH | 234 | SW | Y734TGH | 249 | A | Y749TGH | 266 | BE | PN02XBP |
| 219 | BE | Y819TGH | 235 | SW | Y735TGH | 250 | BE | PL51LDJ | 267 | w | PN02XBR |
| 220 | PL | Y802TGH | 236 | SW | Y736TGH | 251 | PL | PL51LDK | 270 | Q | PN02XBU |
| 221 | A | Y821TGH | 237 | SW | Y737TGH | 252 | A | PL51LDN | 271 | w | PN02XBV |
| 222 | A | Y822TGH | 238 | SW | Y738TGH | 253 | PL | PL51LDO | 272 | Q | PN02XBW |
| 223 | NX | Y823TGH | | | | | | | | | |

## PVL273-354    Volvo B7TL 10m    TransBus President    N41/20D    2002-03

| | | | | | | | | | | | |
|---|---|---|---|---|---|---|---|---|---|---|---|
| 273 | Q | PJ02RAU | 294 | A | PJ02RDZ | 315 | Q | PJ52LVS | 336 | PM | PJ52LWR |
| 274 | Q | PJ02RAX | 295 | A | PJ02REU | 316 | Q | PJ52LVT | 337 | PM | PJ52LWS |
| 275 | Q | PJ02RBF | 296 | A | PJ02RFE | 317 | Q | PJ52LVU | 338 | PM | PJ52LWT |
| 276 | SI | PJ02RBO | 297 | A | PJ02RFF | 318 | Q | PJ52LVV | 339 | PM | PJ52LWU |
| 277 | w | PJ02RBU | 298 | Q | PJ02RFK | 319 | NX | PJ52LVW | 340 | PM | PJ52LWV |
| 278 | Q | PJ02RBV | 299 | Q | PJ02RFL | 320 | NX | PJ52LVX | 341 | PM | PJ52LWW |
| 279 | w | PJ02RBX | 300 | Q | PJ02RFN | 321 | NX | PJ52LVY | 342 | PM | PJ52LWX |
| 280 | w | PJ02RBY | 301 | Q | PJ02RFO | 322 | NX | PJ52LVZ | 343 | NX | PF52WPT |
| 281 | A | PJ02RBZ | 302 | Q | PJ02RFX | 323 | NX | PJ52LWA | 344 | NX | PF52WPU |
| 282 | A | PJ02RCF | 303 | Q | PJ02RFY | 324 | NX | PJ52LWC | 345 | NX | PF52WPV |
| 283 | A | PJ02RCO | 304 | Q | PJ02RFZ | 325 | NX | PJ52LWD | 346 | BX | PF52WPW |
| 284 | A | PJ02RCU | 305 | Q | PJ02RGO | 326 | Q | PJ52LWE | 347 | BX | PF52WPX |
| 285 | A | PJ02RCV | 306 | Q | PJ02RGU | 327 | Q | PJ52LWF | 348 | BX | PF52WPY |
| 286 | A | PJ02RCX | 307 | Q | PJ02RGV | 328 | Q | PJ52LWG | 349 | BX | PF52WPZ |
| 287 | A | PJ02RCY | 308 | Q | PJ02TVN | 329 | PM | PJ52LWH | 350 | BX | PF52WRA |
| 288 | A | PJ02RCZ | 309 | Q | PJ02TVO | 330 | PM | PJ52LWK | 351 | BX | PF52WRC |
| 289 | A | PJ02RDO | 310 | Q | PJ02TVP | 331 | PM | PJ52LWL | 352 | BX | PF52WRD |
| 290 | A | PJ02RDU | 311 | Q | PJ02TVT | 332 | PM | PJ52LWM | 353 | BX | PF52WRE |
| 291 | A | PJ02RDV | 312 | Q | PJ02TVU | 333 | PM | PJ52LWN | 354 | BX | PF52WRG |
| 292 | A | PJ02RDX | 313 | Q | PJ52LVP | 334 | PM | PJ52LWO | | | |
| 293 | A | PJ02RDY | 314 | Q | PJ52LVR | 335 | PM | PJ52LWP | | | |

**London Central names are shown on President PVL241, Y741TGH, as it heads west on route 36. Many in this batch are now withdrawn.**
*Terry Longhurst*

**Go-Ahead London** purchased some four hundred President bodies on Volvo chassis before the Wigan facility closed subsequent to parts of TransBus being purchased by Alexander Dennis Limited (ADL). Seen in Kingston while heading for Sutton is PVL293, PJ02RDY. *Dave Heath*

### PVL355-389

| | | | | | | | | | | |
|---|---|---|---|---|---|---|---|---|---|---|
| | | | Volvo B7TL | 10m | | TransBus President | | N41/20D | 2003-04 | |
| **355** | BX | PL03AGZ | **369** | BX | PJ53SRO | **376** | AL | PJ53NKN | **383** | AL | PJ53NKX |
| **362** | BX | PJ53SOF | **370** | BX | PJ53SRU | **377** | AL | PJ53NKO | **384** | AL | PJ53NKZ |
| **363** | BX | PJ53SOH | **371** | AL | PJ53NKG | **378** | AL | PJ53NKP | **385** | AL | PJ53NLA |
| **364** | BX | PJ53SOU | **372** | AL | PJ53NKH | **379** | AL | PJ53NKR | **386** | AL | PJ53NLC |
| **365** | BX | PJ53SPU | **373** | AL | PJ53NKK | **380** | AL | PJ53NKS | **387** | AL | PJ53NLD |
| **366** | BX | PJ53SPV | **374** | AL | PJ53NKL | **381** | AL | PJ53NKT | **388** | AL | PJ53NLE |
| **367** | BX | PJ53SPX | **375** | AL | PJ53NKM | **382** | AL | PJ53NKW | **389** | AL | PJ53NLF |
| **368** | BX | PJ53SPZ | | | | | | | | |

### PVL390-419

| | | | | | | | | | | |
|---|---|---|---|---|---|---|---|---|---|---|
| | | | Volvo B7TL | 10m | | ADL President | | N41/20D | 2005 | |
| **390** | NX | LX54HAA | **398** | NX | LX54GZK | **406** | NX | LX54GYV | **413** | NX | LX54GZE |
| **391** | NX | LX54HAE | **399** | NX | LX54GZL | **407** | NX | LX54GYW | **414** | NX | LX54GZF |
| **392** | NX | LX54HAO | **400** | NX | LX54GZM | **408** | NX | LX54GYY | **415** | NX | LX54GZU |
| **393** | NX | LX54HAU | **401** | NX | LX54GZN | **409** | NX | LX54GYZ | **416** | NX | LX54GZV |
| **394** | NX | LX54HBA | **402** | NX | LX54GZO | **410** | NX | LX54GZB | **417** | NX | LX54GZW |
| **395** | NX | LX54HBB | **403** | NX | LX54GZP | **411** | NX | LX54GZC | **418** | NX | LX54GZY |
| **396** | NX | LX54GZG | **404** | NX | LX54GZR | **412** | NX | LX54GZD | **419** | NX | LX54GZZ |
| **397** | NX | LX54GZH | **405** | NX | LX54GZT | | | | | |

| | | | | | | | |
|---|---|---|---|---|---|---|---|
| **RM9** | NX | VLT9 | AEC Routemaster R2RH | | Park Royal | B36/28R | 1959 |

### RML2503-2604

| | | | | | | | |
|---|---|---|---|---|---|---|---|
| | | | AEC Routemaster R2RH1 | Park Royal | B40/32R* | 1961-67 | *2318 is O40/32R |
| | | | | | | | *2516 is B40/32R and carries DRM |
| **2305** | AL | CUV305C | **2472** | NX | JJD472D | **2520** | Q | JJD520D | **2604** | AL | NML604E |
| **2318** | NX | CUV318C | **2516** | PL | WLT516 | | | | | |

### SE1-17

| | | | | | | | | | | |
|---|---|---|---|---|---|---|---|---|---|---|
| | | | ADL Dart 4 | 10.2m | | ADL Enviro200 | | N29D | 2007 | |
| **1** | AL | LX07BXH | **6** | AL | LX07BXN | **10** | AL | LX07BXS | **14** | AL | LX07BXY |
| **2** | AL | LX07BXJ | **7** | AL | LX07BXO | **11** | AL | LX07BXU | **15** | AL | LX07BZH |
| **3** | AL | LX07BXK | **8** | AL | LX07BXP | **12** | AL | LX07BXV | **16** | AL | LX07BYA |
| **4** | AL | LX07BXL | **9** | AL | LX07BXR | **13** | AL | LX07BXW | **17** | AL | LX07BYB |
| **5** | AL | LX07BXM | | | | | | | | |

Go-Ahead has chosen the Enviro 200 model for several route tenders recently, including the B16. Pictured in Eltham High Street is SE83, YX60FCV, which is based in Bexleyheath depot. *Richard Godfrey*

### SE18-36

| | | | ADL Dart 4 10.8m | | | ADL Enviro200 | | N32D | 2007-08 | |
|---|---|---|---|---|---|---|---|---|---|---|
| 18 | BE | SK07DZM | 23 | BE | SK07DWK | 28 | BE | SK07DWU | 33 | BE | SK07DWZ |
| 19 | BE | SK07DZN | 24 | BE | SK07DWL | 29 | BE | SK07DWV | 34 | BE | SK07DXA |
| 20 | BE | SK07DZO | 25 | BE | SK07DWM | 30 | BE | SK07DWW | 35 | BE | SK07DXB |
| 21 | BE | SK07DWG | 26 | BE | SK07DWO | 31 | BE | SK07DWX | 36 | BE | YN08DMY |
| 22 | BE | SK07DWJ | 27 | BE | SK07DWP | 32 | BE | SK07DWY | | | |

### SE37-46

| | | | ADL Dart 4 10.2m | | | ADL Enviro200 | | N29D | 2010 | |
|---|---|---|---|---|---|---|---|---|---|---|
| 37 | SI | LX10AUP | 40 | SI | LX10AUU | 43 | SI | LX10AUY | 45 | SI | LX10AVC |
| 38 | SI | LX10AUR | 41 | SI | LX10AUV | 44 | SI | LX10AVB | 46 | SI | LX10AVD |
| 39 | SI | LX10AUT | 42 | SI | LX10AUW | | | | | | |

### SE47-54

| | | | ADL Dart 4 10.8m | | | ADL Enviro200 | | N29D | 2010 | |
|---|---|---|---|---|---|---|---|---|---|---|
| 47 | SW | YX60EOE | 49 | SW | YX60EOG | 51 | SW | YX60EOJ | 53 | SW | YX60EOL |
| 48 | SW | YX60EOF | 50 | SW | YX60EOH | 52 | SW | YX60EOK | 54 | SW | YX60EOO |

### SE55-84

| | | | ADL Dart 4 10.2m | | | ADL Enviro200 | | N29D | 2010 | |
|---|---|---|---|---|---|---|---|---|---|---|
| 55 | BV | YX60DXT | 63 | BV | YX60FSU | 71 | BX | YX60FBZ | 78 | BX | YX60FCL |
| 56 | BV | YX60FSN | 64 | BV | YX60EPP | 72 | BX | YX60FCA | 79 | BX | YX60FCM |
| 57 | BV | YX60DXU | 65 | BV | YX60EPU | 73 | BX | YX60FCC | 80 | BX | YX60FCO |
| 58 | BV | YX60FSO | 66 | BV | YX60EOP | 74 | BX | YX60FCD | 81 | BX | YX60FCP |
| 59 | BV | YX60FSP | 67 | BV | YX60FCZ | 75 | BX | YX60FCE | 82 | BX | YX60FCU |
| 60 | BV | YX60FSS | 68 | BV | YX60FDA | 76 | BX | YX60FCF | 83 | BX | YX60FCV |
| 61 | BV | YX60DXW | 69 | BX | YX60FBU | 77 | BX | YX60FCG | 84 | BX | YX60FCY |
| 62 | BV | YX60EPO | 70 | BX | YX60FBY | | | | | | |

### SE85-93

| | | | ADL Dart 4 9.3m | | | ADL Enviro200 | | N | 2011 | |
|---|---|---|---|---|---|---|---|---|---|---|
| 85 | Q | YX11CPE | 88 | Q | YX11CPN | 90 | Q | YX11CPU | 92 | Q | YX11CPY |
| 86 | Q | YX11CPF | 89 | Q | YX11CPO | 91 | Q | YX11CPV | 93 | Q | YX11CPZ |
| 87 | Q | YX11CPK | | | | | | | | | |

*The London Bus Handbook*

In 2009 Go-Ahead took delivery of forty Darts 4s with Optare Esteem bodywork that were built at the Blackburn factory where East Lancs products were previously constructed. SOE17, LX09AYZ, represents the type as it works route 64. *Terry Longhurst*

### SO1-5

| | | | | | | | | | | | Scania N94 UD 10.6m | East Lancs OmniDekka 4.4m | N45/27D | 2005 | Blue Triangle, 2007 |

| **1** | SI | BV55UCT | **3** | SI | BV55UCW | **4** | SI | BV55UCX | **5** | SI | BV55UCY |
|---|---|---|---|---|---|---|---|---|---|---|---|
| **2** | SI | BV55UCU | | | | | | | | | |

### SOC1-9

Scania OmniCity N230 UD 10.8m Scania — N41/22D — 2008

| **1** | SI | LX08ECD | **4** | SI | LX08ECJ | **6** | SI | LX08ECT | **8** | SI | LX08ECW |
|---|---|---|---|---|---|---|---|---|---|---|---|
| **2** | SI | LX08ECE | **5** | SI | LX08ECN | **7** | SI | LX08ECV | **9** | SI | LX08ECY |
| **3** | SI | LX08ECF | | | | | | | | | |

### SOE1-40

ADL Dart 4 10.4m — Optare Esteem — N29D — 2009

| **1** | AL | LX09AYF | **11** | AL | LX09AYS | **21** | AL | LX09AZD | **31** | A | LX09BXP |
|---|---|---|---|---|---|---|---|---|---|---|---|
| **2** | AL | LX09AYG | **12** | AL | LX09AYT | **22** | AL | LX09AZF | **32** | A | LX09BXR |
| **3** | AL | LX09AYH | **13** | AL | LX09AYU | **23** | AL | LX09AZG | **33** | A | LX09BXS |
| **4** | AL | LX09AYJ | **14** | AL | LX09AYV | **24** | AL | LX09AZJ | **34** | A | LX09EVB |
| **5** | AL | LX09AYK | **15** | AL | LX09AYW | **25** | AL | LX09AZL | **35** | A | LX09EVC |
| **6** | AL | LX09AYL | **16** | AL | LX09AYY | **26** | AL | LX09AZN | **36** | A | LX09EVD |
| **7** | AL | LX09AYM | **17** | AL | LX09AYZ | **27** | AL | LX09AZO | **37** | A | LX09EVF |
| **8** | AL | LX09AYN | **18** | AL | LX09AZA | **28** | AL | LX09AZP | **38** | A | LX09EVG |
| **9** | AL | LX09AYO | **19** | AL | LX09AZB | **29** | A | LX09AZR | **39** | A | LX09EVH |
| **10** | AL | LX09AYP | **20** | AL | LX09AXC | **30** | A | LX09AZT | **40** | A | LX09EVJ |

| **VE1** | AF | LX58CWK | Volvo B9TL 10.4m | ADL Enviro 400 | N41/24D | 2008 | |
|---|---|---|---|---|---|---|---|
| **VE2** | AF | LX58CWL | Volvo B9TL 10.4m | ADL Enviro 400 | N41/24D | 2008 | |
| **VE3** | AF | LX58CWM | Volvo B9TL 10.4m | ADL Enviro 400 | N41/24D | 2008 | |
| **VM1** | SI | BJ11XGZ | Volvo B9TL 10.3m | MCV | N41/22D | 2011 | *development vehicle* |

### VP1-19

Volvo B7TL 10m — Plaxton President — N41/20D* — 2001 — *18/19 N41/23D East Thames, 2009

| **1** | Q | X149FBB | **6** | Q | X157FBB | **11** | Q | X163FBB | **16** | BX | X168FBB |
|---|---|---|---|---|---|---|---|---|---|---|---|
| **2** | Q | X151FBB | **7** | Q | X158FBB | **12** | Q | X164FBB | **17** | BX | X169FBB |
| **3** | Q | X152FBB | **8** | Q | X159FBB | **13** | Q | X165FBB | **18** | Qt | X171FBB |
| **4** | Q | X153FBB | **9** | Q | X161FBB | **14** | Q | X166FBB | **19** | Qt | X172FBB |
| **5** | Q | X154FBB | **10** | Q | X162FBB | **15** | BV | X167FBB | | | |

## VWL1-31 — Volvo B7TL 10.6m — Wrightbus Eclipse Gemini — N43/22D — 2002

| | | | | | | | | | | | |
|---|---|---|---|---|---|---|---|---|---|---|---|
| 1 | Q | LB02YWX | 9 | Q | LB02YXG | 17 | BV | LF52TGO | 25 | BV | LF52THN |
| 2 | Q | LB02YWY | 10 | Q | LB02YXH | 18 | BV | LF52TGU | 26 | BV | LF52THU |
| 3 | Q | LB02YWZ | 11 | BV | LB02YXJ | 19 | BV | LF52TGV | 27 | MW | LF52THV |
| 4 | Q | LB02YXA | 12 | BV | LB02YXK | 20 | BV | LF52TGX | 28 | MW | LF52THX |
| 5 | Q | LB02YXC | 13 | BV | LB02YXL | 21 | BV | LF52TGY | 29 | MW | LF52THZ |
| 6 | Q | LB02YXD | 14 | BV | LB02YXM | 22 | BV | LF52TGZ | 30 | MW | LF52TJO |
| 7 | Q | LB02YXE | 15 | BV | LB02YXN | 23 | BV | LF52THG | 31 | MW | LF52TJU |
| 8 | Q | LB02YXF | 16 | BV | LF52TGN | 24 | BV | LF52THK | | | |

## VWL32-44 — Volvo B7TL 10.6m — Wrightbus Eclipse Gemini — N43/23D — 2004

| | | | | | | | | | | | |
|---|---|---|---|---|---|---|---|---|---|---|---|
| 32 | MW | BX04AZW | 36 | MW | BX04BAA | 39 | MW | BX04BBE | 42 | MW | BX04BKL |
| 33 | MW | BX04AZV | 37 | MW | BX04BAU | 40 | MW | BX04BBF | 43 | MW | BX04BKK |
| 34 | MW | BX04AZU | 38 | MW | BX04BAV | 41 | MW | BX04BBJ | 44 | MW | BX04BKJ |
| 35 | MW | BX04AZZ | | | | | | | | | |

| | | | | | | |
|---|---|---|---|---|---|---|
| WDL1 | SW | LX58CWG | VDL/Wrightbus DL 10.4m | Wrightbus Gemini 2 | N41/24D | 2009 |
| WHD1 | SW | LX58CWJ | VDL DB300 Wrightbus Hybrid | Wrightbus Gemini 2 | N41/24D | 2008 |

## WVL1-121 — Volvo B7TL 10.1m — Wrightbus Eclipse Gemini 4.2m N41/22D 2002-03

| | | | | | | | | | | | |
|---|---|---|---|---|---|---|---|---|---|---|---|
| 1 | SW | LG02KGP | 32 | AF | LF52ZRO | 62 | AF | LF52ZTG | 92 | AL | LF52ZND |
| 2 | SW | LG02KGU | 33 | AF | LF52ZRP | 63 | AF | LF52ZTH | 93 | AL | LF52ZNE |
| 3 | SW | LG02KGV | 34 | AF | LF52ZRR | 64 | AF | LF52ZTJ | 94 | AL | LF52ZNG |
| 4 | SW | LG02KGX | 35 | AF | LF52ZRT | 65 | AF | LF52ZTK | 95 | AL | LF52ZNH |
| 5 | SW | LG02KGY | 36 | AF | LF52ZRU | 66 | AF | LF52ZTL | 96 | AL | LF52ZNJ |
| 6 | SW | LG02KGZ | 37 | AF | LF52ZRV | 67 | AF | LF52ZTM | 97 | AL | LF52ZNK |
| 7 | SW | LG02KHA | 38 | AF | LF52ZRX | 68 | AF | LF52ZTN | 98 | AL | LF52ZNL |
| 8 | SW | LG02KHE | 39 | AF | LF52ZRY | 69 | AF | LF52ZTO | 99 | AL | LF52ZNM |
| 9 | SW | LG02KHF | 40 | AF | LF52ZRZ | 70 | AF | LF52ZTP | 100 | AL | LF52ZNN |
| 10 | SW | LG02KHH | 41 | AF | LF52ZSD | 71 | AF | LF52ZTR | 101 | AL | LF52ZNO |
| 11 | SW | LG02KHJ | 42 | AF | LF52ZPZ | 72 | AL | LF52ZPB | 102 | AL | LF52ZLZ |
| 12 | SW | LG02KHK | 43 | AF | LF52ZRA | 73 | AL | LF52ZPC | 103 | AL | LF52ZMO |
| 13 | SW | LG02KHL | 44 | AF | LF52ZRC | 74 | AL | LF52ZPD | 104 | AL | LF52ZMU |
| 14 | AF | LG02KHM | 45 | AF | LF52ZRD | 75 | AL | LF52ZPE | 105 | SW | LX03EXV |
| 15 | AF | LG02KHO | 46 | AF | LF52ZRE | 76 | AL | LF52ZPG | 106 | SW | LX03EXW |
| 16 | AF | LG02KHP | 47 | AF | LF52ZRG | 77 | AL | LF52ZPH | 107 | SW | LX03EXZ |
| 17 | AF | LG02KHR | 48 | AF | LF52ZRJ | 78 | AL | LF52ZPJ | 108 | SW | LX03EXU |
| 18 | AF | LG02KHT | 49 | AF | LF52ZRK | 79 | AL | LF52ZPK | 109 | SW | LX03EDR |
| 19 | AF | LG02KHU | 50 | AF | LF52ZRL | 80 | AL | LF52ZPL | 110 | SW | LX03EDU |
| 20 | AF | LG02KHV | 51 | AF | LF52ZRN | 81 | AL | LF52ZPM | 111 | SW | LX03EDV |
| 21 | AF | LG02KHW | 52 | AF | LF52ZPN | 82 | AL | LF52ZNP | 112 | SW | LX03EEA |
| 22 | AF | LG02KHX | 53 | AF | LF52ZPO | 83 | AL | LF52ZNR | 113 | SW | LX03EEB |
| 23 | AF | LG02KHY | 54 | AF | LF52ZPP | 84 | AL | LF52ZNS | 114 | SW | LX03EEF |
| 24 | AF | LG02KHZ | 55 | AF | LF52ZPR | 85 | AL | LF52ZNT | 115 | SW | LX03EEG |
| 25 | AF | LG02KJA | 56 | AF | LF52ZPS | 86 | AL | LF52ZNU | 116 | SW | LX03EEH |
| 26 | AF | LG02KJE | 57 | AF | LF52ZPU | 87 | AL | LF52ZNV | 117 | SW | LX03EEJ |
| 27 | AF | LG02KJF | 58 | AF | LF52ZPV | 88 | AL | LF52ZNW | 118 | SW | LX03EEM |
| 28 | AF | LF52ZSO | 59 | AF | LF52ZPW | 89 | AL | LF52ZNX | 119 | SW | LX03ECV |
| 29 | AF | LF52ZSP | 60 | AF | VLT60 | 90 | AL | LF52ZNY | 120 | SW | LX03ECW |
| 30 | AF | LF52ZSR | 61 | AF | LF52ZPY | 91 | AL | LF52ZNZ | 121 | SW | LX03ECY |
| 31 | AF | LF52ZST | | | | | | | | | |

## WVL122-159 — Volvo B7TL 10.1m — Wrightbus Eclipse Gemini 4.2m N41/23D* 2003-04 — *150 is N41/21D

| | | | | | | | | | | | |
|---|---|---|---|---|---|---|---|---|---|---|---|
| 122 | SW | LX53AZP | 132 | SW | LX53AZD | 142 | SW | LX53AYP | 151 | SW | LX53BJU |
| 123 | SW | LX53AZR | 133 | SW | LX53AZF | 143 | SW | LX53AYT | 152 | Q | LX53BEY |
| 124 | SW | LX53AZT | 134 | SW | LX53AZG | 144 | SW | LX53AYU | 153 | AF | LX53BGE |
| 125 | SW | LX53AZU | 135 | SW | LX53AZJ | 145 | SW | LX53AYV | 154 | AF | LX53BFK |
| 126 | SW | LX53AZV | 136 | SW | LX53AZL | 146 | SW | LX53AYW | 155 | AF | LX53BDY |
| 127 | Q | LX53AZW | 137 | SW | LX53AZN | 147 | SW | LX53AYY | 156 | AF | LX53BBZ |
| 128 | Q | LX53AZZ | 138 | SW | LX53AZO | 148 | SW | LX53AYZ | 157 | AF | LX53BAA |
| 129 | SW | LX53AZA | 139 | SW | LX53AYM | 149 | SW | LX53BJK | 158 | AF | LX53BDO |
| 130 | SW | LX53AZB | 140 | SW | LX53AYN | 150 | SW | LX53BJO | 159 | AF | LX53BAO |
| 131 | SW | LX53AZC | 141 | SW | LX53AYO | | | | | | |

## WVL160-211
Volvo B7TL 10.1m  Wrightbus Eclipse Gemini 4.2m N41/23D 2005

| | | | | | | | | | | | |
|---|---|---|---|---|---|---|---|---|---|---|---|
| 160 | AF | LX05FBY | 173 | AF | LX05FBN | 186 | AF | LX05FAU | 199 | AF | LX05EZR |
| 161 | AF | LX05FBZ | 174 | AF | LX05FBO | 187 | AF | LX05FBA | 200 | AF | LX05EZS |
| 162 | AF | LX05FCA | 175 | AF | LX05FBU | 188 | AF | LX05FBB | 201 | AF | LX05EZT |
| 163 | AF | LX05FCC | 176 | AF | LX05EZJ | 189 | AF | LX05FBC | 202 | AF | LX05EZU |
| 164 | AF | LX05FCD | 177 | AF | LX05EYM | 190 | AF | LX05EZV | 203 | AF | LX05EYZ |
| 165 | AF | LX05FCE | 178 | AF | LX05EYO | 191 | AF | LX05EZW | 204 | AF | LX05EZA |
| 166 | AF | LX05FCF | 179 | AF | LX05FBV | 192 | AF | LX05EZZ | 205 | AF | LX05EZB |
| 167 | AF | LX05FBD | 180 | AF | LX05FAA | 193 | AF | LX05EZK | 206 | AF | LX05EZC |
| 168 | AF | LX05FBE | 181 | AF | LX05FAF | 194 | AF | LX05EZL | 207 | AF | LX05EZD |
| 169 | AF | LX05FBF | 182 | AF | LX05FAJ | 195 | AF | LX05EZM | 208 | AF | LX05EZE |
| 170 | AF | LX05FBJ | 183 | AF | LX05FAK | 196 | AF | LX05EZN | 209 | AF | LX05EZF |
| 171 | AF | LX05FBK | 184 | AF | LX05FAM | 197 | AF | LX05EZO | 210 | AF | LX05EZG |
| 172 | AF | LX05FBL | 185 | AF | LX05FAO | 198 | AF | LX05EZP | 211 | AF | LX05EZH |

## WVL212-273
Volvo B7TL 10.1m  Wrightbus Eclipse Gemini 4.2m N41/21D 2006

| | | | | | | | | | | | |
|---|---|---|---|---|---|---|---|---|---|---|---|
| 212 | Q | LX06DYS | 229 | Q | LX06DZM | 244 | Q | LX06EAG | 259 | Q | LX06EBK |
| 213 | Q | LX06DYT | 230 | Q | LX06DZN | 245 | Q | LX06EAJ | 260 | Q | LX06EBL |
| 214 | Q | LX06DYU | 231 | Q | LX06DZO | 246 | Q | LX06EAK | 261 | Q | LX06EBM |
| 215 | Q | LX06DYV | 232 | Q | LX06DZP | 247 | Q | LX06EAL | 262 | Q | LX06EBN |
| 216 | Q | LX06DYW | 233 | Q | LX06DZR | 248 | Q | LX06EAM | 263 | Q | LX06EBO |
| 217 | Q | LX06DYY | 234 | Q | LX06DZS | 249 | Q | LX06EAO | 264 | Q | LX06EBP |
| 218 | Q | LX06DZA | 235 | Q | LX06DZT | 250 | Q | LX06EAP | 265 | Q | LX06EBU |
| 219 | Q | LX06DZB | 236 | Q | LX06DZU | 251 | Q | LX06EAW | 266 | Q | LX06EBV |
| 220 | Q | LX06DZC | 237 | Q | LX06DZV | 252 | Q | LX06EAY | 267 | Q | LX06EBZ |
| 222 | Q | LX06DZE | 238 | Q | LX06DZW | 253 | Q | LX06EBA | 268 | Q | LX06ECA |
| 223 | Q | LX06DZF | 239 | Q | LX06DZY | 254 | Q | LX06EBC | 269 | Q | LX06ECC |
| 224 | Q | LX06DZG | 240 | Q | LX06DZZ | 255 | Q | LX06EBD | 270 | Q | LX06ECD |
| 225 | Q | LX06DZH | 241 | Q | LX06EAA | 256 | Q | LX06EBE | 271 | Q | LX06ECE |
| 226 | Q | LX06DZJ | 242 | Q | LX06EAC | 257 | Q | LX06EBG | 272 | Q | LX06ECF |
| 227 | Q | LX06DZK | 243 | Q | LX06EAF | 258 | Q | LX06EBJ | 273 | Q | LX06ECJ |
| 228 | Q | LX06DZL | | | | | | | | | |

## WVL274-349
Volvo B7TL 10.1m  Wrightbus Eclipse Gemini 2  N39/23D  2009-10

| | | | | | | | | | | | |
|---|---|---|---|---|---|---|---|---|---|---|---|
| 274 | NX | LX59CYL | 293 | NX | LX59CZL | 312 | PM | LX59CZY | 331 | PM | LX59DDF |
| 275 | NX | LX59CYO | 294 | NX | LX59CZM | 313 | PM | LX59CZZ | 332 | PM | LX59DDJ |
| 276 | NX | LX59CYP | 295 | NX | LX59CZN | 314 | PM | LX59DAA | 333 | PM | LX59DDK |
| 277 | NX | LX59CYS | 296 | NX | LX59CZO | 315 | PM | LX59DAO | 334 | BE | LX59DDL |
| 278 | NX | LX59CYT | 297 | NX | LX59CZP | 316 | PM | LX59DAU | 335 | BE, | LX59DDN |
| 279 | NX | LX59CYU | 298 | NX | LX59CZR | 317 | PM | LX59DBO | 336 | BE | LX59DDO |
| 280 | NX | LX59CYV | 299 | NX | LX59CZS | 318 | PM | LX59DBU | 337 | BE | LX59DDU |
| 281 | NX | LX59CYW | 300 | NX | LX59CZT | 319 | PM | LX59DBV | 338 | BE | LX59DDV |
| 282 | NX | LX59CYY | 301 | NX | LX59CZU | 320 | PM | LX59DBY | 339 | BE | LX59DDY |
| 283 | NX | LX59CYZ | 302 | NX | LX59CZV | 321 | PM | LX59DBZ | 340 | BE | LX59DDZ |
| 284 | NX | LX59CZA | 303 | PM | LX59CYA | 322 | PM | LX59DCE | 341 | BE | LX59DEU |
| 285 | NX | LX59CZB | 304 | PM | LX59CYC | 323 | PM | LX59DCF | 342 | BE | LX59DFA |
| 286 | NX | LX59CZC | 305 | PM | LX59CYE | 324 | PM | LX59DCO | 343 | BE | LX59DFC |
| 287 | NX | LX59CZD | 306 | PM | LX59CYF | 325 | PM | LX59DCU | 344 | BE | LX59DFD |
| 288 | NX | LX59CZF | 307 | PM | LX59CYG | 326 | PM | LX59DCV | 345 | BE | LX59DFE |
| 289 | NX | LX59CZG | 308 | PM | LX59CYH | 327 | PM | LX59DCY | 346 | BE | LX59DFF |
| 290 | NX | LX59CZH | 309 | PM | LX59CYJ | 328 | PM | LX59DCZ | 347 | BE | LX59DFG |
| 291 | NX | LX59CZJ | 310 | PM | LX59CYK | 329 | PM | LX59DDA | 348 | BE | LX59DFJ |
| 292 | NX | LX59CZK | 311 | PM | LX59CZW | 330 | PM | LX59DDE | 349 | BE | LX59DFK |

## WVL350-385
Volvo B7TL 10.1m  Wrightbus Eclipse Gemini 2  N39/23D  2010-11

| | | | | | | | | | | | |
|---|---|---|---|---|---|---|---|---|---|---|---|
| 350 | BX | LX60DVY | 359 | BX | LX60DWK | 368 | BX | LX60DWY | 377 | BX | LX60DXH |
| 351 | BX | LX60DVZ | 360 | BX | LX60DWL | 369 | BX | LX60DWZ | 378 | BX | LX60DXJ |
| 352 | BX | LX60DWA | 361 | BX | LX60DWM | 370 | BX | LX60DXA | 379 | BX | LX60DXK |
| 353 | BX | LX60DWC | 362 | BX | LX60DWN | 371 | BX | LX60DXB | 380 | BX | LX60DXM |
| 354 | BX | LX60DWD | 363 | BX | LX60DWO | 372 | BX | LX60DXC | 381 | BX | LX60DXO |
| 355 | BX | LX60DWE | 364 | BX | LX60DWP | 373 | BX | LX60DXD | 382 | BX | LX60DXP |
| 356 | BX | LX60DWF | 365 | BX | LX60DWU | 374 | BX | LX60DXE | 383 | BX | LX60DXR |
| 357 | BX | LX60DWG | 366 | BX | LX60DWV | 375 | BX | LX60DXF | 384 | BX | LX60DXS |
| 358 | BX | LX60DWJ | 367 | BX | LX60DWW | 376 | BX | LX60DXG | 385 | BX | LX60DXT |

WVL336, LX59DDO, is one of sixteen Wrightbus Eclipse Gemini 2 to carry this special livery for the East London Buses operation. It is seen passing through the Thames View Estate while heading for Ilford station.
*Dave Heath*

## WVL386-421    Volvo B7TL 10.1m    Wrightbus Eclipse Gemini 2   N39/23D   2011

| 386 | NX | LX11CVL | 395 | NX | LX11CVV | 404 | NX | LX11CWJ | 413 | SI | LX11CWU |
|-----|----|---------|-----|----|---------|-----|----|---------|-----|----|---------|
| 387 | NX | LX11CVM | 396 | NX | LX11CVW | 405 | NX | LX11CWK | 414 | SI | LX11CWV |
| 388 | NX | LX11CVN | 397 | NX | LX11CVY | 406 | NX | LX11CWL | 415 | SI | LX11CWW |
| 389 | NX | LX11CVO | 398 | NX | LX11CVZ | 407 | NX | LX11CWM | 416 | SI | LX11CWY |
| 390 | NX | LX11CVP | 399 | NX | LX11CWA | 408 | NX | LX11CWN | 417 | SI | LX11CWZ |
| 391 | NX | LX11CVR | 400 | NX | LX11CWC | 409 | NX | LX11CWO | 418 | SI | LX11CXA |
| 392 | NX | LX11CVS | 401 | NX | LX11CWD | 410 | NX | LX11CWP | 419 | SI | LX11CXB |
| 393 | NX | LX11CVT | 402 | NX | LX11CWE | 411 | NX | LX11CWR | 420 | SI | LX11CXC |
| 394 | NX | LX11CVU | 403 | NX | LX11CWG | 412 | NX | LX11CWT | 421 | SI | LX11CXD |

## WVL422-454    Volvo B7TL 10.1m    Wrightbus Eclipse Gemini 2   N39/23D   On order

| 422 | - | LX11 | 431 | - | LX11 | 439 | - | LX11 | 447 | - | LX11 |
|-----|---|------|-----|---|------|-----|---|------|-----|---|------|
| 423 | - | LX11 | 432 | - | LX11 | 440 | - | LX11 | 448 | - | LX11 |
| 424 | - | LX11 | 433 | - | LX11 | 441 | - | LX11 | 449 | - | LX11 |
| 425 | - | LX11 | 434 | - | LX11 | 442 | - | LX11 | 450 | - | LX11 |
| 426 | - | LX11 | 435 | - | LX11 | 443 | - | LX11 | 451 | - | LX11 |
| 427 | - | LX11 | 436 | - | LX11 | 444 | - | LX11 | 452 | - | LX11 |
| 428 | - | LX11 | 437 | - | LX11 | 445 | - | LX11 | 453 | - | LX11 |
| 429 | - | LX11 | 438 | - | LX11 | 446 | - | LX11 | 454 | - | LX11 |
| 430 | - | LX11 | | | | | | | | | |

## WHY1-7    VDL Bus hybrid 10.4m    Wrightbus Electrocity   N26D*   2005-08   *7 is N28D

| 1 | Q | LX06ECN | 3 | Q | LX55EAE | 6 | Q | LX55EAJ | 7 | Q | LX57CLZ |
|---|---|---------|---|---|---------|---|---|---------|---|---|---------|
| 2 | Q | LX55EAC | 4 | Q | LX55EAF | 5 | Q | LX55EAG | | | |

## WHY8-13    VDL Bus hybrid 10.4m    Wrightbus Electrocity   N26D   2011

| 8 | Q | LX11DVA | 10 | Q | LX11DVC | 12 | Q | LX11DVG | 13 | Q | LX11DVH |
|---|---|---------|----|---|---------|----|---|---------|----|---|---------|
| 9 | Q | LX11DVB | 11 | Q | LX11DVF | | | | | | |

Previous registrations:

| 202UXJ | WLT887 | R548LGH | R548LGH, WLT548 |
|--------|--------|---------|------------------|
| LF52ZNG | LF52ZNG, WLT694 | R552LGH | R552LGH, 352CLT |
| LF52ZPX | LF52ZPX, VLT60 | S638JGP | WLT990 |
| P508RYM | P508RYM, 188CLT | S954JGX | WLT311 |
| P509RYM | P509RYM, WLT379 | S955JGX | WLT599 |
| PL51LDY | PL51LDY, 257CLT | V146LGC | V146LGC, 46CLT |

The integral Scania OmniCity double-deck is built in Poland and has been selected by several operators for London services. Go-Ahead operates nine, all from Silvertown depot, including SOC9, LX08ECY. *Dave Heath*

| | | | |
|---|---|---|---|
| R345LGH | R345LGH, 545CLT | V332LGC | V332LGC, WLT532 |
| R370LGH | R370LGH, WLT470 | VLT9 | VLT9, OYM374A |
| R379LGH | R379LGH, VLT179 | VLT110 | PO51WNH |
| R384LGH | R384LGH, VLT284 | W81TJU | 00D88846, W81TJU, V8AEC |
| R387LGH | R387LGH, 197CLT | W425WGH | W425WGH, WLT625 |
| R472LGH | R472LGH, WLT872 | W578DGU | 170CLT |
| R474LGH | R474RGH, 174CLT | WLT516 | CUV283C |
| R476LGH | R476LGH, 176CLT | | |

## Depots and allocations:

### Bexleyheath (Erith Road ) - BX - London Central

| | | | | | | | | |
|---|---|---|---|---|---|---|---|---|
| Dart | LDP91 | LDP107 | LDP113 | | | | | |
| Dart 4 | SE69 | SE70 | SE71 | SE72 | SE73 | SE74 | SE75 | SE76 |
| | SE77 | SE78 | SE79 | SE80 | SE81 | SE82 | SE83 | SE84 |
| SB120 | DW12 | DW13 | DW14 | DW15 | DW16 | DW17 | DW18 | DW19 |
| | DW20 | DW21 | DW22 | DW23 | DW24 | | | |
| Volvo B7TL | PVL56 | PVL57 | PVL58 | PVL71 | PVL72 | PVL73 | PVL88 | PVL89 |
| | PVL90 | PVL91 | PVL171 | PVL175 | PVL176 | PVL178 | PVL210 | PVL211 |
| | PVL217 | PVL346 | PVL347 | PVL348 | PVL349 | PVL350 | PVL351 | PVL352 |
| | PVL353 | PVL354 | PVL355 | PVL356 | PVL357 | PVL358 | PVL359 | PVL360 |
| | PVL361 | PVL362 | PVL363 | PVL364 | PVL365 | PVL366 | PVL367 | PVL368 |
| | PVL369 | PVL370 | VP16 | VP17 | WVL350 | WVL351 | WVL352 | WVL353 |
| | WVL354 | WVL355 | WVL356 | WVL357 | WVL358 | WVL359 | WVL360 | WVL361 |
| | WVL362 | WVL363 | WVL364 | WVL365 | WVL366 | WVL367 | WVL368 | WVL369 |
| | WVL370 | WVL371 | WVL372 | WVL373 | WVL374 | WVL375 | WVL376 | WVL377 |
| | WVL378 | WVL379 | WVL380 | WVL381 | WVL382 | WVL383 | WVL384 | WVL385 |
| Trident 2 | E40 | E41 | E42 | E43 | E44 | E45 | E46 | E47 |
| | E48 | E49 | E50 | E51 | E52 | E53 | E54 | E55 |
| | E56 | | | | | | | |

## Camberwell (Warner Road) - Q - London Central

| | | | | | | | |
|---|---|---|---|---|---|---|---|
| Dart | LDP3 | LDP46 | LDP70 | LDP71 | LDP87 | LDP101 | LDP103 | LDP182 |
| | LDP183 | LDP184 | LDP185 | LDP186 | LDP187 | LDP188 | LDP189 | LDP190 |
| Dart 4 | SE85 | SE86 | SE87 | SE88 | SE89 | SE90 | SE91 | SE92 |
| | SE93 | | | | | | | |
| VDL Hybrid | WHY1 | WHY2 | WHY3 | WHY4 | WHY5 | WHY6 | WHY7 | WHY8 |
| | WHY9 | WHY10 | WHY11 | WHY12 | WHY13 | | | |
| Citaro | MAL1 | MAL12 | MAL62 | MAL63 | MAL64 | MAL65 | MAL66 | MAL67 |
| | MAL68 | MAL69 | MAL70 | MAL71 | MAL72 | MAL73 | MAL74 | MAL75 |
| | MAL76 | MAL77 | MAL78 | MAL79 | MAL80 | MAL81 | MAL82 | MAL83 |
| | MAL84 | MAL85 | MAL86 | MAL87 | MAL88 | MAL89 | MAL90 | MAL91 |
| | MAL92 | MAL93 | MAL94 | MAL120 | | | | |
| Routemaster | RML2520 | | | | | | | |
| Volvo B7TL | VP1 | VP2 | VP3 | VP4 | VP5 | VP6 | VP7 | VP8 |
| | VP9 | VP10 | VP11 | VP12 | VP13 | VP14 | PLV79 | PLV80 |
| | PLV82 | PLV86 | PLV92 | PVL129 | PVL131 | PVL150 | PVL168 | PVL270 |
| | PVL272 | PVL273 | PVL274 | PVL275 | PVL278 | PVL298 | PVL299 | PVL300 |
| | PVL301 | PVL302 | PVL303 | PVL304 | PVL305 | PVL306 | PVL307 | PVL308 |
| | PVL309 | PVL310 | PVL311 | PVL312 | PVL313 | PVL314 | PVL315 | PVL316 |
| | PVL317 | PVL318 | PVL326 | PVL327 | PVL328 | VWL1 | VWL2 | VWL3 |
| | VWL4 | VWL5 | VWL6 | VWL7 | VWL8 | VWL9 | VWL10 | WVL127 |
| | WVL152 | WVL212 | WVL213 | WVL214 | WVL215 | WVL216 | WVL217 | WVL218 |
| | WVL219 | WVL220 | WVL221 | WVL222 | WVL223 | WVL224 | WVL225 | WVL226 |
| | WVL227 | WVL228 | WVL229 | WVL230 | WVL231 | WVL232 | WVL233 | WVL234 |
| | WVL235 | WVL236 | WVL237 | WVL238 | WVL239 | WVL240 | WVL241 | WVL242 |
| | WVL243 | WVL244 | WVL245 | WVL246 | WVL247 | WVL248 | WVL249 | WVL250 |
| | WVL251 | WVL252 | WVL253 | WVL254 | WVL255 | WVL256 | WVL257 | WVL258 |
| | WVL259 | WVL260 | WVL261 | WVL262 | WVL263 | WVL264 | WVL265 | WVL266 |
| | WVL267 | WVL268 | WVL269 | WVL270 | WVL271 | WVL272 | WVL273 | |
| | | | | | | | | |
| Ancillary | PVL7 | PVL17 | PVL30 | PVL37 | PVL38 | PVL59 | PVL60 | PVL62 |
| | PVL75 | PVL76 | PVL120 | PVL123 | PVL130 | PVL132 | PVL133 | PVL134 |
| | PVL135 | PVL136 | PVL137 | PVL138 | PVL139 | PVL140 | PVL141 | PVL142 |
| | PVL143 | VP18 | VP19 | | | | | |

## Merton (High Street) - AL - London General

| | | | | | | | |
|---|---|---|---|---|---|---|---|
| Dart | LDP55 | LDP60 | LDP78 | LDP85 | LDP94 | LDP95 | LDP96 | LDP97 |
| | LDP98 | LDP99 | LDP104 | LDP134 | LDP135 | LDP136 | LDP137 | LDP138 |
| | LDP139 | LDP140 | LDP141 | LDP191 | LDP192 | LDP193 | LDP194 | LDP196 |
| | LDP198 | LDP199 | LDP200 | LDP201 | LDP216 | LDP217 | LDP249 | LDP250 |
| | LDP251 | LDP252 | LDP253 | LDP254 | LDP255 | LDP256 | LDP257 | LDP258 |
| | LDP259 | LDP260 | LDP261 | LDP262 | | | | |
| Dart 4 | SE1 | SE2 | SE3 | SE4 | SE5 | SE6 | SE7 | SE8 |
| | SE9 | SE10 | SE11 | SE12 | SE13 | SE14 | SE15 | SE16 |
| | SE17 | SOE1 | SOE2 | SOE3 | SOE4 | SOE5 | SOE6 | SOE7 |
| | SOE8 | SOE9 | SOE10 | SOE11 | SOE12 | SOE13 | SOE14 | SOE15 |
| | SOE16 | SOE17 | SOE18 | SOE19 | SOE20 | SOE21 | SOE22 | SOE23 |
| | SOE24 | SOE25 | SOE26 | SOE27 | SOE28 | | | |
| Routemaster | RML887 | RML2604 | | | | | | |
| Olympian | NV170 | NV171 | | | | | | |
| Volvo B7TL | PVL61 | PVL62 | PVL63 | PVL64 | PVL66 | PVL67 | PVL68 | PVL69 |
| | PVL74 | PVL75 | PVL76 | PVL77 | PVL78 | PVL80 | PVL81 | PVL84 |
| | PVL85 | PVL86 | PVL87 | PVL92 | PVL93 | PVL95 | PVL96 | PVL97 |
| | PVL98 | PVL99 | PVL100 | PVL101 | PVL102 | PVL103 | PVL104 | PVL105 |
| | PVL106 | PVL107 | PVL108 | PVL109 | PVL110 | PVL111 | PVL112 | PVL113 |
| | PVL114 | PVL115 | PVL116 | PVL117 | PVL118 | PVL119 | PVL121 | PVL122 |
| | PVL123 | PVL124 | PVL125 | PVL126 | PVL127 | PVL128 | PVL130 | PVL132 |
| | PVL144 | PVL145 | PVL146 | PVL147 | PVL148 | PVL149 | PVL150 | PVL151 |
| | PVL152 | PVL153 | PVL154 | PVL155 | PVL160 | PVL161 | PVL162 | PVL163 |
| | PVL164 | PVL165 | PVL166 | PVL167 | PVL168 | PVL195 | PVL197 | PVL251 |
| | PVL253 | PVL281 | PVL371 | PVL372 | PVL373 | PVL374 | PVL375 | PVL376 |
| | PVL377 | PVL378 | PVL379 | PVL380 | PVL381 | PVL382 | PVL383 | PVL384 |
| | PVL385 | PVL386 | PVL387 | PVL388 | PVL389 | | | |

## New Cross (New Cross Road) - NX - London Central

| | | | | | | | | |
|---|---|---|---|---|---|---|---|---|
| Dart | LDP4 | LDP69 | LDP102 | LDP211 | LDP273 | LDP274 | LDP275 | LDP276 |
| | LDP277 | LDP278 | LDP279 | LDP280 | LDP301 | LDP302 | | |
| Dart 4 | ED7 | ED8 | | | | | | |
| SB120 | DW25 | DW26 | DW27 | DW28 | DW29 | DW30 | DW31 | DW32 |
| | DW33 | DW34 | DW35 | DW36 | DW37 | | | |
| MB Citaro O530G | MAL32 | MAL33 | MAL34 | MAL35 | MAL36 | MAL37 | MAL38 | MAL39 |
| | MAL40 | MAL41 | MAL42 | MAL43 | MAL44 | MAL45 | MAL46 | MAL47 |
| | MAL48 | MAL49 | MAL50 | MAL51 | MAL52 | MAL53 | MAL54 | MAL55 |
| | MAL56 | MAL57 | MAL58 | MAL59 | MAL60 | MAL61 | | |
| Routemaster | RM9 | RML2472 | RML2318 | | | | | |
| Trident 2 | E95 | E96 | E97 | E98 | E99 | | | |
| Volvo B7TL | PVL63 | PVL83 | PVL94 | PVL109 | NX111 | PVL156 | PVL157 | PVL158 |
| | PVL159 | PVL208 | PVL212 | PVL213 | PVL215 | PVL216 | PVL223 | PVL225 |
| | PVL227 | PVL228 | PVL248 | PVL264 | PVL319 | PVL320 | PVL321 | PVL322 |
| | PVL323 | PVL324 | PVL325 | PVL343 | PVL344 | PVL345 | PVL390 | PVL391 |
| | PVL392 | PVL393 | PVL394 | PVL395 | PVL396 | PVL397 | PVL398 | PVL399 |
| | PVL400 | PVL401 | PVL402 | PVL403 | PVL404 | PVL405 | PVL406 | PVL407 |
| | PVL408 | PVL409 | PVL410 | PVL411 | PVL412 | PVL413 | PVL414 | PVL415 |
| | PVL416 | PVL417 | PVL418 | PVL419 | WVL274 | WVL275 | WVL276 | WVL277 |
| | WVL278 | WVL279 | WVL280 | WVL281 | WVL282 | WVL283 | WVL284 | WVL285 |
| | WVL286 | WVL287 | WVL288 | WVL289 | WVL290 | WVL291 | WVL292 | WVL293 |
| | WVL294 | WVL295 | WVL296 | WVL297 | WVL298 | WVL299 | WVL300 | WVL301 |
| | WVL302 | WVL386 | WVL387 | WVL388 | WVL389 | WVL390 | WVL391 | WVL392 |
| | WVL393 | WVL394 | WVL395 | WVL396 | WVL397 | WVL398 | WVL399 | WVL400 |
| | WVL401 | WVL402 | WVL403 | WVL404 | WVL405 | WVL406 | WVL407 | WVL408 |
| | WVL409 | WVL410 | WVL411 | WVL412 | | | | |

## Peckham (Blackpool Road) - PM

| | | | | | | | | |
|---|---|---|---|---|---|---|---|---|
| Dart | LDP167 | LDP168 | LDP169 | LDP170 | LDP171 | LDP172 | LDP173 | LDP174 |
| | LDP175 | LDP176 | LDP177 | LDP178 | LDP179 | LDP180 | LDP181 | |
| Volvo B7TL | PVL329 | PVL330 | PVL332 | PVL333 | PVL334 | PVL335 | PVL336 | PVL337 |
| | PVL338 | PVL339 | PVL340 | PVL341 | PVL342 | WVL303 | WVL304 | WVL305 |
| | WVL306 | WVL307 | WVL308 | WVL309 | WVL310 | WVL311 | WVL312 | WVL313 |
| | WVL314 | WVL315 | WVL316 | WVL317 | WVL318 | WVL319 | WVL320 | WVL321 |
| | WVL322 | WVL323 | WVL324 | WVL325 | WVL326 | WVL327 | WVL328 | WVL329 |
| | WVL330 | WVL331 | WVL332 | WVL333 | | | | |
| Trident 2 | E16 | E17 | E18 | E19 | E20 | E21 | E22 | E23 |
| | E24 | E25 | E26 | E27 | E28 | E29 | E30 | E31 |
| | E32 | E33 | E34 | E35 | E36 | E37 | | |

## Putney (Chelverton Road) - AF - London General

| | | | | | | | | |
|---|---|---|---|---|---|---|---|---|
| Dart | LDP281 | LDP282 | LDP283 | LDP284 | LDP285 | LDP286 | | |
| Volvo B7TL | WVL14 | WVL15 | WVL16 | WVL17 | WVL18 | WVL19 | WVL20 | WVL21 |
| | WVL22 | WVL23 | WVL24 | WVL25 | WVL26 | WVL27 | WVL28 | WVL29 |
| | WVL30 | WVL31 | WVL32 | WVL33 | WVL34 | WVL35 | WVL36 | WVL37 |
| | WVL38 | WVL39 | WVL40 | WVL41 | WVL42 | WVL43 | WVL44 | WVL45 |
| | WVL46 | WVL47 | WVL48 | WVL49 | WVL50 | WVL51 | WVL52 | WVL53 |
| | WVL54 | WVL55 | WVL56 | WVL57 | WVL58 | WVL59 | WVL60 | WVL61 |
| | WVL62 | WVL63 | WVL64 | WVL65 | WVL66 | WVL67 | WVL68 | WVL69 |
| | WVL70 | WVL71 | WVL153 | WVL154 | WVL155 | WVL156 | WVL157 | WVL158 |
| | WVL159 | WVL160 | WVL161 | WVL162 | WVL163 | WVL164 | WVL165 | WVL166 |
| | WVL167 | WVL168 | WVL169 | WVL170 | WVL171 | WVL172 | WVL173 | WVL174 |
| | WVL175 | WVL176 | WVL177 | WVL178 | WVL179 | WVL180 | WVL181 | WVL182 |
| | WVL183 | WVL184 | WVL185 | WVL186 | WVL187 | WVL188 | WVL189 | WVL190 |
| | WVL191 | WVL192 | WVL193 | WVL194 | WVL195 | WVL196 | WVL197 | WVL198 |
| | WVL199 | WVL200 | WVL201 | WVL202 | WVL203 | WVL204 | WVL205 | WVL206 |
| | WVL207 | WVL208 | WVL209 | WVL210 | WVL211 | | | |
| Volvo B9TL | VE1 | VE2 | VE3 | | | | | |

## Rainham (Ferry Lane)  -  BE - Blue Triangle

| | | | | | | | | |
|---|---|---|---|---|---|---|---|---|
| Dart | DP192 | DP206 | DP207 | DP209 | | | | |
| Dart 4 | ED9 | ED10 | ED11 | ED12 | ED13 | ED14 | ED15 | ED16 |
| | ED17 | SE18 | SE19 | SE20 | SE21 | SE22 | SE23 | SE24 |
| | SE25 | SE26 | SE27 | SE28 | SE29 | SE30 | SE31 | SE32 |
| | SE33 | SE34 | SE35 | SE36 | | | | |
| Volvo B7TL | PVL64 | PVL66 | PVL67 | PVL68 | PVL69 | PVL70 | PVL95 | PVL96 |
| | PVL97 | PVL110 | PVL180 | PVL182 | PVL183 | PVL185 | PVL186 | PVL208 |
| | PVL219 | PVL250 | PVL254 | PVL258 | PVL259 | PVL260 | PVL266 | |
| Volvo B9TL | WVL334 | WVL335 | WVL336 | WVL337 | WVL338 | WVL339 | WVL340 | WVL341 |
| | WVL342 | WVL343 | WVL344 | WVL345 | WVL346 | WVL347 | WVL348 | WVL349 |

## Silvertown (Factory Road)  -  SI - Docklands Buses

| | | | | | | | | |
|---|---|---|---|---|---|---|---|---|
| Dart | LDP295 | LDP296 | LDP297 | LDP298 | LDP299 | LDP300 | | |
| Dart 4 | ED17 | ED18 | ED19 | ED20 | ED21 | ED22 | ED23 | ED24 |
| | ED25 | ED26 | ED27 | ED28 | SE37 | SE38 | SE39 | SE40 |
| | SE41 | SE42 | SE43 | SE44 | SE45 | SE46 | | |
| Trident | PDL19 | PDL20 | TL910 | TL911 | TL912 | TL913 | TL914 | TL915 |
| | TL917 | TL918 | TL919 | TL920 | TL921 | TL922 | TL923 | TPL926 |
| | TPL927 | | | | | | | |
| Volvo B7TL | PVL179 | PVL181 | PVL184 | PVL187 | PVL276 | | | |
| Volvo B9TL | WVL413 | WVL414 | WVL415 | WVL416 | WVL417 | WVL418 | WVL419 | WVL420 |
| | WVL421 | | | | | | | |
| Scania OmniDekka | SO1 | SO2 | SO3 | SO4 | SO5 | SOC1 | SOC2 | SOC3 |
| | SOC4 | SOC5 | SOC6 | SOC7 | SOC8 | SOC9 | | |

## Southwark (Mandela Way)  -  MW

| | | | | | | | | |
|---|---|---|---|---|---|---|---|---|
| MB Citaro O530G | MAL95 | MAL96 | MAL97 | MAL98 | MAL99 | MAL100 | MAL101 | MAL102 |
| | MAL103 | MAL104 | MAL105 | MAL106 | MAL107 | MAL108 | MAL109 | MAL110 |
| | MAL111 | MAL112 | MAL113 | MAL114 | MAL115 | MAL116 | MAL117 | MAL118 |
| | MAL119 | | | | | | | |
| Volvo B7TL | VWL27 | VWL28 | VWL29 | VWL30 | VWL31 | VWL32 | VWL33 | VWL34 |
| | VWL35 | VWL36 | VWL37 | VWL38 | VWL39 | VWL40 | VWL41 | VWL42 |
| | VWL43 | VWL44 | | | | | | |

## Stockwell (Binfield Road) - SW

| | | | | | | | | |
|---|---|---|---|---|---|---|---|---|
| Dart | DP193 | DP194 | DP195 | DP196 | DP197 | DP198 | DP199 | DP200 |
| | DP201 | DP202 | DP203 | DP204 | DP205 | LDP2 | LDP287 | LDP288 |
| | LDP289 | LDP290 | LDP291 | SE47 | SE48 | SE49 | SE50 | SE51 |
| | SE52 | SE53 | SE54 | | | | | |
| Trident | PDL24 | PDL28 | PDL31 | PDL33 | PDL34 | PDL35 | PDL36 | PDL37 |
| | PDL38 | PDL39 | PDL40 | PDL41 | PDL42 | PDL43 | PDL44 | PDL45 |
| | PDL46 | PDL47 | PDL48 | PDL49 | PDL50 | | | |
| Trident 2 | E1 | E2 | E3 | E4 | E5 | E6 | E7 | E8 |
| | E9 | E10 | E11 | E12 | E13 | E14 | E15 | E38 |
| | E39 | E57 | E62 | E63 | E64 | E65 | E66 | E67 |
| | E68 | E69 | E70 | E71 | E72 | E73 | E74 | E75 |
| | E76 | E77 | E78 | E79 | E80 | E81 | E82 | E83 |
| | E84 | E85 | E86 | E87 | E88 | E89 | E90 | E91 |
| | E92 | E93 | E100 | E101 | E102 | E103 | E104 | E105 |
| | E106 | E107 | E108 | E109 | E110 | E111 | E112 | E113 |
| | E114 | E115 | E116 | E117 | E118 | E119 | E120 | E121 |
| | E122 | E123 | E124 | E125 | E126 | E127 | E128 | E129 |
| | E130 | E131 | E132 | E133 | E134 | E135 | E136 | E137 |
| | E151 | E152 | E153 | E154 | E155 | E156 | E157 | E158 |
| | E159 | E160 | E161 | E162 | | | | |
| Trident E400H | EH1 | EH2 | EH3 | EH4 | EH5 | | | |
| VDL/Wrightbus | WDL1 | WHD1 | | | | | | |

| Volvo B7TL | EVL5 | EVL15 | EVL17 | PVL168 | PVL188 | PVL189 | PVL190 | PVL191 |
|---|---|---|---|---|---|---|---|---|
| | PVL192 | PVL193 | PVL194 | PVL198 | PVL199 | PVL200 | PVL201 | PVL202 |
| | PVL203 | PVL204 | PVL205 | PVL206 | PVL207 | PVL214 | PVL230 | PVL232 |
| | PVL233 | PVL234 | PVL235 | PVL236 | PVL237 | WVL1 | WVL2 | WVL3 |
| | WVL4 | WVL5 | WVL6 | WVL7 | WVL8 | WVL9 | WVL10 | WVL11 |
| | WVL12 | WVL13 | WVL105 | WVL106 | WVL107 | WVL108 | WVL109 | WVL110 |
| | WVL111 | WVL112 | WVL113 | WVL114 | WVL115 | WVL116 | WVL117 | WVL118 |
| | WVL119 | WVL120 | WVL122 | WVL123 | WVL125 | WVL126 | WVL127 | WVL128 |
| | WVL129 | WVL130 | WVL131 | WVL132 | WVL133 | WVL134 | WVL135 | WVL136 |
| | WVL139 | WVL140 | WVL141 | WVL142 | WVL143 | WVL144 | WVL145 | WVL146 |
| | WVL147 | WVL148 | WVL149 | WVL151 | | | | |

## Sutton (Bushey Road) - A

| Dart | LDP203 | LDP204 | LDP205 | LDP206 | LDP207 | LDP208 | LDP209 | LDP210 |
|---|---|---|---|---|---|---|---|---|
| Dart 4 | SOE29 | SOE30 | SOE31 | SOE32 | SOE33 | SOE34 | SOE35 | SOE36 |
| | SOE37 | SOE38 | SOE39 | SOE40 | | | | |
| Trident 2 | DOE1 | DOE2 | DOE3 | DOE4 | DOE5 | DOE6 | DOE7 | DOE8 |
| | DOE8 | DOE10 | DOE11 | DOE12 | DOE13 | DOE14 | DOE15 | DOE16 |
| | DOE17 | DOE18 | DOE19 | DOE20 | DOE21 | DOE22 | DOE23 | DOE24 |
| | DOE25 | DOE26 | DOE27 | DOE28 | DOE29 | DOE30 | DOE31 | DOE32 |
| | DOE33 | DOE34 | DOE35 | DOE36 | DOE37 | DOE38 | DOE39 | DOE40 |
| | DOE41 | DOE42 | DOE43 | DOE44 | DOE45 | DOE46 | DOE47 | DOE48 |
| | DOE49 | DOE50 | DOE51 | DOE52 | DOE53 | E58 | E59 | E60 |
| | E61 | | | | | | | |
| Volvo B7TL | PVL218 | PVL221 | PVL222 | PVL224 | PVL226 | PVL229 | PVL231 | PVL245 |
| | PVL247 | PVL249 | PVL252 | PVL263 | PVL265 | PVL281 | PVL282 | PVL283 |
| | PVL284 | PVL285 | PVL286 | PVL287 | PVL288 | PVL289 | PVL290 | PVL291 |
| | PVL292 | PVL293 | PVL294 | PVL295 | PVL296 | PVL297 | | |

## Waterloo (Cornwall Street) - RA

| MB Citaro O530 | MEC1 | MEC2 | MEC3 | MEC4 | MEC5 | MEC6 | MEC7 | MEC8 |
|---|---|---|---|---|---|---|---|---|
| | MEC9 | MEC10 | MEC11 | MEC12 | MEC13 | MEC14 | MEC15 | MEC16 |
| | MEC17 | MEC18 | MEC19 | MEC20 | MEC21 | MEC22 | MEC23 | MEC24 |
| | MEC25 | MEC26 | MEC27 | MEC28 | MEC29 | MEC30 | MEC31 | MEC32 |
| | MEC33 | MEC34 | MEC35 | MEC36 | MEC37 | MEC38 | MEC39 | MEC40 |
| | MEC41 | MEC42 | MEC43 | MEC44 | MEC45 | MEC46 | MEC47 | MEC48 |
| | MEC49 | MEC50 | | | | | | |

## Wimbledon (Plough Lane) - PL  - London General

| Dart | LDP186 | LDP212 | LDP213 | LDP214 | LDP215 | LDP216 | LDP217 | LDP218 |
|---|---|---|---|---|---|---|---|---|
| | LDP219 | LDP220 | LDP221 | LDP222 | LDP223 | LDP224 | LDP225 | LDP226 |
| | LDP227 | LDP263 | LDP264 | LDP265 | LDP266 | LDP267 | LDP268 | LDP269 |
| | LDP270 | LDP271 | LDP272 | | | | | |
| Olympian | NV176 | | | | | | | |
| Routemaster | RML2516 | | | | | | | |
| Volvo B7TL | PVL244 | PVL246 | PVL251 | PVL253 | | | | |

## unallocated/stored/refurbishing - u/w

remainder

# HACKNEY CT

CT Plus Ltd, Ash Grove Depot, Mare Street, Hackney, E8 4RH

| | | | | | | | | | | |
|---|---|---|---|---|---|---|---|---|---|---|
| BT1 | HK | YX10AYD | Volkswagen T5 | | Bluebird Tucana | | N12F | 2010 | | |
| BT2 | HK | YX10AYF | Volkswagen T5 | | Bluebird Tucana | | N12F | 2010 | | |
| BT3 | HK | YX10FFW | Volkswagen T5 | | Bluebird Tucana | | N12F | 2010 | | |
| DA1 | HK | MX10DXR | ADL Dart 4 10.8m | | ADL Enviro 200 | | N37F | 2010 | | |
| DAS1 | HK | SN57DWE | ADL Dart 4 8.9m | | ADL Enviro 200 | | N26F | 2007 | | |
| DAS2 | HK | SN57DWF | ADL Dart 4 8.9m | | ADL Enviro 200 | | N26F | 2007 | | |

### DCS1-9

| | | | | | | | | | | |
|---|---|---|---|---|---|---|---|---|---|---|
| | | | TransBus Dart 8.9m | | Caetano Slimbus | | N30F | 2003 | | |
| 1 | HK | KV03ZFE | 4 | HK | KV03ZFH | 6 | HK | HX03MGU | 8 | HK | HX03MGY |
| 2 | HK | KV03ZFF | 5 | HK | HX03MGV | 7 | HK | HX03MGJ | 9 | HK | HX03MGZ |
| 3 | HK | KV03ZFG | | | | | | | | | |

### DE1-6

| | | | | | | | | | | |
|---|---|---|---|---|---|---|---|---|---|---|
| | | | ADL Dart 4 9.4m | | East Lancs Esteem | | N28D | 2007 | | |
| 1 | HK | PN07KPY | 3 | HK | PN07KRD | 5 | HK | PN07KRF | 6 | HK | PN07KRG |
| 2 | HK | PN07KPZ | 4 | HK | PN07KRE | | | | | | |

| | | | | | | | | | | |
|---|---|---|---|---|---|---|---|---|---|---|
| DPS1 | HK | P508RYM | Dennis Dart 9.2m | | Plaxton Pointer | | N32F | 1996 | | |
| DPS2 | AW | BU05HFG | ADL Dart 8.8m | | ADL Mini Pointer | | N29F | 2005 | | |
| EO1 | HK | PN08SWJ | ADL Trident 2 10.3m | | East Lancs Olympus | | N43/21D | 2008 | | |

### HDC1-11

| | | | | | | | | | | |
|---|---|---|---|---|---|---|---|---|---|---|
| | | | Dennis Dart SLF 10.5m | | Caetano Nimbus | | N24D | 2001 | | |
| 1 | HK | X584ORV | 4 | HK | X587ORV | 7 | HK | X591ORV | 10 | HK | X594ORV |
| 2 | HK | X585ORV | 5 | HK | X588ORV | 8 | HK | X592ORV | 11 | HK | X595ORV |
| 3 | HK | X586ORV | 6 | HK | X589ORV | 9 | HK | X593ORV | | | |

| | | | | | | | | | |
|---|---|---|---|---|---|---|---|---|---|
| HDC12 | HK | T433LGP | Dennis Dart SLF 10.7m | | Caetano Compass | | N30D | 1999 | Travel London, 2006 |

**The HCT Group is an award winning and rapidly growing provider of public transport and related training services in several parts of Britain and was originally founded in 1982. The London operation is based at the Ash Grove depot in Hackney with another base in Walthamstow. Optare Solo OS4, YJ10EYF, is seen in Woodford.** *Mark Lyons*

HCT operates route 388 on which HTL1, LR52LTO, is shown. This is a TransBus Trident with East Lancs
Myllenium Lolyne bodywork. All this class have been refurbished recently and now feature the front blind
boxes as shown here. *Richard Godfrey*

### HTL1-13

TransBus Trident 10m    East Lancs Myllenium Lolyne  N45/17D  2003

| | | | | | | | | | | | |
|---|---|---|---|---|---|---|---|---|---|---|---|
| **1** | HK | LR52LTO | **5** | HK | LR52LWE | **8** | HK | LR52LWH | **11** | HK | PF52TGZ |
| **2** | HK | LR52LTN | **6** | HK | LR52LTK | **9** | HK | LR52LWJ | **12** | HK | LR52LYC |
| **3** | HK | LR52LTJ | **7** | HK | LR52LWF | **10** | HK | PF52TFX | **13** | HK | LR52LYJ |
| **4** | HK | LR52LTF | | | | | | | | | |

| | | | | | | |
|---|---|---|---|---|---|---|
| **HTP3** | HK | PN03UMB | TransBus Trident 9.9m | TransBus President | N41/23D | 2003 | Go-Ahead London, 2009 |
| **HTP4** | HK | PN03UMK | TransBus Trident 9.9m | TransBus President | N41/23D | 2003 | Go-Ahead London, 2009 |
| **HTP6** | AW | PN03ULY | TransBus Trident 9.9m | TransBus President | N41/23D | 2003 | Go-Ahead London, 2009 |

### LFO1-6

Optare Alero    Optare    BC13F*    2003-04  *seating varies

| | | | | | | | | | |
|---|---|---|---|---|---|---|---|---|---|
| **1** | HK | YN53ENE | **3** | HK | YN53ENH | **5** | HK | YN54LLA | **6** | HK | YN54LKU |
| **2** | HK | YN53ENF | **4** | HK | YN53ENM | | | | | |

| | | | | | | |
|---|---|---|---|---|---|---|
| **OS1** | HK | YJ08XDH | Optare Solo M950 | Optare | N33F | 2008 |

### OS2-8

Optare Solo M780 SE    Optare    N21F    2010-11

| | | | | | | | | | |
|---|---|---|---|---|---|---|---|---|---|
| **2** | AW | YJ59NRN | **4** | AW | YJ10EYF | **6** | AW | YJ10EYH | **8** | AW | YJ10EYL |
| **3** | AW | YJ59NRO | **5** | AW | YJ10EYG | **7** | AW | YJ10EYK | | | |

### OS9-18

Optare Solo M880    Optare    N23F    2011

| | | | | | | | | | |
|---|---|---|---|---|---|---|---|---|---|
| **9** | HK | YJ11PFA | **12** | HK | YJ11PFF | **15** | HK | YJ11PFN | **17** | HK | YJ60LRX |
| **10** | HK | YJ11PFD | **13** | HK | YJ11PFG | **16** | HK | YJ11PFO | **18** | HK | YJ60LRY |
| **11** | HK | YJ11PFE | **14** | HK | YJ11PFK | | | | | |

**Two short Enviro 200 Darts joined the HCT fleet in 2007. Seen in London's N1 district is DAS1, SN57DWE.**
*Mark Lyons*

### SD1-10

| | | | Scania N230 UD 10.8m | | | East Lancs OmniDekka | | N41/22D | 2010 | | |
|---|---|---|---|---|---|---|---|---|---|---|---|
| **1** | AW | YR59NPA | **4** | AW | YR59NPF | **7** | AW | YR59NPN | **9** | AW | YR59NPK |
| **2** | AW | YR59NPC | **5** | AW | YR59NPG | **8** | AW | YR59NPE | **10** | AW | YR59NPO |
| **3** | AW | YR59NPD | **6** | AW | YR59NPJ | | | | | | |

Ancillary vehicles:

| | | | | | |
|---|---|---|---|---|---|
| - | HK | HV02OZT | Dennis Dart SLF | Caetano Nimbus | N31D | 2002 |
| - | HK | HV02PDO | Dennis Dart SLF | Caetano Nimbus | N31D | 2002 |

**Note:** The operator also provides over forty non-PCV vehicles for welfare related work in London using the CT Plus name. Its associate, Hackney Community Transport, operates more than thirty similar vehicles. There is also an extensive operation in West Yorkshire.

*The London Bus Handbook*

Transport for London, Dial-a-Ride, 5 Mandela Way, London, SE1 5SS

### D7001-7068 · Volkswagen T5 · Bluebird Tucana · N8F · 2008

| | | | | | | | | | | | |
|---|---|---|---|---|---|---|---|---|---|---|---|
| 7001 | DR | YX57HBZ | 7018 | DR | YX08GVT | 7035 | DR | YX58EGD | 7052 | DR | YX58EEZ |
| 7002 | DR | YX08FKE | 7019 | DR | YX08GVU | 7036 | DR | YX08KXT | 7053 | DR | YX58EFC |
| 7003 | DR | YX08FKF | 7020 | DR | YX08GWF | 7037 | DR | YX08KXW | 7054 | DR | YX58EHB |
| 7004 | DR | YX08FKO | 7021 | DR | YX08GVW | 7038 | DR | YX58EGE | 7055 | DR | YX58EFA |
| 7005 | DR | YX08FKP | 7022 | DR | YX08GVY | 7039 | DR | YX58EGF | 7056 | DR | YX58EHG |
| 7006 | DR | YX08FKR | 7023 | DR | YX08GVZ | 7040 | DR | YX58EGJ | 7057 | DR | YX58EHH |
| 7007 | DR | YX08FKS | 7024 | DR | YX08GWA | 7041 | DR | YX58EGZ | 7058 | DR | YX58EHJ |
| 7008 | DR | YX08FKU | 7025 | DR | YX08GWC | 7042 | DR | YX58EFD | 7059 | DR | YX58EHK |
| 7009 | DR | YX08FKT | 7026 | DR | YX08GVV | 7043 | DR | YX58EFE | 7060 | DR | YX58EHL |
| 7010 | DR | YX08FKZ | 7027 | DR | YX08GWG | 7044 | DR | YX58EFF | 7061 | DR | YX58EHR |
| 7011 | DR | YX08FKV | 7028 | DR | YX08KXJ | 7045 | DR | YX58EFO | 7062 | DR | YX58GSO |
| 7012 | DR | YX08FKW | 7029 | DR | YX08KXK | 7046 | DR | YX58EFN | 7063 | DR | YX58GSY |
| 7013 | DR | YX08FKG | 7030 | DR | YX08KXL | 7047 | DR | YX58EEU | 7064 | DR | YX58GSZ |
| 7014 | DR | YX08FKK | 7031 | DR | YX08KXP | 7048 | DR | YX58EET | 7065 | DR | YX58GTF |
| 7015 | DR | YX08FKJ | 7032 | DR | YX08KXR | 7049 | DR | YX58EEW | 7066 | DR | YX58GTU |
| 7016 | DR | YX08FKL | 7033 | DR | YX08KXM | 7050 | DR | YX58EEV | 7067 | DR | YX58GTY |
| 7017 | DR | YX08FKM | 7034 | DR | YX08KXN | 7051 | DR | YX58EEY | 7068 | DR | YX58GTZ |

### D7069-7104 · Volkswagen T5 · Bluebird Tucana · N8F · 2009

| | | | | | | | | | | | |
|---|---|---|---|---|---|---|---|---|---|---|---|
| 7069 | DR | YX09ETA | 7078 | DR | YX09ETR | 7087 | DR | YX09EUH | 7096 | DR | YX09EUZ |
| 7070 | DR | YX09ETD | 7079 | DR | YX09ETU | 7088 | DR | YX09EUJ | 7097 | DR | YX09EVB |
| 7071 | DR | YX09ETE | 7080 | DR | YX09ETV | 7089 | DR | YX09EUK | 7098 | DR | YX09EVC |
| 7072 | DR | YX09ETF | 7081 | DR | YX09ETY | 7090 | DR | YX09EUL | 7099 | DR | YX09EVF |
| 7073 | DR | YX09ESY | 7082 | DR | YX09ETZ | 7091 | DR | YX09EUP | 7100 | DR | YX09EVK |
| 7074 | DR | YX09ETJ | 7083 | DR | YX09EUA | 7092 | DR | YX09EUR | 7101 | DR | YX09HRL |
| 7075 | DR | YX09ETK | 7084 | DR | YX09EUB | 7093 | DR | YX09EUT | 7102 | DR | YX09HRM |
| 7076 | DR | YX09ETL | 7085 | DR | YX09EUC | 7094 | DR | YX09EUW | 7103 | DR | YX09HRN |
| 7077 | DR | YX09ETO | 7086 | DR | YX09EUF | 7095 | DR | YX09EUY | 7104 | DR | YX09HRO |

Transport for London provides a Dial-a-Ride service for which a fleet of Bluebird Tucana minibuses is used. Illustrating the type is D7008, YX08FKU.
*Mark Lyons*

As we go to press further new Dial-A-Ride buses are being added to the operation . These provides free transport for disabled people unable to use normal public transport. D7099, YX09EVF, is shown. *Keith Grimes*

### D7105-7141 — Volkswagen T5 — Bluebird Tucana — N8F — 2009-10

| | | | | | | | | | |
|---|---|---|---|---|---|---|---|---|---|
| 7105 | DR | YX59AAO | 7115 | DR | YX59ACY | 7124 | DR | YX10FGA | 7133 | DR | YX60CJV |
| 7106 | DR | YX59ABN | 7116 | DR | YX59ADO | 7125 | DR | YX10FGD | 7134 | DR | YX60CJY |
| 7107 | DR | YX59ABV | 7117 | DR | YX59ADU | 7126 | DR | YX10FGC | 7135 | DR | YX60CJE |
| 7108 | DR | YX59ABU | 7118 | DR | YX59ADV | 7127 | DR | YX10FGE | 7136 | DR | YX60CKG |
| 7109 | DR | YX59ABZ | 7119 | DR | YX59ADZ | 7128 | DR | YX10FGF | 7137 | DR | YX60CKJ |
| 7110 | DR | YX59ACF | 7120 | DR | YX59AEA | 7129 | DR | YX10FGG | 7138 | DR | YX60CJF |
| 7111 | DR | YX59ACJ | 7121 | DR | YX59AEB | 7130 | DR | YX60CJJ | 7139 | DR | YX60CKK |
| 7112 | DR | YX59ACO | 7122 | DR | YX10FFY | 7131 | DR | YX60CJO | 7140 | DR | YX60CKU |
| 7113 | DR | YX59ACU | 7123 | DR | YX10FFZ | 7132 | DR | YX60CJU | 7141 | DR | YX60CKV |
| 7114 | DR | YX59ACV | | | | | | | | | |

### D7142-7161 — Volkswagen T5 — Bluebird Tucana — N8F — 2011

| | | | | | | | | | |
|---|---|---|---|---|---|---|---|---|---|
| 7142 | DR | YX60DYN | 7147 | DR | YX60DYU | 7152 | DR | YX60DZF | 7157 | DR | YX11EVG |
| 7143 | DR | YX60DYO | 7148 | DR | YX60DYY | 7153 | DR | YX60DZG | 7158 | DR | YX11CVV |
| 7144 | DR | YX60DYP | 7149 | DR | YX60DZA | 7154 | DR | YX60DZJ | 7159 | DR | YX11CVW |
| 7145 | DR | YX60DYS | 7150 | DR | YX60CLY | 7155 | DR | YX60DZL | 7160 | DR | YX11CVY |
| 7146 | DR | YX60DYT | 7151 | DR | YX60CLV | 7156 | DR | YX60EVR | 7161 | DR | YX11 |

**Note:** Also operated is a fleet of Mercedes-Benz minibuses that are in the process of being replaced and are not listed here.

*The London Bus Handbook*

# LONDON DUCK TOURS

London Duck Tours Ltd, 55 York Road, Waterloo, SE1 7NJ

| | | | | | |
|---|---|---|---|---|---|
| BSK157 | General Motors DUKW | Tanmill | -30R | 1944 | |
| ESL636 | General Motors DUKW | Tanmill | -30R | 1944 | Frog Tours, 2002 |
| ESL660 | General Motors DUKW | Tanmill | -30R | 1944 | Frog Tours, 2002 |
| ESL679 | General Motors DUKW | Tanmill | -30R | 1944 | Frog Tours, 2002 |
| OAY770P | General Motors DUKW | Tanmill | -30R | 1944 | |
| RSL602 | General Motors DUKW | Tanmill | -30R | 1944 | Frog Tours, 2002 |
| VSL143 | General Motors DUKW | Tanmill | -30R | 1944 | Frog Tours, 2002 |

**Named vehicles:** BSK157, *Rosalind*; ESL636, *Mistress Quickly*; ESL660, *Beatrice*; ESL679, *Cleopatra*; OAY770P, *Portia*; RSL602, *Titania*; VSL143 *Desdemona*. **Depot:** Tideway Industrial Estate, Kirtling Street, Nine Elms, SW8

**London Duck Tours add an unusual dimension to the London Tourist services. Cleopatra, ESL679, is seen turning at Parliament Square.** *Keith Grimes*

# LONDON SOVEREIGN

London Sovereign Ltd, Approach Road, Edgware, HA8 7AN

### DE50-56    ADL Dart 4 10.2m    ADL Enviro 200    N29D    2008-09

| | | | | | | | | | | | |
|---|---|---|---|---|---|---|---|---|---|---|---|
| 50 | SO | YX59BYA | 52 | SO | YX59BYC | 54 | SO | YX59BYF | 56 | SO | YX59BYH |
| 51 | SO | YX59BYB | 53 | SO | YX59BYD | 55 | SO | YX59BYG | | | |

### DE57-99    ADL Dart 4 10.2m    ADL Enviro 200    N29D    On order

| | | | | | | | | | | |
|---|---|---|---|---|---|---|---|---|---|---|
| 57 | BT | - | 68 | SO | - | 79 | SO | - | 90 | SO | - |
| 58 | BT | - | 69 | SO | - | 80 | SO | - | 91 | SO | - |
| 59 | BT | - | 70 | SO | - | 81 | SO | - | 92 | SO | - |
| 60 | BT | - | 71 | SO | - | 82 | SO | - | 93 | SO | - |
| 61 | BT | - | 72 | SO | - | 83 | SO | - | 94 | SO | - |
| 62 | BT | - | 73 | SO | - | 84 | SO | - | 95 | SO | - |
| 63 | BT | - | 74 | SO | - | 85 | SO | - | 96 | SO | - |
| 64 | BT | - | 75 | SO | - | 86 | SO | - | 97 | SO | - |
| 65 | BT | - | 76 | SO | - | 87 | SO | - | 98 | SO | - |
| 66 | BT | - | 77 | SO | - | 88 | SO | - | 99 | SO | - |
| 67 | BT | - | 78 | SO | - | 89 | SO | - | | | |

| | | | | | | | |
|---|---|---|---|---|---|---|---|
| DPS1 | SO | V801KAG | Dennis Dart SLF 10.1m | Plaxton Pointer 2 | N27D | 1999 | |
| DPS2 | SO | V802KAG | Dennis Dart SLF 10.1m | Plaxton Pointer 2 | N27D | 1999 | |

### DPS511-533    Dennis Dart SLF 10.1m    Plaxton Pointer 2    N27D    2000

| | | | | | | | | | | |
|---|---|---|---|---|---|---|---|---|---|---|
| 511 | SO | X511UAT | 517 | SO | X517UAT | 523 | SO | X523UAT | 529 | SO | X529UAT |
| 512 | SO | X512UAT | 518 | SO | X518UAT | 524 | SO | X524UAT | 531 | SO | X531UAT |
| 513 | SO | X513UAT | 519 | SO | X519UAT | 526 | SO | X526UAT | 532 | SO | X532UAT |
| 514 | SO | X514UAT | 521 | SO | X521UAT | 527 | SO | X527UAT | 533 | SO | X533UAT |
| 516 | SO | X516UAT | 522 | SO | X522UAT | | | | | | |

### DPS534-548    Dennis Dart SLF 10.1m    Plaxton Pointer 2    N27D*    2001    *seating varies

| | | | | | | | | | | |
|---|---|---|---|---|---|---|---|---|---|---|
| 534 | SO | Y534XAG | 543 | SO | Y543XAG | 546 | SO | Y546XAG | 548 | SO | Y548XAG |
| 536 | SO | Y536XAG | 544 | SO | Y544XAG | 547 | SO | Y547XAG | | | |

| | | | | | | | |
|---|---|---|---|---|---|---|---|
| DPS599 | SO | SN51TBX | Dennis Dart SLF 10.1m | Alexander ALX200 | N30D | 2001 | |

**On March 3rd 2011 the merger of French operators Veolia Transport and Transdev was approved by the French Commission on State Shareholdings and Transfers. The result has split the London Transdev operation. Colindale is the location for this view of Enviro 200 SDE21, YX60BZD.** *Richard Godfrey*

Following on from two batches of Scania N94UDs with East Lancs OmniDekka bodywork, a batch of the integral Scania OmniCity CN230 arrived in 2009. Illustrating the type is SP83, YT59RYJ. *Terry Longhurst*

### DPS627-640

| | | | | TransBus Dart 10.1m | | TransBus Pointer | | N27F* | | 2002 | | *seating varies |
|---|---|---|---|---|---|---|---|---|---|---|---|---|
| 627 | SO | SK02XGW | 632 | SO | SK02XHG | 635 | SO | SK02XHL | 638 | SO | SK02XHO |
| 628 | SO | SK02XGX | 633 | SO | SK02XHH | 636 | SO | SK02XHM | 639 | SO | SK02XHP |
| 629 | SO | SK02XHD | 634 | SO | SK02XHJ | 637 | SO | SK02XHN | 640 | SO | SK02XHR |
| 630 | SO | SK02XHE | | | | | | | | | |

### SDE18-24

| | | | | ADL Dart 4 8.9m | | ADL Enviro 200 | | N26F | | 2010 |
|---|---|---|---|---|---|---|---|---|---|---|
| 18 | BT | YX60BZA | 20 | BT | YX60BZC | 22 | BT | YX60BZE | 24 | BT | YX60BZG |
| 19 | BT | YX60BZB | 21 | BT | YX60BZD | 23 | BT | YX60BZF |

### SLE1-6

| | | | | Scania N94UD 10.8m | | East Lancs OmniDekka | | N49/27D | | 2004 |
|---|---|---|---|---|---|---|---|---|---|---|
| 1 | BT | YN54OAA | 3 | BT | YN54OAC | 5 | BT | YN54OAG | 6 | BT | YN54OAH |
| 2 | BT | YN54OAB | 4 | BT | YN54OAE |

### SLE21-42

| | | | | Scania N94UD 10.8m | | East Lancs OmniDekka | | N45/27D | | 2005 |
|---|---|---|---|---|---|---|---|---|---|---|
| 21 | BT | YN55NHT | 27 | BT | YN55NJE | 33 | BT | YN55NKA | 38 | BT | YN55NKG |
| 22 | BT | YN55NHU | 28 | BT | YN55NJF | 34 | BT | YN55NKC | 39 | BT | YN55NKH |
| 23 | BT | YN55NHV | 29 | BT | YN55NJJ | 35 | BT | YN55NKD | 40 | BT | YN55NKJ |
| 24 | BT | YN55NHX | 30 | BT | YN55NJK | 36 | BT | YN55NKE | 41 | BT | YN55NKK |
| 25 | BT | YN55NHY | 31 | BT | YN55NJU | 37 | BT | YN55NKF | 42 | BT | YN55NKL |
| 26 | BT | YN55NHZ | 32 | BT | YN55NJV |

### SP68-87

| | | | | Scania OmniCity CN230 UD | | Scania | | N41/22D | | 2009 |
|---|---|---|---|---|---|---|---|---|---|---|
| 68 | BT | YT59RXR | 73 | BT | YT59RXX | 78 | BT | YT59RYC | 83 | BT | YT59RYJ |
| 69 | BT | YT59RXS | 74 | BT | YT59RXY | 79 | BT | YT59RYD | 84 | BT | YT59RYK |
| 70 | BT | YT59RXU | 75 | BT | YT59RXZ | 80 | BT | YT59RYF | 85 | BT | YT59RYM |
| 71 | BT | YT59RXV | 76 | BT | YT59RYA | 81 | BT | YT59RYG | 86 | BT | YT59RYN |
| 72 | BT | YT59RXW | 77 | BT | YT59RYB | 82 | BT | YT59RYH | 87 | BT | YT59RYO |

| VA17 | BTt | XDZ5917 | Volvo Olympian | | Alexander RH | | B47/25D | | 1997 |
|---|---|---|---|---|---|---|---|---|---|

### VLE27-39

Volvo B7TL 11m | East Lancs Mylennium Vyking N47/22D | 2004

| 27 | BT | PA04CYK | 31 | BT | PA04CYT | 34 | BT | PO54ACJ | 37 | BT | PO54ACX |
| 28 | BT | PA04CYL | 32 | BT | PO54ABZ | 35 | BT | PO54ACU | 38 | BT | PO54ACY |
| 29 | BT | PA04CYP | 33 | BT | PO54ACF | 36 | BT | PO54ACV | 39 | BT | PO54ACZ |
| 30 | BT | PA04CYS | | | | | | | | | |

### VLP18-27

Volvo B7TL 10.6m | TransBus President 4.4m | N45/23D | 2003

| 18 | BT | PJ53OUN | 21 | BT | PJ53OUU | 24 | BT | PJ53OUX | 26 | BT | PJ53OVA |
| 19 | BT | PJ53OUO | 22 | BT | PJ53OUV | 25 | BT | PJ53OUY | 27 | BT | PJ53OVB |
| 20 | BT | PJ53OUP | 23 | u | PJ53OUW | | | | | | |

## Depots and allocations:

### Edgware (Station Road) - BT

| Dart 4 | SDE18 | SDE19 | SDE20 | SDE21 | SDE22 | SDE23 | SDE24 | DE57 |
| | DE58 | DE59 | DE60 | DE61 | DE62 | DE63 | DE64 | DE65 |
| | DE66 | DE67 | DE68 | DE69 | | | | |
| Scania DD | SLE1 | SLE2 | SLE3 | SLE4 | SLE5 | SLE6 | SLE21 | SLE22 |
| | SLE23 | SLE24 | SLE25 | SLE26 | SLE27 | SLE28 | SLE29 | SLE30 |
| | SLE31 | SLE32 | SLE33 | SLE34 | SLE35 | SLE36 | SLE37 | SLE38 |
| | SLE39 | SLE40 | SLE41 | SLE42 | SP68 | SP69 | SP70 | SP71 |
| | SP72 | SP73 | SP74 | SP75 | SP76 | SP77 | SP78 | SP79 |
| | SP80 | SP81 | SP82 | SP83 | SP84 | SP85 | SP86 | SP87 |
| | | | | | | | | |
| Ancillary | VA17 | | | | | | | |

### Harrow (Pinner Road) - SO

| Dart | DPS1 | DPS2 | DPS511 | DPS512 | DPS513 | DPS514 | DPS515 | DPS516 |
| | DPS517 | DPS518 | DPS519 | DPS520 | DPS521 | DPS522 | DPS523 | DPS524 |
| | DPS525 | DPS526 | DPS527 | DPS528 | DPS529 | DPS530 | DPS531 | DPS532 |
| | DPS533 | DPS534 | DPS535 | DPS536 | DPS537 | DPS538 | DPS539 | DPS540 |
| | DPS541 | DPS542 | DPS543 | DPS544 | DPS545 | DPS546 | DPS547 | DPS548 |
| | DPS599 | DPS627 | DPS628 | DPS629 | DPS630 | DPS631 | DPS632 | DPS633 |
| | DPS634 | DPS635 | DPS636 | DPS637 | DPS638 | DPS639 | DPS640 | |
| Dart 4 | DE50 | DE51 | DE52 | DE53 | DE54 | DE55 | DE56 | DE70 |
| | DE71 | DE72 | DE73 | DE74 | DE75 | DE76 | DE77 | DE78 |
| | DE79 | DE80 | DE81 | DE82 | DE83 | DE84 | DE85 | DE86 |
| | DE87 | DE88 | DE89 | DE90 | DE91 | DE92 | DE93 | DE95 |
| | DE96 | DE97 | DE98 | DE99 | | | | |

**All of Sovereign's East Lancs Myllennium Vyking-bodied Volvo B7TLs are allocated to Edgware depot. VLE33, PO54ACF, illustrates the type as it operates route 114 in Harrow town centre.**
*Terry Longhurst*

# LONDON TRAMLINK

First Tram Operations Ltd, Tramlink Depot, Coomber Way, Croydon, CR0 4TQ

**2530-2553**  Bombardier Eurorail CR-4000  Bombardier  AB70T  1998-99

| 2530 | 2533 | 2536 | 2539 | 2542 | 2544 | 2546 | 2548 | 2550 | 2552 |
| 2531 | 2534 | 2537 | 2540 | 2543 | 2545 | 2547 | 2549 | 2551 | 2553 |
| 2532 | 2535 | 2538 | 2541 | | | | | | |

**Depot:** Coomer Way, Croydon

London Tramlink began operation in May 2000 and features Croydon as its central point. A division of the First Group operates the system on behalf of London Translink with a fleet now painted into a new livery. Illustrating the scheme is 2553. *Mark Lyons*

# LONDON UNITED - RATP Group

London United Busways Ltd, Busways House, Wellington Road, Twickenham, TW2 5NX

## ADH1-22   ADL Trident E400H 10.1m   ADL Enviro 400   N37/24D*   2009-10   *1/2 are N37/26D

| | | | | | | | | | | | |
|---|---|---|---|---|---|---|---|---|---|---|---|
| 1 | HH | SN58EOR | 7 | S | SN60BYB | 13 | S | SN60BYJ | 18 | S | SN60BYP |
| 2 | HH | SN58EOS | 8 | S | SN60BYC | 14 | S | SN60BYK | 19 | S | SN60BYR |
| 3 | S | SN60BXX | 9 | S | SN60BYD | 15 | S | SN60BYL | 20 | S | SN60BYS |
| 4 | S | SN60BXY | 10 | S | SN60BYF | 16 | S | SN60BYM | 21 | S | SN60BYT |
| 5 | S | SN60BXZ | 11 | S | SN60BYG | 17 | S | SN60BYO | 22 | S | SN60BYU |
| 6 | S | SN60BYA | 12 | S | SN60BYH | | | | | | |

## DE1-49   ADL Dart 4 10.2m   ADL Enviro 200   N29D   2008-09

| | | | | | | | | | | | |
|---|---|---|---|---|---|---|---|---|---|---|---|
| 1 | HH | YX58DVA | 14 | HH | YX58DVR | 26 | FW | YX09HJU | 38 | S | YX09HKT |
| 2 | HH | YX58DVB | 15 | HH | YX58DVT | 27 | FW | YX09HJV | 39 | S | YX09HKH |
| 3 | HH | YX58DVC | 16 | HH | YX58DVU | 28 | FW | YX09HJY | 40 | S | YX09HKJ |
| 4 | HH | YX58DVF | 17 | HH | YX58DVV | 29 | FW | YX09HJZ | 41 | S | YX09HKK |
| 5 | HH | YX58DVG | 18 | HH | YX58DVW | 30 | FW | YX09HKZ | 42 | S | YX09HKL |
| 6 | HH | YX58DVH | 19 | HH | YX58DUV | 31 | FW | YX09HLA | 43 | S | YX09HKM |
| 7 | HH | YX58DVJ | 20 | HH | YX58DUY | 32 | S | YX09HKA | 44 | S | YX09HKN |
| 8 | HH | YX58DVK | 21 | HH | YX58DWK | 33 | S | YX09HKB | 45 | S | YX09HKO |
| 9 | HH | YX58DVL | 22 | FW | YX09HJJ | 34 | S | YX09HKC | 46 | S | YX09HKP |
| 10 | HH | YX58DVM | 23 | FW | YX09HJK | 35 | S | YX09HKD | 47 | S | YX09HKT |
| 11 | HH | YX58DVN | 24 | FW | YX09HJN | 36 | S | YX09HKE | 48 | S | YX09HKU |
| 12 | HH | YX58DVO | 25 | FW | YX09HJO | 37 | S | YX09HKR | 49 | S | YX09HKV |
| 13 | HH | YX58DVP | | | | | | | | | |

## DE57-92   ADL Dart 4 10.2m   ADL Enviro 200   N29D   2008   NCP, London, 2010

| | | | | | | | | | | | |
|---|---|---|---|---|---|---|---|---|---|---|---|
| 57 | NC | SK07DXE | 66 | NC | SK07DXR | 75 | PK | SK07DYC | 84 | PK | SK07DYP |
| 58 | NC | SK07DXF | 67 | NC | SK07DXS | 76 | PK | SK07DYD | 85 | PK | SK07DYS |
| 59 | NC | SK07DXG | 68 | NC | SK07DXT | 77 | PK | SK07DYF | 86 | PK | SK07DYT |
| 60 | NC | SK07DXH | 69 | NC | SK07DXU | 78 | PK | SK07DYG | 87 | PK | SK07DYU |
| 61 | NC | SK07DXJ | 70 | NC | SK07DXV | 79 | PK | SK07DYH | 88 | PK | SK07DYV |
| 62 | NC | SK07DXL | 71 | NC | SK07DXW | 80 | PK | SK07DYJ | 89 | PK | SK07DYW |
| 63 | NC | SK07DXM | 72 | NC | SK07DXX | 81 | PK | SK07DYM | 90 | PK | SK07DYX |
| 64 | NC | SK07DXO | 73 | NC | SK07DXY | 82 | PK | SK07DYN | 91 | PK | SK07DYY |
| 65 | NC | SK07DXP | 74 | NC | SK07DXZ | 83 | PK | SK07DYO | 92 | PK | VX58DXA |

## DE93-128   ADL Dart 4 10.2m   ADL Enviro 200   N29D   2010

| | | | | | | | | | | | |
|---|---|---|---|---|---|---|---|---|---|---|---|
| 93 | PK | SN10CAV | 102 | PK | SN10CCD | 111 | NC | YX60CAO | 120 | NC | YX60CCD |
| 94 | PK | SN10CAX | 103 | PK | SN10CCE | 112 | NC | YX60CAU | 121 | NC | YX60CCE |
| 95 | PK | SN10CBF | 104 | PK | SN10CCF | 113 | NC | YX60CAV | 122 | NC | YX60CCF |
| 96 | PK | SN10CBO | 105 | PK | SN10CCJ | 114 | NC | YX60CBF | 123 | NC | YX60CCJ |
| 97 | PK | SN10CBU | 106 | PK | SN10CCK | 115 | NC | YX60CBO | 124 | NC | YX60CCK |
| 98 | PK | SN10CBV | 107 | PK | SN10CCO | 116 | NC | YX60CBU | 125 | NC | YX60CCN |
| 99 | PK | SN10CBX | 108 | PK | SN10CCU | 117 | NC | YX60CBV | 126 | NC | YX60CCO |
| 100 | PK | SN10CBY | 109 | NC | YX60CAA | 118 | NC | YX60CBY | 127 | NC | YX60BZH |
| 101 | PK | SN10CCA | 110 | NC | YX60CAE | 119 | NC | YX60CCA | 128 | NC | YX60BZJ |

## DLE1-25   ADL Dart 4 10.8m   ADL Enviro 200   N32D   2011

| | | | | | | | | | | | |
|---|---|---|---|---|---|---|---|---|---|---|---|
| 1 | AV | SN60EAX | 8 | AV | SN60EBJ | 14 | HH | SN60EBU | 20 | AV | SN60ECD |
| 2 | AV | SN60EAY | 9 | AV | SN60EBK | 15 | HH | SN60EBV | 21 | AV | SN60ECE |
| 3 | AV | SN60EBA | 10 | HH | SN60EBL | 16 | HH | SN60EBX | 22 | AV | SN60ECF |
| 4 | AV | SN60EBC | 11 | AV | SN60EBM | 17 | HH | SN60EBZ | 23 | AV | SN60ECJ |
| 5 | AV | SN60EBD | 12 | HH | SN60EBO | 18 | HH | SN60ECA | 24 | AV | SN60ECT |
| 6 | AV | SN60EBF | 13 | HH | SN60EBP | 19 | AV | SN60ECC | 25 | AV | SN60ECV |
| 7 | AV | SN60EBG | | | | | | | | | |

## DP1-11   Dennis Dart SLF 10.7m   Plaxton Pointer 2   N36F   1998

| | | | | | | | | | | | |
|---|---|---|---|---|---|---|---|---|---|---|---|
| 1 | FW | S301MKH | 7 | Vt | S307MKH | 10 | Vt | S310MKH | 11 | FW | S311MKH |
| 6 | Vt | S306MKH | | | | | | | | | |

The French-based RATP operates in four European countries, France, United Kingdom, Italy and Switzerland. In England its operations are London United and Yellow Buses in Bournemouth. From the 2008 order for Enviro 200s, DE20, YX58DUY, passes The Holiday Inn hotel on Bath Road en route for Heathrow Central. *Mark Lyons*

## DP34-99

| | | | | | | | | | | | | | | | |
|---|---|---|---|---|---|---|---|---|---|---|---|---|---|---|---|
| | | Dennis Dart SLF | 10.7m | | | Plaxton Pointer 2 | | | N31D* | | 1999 | | *seating varies | | |
| 34 | PK | T334PRH | 51 | PK | T351PRH | 68 | AV | T368PRH | 84 | w | V784FKH | | | | |
| 35 | PK | T335PRH | 52 | PK | T352PRH | 69 | AV | T369PRH | 85 | PK | V785FKH | | | | |
| 36 | PK | T336PRH | 53 | PK | T353PRH | 70 | AV | T370PRH | 86 | PK | V886FKH | | | | |
| 37 | PK | T337PRH | 54 | PK | T354PRH | 71 | u | T371PRH | 87 | w | V787FKH | | | | |
| 38 | AV | T338PRH | 55 | HH | T455PRH | 72 | u | T372PRH | 88 | PK | V788FKH | | | | |
| 39 | AV | T339PRH | 56 | AV | T356PRH | 73 | AV | T373PRH | 89 | w | V789FKH | | | | |
| 40 | AV | T340PRH | 57 | AV | T357PRH | 74 | AV | T374PRH | 90 | w | V790FKH | | | | |
| 41 | AV | T341PRH | 58 | TV | T358PRH | 75 | AV | T375PRH | 91 | w | V791FKH | | | | |
| 42 | AV | T342PRH | 59 | AV | T359PRH | 76 | AV | T976SRH | 92 | w | V792FKH | | | | |
| 43 | PK | T343PRH | 60 | AV | T360PRH | 77 | AV | T977SRH | 93 | AV | V793FKH | | | | |
| 44 | PK | T344PRH | 61 | PK | T361PRH | 78 | AV | T978SRH | 94 | w | V794FKH | | | | |
| 45 | PK | T345PRH | 62 | AV | T362PRH | 79 | w | T979SRH | 95 | w | V795FKH | | | | |
| 46 | AV | T346PRH | 63 | AV | T363PRH | 80 | PK | T980SRH | 96 | w | V796FKH | | | | |
| 47 | AV | T347PRH | 64 | AV | T364PRH | 81 | w | V781FKH | 97 | PK | V797FKH | | | | |
| 48 | u | T348PRH | 65 | AV | T365PRH | 82 | w | V782FKH | 98 | PK | V798FKH | | | | |
| 49 | u | T349PRH | 66 | AV | T366PRH | 83 | PK | V783FKH | 99 | w | V799FKH | | | | |
| 50 | PK | T350PRH | 67 | AV | T367PRH | | | | | | | | | | |

## DPS3-16

| | | | | | | | | | | | |
|---|---|---|---|---|---|---|---|---|---|---|---|
| | | Dennis Dart SLF | 10.1m | | | Plaxton Pointer 2 | | | N27D | 1999 | |
| 3 | PK | V803KAG | 7 | PK | V807KAG | 11 | PK | V811KAG | 14 | PK | V814KAG |
| 4 | PK | V904KAG | 8 | TV | V808KAG | 12 | PK | V812KAG | 15 | PK | V815KAG |
| 5 | PK | V805KAG | 9 | PK | V809KAG | 13 | PK | V813KAG | 16 | PK | V816KAG |
| 6 | PK | V806KAG | 10 | PK | V810KAG | | | | | | |

## DPS537-557

| | | | | | | | | | | | |
|---|---|---|---|---|---|---|---|---|---|---|---|
| | | Dennis Dart SLF | 10.1m | | | Plaxton Pointer 2 | | | N27D* | 2001 | *seating varies |
| 537 | TV | Y537XAG | 541 | TV | Y541XAG | 551 | TV | Y551XAG | 554 | TV | Y554XAG |
| 538 | TV | Y538XAG | 542 | TV | Y542XAG | 552 | TV | Y552XAG | 556 | TV | Y556XAG |
| 539 | TV | Y539XAG | 549 | TV | Y549XAG | 553 | TV | Y553XAG | 557 | TV | Y557XAG |

Recently introduced to Route H37 are a batch of Optare Tempo buses. Illllustrating the model is OT4, YJ11EHL. It is seen in Isleworth while heading for Hounslow. *Mark Lyons*

### DPS579-602

Dennis Dart SLF 10.1m     Alexander ALX200     N30D     2001

| | | | | | | | | | | | |
|---|---|---|---|---|---|---|---|---|---|---|---|
| 579 | FW | SN51TAU | 585 | FW | SN51TCX | 591 | TV | SN51TBU | 597 | TV | SN51TDO |
| 580 | FW | SN51TBY | 586 | FW | SN51TDX | 592 | AV | SN51TCK | 598 | TV | SN51TEO |
| 581 | NC | SN51TCV | 587 | FW | SN51TBO | 593 | TV | SN51TCZ | 600 | TV | SN51TCU |
| 582 | FW | SN51TDV | 588 | AV | SN51TCJ | 594 | TV | SN51TEJ | 601 | TV | SN51TDU |
| 583 | FW | SN51TAV | 589 | AV | SN51TCY | 595 | NC | SN51TBV | 602 | TV | SN51TEU |
| 584 | FW | SN51TBZ | 590 | AV | SN51TDZ | 596 | NC | SN51TCO | | | |

| | | | | | | | |
|---|---|---|---|---|---|---|---|
| DPK613 | TV | SN51SXG | Dennis Dart SLF | 8.8m | Plaxton Pointer MPD | N29F | 2001 |
| DPK614 | TV | SN51SXH | Dennis Dart SLF | 8.8m | Plaxton Pointer MPD | N29F | 2001 |
| DPK615 | TV | SN51SXJ | Dennis Dart SLF | 8.8m | Plaxton Pointer MPD | N29F | 2001 |
| DPK616 | TV | LG02FEX | TransBus Dart 8.8m | | TransBus Mini Pointer | N29F | 2002 |
| DPK617 | TV | LG02FFA | TransBus Dart 8.8m | | TransBus Mini Pointer | N29F | 2002 |
| DPK618 | TV | LG02FFB | TransBus Dart 8.8m | | TransBus Mini Pointer | N29F | 2002 |
| DPK624 | TV | SN06JPV | ADL Dart 8.8m | | ADL Mini Pointer | N23F | 2006 |
| DPK625 | TV | SN06JPX | ADL Dart 8.8m | | ADL Mini Pointer | N23F | 2006 |

### DPS624-680

TransBus Dart 10.1m     TransBus Pointer     N27F*     2002     *seating varies

| | | | | | | | | | | | |
|---|---|---|---|---|---|---|---|---|---|---|---|
| 624 | HH | SK02XGT | 649 | TV | LG02FFT | 660 | AV | LG02FGF | 671 | HH | LG02FHA |
| 625 | TV | SK02XGU | 650 | TV | LG02FFU | 661 | HH | LG02FGJ | 672 | HH | LG02FHB |
| 626 | TV | SK02XGV | 651 | TV | LG02FFV | 662 | AV | LG02FGK | 673 | HH | LG02FHC |
| 641 | TV | LG02FFK | 652 | TV | LG02FFW | 663 | AV | LG02FGM | 674 | HH | LG02FHD |
| 642 | TV | LG02FFL | 653 | TV | LG02FFX | 664 | AV | LG02FGN | 675 | HH | LG02FHE |
| 643 | TV | LG02FFM | 654 | FW | LG02FFY | 665 | AV | LG02FGO | 676 | HH | LG02FHF |
| 644 | TV | LG02FFN | 655 | FW | LG02FFZ | 666 | AV | LG02FGP | 677 | HH | LG02FHH |
| 645 | TV | LG02FFO | 656 | AV | LG02FGA | 667 | AV | LG02FGU | 678 | HH | LG02FHJ |
| 646 | TV | LG02FFP | 657 | AV | LG02FGC | 668 | AV | LG02FGV | 679 | HH | LG02FHK |
| 647 | TV | LG02FFR | 658 | AV | LG02FGD | 669 | AV | LG02FGX | 680 | HH | LG02FHL |
| 648 | TV | LG02FFS | 659 | AV | LG02FGE | 670 | TV | LG02FGZ | | | |

### DPS681-694

TransBus Dart SLF 10.1m     TransBus Pointer     N27D*     2003     *seating varies

| | | | | | | | | | | | |
|---|---|---|---|---|---|---|---|---|---|---|---|
| 681 | AV | SN03LDY | 685 | AV | SN03LEV | 689 | FW | SN03LFE | 692 | FW | SN03LFH |
| 682 | AV | SN03LDZ | 686 | FW | SN03LFA | 690 | FW | SN03LFF | 693 | FW | SN03LFJ |
| 683 | AV | SN03LEF | 687 | FW | SN03LFB | 691 | FW | SN03LFG | 694 | AV | SN03LFK |
| 684 | AV | SN03LEJ | 688 | S | SN03LFD | | | | | | |

*The London Bus Handbook*

New arrivals with London United are twenty-five 10.8 metre dual-door Enviro 200 Darts. Seen shortly after delivery, DLE4, SN60EBC, is seen on the Hounslow network of routes. *Richard Godfrey*

### DPS701-727

| | | | | | | | | | | | | | |
|---|---|---|---|---|---|---|---|---|---|---|---|---|---|
| | | | ADL Dart SLF 10.1m | | | ADL Pointer | | | N28D | | 2005 | NCP, London, 2010 | |
| **701** | NC | SN55HKD | **708** | HH | SN55HKL | **715** | HH | SN55HKW | **722** | AV | SN55HLC | | |
| **702** | NC | SN55HKE | **709** | HH | SN55HKM | **716** | HH | SN55HKX | **723** | AV | SN55DVR | | |
| **703** | NC | SN55HKF | **710** | HH | SN55HKO | **717** | HH | SN55HKY | **724** | AV | SN55DVT | | |
| **704** | NC | SN55HKG | **711** | HH | SN55HKP | **718** | HH | SN55HSD | **725** | AV | SN55DVU | | |
| **705** | NC | SN55HKH | **712** | HH | SN55HKY | **719** | AV | SN55HSE | **726** | AV | SN55DVV | | |
| **706** | NC | SN55HKJ | **713** | HH | SN55HKU | **720** | AV | SN55HKZ | **727** | NC | SN55DVW | | |
| **707** | HH | SN55HKK | **714** | HH | SN55HKV | **721** | AV | SN55HLA | | | | | |

| | | | | | | | | |
|---|---|---|---|---|---|---|---|---|
| **DRL107** | u | K107SAG | Dennis Dart 9m | | Plaxton Pointer | B28F | 1993 | |
| **RML880** | FW | WLT880 | AEC Routemaster RH2H1 | | Park Royal | B40/32R | 1961 | |

### HDE1-5

| | | | | | | | | | | | |
|---|---|---|---|---|---|---|---|---|---|---|---|
| | | | ADL Hybrid Dart 10.2m | | | ADL Enviro 200 | | N29F | 2009 | | |
| **1** | FW | SN09CHC | **3** | FW | SN09CHF | **4** | FW | SN09CHG | **5** | FW | SN09CHH |
| **2** | FW | SN09CHD | | | | | | | | | |

### MV1-8

| | | | | | | | | | | | |
|---|---|---|---|---|---|---|---|---|---|---|---|
| | | | MAN 11.190 | | | Optare Vecta | | N42F | 1995 | | |
| **1** | Vt | N281DWY | **3** | w | N283DWY | **5** | Vt | N285DWY | **8** | Vt | N288DWY |
| **2** | Vt | N282DWY | **4** | Vt | N284DWY | **6** | Vt | N286DWY | | | |

### OT1-16

| | | | | | | | | | | | |
|---|---|---|---|---|---|---|---|---|---|---|---|
| | | | Optare Tempo X1200 | | | Optare | | N34D | 2011 | | |
| **1** | AV | YJ11EHG | **5** | AV | YJ11EHM | **9** | AV | YJ11EHR | **13** | AV | YJ11EHV |
| **2** | AV | YJ11EHH | **6** | AV | YJ11EHN | **10** | AV | YJ11EHS | **14** | AV | YJ11EHW |
| **3** | AV | YJ11EHK | **7** | AV | YJ11EHO | **11** | AV | YJ11EHT | **15** | AV | YJ11EHX |
| **4** | AV | YJ11EHL | **8** | AV | YJ11EHP | **12** | AV | YJ11EHU | **16** | AV | YJ11EHZ |

### OV1-19

| | | | | | | | | | | | |
|---|---|---|---|---|---|---|---|---|---|---|---|
| | | | Optare Versa V1040 | | | Optare | | N27D | 2008-09 | | |
| **1** | V | YJ58VBA | **6** | V | YJ58VBF | **11** | V | YJ58VBN | **16** | V | YJ58VBV |
| **2** | V | YJ58VBB | **7** | V | YJ58VBG | **12** | V | YJ58VBO | **17** | V | YJ58VBX |
| **3** | V | YJ58VBC | **8** | V | YJ58VBK | **13** | V | YJ58VBP | **18** | V | YJ58VBY |
| **4** | V | YJ58VBD | **9** | V | YJ58VBL | **14** | V | YJ58VBT | **19** | V | YJ58VBZ |
| **5** | V | YJ58VBE | **10** | V | YJ58VBM | **15** | V | YJ58VBU | | | |

With Knightsbridge as a background, SP142, YP59OEA, is one of almost two hundred of the Scania OmniCity double-deck model operated by London United. The SP class were the first to gain the RAPT logos in place of their Transdev names. *Richard Godfrey*

### OV50-66

Optare Versa V1040 — Optare — N27D — 2009

| | | | | | | | | | | | | |
|---|---|---|---|---|---|---|---|---|---|---|---|---|
| 50 | PK | YJ58PHY | 55 | PK | YJ09EZF | 59 | PK | YJ09EYW | 63 | PK | YJ09EZA |
| 51 | PK | YJ58PHZ | 56 | PK | YJ09EYT | 60 | PK | YJ09EYX | 64 | PK | YJ09EZB |
| 52 | PK | YJ58PJO | 57 | PK | YJ09EYU | 61 | PK | YJ09EYY | 65 | PK | YJ09EZC |
| 53 | PK | YJ58PJU | 58 | PK | YJ09EYV | 62 | PK | YJ09EYZ | 66 | PK | YJ09EZD |
| 54 | PK | YJ09EZE | | | | | | | | | |

### SDE1-10

ADL Dart 4 8.9m — ADL Enviro 200 — N26F — 2008

| | | | | | | | | | | | | |
|---|---|---|---|---|---|---|---|---|---|---|---|---|
| 1 | TV | YX08MFO | 4 | TV | YX08MDZ | 7 | TV | YX08MEV | 9 | TV | YX08MHM |
| 2 | TV | YX08MDV | 5 | TV | YX08MFN | 8 | TV | YX08MFA | 10 | TV | YX08MFK |
| 3 | TV | YX08MDY | 6 | TV | YX08MEU | | | | | | |

### SDE11-17

ADL Dart 4 8.9m — ADL Enviro 200 — N26F — 2007 — NCP, London, 2010

| | | | | | | | | | | |
|---|---|---|---|---|---|---|---|---|---|---|
| 11 | PK | SK07HLM | 13 | PK | SK07HLO | 15 | PK | SK07HLR | 17 | PK | SK07HLV |
| 12 | PK | SK07HLN | 14 | PK | SK07HLP | 16 | PK | SK07HLU | | | |

### SLE7-20

Scania N94UD 10.8m — East Lancs OmniDekka — N45/27D — 2005

| | | | | | | | | | | | | |
|---|---|---|---|---|---|---|---|---|---|---|---|---|
| 7 | FW | YN55NHA | 11 | FW | YN55NHE | 15 | FW | YN55NHJ | 18 | FW | YN55NHM |
| 8 | FW | YN55NHB | 12 | FW | YN55NHF | 16 | FW | YN55NHK | 19 | FW | YN55NHO |
| 9 | FW | YN55NHC | 13 | FW | YN55NHG | 17 | FW | YN55NHL | 20 | FW | YN55NHP |
| 10 | FW | YN55NHD | 14 | FW | YN55NHH | | | | | | |

### SLE43-64

Scania N94UD 10.8m — East Lancs OmniDekka — N45/26D — 2005

| | | | | | | | | | | | | |
|---|---|---|---|---|---|---|---|---|---|---|---|---|
| 43 | V | YN55NKM | 49 | V | YN55NKU | 55 | V | YN55NLD | 60 | V | YN55NLL |
| 44 | V | YN55NKO | 50 | V | YN55NKW | 56 | V | YN55NLE | 61 | V | YN55NLM |
| 45 | V | YN55NKP | 51 | V | YN55NKX | 57 | V | YN55NLG | 62 | V | YN55NLO |
| 46 | V | YN55NKR | 52 | V | YN55NKZ | 58 | V | YN55NLJ | 63 | V | YN55NLP |
| 47 | V | YN55NKS | 53 | V | YN55NLA | 59 | V | YN55NLK | 64 | V | YN55NLR |
| 48 | V | YN55NKT | 54 | V | YN55NLC | | | | | | |

### SP1-15

Scania OmniCity CN94 UD 10.7m Scania — N41/23D — 2006-07

| | | | | | | | | | | | | |
|---|---|---|---|---|---|---|---|---|---|---|---|---|
| 1 | HH | YN56FCA | 5 | AV | YN56FCF | 9 | AV | YN56FBB | 13 | AV | YN56FBX |
| 2 | HH | YN56FCC | 6 | AV | YN56FCG | 10 | AV | YN56FBO | 14 | AV | YN56FBY |
| 3 | HH | YN56FCD | 7 | AV | YN56FCJ | 11 | AV | YN56FBU | 15 | AV | YN56FBZ |
| 4 | HH | YN56FCE | 8 | AV | YN56FBA | 12 | AV | YN56FBV | | | |

### SP16-37
Scania OmniCity CN230 UD 10.8m Scania — N41/22D — 2008

| | | | | | | | | | | | |
|---|---|---|---|---|---|---|---|---|---|---|---|
| 16 | HH | YN08DEU | 22 | HH | YN08DHG | 28 | FW | YN08DHP | 33 | S | YN08DHZ |
| 17 | HH | YN08DHA | 23 | AV | YN08DHJ | 29 | S | YN08DHU | 34 | S | YN08MRU |
| 18 | HH | YN08DHC | 24 | AV | YN08DHK | 30 | S | YN08DHV | 35 | S | YN08MRV |
| 19 | HH | YN08DHD | 25 | FW | YN08DHL | 31 | S | YN08DHX | 36 | S | YN08MRX |
| 20 | HH | YN08DHE | 26 | FW | YN08DHM | 32 | S | YN08DHY | 37 | S | YN08MRY |
| 21 | HH | YN08DHF | 27 | FW | YN08DHO | | | | | | |

### SP38-67
Scania OmniCity CN230 UD — Scania — N41/22D — 2009

| | | | | | | | | | | | |
|---|---|---|---|---|---|---|---|---|---|---|---|
| 38 | AV | YP58ACF | 46 | AV | YT09BNA | 54 | FW | YT09BNN | 61 | FW | YT09ZCL |
| 39 | S | YP58ACJ | 47 | AV | YT09BNB | 55 | FW | YT09BJU | 62 | FW | YT09ZCN |
| 40 | S | YP58ACO | 48 | AV | YT09BND | 56 | FW | YT09ZCA | 63 | FW | YT09ZCO |
| 41 | AV | YT09BKA | 49 | AV | YT09BNE | 57 | FW | YT09ZCE | 64 | FW | YT09ZCU |
| 42 | AV | YT09BMO | 50 | AV | YT09BNF | 58 | FW | YT09ZCF | 65 | FW | YT09BJV |
| 43 | AV | YT09BMU | 51 | AV | YT09BNJ | 59 | FW | YT09ZCJ | 66 | FW | YT09BJX |
| 44 | AV | YT09BMY | 52 | FW | YT09BNK | 60 | FW | YT09ZCK | 67 | FW | YT09BJY |
| 45 | AV | YT09BMZ | 53 | FW | YT09BNL | | | | | | |

### SP88-108
Scania OmniCity CN230 UD — Scania — N41/22D — 2009

| | | | | | | | | | | | |
|---|---|---|---|---|---|---|---|---|---|---|---|
| 88 | FW | YT59SFK | 94 | FW | YT59SFY | 99 | FW | YT59SGX | 104 | FW | YT59SFF |
| 89 | FW | YT59SFN | 95 | FW | YT59SFZ | 100 | FW | YT59SGY | 105 | FW | YT59DXY |
| 90 | FW | YT59SFO | 96 | FW | YT59SGO | 101 | FW | YT59SGZ | 106 | FW | YT59DXZ |
| 91 | FW | YT59SFU | 97 | FW | YT59SGU | 102 | FW | YT59SHJ | 107 | FW | YT59DYX |
| 92 | FW | YT59SFV | 98 | FW | YT59SGV | 103 | FW | YT59SHV | 108 | FW | YT59DYY |
| 93 | FW | YT59SFX | | | | | | | | | |

### SP109-125
Scania OmniCity CN230 UD — Scania — N41/22D — 2009

| | | | | | | | | | | | |
|---|---|---|---|---|---|---|---|---|---|---|---|
| 109 | S | YR59FYO | 114 | S | YR59FYV | 118 | S | YR59FYZ | 122 | S | YR59FZD |
| 110 | S | YR59FYP | 115 | S | YR59FYW | 119 | S | YR59FZA | 123 | S | YR59FZE |
| 111 | S | YR59FYS | 116 | S | YR59FYX | 120 | S | YR59FZB | 124 | S | YR59FZF |
| 112 | S | YR59FYT | 117 | S | YR59FYY | 121 | S | YR59FZC | 125 | S | YR59FZG |
| 113 | S | YR59FYU | | | | | | | | | |

### SP126-164
Scania OmniCity CN230 UD — Scania — N41/22D — 2009-10

| | | | | | | | | | | | |
|---|---|---|---|---|---|---|---|---|---|---|---|
| 126 | S | YT59PBF | 136 | S | YP59ODS | 146 | V | YP59OEE | 156 | V | YP59OER |
| 127 | S | YT59PBO | 137 | V | YP59ODT | 147 | V | YP59OEF | 157 | V | YP59OES |
| 128 | S | YT59PBV | 138 | V | YP59ODU | 148 | V | YP59OEG | 158 | V | YP59OET |
| 129 | S | YT59PBX | 139 | V | YP59ODV | 149 | V | YP59OEH | 159 | V | YP59OEU |
| 130 | S | YT59PBY | 140 | V | YP59ODW | 150 | V | YP59OEJ | 160 | V | YP59OEV |
| 131 | S | YT59PBZ | 141 | V | YP59ODX | 151 | V | YP59OEK | 161 | V | YP59OEW |
| 132 | S | YT59PCF | 142 | V | YP59OEA | 152 | V | YP59OEL | 162 | V | YP59OEX |
| 133 | S | YT59PCO | 143 | V | YP59OEB | 153 | V | YP59OEM | 163 | V | YP59OEY |
| 134 | S | YT59PCU | 144 | V | YP59OEC | 154 | V | YP59OEN | 164 | V | YP59OEZ |
| 135 | S | YT59BPU | 145 | V | YP59OED | 155 | V | YP59OEO | | | |

### SP165-206
Scania OmniCity CN230 UD — Scania — N41/22D — 2010

| | | | | | | | | | | | |
|---|---|---|---|---|---|---|---|---|---|---|---|
| 165 | AV | YT10UWA | 176 | AV | YT10XBZ | 187 | AV | YT10XCL | 197 | HH | YR10FGD |
| 166 | AV | YT10UWB | 177 | AV | YT10XCA | 188 | AV | YT10XCM | 198 | HH | YR10FGE |
| 167 | AV | YT10UWD | 178 | AV | YT10XCB | 189 | AV | YT10XCN | 199 | HH | YR10FGF |
| 168 | AV | YT10UWF | 179 | AV | YT10XCC | 190 | AV | YT10XCO | 200 | HH | YR10FGG |
| 169 | AV | YT10UWG | 180 | AV | YT10XCD | 191 | HH | YR10FFW | 201 | HH | YR10FGJ |
| 170 | AV | YT10UWH | 181 | AV | YT10XCE | 192 | HH | YR10FFX | 202 | HH | YR10FGK |
| 171 | AV | YT10XBU | 182 | AV | YT10XCF | 193 | HH | YR10FFY | 203 | PK | YR10FGM |
| 172 | AV | YT10XBV | 183 | AV | YT10XCG | 194 | HH | YR10FFZ | 204 | HH | YR10FGN |
| 173 | AV | YT10XBW | 184 | AV | YT10XCH | 195 | HH | YR10FGA | 205 | HH | YR10FGO |
| 174 | AV | YT10XBX | 185 | AV | YT10XCJ | 196 | HH | YR10FGC | 206 | HH | YR10FGP |
| 175 | AV | YT10XBY | 186 | AV | YT10XCK | | | | | | |

### TA201-225
Dennis Trident 9.9m — Alexander ALX400 4.4m — N43/20D — 2000-01

| | | | | | | | | | | | |
|---|---|---|---|---|---|---|---|---|---|---|---|
| 201 | w | X201UMS | 208 | FW | SN51SYG | 214 | TV | SN51SYT | 220 | FW | SN51SYZ |
| 202 | w | X202UMS | 209 | FW | SN51SYH | 215 | FW | SN51SYV | 221 | FW | SN51SZC |
| 203 | w | X203UMS | 210 | FW | SN51SYJ | 216 | FW | SN51SYV | 222 | FW | SN51SZD |
| 204 | FW | SN51SYA | 211 | FW | SN51SYO | 217 | FW | SN51SYW | 223 | FW | SN51SZE |
| 205 | FW | SN51SYC | 212 | FW | SN51SYR | 218 | FW | SN51SYX | 224 | FW | SN51SZT |
| 206 | FW | SN51SYE | 213 | TV | SN51SYS | 219 | FW | SN51SYY | 225 | FW | SN51SZU |
| 207 | FW | SN51SYF | | | | | | | | | |

The caption on page 92 referred to the new Alexander Dennis name and here we see the TransBus badge on ALX400 TLA25, SN53KJA. The TLA class designates the longer version of the Trident. The vehicle is seen on route 94 which requires thirty buses from Shepherd's Bush. *Mark Lyons*

## TA229-250
TransBus Trident 9.9m    TransBus ALX400 4.4m    N43/19D    2002

| | | | | | | | | | | | |
|---|---|---|---|---|---|---|---|---|---|---|---|
| 229 | TV | LG02FAA | 235 | TV | LG02FAU | 241 | TV | LG02FBF | 246 | TV | LG02FBO |
| 230 | TV | LG02FAF | 236 | TV | LG02FBA | 242 | TV | LG02FBJ | 247 | TV | LG02FBU |
| 231 | TV | LG02FAJ | 237 | TV | LG02FBB | 243 | TV | LG02FBK | 248 | TV | LG02FBV |
| 232 | TV | LG02FAK | 238 | TV | LG02FBC | 244 | TV | LG02FBL | 249 | TV | LG02FBX |
| 233 | TV | LG02FAM | 239 | TV | LG02FBD | 245 | TV | LG02FBN | 250 | TV | LG02FBY |
| 234 | TV | LG02FAO | 240 | TV | LG02FBE | | | | | | |

## TA281-286
TransBus Trident 9.9m    TransBus ALX400 4.4m    N43/19D    2002

| | | | | | | | | |
|---|---|---|---|---|---|---|---|---|
| 281 | TV | LG02FDY | 283 | TV | LG02FEF | 285 | TV | LG02FEJ | 286 | TV | LG02FEK |
| 282 | TV | LG02FDZ | 284 | TV | LG02FEH | | | |

## TA312-346
TransBus Trident 9.9m    TransBus ALX400 4.4m    N43/19D    2003

| | | | | | | | | | | | |
|---|---|---|---|---|---|---|---|---|---|---|---|
| 312 | TV | SN03DZJ | 321 | FW | SN03DZX | 330 | FW | SN03EAW | 339 | FW | SN03EBL |
| 313 | FW | SN03DZK | 322 | FW | SN03EAA | 331 | FW | SN03EAX | 340 | FW | SN03EBM |
| 314 | FW | SN03DZM | 323 | FW | SN03EAC | 332 | FW | SN03EBA | 341 | FW | SN03LFL |
| 315 | FW | SN03DZP | 324 | FW | SN03EAE | 333 | FW | SN03EBC | 342 | FW | SN03LFM |
| 316 | FW | SN03DZR | 325 | FW | SN03EAF | 334 | FW | SN03EBD | 343 | FW | SN03LFP |
| 317 | FW | SN03DZS | 326 | FW | SN03EAG | 335 | FW | SN03EBF | 344 | FW | SN03LFR |
| 318 | FW | SN03DZT | 327 | FW | SN03EAJ | 336 | FW | SN03EBG | 345 | FW | SN03LFS |
| 319 | FW | SN03DZV | 328 | FW | SN03EAM | 337 | FW | SN03EBJ | 346 | FW | SN03LFT |
| 320 | TV | SN03DZW | 329 | FW | SN03EAP | 338 | FW | SN03EBK | | | |

## TLA1-32
TransBus Trident 10.5m    TransBus ALX400    N45/22D    2003-04

| | | | | | | | | | | | |
|---|---|---|---|---|---|---|---|---|---|---|---|
| 1 | S | SN53EUF | 9 | S | SN53EUR | 17 | FW | SN53KHR | 25 | S | SN53KJA |
| 2 | S | SN53EUH | 10 | S | SN53EUT | 18 | FW | SN53KHT | 26 | S | SN53KJE |
| 3 | S | SN53EUJ | 11 | S | SN53EUU | 19 | FW | SN53KHU | 27 | S | SN53KJF |
| 4 | S | SN53EUK | 12 | S | SN53EUV | 20 | FW | SN53KHV | 28 | S | SN53KJJ |
| 5 | S | SN53EUL | 13 | S | SN53EUW | 21 | FW | SN53KHW | 29 | S | SN53KJK |
| 6 | S | SN53EUM | 14 | S | SN53EUX | 22 | S | SN53KHX | 30 | S | SN53KJO |
| 7 | S | SN53EUO | 15 | S | SN53EUY | 23 | FW | SN53KHY | 31 | S | SN53KJU |
| 8 | S | SN53EUP | 16 | S | SN53EUZ | 24 | S | SN53KHZ | 32 | S | SN53KJV |

*The London Bus Handbook*

London United ordered the Alexander ALX400 model on both Volvo and Dennis chassis. Seen with Transdev names is VA85, V208OOE as it heads for Hounslow. Several examples of this model have now been displaced from the fleet as newer buses enter service. *Mark Lyons*

### VA6-10

| | | | | | | | | | | | |
|---|---|---|---|---|---|---|---|---|---|---|---|
| | | | Volvo Olympian | | | Alexander RH | | B45/29F | 1996 | | |
| 6 | FW | N136YRW | 8 | FW | N138YRW | 9 | FW | N139YRW | 10 | FW | N140YRW |
| 7 | FW | N137YRW | | | | | | | | | |

### VA45-54

| | | | | | | | | | | | |
|---|---|---|---|---|---|---|---|---|---|---|---|
| | | | Volvo Olympian | | | Alexander RH | | B47/25D | 1998 | | |
| 45 | FW | R945YOV | 49 | FW | R949YOV | 51 | Vt | R951YOV | 53 | Vt | R953YOV |
| 46 | FW | R946YOV | 50 | Vt | R950YOV | 52 | Vt | R952YOV | 54 | FW | R954YOV |
| 48 | FW | R948YOV | | | | | | | | | |

### VA60-104

| | | | | | | | | | | | |
|---|---|---|---|---|---|---|---|---|---|---|---|
| | | | Volvo B7TL 10.1m | | | Alexander ALX400 4.4m | | N43/17D | 2000 | *Seating varies | |
| 60 | HH | V176OOE | 74 | AV | V190OOE | 84 | HH | V207OOE | 94 | AV | W128EON |
| 61 | HH | V177OOE | 75 | AV | V191OOE | 85 | AV | V208OOE | 95 | AV | W129EON |
| 62 | S | V178OOE | 76 | AV | V192OOE | 86 | AV | W116EON | 96 | AV | W131EON |
| 63 | S | V179OOE | 77 | AV | V193OOE | 87 | PK | W117EON | 97 | AV | W132EON |
| 64 | S | V180OOE | 78 | PK | V194OOE | 88 | PK | W118EON | 98 | PK | W133EON |
| 65 | S | V181OOE | 79 | PK | V202OOE | 89 | PK | W119EON | 99 | AV | W134EON |
| 66 | HH | V182OOE | 80 | AV | V203OOE | 90 | S | W122EON | 101 | AV | W137EON |
| 71 | AV | V187OOE | 81 | HH | V204OOE | 91 | S | W124EON | 102 | AV | W138EON |
| 72 | AV | V188OOE | 82 | PK | V205OOE | 92 | S | W126EON | 103 | AV | W139EON |
| 73 | HH | V189OOE | 83 | PK | V206OOE | 93 | AV | W127EON | 104 | AV | W141EON |

### VP105-112

| | | | | | | | | | | | |
|---|---|---|---|---|---|---|---|---|---|---|---|
| | | | Volvo B7TL 10m | | | Plaxton President 4.4m | | N41/19D* | 2000 | *seating varies | |
| 105 | AV | W448BCW | 107 | AV | W451BCW | 109 | AV | W453BCW | 111 | AV | W457BCW |
| 106 | AV | W449BCW | 108 | AV | W452BCW | 110 | AV | W454BCW | 112 | w | W458BCW |

### VA293-311

| | | | | | | | | | | | |
|---|---|---|---|---|---|---|---|---|---|---|---|
| | | | Volvo B7TL 10.1m | | | TransBus ALX400 4.4m | | N45/20D | 2002-03 | | |
| 293 | AV | SK52MKV | 298 | S | SK52MPY | 303 | AV | SK52URZ | 308 | AV | SK52USG |
| 294 | AV | SK52MSO | 299 | S | SK52URV | 304 | AV | SK52USB | 309 | AV | SK52USH |
| 295 | AV | SK52MPU | 300 | S | SK52URW | 305 | AV | SK52USC | 310 | S | SK52USJ |
| 296 | S | SK52MPV | 301 | S | SK52URX | 306 | AV | SK52USD | 311 | S | SK52USL |
| 297 | S | SK52MPX | 302 | S | SK52URY | 307 | AV | SK52USF | | | |

*The London Bus Handbook*

## VE1-10 — Volvo B7TL 10.4m — East Lancs Myllennium Vyking N45/19D — 2004

| | | | | | | | | | | | |
|---|---|---|---|---|---|---|---|---|---|---|---|
| 1 | S | PG04WGN | 4 | S | PG04WGV | 7 | S | PG04WGY | 9 | S | PG04WHA |
| 2 | S | PG04WGP | 5 | S | PG04WGW | 8 | S | PG04WGZ | 10 | S | PG04WHB |
| 3 | S | PG04WGU | 6 | S | PG04WGX | | | | | | |

## VLE1-45 — Volvo B7TL 11m — East Lancs Myllennium Vyking N47/22D — 2004

| | | | | | | | | | | | |
|---|---|---|---|---|---|---|---|---|---|---|---|
| 1 | V | PG04WHC | 9 | V | PG04WHM | 17 | V | PG04WHW | 25 | V | PA04CYH |
| 2 | V | PG04WHD | 10 | V | PG04WHN | 18 | V | PG04WHX | 26 | V | PA04CYJ |
| 3 | u | PG04WHE | 11 | V | PG04WHP | 19 | V | PG04WHY | 40 | V | PO54ADU |
| 4 | V | PG04WHF | 12 | V | PG04WHR | 20 | V | PG04WJA | 41 | V | PO54ADV |
| 5 | V | PG04WHH | 13 | V | PG04WHS | 21 | V | PA04CYC | 42 | V | PO54OOD |
| 6 | V | PG04WHJ | 14 | V | PG04WHT | 22 | V | PA04CYE | 43 | V | PO54OOE |
| 7 | V | PG04WHK | 15 | V | PG04WHU | 23 | V | PA04CYF | 44 | V | PO54OOF |
| 8 | V | PG04WHL | 16 | V | PG04WHV | 24 | V | PA04CYG | 45 | V | PO54OOG |

| | | | | | | |
|---|---|---|---|---|---|---|
| VR226 | S | BD51YCR | Volvo B7TL 10.1m | Wrightbus Eclipse Gemini | N41/23D | 2002 |
| VR227 | S | BD51YCS | Volvo B7TL 10.1m | Wrightbus Eclipse Gemini | N41/23D | 2002 |
| VR228 | V | BD51YCT | Volvo B7TL 10.1m | Wrightbus Eclipse Gemini | N41/23D | 2002 |

## Depots and allocations:

### Fulwell (Wellington Road) - FW

| | | | | | | | | |
|---|---|---|---|---|---|---|---|---|
| Dart | DP1 | DP11 | DPS579 | DPS580 | DPS582 | DPS583 | DPS584 | DPS585 |
| | DPS586 | DPS587 | DPS686 | DPS687 | DPS689 | DPS690 | DPS691 | DPS692 |
| | DPS693 | | | | | | | |
| Dart 4 | DE22 | DE23 | DE24 | DE25 | DE26 | DE27 | DE28 | DE29 |
| | DE30 | DE31 | | | | | | |
| Dart Hybrid | HDE1 | HDE2 | HDE3 | HDE4 | HDE5 | | | |
| Routemaster | RML880 | | | | | | | |
| Olympian | VA6 | VA7 | VA8 | VA9 | VA10 | VA45 | VA46 | VA48 |
| | VA49 | VA54 | | | | | | |
| Trident | TAL18 | TAL19 | TAL20 | TAL21 | TAL23 | TA202 | TA204 | TA205 |
| | TA206 | TA207 | TA208 | TA209 | TA210 | TA211 | TA212 | TA213 |
| | TA215 | TA216 | TA217 | TA218 | TA219 | TA220 | TA221 | TA222 |
| | TA223 | TA224 | TA225 | TA313 | TA314 | TA318 | TA319 | TA320 |
| | TA321 | TA322 | TA323 | TA324 | TA325 | TA326 | TA327 | TA328 |
| | TA329 | TA330 | TA331 | TA332 | TA333 | TA334 | TA335 | TA336 |
| | TA337 | TA338 | TA339 | TA340 | TA341 | TA342 | TA343 | TA344 |
| | TA345 | TA346 | | | | | | |
| Scania DD | SLE7 | SLE8 | SLE9 | SLE10 | SLE11 | SLE12 | SLE13 | SLE14 |
| | SLE15 | SLE16 | SLE17 | SLE18 | SLE19 | SLE20 | SP25 | SP26 |
| | SP27 | SP28 | SP52 | SP53 | SP54 | SP55 | SP56 | SP57 |
| | SP58 | SP59 | SP60 | SP61 | SP62 | SP63 | SP64 | SP65 |
| | SP66 | SP67 | SP88 | SP89 | SP90 | SP91 | SP92 | SP93 |
| | SP94 | SP95 | SP96 | SP97 | SP98 | SP99 | SP100 | SP101 |
| | SP102 | SP103 | SP104 | SP105 | SP106 | SP107 | SP108 | |

### Hounslow (Kingsley Road) - AV

| | | | | | | | | |
|---|---|---|---|---|---|---|---|---|
| Dart | DP38 | DP39 | DP40 | DP41 | DP42 | DP46 | DP47 | DP56 |
| | DP57 | DP58 | DP59 | DP60 | DP61 | DP62 | DP63 | DP64 |
| | DP65 | DP66 | DP67 | DP68 | DP69 | DP70 | DP71 | DP72 |
| | DP73 | DP74 | DP75 | DP76 | DP77 | DP79 | DP588 | DP589 |
| | DP590 | DP592 | DPS656 | DPS657 | DPS658 | DPS659 | DPS660 | DPS662 |
| | DPS663 | DPS664 | DPS665 | DPS666 | DPS667 | DPS668 | DPS669 | DPS681 |
| | DSP682 | DPS683 | DPS684 | DPS685 | DPS694 | DPS719 | DPS720 | DPS721 |
| | DPS722 | DPS723 | DPS724 | DPS725 | | | | |
| Dart 4 | DLE1 | DLE2 | DLE3 | DLE4 | DLE5 | DLE6 | DLE7 | DLE8 |
| | DLE9 | DLE10 | DLE11 | DLE12 | DLE13 | DLE14 | DLE15 | DLE16 |
| | DLE17 | DLE18 | DLE19 | DLE20 | DLE21 | DLE22 | DLE23 | DLE24 |
| | DLE25 | | | | | | | |
| Tempo | OT1 | OT2 | OT3 | OT4 | OT5 | OT6 | OT7 | OT8 |
| | OT9 | OT10 | OT11 | OT12 | OT13 | OT14 | OT15 | OT16 |
| Trident | TA201 | | | | | | | |
| Volvo B7TL | VA71 | VA72 | VA74 | VA75 | VA76 | VA77 | VA80 | VA85 |
| | VA86 | VA93 | VA94 | VA95 | VA96 | VA97 | VA99 | VA101 |

Hybrid single-deck buses continue to be developed. Pictured in Church Road, Richmond is HDE4, SN09CHG, one of five Hybrid versions of the Dart with Enviro 200 bodywork. A new model, the Enviro 350H is currently under development with early examples in use in Australia and elsewhere. *Mark Lyons*

|         |        |        |        |        |        |        |        |        |
|---------|--------|--------|--------|--------|--------|--------|--------|--------|
|         | VA102  | VP103  | VP104  | VP105  | VP106  | VP107  | VP108  | VP109  |
|         | VP110  | VP111  | VA293  | VA294  | VA295  | VA303  | VA304  | VA305  |
|         | VA306  | VA307  | VA308  | VA309  |        |        |        |        |
| Scania  | SP5    | SP6    | SP7    | SP8    | SP9    | SP10   | SP11   | SP12   |
|         | SP13   | SP14   | SP15   | SP23   | SP24   | SP38   | SP41   | SP42   |
|         | SP43   | SP44   | SP45   | SP46   | SP47   | SP48   | SP49   | SP50   |
|         | SP51   | SP165  | SP166  | SP167  | SP168  | SP169  | SP170  | SP171  |
|         | SP172  | SP173  | SP174  | SP175  | SP176  | SP177  | SP178  | SP179  |
|         | SP180  | SP181  | SP182  | SP183  | SP184  | SP185  | SP186  | SP187  |
|         | SP188  | SP189  | SP190  |        |        |        |        |        |

## Hounslow Heath (Pulborough Way) - HH

|                    |        |        |        |        |        |        |        |        |
|--------------------|--------|--------|--------|--------|--------|--------|--------|--------|
| Dart               | DP48   | DP49   | DP55   | DP71   | DP72   | DPS671 | DPS672 | DPS673 |
|                    | DPS674 | DPS675 | DPS676 | DPS677 | DPS678 | DPS679 | DPS680 | DPS688 |
|                    | DPS707 | DPS708 | DPS709 | DPS710 | DPS711 | DPS712 | DPS713 | DPS714 |
|                    | DPS715 | DPS716 | DPS717 | DPS718 |        |        |        |        |
| Dart 4             | DE1    | DE2    | DE3    | DE4    | DE5    | DE6    | DE7    | DE8    |
|                    | DE9    | DE10   | DE11   | DE12   | DE13   | DE14   | DE15   | DE16   |
|                    | DE17   | DE18   | DE19   | DE20   | DE21   | DLE12  | DLE13  | DLE14  |
|                    | DLE15  | DLE16  | DLE17  | DLE18  |        |        |        |        |
| Volvo B7TL         | VA60   | VA61   | VA66   | VA68   | VA73   | VA81   | VA84   | VA101  |
| Scania OmniCity DD | SP1    | SP2    | SP3    | SP4    | SP16   | SP17   | SP18   | SP19   |
|                    | SP20   | SP21   | SP22   | SP23   | SP24   | SP191  | SP192  | SP193  |
|                    | SP194  | SP195  | SP196  | SP197  | SP198  | SP199  | SP200  | SP204  |
|                    | SP205  | SP206  |        |        |        |        |        |        |
| Trident E400H      | ADH1   | ADH2   |        |        |        |        |        |        |

## Park Royal (Atlas Road) - PK

|        |        |        |        |        |        |        |        |        |
|--------|--------|--------|--------|--------|--------|--------|--------|--------|
| Dart   | DPS3   | DPS4   | DPS5   | DPS6   | DPS7   | DPS9   | DPS10  | DPS11  |
|        | DPS12  | DPS13  | DPS14  | DPS15  | DPS16  | DP34   | DP35   | DP36   |
|        | DP37   | DP50   | DP51   | DP52   | DP53   | DP54   | DP61   | DP80   |
|        | DP83   | DP85   | DP86   | DP88   | DP97   | DP98   |        |        |
| Dart 4 | DE75   | DE76   | DE77   | DE78   | DE79   | DE80   | DE81   | DE82   |
|        | DE83   | DE84   | DE85   | DE86   | DE87   | DE88   | DE89   | DE90   |

| | | | | | | | | |
|---|---|---|---|---|---|---|---|---|
| | DE91 | DE92 | DE93 | DE94 | DE95 | DE96 | DE97 | DE98 |
| | DE99 | DE100 | DE101 | DE102 | DE103 | DE104 | DE105 | DE106 |
| | DE107 | SDE11 | SDE12 | SDE13 | SDE14 | SDE15 | SDE16 | SDE17 |
| Optare Versa | OV50 | OV51 | OV52 | OV53 | OV54 | OV55 | OV56 | OV57 |
| | OV58 | OV59 | OV60 | OV61 | OV62 | OV63 | OV64 | OV65 |
| | OV66 | | | | | | | |
| Volvo B7TL | VA78 | VA79 | VA82 | VA83 | VA87 | VA88 | VA89 | VA98 |
| Scania DD | SP203 | | | | | | | |

## Shepherd's Bush (Wells Road) - S

| | | | | | | | | |
|---|---|---|---|---|---|---|---|---|
| Dart | DPS624 | DPS688 | | | | | | |
| Dart 4 | DE32 | DE33 | DE34 | DE35 | DE36 | DE37 | DE38 | DE39 |
| | DE40 | DE41 | DE42 | DE43 | DE44 | DE45 | DE46 | DE47 |
| | DE48 | DE49 | | | | | | |
| Trident | TLA1 | TLA2 | TLA3 | TLA4 | TLA5 | TLA6 | TLA7 | TLA8 |
| | TLA9 | TLA10 | TLA11 | TLA12 | TLA13 | TLA14 | TLA15 | TLA16 |
| | TLA17 | TLA22 | TLA24 | TLA25 | TLA26 | TLA27 | TLA28 | TLA29 |
| | TLA30 | TLA31 | TLA32 | | | | | |
| Trident 2 | ADH3 | ADH4 | ADH5 | ADH6 | ADH7 | ADH8 | ADH9 | ADH10 |
| | ADH11 | ADH12 | ADH13 | ADH14 | ADH15 | ADH16 | ADH17 | ADH18 |
| | ADH19 | ADH20 | ADH21 | ADH22 | | | | |
| Volvo B7TL | VE1 | VE2 | VE3 | VE4 | VE5 | VE6 | VE7 | VE8 |
| | VE9 | VE10 | VA62 | VA63 | VA64 | VA66 | VA90 | VA91 |
| | VA92 | VR226 | VR227 | VA296 | VA297 | VA298 | VA299 | VA300 |
| | VA301 | VA302 | VA310 | VA311 | | | | |
| Scania | SP29 | SP30 | SP31 | SP32 | SP33 | SP34 | SP35 | SP36 |
| | SP37 | SP39 | SP40 | SP109 | SP110 | SP111 | SP112 | SP113 |
| | SP114 | SP115 | SP116 | SP117 | SP118 | SP119 | SP120 | SP121 |
| | SP122 | SP123 | SP124 | SP125 | SP126 | SP127 | SP128 | SP129 |
| | SP130 | SP131 | SP132 | SP133 | SP134 | SP135 | SP136 | |

## Stamford Brook (Chiswick High Road, Chiswick) - V

| | | | | | | | | |
|---|---|---|---|---|---|---|---|---|
| Versa | OV1 | OV2 | OV3 | OV4 | OV5 | OV6 | OV7 | OV8 |
| | OV9 | OV10 | OV11 | OV12 | OV13 | OV14 | OV15 | OV16 |
| | OV17 | OV18 | OV19 | | | | | |
| Volvo B7TL | VLE1 | VLE2 | VLE3 | VLE4 | VLE5 | VLE6 | VLE7 | VLE8 |
| | VLE9 | VLE10 | VLE11 | VLE12 | VLE13 | VLE14 | VLE15 | VLE16 |
| | VLE17 | VLE18 | VLE19 | VLE20 | VLE21 | VLE22 | VLE23 | VLE24 |
| | VLE25 | VLE26 | VLE40 | VLE41 | VLE42 | VLE43 | VLE44 | VLE45 |
| | VR228 | | | | | | | |
| Scania | SLE43 | SLE44 | SLE45 | SLE46 | SLE47 | SLE48 | SLE49 | SLE50 |
| | SLE51 | SLE52 | SLE53 | SLE54 | SLE55 | SLE56 | SLE57 | SLE58 |
| | SLE59 | SLE60 | SLE61 | SLE62 | SLE63 | SLE64 | SP137 | SP138 |
| | SP139 | SP140 | SP141 | SP142 | SP143 | SP144 | SP145 | SP146 |
| | SP147 | SP148 | SP149 | SP150 | SP151 | SP152 | SP153 | SP154 |
| | SP155 | SP156 | SP157 | SP158 | SP159 | SP160 | SP161 | SP162 |
| | SP163 | SP164 | | | | | | |
| *Ancillary* | *DP6* | *DP7* | *DP10* | *MV1* | *MV2* | *MV3* | *MV4* | *MV5* |
| | *MV6* | *MV8* | *VA50* | *VA51* | *VA52* | *VA53* | | |

## Tolworth (Day's Yard, Kingston Road) - TV

| | | | | | | | | |
|---|---|---|---|---|---|---|---|---|
| Dart | DPS537 | DPS538 | DPS539 | DPS541 | DPS542 | DPS549 | DPS551 | |
| | DPS552 | DPS553 | DPS554 | DPS556 | DPS557 | DPS591 | DPS593 | DPS594 |
| | DPS597 | DPS598 | DPS600 | DPS601 | DPK602 | DPK613 | DPK614 | DPK615 |
| | DPK616 | DPK617 | DPK618 | DPK624 | DPK625 | DPS625 | DPS626 | DPS641 |
| | DPS642 | DPS643 | DPS644 | DPS645 | DPS646 | DPS647 | DPS648 | DPS649 |
| | DPS650 | DPS651 | DPS652 | DPS653 | DPS670 | | | |
| Dart 4 | SDE1 | SDE2 | SDE3 | SDE4 | SDE5 | SDE6 | SDE7 | SDE8 |
| | SDE9 | SDE10 | | | | | | |
| Trident | TA213 | TA214 | TA229 | TA230 | TA231 | TA232 | TA233 | TA234 |
| | TA235 | TA236 | TA237 | TA238 | TA239 | TA240 | TA241 | TA242 |
| | TA243 | TA244 | TA245 | TA246 | TA247 | TA248 | TA249 | TA250 |
| | TA281 | TA282 | TA283 | TA284 | TA285 | TA286 | TA312 | |

*The London Bus Handbook*

# METROBUS

Metrobus Ltd,  Wheatstone Close, Crawley, RH10 9UA

| | | | | | | | | | |
|---|---|---|---|---|---|---|---|---|---|
| 101 | MB | YJ56WVF | Optare Solo M710 SE | | Optare | | N17F | 2006 | |
| 102 | MB | YJ56WVG | Optare Solo M710 SE | | Optare | | N17F | 2006 | |

### 133-147
TransBus Dart 8.9m — Marshall Capital — N25F — 2002 — FirstBus, 2007

| | | | | | | | | | | | |
|---|---|---|---|---|---|---|---|---|---|---|---|
| 133 | MB | LT02ZDC | 137 | MB | LT02ZDG | 141 | MB | LT02ZDP | 145 | MB | LT02ZDV |
| 134 | MB | LT02ZDD | 138 | MB | LT02ZDM | 142 | MB | LT02ZDR | 146 | MB | LT02ZDW |
| 135 | MB | LT02ZDE | 139 | MB | LT02ZDN | 143 | MB | LT02ZDS | 147 | MB | LT02ZDX |
| 136 | MB | LT02ZDF | 140 | MB | LT02ZDO | 144 | MB | LT02ZDU | | | |

### 148-162
ADL Dart 4 8.9m — ADL Enviro 200 — N26F — 2011

| | | | | | | | | | | | |
|---|---|---|---|---|---|---|---|---|---|---|---|
| 148 | MB | YX60FTO | 152 | MB | YX60FTV | 156 | MB | YX60FUW | 160 | MB | YX60FVC |
| 149 | MB | YX60FTP | 153 | MB | YX60FTY | 157 | MB | YX60FUY | 161 | MB | YX60FVD |
| 150 | MB | YX60FTT | 154 | MB | YX60FTZ | 158 | MB | YX60FVA | 162 | MB | YX60FVE |
| 151 | MB | YX60FTU | 155 | MB | YX60FUV | 159 | MB | YX60FVB | | | |

### 163-178
ADL Dart 4 8.9m — ADL Enviro 200 — N26F — On order

| | | | | | | | | | | | |
|---|---|---|---|---|---|---|---|---|---|---|---|
| 163 | - | - | 167 | - | - | 171 | - | - | 175 | - | - |
| 164 | - | - | 168 | - | - | 172 | - | - | 176 | - | - |
| 165 | - | - | 169 | - | - | 173 | - | - | 177 | - | - |
| 166 | - | - | 170 | - | - | 174 | - | - | 178 | - | - |

### 201-219
TransBus Dart 10.7m — TransBus Pointer — N36D* — 2003 — *seating varies

| | | | | | | | | | | | |
|---|---|---|---|---|---|---|---|---|---|---|---|
| 201 | CY | SN03WKU | 206 | CY | SN03WLH | 212 | C | SN03WMC | 216 | C | SN03WMP |
| 202 | CY | SN03WKY | 207 | CY | SN03WLL | 213 | C | SN03WMF | 217 | CY | SN03WMT |
| 203 | CY | SN03WLA | 210 | C | SN03WLX | 214 | C | SN03WMG | 218 | CY | SN03WMV |
| 204 | CY | SN03WLE | 211 | C | SN03WLZ | 215 | C | SN03WMK | 219 | C | SN03WMY |
| 205 | CY | SN03WLF | | | | | | | | | |

### 220-225
ADL Dart 4 10.1m — ADL Enviro 200 — N29D — 2007 — Arriva Southern Counties, '09

| | | | | | | | | | | | |
|---|---|---|---|---|---|---|---|---|---|---|---|
| 220 | CY | GN07AVR | 222 | CY | GN07AVU | 224 | CY | GN07AVW | 225 | CY | GN07AUY |
| 221 | CY | GN07AVT | 223 | CY | GN07AVV | | | | | | |

**Metrobus operates buses both on TfL contracts where they use the red livery and on routes outside the TfL area where a blue scheme is used.  Representing the latest batch of short Enviro 200 buses is 155, YX60FUV.**
*Richard Godfrey*

### 228-236 — ADL Dart 4 9.1m — East Lancs Esteem — N24F — 2006

| 228 | MB | PO56JEU | 231 | MB | PO56JFF | 233 | MB | PO56JFJ | 235 | MB | PO56JFN |
|---|---|---|---|---|---|---|---|---|---|---|---|
| 229 | MB | PO56JFA | 232 | MB | PO56JFG | 234 | MB | PO56JFK | 236 | MB | PO56JFU |
| 230 | MB | PO56JFE | | | | | | | | | |

### 241-247 — Dennis Dart SLF 10m — Plaxton Pointer — N35F* — 1998 — *241 is N32F

| 241 | CY | R741BMY | 243 | CY | R743BMY | 245 | CY | R745BMY | 247 | CY | R747FGX |
|---|---|---|---|---|---|---|---|---|---|---|---|
| 242 | CY | R742BMY | 244 | CY | R744BMY | 246 | CY | R746FGX | | | |

### 251-256 — ADL Dart 8.8m — ADL Mini Pointer — N23F — 2004

| 251 | MB | SN54GPV | 253 | MB | SN54GPY | 255 | MB | SN54GRF | 256 | MB | SN54GRK |
|---|---|---|---|---|---|---|---|---|---|---|---|
| 252 | MB | SN54GPX | 254 | MB | SN54GPZ | | | | | | |

### 257-268 — ADL Dart 9m — East Lancs Myllennium* — N24F — 2006 — *Esteem fronts are fitted

| 257 | MB | PN06UYL | 260 | MB | PN06UYP | 263 | MB | PN06UYT | 266 | MB | PN06UYW |
|---|---|---|---|---|---|---|---|---|---|---|---|
| 258 | MB | PN06UYM | 261 | MB | PN06UYR | 264 | MB | PN06UYU | 267 | MB | PN06UYX |
| 259 | MB | PN06UYO | 262 | MB | PN06UYS | 265 | MB | PN06UYV | 268 | MB | PN06UYY |

### 271-289 — TransBus Dart 8.8m — TransBus Mini Pointer — N23F* — 2003 — *287-9 are N29F

| 271 | MB | SN03YBA | 276 | MB | SN03YBK | 281 | MB | SN03YBY | 286 | MB | SN03YCK |
|---|---|---|---|---|---|---|---|---|---|---|---|
| 272 | MB | SN03YBB | 277 | MB | SN03YBR | 282 | MB | SN03YBZ | 287 | CY | SN03YCL |
| 273 | MB | SN03YBC | 278 | MB | SN03YBS | 283 | MB | SN03YCD | 288 | CY | SN03YCM |
| 274 | MB | SN03YBG | 279 | MB | SN03YBT | 284 | MB | SN03YCE | 289 | CY | SN03YCT |
| 275 | MB | SN03YBH | 280 | MB | SN03YBX | 285 | MB | SN03YCF | | | |

| 309 | CY | T309SMV | Dennis Dart SLF 10.2m | Alexander ALX200 | N32F | 1999 | |
|---|---|---|---|---|---|---|---|
| 310 | CY | T310SMV | Dennis Dart SLF 10.2m | Alexander ALX200 | N32F | 1999 | |
| 311 | CY | T311SMV | Dennis Dart SLF 10.2m | Alexander ALX200 | N32F | 1999 | |
| 320 | CY | LX03OJP | TransBus Dart SLF 10.7m | TransBus Pointer | N37F | 2003 | |
| 321 | CY | LX03OJN | TransBus Dart SLF 10.7m | TransBus Pointer | N37F | 2003 | |

### 322-334 — Dennis Dart SLF 10.7m — Plaxton Pointer 2 — N31D — 1999-2000

| 322 | C | V322KMY | 325 | C | V325KMY | 328 | C | V328KMY | 331 | C | V331KMY |
|---|---|---|---|---|---|---|---|---|---|---|---|
| 323 | C | V323KMY | 326 | C | V326KMY | 329 | C | V329KMY | 332 | C | W332VGX |
| 324 | C | V324KMY | 327 | C | V327KMY | 330 | C | V330KMY | 334 | C | W334VGX |

### 344-356 — Dennis Dart SLF 8.8m — Plaxton Pointer MPD — N21F* — 2000-01 — *344 N29F; 356 is N27F

| 344 | CY | X344YGU | 351 | MB | Y351HMY | 352 | MB | Y352HMY | 356 | MB | Y356HMY |
|---|---|---|---|---|---|---|---|---|---|---|---|
| 348 | MB | Y348HMY | | | | | | | | | |

### 359-376 — Dennis Dart SLF 11m — Caetano Nimbus — N38F — 2001

| 359 | CY | Y359HMY | 364 | CY | Y364HMY | 368 | CY | Y368HMY | 373 | CY | Y373HMY |
|---|---|---|---|---|---|---|---|---|---|---|---|
| 361 | CY | Y361HMY | 365 | CY | Y365HMY | 369 | CY | Y369HMY | 374 | CY | Y374HMY |
| 362 | CY | Y362HMY | 366 | CY | Y366HMY | 371 | CY | Y371HMY | 376 | CY | Y376HMY |
| 363 | CY | Y363HMY | 367 | CY | Y367HMY | 372 | CY | Y372HMY | | | |

| 377 | CY | Y377HMY | Dennis Dart SLF 10m | Caetano Nimbus | N34F | 2001 | |
|---|---|---|---|---|---|---|---|
| 378 | CY | Y378HMY | Dennis Dart SLF 10m | Caetano Nimbus | N34F | 2001 | |
| 379 | CY | Y379HMY | Dennis Dart SLF 10m | Caetano Nimbus | N34F | 2001 | |
| 381 | MB | LK51JYL | Dennis Dart SLF 10.2m | Marshall Capital | N28D | 2001 | FirstBus, 2007 |
| 382 | MB | LK51JYN | Dennis Dart SLF 10.2m | Marshall Capital | N28D | 2001 | FirstBus, 2007 |
| 387 | MB | S112EGK | Dennis Dart SLF 10.1m | Plaxton Pointer 2 | N29D | 1998 | On loan |
| 388 | MB | S638JGP | Dennis Dart SLF 10.1m | Plaxton Pointer 2 | N29D | 1998 | On loan |
| 390 | CY | P380FPK | Dennis Dart SLF 10.7m | Plaxton Pointer | B39F | 1997 | Arriva Southern Counties, '09 |
| 393 | CY | P283FPK | Dennis Dart SLF 10.7m | Plaxton Pointer | B39F | 1997 | Arriva Southern Counties, '09 |
| 394 | CY | P274FPK | Dennis Dart SLF 10.7m | Plaxton Pointer | B39F | 1997 | Arriva Southern Counties, '09 |
| 395 | CY | P285FPK | Dennis Dart SLF 10.7m | Plaxton Pointer | B39F | 1997 | Arriva Southern Counties, '09 |
| 396 | CY | N232TPK | Dennis Dart SLF 10.2m | Plaxton Pointer | B35F | 1996 | Arriva Southern Counties, '09 |
| 398 | CY | P278FPK | Dennis Dart SLF 10.7m | Plaxton Pointer | B39F | 1997 | Arriva Southern Counties, '09 |

### 431-447 — Scania N94UD OmniDekka 10.6m East Lancs 4.4m — N45/29D* — 2003 — *several N45/27D

| 431 | C | YV03PZW | 436 | C | YV03PZF | 440 | C | YV03PZK | 444 | C | YV03RCZ |
|---|---|---|---|---|---|---|---|---|---|---|---|
| 432 | C | YV03PZX | 437 | C | YV03PZG | 441 | C | YV03PZL | 445 | C | YV03RAU |
| 433 | C | YV03PZY | 438 | C | YV03PZH | 442 | C | YV03PZM | 446 | C | YV03RAX |
| 434 | C | YV03PZZ | 439 | C | YV03PZJ | 443 | C | YV03RCY | 447 | C | YV03RBF |
| 435 | C | YV03PZE | | | | | | | | | |

The standard double-deck for Metrobus fleet is based on the Scania product, initally with East Lancs bodywork and latterly with Scania's own body. Illustrating the East Lancs model is 493, YN53RZF, seen heading for Horsham. *Dave Heath*

### 451-471

Scania N94UD OmniDekka 10.6m East Lancs  4.4m    N45/27D*  2003    *469-71 are N45/29D

| 451 | C  | YU52XVK | 459 | MB | YN03DFE | 464 | MB | YN03DFP | 468 | MB | YN03DFY |
|-----|----|---------|-----|----|---------|-----|----|---------|-----|----|---------|
| 455 | C  | YN03DFA | 460 | MB | YN03DFG | 465 | MB | YN03DFU | 469 | CY | YV03RBU |
| 456 | C  | YN03DFC | 461 | MB | YN03DFJ | 466 | MB | YN03DFV | 470 | CY | YV03RBX |
| 457 | MB | YU52XVR | 462 | MB | YN03DFK | 467 | MB | YN03DFX | 471 | CY | YN53USG |
| 458 | MB | YN03DFD | 463 | MB | YN03DFL |     |    |         |     |    |         |

### 472-497

Scania N94UD OmniDekka 10.6m East Lancs  4.4m    N45/29D*  2003-05    *480/1 are N45/27D

| 472 | CY | YN53RYA | 479 | MB | YN53RYM | 486 | CY | YN53RYY | 492 | CY | YN53RZE |
|-----|----|---------|-----|----|---------|-----|----|---------|-----|----|---------|
| 473 | CY | YN53RYB | 480 | C  | YN53RYP | 487 | CY | YN53RYZ | 493 | CY | YN53RZF |
| 474 | CY | YN53RYC | 481 | C  | YN53RYR | 488 | CY | YN53RZA | 494 | CY | YN54AJU |
| 475 | CY | YN53RYD | 482 | CY | YN53RYT | 489 | CY | YN53RZB | 495 | CY | YN54AJV |
| 476 | CY | YN53RYF | 483 | CY | YN53RYV | 490 | CY | YN53RZC | 496 | CY | YN54AJX |
| 477 | CY | YN53RYH | 484 | CY | YN53RYW | 491 | CY | YN53RZD | 497 | CY | YN54AJY |
| 478 | CY | YN53RYK | 485 | CY | YN53RYX |     |    |         |     |    |         |

| 513 | CY | YP52CTO | Scania OmniCity CN94 UB 12m | Scania | | N42F | 2002 |

### 514-530

Scania OmniCity CN94 UB 12m  Scania    N32D  2003

| 514 | MB | YN53RXF | 519 | MB | YN53RXL | 523 | MB | YN53RXR | 527 | MB | YN53RXW |
|-----|----|---------|-----|----|---------|-----|----|---------|-----|----|---------|
| 515 | MB | YN53RXG | 520 | MB | YN53RXM | 524 | MB | YN53RXT | 528 | MB | YN53RXX |
| 516 | MB | YN53RXH | 521 | MB | YN53RXO | 525 | MB | YN53RXU | 529 | MB | YN53RXY |
| 517 | MB | YN53RXJ | 522 | MB | YN53RXP | 526 | MB | YN53RXV | 530 | MB | YN53RXZ |
| 518 | MB | YN53RXK |     |    |         |     |    |         |     |    |         |

### 531-545

Scania OmniCity CN94 UB 12m  Scania    N32D*  2003-05    *seating varies

| 531 | CY | YN03UWU | 535 | CY | YN03WPR | 539 | C | YN03WRL | 543 | C | YN05HFG |
|-----|----|---------|-----|----|---------|-----|---|---------|-----|---|---------|
| 532 | CY | YN03UWY | 536 | C  | YN03WRF | 540 | C | YN03WRP | 544 | C | YN05HFH |
| 533 | CY | YN03UPM | 537 | C  | YN03WRG | 541 | C | YN05HFE | 545 | C | YN05HFJ |
| 534 | CY | YN03WPP | 538 | C  | YN03WRJ | 542 | C | YN05HFF |     |   |         |

**Metrobus operates several batches of the Scania OmniCity low-floor integral single-deck bus. Seen en route for Epsom General Hospital, 567, YN08OAZ, illustrates the model in dual-door format.** *Richard Godfrey*

### 546-558

Scania OmniCity CN94 UB 12m   Scania     N37D*   2005   *seating varies

| 546 | CY | YN05HCA | 550 | CY | YN05HCF | 553 | CY | YN55PWK | 556 | CY | YN55PWU |
| 547 | CY | YN05HCC | 551 | CY | YN05HCG | 554 | CY | YN55PWL | 557 | CY | YN55PWV |
| 548 | CY | YN05HCD | 552 | CY | YN55PWJ | 555 | CY | YN55PWO | 558 | CY | YN55PWX |
| 549 | CY | YN05HCE | | | | | | | | | |

### 559-567

Scania OmniCity CN230 UB 12m  Scania     N33D*   2007-08  *seating varies

| 559 | CY | YN07LKF | 562 | C | YN08OAU | 564 | C | YN08OAW | 566 | C | YN08OAY |
| 560 | CY | YN07LKG | 563 | C | YN08OAV | 565 | C | YN08OAX | 567 | C | YN08OAZ |
| 561 | C | YN08OAS | | | | | | | | | |

### 568-581

Scania OmniCity CN230 UB 12m  Scania     N36D   2009

| 568 | CY | YT09BKD | 572 | CY | YT09BKJ | 576 | CY | YT09BKO | 579 | CY | YT09BKX |
| 569 | CY | YT09BKE | 573 | CY | YT09BKK | 577 | CY | YT09BKU | 580 | CY | YT09BKY |
| 570 | CY | YT09BKF | 574 | CY | YT09BKL | 578 | CY | YT09BKV | 581 | CY | YT09BKZ |
| 571 | CY | YT09BKG | 575 | CY | YT09BKN | | | | | | |

### 601-623

Scania OmniTown N94 UB 10.6m East Lancs Myllennium*   N29D   2006   *Esteem fronts are fitted

| 601 | MB | YM55SWU | 607 | MB | YM55SXA | 613 | MB | YN06JXT | 619 | MB | YM55SXO |
| 602 | MB | YM55SWV | 608 | MB | YM55SXB | 614 | MB | YM55SXH | 620 | MB | YM55SXP |
| 603 | MB | YN06JXR | 609 | MB | YM55SXC | 615 | MB | YN06JXU | 621 | MB | YM55SXR |
| 604 | MB | YM55SWX | 610 | MB | YM55SXD | 616 | MB | YN06JXV | 622 | MB | YN06JXY |
| 605 | MB | YM55SWY | 611 | MB | YM55SXE | 617 | MB | YN06JXW | 623 | MB | YN06JXZ |
| 606 | MB | YN06JXS | 612 | MB | YM55SXF | 618 | MB | YN06JXX | | | |

### 624-633

Scania OmniCity N230 UB 10.9m  Scania     N33F   2008

| 624 | CY | YN08DFJ | 627 | CY | YN08DFO | 630 | CY | YN08DFV | 632 | CY | YN08DFY |
| 625 | CY | YN08DFK | 628 | CY | YN08DFP | 631 | CY | YN08DFX | 633 | CY | YN08DFZ |
| 626 | CY | YN08DFL | 629 | CY | YN08DFU | | | | | | |

### 701-705

MAN 12.240 10.3m      East Lancs Esteem     N27D   2007

| 701 | MB | PN07KRK | 703 | MB | PN07KRU | 704 | MB | PN07KRV | 705 | C | PN07KRX |
| 702 | MB | PN07KRO | | | | | | | | | |

| 706 | C | YX58DXB | MAN 14.240 | 10.8m | ADL Enviro 200 | N34D | 2009 |
| 707 | C | YX58DXC | MAN 14.240 | 10.8m | ADL Enviro 200 | N34D | 2009 |
| 708 | C | YX58DXD | MAN 14.240 | 10.8m | ADL Enviro 200 | N34D | 2009 |

## 709-723

MAN 14.240 10.8m  MCV Evolution  N28D  2009

| | | | | | | | | | | | | |
|---|---|---|---|---|---|---|---|---|---|---|---|---|
| 709 | C | AE09DHG | 713 | C | AE09DHP | 717 | C | AJ58WBG | 721 | C | AJ58WBK |
| 710 | C | AE09DHK | 714 | C | AJ58WBE | 718 | C | AE09DHU | 722 | C | AJ58WBF |
| 711 | C | AJ58WBD | 715 | C | AE09DHJ | 719 | C | AE09DHN | 723 | C | AE09DHV |
| 712 | C | AE09DHM | 716 | C | AE09DHO | 720 | C | AE09DHL | | | |

## 870-899

Scania OmniCity N230 UD 10.8m  Optare Olympus  N45/23D  2009

| | | | | | | | | | | | | |
|---|---|---|---|---|---|---|---|---|---|---|---|---|
| 870 | C | PN09EKR | 878 | C | PN09ELU | 886 | MB | PN09ENC | 893 | MB | PN09ENO |
| 871 | C | PN09EKT | 879 | C | PN09ELV | 887 | MB | PN09ENE | 894 | MB | PN09ENP |
| 872 | C | PN09EKU | 880 | C | PN09ELW | 888 | MB | PN09ENF | 895 | MB | PN09ENR |
| 873 | C | PN09EKV | 881 | C | PN09ELX | 889 | MB | PN09ENH | 896 | MB | PN09ENT |
| 874 | C | PN09EKW | 882 | C | PN09EMF | 890 | MB | PN09ENK | 897 | MB | PN09ENU |
| 875 | C | PN09EKX | 883 | C | PN09EMK | 891 | MB | PN09ENL | 898 | MB | PN09ENV |
| 876 | C | PN09EKY | 884 | C | PN09EMV | 892 | MB | PN09ENM | 899 | MB | PN09ENW |
| 877 | C | PN09ELO | 885 | MB | PN09EMX | | | | | | |

## 901-927

Scania N94 UD 10.6m  East Lancs OmniDekka  N45/26D  2006

| | | | | | | | | | | | | |
|---|---|---|---|---|---|---|---|---|---|---|---|---|
| 901 | MB | YN55PZC | 908 | MB | YN55PZL | 915 | MB | YN55PZW | 922 | C | YN06JYG |
| 902 | MB | YN55PZD | 909 | MB | YN55PZM | 916 | MB | YN55PZX | 923 | C | YN06JYH |
| 903 | MB | YN55PZE | 910 | MB | YN55PZO | 917 | C | YN06JYB | 924 | C | YN06JYJ |
| 904 | MB | YN55PZF | 911 | MB | YN55PZP | 918 | C | YN06JYC | 925 | C | YN06JYK |
| 905 | MB | YN55PZG | 912 | MB | YN55PZR | 919 | C | YN06JYD | 926 | C | YN06JYL |
| 906 | MB | YN55PZH | 913 | MB | YN55PZU | 920 | C | YN06JYE | 927 | C | YN06JYO |
| 907 | MB | YN55PZJ | 914 | MB | YN55PZV | 921 | C | YN06JYF | | | |

## 928-946

Scania N94 UD 10.6m  East Lancs OmniDekka  N45/26D  2006

| | | | | | | | | | | | | |
|---|---|---|---|---|---|---|---|---|---|---|---|---|
| 928 | C | YN56FDA | 933 | MB | YN56FDG | 938 | MB | YN56FDO | 943 | MB | YN56FDY |
| 929 | C | YN56FDC | 934 | MB | YN56FDJ | 939 | MB | YN56FDP | 944 | MB | YN56FDZ |
| 930 | MB | YN56FDD | 935 | MB | YN56FDK | 940 | MB | YN56FDU | 945 | MB | YN56FEF |
| 931 | MB | YN56FDE | 936 | MB | YN56FDL | 941 | MB | YN56FDV | 946 | MB | YN56FEG |
| 932 | MB | YN56FDF | 937 | MB | YN56FDM | 942 | MB | YN56FDX | | | |

## 947-952

Scania N230 UD 10.8m  East Lancs OmniDekka  N43/23D  2007

| | | | | | | | | | | | | |
|---|---|---|---|---|---|---|---|---|---|---|---|---|
| 947 | C | YN07EXF | 949 | C | YN07EXH | 951 | C | YN07EXM | 952 | C | YN07EXO |
| 948 | C | YN07EXG | 950 | C | YN07EXK | | | | | | |

## 953-978

Scania OmniCity N230 UD  Scania  N47/31F  2008-10  *955-78 are N41/22D

| | | | | | | | | | | | | |
|---|---|---|---|---|---|---|---|---|---|---|---|---|
| 953 | CY | YN08OBP | 960 | C | YT59DYC | 967 | C | YT59DYM | 973 | C | YT59DYW |
| 954 | CY | YN08OBR | 961 | C | YT59DYD | 968 | C | YT59DYO | 974 | MB | YR10BCE |
| 955 | C | YR58SNY | 962 | C | YT59DYF | 969 | C | YT59DYP | 975 | MB | YR10BCF |
| 956 | C | YR58SNZ | 963 | C | YT59DYG | 970 | C | YT59DYS | 976 | MB | YR10BCK |
| 957 | C | YP58UFV | 964 | C | YT59DYH | 971 | C | YT59DYU | 977 | MB | YR10BCO |
| 958 | C | YT59DYA | 965 | C | YT59DYN | 972 | C | YT59DYV | 978 | MB | YR10BCU |
| 959 | C | YT59DYB | 966 | C | YT59DYJ | | | | | | |

Ancillary vehicles:

| | | | | | | | | |
|---|---|---|---|---|---|---|---|---|
| 7208 | LRt | SN03WLP | TransBus Dart 10.7m | TransBus Pointer | TV | 2003 | |
| 7209 | CYt | SN03WLU | TransBus Dart 10.7m | TransBus Pointer | TV | 2003 | |
| 7380 | CYt | LK51JYL | Dennis Dart SLF 10.2m | Marshall Capital | N28D | 2001 | FirstBus, 2007 |
| 7764 | LRt | M516VJO | Dennis Dart 9.8m | Marshall C37 | TV | 1995 | Oxford Citybus, 2004 |
| 7765 | LRt | M520VJO | Dennis Dart 9.8m | Marshall C37 | TV | 1995 | Oxford Citybus, 2004 |
| 7766 | LRt | M506VJO | Dennis Dart 9.8m | Marshall C37 | TV | 1995 | Oxford Citybus, 2004 |
| 7767 | CYt | M507VJO | Dennis Dart 9.8m | Marshall C37 | TV | 1995 | Oxford Citybus, 2004 |
| 7768 | CYt | M508VJO | Dennis Dart 9.8m | Marshall C37 | TV | 1995 | Oxford Citybus, 2004 |

## Depots and allocations:

### Crawley (Wheatstone Close) - CY

| | | | | | | | | | |
|---|---|---|---|---|---|---|---|---|---|
| Dart | | 201 | 202 | 203 | 204 | 205 | 206 | 207 | 217 |
| | | 218 | 241 | 242 | 243 | 244 | 245 | 246 | 247 |
| | | 287 | 288 | 289 | 309 | 310 | 311 | 320 | 321 |
| | | 344 | 359 | 361 | 362 | 363 | 364 | 365 | 366 |
| | | 367 | 368 | 369 | 371 | 372 | 373 | 374 | 375 |
| | | 376 | 377 | 378 | 379` | 390 | 393 | 394 | 395 |
| | | 396 | 398 | | | | | | |
| Dart 4 | | 220 | 221 | 222 | 223 | 224 | 225 | | |

| Scania sd | 513 | 531 | 532 | 533 | 534 | 535 | 546 | 547 |
| | 548 | 549 | 550 | 551 | 552 | 553 | 554 | 555 |
| | 556 | 557 | 558 | 559 | 560 | 568 | 569 | 570 |
| | 571 | 572 | 573 | 574 | 575 | 576 | 577 | 578 |
| | 579 | 580 | 581 | 624 | 625 | 626 | 627 | 628 |
| | 629 | 630 | 631 | 632 | 633 | | | |
| Scania dd | 469 | 470 | 471 | 472 | 473 | 474 | 475 | 476 |
| | 477 | 482 | 483 | 484 | 485 | 486 | 487 | 488 |
| | 489 | 490 | 491 | 492 | 493 | 494 | 495 | 496 |
| | 497 | 953 | 954 | | | | | |
| *Ancillary* | *7209* | *7380* | *7767* | *7768* | | | | |

## Croydon (Beddington Lane) - C

| Dart | 210 | 211 | 212 | 213 | 214 | 215 | 216 | 219 |
| | 322 | 323 | 324 | 325 | 326 | 327 | 328 | 328 |
| | 330 | 331 | 332 | 334 | 358 | | | |
| MAN 12.240 | 705 | 706 | 707 | 708 | 709 | 710 | 711 | 712 |
| | 713 | 714 | 715 | 716 | 717 | 718 | 719 | 720 |
| | 721 | 722 | 723 | | | | | |
| Scania sd | 536 | 537 | 538 | 539 | 540 | 541 | 542 | 543 |
| | 544 | 545 | 561 | 562 | 563 | 564 | 565 | 566 |
| | 567 | | | | | | | |
| Scania dd | 431 | 432 | 433 | 434 | 435 | 436 | 437 | 438 |
| | 439 | 440 | 441 | 442 | 443 | 444 | 445 | 446 |
| | 447 | 455 | 456 | 480 | 481 | 870 | 871 | 872 |
| | 873 | 874 | 875 | 876 | 877 | 878 | 879 | 880 |
| | 881 | 882 | 883 | 884 | 917 | 918 | 919 | 920 |
| | 921 | 922 | 923 | 924 | 925 | 926 | 927 | 947 |
| | 948 | 949 | 950 | 951 | 952 | 928 | 929 | 955 |
| | 956 | 957 | 958 | 959 | 960 | 961 | 962 | 963 |
| | 964 | 965 | 966 | 967 | 968 | 969 | 970 | 971 |
| | 972 | 973 | | | | | | |

## Orpington (Farnborough Hill, Green Street Green) - MB

| Solo | 101 | 102 | | | | | | |
| Dart | 133 | 134 | 135 | 136 | 137 | 138 | 139 | 140 |
| | 141 | 142 | 143 | 144 | 145 | 146 | 147 | 251 |
| | 252 | 253 | 254 | 255 | 256 | 257 | 258 | 259 |
| | 260 | 261 | 262 | 263 | 264 | 265 | 266 | 267 |
| | 268 | 271 | 272 | 273 | 274 | 275 | 276 | 277 |
| | 278 | 279 | 280 | 281 | 282 | 283 | 284 | 285 |
| | 286 | 348 | 349 | 351 | 352 | 356 | 381 | 382 |
| | 387 | 388 | | | | | | |
| Dart 4 | 148 | 149 | 150 | 151 | 152 | 153 | 154 | 155 |
| | 156 | 157 | 158 | 159 | 160 | 161 | 162 | 228 |
| | 229 | 230 | 231 | 232 | 233 | 234 | 235 | 236 |
| MAN 12.240 | 701 | 702 | 703 | 704 | | | | |
| Scania OmniCity | 514 | 515 | 516 | 517 | 518 | 519 | 520 | 521 |
| | 522 | 523 | 524 | 525 | 526 | 527 | 528 | 529 |
| | 530 | | | | | | | |
| Scania OmniTown | 601 | 602 | 603 | 604 | 605 | 606 | 607 | 608 |
| | 609 | 610 | 611 | 612 | 613 | 614 | 615 | 616 |
| | 617 | 618 | 619 | 620 | 621 | 622 | 623 | |
| Scania OmniDekka | 457 | 458 | 459 | 460 | 461 | 462 | 463 | 464 |
| | 465 | 466 | 467 | 468 | 479 | 885 | 886 | 887 |
| | 888 | 889 | 890 | 891 | 892 | 893 | 894 | 895 |
| | 896 | 897 | 898 | 899 | 901 | 902 | 903 | 904 |
| | 905 | 906 | 907 | 908 | 909 | 910 | 911 | 912 |
| | 913 | 914 | 915 | 916 | 930 | 931 | 932 | 933 |
| | 934 | 939 | 941 | 942 | 944 | 945 | 946 | 974 |
| | 975 | 976 | 977 | 978 | | | | |

## Orpington (Lagoon Road, St Mary Cray) - LR - Training school

| Ancillary | 7208 | 7764 | 7765 | 7766 |

*The London Bus Handbook*

# METROLINE

Metroline Travel Ltd, Comfort Delgro House, 329 Edgware Road, London NW2 6JP

### DP12-49
Dennis Dart SLF 10.1m · Plaxton Pointer 2 · N27D* · 2000 · Centra, Heathrow, 2006 · *seating varies

| | | | | | | | | | | | |
|---|---|---|---|---|---|---|---|---|---|---|---|
| 12 | PV | W112WGT | 19 | PV | W119WGT | 28 | AH | W128WGT | 37 | AH | W137WGT |
| 14 | PV | W114WGT | 22 | AH | W122WGT | 32 | AH | W132WGT | 38 | u | W138WGT |
| 16 | PV | W116WGT | 24 | AH | W124WGT | 33 | AH | W133WGT | 43 | AH | W143WGT |
| 17 | PV | W117WGT | 26 | PV | W126WGT | 34 | PV | W134WGT | 49 | u | W149WGT |
| 18 | PV | W118WGT | 27 | AH | W127WGT | 36 | AH | W136WGT | | | |

### DLD86-98
Dennis Dart SLF 10.1m · Plaxton Pointer 2 · N25D · 1998

| | | | | | | | | | | | |
|---|---|---|---|---|---|---|---|---|---|---|---|
| 86 | w | S286JLP | 89 | w | S289JLP | 93 | w | S293JLP | 97 | w | S297JLP |
| 87 | w | S287JLP | 90 | w | S290JLP | 94 | w | S294JLP | 98 | w | S298JLP |
| 88 | w | S288JLP | 92 | w | S292JLP | | | | | | |

### DLD108-132
Dennis Dart SLF 10.1m · Plaxton Pointer 2 · N29D* · 1999 · *seating varies

| | | | | | | | | | | | |
|---|---|---|---|---|---|---|---|---|---|---|---|
| 108 | w | T48KLD | 118 | KC | V118GBY | 123 | KC | V133GBY | 128 | KC | V128GBY |
| 109 | w | T49KLD | 119 | KC | V119GBY | 124 | KC | V124GBY | 129 | KC | V129GBY |
| 110 | PV | T39KLD | 120 | KC | V120GBY | 125 | KC | V125GBY | 130 | KC | V130GBY |
| 113 | w | T53KLD | 121 | KC | V134GBY | 126 | KC | V126GBY | 131 | KC | V131GBY |
| 115 | PV | T35KLD | 122 | KC | V122GBY | 127 | KC | V127GBY | 132 | KC | V132GBY |

### DLD133-149
Dennis Dart SLF 10.1m · Plaxton Pointer 2 · N27D* · 2000 · *seating varies

| | | | | | | | | | | | |
|---|---|---|---|---|---|---|---|---|---|---|---|
| 133 | KC | W133ULR | 138 | W | W138ULR | 142 | PV | W142ULR | 146 | PV | W146ULR |
| 134 | KC | W134ULR | 139 | PV | W139ULR | 143 | PV | W143ULR | 147 | PB | W147ULR |
| 135 | KC | W151ULR | 140 | PV | W152ULR | 144 | PV | W144ULR | 148 | PB | W148ULR |
| 136 | KC | W136ULR | 141 | PV | W141ULR | 145 | PV | W153ULR | 149 | KC | W149ULR |
| 137 | W | W137ULR | | | | | | | | | |

| | | | | | |
|---|---|---|---|---|---|
| DLM152 | PB | Y252NLK | Dennis Dart SLF 8.8m | Plaxton Pointer MPD | N25F | 2001 |
| DLM158 | PB | Y258NLK | Dennis Dart SLF 8.8m | Plaxton Pointer MPD | N25F | 2001 |

**Since March 2000, Metroline has been a wholly owned subsidiary of Comfort DelGro, a major world transport company that is based in Singapore. In March 2009 the company opened a new depot and head office at Cricklewood. Pictured in Ealing is Plaxton Pointer-bodied Dart DP36, W136WGT.** *Terry Longhurst*

Metroline currently has a paint programme during which the blue skirt is being displaced and the ComfortDelgro name added as shown by Dart DP1015, RL51DOU, seen operating route 117. *Terry Longhurst*

### DLD161-197

| | | | | | | | | | | Dennis Dart SLF 10.1m | | Plaxton Pointer 2 | | N27D* | | 2001 | | *seating varies |
|---|---|---|---|---|---|---|---|---|

| 161 | KC | Y661NLO | 171 | KC | Y671NLO | 180 | KC | Y158NLK | 189 | PB | Y249NLK |
|---|---|---|---|---|---|---|---|---|---|---|---|
| 162 | KC | Y662NLO | 172 | KC | Y672NLO | 181 | PV | Y659NLO | 190 | PB | Y154NLK |
| 163 | KC | Y663NLO | 173 | KC | Y673NLO | 182 | PV | Y652NLO | 191 | PB | Y261NLK |
| 164 | KC | Y664NLO | 174 | KC | Y674NLO | 183 | PV | Y653NLO | 192 | PB | Y262NLK |
| 165 | KC | Y665NLO | 175 | KC | Y675NLO | 184 | PV | Y654NLO | 193 | PB | Y263NLK |
| 166 | KC | Y161NLK | 176 | KC | Y153NLK | 185 | PV | Y658NLO | 194 | PB | Y264NLK |
| 167 | KC | Y667NLO | 177 | KC | Y237NLK | 186 | PB | Y656NLO | 195 | PB | Y265NLK |
| 168 | KC | Y668NLO | 178 | KC | Y238NLK | 187 | PB | Y657NLO | 196 | PB | Y159NLK |
| 169 | KC | Y669NLO | 179 | KC | Y239NLK | 188 | PB | Y248NLK | 197 | PB | Y157NLK |
| 170 | KC | Y152NLK | | | | | | | | | |

### DLD198-207

| | | | | | | | | | | Dennis Dart SLF 10.1m | | Plaxton Pointer 2 | | N30D* | | 2002 | | *seating varies |
|---|---|---|---|---|---|---|---|---|

| 198 | PVt | LN51KXD | 201 | PVt | LN51KXG | 204 | PVt | LN51KXK | 206 | PVt | LN51KXM |
|---|---|---|---|---|---|---|---|---|---|---|---|
| 199 | w | LN51KXE | 202 | PVt | LN51KXH | 205 | PVt | LN51KXL | 207 | w | LN51KXO |
| 200 | PVt | LN51KXF | 203 | PVt | LN51KXJ | | | | | | |

### DSD208-217

| | | | | | | | | | | TransBus Dart 9.3m | | TransBus Pointer | | N24D | | 2002 | |
|---|---|---|---|---|---|---|---|---|

| 208 | PB | LR02BDV | 211 | PB | LR02BDZ | 214 | PB | LR02BEU | 216 | PB | LR02BFA |
|---|---|---|---|---|---|---|---|---|---|---|---|
| 209 | PB | LR02BDX | 212 | PB | LR02BEJ | 215 | PB | LR02BEY | 217 | PB | LR02BFE |
| 210 | PB | LR02BDY | 213 | PB | LR02BEO | | | | | | |

### DP1001-1016

| | | | | | | | | | | Dennis Dart SLF 10.1m | | Plaxton Pointer 2 | | N27D | | 2001-02 | |
|---|---|---|---|---|---|---|---|---|

| 1001 | AH | RX51FNP | 1005 | AH | RX51FNW | 1009 | AH | RL51DOA | 1013 | AH | RL51DNY |
|---|---|---|---|---|---|---|---|---|---|---|---|
| 1002 | AH | RX51FNS | 1006 | AH | RX51FNV | 1010 | AH | RL51DNX | 1014 | AH | RL51DNV |
| 1003 | AH | RX51FNT | 1007 | AH | RX51FNU | 1011 | AH | RL51DOJ | 1015 | AH | RL51DOU |
| 1004 | AH | Y63LTF | 1008 | AH | RX51FNY | 1012 | AH | RL51DOH | 1016 | AH | RL51DNU |

| DP1049 | AH | KX54NJO | ADL Dart 10.1m | | | ADL Pointer | | N27D | 2004 | |
|---|---|---|---|---|---|---|---|---|---|---|

**Former Routemaster index marks continue to be allocated to the current fleet. Seen heading for London Bridge is Dennis Trident TP2, now with carrying WLT826.** *Terry Longhurst*

### TP1-65

| | | | | | | | | | | | | |
|---|---|---|---|---|---|---|---|---|---|---|---|---|
| | | | | | Dennis Trident 9.9m | | Plaxton President 4.4m | | N41/21D* | 1999 | *seating varies | |
| 1 | HT | T101KLD | 18 | HT | T118KLD | 34 | HT | T134CLO | 50 | HT | V750HBY | | |
| 2 | HT | WLT826 | 19 | HT | T119KLD | 35 | HT | T135CLO | 51 | HT | V751HBY | | |
| 3 | HT | T103KLD | 20 | HT | T120KLD | 36 | HT | T136CLO | 52 | HT | V752HBY | | |
| 4 | HT | T104KLD | 21 | HT | T71KLD | 37 | HT | T137CLO | 53 | HT | V753HBY | | |
| 5 | HT | T105KLD | 22 | HT | T122KLD | 38 | HT | T138CLO | 54 | HT | V754HBY | | |
| 6 | HT | T106KLD | 23 | HT | T73KLD | 39 | HT | T139CLO | 55 | HT | V755HBY | | |
| 7 | HT | T107KLD | 24 | HT | T124KLD | 40 | HT | T140CLO | 56 | HT | V756HBY | | |
| 8 | HT | T108KLD | 25 | HT | T125KLD | 41 | HT | T141CLO | 57 | HT | V757HBY | | |
| 9 | HT | T109KLD | 26 | HT | T126KLD | 42 | HT | T142CLO | 58 | HT | V758HBY | | |
| 10 | HT | T110KLD | 27 | HT | T127KLD | 43 | HT | T143CLO | 59 | HT | V759HBY | | |
| 11 | HT | T81KLD | 28 | HT | T128KLD | 44 | HT | T144CLO | 60 | HT | V760HBY | | |
| 12 | HT | T112KLD | 29 | HT | T129KLD | 45 | HT | T145CLO | 61 | HT | V761HBY | | |
| 13 | HT | T113KLD | 30 | HT | T97KLD | 46 | HT | T146CLO | 62 | HT | V762HBY | | |
| 14 | HT | T114KLD | 31 | HT | T98KLD | 47 | HT | V307GLB | 63 | HT | V763HBY | | |
| 15 | HT | T115KLD | 32 | HT | T132CLO | 48 | HT | T148CLO | 64 | HT | V764HBY | | |
| 16 | HT | T116KLD | 33 | HT | T133CLO | 49 | HT | V749HBY | 65 | HT | V765HBY | | |
| 17 | HT | T117KLD | | | | | | | | | | | |

### TA67-114

| | | | | | | | | | | | | |
|---|---|---|---|---|---|---|---|---|---|---|---|---|
| | | | | | Dennis Trident 9.9m | | Alexander ALX400 4.4m | | N45/18D | 1999 | | |
| 67 | W | T67KLD | 73 | W | T43KLD | 91 | w | T191CLO | 102 | w | T202CLO | | |
| 68 | W | T68KLD | 74 | W | T74KLD | 92 | w | T192CLO | 105 | w | T205CLO | | |
| 69 | W | T69KLD | 76 | W | T76KLD | 93 | w | T193CLO | 108 | w | T208CLO | | |
| 70 | u | T37KLD | 78 | W | T78KLD | 99 | W | T199CLO | 109 | w | T209CLO | | |
| 71 | W | T41KLD | 79 | W | T79KLD | 100 | W | T218CLO | 114 | W | V314GLB | | |
| 72 | W | T72KLD | 82 | W | T182CLO | | | | | | | | |

### TAL118-134

| | | | | | | | | | | | | |
|---|---|---|---|---|---|---|---|---|---|---|---|---|
| | | | | | Dennis Trident 10.5m | | Alexander ALX400 4.4m | | N45/23D | 2000 | | |
| 118 | W | X341HLL | 123 | W | X343HLL | 127 | W | X327HLL | 131 | W | X331HLL | | |
| 119 | W | X319HLL | 124 | W | X324HLL | 128 | W | X338HLL | 132 | W | X332HLL | | |
| 120 | W | X336HLL | 125 | W | X335HLL | 129 | W | X329HLL | 133 | W | X339HLL | | |
| 121 | W | X337HLL | 126 | W | X326HLL | 130 | W | X342HLL | 134 | W | X334HLL | | |
| 122 | W | X322HLL | | | | | | | | | | | |

## VPL135-161

Volvo B7TL 10.6m    Plaxton President 4.4m    N43/23D    2000-01

| | | | | | | | | | | | |
|---|---|---|---|---|---|---|---|---|---|---|---|
| 135 | HT | X635LLX | 142 | HT | X642LLX | 149 | EW | X649LLX | 156 | EW | X656LLX |
| 136 | HT | X636LLX | 143 | HT | X643LLX | 150 | EW | X663LLX | 157 | EW | X657LLX |
| 137 | HT | X637LLX | 144 | HT | X644LLX | 151 | EW | X651LLX | 158 | EW | X658LLX |
| 138 | HT | X638LLX | 145 | HT | X645LLX | 152 | EW | X652LLX | 159 | EW | X659LLX |
| 139 | HT | X639LLX | 146 | EW | X646LLX | 153 | EW | X653LLX | 160 | EW | X662LLX |
| 140 | HT | X664LLX | 147 | EW | X647LLX | 154 | EW | X654LLX | 161 | EW | X661LLX |
| 141 | HT | X641LLX | 148 | EW | X648LLX | 155 | EW | X665LLX | | | |

## VPL162-236

Volvo B7TL 10.6m    Plaxton President 4.4m    N43/23D    2001

| | | | | | | | | | | | |
|---|---|---|---|---|---|---|---|---|---|---|---|
| 162 | EW | Y162NLK | 181 | AC | Y181NLK | 200 | EW | Y149NLK | 219 | EW | LK51XGO |
| 163 | EW | Y163NLK | 182 | AC | Y182NLK | 201 | EW | Y201NLK | 220 | EW | LK51XGP |
| 164 | EW | Y164NLK | 183 | AC | Y183NLK | 202 | EW | Y202NLK | 221 | EW | LK51XGR |
| 165 | EW | Y165NLK | 184 | AC | Y184NLK | 203 | EW | Y203NLK | 222 | HT | LK51XGS |
| 166 | EW | Y166NLK | 185 | AC | Y185NLK | 204 | EW | Y204NLK | 223 | HT | LK51XGT |
| 167 | EW | Y167NLK | 186 | AC | Y186NLK | 205 | EW | LK51XGD | 224 | HT | LK51XGU |
| 168 | AC | Y168NLK | 187 | AC | Y187NLK | 206 | EW | Y246NLK | 225 | HT | LK51XGV |
| 169 | AC | Y169NLK | 188 | AC | Y188NLK | 207 | HD | Y207NLK | 226 | HT | LK51XGW |
| 170 | AC | Y196NLK | 189 | AC | Y189NLK | 208 | HD | Y208NLK | 227 | HT | LK51XGX |
| 171 | AC | Y171NLK | 190 | AC | Y198NLK | 209 | AC | Y209NLK | 228 | HT | LK51XGY |
| 172 | AC | Y172NLK | 191 | AC | Y191NLK | 210 | EW | Y143NLK | 229 | HT | LK51XGZ |
| 173 | AC | Y173NLK | 192 | AC | Y192NLK | 211 | EW | LK51XGE | 230 | HT | LK51XHA |
| 174 | EW | Y174NLK | 193 | AC | Y193NLK | 213 | EW | LK51XGG | 231 | HT | LK51XHB |
| 175 | AC | Y195NLK | 194 | AC | Y194NLK | 214 | EW | LK51XGH | 232 | HT | Y232NLK |
| 176 | AC | Y176NLK | 195 | AC | Y144NLK | 215 | EW | LK51XGJ | 233 | HT | Y233NLK |
| 177 | AC | Y177NLK | 196 | AC | Y146NLK | 216 | EW | LK51XGL | 234 | HT | Y234NLK |
| 178 | AC | Y178NLK | 197 | AC | Y147NLK | 217 | EW | LK51XGM | 235 | HT | Y235NLK |
| 179 | AC | Y179NLK | 198 | EW | Y148NLK | 218 | EW | LK51XGN | 236 | HT | Y236NLK |
| 180 | AC | Y197NLK | 199 | EW | Y199NLK | | | | | | |

## TPL237-296

Dennis Trident 10.6m    Plaxton President 4.4m    N43/23D    2002

| | | | | | | | | | | | |
|---|---|---|---|---|---|---|---|---|---|---|---|
| 237 | HD | LN51KXP | 252 | PB | LN51KYH | 267 | HT | LN51KZB | 282 | PB | LR02BBX |
| 238 | HD | LN51KXR | 253 | PB | LN51KYJ | 268 | u | LN51KZC | 283 | PB | LR02BBZ |
| 239 | HD | LN51KXS | 254 | PB | LN51KYK | 269 | HT | LN51KZD | 284 | PB | LR02BCE |
| 240 | PB | LN51KXT | 255 | HT | LN51KYO | 270 | HT | LR02BAA | 285 | PB | LR02BCF |
| 241 | W | LN51KXU | 256 | HT | LN51KYP | 271 | W | LR02BAO | 286 | PB | LR02BCK |
| 242 | HT | LN51KXV | 257 | HT | LN51KYR | 272 | HT | LR02BAU | 287 | PB | LR02BCO |
| 243 | HT | LN51KXW | 258 | HT | LN51KYS | 273 | W | LR02BAV | 288 | PB | LR02BCU |
| 244 | HT | LN51KXY | 259 | u | LN51KYT | 274 | W | LR02BBE | 289 | PB | LR02BCV |
| 245 | HT | LN51KXZ | 260 | HT | LN51KYU | 275 | W | LR02BBF | 290 | PB | LR02BCX |
| 246 | HT | LN51KYA | 261 | W | LN51KYV | 276 | PB | LR02BBJ | 291 | PB | LR02BCY |
| 247 | PB | LN51KYB | 262 | W | LN51KYW | 277 | PB | LR02BBK | 292 | PB | LR02BCZ |
| 248 | PB | LN51KYC | 263 | HT | LN51KYX | 278 | PB | LR02BBN | 293 | PB | LR02BDE |
| 249 | PB | LN51KYE | 264 | HT | LN51KYY | 279 | PB | LR02BBO | 294 | PB | LR02BDF |
| 250 | PB | LN51KYF | 265 | HT | LN51KYZ | 280 | PB | LR02BBU | 295 | PB | LR02BDO |
| 251 | PB | LN51KYG | 266 | W | LN51KZA | 281 | PB | LR02BBV | 296 | PB | LR02BDU |

## VP317-347

Volvo B7TL 10m    Plaxton President 4.4m    N39/20D    2002

| | | | | | | | | | | | |
|---|---|---|---|---|---|---|---|---|---|---|---|
| 317 | HD | LR52BLK | 325 | HD | LR52BMY | 333 | HD | LR52BNK | 341 | HD | LR52BNZ |
| 318 | HD | LR52BLN | 326 | HD | LR52BMZ | 334 | HD | LR52BNL | 342 | HD | LR52BOF |
| 319 | HD | LR52BLV | 327 | HD | LR52BNA | 335 | HD | LR52BNN | 343 | HD | LR52BOH |
| 320 | HD | LR52BLX | 328 | HD | LR52BNB | 336 | HD | LR52BNO | 344 | HD | LR52BOJ |
| 321 | HD | LR52BLZ | 329 | HD | LR52BND | 337 | HD | LR52BNU | 345 | HD | LR52BOU |
| 322 | HD | LR52BMO | 330 | HD | LR52BNE | 338 | HD | LR52BNV | 346 | HD | LR52BOV |
| 323 | HD | LR52BMU | 331 | HD | LR52BNF | 339 | HD | LR52BNX | 347 | HD | LR52BPE |
| 324 | HD | LR52BMV | 332 | HD | LR52BNJ | 340 | HD | LR52BNY | | | |

## TP403-428

TransBus Trident 9.9m    TransBus President 4.4m    N39/20D*    2003    *seating varies

| | | | | | | | | | | | |
|---|---|---|---|---|---|---|---|---|---|---|---|
| 403 | HT | LK03CEJ | 410 | HT | LK03CDD | 417 | HT | LK03CDN | 423 | HT | LK03CDZ |
| 404 | HT | LK03CEN | 411 | AH | LK03CDE | 418 | HT | LK03CDP | 424 | HT | LK03CGE |
| 405 | HT | LK03CEU | 412 | AH | LK03CDF | 419 | HT | LK03CDU | 425 | HT | LK03CGF |
| 406 | HT | LK03CEV | 413 | AH | LK03CDG | 420 | HT | LK03CDV | 426 | HD | LK03CGG |
| 407 | HT | LK03CEX | 414 | HT | LK03CDJ | 421 | HT | LK03CDX | 427 | HD | LK03CGU |
| 408 | HT | LK03CEY | 415 | HT | LK03CDL | 422 | HT | LK03CDY | 428 | HD | LK03CGV |
| 409 | HT | LK03CDA | 416 | HT | LK03CDM | | | | | | |

The Wigan-built Plaxton President dominated the early low-floor purchases for Metroline with the product being assembled on both Dennis Trident and Volvo B7TL chassis. Seen operating route 6 is Volvo VP510, LK53LYF, which now carries the latest all-red livery. *Terry Longhurst*

### TP429-465

TransBus Trident 9.9m          TransBus President 4.4m          N39/20D          2003

| 429 | HD | LK03GFU | 439 | PB | LK03GGV | 448 | PB | LK03GHH | 457 | PB | LK03GJG |
|-----|----|---------|-----|----|---------|-----|----|---------|-----|----|---------|
| 430 | HD | LK03GFV | 440 | PB | LK03GGX | 449 | PB | LK03GHJ | 458 | PB | LK03GJU |
| 431 | HD | LK03GFX | 441 | PB | LK03GGY | 450 | PB | LK03GHN | 459 | PB | LK03GJV |
| 432 | HT | LK03GFY | 442 | PB | LK03GGZ | 451 | PB | LK03GHU | 460 | PB | LK03GJX |
| 433 | u  | LK03GFZ | 443 | PB | LK03GHA | 452 | PB | LK03GHV | 461 | PB | LK03GJY |
| 434 | HT | LK03GGA | 444 | PB | LK03GHB | 453 | PB | LK03GHX | 462 | PB | LK03GJZ |
| 435 | PB | LK03GGF | 445 | PB | LK03GHD | 454 | PB | LK03GHY | 463 | PB | LK03GKA |
| 436 | PB | LK03GGJ | 446 | PB | LK03GHF | 455 | PB | LK03GHZ | 464 | PB | LK03GKC |
| 437 | PB | LK03GGP | 447 | PB | LK03GHG | 456 | PB | LK03GJF | 465 | PB | LK03GKD |
| 438 | PB | LK03GGU |     |    |         |     |    |         |     |    |         |

### VP466-511

Volvo B7TL 10m          TransBus President 4.4m          N39/20D          2003

| 466 | HD | LK03GKE | 478 | AC | LK03GLF | 490 | AC | LK03GMZ | 501 | AC | LK53LXU |
|-----|----|---------|-----|----|---------|-----|----|---------|-----|----|---------|
| 467 | HD | LK03GKF | 479 | AC | LK03GLJ | 491 | AC | LK03GNF | 502 | AC | LK53LXV |
| 468 | HD | LK03GKG | 480 | AC | LK03GLV | 492 | AC | LK03GNJ | 503 | AC | LK53LXW |
| 469 | HD | LK03GKJ | 481 | AC | LK03GLY | 493 | AC | LK03GNN | 504 | AC | LK53LXX |
| 470 | AC | LK03GKL | 482 | AC | LK03GLZ | 494 | AC | LK03GNP | 505 | AC | LK53LXY |
| 471 | AC | LK03GKN | 483 | AC | LK03GME | 495 | AC | LK53LXM | 506 | AC | LK53LXZ |
| 472 | AC | LK03GKP | 484 | AC | LK03GMF | 496 | AC | LK53LXN | 507 | AC | LK53LYA |
| 473 | AC | LK03GKU | 485 | HD | LK03GMG | 497 | AC | LK53LXO | 508 | AC | LK53LYC |
| 474 | AC | LK03GKV | 486 | HD | LK03GMU | 498 | AC | LK53LXP | 509 | AC | LK53LYD |
| 475 | AC | LK03GKX | 487 | HD | LK03GMV | 499 | AC | LK53LXR | 510 | AC | LK53LYF |
| 476 | AC | LK03GKY | 488 | HD | LK03GMX | 500 | AC | LK53LXT | 511 | AC | LK53LYG |
| 477 | AC | LK03GKZ | 489 | AC | LK03GMY |     |    |         |     |    |         |

2007 saw the arrival of twenty-six Scania OmniDekka N230 UDs with the latest East Lancs Olympus bodywork. Unlike the earlier OmniDekka buses they do not feature the Scania front. SEL745, LK07BAU, is seen at Marble Arch while working route 7. *Richard Godfrey*

## VP512-580

Volvo B7TL 10m TransBus President 4.4m N39/20D 2004

| | | | | | | | | | | | | |
|---|---|---|---|---|---|---|---|---|---|---|---|
| 512 | AC | LK04CPY | 530 | AC | LK04CTZ | 547 | AC | LK04CVH | 564 | AC | LK04EKY |
| 513 | AC | LK04CPZ | 531 | AC | LK04CUA | 548 | AC | LK04CVJ | 565 | AC | LK04EKZ |
| 514 | AC | LK04CRF | 532 | AC | LK04CUC | 549 | AC | LK04CVL | 566 | AC | LK04ELC |
| 515 | AC | LK04CRJ | 533 | AC | LK04CUG | 550 | AC | LK04CVM | 567 | AC | LK04ELH |
| 516 | AC | LK04CRU | 534 | AC | LK04CUH | 551 | AC | LK04CVN | 568 | AC | LK04ELJ |
| 517 | AC | LK04CRV | 535 | AC | LK04CUJ | 552 | AC | LK04CVP | 569 | AC | LK04ELU |
| 518 | AC | LK04CRZ | 536 | AC | LK04CUU | 553 | AC | LK04CVR | 570 | AC | LK04ELV |
| 519 | AC | LK04CSF | 537 | AC | LK04CUW | 554 | AC | LK04CVS | 571 | AC | LK04ELW |
| 520 | AC | LK04CSU | 538 | AC | LK04CUX | 555 | AC | LK04CVT | 572 | AC | LK04ELX |
| 521 | AC | LK04CSX | 539 | AC | LK04CUY | 556 | AC | LK04CVU | 573 | AC | LK04EMF |
| 522 | AC | LK04CSY | 540 | AC | LK04CVA | 557 | AC | LK04CVV | 574 | AC | LK04EMJ |
| 523 | AC | LK04CSY | 541 | AC | LK04CVB | 558 | AC | LK04CVW | 575 | AC | LK04EMV |
| 524 | AC | LK04CSZ | 542 | AC | LK04CVC | 559 | AC | LK04CVX | 576 | AC | LK04EMX |
| 525 | AC | LK04CTE | 543 | AC | LK04CVD | 560 | AC | LK04EKU | 577 | AC | LK04ENE |
| 526 | AC | LK04CTF | 544 | AC | LK04CVE | 561 | AC | LK04EKV | 578 | AC | LK04ENF |
| 527 | AC | LK04CTU | 545 | AC | LK04CVF | 562 | AC | LK04EKW | 579 | AC | LK04ENH |
| 528 | AC | LK04CTV | 546 | AC | LK04CVG | 563 | AC | LK04EKX | 580 | AC | LK04ENJ |
| 529 | AC | LK04CTX | | | | | | | | | |

## VPL581-603

Volvo B7TL 10.6m TransBus President 4.4m N43/23D 2004

| | | | | | | | | | | | | |
|---|---|---|---|---|---|---|---|---|---|---|---|
| 581 | HT | LK04NLZ | 587 | HT | LK04NMU | 593 | HT | LK04NNB | 599 | HT | LK04NNH |
| 582 | HT | LK04NMA | 588 | HT | LK04NMV | 594 | HT | LK04NNC | 600 | HT | LK04NNJ |
| 583 | HT | LK04NME | 589 | HT | LK04NMX | 595 | HT | LK04NND | 601 | HT | LK04NNL |
| 584 | HT | LK04NMF | 590 | HT | LK04NMY | 596 | HT | LK04NNE | 602 | HT | LK04NNM |
| 585 | HT | LK04NMJ | 591 | HT | LK04NMZ | 597 | HT | LK04NNF | 603 | HT | LK04NNP |
| 586 | HT | LK04NMM | 592 | HT | LK04NNA | 598 | HT | LK04NNG | | | |

## VP604-628

Volvo B7TL 10m     TransBus President 4.4m     N39/20D     2004

| 604 | HD | LK04UWJ | 611 | HD | LK04UWT | 617 | HD | LK04UWZ | 623 | HD | LK04UXF |
|---|---|---|---|---|---|---|---|---|---|---|---|
| 605 | HD | LK04UWL | 612 | HD | LK04UWU | 618 | HD | LK04UXA | 624 | HD | LK04UXG |
| 606 | HD | LK04UWM | 613 | HD | LK04UWV | 619 | HD | LK04UXB | 625 | HD | LK04UXH |
| 607 | HD | LK04UWN | 614 | HD | LK04UWW | 620 | HD | LK04UXC | 626 | HD | LK54FWE |
| 608 | HD | LK04UWP | 615 | HD | LK04UWX | 621 | HD | LK04UXD | 627 | HD | LK54FWF |
| 609 | HD | LK04UWR | 616 | HD | LK04UWY | 622 | HD | LK04UXE | 628 | HD | LK54FWG |
| 610 | HD | LK04UWS | | | | | | | | | |

## VP629-637

Volvo B7TL 10.6m     ADL President 4.4m     N43/23D     2005

| 629 | HT | LK54FWH | 632 | HT | LK54FWM | 634 | HT | LK54FWO | 636 | HT | LK54FWR |
|---|---|---|---|---|---|---|---|---|---|---|---|
| 630 | HT | LK54FWJ | 633 | HT | LK54FWN | 635 | HT | LK54FWP | 637 | HT | LK54FWT |
| 631 | HT | LK54FWL | | | | | | | | | |

## TA638-659

ADL Trident 9.9m     ADL ALX400 4.4m     N41/19D     2005

| 638 | W | LK05GFO | 644 | W | LK05GGE | 650 | W | LK05GGV | 655 | W | LK05GHB |
|---|---|---|---|---|---|---|---|---|---|---|---|
| 639 | W | LK05GFV | 645 | W | LK05GGF | 651 | W | LK05GGX | 656 | W | LK05GHD |
| 640 | W | LK05GFX | 646 | W | LK05GGJ | 652 | W | LK05GGY | 657 | W | LK05GHF |
| 641 | W | LK05GFY | 647 | W | LK05GGO | 653 | W | LK05GGZ | 658 | W | LK05GHG |
| 642 | W | LK05GFZ | 648 | W | LK05GGP | 654 | W | LK05GHA | 659 | W | LK05GHH |
| 643 | W | LK05GGA | 649 | W | LK05GGU | | | | | | |

## TE665-692

ADL Trident 2 10.1m     ADL Enviro 400 4.4m     N41/26D     2005-06

| 665 | HT | LK55KJV | 672 | HT | LK55KKD | 679 | HT | LK55KKM | 686 | HT | LK55KKV |
|---|---|---|---|---|---|---|---|---|---|---|---|
| 666 | HT | LK55KJX | 673 | HT | LK55KKE | 680 | HT | LK55KKO | 687 | HT | LK06FLA |
| 667 | HT | LK55KJY | 674 | HT | LK55KKF | 681 | HT | LK55KKP | 688 | HT | LK55KKY |
| 668 | HT | LK55KJZ | 675 | HT | LK55KKG | 682 | HT | LK55KKR | 689 | HT | LK55KKZ |
| 669 | HT | LK55KKA | 676 | HT | LK55KKH | 683 | HT | LK55KKS | 690 | HT | LK55KLA |
| 670 | HT | LK55KKB | 677 | HT | LK55KKJ | 684 | HT | LK55KKT | 691 | HT | LK06FLB |
| 671 | HT | LK55KKC | 678 | HT | LK55KKL | 685 | HT | LK55KKU | 692 | HT | LK06FLC |

## DLD693-711

ADL Dart 10.1m     ADL Pointer     N28D     2005-06

| 693 | KC | LK55KLE | 698 | KC | LK55KLO | 703 | KC | LK55KLX | 708 | KC | LK55KMG |
|---|---|---|---|---|---|---|---|---|---|---|---|
| 694 | KC | LK55KLF | 699 | KC | LK55KLP | 704 | KC | LK55KLZ | 709 | KC | LK55KMJ |
| 695 | KC | LK55KLJ | 700 | KC | LK55KLS | 705 | KC | LK55KMA | 710 | KC | LK55KMM |
| 696 | KC | LK55KLL | 701 | KC | LK55KLU | 706 | KC | LK55KME | 711 | KC | LK55KMO |
| 697 | KC | LK55KLM | 702 | KC | LK55KLV | 707 | KC | LK55KMF | | | |

## TE712-723

ADL Trident 2 10.1m     ADL Enviro 400 4.4m     N41/26D     2006

| 712 | EW | LK56FHE | 715 | EW | LK56FHH | 718 | EW | LK56FHN | 721 | EW | LK56FHR |
|---|---|---|---|---|---|---|---|---|---|---|---|
| 713 | EW | LK56FHF | 716 | EW | LK56FHJ | 719 | EW | LK56FHO | 722 | EW | LK56FHS |
| 714 | EW | LK56FHG | 717 | EW | LK56FHM | 720 | EW | LK56FHP | 723 | EW | LK56FHT |

## TE724-738

ADL Trident 2 10.1m     ADL Enviro 400 4.4m     N41/26D     2007

| 724 | EW | LK07AYZ | 728 | EW | LK07AZD | 732 | EW | LK07AZL | 736 | EW | LK07AZR |
|---|---|---|---|---|---|---|---|---|---|---|---|
| 725 | EW | LK07AZA | 729 | EW | LK07AZF | 733 | EW | LK07AZN | 737 | EW | LK07AZT |
| 726 | EW | LK07AZB | 730 | EW | LK07AZG | 734 | EW | LK07AZO | 738 | EW | LK07AZU |
| 727 | EW | LK07AZC | 731 | EW | LK07AZJ | 735 | EW | LK07AZP | | | |

## SEL739-764

Scania OmniDekka N230 UD     East Lancs Olympus     N45/23D     2007

| 739 | PV | LK07AZV | 746 | PV | LK07BBE | 753 | PV | LK07BBX | 759 | PV | LK07BCV |
|---|---|---|---|---|---|---|---|---|---|---|---|
| 740 | PV | LK07AZW | 747 | PV | LK07BBF | 754 | PV | LK07BBZ | 760 | PV | LK07BCX |
| 741 | PV | LK07AZX | 748 | PV | LK07BBJ | 755 | PV | LK07BCE | 761 | PV | LK07BCY |
| 742 | PV | LK07AZZ | 749 | PV | LK07BBN | 756 | PV | LK07BCF | 762 | PV | LK07BCZ |
| 743 | PV | LK07BAA | 750 | PV | LK07BBO | 757 | PV | LK07BCO | 763 | PV | LK07BDE |
| 744 | PV | LK07BAO | 751 | PV | LK07BBU | 758 | PV | LK07BCU | 764 | PV | LK57KAU |
| 745 | PV | LK07BAU | 752 | PV | LK07BBV | | | | | | |

## MM771-790

MAN 12.240 10.4m     MCV Evolution     N26D     2007

| 771 | PV | LK07ELH | 776 | PV | LK07AYG | 781 | PV | LK07AYN | 786 | PV | LK57EHW |
|---|---|---|---|---|---|---|---|---|---|---|---|
| 772 | PV | LK07AYC | 777 | PV | LK07AYH | 782 | PV | LK57EHS | 787 | PV | LK57EJA |
| 773 | PV | LK07AYD | 778 | PV | LK07AYJ | 783 | PV | LK57EHT | 788 | PV | LK57EHX |
| 774 | PV | LK07AYE | 779 | PV | LK07AYL | 784 | PV | LK57EHU | 789 | PV | LK57EHY |
| 775 | PV | LK07AYF | 780 | PV | LK07AYM | 785 | PV | LK57EHV | 790 | PV | LK57EHZ |

Two batches of MCV Evolution-bodied MAN single-deck buses joined Metroline in 2007. All are allocated to Alperton Lane depot in Perivale Park. From the second batch, MM824, LK57AYV, is seen in Harlington High Street in March 2011. *Richard Godfrey*

### DES791-802

ADL Dart 4 8.9m | ADL Enviro 200 | N26F | 2007

| | | | | | | | | | | | |
|---|---|---|---|---|---|---|---|---|---|---|---|
| 791 | PB | LK07BDO | 794 | PB | LK07BDX | 797 | PB | LK07BEJ | 800 | PB | LK07BEY |
| 792 | PB | LK07BDU | 795 | PB | LK07BDY | 798 | PB | LK07BEO | 801 | PB | LK07ELJ |
| 793 | PB | LK07BDV | 796 | PB | LK07BDZ | 799 | PB | LK07BEU | 802 | PB | LK07ELO |

### SEL803-809

Scania N230 UD 10.8m | East Lancs Olympus | N45/23D | 2007-08

| | | | | | | | | | | | |
|---|---|---|---|---|---|---|---|---|---|---|---|
| 803 | PV | LK57KAX | 805 | PA | LK57KBF | 807 | PA | LK57KBN | 809 | PA | LK08DVY |
| 804 | PA | LK57KBE | 806 | PA | LK57KBJ | 808 | PA | LK57KBO | | | |

### MM810-827

MAN 12.240 10.4m | MCV Evolution | N26D | 2007

| | | | | | | | | | | | |
|---|---|---|---|---|---|---|---|---|---|---|---|
| 810 | PV | LK57AYD | 815 | PV | LK57AYJ | 820 | PV | LK57AYP | 824 | PV | LK57AYV |
| 811 | PV | LK57AYE | 816 | PV | LK57AYL | 821 | PV | LK57AYS | 825 | PV | LK57AYW |
| 812 | PV | LK57AYF | 817 | PV | LK57AYM | 822 | PV | LK57AYT | 826 | PV | LK57AYX |
| 813 | PV | LK57AYG | 818 | PV | LK57AYN | 823 | PV | LK57AYU | 827 | PV | LK57AYY |
| 814 | PV | LK57AYH | 819 | PV | LK57AYO | | | | | | |

### TE828-847

ADL Trident 2 10.1m | ADL Enviro 400 4.4m | N41/26D | 2007

| | | | | | | | | | | | |
|---|---|---|---|---|---|---|---|---|---|---|---|
| 828 | EW | LK57AXF | 833 | W | LK57AXN | 838 | W | LK57AXT | 843 | EW | LK57AXY |
| 829 | W | LK57AXG | 834 | W | LK57AXO | 839 | W | LK57AXU | 844 | EW | LK57AXZ |
| 830 | W | LK57AXH | 835 | W | LK57AXP | 840 | EW | LK57AXV | 845 | EW | LK57AYA |
| 831 | W | LK57AXJ | 836 | W | LK57AXR | 841 | EW | LK57AXW | 846 | EW | LK57AYB |
| 832 | W | LK57AXM | 837 | W | LK57AXS | 842 | EW | LK57AXX | 847 | EW | LK57AYC |

### DEL848-858

ADL Dart 4 10.8m | ADL Enviro 200 | N37F | 2008

| | | | | | | | | | | | |
|---|---|---|---|---|---|---|---|---|---|---|---|
| 848 | PB | LK08DVZ | 851 | PB | LK08DWD | 854 | PB | LK08DWG | 857 | PB | LK08DWM |
| 849 | PB | LK08DWA | 852 | PB | LK08DWE | 855 | PB | LK08DWJ | 858 | PB | LK08DWN |
| 850 | PB | LK08DWC | 853 | PB | LK08DWF | 856 | PB | LK08DWL | | | |

### DEL859-877

ADL Dart 4 10.2m | ADL Enviro 200 | N29D | 2008

| | | | | | | | | | | | |
|---|---|---|---|---|---|---|---|---|---|---|---|
| 859 | PA | LK08DWO | 864 | PA | LK08DWX | 869 | PA | LK08DXC | 874 | PA | LK08DXH |
| 860 | PA | LK08DWP | 865 | PA | LK08DWY | 870 | PA | LK08DXD | 875 | PA | LK58CMZ |
| 861 | PA | LK08DWU | 866 | PA | LK08DWZ | 871 | PA | LK08DXE | 876 | PA | LK58CNA |
| 862 | W | LK08DWV | 867 | PA | LK08DXA | 872 | PA | LK08DXF | 877 | PA | LK58CNC |
| 863 | PA | LK08DWW | 868 | PA | LK08DXB | 873 | PA | LK08DXG | | | |

The 2008 deliveries for Metroline were all supplied by Alexander Dennis. The first of of the 2008 batch of five Enviro 400 Hybrid buses, TEH915, SN08AAO, is seen at Hyde Park Corner while operating route 16.
*Dave Heath*

### TE878-914

ADL Trident 2 10.1m — ADL Enviro 400 4.4m — N41/26D — 2008

| No. | Dep | Reg | No. | Dep | Reg | No. | Dep | Reg | No. | Dep | Reg |
|---|---|---|---|---|---|---|---|---|---|---|---|
| 878 | W | LK08DXO | 888 | W | LK08DZA | 897 | PA | LK08NVN | 906 | PA | LK58CNX |
| 879 | W | LK08DXP | 889 | W | LK08NVD | 898 | PA | LK08NVO | 907 | PA | LK58CNY |
| 880 | W | LK08DXR | 890 | W | LK08NVE | 899 | PA | LK08NVP | 908 | PA | LK58CNZ |
| 881 | W | LK08DXS | 891 | W | LK08NVF | 900 | PA | LK58CNE | 909 | HT | LK58COA |
| 882 | W | LK08DXU | 892 | W | LK08NVG | 901 | PA | LK58CNF | 910 | HT | LK58COH |
| 883 | W | LK08DXV | 893 | W | LK08NVH | 902 | PA | LK58CNN | 911 | HT | LK58COJ |
| 884 | W | LK08DXW | 894 | W | LK08NVJ | 903 | PA | LK58CNO | 912 | HT | LK58COU |
| 885 | W | LK08DXX | 895 | W | LK08NVL | 904 | PA | LK58CNU | 913 | HT | LK58CPE |
| 886 | W | LK08DXY | 896 | W | LK08NVM | 905 | PA | LK58CNV | 914 | HT | LK58CPF |
| 887 | W | LK08DXZ | | | | | | | | | |

### TEH915-919

ADL Trident E400H Hybrid — ADL Enviro 400 4.4m — N37/26D — 2008

| No. | Dep | Reg | No. | Dep | Reg | No. | Dep | Reg | No. | Dep | Reg |
|---|---|---|---|---|---|---|---|---|---|---|---|
| 915 | W | SN08AAO | 917 | W | LK58CPO | 918 | W | LK58CPU | 919 | W | LK58CPV |
| 916 | W | LK58CPN | | | | | | | | | |

### TE920-951

ADL Trident 2 10.1m — ADL Enviro 400 4.4m — N41/26D — 2009

| No. | Dep | Reg | No. | Dep | Reg | No. | Dep | Reg | No. | Dep | Reg |
|---|---|---|---|---|---|---|---|---|---|---|---|
| 920 | HT | LK58KFW | 928 | HT | LK58KGJ | 936 | PB | LK09EKR | 944 | PB | LK09EHU |
| 921 | HT | LK58KFX | 929 | HT | LK58KGN | 937 | PB | LK09EKT | 945 | PB | LK58KHL |
| 922 | HT | LK58KFY | 930 | HT | LK58KGO | 938 | PB | LK58KHC | 946 | PB | LK58KHM |
| 923 | HT | LK58KFZ | 931 | HT | LK09EKO | 939 | PB | LK58KHD | 947 | PB | LK58KHO |
| 924 | HT | LK58KGA | 932 | HT | LK58KGU | 940 | PB | LK58KHE | 948 | PB | LK58KHP |
| 925 | HT | LK58KGE | 933 | HT | LK58KGV | 941 | PB | LK58KHF | 949 | PB | LK58KHR |
| 926 | HT | LK58KGF | 934 | HT | LK58KGW | 942 | PB | LK58KHG | 950 | PB | LK58KHT |
| 927 | HT | LK58KGG | 935 | PB | LK09EKP | 943 | PB | LK58KHH | 951 | PB | LK58KHU |

### DE952-960

ADL Dart 4 10.2m — ADL Enviro 200 — N29D — 2008

| No. | Dep | Reg | No. | Dep | Reg | No. | Dep | Reg | No. | Dep | Reg |
|---|---|---|---|---|---|---|---|---|---|---|---|
| 952 | PA | LK58CSX | 955 | PA | LK58CTE | 957 | PA | LK58CTO | 959 | PA | LK58CTV |
| 953 | PA | LK58CSY | 956 | PA | LK58CTF | 958 | PA | LK58CTU | 960 | PA | LK58CTX |
| 954 | PA | LK58CSZ | | | | | | | | | |

In 2009, Metroline took delivery of five Optare Tempo X1060 Hybrids for use in the Brentford area. Representing the type here is OTH975, LK09EKH. *Mark Lyons*

### DM961-970

| | | ADL Dart 4 10.4m | | | MCV Evolution | | | N29D | | 2009 | |
|---|---|---|---|---|---|---|---|---|---|---|---|
| **961** | AH | LK58CRF | **964** | AH | LK58CRV | **967** | AH | LK58CSF | **969** | AH | LK58CSU |
| **962** | AH | LK09EKJ | **965** | AH | LK58CRX | **968** | AH | LK09EKM | **970** | AH | LK09EKN |
| **963** | AH | LK09EKL | **966** | AH | LK58CRZ | | | | | | |

### OTH971-975

| | | Optare Tempo X1060 Hybrid | | | Optare | | | N28D | | 2009 | |
|---|---|---|---|---|---|---|---|---|---|---|---|
| **971** | AH | LK58CTY | **973** | AH | LK58CUA | **974** | AH | LK09EKG | **975** | AH | LK09EKH |
| **972** | AH | LK58CTZ | | | | | | | | | |

### TE976-992

| | | ADL Trident 2 10.1m | | | ADL Enviro 400 | | | N41/26D | | 2009 | |
|---|---|---|---|---|---|---|---|---|---|---|---|
| **976** | W | LK09EKV | **981** | W | LK09ELC | **985** | W | LK09ELU | **989** | W | LK09EMF |
| **977** | W | LK09EKW | **982** | W | LK09ELH | **986** | W | LK09ELV | **990** | W | LK09EMJ |
| **978** | W | LK09EKX | **983** | W | LK09ELJ | **987** | W | LK09ELW | **991** | W | LK09EMV |
| **979** | W | LK09EKY | **984** | W | LK09ELO | **988** | W | LK09ELX | **992** | W | LK09EMX |
| **980** | W | LK09EKZ | | | | | | | | | |

### DE993-1014

| | | ADL Dart 4 10.2m | | | ADL Enviro 200 | | | N29D | | 2009 | |
|---|---|---|---|---|---|---|---|---|---|---|---|
| **993** | AH | LK09ENC | **999** | PA | LK09ENM | **1005** | W | LK09ENU | **1010** | W | LK09EOA |
| **994** | AH | LK09ENE | **1000** | PA | LK09ENN | **1006** | W | LK09ENV | **1011** | W | LK09EOB |
| **995** | AH | LK09ENF | **1001** | PA | LK09ENO | **1007** | W | LK09ENW | **1012** | W | LK09EOC |
| **996** | AH | LK09ENH | **1002** | PA | LK09ENP | **1008** | W | LK09ENX | **1013** | W | LK09EOD |
| **997** | AH | LK09ENJ | **1003** | PA | LK09ENR | **1009** | W | LK09ENY | **1014** | W | LK09EOE |
| **998** | AH | LK09ENL | **1004** | W | LK09ENT | | | | | | |

### DE1015-1033

| | | ADL Dart 4 10.2m | | | ADL Enviro 200 | | | N29D | | 2009 | |
|---|---|---|---|---|---|---|---|---|---|---|---|
| **1015** | W | LK59AUW | **1020** | W | LK59AVF | **1025** | W | LK59AVN | **1030** | W | LK59AVU |
| **1016** | W | LK59AUY | **1021** | W | LK59AVG | **1026** | W | LK59AVO | **1031** | W | LK59AVV |
| **1017** | W | LK59AVB | **1022** | W | LK59AVJ | **1027** | W | LK59AVP | **1032** | W | LK59AVW |
| **1018** | W | LK59AVC | **1023** | W | LK59AVL | **1028** | W | LK59AVR | **1033** | W | LK59AVX |
| **1019** | W | LK59AVD | **1024** | W | LK59AVM | **1029** | W | LK59AVT | | | |

**More recent arrivals are further batches of Enviro 400 buses. Seen arriving at Waterloo on route 139 is TE1094, LK60AHA.** *Dave Heath*

### VW1034-1072 — Volvo B9TL 10.4m — Wrightbus Eclipse Gemini 2 — N39/23D — 2010

| | | | | | | | | | | |
|---|---|---|---|---|---|---|---|---|---|---|
| 1034 | AH | LK59JJU | 1044 | AH | LK10BXN | 1054 | AH | LK10BXZ | 1064 | AH | LK60AEL |
| 1035 | AH | LK10BXC | 1045 | AH | LK10BXO | 1055 | AH | LK10BYA | 1065 | AH | LK60AEM |
| 1036 | AH | LK10BXD | 1046 | AH | LK10BXP | 1056 | AH | LK60AEA | 1066 | AH | LK60AEN |
| 1037 | AH | LK10BXE | 1047 | AH | LK10BXR | 1057 | AH | LK60AEB | 1067 | AH | LK60AEO |
| 1038 | AH | LK10BXF | 1048 | AH | LK10BXS | 1058 | AH | LK60AEC | 1068 | AH | LK60AEP |
| 1039 | AH | LK10BXG | 1049 | AH | LK10BXU | 1059 | AH | LK60AED | 1069 | AH | LK60AET |
| 1040 | AH | LK10BXH | 1050 | AH | LK10BXV | 1060 | AH | LK60AEE | 1070 | AH | LK60AEU |
| 1041 | AH | LK10BXJ | 1051 | AH | LK10BXW | 1061 | AH | LK60AEF | 1071 | AH | LK60AEV |
| 1042 | AH | LK10BXL | 1052 | AH | LK10BXX | 1062 | AH | LK60AEG | 1072 | AH | LK60AEW |
| 1043 | AH | LK10BXM | 1053 | AH | LK10BXY | 1063 | AH | LK60AEJ | | | |

### TE1073-1104 — ADL Trident 2 10.1m — ADL Enviro 400 — N41/24D* — 2010 — *1073-5 are N41/26D

| | | | | | | | | | | |
|---|---|---|---|---|---|---|---|---|---|---|
| 1073 | W | LK10BZV | 1081 | W | LK60AFF | 1089 | W | LK60AGO | 1097 | W | LK60AHE |
| 1074 | W | LK10BZX | 1082 | W | LK60AFN | 1090 | W | LK60AGU | 1098 | W | LK60AHG |
| 1075 | W | LK10BZY | 1083 | W | LK60AFO | 1091 | W | LK60AGV | 1099 | W | LK60AHJ |
| 1076 | W | LK60AEX | 1084 | W | LK60AFU | 1092 | W | LK60AGY | 1100 | W | LK60AHL |
| 1077 | W | LK60AEY | 1085 | W | LK60AFV | 1093 | W | LK60AGZ | 1101 | W | LK60AHN |
| 1078 | W | LK60AEZ | 1086 | W | LK60AFX | 1094 | W | LK60AHA | 1102 | W | LK60AHO |
| 1079 | W | LK60AFA | 1087 | W | LK60AFY | 1095 | W | LK60AHC | 1103 | W | LK60AHP |
| 1080 | W | LK60AFE | 1088 | W | LK60AFZ | 1096 | W | LK60AHD | 1104 | W | LK60AHU |

### TE1105-1114 — ADL Trident E400H 10.1m — ADL Enviro 400 — N34/24D — 2010

| | | | | | | | | | | |
|---|---|---|---|---|---|---|---|---|---|---|
| 1105 | W | LK60AHV | 1108 | W | LK60AHZ | 1111 | W | LK60AJV | 1113 | W | LK60AJY |
| 1106 | W | LK60AHX | 1109 | W | LK60AJO | 1112 | W | LK60AJX | 1114 | W | LK60AKF |
| 1107 | W | LK60AHY | 1110 | W | LK60AJU | | | | | | |

### DE1115-1151 — ADL Dart 4 10.2m — ADL Enviro 200 — N29D — 2010

| | | | | | | | | | | |
|---|---|---|---|---|---|---|---|---|---|---|
| 1115 | PA | LK10BYB | 1125 | PA | LK10BYR | 1134 | PA | LK10BZA | 1143 | PA | LK10BZL |
| 1116 | PA | LK10BYC | 1126 | PA | LK10BYS | 1135 | PA | LK10BZB | 1144 | PA | LK10BZM |
| 1117 | PA | LK10BYD | 1127 | PA | LK10BYT | 1136 | PA | LK10BZC | 1145 | PA | LK10BZN |
| 1118 | PA | LK10BYG | 1128 | PA | LK10BYU | 1137 | PA | LK10BZD | 1146 | PA | LK10BZO |
| 1119 | PA | LK10BYJ | 1129 | PA | LK10BYV | 1138 | PA | LK10BZE | 1147 | PA | LK10BZP |
| 1120 | PA | LK10BYL | 1130 | PA | LK10BYW | 1139 | PA | LK10BZF | 1148 | PA | LK10BZR |
| 1121 | PA | LK10BYM | 1131 | PA | LK10BYX | 1140 | PA | LK10BZG | 1149 | PA | LK10BZS |
| 1122 | PA | LK10BYN | 1132 | PA | LK10BYY | 1141 | PA | LK10BZH | 1150 | PA | LK10BZT |
| 1123 | PA | LK10BYO | 1133 | PA | LK10BYZ | 1142 | PA | LK10BZJ | 1151 | PA | LK10BZU |
| 1124 | PA | LK10BYP | | | | | | | | | |

In 2010 the first Volvo B9TLs with Wrightbus Eclipse Gemini 2 bodywork for Metroline were placed in service at Brentford, with a second batch currently in course of delivery. VW1038, LK10BXF, is seen at Isleworth while operating route 237. *Richard Godfrey*

### DE1152-1174

ADL Dart 4 10.2m   ADL Enviro 200   N29D   2011

| | | | | | | | | | | | |
|---|---|---|---|---|---|---|---|---|---|---|---|
| 1152 | KC | LK11CWF | 1158 | KC | LK11CWO | 1164 | KC | LK11CWW | 1170 | KC | LK11CXC |
| 1153 | KC | LK11CWG | 1159 | KC | LK11CWP | 1165 | KC | LK11CWX | 1171 | AH | LK11CXD |
| 1154 | KC | LK11CWJ | 1160 | KC | LK11CWR | 1166 | KC | LK11CWY | 1172 | AH | LK11CXE |
| 1155 | KC | LK11CWL | 1161 | KC | LK11CWT | 1167 | KC | LK11CWZ | 1173 | AH | LK11CXF |
| 1156 | KC | LK11CWM | 1162 | KC | LK11CWU | 1168 | KC | LK11CXA | 1174 | AH | LK11CXG |
| 1157 | KC | LK11CWN | 1163 | KC | LK11CWV | 1169 | KC | LK11CXB | | | |

### VW1175-1204

Volvo B9TL 10.4m   Wrightbus Eclipse Gemini 2   N39/23D   2011

| | | | | | | | | | |
|---|---|---|---|---|---|---|---|---|---|
| 1175 | - | LK11CXJ | 1183 | - | LK11CXT | 1191 | - | LK11CYE | 1198 | - | LK11 |
| 1176 | - | LK11CXL | 1184 | - | LK11CXU | 1192 | - | LK11CYF | 1199 | - | LK11 |
| 1177 | - | LK11CXK | 1185 | - | LK11CXV | 1193 | - | LK11 | 1200 | - | LK11 |
| 1178 | - | LK11CXN | 1186 | - | LK11CXW | 1194 | - | LK11 | 1201 | - | LK11 |
| 1179 | - | LK11CXO | 1187 | - | LK11CXX | 1195 | - | LK11 | 1202 | - | LK11 |
| 1180 | - | LK11CXP | 1188 | - | LK11CXY | 1196 | - | LK11 | 1203 | - | LK11 |
| 1181 | - | LK11CXR | 1189 | - | LK11CXZ | 1197 | - | LK11 | 1204 | - | LK11 |
| 1182 | - | LK11CXS | 1190 | - | LK11CYA | | | | | | |

### TEH1205-1230*

ADL Hybrid   ADL   On order

| | | | | | | | | | | | |
|---|---|---|---|---|---|---|---|---|---|---|---|
| 1205 | - | - | 1212 | - | - | 1219 | - | - | 1225 | - | - |
| 1206 | - | - | 1213 | - | - | 1220 | - | - | 1226 | - | - |
| 1207 | - | - | 1214 | - | - | 1221 | - | - | 1227 | - | - |
| 1208 | - | - | 1215 | - | - | 1222 | - | - | 1228 | - | - |
| 1209 | - | - | 1216 | - | - | 1223 | - | - | 1229 | - | - |
| 1210 | - | - | 1217 | - | - | 1224 | - | - | 1230 | - | - |
| 1211 | - | - | 1218 | - | - | | | | | | |

Special event vehicles (with original operator's name):

| | | | | | | |
|---|---|---|---|---|---|---|
| **RM644** | HT | WLT644 | AEC Routemaster RH2H | Park Royal | O36/28RD | 1961 | London Transport |
| **RML903** | HT | WLT903 | AEC Routemaster RH2H/1 | Park Royal | B40/32R | 1962 | London Transport |
| **RMC1513** | HT | 513CLT | AEC Routemaster RH2H | Park Royal | B32/25RD | 1962 | London Transport |

Ancillary vehicles:

| | | | | | | | |
|---|---|---|---|---|---|---|---|
| **AV33** | ACt | 33LUG | Volvo Olympian | Alexander RH | TV | 1998 | |
| **DP274** | PV | P674MLE | Dennis Dart 9m | Plaxton Pointer | Staff | 1997 | |
| **DP275** | PV | P675MLE | Dennis Dart 9m | Plaxton Pointer | Staff | 1997 | |

Previous registrations:

| | | | |
|---|---|---|---|
| 33LUG | S133RLE | WLT826 | T102KLD |

## Depots and allocations:

### Brentford (Commerce Road) - AH

| | | | | | | | | |
|---|---|---|---|---|---|---|---|---|
| Dart | DP19 | DP22 | DP24 | DP27 | DP28 | DP32 | DP33 | DP36 |
| | DP37 | DP43 | DP1001 | DP1002 | DP1003 | DP1004 | DP1005 | DP1006 |
| | DP1007 | DP1008 | DP1009 | DP1010 | DP1011 | DP1012 | DP1013 | DP1014 |
| | DP1049 | | | | | | | |
| Dart 4 | DM961 | DM962 | DM963 | DM964 | DM965 | DM966 | DM967 | DM968 |
| | DM968 | DM970 | DE993 | DE994 | DE995 | DE996 | DE997 | DE998 |
| | DE999 | DE1000 | | | | | | |
| Tempo | OTH971 | OTH972 | OTH973 | OTH974 | OTH975 | | | |
| Trident | TP423 | | | | | | | |
| Volvo B9TL | VW1034 | VW1035 | VW1036 | VW1037 | VW1038 | VW1039 | VW1040 | VW1041 |
| | VW1042 | VW1043 | VW1044 | VW1045 | VW1046 | VW1047 | VW1048 | VW1049 |
| | VW1050 | VW1051 | VW1052 | VW1053 | VW1054 | VW1055 | VW1056 | VW1057 |
| | VW1058 | VW1059 | VW1060 | VW1061 | VW1062 | VW1063 | VW1064 | VW1065 |
| | VW1066 | VW1067 | VW1068 | VW1069 | VW1070 | VW1071 | VW1072 | |

### Cricklewood (Edgware Road) - W

| | | | | | | | | |
|---|---|---|---|---|---|---|---|---|
| Dart | DLD137 | DLD138 | | | | | | |
| Dart 4 | DE1004 | DE1005 | DE1006 | DE1007 | DE1008 | DE1009 | DE1010 | DE1011 |
| | DE1012 | DE1013 | DE1014 | DE1015 | DE1016 | DE1017 | DE1018 | DE1019 |
| | DE1020 | DE1021 | DE1022 | DE1023 | DE1024 | DE1025 | DE1026 | DE1027 |
| | DE1028 | DE1029 | DE1030 | DE1031 | DE1032 | DE1033 | | |
| Trident | TA67 | TA68 | TA69 | TA71 | TA72 | TA73 | TA74 | TA76 |
| | TA78 | TA79 | TA91 | TA92 | TA93 | TA99 | TA100 | TA102 |
| | TA103 | TA109 | TA114 | TAL118 | TAL119 | TAL120 | TAL121 | TAL122 |
| | TAL123 | TAL124 | TAL125 | TAL126 | TAL127 | TAL128 | TAL129 | TAL130 |
| | TAL131 | TAL132 | TAL133 | TAL134 | TPL241 | TPL261 | TPL262 | TPL266 |
| | TA638 | TA639 | TA640 | TA641 | TA642 | TA643 | TA644 | TA645 |
| | TA646 | TA647 | TA648 | TA649 | TA650 | TA651 | TA652 | TA653 |
| | TA654 | TA655 | TA656 | TA657 | TA658 | TA659 | | |
| Trident 2 | TE829 | TE830 | TE831 | TE832 | TE833 | TE834 | TE835 | TE836 |
| | TE837 | TE838 | TE839 | TE878 | TE879 | TE880 | TE881 | TE882 |
| | TE883 | TE884 | TE885 | TE886 | TE887 | TE888 | TE889 | TE890 |
| | TE896 | TEH915 | TEH916 | TEH917 | TEH918 | TEH919 | TE976 | TE977 |
| | TE978 | TE979 | TE980 | TE981 | TE982 | TE983 | TE984 | TE985 |
| | TE986 | TE987 | TE988 | TE989 | TE990 | TE991 | TE992 | TE1073 |
| | TE1074 | TE1075 | TE1076 | TE1077 | TE1078 | TE1079 | TE1080 | TE1081 |
| | TE1082 | TE1083 | TE1084 | TE1085 | TE1086 | TE1087 | TE1088 | TE1089 |
| | TE1090 | TE1091 | TE1092 | TE1093 | TE1094 | TE1095 | TE1096 | TE1097 |
| | TE1098 | TE1099 | TE1100 | TE1101 | TE1102 | TE1103 | TE1104 | |
| ADL E400H | TE1105 | TE1106 | TE1107 | TE1108 | TE1109 | TE1110 | TE1111 | TE1112 |
| | TE1113 | TE1114 | | | | | | |

## Edgware (Station Road) - EW

| Volvo B7TL | VPL146 | VPL147 | VPL148 | VPL149 | VPL150 | VPL151 | VPL152 | VPL153 |
| --- | --- | --- | --- | --- | --- | --- | --- | --- |
| | VPL154 | VPL155 | VPL156 | VPL157 | VPL158 | VPL159 | VPL160 | VPL161 |
| | VPL162 | VPL163 | VPL164 | VPL165 | VPL166 | VPL167 | VPL198 | VPL199 |
| | VPL200 | VPL201 | VPL202 | VPL203 | VPL204 | VPL205 | VPL206 | VPL210 |
| | VPL211 | VPL212 | VPL213 | VPL214 | VPL215 | VPL216 | VPL217 | VPL218 |
| | VPL219 | VPL220 | VPL221 | | | | | |
| Trident 2 | TE712 | TE713 | TE714 | TE715 | TE716 | TE717 | TE718 | TE719 |
| | TE720 | TE721 | TE722 | TE723 | TE724 | TE725 | TE726 | TE727 |
| | TE728 | TE729 | TE730 | TE731 | TE732 | TE733 | TE734 | TE735 |
| | TE736 | TE737 | TE738 | TE840 | TE841 | TE842 | TE843 | TE844 |
| | TE845 | TE846 | TE847 | | | | | |

## Harrow Weald (High Road) - HD

| Volvo B7TL | VPL207 | VPL208 | VP317 | VP318 | VP319 | VP320 | VP321 | |
| --- | --- | --- | --- | --- | --- | --- | --- | --- |
| | VP322 | VP323 | VP324 | VP325 | VLP326 | VP327 | VP328 | VP329 |
| | VP330 | VP331 | VP332 | VP333 | VP334 | VP335 | VP336 | VP337 |
| | VP338 | VP339 | VP340 | VP341 | VP342 | VP343 | VP344 | VP345 |
| | VP346 | VP347 | VP466 | VP467 | VP468 | VP469 | VP604 | VP605 |
| | VP606 | VP607 | VP608 | VP609 | VP610 | VP611 | VP612 | VP613 |
| | VP614 | VP615 | VP616 | VP619 | VP620 | VP621 | VP622 | |
| | VP623 | VP624 | VP625 | VP626 | VP627 | VP628 | | |
| Trident | TP237 | TP238 | TP239 | TP426 | TP427 | TP428 | TP429 | TP430 |
| | TP431 | | | | | | | |

## Holloway (Pemberton Gardens) - HT

| Trident | TP1 | TP2 | TP3 | TP4 | TP5 | TP6 | TP7 | TP8 |
| --- | --- | --- | --- | --- | --- | --- | --- | --- |
| | TP9 | TP10 | TP11 | TP12 | TP13 | TP14 | TP15 | TP16 |
| | TP17 | TP18 | TP19 | TP20 | TP21 | TP22 | TP23 | TP24 |
| | TP25 | TP26 | TP27 | TP28 | TP29 | TP30 | TP31 | TP32 |
| | TP33 | TP34 | TP35 | TP36 | TP37 | TP38 | TP39 | TP40 |
| | TP41 | TP42 | TP43 | TP44 | TP45 | TP46 | TP47 | TP48 |
| | TP49 | TP50 | TP51 | TP52 | TP53 | TP54 | TP55 | TP56 |
| | TP57 | TP58 | TP59 | TP60 | TP61 | TP62 | TP63 | TP64 |
| | TP65 | TPL242 | TPL243 | TPL244 | TPL245 | TPL246 | TPL255 | TPL256 |
| | TPL257 | TPL258 | TPL259 | TPL260 | TPL263 | TPL264 | TPL265 | TPL267 |
| | TPL268 | TPL269 | TPL270 | TPL272 | TP403 | TP404 | TP405 | TP406 |
| | TP407 | TP408 | TP409 | TP410 | TP414 | TP415 | TP416 | TP417 |
| | TP418 | TP419 | TP420 | TP421 | TP422 | TP423 | TP424 | TP425 |
| | TP426 | TP427 | TP428 | TP429 | TP430 | TP431 | TP434 | |
| Trident 2 | TE665 | TE666 | TE667 | TE668 | TE669 | TE670 | TE671 | TE672 |
| | TE673 | TE674 | TE675 | TE676 | TE677 | TE678 | TE679 | TE680 |
| | TE681 | TE682 | TE683 | TE684 | TE685 | TE686 | TE687 | TE688 |
| | TE689 | TE690 | TE691 | TE692 | TE909 | TE910 | TE911 | TE912 |
| | TE913 | TE914 | TE920 | TE921 | TE922 | TE923 | TE924 | TE925 |
| | TE926 | TE927 | TE928 | TE929 | TE930 | TE931 | TE932 | TE933 |
| | TE934 | | | | | | | |
| Volvo B7TL | VPL135 | VPL136 | VPL137 | VPL138 | VPL139 | VPL140 | VPL141 | VPL142 |
| | VPL143 | VPL144 | VPL145 | VPL222 | VPL223 | VPL224 | VPL225 | VPL226 |
| | VPL227 | VPL228 | VPL229 | VPL230 | VPL231 | VPL232 | VPL233 | VPL234 |
| | VPL235 | VPL236 | VP466 | VP467 | VP468 | VP469 | VP485 | VP486 |
| | VP487 | VP488 | VPL581 | VPL582 | VPL583 | VPL584 | VPL585 | VPL586 |
| | VPL587 | VPL588 | VPL589 | VPL590 | VPL591 | VPL592 | VPL593 | VPL594 |
| | VPL595 | VPL596 | VPL597 | VPL598 | VPL599 | VPL600 | VPL601 | VPL602 |
| | VPL603 | VP629 | VP630 | VP631 | VP632 | VP633 | VP634 | VP635 |
| | VP636 | VP637 | | | | | | |

*The London Bus Handbook*

Illustrating the latest application of branding for the hybrid buses is TEH1110, LK60AJU, which is one of ten of the model that entered service at Cricklewood in 2011. It is seen on route 139 in April shortly after entering service. *Mark Lyons*

## King's Cross (York Way) - KX *(Managed from Holloway)*

| Dart | | | | | | | |
|---|---|---|---|---|---|---|---|
| DLD118 | DLD119 | DLD120 | DLD121 | DLD122 | DLD123 | DLD124 | DLD125 |
| DLD126 | DLD127 | DLD128 | DLD129 | DLD130 | DLD131 | DLD132 | DLD133 |
| DLD134 | DLD135 | DLD136 | DLD149 | DLD161 | DLD162 | DLD163 | DLD164 |
| DLD165 | DLD166 | DLD167 | DLD168 | DLD169 | DLD170 | DLD171 | DLD172 |
| DLD173 | DLD174 | DLD175 | DLD176 | DLD177 | DLD178 | DLD179 | DLD179 |
| DLD693 | DLD694 | DLD695 | DLD696 | DLD697 | DLD698 | DLD699 | DLD700 |
| DLD701 | DLD702 | DLD703 | DLD704 | DLD705 | DLD706 | DLD707 | DLD708 |
| DLD709 | DLD710 | DLD711 | | | | | |

## Perivale Park (Alperton Lane) - PV

| Dart | DP12 | DP14 | DP16 | DP17 | DP18 | DP26 | DP34 | DLD110 |
|---|---|---|---|---|---|---|---|---|
| | DLD110 | DLD113 | DLD115 | DLD139 | DLD140 | DLD141 | DLD142 | DLD143 |
| | DLD144 | DLD145 | DLD146 | DLD181 | DLD182 | DLD183 | DLD184 | DLD185 |
| MAN/Evolution | MM771 | MM772 | MM773 | MM774 | MM775 | MM776 | MM777 | MM778 |
| | MM779 | MM780 | MM781 | MM782 | MM783 | MM784 | MM785 | MM786 |
| | MM787 | MM788 | MM789 | MM790 | MM810 | MM811 | MM812 | MM813 |
| | MM814 | MM815 | MM816 | MM817 | MM818 | MM819 | MM820 | MM821 |
| | MM822 | MM823 | MM824 | MM825 | MM826 | MM827 | | |
| OmniDekka | SEL739 | SEL740 | SEL741 | SEL742 | SEL743 | SEL744 | SEL745 | SEL746 |
| | SEL747 | SEL748 | SEL749 | SEL750 | SEL751 | SEL752 | SEL753 | SEL754 |
| | SEL755 | SEL756 | SEL757 | SEL758 | SEL759 | SEL760 | SEL761 | SEL762 |
| | SEL763 | SEL764 | SEL803 | | | | | |
| *Ancillary* | *DLD198* | *DLD200* | *DLD201* | *DLD202* | *DLD203* | *DLD204* | *DLD205* | *DLD206* |

## Perivale (Horsenden Lane South) - PA

| Dart 4 | DEL859 | DEL860 | DEL861 | DEL862 | DEL863 | DEL864 | DEL865 | DEL866 |
|---|---|---|---|---|---|---|---|---|
| | DEL867 | DEL868 | DEL869 | DEL870 | DEL871 | DEL872 | DEL873 | DEL874 |
| | DEL875 | DEL876 | DEL877 | DE952 | DE953 | DE954 | DE955 | DE956 |
| | DE957 | DE958 | DE959 | DE960 | DE999 | DE1000 | DE1001 | DE1002 |
| | DE1003 | DE1115 | DE1116 | DE1117 | DE1118 | DE1119 | DE1120 | DE1121 |
| | DE1122 | DE1123 | DE1124 | DE1125 | DE1126 | DE1127 | DE1128 | DE1129 |
| | DE1130 | DE1131 | DE1132 | DE1133 | DE1134 | DE1135 | DE1136 | DE1137 |
| | DE1138 | DE1139 | DE1140 | DE1141 | DE1142 | DE1143 | DE1144 | DE1145 |
| | DE1146 | DE1147 | DE1148 | DE1149 | DE1150 | DE1151 | | |
| Trident 2 | TE897 | TE898 | TE899 | TE900 | TE901 | TE902 | TE903 | TE904 |
| | TE905 | TE906 | TE907 | TE908 | | | | |
| Scania dd | SEL804 | SEL805 | SEL806 | SEL807 | SEL808 | SEL809 | | |

## Potters Bar (High Street) - PB

| Dart | DLD147 | DLD148 | DLD186 | DLD187 | DLD188 | DLD189 | DLD190 | DLD191 |
|---|---|---|---|---|---|---|---|---|
| | DLD192 | DLD193 | DLD194 | DLD195 | DLD196 | DLD197 | DSD208 | DSD209 |
| | DSD210 | DSD211 | DSD212 | DSD213 | DSD214 | DSD215 | DSD216 | DSD217 |
| Dart 4 | DES791 | DES792 | DES793 | DES794 | DES795 | DES796 | DES797 | DES798 |
| | DES799 | DES800 | DES801 | DES802 | DEL848 | DEL849 | DEL850 | DEL851 |
| | DEL852 | DEL853 | DEL854 | DEL855 | DEL856 | DEL857 | DEL858 | |
| Trident | TPL247 | TPL248 | TPL249 | TPL250 | TPL251 | TPL252 | TPL253 | TPL254 |
| | TPL278 | TPL279 | TPL280 | TPL281 | TPL282 | TPL283 | TPL284 | TPL285 |
| | TPL286 | TPL287 | TPL288 | TPL289 | TPL290 | TPL291 | TPL292 | TPL293 |
| | TPL294 | TPL295 | TPL296 | TP299 | TP437 | TP438 | TP439 | TP440 |
| | TP441 | TP442 | TP443 | TP444 | TP445 | TP446 | TP447 | TP448 |
| | TP449 | TP450 | TP451 | TP452 | TP453 | TP454 | TP455 | TP456 |
| | TP457 | TP458 | TP459 | TP460 | TP461 | TP462 | TP463 | TP464 |
| | TP465 | | | | | | | |
| Trident 2 | TE939 | TE940 | TE941 | TE942 | TE943 | TE944 | TE945 | TE946 |
| | TE947 | TE948 | TE949 | TE950 | TE951 | | | |

## Willesden (High Road) - AC

| Volvo B7TL | VPL168 | VPL169 | VPL170 | VPL171 | VPL172 | VPL173 | VPL174 | VPL175 |
|---|---|---|---|---|---|---|---|---|
| | VPL176 | VPL177 | VPL178 | VPL179 | VPL180 | VPL181 | VPL182 | VPL183 |
| | VPL184 | VPL185 | VPL186 | VPL187 | VPL188 | VPL189 | VPL190 | VPL191 |
| | VPL192 | VPL193 | VPL194 | VPL195 | VPL196 | VPL197 | VP209 | VP470 |
| | VP471 | VP472 | VP473 | VP474 | VP475 | VP476 | VP477 | VP478 |
| | VP479 | VP480 | VP481 | VP482 | VP483 | VP484 | VP489 | VP490 |
| | VP491 | VP492 | VP493 | VP494 | VP495 | VP496 | VP497 | VP498 |
| | VP499 | VP500 | VP501 | VP502 | VP503 | VP504 | VP505 | VP506 |
| | VP507 | VP508 | VP509 | VP510 | VP512 | VP512 | VP513 | VP514 |
| | VP515 | VP516 | VP517 | VP518 | VP519 | VP520 | VP521 | VP522 |
| | VP523 | VP524 | VP525 | VP526 | VP527 | VP528 | VP529 | VP530 |
| | VP531 | VP532 | VP533 | VP534 | VP535 | VP536 | VP537 | VP538 |
| | VP539 | VP540 | VP541 | VP542 | VP543 | VP544 | VP545 | VP546 |
| | VP547 | VP548 | VP549 | VP550 | VP551 | VP552 | VP553 | VP554 |
| | VP555 | VP556 | VP557 | VP558 | VP559 | VP560 | VP561 | VP562 |
| | VP563 | VP564 | VP565 | VP566 | VP567 | VP568 | VP569 | VP570 |
| | VP571 | VP572 | VP573 | VP574 | VP575 | VP576 | VP577 | VP578 |
| | VP579 | VP580 | | | | | | |

## Unallocated and reserve - u/w

Remainder

# QUALITY LINE

HR Richmond Ltd, Blenheim Road, Epsom, KT19 9AF

### OP01-11

Optare Solo M850 — Optare — N25F — 2002

| No. | | Reg | | | Reg | No. | | Reg | No. | | Reg |
|---|---|---|---|---|---|---|---|---|---|---|---|
| 01 | EB | YE52FHH | 04 | EB | YE52FHL | 07 | EB | YE52FHO | 10 | EB | YE52FHS |
| 02 | EB | YE52FHJ | 05 | EB | YE52FHM | 08 | EB | YE52FHP | 11 | EB | YE52FGU |
| 03 | EB | YE52FHK | 06 | EB | YE52FHN | 09 | EB | YE52FHR | | | |

| OP12 | EB | YN03ZXF | Optare Solo M850 | Optare | N25F | 2003 |
|---|---|---|---|---|---|---|
| OP13 | EB | YN53SWF | Optare Solo M850 | Optare | N25F | 2003 |

### OP14-21

Optare Solo M850 — Optare — N25F — 2004

| 14 | EB | YN53SUF | 16 | EB | YN53SVL | 18 | EB | YN53SVP | 20 | EB | YN53ZXA |
|---|---|---|---|---|---|---|---|---|---|---|---|
| 15 | EB | YN53SVK | 17 | EB | YN53SVO | 19 | EB | YN53SVR | 21 | EB | YN53ZXB |

### OP23-30

Optare Solo M850 — Optare — N28F — 2009

| 23 | EB | YJ09MHK | 25 | EB | YJ09MHM | 27 | EB | YJ09MHO | 29 | EB | YJ09MHV |
|---|---|---|---|---|---|---|---|---|---|---|---|
| 24 | EB | YJ09MHL | 26 | EB | YJ09MHN | 28 | EB | YJ09MHU | 30 | EB | YJ09MHX |

| OP31 | EB | - | Optare Solo M850 | Optare | N25F | On order | |
|---|---|---|---|---|---|---|---|
| OP32 | EB | - | Optare Solo M850 | Optare | N25F | On order | |
| OP33 | EB | - | Optare Solo M850 | Optare | N25F | On order | |
| ET01 | EBt | HV52WSZ | Dennis Dart SLF 8.9m | Caetano Nimbus | N31D | 2002 | Mitcham Belle |
| SD26 | EB | W874VGT | Dennis Dart SLF 8.9m | Alexander ALX200 | N28F | 2000 | |
| SD27 | EB | W875VGT | Dennis Dart SLF 8.9m | Alexander ALX200 | N28F | 2000 | |
| SD28 | EB | W876VGT | Dennis Dart SLF 8.9m | Alexander ALX200 | N28F | 2000 | |
| SD33 | EB | SN51UCO | Dennis Dart SLF 8.9m | Alexander ALX200 | N28F | 2000 | |

### SD38-42

ADL Dart SLF 9m — East Lancs Myllennium — N26F — 2005

| 38 | EB | PL05PLN | 40 | EB | PL05PLU | 41 | EB | PL05PLV | 42 | EB | PL05PLX |
|---|---|---|---|---|---|---|---|---|---|---|---|
| 39 | EB | PL05PLO | | | | | | | | | |

**Quality Line is the bus division of Epsom Coaches. Pictured outside Hampton Court Palace is OV3, YJ60KGF, one of the shorter 10.4 metre models of the Optare Versa.** *Richard Godfrey*

The Alexander Dennis Dart is bodied by several coachbuilders in addition to the Enviro 200 body assembled at ADL's own facilities in Scarborough and Falkirk. Belmont is the location for this view of Quality Line SD44, **PE56UFJ**. *Richard Godfrey*

### SD43-51

ADL Dart 4 9.5m — East Lancs Esteem — N25D — 2007

| | | | | | | | | | | | |
|---|---|---|---|---|---|---|---|---|---|---|---|
| **43** | EB | PE56UFH | **46** | EB | PE56UFL | **48** | EB | PE56UFN | **50** | EB | PE56UFR |
| **44** | EB | PE56UFJ | **47** | EB | PE56UFM | **49** | EB | PE56UFP | **51** | EB | PE56UFS |
| **45** | EB | PE56UFK | | | | | | | | | |

| | | | | | | |
|---|---|---|---|---|---|---|
| **SD52** | EB | PN07KRZ | ADL Dart 4 9m | East Lancs Esteem | N23F | 2007 |
| **SD53** | EB | PN07KSE | ADL Dart 4 9m | East Lancs Esteem | N23F | 2007 |
| **SD54** | EB | LJ08RJY | ADL Dart 4 8.9m | ADL Enviro 200 | N26F | 2008 |
| **MCL1** | EB | BW03ZMZ | Mercedes-Benz Citaro O530 | | N38D | 2003 |

### OV1-8

Optare Versa V1040 — Optare — N30D — 2010

| | | | | | | | | | | | |
|---|---|---|---|---|---|---|---|---|---|---|---|
| **1** | EB | YJ60KGA | **3** | EB | YJ60KGF | **5** | EB | YJ60KGK | **7** | EB | YJ60KGO |
| **2** | EB | YJ60KGE | **4** | EB | YJ60KGG | **6** | EB | YJ60KGN | **8** | EB | YJ60KGP |

### DD01-10

ADL Trident 2 — ADL Enviro 400 — N41/26D — 2007

| | | | | | | | | | | | |
|---|---|---|---|---|---|---|---|---|---|---|---|
| **01** | EB | SK07DZA | **04** | EB | SK07DZD | **07** | EB | SK07DZG | **09** | EB | SK07DZJ |
| **02** | EB | SK07DZB | **05** | EB | SK07DZE | **08** | EB | SK07DZH | **10** | EB | SK07DZL |
| **03** | EB | SK07DZC | **06** | EB | SK07DZF | | | | | | |

| | | | | | | |
|---|---|---|---|---|---|---|
| **DD11** | EB | - | ADL Trident 2 | ADL Enviro 400 | N41/26D | 2011 |
| **DD12** | EB | - | ADL Trident 2 | ADL Enviro 400 | N41/26D | 2011 |

## Depot with allocations:

### Epsom (Blenheim Road) - EB

| | | | | | | | | |
|---|---|---|---|---|---|---|---|---|
| Solo | OP01 | OP02 | OP03 | OP04 | OP05 | OP06 | OP07 | OP08 |
| | OP09 | OP10 | OP11 | OP12 | OP13 | OP14 | OP15 | OP16 |
| | OP17 | OP18 | OP19 | OP20 | OP21 | OP23 | OP24 | OP25 |
| | OP26 | OP27 | OP29 | OP30 | OP31 | OP32 | OP33 | |
| Dart | ET01 | SD26 | SD27 | SD28 | SD33 | SD38 | SD39 | SD40 |
| | SD41 | SD42 | | | | | | |
| Dart 4 | SD43 | SD44 | SD45 | SD46 | SD47 | SD48 | SD49 | SD50 |
| | SD51 | SD52 | SD53 | SD54 | | | | |
| Versa | OV1 | OV2 | OV3 | OV4 | OV5 | OV6 | OV7 | OV8 |
| Citaro | MCL1 | | | | | | | |
| Trident 2 | DD01 | DD02 | DD03 | DD04 | DD05 | DD06 | DD07 | DD08 |
| | DD09 | DD10 | DD11 | DD12 | | | | |

# STAGECOACH LONDON

## East London - Selkent - Thameside

East London Buses Ltd; South East London & Kent Bus Co Ltd
Stephenson Street, Canning Town, London, E16 4SA

### 12128-12153   ADL Trident E400H 10.1m   ADL Enviro 400H   N49/31F   On order for 2011-12

| | | | | | | |
|---|---|---|---|---|---|
| 12128 - - | 12135 - - | 12142 - - | 12148 - - |
| 12129 - - | 12136 - - | 12143 - - | 12149 - - |
| 12130 - - | 12137 - - | 12144 - - | 12150 - - |
| 12131 - - | 12138 - - | 12145 - - | 12151 - - |
| 12132 - - | 12139 - - | 12146 - - | 12152 - - |
| 12133 - - | 12140 - - | 12147 - - | 12153 - - |
| 12134 - - | 12141 - - | | |

### 15001-15096   Scania OmniCity N230 UB 10.6m   N41/22D   2008-09

| | | | |
|---|---|---|---|
| 15001 RM LX58CDV | 15025 WH LX58CFU | 15049 PD LX09ABU | 15073 PD LX09AEW |
| 15002 RM LX58CDY | 15026 WH LX58CFV | 15050 PD LX09ABV | 15074 PD LX09AEY |
| 15003 RM LX58CDZ | 15027 WH LX58CFY | 15051 PD LX09ABZ | 15075 PD LX09AEZ |
| 15004 RM LX58CEA | 15028 WH LX58CFZ | 15052 PD LX09ACF | 15076 PD LX09AFA |
| 15005 RM LX58CEF | 15029 WH LX58CGE | 15053 PD LX09ACJ | 15077 PD LX09AFE |
| 15006 RM LX58CEJ | 15030 WH LX58CGF | 15054 PD LX09ACO | 15078 PD LX09AFF |
| 15007 RM LX58CEK | 15031 WH LX58CGG | 15055 PD LX09ADZ | 15079 PD LX09AFJ |
| 15008 RM LX58CEN | 15032 WH LX58CGK | 15056 PD LX09AEA | 15080 PD LX09AFK |
| 15009 RM LX58CEO | 15033 WH LX58CGO | 15057 PD LX09AEB | 15081 PD LX09AFN |
| 15010 RM LX58CEU | 15034 WH LX58CGU | 15058 PD LX09AEC | 15082 PD LX09AFO |
| 15011 RM LX58CEV | 15035 WH LX58CGV | 15059 PD LX09AED | 15083 PD LX09AFU |
| 15012 RM LX58CEY | 15036 PD LX58CGY | 15060 PD LX09AEE | 15084 PD LX09AFV |
| 15013 RM LX58CFA | 15037 PD LX58CGZ | 15061 PD LX09AEF | 15085 PD LX09AFY |
| 15014 RM LX58CFD | 15038 PD LX58CHC | 15062 PD LX09AEG | 15086 PD LX09AFZ |
| 15015 RM LX58CFE | 15039 PD LX58CHD | 15063 PD LX09AEJ | 15087 PD LX09AGO |
| 15016 WH LX58CFF | 15040 PD LX09AAO | 15064 PD LX09AEK | 15088 PD LX09AGU |
| 15017 WH LX58CFG | 15041 PD LX09AAU | 15065 PD LX09AEL | 15089 PD LX09AGV |
| 15018 WH LX58CFJ | 15042 PD LX09AAV | 15066 PD LX09AEM | 15090 PD LX09AGY |
| 15019 WH LX58CFK | 15043 PD LX09AAY | 15067 PD LX09AEN | 15091 PD LX09AGZ |
| 15020 WH LX58CFL | 15044 PD LX09AAZ | 15068 PD LX09AEO | 15092 PD LX09AHA |
| 15021 WH LX58CFM | 15045 PD LX09ABF | 15069 PD LX09AEP | 15093 PD LX09AHC |
| 15022 WH LX58CFN | 15046 PD LX09ABK | 15070 PD LX09AET | 15094 PD LX09AHD |
| 15023 WH LX58CFO | 15047 PD LX09ABN | 15071 PD LX09AEU | 15095 PD LX09AHE |
| 15024 WH LX58CFP | 15048 PD LX09ABO | 15072 PD LX09AEV | 15096 PD LX09AHF |

In a move which surprised many, Stagecoach re-entered the London bus market in October 2010 when it acquired from its administrators the East London operation that it had sold to Macquarie in 2006. 174 integral Scania OmniCity double-deck buses had been taken into stock including 15076, LX09AFA, seen here outside Plumstead depot.
*Dave Heath*

Illustrating the nearside of the Scania OmniCity double-deck is 15139, LX59CNE, allocated to Leyton depot. It is seen at Whipps Cross, one of twenty-one vehicles required for route 56. *Mark Lyons*

### 15097-15124

Scania OmniCity N230 UB 10.6m    N41/22D    2009

| | | | | | | | | | | |
|---|---|---|---|---|---|---|---|---|---|---|
| 15097 | BW | LX09FYS | 15104 | BW | LX09FZA | 15111 | BW | LX09FZH | 15118 | BW | LX09FZP |
| 15098 | BW | LX09FYT | 15105 | BW | LX09FZB | 15112 | BW | LX09FZJ | 15119 | BW | LX09FZR |
| 15099 | BW | LX09FYU | 15106 | BW | LX09FZC | 15113 | BW | LX09FZK | 15120 | BW | LX09FZS |
| 15100 | BW | LX09FYV | 15107 | BW | LX09FZD | 15114 | BW | LX09FZL | 15121 | BW | LX09FZT |
| 15101 | BW | LX09FYW | 15108 | BW | LX09FZE | 15115 | BW | LX09FZM | 15122 | BW | LX09FZU |
| 15102 | BW | LX09FYY | 15109 | BW | LX09FZF | 15116 | BW | LX09FZN | 15123 | BW | LX09FZV |
| 15103 | BW | LX09FYZ | 15110 | BW | LX09FZG | 15117 | BW | LX09FZO | 15124 | BW | LX09FZW |

### 15125-15174

Scania OmniCity N230 UB 10.6m    N41/22D    2009-10

| | | | | | | | | | | |
|---|---|---|---|---|---|---|---|---|---|---|
| 15125 | T | LX59CLU | 15138 | T | LX59CNC | 15151 | T | LX59COJ | 15163 | T | LX59CRJ |
| 15126 | T | LX59CLV | 15139 | T | LX59CNE | 15152 | T | LX59COU | 15164 | T | LX59CRK |
| 15127 | T | LX59CLY | 15140 | T | LX59CNF | 15153 | T | LX59CPE | 15165 | T | LX59CRU |
| 15128 | T | LX59CLZ | 15141 | T | LX59CNJ | 15154 | T | LX59CPF | 15166 | T | LX59CRV |
| 15129 | T | LX59CME | 15142 | T | LX59CNK | 15155 | T | LX59CPK | 15167 | T | LX59CRZ |
| 15130 | T | LX59CMF | 15143 | T | LX59CNN | 15156 | T | LX59CPN | 15168 | T | LX59CSF |
| 15131 | T | LX59CMK | 15144 | T | LX59CNO | 15157 | T | LX59CPO | 15169 | T | LX59CSO |
| 15132 | T | LX59CMO | 15145 | T | LX59CNU | 15158 | T | LX59CPU | 15170 | T | LX10AUC |
| 15133 | T | LX59CMU | 15146 | T | LX59CNV | 15159 | T | LX59CPV | 15171 | T | LX10AUE |
| 15134 | T | LX59CMV | 15147 | T | LX59CNY | 15160 | T | LX59CPY | 15172 | T | LX10AUF |
| 15135 | T | LX59CMY | 15148 | T | LX59CNZ | 15161 | T | LX59CPZ | 15173 | T | LX10AUH |
| 15136 | T | LX59CMZ | 15149 | T | LX59COA | 15162 | T | LX59CRF | 15174 | T | LX10AUJ |
| 15137 | T | LX59CNA | 15150 | T | LX59COH | | | | | | |

| 17001 | T | S801BWC | Dennis Trident 10.5m | Alexander ALX400 4.2m | N51/22D | 1999 | *displays fleet number TA1* |
|---|---|---|---|---|---|---|---|

Stagecoach London is currently receiving some 140 new Enviro 400-bodied Trident 2s for the services and these are allowing earlier Tridents to be displaced. Many are being transferred within the group with Merseyside an initial destination. Barking's 17130, V130MEV, is seen in the town while working route 169 and represents one of these that are now due for replacement. *Dave Heath*

### 17100-17222

Dennis Trident 10.5m    Alexander ALX400 4.4m    N47/23D    1999-2000

| | | | | | | | | | | | |
|---|---|---|---|---|---|---|---|---|---|---|---|
| 17100 | w | V474KJN | 17143 | u | V143MEV | 17177 | BW | V177MEV | 17202 | BW | V202MEV |
| 17101 | w | V475KJN | 17144 | u | V144MEV | 17178 | BW | V178MEV | 17203 | u | V203MEV |
| 17102 | w | V102MEV | 17149 | BW | V149MEV | 17180 | BW | W187CNO | 17204 | PD | V204MEV |
| 17103 | u | V103MEV | 17151 | BW | V151MEV | 17181 | T | V181MEV | 17205 | u | V205MEV |
| 17104 | u | V104MEV | 17152 | u | V152MEV | 17182 | T | V182MEV | 17206 | u | V206MEV |
| 17105 | u | V105MEV | 17153 | u | V153MEV | 17183 | T | V183MEV | 17207 | u | V207MEV |
| 17109 | RMt | V109MEV | 17157 | PD | V157MEV | 17184 | T | V184MEV | 17208 | u | V208MEV |
| 17111 | RMt | V477KJN | 17159 | PD | V159MEV | 17185 | u | V185MEV | 17209 | u | V209MEV |
| 17112 | TLt | V112MEV | 17161 | PD | V161MEV | 17186 | BK | V186MEV | 17211 | BK | V211MEV |
| 17113 | TLt | V113MEV | 17162 | PD | V162MEV | 17190 | u | V190MEV | 17212 | w | V212MEV |
| 17126 | w | V126MEV | 17164 | PD | V164MEV | 17192 | w | V192MEV | 17214 | PD | V214MEV |
| 17127 | u | V127MEV | 17165 | u | V165MEV | 17193 | PD | V193MEV | 17215 | PD | V215MEV |
| 17128 | w | V128MEV | 17166 | PD | V166MEV | 17194 | w | V194MEV | 17216 | PD | V216MEV |
| 17129 | BW | V129MEV | 17167 | BW | V167MEV | 17195 | PD | V195MEV | 17217 | PD | V217MEV |
| 17130 | u | V130MEV | 17170 | w | V170MEV | 17196 | BW | V196MEV | 17218 | PD | V218MEV |
| 17134 | BW | V134MEV | 17171 | BW | V171MEV | 17197 | BW | V197MEV | 17219 | u | V219MEV |
| 17136 | u | V136MEV | 17172 | BW | V172MEV | 17198 | BW | V198MEV | 17220 | U | V220MEV |
| 17140 | u | V140MEV | 17174 | BK | V174MEV | 17199 | BW | V199MEV | 17221 | PD | V221MEV |
| 17141 | u | V141MEV | 17175 | BW | V175MEV | 17200 | BW | V363OWC | 17222 | PD | V364OWC |

### 17224-17260

Dennis Trident 9.9m    Alexander ALX400 4.4m    N43/20D    2000

| | | | | | | | | | | | |
|---|---|---|---|---|---|---|---|---|---|---|---|
| 17224 | WH | X362NNO | 17234 | u | X234NNO | 17245 | BW | X371NNO | 17253 | WH | X253NNO |
| 17226 | u | X364NNO | 17238 | u | X238NNO | 17246 | BW | X246NNO | 17254 | WH | X254NNO |
| 17227 | u | X365NNO | 17239 | BW | X239NNO | 17247 | u | X247NNO | 17255 | WH | X373NNO |
| 17228 | u | X366NNO | 17240 | BW | X368NNO | 17248 | u | X248NNO | 17256 | WH | X256NNO |
| 17229 | u | X229NNO | 17241 | BW | X241NNO | 17249 | w | X249NNO | 17257 | WH | X257NNO |
| 17230 | T | X367NNO | 17242 | BW | X242NNO | 17250 | w | X372NNO | 17258 | WH | X258NNO |
| 17231 | U | X231NNO | 17243 | U | X243NNO | 17251 | WH | X251NNO | 17259 | WH | X259NNO |
| 17232 | U | X232NNO | 17244 | BW | X369NNO | 17252 | WH | X252NNO | 17260 | WH | WLT575 |
| 17233 | U | X233NNO | | | | | | | | | |

*The London Bus Handbook*

## 17261-17358 — Dennis Trident 10.5m — Alexander ALX400 4.4m — N47/23D* — 2000 — *seating varies

| No. | | Reg | No. | | Reg | No. | | Reg | No. | | Reg |
|---|---|---|---|---|---|---|---|---|---|---|---|
| 17261 | BK | X261NNO | 17293 | BW | X293NNO | 17312 | PD | X312NNO | 17341 | TB | X341NNO |
| 17262 | w | X262NNO | 17294 | BW | X294NNO | 17313 | PD | X313NNO | 17342 | TL | X342NNO |
| 17263 | BK | X263NNO | 17295 | BW | X295NNO | 17314 | PD | X314NNO | 17343 | TL | X343NNO |
| 17267 | w | X267NNO | 17296 | BW | X296NNO | 17315 | PD | X315NNO | 17344 | TB | X344NNO |
| 17268 | PD | X268NNO | 17297 | BW | X297NNO | 17316 | PD | X385NNO | 17345 | TL | X396NNO |
| 17270 | BK | X376NNO | 17298 | BW | X298NNO | 17317 | TL | X317NNO | 17346 | TB | X346NNO |
| 17277 | BW | X277NNO | 17299 | BW | X299NNO | 17318 | TL | X386NNO | 17347 | TB | X347NNO |
| 17278 | PD | X278NNO | 17300 | NS | X381NNO | 17319 | TL | X319NNO | 17348 | TB | X348NNO |
| 17279 | u | X279NNO | 17301 | w | X301NNO | 17321 | TL | X388NNO | 17349 | TB | X349NNO |
| 17280 | u | X378NNO | 17302 | u | X302NNO | 17322 | w | X322NNO | 17350 | TL | X397NNO |
| 17281 | w | X281NNO | 17303 | PD | X303NNO | 17323 | TL | X389NNO | 17351 | TB | X351NNO |
| 17282 | WH | X282NNO | 17304 | PD | X304NNO | 17324 | TB | X324NNO | 17352 | TB | X352NNO |
| 17285 | u | X285NNO | 17305 | PD | X382NNO | 17326 | NS | X326NNO | 17353 | PD | X353NNO |
| 17286 | TB | X286NNO | 17306 | PD | X383NNO | 17328 | w | X392NNO | 17354 | TB | X354NNO |
| 17288 | NS | X288NNO | 17307 | PD | X307NNO | 17336 | w | X336NNO | 17355 | TB | X398NNO |
| 17289 | BK | X289NNO | 17308 | PD | X308NNO | 17338 | TL | X338NNO | 17356 | TB | X356NNO |
| 17290 | BK | X379NNO | 17309 | PD | X309NNO | 17339 | TB | X339NNO | 17357 | TB | X357NNO |
| 17291 | u | X291NNO | 17310 | PD | X384NNO | 17340 | TB | X395NNO | 17358 | TB | X358NNO |
| 17292 | BW | X292NNO | 17311 | PD | X311NNO | | | | | | |

## 17359-17435 — Dennis Trident 10.5m — Alexander ALX400 4.4m — N45/22D — 2001

| No. | | Reg | No. | | Reg | No. | | Reg | No. | | Reg |
|---|---|---|---|---|---|---|---|---|---|---|---|
| 17359 | BK | Y359NHK | 17380 | BK | Y512NHK | 17399 | PDt | LX51FHP | 17418 | TB | LX51FJF |
| 17360 | BK | Y508NHK | 17381 | BK | Y381NHK | 17400 | BW | Y514NHK | 17419 | TB | LX51FJJ |
| 17361 | BK | Y361NHK | 17382 | BK | Y382NHK | 17401 | BW | Y401NHK | 17420 | TL | LX51FJK |
| 17362 | NS | Y362NHK | 17383 | BK | LX51FPF | 17403 | BW | LX51FHS | 17421 | TB | LX51FJN |
| 17363 | BK | Y363NHK | 17384 | BK | Y384NHK | 17404 | BW | Y404NHK | 17422 | TB | LX51FJO |
| 17364 | u | Y364NHK | 17385 | BK | Y385NHK | 17405 | BW | LX51FHT | 17423 | NS | LX51FJP |
| 17366 | BW | Y366NHK | 17386 | BK | Y386NHK | 17406 | BW | Y517NHK | 17424 | RM | LX51FJV |
| 17367 | BW | Y367NHK | 17387 | BK | LX51FPC | 17407 | BW | Y407NHK | 17425 | T | LX51FJZ |
| 17368 | PD | Y368NHK | 17388 | BK | Y388NHK | 17408 | PD | LX51FHU | 17426 | u | LX51FJY |
| 17370 | BK | Y509NHK | 17389 | BK | Y389NHK | 17409 | T | Y409NHK | 17427 | PD | LX51FKA |
| 17371 | BK | Y371NHK | 17390 | BK | LX51FPD | 17410 | w | LX51FHV | 17428 | TB | LX51FKB |
| 17372 | PD | Y372NHK | 17391 | RM | Y391NHK | 17411 | w | LX51FHW | 17429 | TB | Y429NHK |
| 17373 | BK | Y373NHK | 17392 | RM | Y392NHK | 17412 | TL | LX51FHY | 17430 | TB | LX51FKD |
| 17374 | BK | Y374NHK | 17393 | RM | Y393NHK | 17413 | TL | LX51FHZ | 17431 | PD | LX51FKE |
| 17375 | BK | Y511NHK | 17394 | NS | LX51FHN | 17414 | TL | LX51FJA | 17432 | u | LX51FKF |
| 17376 | BK | Y376NHK | 17395 | TBt | Y395NHK | 17415 | TL | LX51FJC | 17433 | WH | LX51FKG |
| 17377 | BK | Y377NHK | 17396 | RMt | LX51FHO | 17416 | TL | LX51FJD | 17434 | PD | Y434NHK |
| 17378 | BK | Y378NHK | 17397 | RMt | Y367NHK | 17417 | NS | LX51FJE | 17435 | TL | LX51FKJ |
| 17379 | BK | Y379NHK | 17398 | RMt | Y368NHK | | | | | | |

February 2011 and Trident 17355, X398NNO, is seen on route 269 at Queen Mary's Hospital in Sidcup.
*Richard Godfrey*

## 17436-17534    Dennis Trident 9.9m    Alexander ALX400    N43/19D    2001

| | | | | | | | | | | | |
|---|---|---|---|---|---|---|---|---|---|---|---|
| 17436 | TB | Y436NHK | 17461 | U | LX51FKW | 17486 | T | LX51FME | 17510 | T | LX51FNN |
| 17437 | TB | Y437NHK | 17462 | U | Y462NHK | 17487 | WH | LX51FMF | 17511 | PD | LX51FNO |
| 17438 | TB | Y438NHK | 17463 | U | LX51FKZ | 17488 | WH | LX51FMG | 17512 | PD | LX51FNP |
| 17439 | TB | LX51FKL | 17464 | U | Y464NHK | 17489 | WH | LX51FMJ | 17513 | NS | LX51FNR |
| 17440 | TB | Y522NHK | 17465 | T | LX51FLB | 17490 | WH | LX51FMK | 17514 | WH | LX51FNS |
| 17441 | TB | Y441NHK | 17466 | u | LX51FLC | 17491 | WH | LX51FML | 17515 | WH | LX51FNT |
| 17442 | TB | Y442NHK | 17467 | TL | LX51FLD | | | | 17516 | WH | LX51FNU |
| 17443 | u | Y443NHK | 17468 | TL | LX51FLE | 17493 | WH | LX51FMO | 17517 | WH | LX51FNV |
| 17444 | u | LX51FKO | 17469 | TL | LX51FLF | 17494 | WH | LX51FMP | 17518 | WH | LX51FNW |
| 17445 | u | Y445NHK | 17470 | TL | Y531NHK | 17495 | U | LX51FMU | 17519 | WH | LX51FNY |
| 17446 | u | Y446NHK | 17471 | TL | LX51FLG | 17496 | U | LX51FMV | 17520 | WH | LX51FNZ |
| 17447 | u | Y447NHK | 17472 | TL | LX51FLH | 17497 | U | LX51FMY | 17521 | WH | LX51FOA |
| 17448 | u | Y448NHK | 17473 | TL | LX51FLJ | 17498 | U | LX51FMZ | 17522 | WH | LX51FOC |
| 17449 | u | Y449NHK | 17474 | TL | LX51FLK | 17499 | U | LX51FNA | 17523 | RM | LX51FOD |
| 17450 | u | Y524NHK | 17475 | TL | LX51FLL | 17500 | U | LX51FNC | 17524 | RM | LX51FOF |
| 17451 | WH | LX51FKR | 17476 | TL | LX51FLM | 17501 | U | LX51FND | 17525 | RM | LX51FOH |
| 17452 | NS | Y452NHK | 17477 | TL | LX51FLN | 17502 | PD | LX51FNE | 17526 | RM | LX51FOJ |
| 17453 | u | Y453NHK | 17478 | TL | LX51FLP | 17503 | PD | LX51FNF | 17527 | RM | LX51FOK |
| 17454 | u | Y454NHK | 17479 | TL | LX51FLR | 17504 | T | LX51FNG | 17528 | U | LX51FOM |
| 17455 | NS | Y526NHK | 17480 | PD | LX51FLV | 17505 | T | LX51FNH | 17529 | U | LX51FON |
| 17456 | U | Y527NHK | 17481 | PD | LX51FLW | 17506 | T | LX51FNJ | 17530 | WH | LX51FOP |
| 17457 | U | LX51FKT | 17482 | T | LX51FLZ | 17507 | T | LX51FNK | 17531 | WH | LX51FOT |
| 17458 | U | Y458NHK | 17483 | NS | LX51FMA | 17508 | PD | LX51FNL | 17533 | NS | LX51FOV |
| 17459 | RM | LX51FKU | 17484 | NS | LX51FMC | 17509 | WH | LX51FNM | 17534 | NS | LX51FPA |
| 17460 | U | Y529NHK | 17485 | T | LX51FMD | | | | | | |

## 17535-17591    Dennis Trident 9.9m    Alexander ALX400    N43/20D    2002

| | | | | | | | | | | | |
|---|---|---|---|---|---|---|---|---|---|---|---|
| 17535 | U | LY02OAA | 17550 | U | LY02OBB | 17564 | NS | LV52HDX | 17578 | NS | LV52HFL |
| 17536 | U | LY02OAB | 17551 | U | LY02OBC | 17565 | NS | LV52HDY | 17579 | WH | LV52HFM |
| 17537 | NS | LY02OAC | 17552 | U | LY02OBD | 17566 | NS | LV52HDZ | 17580 | U | LV52HFN |
| 17538 | NS | LY02OAD | 17553 | U | LY02OBE | 17567 | NS | LV52HEJ | 17581 | U | LV52HFO |
| 17539 | NS | LY02OAE | 17554 | U | LY02OBF | 17568 | NS | LV52HFU | 17582 | U | LV52HFP |
| 17540 | NS | LY02OAG | 17555 | U | LY02OBG | 17569 | NS | LV52HFA | 17583 | U | LV52HFR |
| 17541 | NS | LY02OAN | 17556 | U | LY02OBH | 17570 | PD | LV52HFB | 17584 | U | LV52HFS |
| 17543 | NS | LY02OAP | 17557 | U | LY02OBJ | 17571 | PD | LV52HFC | 17585 | U | LV52HFT |
| 17544 | NS | LY02OAS | 17558 | U | LY02OBK | 17572 | PD | LV52HFD | 17586 | U | LV52HFU |
| 17545 | U | LY02OAU | 17559 | NS | LY02OBL | 17573 | PD | LV52HFE | 17587 | U | LV52HFW |
| 17546 | U | LY02OAV | 17560 | PD | LY02OBM | 17574 | NS | LV52HFF | 17588 | U | LV52HFX |
| 17547 | U | LY02OAW | 17561 | WH | LV52USV | 17575 | T | LV52HFH | 17589 | U | LV52HFY |
| 17548 | U | LY02OAX | 17562 | NS | LV52HDO | 17576 | TL | LV52HFJ | 17590 | U | LV52HFZ |
| 17549 | U | LY02OAZ | 17563 | PD | LV52HDU | 17577 | NS | LV52HFK | 17591 | U | LV52HGA |

**Also seen on route 269 is 17440, Y522NHK. Operated from Bromley, route 269 runs through to Bexleyheath.**
*Terry Longhurst*

Stagecoach London's 17823, LX03BXV, is seen at Whipps Cross. Leading towards Walthemstow on route 230. This Leyton-bused route was the last single-deck service operated by Leyton prior to its conversion to Trident. *Mark Lyons*

## 17740-17853     TransBus Trident 10.5m     TransBus ALX400 4.4m     N45/22D     2003

| | | | | | | | | | | | |
|---|---|---|---|---|---|---|---|---|---|---|---|
| 17740 | WH | LY52ZDX | 17770 | NS | LX03BVF | 17798 | T | LX03BWM | 17826 | T | LX03BXZ |
| 17741 | WH | LY52ZDZ | 17771 | NS | LX03BVG | 17799 | T | LX03BWN | 17827 | T | LX03BYA |
| 17742 | WH | LY52ZFA | 17772 | NS | LX03BVH | 17800 | T | LX03BWP | 17828 | T | LX03BYB |
| 17743 | WH | LY52ZFB | 17773 | NS | LX03BVJ | 17801 | T | LX03BWU | 17829 | NS | LX03BYC |
| 17744 | WH | LY52ZFC | 17774 | NS | LX03BVK | 17802 | T | LX03BWV | 17830 | NS | LX03BYD |
| 17745 | T | LY52ZFD | 17775 | NS | LX03BVL | 17803 | T | LX03BWW | 17831 | U | LX03BYF |
| 17746 | T | LY52ZFE | 17776 | NS | LX03BVM | 17804 | T | LX03BWY | 17832 | WH | LX03BYG |
| 17747 | T | LY52ZFF | 17777 | NS | LX03BVN | 17805 | T | LX03BWZ | 17833 | U | LX03BYH |
| 17748 | NS | LY52ZFG | 17778 | NS | LX03BVP | 17806 | T | LX03BXA | 17834 | U | LX03BYJ |
| 17749 | T | LY52ZFH | 17779 | U | LX03BVR | 17807 | T | LX03BXB | 17835 | NS | LX03BYL |
| 17750 | WH | LX03BTE | 17780 | U | LX03BVS | 17808 | T | LX03BXC | 17836 | PD | LX03BYM |
| 17751 | WH | LX03BTF | 17781 | WH | LX03BVT | 17809 | T | LX03BXD | 17837 | PD | LX03BYN |
| 17752 | WH | LX03BTU | 17782 | WH | LX03BVU | 17810 | T | LX03BXE | 17838 | PD | LX03BYP |
| 17753 | WH | LX03BTV | 17783 | WH | LX03BVV | 17811 | T | LX03BXF | 17839 | PD | LX03BYR |
| 17754 | WH | LX03BTY | 17784 | WH | LX03BVW | 17812 | T | LX03BXG | 17840 | PD | LX03BYS |
| 17755 | WH | LX03BTZ | 17785 | WH | LX03BVY | 17813 | T | LX03BXH | 17841 | T | LX03BYT |
| 17756 | WH | LX03BUA | 17786 | WH | LX03BVZ | 17814 | T | LX03BXJ | 17842 | U | LX03BYU |
| 17757 | WH | LX03BUE | 17787 | WH | LX03BWA | 17815 | T | LX03BXK | 17843 | U | LX03BYV |
| 17759 | NS | LX03BUH | 17788 | U | LX03BWB | 17816 | T | LX03BXL | 17844 | U | LX03BYW |
| 17760 | NS | LX03BUJ | 17789 | PD | LX03BWC | 17817 | T | LX03BXM | 17845 | U | LX03BYY |
| 17761 | NS | LX03BUP | 17790 | PD | LX03BWD | 17818 | WH | LX03BXN | 17846 | WH | LX03BYZ |
| 17762 | NS | LX03BUU | 17791 | NS | LX03BWE | 17819 | WH | LX03BXP | 17847 | U | LX03BZA |
| 17763 | NS | LX03BUV | 17792 | NS | LX03BWF | 17820 | T | LX03BXR | 17848 | U | LX03BZB |
| 17764 | NS | LX03BUW | 17793 | NS | LX03BWG | 17821 | T | LX03BXS | 17849 | U | LX03BZC |
| 17765 | NS | LX03BVA | 17794 | WH | LX03BWH | 17822 | T | LX03BXU | 17850 | U | LX03BZD |
| 17766 | NS | LX03BVB | 17795 | WH | LX03BWJ | 17823 | T | LX03BXV | 17851 | T | LX03BZE |
| 17767 | u | LX03BVC | 17796 | T | LX03BWK | 17824 | T | LX03BXW | 17852 | T | LX03BZF |
| 17768 | NS | LX03BVD | 17797 | T | LX03BWL | 17825 | T | LX03BXY | 17853 | T | LX03BZG |
| 17769 | NS | LX03BVE | | | | | | | | | |

| | | | | | | | | |
|---|---|---|---|---|---|---|---|---|
| 17854 | NS | LX03BZH | TransBus Trident 9.9m | | TransBus ALX400 4.4m | N43/21D | 2003 | |

Seen shortly after refurbishment, 17915, LX03OSL, is allocated to West Ham. Pictured on route 15 which needs twenty-four vehicles along with five Routemasters for the ISH heritage route. Aldwych is the setting. *Terry Longhurst*

### 17855-17933

TransBus Trident 10.5m    TransBus ALX400 4.4m    N45/23D    2003

| | | | | | | | | | | | |
|---|---|---|---|---|---|---|---|---|---|---|---|
| 17855 | WH | LX03NEU | 17876 | T | LX03NGE | 17896 | BK | LX03ORJ | 17915 | WH | LX03OSL |
| 17856 | u | LX03NEY | 17877 | T | LX03NGF | 17897 | BK | LX03ORK | 17916 | WH | LX03OSM |
| 17857 | BK | LX03NFA | 17878 | T | LX03NGJ | 17898 | BK | LX03ORN | 17917 | WH | LX03OSN |
| 17858 | BK | LX03NFC | 17879 | WH | 527CLT | 17899 | BK | LX03ORP | 17918 | WH | LX03OSP |
| 17859 | BK | LX03NFD | 17880 | BK | LX03NGU | 17900 | BK | LX03ORS | 17919 | WH | LX03OSR |
| 17860 | BK | LX03NFE | 17881 | BK | LX03NGV | 17901 | BK | LX03ORT | 17920 | WH | LX03OSU |
| 17861 | BK | LX03NFF | 17882 | BK | LX03NGY | 17902 | BK | LX03ORU | 17921 | WH | LX03OSV |
| 17862 | BK | LX03NFG | 17883 | BK | LX03NGZ | 17903 | U | LX03ORV | 17922 | WH | LX03OSW |
| 17863 | BK | LX03NFH | 17884 | BK | LX03NHA | 17904 | BK | LX03ORW | 17923 | WH | LX03OSY |
| 17864 | U | LX03NFJ | 17885 | BK | LX03OPT | 17905 | T | LX03ORY | 17924 | WH | LX03OSZ |
| 17865 | U | LX03NFK | 17886 | BK | LX03OPU | 17906 | T | LX03ORZ | 17925 | WH | LX03OTA |
| 17866 | PD | LX03NFL | 17887 | BK | LX03OPV | 17907 | T | LX03OSA | 17926 | WH | LX03OTB |
| 17867 | NS | LX03NFM | 17888 | BK | LX03OPW | 17908 | T | LX03OSB | 17927 | WH | LX03OTC |
| 17868 | NS | LX03NFN | 17889 | U | LX03OPY | 17909 | WH | LX03OSC | 17928 | WH | LX03OTD |
| 17869 | NS | LX03NFP | 17890 | U | LX03OPZ | 17910 | WH | LX03OSD | 17929 | WH | LX03OTE |
| 17870 | NS | LX03NFR | 17891 | U | LX03ORA | 17911 | WH | LX03OSE | 17930 | WH | LX03OTF |
| 17871 | T | LX03NFT | 17892 | BK | LX03ORC | 17912 | WH | LX03OSG | 17931 | WH | LX03OTG |
| 17873 | T | LX03NFV | 17893 | BK | LX03ORF | 17913 | WH | LX03OSJ | 17932 | u | LX03OTH |
| 17874 | NS | LX03NFY | 17894 | BK | LX03ORG | 17914 | WH | LX03OSK | 17933 | WH | LX03OTJ |
| 17875 | T | LX03NFZ | 17895 | BK | LX03ORH | | | | | | |

### 17934-17975

TransBus Trident 10.5m    TransBus ALX400    N45/23D    2003

| | | | | | | | | | | | |
|---|---|---|---|---|---|---|---|---|---|---|---|
| 17934 | U | LX53JXU | 17945 | PD | LX53JYH | 17956 | PD | LX53JYW | 17966 | TB | LX53JZJ |
| 17935 | U | LX53JXV | 17946 | PD | LX53JYJ | 17957 | PD | LX53JYY | 17967 | TB | LX53JZK |
| 17936 | U | LX53JXW | 17947 | PD | LX53JYK | 17958 | PD | LX53JYZ | 17968 | TB | LX53JZL |
| 17937 | U | LX53JXY | 17948 | PD | LX53JYL | 17959 | PD | LX53JZA | 17969 | TB | LX53JZM |
| 17938 | U | LX53JYA | 17949 | PD | LX53JYN | 17960 | PD | LX53JZC | 17970 | TB | LX53JZN |
| 17939 | U | LX53JYB | 17950 | PD | LX53JYO | 17961 | PD | LX53JZD | 17971 | TB | LX53JZO |
| 17940 | U | LX53JYC | 17951 | PD | LX53JYP | 17962 | PD | LX53JZE | 17972 | TB | LX53JZP |
| 17941 | U | LX53JYD | 17952 | PD | LX53JYR | 17963 | PD | LX53JZF | 17973 | TB | LX53JZR |
| 17942 | U | LX53JYE | 17953 | PD | LX53JYT | 17964 | PD | LX53JZG | 17974 | TB | LX53JZT |
| 17943 | U | LX53JYF | 17954 | PD | LX53JYU | 17965 | TB | LX53JZH | 17975 | TB | LX53JZU |
| 17944 | U | LX53JYG | 17955 | PD | LX53JYV | | | | | | |

Chislehurst Pond in February 2011and 19140, LX56EBA, from the initial batch of Trident 2s for London that were supplied under Stagecoach ownership. Is seen on route 61. *Richard Godfrey*

## 17976-17999

TransBus Trident 9.9m TransBus ALX400 N43/20D 2004

| | | | | | | | | | |
|---|---|---|---|---|---|---|---|---|---|
| 17976 | NS | LX53JZV | 17982 | NS | LX53KAU | 17988 | NS | LX53KBO | 17994 | NS | LX53KCC |
| 17977 | NS | LX53JZW | 17983 | NS | LX53KBE | 17989 | NS | LX53KBP | 17995 | NS | LX53KCE |
| 17978 | NS | LX53KAE | 17984 | NS | LX53KBF | 17990 | NS | LX53KBV | 17996 | NS | LX53KCF |
| 17979 | NS | LX53KAJ | 17985 | NS | LX53KBJ | 17991 | NS | LX53KBW | 17997 | NS | LX53KCG |
| 17980 | NS | LX53KAK | 17986 | NS | LX53KBK | 17992 | NS | LX53KBZ | 17998 | NS | LX53KCJ |
| 17981 | NS | LX53KAO | 17987 | NS | LX53KBN | 17993 | NS | LX53KCA | 17999 | NS | LX53KCK |

## 18201-18265

TransBus Trident 10.5m TransBus ALX400 N45/22D* 2004 *seating varies

| | | | | | | | | | |
|---|---|---|---|---|---|---|---|---|---|
| 18201 | BW | LX04FWL | 18218 | BW | LX04FXF | 18234 | BW | LX04FYA | 18250 | WH | LX04FYT |
| 18202 | BW | LX04FWM | 18219 | BW | LX04FXG | 18235 | BW | LX04FYB | 18251 | WH | LX04FYU |
| 18203 | BW | LX04FWN | 18220 | BW | LX04FXH | 18236 | BW | LX04FYC | 18252 | WH | LX04FYV |
| 18204 | BW | LX04FWP | 18221 | BW | LX04FXJ | 18237 | BW | LX04FYD | 18253 | WH | LX04FYW |
| 18205 | BW | LX04FWR | 18222 | BW | LX04FXK | 18238 | BW | LX04FYE | 18254 | WH | LX04FYY |
| 18206 | BW | LX04FWS | 18223 | BW | LX04FXL | 18239 | WH | LX04FYF | 18255 | WH | LX04FYZ |
| 18207 | BW | LX04FWT | 18224 | BW | LX04FXM | 18240 | WH | LX04FYG | 18256 | WH | LX04FZA |
| 18208 | BW | LX04FWU | 18225 | BW | LX04FXP | 18241 | WH | LX04FYH | 18257 | U | LX04FZB |
| 18209 | BW | LX04FWV | 18226 | BW | LX04FXR | 18242 | WH | LX04FYK | 18258 | U | LX04FZC |
| 18210 | BW | LX04FWW | 18227 | BW | LX04FXS | 18243 | WH | LX04FYL | 18259 | U | LX04FZD |
| 18211 | BW | LX04FWY | 18228 | BW | LX04FXT | 18244 | WH | LX04FYM | 18260 | U | LX04FZE |
| 18212 | BW | LX04FWZ | 18229 | BW | LX04FXU | 18245 | WH | LX04FYN | 18261 | U | LX04FZF |
| 18213 | BW | LX04FXA | 18230 | BW | LX04FXV | 18246 | WH | LX04FYP | 18262 | U | LX04FZG |
| 18214 | BW | LX04FXB | 18231 | BW | LX04FXW | 18247 | WH | LX04FYR | 18263 | U | LX04FZH |
| 18215 | BW | LX04FXC | 18232 | BW | LX04FXY | 18248 | WH | LX04FYS | 18264 | U | LX04FZJ |
| 18216 | BW | LX04FXD | 18233 | BW | LX04FXZ | 18249 | WH | LX04FYT | 18265 | U | LX04FZK |
| 18217 | BW | LX04FXE | | | | | | | | | |

## 18266-18277

ADL Trident 10.5m ADL ALX400 N45/23D 2005

| | | | | | | | | | |
|---|---|---|---|---|---|---|---|---|---|
| 18266 | T | LX05BVY | 18269 | T | LX05BWB | 18272 | T | LX05BWE | 18275 | T | LX05BWH |
| 18267 | T | LX05BVZ | 18270 | T | LX05BWC | 18273 | T | LX05BWF | 18276 | T | LX05BWJ |
| 18268 | T | LX05BWA | 18271 | T | LX05BWD | 18274 | T | LX05BWG | 18277 | T | LX05BWK |

Having re-acquired the London operations, Stagecoach has begun a large vehicle investment programme. The first vehicle of this new order is 19711, LX11AYS, seen on route 174 while heading for Dagenham.
*Richard Godfrey*

### 18451-18499     ADL Trident 10.5m     ADL ALX400     N45/22D     2005-06

| | | | | | | | | | | | |
|---|---|---|---|---|---|---|---|---|---|---|---|
| 18451 | NS | LX05LLM | 18464 | TL | LX55EPO | 18476 | WH | LX55ERZ | 18488 | TL | LX06AFY |
| 18452 | NS | LX05LLN | 18465 | WH | LX55EPP | 18477 | WH | LX55ESF | 18489 | TL | LX06AFZ |
| 18453 | NS | LX05LLO | 18466 | WH | LX55EPU | 18478 | WH | LX55ESG | 18490 | TL | LX06AGO |
| 18454 | NS | LX05LLP | 18467 | WH | LX55EPV | 18479 | WH | LX55ESN | 18491 | TL | LX06AGU |
| 18455 | TL | LX55EPA | 18468 | WH | LX55EPY | 18480 | WH | LX55ESO | 18492 | TL | LX06AGV |
| 18456 | PD | LX55EPC | 18469 | WH | LX55EPZ | 18481 | TL | LX06AFF | 18493 | TL | LX06AGY |
| 18457 | U | LX55EPD | 18470 | WH | LX55ERJ | 18482 | TL | LX06AFJ | 18494 | TL | LX06AGZ |
| 18458 | U | LX55EPE | 18471 | WH | LX55ERK | 18483 | TL | LX06AFK | 18495 | TL | LX06AHA |
| 18459 | U | LX55EPF | 18472 | WH | LX55ERO | 18484 | TL | LX06AFN | 18496 | TL | LX06AHC |
| 18460 | U | LX55EPJ | 18473 | WH | LX55ERU | 18485 | TL | LX06AFO | 18497 | TL | LX06AHD |
| 18461 | U | LX55EPK | 18474 | WH | LX55ERV | 18486 | TL | LX06AFU | 18498 | TL | LX06AHE |
| 18462 | U | LX55EPL | 18475 | WH | LX55ERY | 18487 | TL | LX06AFV | 18499 | TL | LX06AHF |
| 18463 | TL | LX55EPN | | | | | | | | | |

| 19000 | WH | LX55HGC | ADL Trident 2 10.9m | | ADL Enviro 400 | | N51/30D | 2006 | ADL development vehicle |
|---|---|---|---|---|---|---|---|---|---|

### 19131-19140     ADL Trident 2 10.9m     ADL Enviro 400     N45/30D     2006

| | | | | | | | | | | | |
|---|---|---|---|---|---|---|---|---|---|---|---|
| 19131 | TB | LX56EAF | 19134 | TB | LX56EAK | 19137 | TB | LX56EAP | 19139 | TB | LX56EAY |
| 19132 | TB | LX56EAG | 19135 | TB | LX56EAM | 19138 | TB | LX56EAW | 19140 | TB | LX56EBA |
| 19133 | TB | LX56EAJ | 19136 | TB | LX56EAO | | | | | | |

### 19711-19741     ADL Trident 2 10.2m     ADL Enviro 400     N41/24D     2011

| | | | | | | | | | | | |
|---|---|---|---|---|---|---|---|---|---|---|---|
| 19711 | RM | LX11AYS | 19719 | RM | LX11AZB | 19727 | RM | LX11AZO | 19735 | NS | LX11BAA |
| 19712 | RM | LX11AYT | 19720 | RM | LX11AZC | 19728 | RM | LX11AZP | 19736 | NS | LX11BAO |
| 19713 | RM | LX11AYU | 19721 | RM | LX11AZD | 19729 | RM | LX11AZR | 19737 | NS | LX11BAU |
| 19714 | RM | LX11AYV | 19722 | RM | LX11AZF | 19730 | RM | LX11AZT | 19738 | NS | LX11BAV |
| 19715 | RM | LX11AYW | 19723 | RM | LX11AZG | 19731 | RM | LX11AZU | 19739 | NS | LX11BBE |
| 19716 | RM | LX11AYY | 19724 | RM | LX11AZJ | 19732 | RM | LX11AZV | 19740 | NS | LX11BBF |
| 19717 | RM | LX11AYZ | 19725 | RM | LX11AZL | 19733 | RM | LX11AZW | 19741 | NS | LX11BBJ |
| 19718 | RM | LX11AZA | 19726 | RM | LX11AZN | 19734 | NS | LX11AZZ | | | |

As we go press the order for new buses is still in build, and a further twenty-six hybrid Enviro 400s are due towards the end of 2011 for route 15. One of the batch fitted with Telematics for route 99 and based at Plumstead is 19743, **LX11BBN**. *Richard Godfrey*

### 19742-19755
ADL Trident 2 10.2m | ADL Enviro 400 | N41/24D | 2011

| | | | | | | | | | | |
|---|---|---|---|---|---|---|---|---|---|---|
| 19742 | PD | LX11BBK | 19746 | PD | LX11BBZ | 19750 | PD | LX11BCO | 19753 | PD | LX11BCY |
| 19743 | PD | LX11BBN | 19747 | PD | LX11BCE | 19751 | PD | LX11BCU | 19754 | PD | LX11BCZ |
| 19744 | PD | LX11BBO | 19748 | PD | LX11BCF | 19752 | PD | LX11BCV | 19755 | PD | LX11BDE |
| 19745 | PD | LX11BBV | 19749 | PD | LX11BCK | | | | | | |

### 19756-19805
ADL Trident 2 10.2m | ADL Enviro 400 | N41/24D | 2011

| | | | | | | | | | | |
|---|---|---|---|---|---|---|---|---|---|---|
| 19756 | BK | LX11BDF | 19769 | BK | LX11BFK | 19782 | BK | LX11BGO | 19794 | BK | LX11BHN |
| 19757 | BK | LX11BDO | 19770 | BK | LX11BFL | 19783 | BK | LX11BGU | 19795 | BK | LX11BHO |
| 19758 | BK | LX11BDU | 19771 | BK | LX11BFM | 19784 | BK | LX11BGV | 19796 | BK | LX11BHP |
| 19759 | BK | LX11BDV | 19772 | BK | LX11BFN | 19785 | BK | LX11BGY | 19797 | BK | LX11BHU |
| 19760 | BK | LX11BDY | 19773 | BK | LX11BFO | 19786 | NS | LX11BGZ | 19798 | BK | LX11BHV |
| 19761 | BK | LX11BDZ | 19774 | BK | LX11BFP | 19787 | NS | LX11BHA | 19799 | BK | LX11BHW |
| 19762 | BK | LX11BEJ | 19775 | BK | LX11BFU | 19788 | NS | LX11BHD | 19800 | BK | LX11BHY |
| 19763 | BK | LX11BEO | 19776 | BK | LX11BFV | 19789 | NS | LX11BHE | 19801 | BK | LX11BHZ |
| 19764 | BK | LX11BEU | 19777 | BK | LX11BFY | 19790 | NS | LX11BHF | 19802 | BK | LX11BJE |
| 19765 | BK | LX11BEY | 19778 | BK | LX11BFZ | 19791 | NS | LX11BHJ | 19803 | BK | LX11BJF |
| 19766 | BK | LX11BFA | 19779 | BK | LX11BGE | 19792 | NS | LX11BHK | 19804 | BK | LX11BJJ |
| 19767 | BK | LX11BFF | 19780 | BK | LX11BGF | 19793 | NS | LX11BHL | 19805 | PD | LX11BJK |
| 19768 | BK | LX11BFJ | 19781 | BK | LX11BGK | | | | | | |

### 19806-19834
ADL Trident 2 10.2m | ADL Enviro 400 | N41/24D | 2011

| | | | | | | | | | | |
|---|---|---|---|---|---|---|---|---|---|---|
| 19806 | PD | LX11BJO | 19814 | PD | LX11BKF | 19821 | PD | LX11BKU | 19828 | PD | LX11BLN |
| 19807 | PD | LX11BJU | 19815 | PD | LX11BKG | 19822 | PD | LX11BKV | 19829 | PD | LX11BLV |
| 19808 | PD | LX11BJV | 19816 | PD | LX11BKJ | 19823 | PD | LX11BKY | 19830 | PD | LX11BLZ |
| 19809 | PD | LX11BJY | 19817 | PD | LX11BKK | 19824 | PD | LX11BKZ | 19831 | PD | LX11BMO |
| 19810 | PD | LX11BJZ | 19818 | PD | LX11BKL | 19825 | PD | LX11BLF | 19832 | PD | LX11BMU |
| 19811 | PD | LX11BKA | 19819 | PD | LX11BKN | 19826 | PD | LX11BLJ | 19833 | PD | LX11BMV |
| 19812 | PD | LX11BKD | 19820 | PD | LX11BKO | 19827 | PD | LX11BLK | 19834 | PD | LX11BMY |
| 19813 | PD | LX11BKE | | | | | | | | | |

The Routemasters operated by Stagecoach London include seven from TfL for route 15 and the company's own four. All are based at West Ham depot. Seen passing St Paul's is 19966 (RM1968), ALD968B. Since rejoining the main fleet the Routemasters are numbered in the 199xx series as the Enviro 400 hybrids occupy the 12000 numbers previously used. *Mark Lyons*

### 19835-19846

| | ADL Trident 2 10.2m | ADL Enviro 400 | N41/24D | On order |
|---|---|---|---|---|
| 19835 - - | 19838 - - | 19841 - - | 19844 - - |
| 19836 - - | 19839 - - | 19842 - - | 19845 - - |
| 19837 - - | 19840 - - | 19843 - - | 19846 - - |

*Note: Routemasters display their former London Transport numbers.* Special event vehicles,19960-3, are often used in normal service.

| | | | | | | |
|---|---|---|---|---|---|---|
| 19960 | WHp | SMK760F | AEC Routemaster R2RH/1 | Park Royal | B40/32R | 1968 |
| 19961 | WH | WLT324 | AEC Routemaster R2RH | Park Royal | B36/28R | 1960 |
| 19962 | WH | WLT652 | AEC Routemaster R2RH | Park Royal | B36/28R | 1961 |
| 19963 | WH | WLT871 | AEC Routemaster R2RH | Park Royal | B36/28R | 1962 |
| 19964 | WH | ALD933B | AEC Routemaster 2R2RH | Park Royal | B36/28R | 1964 |
| 19965 | WH | ALD941B | AEC Routemaster 2R2RH | Park Royal | B36/28R | 1964 |
| 19966 | WH | ALD968B | AEC Routemaster 2R2RH | Park Royal | B36/28R | 1964 |
| 19967 | WH | ALD50B | AEC Routemaster 2R2RH | Park Royal | B36/28R | 1965 |
| 19968 | WH | ALD60B | AEC Routemaster 2R2RH | Park Royal | B36/28R | 1965 |
| 19969 | WH | ALD71B | AEC Routemaster 2R2RH | Park Royal | B36/28R | 1965 |
| 19970 | WH | ALD89B | AEC Routemaster 2R2RH | Park Royal | B36/28R | 1964 |

### 23019-23035

| | Mercedes-Benz Citaro O530 G | | AN49D | 2003 |
|---|---|---|---|---|
| 23019 | WH | LX03HDC | 23029 | WH | LX03HDU | 23032 | WH | LX03HDZ | 23034 | WH | LX03HEU |
| 23027 | WH | LX03HDL | 23031 | WH | LX03HDY | 23033 | WH | LX03HEJ | 23035 | WH | LX03HEV |
| 23028 | WH | LX03HDN | | | | | | | | | |

### 23036-23077

| | Mercedes-Benz Citaro O530 G | | AN49D | 2004 |
|---|---|---|---|---|
| 23036 | WH | LX04KZG | 23047 | WH | LX04KZV | 23058 | WH | LX04LBN | 23068 | WH | LX04LCG |
| 23037 | WH | LX04KZJ | 23048 | WH | LX04KZW | 23059 | WH | LX04LBP | 23069 | WH | LX04LCJ |
| 23038 | WH | LX04KZK | 23049 | WH | LX04KZY | 23060 | WH | LX04LBU | 23070 | WH | LX04LCK |
| 23039 | WH | LX04KZL | 23050 | WH | LX04KZZ | 23061 | WH | LX04LBV | 23071 | WH | LX04LCM |
| 23040 | WH | LX04KZM | 23051 | WH | LX04LBA | 23062 | WH | LX04LBY | 23072 | WH | LX04LCN |
| 23041 | WH | LX04KZN | 23052 | WH | LX04LBE | 23063 | WH | 630DYE | 23073 | WH | LX04LCP |
| 23042 | WH | LX04KZP | 23053 | WH | LX04LBF | 23064 | WH | LX04LCA | 23074 | WH | LX04LCT |
| 23043 | WH | LX04KZR | 23054 | WH | LX04LBG | 23065 | WH | LX04LCC | 23075 | WH | LX04LCU |
| 23044 | WH | LX04KZS | 23055 | WH | LX04LBJ | 23066 | WH | LX04LCE | 23076 | WH | LX04LCV |
| 23045 | WH | LX04KZT | 23056 | WH | LX04LBK | 23067 | WH | LX04LCF | 23077 | WH | VLT240 |
| 23046 | WH | LX04KZU | 23057 | WH | LX04LBL | | | | | | |

**25111-25115**  Optare Tempo X1060H 10.6m  Optare  N28D  2009

| | | | | | | | | | |
|---|---|---|---|---|---|---|---|---|---|
| 25111 | WH | VLT14 | 25113 | WH | LX09BGK | 25114 | WH | LX09BGU | 25115 WH LX09BGV |
| 25112 | WH | WLT461 | | | | | | | |

**25301-25314**  Optare Versa V1040  Optare  N27D  2009

| | | | | | | | | | | | |
|---|---|---|---|---|---|---|---|---|---|---|---|
| 25301 | PD | LX58CHF | 25305 | PD | LX58CHK | 25309 | PD | LX58CHV | 25312 | BK | LX09AAJ |
| 25302 | PD | LX58CHG | 25306 | PD | LX58CHL | 25310 | BK | LX09AAE | 25313 | BK | LX09AAF |
| 25303 | PD | LX58CHH | 25307 | PD | LX58CHN | 25311 | BK | LX09AAK | 25314 | BK | LX09AAN |
| 25304 | PD | LX58CHJ | 25308 | PD | LX58CHO | | | | | | |

| | | | | | | |
|---|---|---|---|---|---|---|
| 34162 | PD | V162MXV | Dennis Dart SLF 9.3m | Plaxton Pointer 2 | N24D | 1999 |
| 34163 | PD | V163MXV | Dennis Dart SLF 9.3m | Plaxton Pointer 2 | N24D | 1999 |

**34224-34236**  Dennis Dart SLF 11.3m  Plaxton Pointer SPD  N35D  2000

| | | | | | | | | | | | |
|---|---|---|---|---|---|---|---|---|---|---|---|
| 34224 | TB | X224WNO | 34228 | TB | X228WNO | 34231 | TB | X231WNO | 34234 | TB | X234WNO |
| 34225 | TB | X237WNO | 34229 | TB | X229WNO | 34232 | TB | X232WNO | 34235 | TB | X235WNO |
| 34226 | TB | X226WNO | 34230 | TB | X238WNO | 34233 | TB | X233WNO | 34236 | TB | X236WNO |
| 34227 | TB | X227WNO | | | | | | | | | |

**34237-34253**  Dennis Dart SLF 8.9m  Alexander ALX200  N23F  2001

| | | | | | | | | | | | |
|---|---|---|---|---|---|---|---|---|---|---|---|
| 34237 | u | Y237FJN | 34242 | TL | Y242FJN | 34246 | TL | Y246FJN | 34250 | TL | Y349FJN |
| 34238 | u | Y238FJN | 34243 | TL | Y243FJN | 34247 | TL | Y247FJN | 34251 | TL | Y251FJN |
| 34239 | u | Y239FJN | 34244 | TL | Y244FJN | 34248 | TL | Y248FJN | 34252 | TL | Y252FJN |
| 34240 | TL | Y347FJN | 34245 | TL | Y348FJN | 34249 | TL | Y249FJN | 34253 | TL | Y253FJN |
| 34241 | TL | Y241FJN | | | | | | | | | |

**34255-34272**  Dennis Dart SLF 10.2m  Alexander ALX200  N30D*  2001  *34255 is N26D

| | | | | | | | | | | | |
|---|---|---|---|---|---|---|---|---|---|---|---|
| 34255 | WH | Y351FJN | 34267 | BK | Y267FJN | 34269 | BK | Y269FJN | 34271 | WH | Y271FJN |
| 34262 | U | Y262FJN | 34268 | BK | Y268FJN | 34270 | BK | Y353FJN | 34272 | BK | Y272FJN |
| 34265 | w | Y265FJN | | | | | | | | | |

**34273-34327**  Dennis Dart SLF 10m  Alexander ALX200  N30D  2001

| | | | | | | | | | | | |
|---|---|---|---|---|---|---|---|---|---|---|---|
| 34273 | WH | Y273FJN | 34285 | w | Y285FJN | 34294 | U | Y294FJN | 34317 | TB | LX51FHG |
| 34277 | w | Y277FJN | 34286 | w | Y286FJN | 34295 | U | Y295FJN | 34318 | U | LX51FHB |
| 34278 | BK | LX51FPE | 34287 | TB | Y287FJN | 34296 | U | Y296FJN | 34319 | U | LX51FHA |
| 34279 | w | Y279FJN | 34288 | BK | Y671JSG | 34310 | TB | LX51FGV | 34323 | TB | LX51FHF |
| 34280 | w | Y356FJN | 34289 | BK | Y289FJN | 34311 | TB | LX51FGJ | 34324 | U | LX51FHK |
| 34281 | BK | Y281FJN | 34290 | BK | LX51FFW | 34312 | TB | LX51FGN | 34325 | U | LX51FHL |
| 34282 | w | Y282FJN | 34291 | BK | Y291FJN | 34313 | BK | LX51FGO | 34326 | U | LX51FHH |
| 34283 | BK | Y283FJN | 34292 | BK | Y292FJN | 34315 | BK | LX51FGU | 34327 | U | LX51FHJ |
| 34284 | BK | Y284FJN | 34293 | BK | Y293FJN | | | | | | |

**34329-34346**  Dennis Dart SLF 10.8m  Alexander ALX200  N29D  2001

| | | | | | | | | | | | |
|---|---|---|---|---|---|---|---|---|---|---|---|
| 34329 | WH | Y329FJN | 34334 | WH | Y334FJN | 34339 | WH | Y339FJN | 34343 | WH | Y343FJN |
| 34330 | WH | Y372FJN | 34335 | WH | Y335FJN | 34340 | WH | Y374FJN | 34344 | WH | Y344FJN |
| 34331 | WH | Y331FJN | 34336 | WH | Y336FJN | 34341 | WH | LX51FFO | 34345 | WH | Y376FJN |
| 34332 | WH | Y332FJN | 34337 | WH | Y337FJN | 34342 | WH | Y342FJN | 34346 | TB | Y346FJN |
| 34333 | WH | Y373FJN | 34338 | WH | Y338FJN | | | | | | |

**34347-34365**  Dennis Dart SLF 10.1m  TransBus Pointer  N31D  2002

| | | | | | | | | | | | |
|---|---|---|---|---|---|---|---|---|---|---|---|
| 34347 | BK | LV52HJY | 34352 | BK | LV52HKD | 34357 | TB | LV52HKJ | 34362 | TB | LV52HKO |
| 34348 | BK | LV52HJZ | 34353 | TL | LV52HKE | 34358 | TB | LV52HKK | 34363 | TB | LV52HKP |
| 34349 | BK | LV52HKA | 34354 | TB | LV52HKF | 34359 | TB | LV52HKL | 34364 | TB | LV52HKT |
| 34350 | BK | LV52HKB | 34355 | TB | LV52HKG | 34360 | TB | LV52HKM | 34365 | TB | LV52HKU |
| 34351 | BK | LV52HKC | 34356 | TB | LV52HKH | 34361 | TB | LV52HKN | | | |

**34366-34376**  TransBus Dart 8.8m  TransBus Pointer  N28F  2003

| | | | | | | | | | | | |
|---|---|---|---|---|---|---|---|---|---|---|---|
| 34366 | TL | LV52HGC | 34369 | TL | LV52HGF | 34372 | TL | LV52HGK | 34375 | TL | LV52HGN |
| 34367 | TL | LV52HGD | 34370 | TL | LV52HGG | 34373 | TL | LV52HGL | 34376 | TL | LV52HGO |
| 34368 | w | LV52HGE | 34371 | TL | LV52HGJ | 34374 | TL | LV52HGM | | | |

Illustrating the Alexander ALX200 body is 34270, Y353FJN, seen opposite Barking station entrance while heading for East Beckton. Route 366 is now converted to the new Enviro 200s *Richard Godfrey*

### 34377-34386
TransBus Dart 9.3m   TransBus Pointer   N31F   2003

| 34377 | TL | LX03BZJ | 34380 | PD | LX03BZM | 34383 | PD | LX03BZR | 34385 | PD | LX03BZT |
| 34378 | u | LX03BZK | 34381 | PD | LX03BZN | 34384 | PD | LX03BZS | 34386 | PD | LX03BZU |
| 34379 | TL | LX03BZL | 34382 | PD | LX03BZP | | | | | | |

### 34387-34397
TransBus Dart 10.2m   TransBus Pointer   N31D   2003

| 34387 | BK | LX03BZV | 34390 | TL | LX03CAA | 34393 | TL | LX03CAV | 34396 | TL | LX03CBV |
| 34388 | TL | LX03BZW | 34391 | TL | LX03CAE | 34394 | TL | LX03CBF | 34397 | TL | LX03CBY |
| 34389 | TL | LX03BZY | 34392 | TL | LX03CAU | 34395 | TL | LX03CBU | | | |

### 34551-34560
TransBus Dart 10.2m   TransBus Pointer   N27D   2003

| 34551 | TL | LX53LGF | 34554 | TL | LX53LGK | 34557 | TL | LX53LGO | 34559 | TL | LX53LGV |
| 34552 | TL | LX53LGG | 34555 | TL | LX53LGL | 34558 | TL | LX53LGU | 34560 | TL | LX53LGW |
| 34553 | TL | LX53LGJ | 34556 | TL | LX53LGN | | | | | | |

### 36261-36299
ADL Dart 4 10.2m   ADL Enviro 200   N29D   2011

| 36261 | NS | LX11AVP | 36271 | BK | LX11AWG | 36281 | BK | LX11AWW | 36291 | BK | LX11AXJ |
| 36262 | NS | LX11AVR | 36272 | BK | LX11AWH | 36282 | BK | LX11AWY | 36292 | BK | LX11AXK |
| 36263 | NS | LX11AVT | 36273 | BK | LX11AWJ | 36283 | BK | LX11AWZ | 36293 | BK | LX11AXM |
| 36264 | NS | LX11AVU | 36274 | BK | LX11AWM | 36284 | BK | LX11AXA | 36294 | BK | LX11AXN |
| 36265 | NS | LX11AVV | 36275 | BK | LX11AWN | 36285 | BK | LX11AXB | 36295 | BK | LX11AXO |
| 36266 | NS | LX11AVW | 36276 | BK | LX11AWO | 36286 | BK | LX11AXC | 36296 | BK | LX11AXP |
| 36267 | NS | LX11AVY | 36277 | BK | LX11AWP | 36287 | BK | LX11AXD | 36297 | BK | LX11AXR |
| 36268 | BK | LX11AVZ | 36278 | BK | LX11AWR | 36288 | BK | LX11AXF | 36298 | BK | LX11AXS |
| 36269 | BK | LX11AWC | 36279 | BK | LX11AWU | 36289 | BK | LX11AXG | 36299 | BK | LX11AXT |
| 36270 | BK | LX11AWF | 36280 | BK | LX11AWV | 36290 | BK | LX11AXH | | | |

### 36301-36308
ADL Dart 4 8.9m   ADL Enviro 200   N26F   2006

| 36301 | TL | LX56DZU | 36303 | TL | LX56DZW | 36305 | TL | LX56DZZ | 36307 | TL | LX56EAC |
| 36302 | TL | LX56DZV | 36304 | TL | LX56DZY | 36306 | TL | LX56EAA | 36308 | TL | LX56EAE |

## 36309-36313    ADL Dart 4 10.7m    ADL Enviro 200    N32D    2008

| | | | | | | | | | | | |
|---|---|---|---|---|---|---|---|---|---|---|---|
| 36309 | TB | LX58BZW | 36311 | TB | LX58CAA | 36312 | TB | LX58CAE | 36313 | TB | LX58CAO |
| 36310 | TB | LX58BZY | | | | | | | | | |

## 36314-36326    ADL Dart 4 8.9m    ADL Enviro 200    N26F    2008

| | | | | | | | | | | | |
|---|---|---|---|---|---|---|---|---|---|---|---|
| 36314 | TB | LX58CAU | 36318 | TB | LX58CBU | 36321 | TL | LX58CCA | 36324 | TL | LX58CCF |
| 36315 | TB | LX58CAV | 36319 | TB | LX58CBV | 36322 | TL | LX58CCD | 36325 | TL | LX58CCJ |
| 36316 | TB | LX58CBF | 36320 | TL | LX58CBY | 36323 | TL | LX58CCE | 36326 | TL | LX58CCK |
| 36317 | TB | LX58CBO | | | | | | | | | |

## 36327-36337    ADL Dart 4 9.3m    ADL Enviro 200    N24D    2008

| | | | | | | | | | | | |
|---|---|---|---|---|---|---|---|---|---|---|---|
| 36327 | PD | LX58CCN | 36330 | PD | LX58CCV | 36333 | PD | LX58CDF | 36336 | PD | LX58CDO |
| 36328 | PD | LX58CCO | 36331 | PD | LX58CCY | 36334 | PD | LX58CDK | 36337 | PD | LX58CDU |
| 36329 | PD | LX58CCU | 36332 | PD | LX58CDE | 36335 | PD | LX58CDN | | | |

## 36338-36344    ADL Dart 4 10.8m    ADL Enviro 200    N32D    2009

| | | | | | | | | | | | |
|---|---|---|---|---|---|---|---|---|---|---|---|
| 36338 | RM | LX09ACU | 36340 | RM | LX09ACY | 36342 | RM | LX09ADO | 36344 | RM | LX09ADV |
| 36339 | RM | LX09ACV | 36341 | RM | LX09ACZ | 36343 | RM | LX09ADU | | | |

## 36345-36375    ADL Dart 4 10.2m    ADL Enviro 200    N29D    2009-10

| | | | | | | | | | | | |
|---|---|---|---|---|---|---|---|---|---|---|---|
| 36345 | WH | LX59ANF | 36353 | WH | LX59AOD | 36361 | WH | LX59AOM | 36369 | WH | LX59ECZ |
| 36346 | WH | LX59ANP | 36354 | WH | LX59AOE | 36362 | WH | LX59ECF | 36370 | WH | LX59EDC |
| 36347 | WH | LX59ANR | 36355 | WH | LX59AOF | 36363 | WH | LX59ECJ | 36371 | WH | LX59EDF |
| 36348 | WH | LX59ANU | 36356 | WH | LX59AOG | 36364 | WH | LX59ECN | 36372 | WH | LX59EDJ |
| 36349 | WH | LX59ANV | 36357 | WH | LX59AOH | 36365 | WH | LX59ECT | 36373 | WH | LX59EDK |
| 36350 | WH | LX59AOA | 36358 | WH | LX59AOJ | 36366 | WH | LX59ECV | 36374 | WH | LX59EDL |
| 36351 | WH | LX59AOB | 36359 | WH | LX59AOK | 36367 | WH | LX59ECW | 36375 | WH | LX59EDO |
| 36352 | WH | LX59AOC | 36360 | WH | LX59AOL | 36368 | WH | LX59ECY | | | |

Previous registrations:

| | | | |
|---|---|---|---|
| 527CLT | LX03NGN | VLT240 | LX04LCW |
| 630DYE | LX04LBZ | WLT461 | LX09BGF |
| LX04LCV | LX04LCV, WLT886 | WLT575 | X374NNO |
| V474KJN | V474KJN, WLT491 | WLT886 | LX04LCV |
| V475KJN | V475KJN, WLT461 | | |
| VLT14 | YJ58PGO | | |

## Depots and allocations:

### Barking (Longbridge Road, IG11 8UE) - BK

| | | | | | | | | |
|---|---|---|---|---|---|---|---|---|
| Trident | 17186 | 17211 | 17261 | 17263 | 17270 | 17290 | 17359 | 17360 |
| | 17361 | 17363 | 17370 | 17371 | 17373 | 17374 | 17375 | 17376 |
| | 17377 | 17378 | 17379 | 17380 | 17381 | 17382 | 17383 | 17384 |
| | 17385 | 17386 | 17387 | 17389 | 17390 | 17857 | 17858 | 17859 |
| | 17860 | 17861 | 17862 | 17863 | 17880 | 17881 | 17882 | 17883 |
| | 17884 | 17885 | 17886 | 17887 | 17888 | 17892 | 17893 | 17894 |
| | 17895 | 17896 | 17897 | 17898 | 17899 | 17900 | 17901 | 17902 |
| | 17094 | | | | | | | |
| Trident 2 | 19756 | 19757 | 19758 | 19759 | 19760 | 19761 | 19762 | 19763 |
| | 19764 | 19765 | 19766 | 19767 | 19768 | 19769 | 19770 | 19771 |
| | 19772 | 19777 | | | | | | |
| Optare Versa | 25310 | 25311 | 25312 | 25313 | 25314 | | | |
| Dart SLF | 34267 | 34268 | 34272 | 34278 | 34281 | 34283 | 34284 | 34287 |
| | 34288 | 34289 | 34290 | 34291 | 34292 | 34293 | 34313 | 34315 |
| | 34347 | 34348 | 34349 | 34350 | 34351 | 34352 | | |
| Dart 4 | 36268 | 36269 | 36271 | 36275 | 36276 | 36277 | 36281 | 36282 |
| | 36283 | 36284 | | | | | | |

### Bow (Fairfield Road, E3 2QP) - BW

| | | | | | | | | |
|---|---|---|---|---|---|---|---|---|
| Scania CN230 | 15097 | 15098 | 15099 | 15100 | 15101 | 15102 | 15103 | 15104 |
| | 15105 | 15106 | 15107 | 15108 | 15109 | 15110 | 15111 | 15112 |
| | 15113 | 15114 | 15115 | 15116 | 15117 | 15118 | 15119 | 15120 |
| | 15121 | 15122 | 15123 | 15124 | | | | |

During the Maguire ownership fourteen Optare Versa V1040 buses joined the fleet at Plumstead. Cranbrook Road in Ilford provides the background to 25312, LX09AAJ, as it heads for Ilford Broadway. *Richard Godfrey*

| Trident | | | | | | | | |
|---------|-------|-------|-------|-------|-------|-------|-------|-------|
| | 17129 | 17134 | 17149 | 17151 | 17167 | 17171 | 17172 | 17174 |
| | 17175 | 17177 | 17178 | 17180 | 17196 | 17197 | 17198 | 17199 |
| | 17200 | 17202 | 17239 | 17240 | 17241 | 17242 | 17244 | 17245 |
| | 17246 | 17277 | 17289 | 17292 | 17293 | 17294 | 17295 | 17296 |
| | 17297 | 17298 | 17299 | 17366 | 17367 | 17400 | 17401 | 17403 |
| | 17404 | 17405 | 17406 | 17407 | 18201 | 18202 | 18203 | 18204 |
| | 18205 | 18206 | 18207 | 18208 | 18209 | 18210 | 18211 | 18212 |
| | 18213 | 18214 | 18215 | 18216 | 18217 | 18218 | 18219 | 18220 |
| | 18221 | 18222 | 18223 | 18224 | 18225 | 18226 | 18227 | 18228 |
| | 18229 | 18230 | 18231 | 18232 | 18233 | 18234 | 18235 | 18236 |
| | 18237 | 18238 | | | | | | |

## Bromley (Hastings Road, BR2 8NH) - TB

| Trident | | | | | | | | |
|---------|-------|-------|-------|-------|-------|-------|-------|-------|
| | 17286 | 17324 | 17339 | 17340 | 17341 | 17344 | 17346 | 17347 |
| | 17348 | 17349 | 17351 | 17352 | 17354 | 17355 | 17356 | 17357 |
| | 17358 | 17418 | 17419 | 17421 | 17422 | 17428 | 17429 | 17430 |
| | 17436 | 17437 | 17438 | 17439 | 17440 | 17441 | 17442 | 17965 |
| | 17966 | 17967 | 17968 | 17969 | 17970 | 17971 | 17972 | 17973 |
| | 17974 | 17975 | | | | | | |
| Trident 2 | 19131 | 19132 | 19133 | 19134 | 19135 | 19136 | 19137 | 19138 |
| | 19139 | 19140 | | | | | | |
| Dart SLF | 34224 | 34225 | 34226 | 34227 | 34228 | 34229 | 34230 | 34231 |
| | 34232 | 34233 | 34234 | 34235 | 34236 | 34310 | 34311 | 34312 |
| | 34317 | 34323 | 34346 | 34354 | 34355 | 34356 | 34357 | 34358 |
| | 34359 | 34360 | 34361 | 34362 | 34363 | 34364 | 34365 | |
| Dart 4 | 36309 | 36310 | 36311 | 36312 | 36313 | 36314 | 36315 | 36316 |
| | 36317 | 36318 | 36319 | | | | | |

## Catford (Bromley Road, SE6 2XA) - TL

| | | | | | | | | |
|---|---|---|---|---|---|---|---|---|
| Trident | 17225 | 17317 | 17318 | 17319 | 17321 | 17323 | 17338 | 17342 |
| | 17343 | 17345 | 17350 | 17362 | 17412 | 17413 | 17414 | 17415 |
| | 17416 | 17417 | 17420 | 17435 | 17467 | 17468 | 17469 | 17470 |
| | 17471 | 17472 | 17473 | 17474 | 17475 | 17476 | 17477 | 17478 |
| | 17479 | 17576 | 18455 | 18463 | 18464 | 18481 | 18482 | 18483 |
| | 18484 | 18485 | 18486 | 18487 | 18488 | 18489 | 18490 | 18491 |
| | 18492 | 18493 | 18494 | 18495 | 18496 | 18497 | 18498 | 18499 |
| Dart SLF | 34240 | 34241 | 34242 | 34243 | 34244 | 34245 | 34246 | 34247 |
| | 34249 | 34250 | 34251 | 34252 | 34253 | 34353 | 34366 | 34367 |
| | 34369 | 34370 | 34371 | 34372 | 34373 | 34374 | 34375 | 34376 |
| | 34377 | 34379 | 34388 | 34389 | 34390 | 34391 | 34392 | 34393 |
| | 34394 | 34395 | 34396 | 34397 | 34551 | 34552 | 34553 | 34554 |
| | 34555 | 34556 | 34557 | 34558 | 34559 | 34560 | | |
| Dart 4 | 36301 | 36302 | 36303 | 36304 | 36305 | 36306 | 36307 | 36308 |
| | 36320 | 36321 | 36322 | 36323 | 36324 | 36325 | 36326 | |

## Leyton (High Road, E10 6AD) - T

| | | | | | | | | |
|---|---|---|---|---|---|---|---|---|
| Scania CN230 | 15125 | 15126 | 15127 | 15128 | 15129 | 15130 | 15131 | 15132 |
| | 15133 | 15134 | 15135 | 15136 | 15137 | 15138 | 15139 | 15140 |
| | 15141 | 15142 | 15143 | 15144 | 15145 | 15146 | 15147 | 15148 |
| | 15149 | 15150 | 15151 | 15152 | 15153 | 15154 | 15155 | 15156 |
| | 15157 | 15158 | 15159 | 15160 | 15161 | 15162 | 15163 | 15164 |
| | 15165 | 15166 | 15167 | 15168 | 15169 | 15170 | 15171 | 15172 |
| | 15173 | 15174 | | | | | | |
| Trident | 17001 | 17181 | 17182 | 17183 | 17184 | 17409 | 17425 | 17482 |
| | 17485 | 17486 | 17504 | 17505 | 17506 | 17507 | 17510 | 17575 |
| | 17745 | 17746 | 17747 | 17749 | 17796 | 17797 | 17798 | 17799 |
| | 17800 | 17801 | 17802 | 17803 | 17804 | 17805 | 17806 | 17807 |
| | 17808 | 17809 | 17810 | 17811 | 17812 | 17813 | 17814 | 17815 |
| | 17816 | 17817 | 17820 | 17821 | 17822 | 17823 | 17824 | 17825 |
| | 17826 | 17827 | 17828 | 17841 | 17851 | 17852 | 17853 | 17871 |
| | 17873 | 17875 | 17876 | 17877 | 17878 | 17905 | 17906 | 17907 |
| | 17908 | 18266 | 18267 | 18268 | 18269 | 18270 | 18271 | 18272 |
| | 18273 | 18274 | 18275 | 18276 | 18277 | | | |

## Plumstead (Pettman Crescent, SE28 0BJ) - PD

| | | | | | | | | |
|---|---|---|---|---|---|---|---|---|
| Scania CN230 | 15036 | 15037 | 15038 | 15039 | 15040 | 15041 | 15042 | 15043 |
| | 15044 | 15045 | 15046 | 15047 | 15048 | 15049 | 15050 | 15051 |
| | 15052 | 15053 | 15054 | 15055 | 15056 | 15057 | 15058 | 15059 |
| | 15060 | 15061 | 15062 | 15063 | 15064 | 15065 | 15066 | 15067 |
| | 15068 | 15069 | 15070 | 15071 | 15072 | 15073 | 15074 | 15075 |
| | 15076 | 15077 | 15078 | 15079 | 15080 | 15081 | 15082 | 15083 |
| | 15084 | 15085 | 15086 | 15087 | 15088 | 15089 | 15090 | 15091 |
| | 15092 | 15093 | 15094 | 15095 | 15096 | | | |
| Trident | 17157 | 17159 | 17161 | 17162 | 17164 | 17166 | 17193 | 17195 |
| | 17214 | 17215 | 17216 | 17217 | 17218 | 17221 | 17222 | 17268 |
| | 17278 | 17303 | 17304 | 17305 | 17306 | 17307 | 17308 | 17309 |
| | 17310 | 17311 | 17312 | 17313 | 17314 | 17315 | 17316 | 17353 |
| | 17368 | 17372 | 17408 | 17427 | 17431 | 17434 | 17480 | 17481 |
| | 17502 | 17503 | 17508 | 17511 | 17512 | 17560 | 17563 | 17570 |
| | 17571 | 17572 | 17573 | 17789 | 17790 | 17836 | 17837 | 17838 |
| | 17839 | 17840 | 17866 | 17945 | 17946 | 17947 | 17948 | 17949 |
| | 17950 | 17951 | 17952 | 17953 | 17954 | 17955 | 17956 | 17957 |
| | 17958 | 17959 | 17960 | 17961 | 17962 | 17963 | 17964 | 18456 |
| Trident 2 | 19742 | 19743 | 19744 | 19745 | 19746 | 19747 | 19748 | 19749 |
| | 19750 | 19751 | 19752 | 19753 | 19754 | 19755 | 19806 | 19807 |
| | 19808 | 19809 | 19810 | 19811 | 19812 | 19813 | 19814 | 19815 |
| | 19816 | 19817 | 19818 | 19819 | 19820 | 19821 | 19822 | 19823 |
| | 19824 | 19825 | 19826 | 19827 | 19828 | 19829 | 19830 | 19831 |
| | 19832 | 19833 | 19834 | | | | | |

| Optare Versa | 25301 | 25302 | 25303 | 25304 | 25305 | 25306 | 25307 | 25308 |
| | 25309 | | | | | | | |
| Dart SLF | 34162 | 34163 | 34378 | 34380 | 34381 | 34382 | 34383 | 34384 |
| | 34385 | 34386 | | | | | | |
| Dart 4 | 36327 | 36328 | 36329 | 36330 | 36331 | 36332 | 36333 | 36334 |
| | 36335 | 36336 | 36337 | | | | | |

## Rainham (Albright Industrial Estate, Ferry Lane, RM13 9BU) - RM

| Scania CN230 | 15001 | 15002 | 15003 | 15004 | 15005 | 15006 | 15007 | 15008 |
| | 15009 | 15010 | 15011 | 15012 | 15013 | 15014 | 15015 | |
| Trident | 17391 | 17392 | 17393 | 17459 | 17523 | 17524 | 17525 | 17526 |
| | 17527 | | | | | | | |
| Trident 2 | 19711 | 19712 | 19713 | 19714 | 19715 | 19716 | 19717 | 19718 |
| | 19719 | 19720 | 19721 | 19722 | 19723 | 19724 | 19725 | 19726 |
| | 19727 | 19728 | 19729 | 19730 | 19731 | 19732 | 19733 | |
| Dart 4 | 36338 | 36339 | 36340 | 36341 | 36342 | 36343 | 36344 | |

## Romford (North Street, RM1 1DS) - NS

| Trident | 17288 | 17300 | 17328 | 17394 | 17455 | 17465 | 17483 | 17484 |
| | 17513 | 17533 | 17534 | 17537 | 17538 | 17539 | 17540 | 17541 |
| | 17543 | 17544 | 17559 | 17562 | 17564 | 17565 | 17566 | 17567 |
| | 17568 | 17569 | 17574 | 17577 | 17578 | 17748 | 17759 | 17760 |
| | 17761 | 17762 | 17763 | 17764 | 17765 | 17766 | 17778 | 17769 |
| | 17770 | 17771 | 17772 | 17773 | 17774 | 17775 | 17776 | 17777 |
| | 17778 | 17791 | 17792 | 17793 | 17829 | 17830 | 17835 | 17854 |
| | 17867 | 17868 | 17869 | 17870 | 17874 | 17976 | 17977 | 17978 |
| | 17979 | 17980 | 17981 | 17982 | 17983 | 17984 | 17985 | 17986 |
| | 17987 | 17988 | 17989 | 17990 | 17991 | 17992 | 17993 | 17994 |
| | 17995 | 17996 | 17997 | 17998 | 17999 | 18451 | 18452 | 18453 |
| | 18454 | | | | | | | |
| Trident 2 | 19734 | 19735 | 19736 | 19737 | 19738 | 19739 | 19740 | 19741 |
| | 19786 | 19787 | 19788 | 19789 | 19790 | 19791 | 19792 | 19793 |
| Dart 4 | 36261 | 36262 | 36263 | 36264 | 36265 | 36266 | 36267 | |

## Upton Park (Redclyffe Road, E6 1DS) - U

| Trident | 17141 | 17220 | 17231 | 17232 | 17233 | 17243 | 17456 | 17457 |
| | 17458 | 17460 | 17461 | 17462 | 17463 | 17464 | 17495 | 17496 |
| | 17497 | 17498 | 17499 | 17500 | 17501 | 17528 | 17529 | 17535 |
| | 17536 | 17545 | 17546 | 17547 | 17548 | 17549 | 17550 | 17551 |
| | 17552 | 17553 | 17554 | 17555 | 17556 | 17557 | 17558 | 17580 |
| | 17581 | 17582 | 17583 | 17584 | 17585 | 17586 | 17587 | 17588 |
| | 17589 | 17590 | 17591 | 17779 | 17780 | 17788 | 17831 | 17833 |
| | 17834 | 17842 | 17843 | 17844 | 17845 | 17847 | 17848 | 17849 |
| | 17850 | 17864 | 17865 | 17889 | 17890 | 17891 | 17903 | 17934 |
| | 17935 | 17936 | 17937 | 17938 | 17939 | 17940 | 17941 | 17942 |
| | 17943 | 17944 | 18257 | 18258 | 18259 | 18260 | 18261 | 18262 |
| | 18263 | 18264 | 18265 | 18457 | 18458 | 18459 | 18460 | 18461 |
| | 18462 | | | | | | | |
| Dart SLF | 34262 | 34294 | 34295 | 34296 | 34318 | 34319 | 34324 | 34325 |
| | 34326 | 34327 | | | | | | |

## West Ham (Stephenson Street, Canning Town, E6 4SA) - WH

| | | | | | | | | |
|---|---|---|---|---|---|---|---|---|
| Scania CN230 | 15016 | 15017 | 15018 | 15019 | 15020 | 15021 | 15022 | 15023 |
| | 15024 | 15025 | 15026 | 15027 | 15028 | 15029 | 15030 | 15031 |
| | 15032 | 15033 | 15034 | 15035 | | | | |
| Trident | 17224 | 17251 | 17252 | 17253 | 17254 | 17255 | 17256 | 17257 |
| | 17258 | 17259 | 17260 | 17282 | 17433 | 17451 | 17452 | 17487 |
| | 17488 | 17489 | 17490 | 17491 | 17493 | 17494 | 17509 | 17514 |
| | 17515 | 17516 | 17517 | 17518 | 17519 | 17520 | 17521 | 17522 |
| | 17530 | 17531 | 17561 | 17579 | 17740 | 17741 | 17742 | 17743 |
| | 17744 | 17750 | 17751 | 17752 | 17753 | 17754 | 17755 | 17756 |
| | 17757 | 17781 | 17782 | 17783 | 17784 | 17785 | 17786 | 17787 |
| | 17794 | 17795 | 17818 | 17819 | 17832 | 17846 | 17855 | 17879 |
| | 17909 | 17910 | 17911 | 17912 | 17913 | 17914 | 17915 | 17916 |
| | 17917 | 17918 | 17919 | 17920 | 17921 | 17922 | 17923 | 17924 |
| | 17925 | 17926 | 17927 | 17928 | 17929 | 17930 | 17931 | 17933 |
| | 18239 | 18240 | 18241 | 18242 | 18243 | 18244 | 18245 | 18246 |
| | 18247 | 18248 | 18249 | 18250 | 18251 | 18252 | 18253 | 18254 |
| | 18255 | 18256 | 18465 | 18466 | 18467 | 18468 | 18469 | 18470 |
| | 18471 | 18472 | 18473 | 18474 | 18475 | 18476 | 18477 | 18478 |
| | 18479 | 18480 | | | | | | |
| Trident 2 | 19000 | | | | | | | |
| Routemaster | 19960 | 19961 | 19962 | 19963 | 19964 | 19965 | 19966 | 19967 |
| | 19968 | 19969 | 19970 | | | | | |
| Citaro Artic | 23019 | 23027 | 23028 | 23029 | 23031 | 23032 | 23033 | 23034 |
| | 23035 | 23036 | 23037 | 23038 | 23039 | 23040 | 23041 | 23042 |
| | 23043 | 23044 | 23045 | 23046 | 23047 | 23048 | 23049 | 23050 |
| | 23051 | 23052 | 23053 | 23054 | 23055 | 23056 | 23057 | 23058 |
| | 23059 | 23060 | 23061 | 23062 | 23063 | 23064 | 23065 | 23066 |
| | 23067 | 23068 | 23069 | 23070 | 23071 | 23072 | 23073 | 23074 |
| | 23075 | 23076 | 23077 | | | | | |
| Optare Tempo | 25111 | 25112 | 25113 | 25114 | 25115 | | | |
| Dart SLF | 34255 | 34271 | 34273 | 34329 | 32330 | 32331 | 32332 | 32333 |
| | 32334 | 32335 | 32336 | 32337 | 32339 | 32340 | 32341 | 32342 |
| | 32343 | 32344 | 32345 | | | | | |
| Dart 4 | 36345 | 36346 | 36347 | 36348 | 36349 | 36350 | 36351 | 36352 |
| | 36353 | 36354 | 36355 | 36356 | 36357 | 36358 | 36359 | 36360 |
| | 36361 | 36362 | 36363 | 36364 | 36365 | 36366 | 36367 | 36368 |
| | 36369 | 36370 | 36371 | 36372 | 36373 | 36374 | 36375 | |

## London unallocated and stored - LN

Remainder

# Vehicle Index

| Reg | Operator | Reg | Operator | Reg | Operator | Reg | Operator |
|---|---|---|---|---|---|---|---|
| 33LUG | Metroline | AE09DHU | Metrobus | BD09ZWF | Go-Ahead London | BF60UUA | First London |
| 70CLT | Arriva London | AE09DHV | Metrobus | BD09ZWG | Go-Ahead London | BF60UUB | First London |
| 185CLT | Arriva London | AE56OUH | Go-Ahead London | BD09ZWH | Go-Ahead London | BF60UUC | First London |
| 201KYD | Arriva Original Tour | AE56OUJ | Go-Ahead London | BD51YCR | London United | BF60UUD | First London |
| 204CLT | First London | AE56OUK | Go-Ahead London | BD51YCS | London United | BF60UUE | First London |
| 205CLT | Arriva London | AE56OUL | Go-Ahead London | BD51YCT | London United | BF60UUG | First London |
| 217CLT | Arriva London | AE56OUM | Go-Ahead London | BD52LMO | Go-Ahead London | BF60UUH | First London |
| 218CLT | First London | AE56OUN | Go-Ahead London | BD52LMU | Go-Ahead London | BF60UUJ | First London |
| 280CLT | First London | AE56OUO | Go-Ahead London | BD52LMV | Go-Ahead London | BF60UUK | First London |
| 319CLT | Arriva London | AE56OUP | Go-Ahead London | BD52LMX | Go-Ahead London | BF60UUL | First London |
| 324CLT | Arriva London | AE56OUS | Go-Ahead London | BD52LMY | Go-Ahead London | BF60UUM | First London |
| 330CLT | Arriva London | AJ58WBD | Metrobus | BD52LNA | Go-Ahead London | BF60UUN | First London |
| 361CLT | Arriva London | AJ58WBE | Metrobus | BD52LNC | Go-Ahead London | BF60UUO | First London |
| 398CLT | Arriva London | AJ58WBF | Metrobus | BD52LNE | Go-Ahead London | BF60UUP | First London |
| 453CLT | Arriva London | AJ58WBG | Metrobus | BD52LNF | Go-Ahead London | BF60UUR | First London |
| 464CLT | Arriva London | AJ58WBK | Metrobus | BD52LNG | Go-Ahead London | BF60UUS | First London |
| 510CLT | First London | ALD50B | Stagecoach | BD52LNO | Go-Ahead London | BF60UUT | First London |
| 513CLT | Metroline | ALD60B | Stagecoach | BD52LNP | Go-Ahead London | BF60UUV | First London |
| 519CLT | Arriva London | ALD71B | Stagecoach | BD52LNR | Go-Ahead London | BF60UUW | First London |
| 527CLT | Stagecoach | ALD89B | Stagecoach | BD52LNT | Go-Ahead London | BF60UUX | First London |
| 562CLT | First London | ALD913B | First London | BD52LNU | Go-Ahead London | BF60UUY | First London |
| 593CLT | Arriva London | ALD933B | Stagecoach | BD57OXJ | Go-Ahead London | BF60UUZ | First London |
| 627DYE | First London | ALD941B | Stagecoach | BD57OXK | Go-Ahead London | BF60UVA | First London |
| 630DYE | Stagecoach | ALD968B | Stagecoach | BD57OXM | Go-Ahead London | BF60UVB | First London |
| 640DYE | First London | B14BUS | Big Bus Company | BD57OXN | Go-Ahead London | BF60UVD | First London |
| 650DYE | First London | B15BUS | Big Bus Company | BD57OXP | Go-Ahead London | BF60UVE | First London |
| 656DYE | Arriva London | B16BUS | Big Bus Company | BD57UYE | Go-Ahead London | BF60UVG | First London |
| 725DYE | Arriva London | B20DMS | Big Bus Company | BD57UYF | Go-Ahead London | BF60UVH | First London |
| 734DYE | Arriva London | BD09ZPR | Go-Ahead London | BD57UYG | Go-Ahead London | BF60UVO | First London |
| 735DYE | First London | BD09ZPS | Go-Ahead London | BD57UYH | Go-Ahead London | BF60VHP | First London |
| 776DYE | First London | BD09ZPT | Go-Ahead London | BD57UYJ | Go-Ahead London | BF60VHR | First London |
| 801DYE | Arriva London | BD09ZPU | Go-Ahead London | BD57UYK | Go-Ahead London | BF60VHU | First London |
| 822DYE | Arriva London | BD09ZPV | Go-Ahead London | BD57UYL | Go-Ahead London | BF60VHV | First London |
| A638THV | Big Bus Company | BD09ZPW | Go-Ahead London | BD57WCY | Go-Ahead London | BF60VHW | First London |
| A735WEV | Arriva Original Tour | BD09ZPX | Go-Ahead London | BD57WCZ | Go-Ahead London | BF60VHX | First London |
| A737WEV | Arriva Original Tour | BD09ZPY | Go-Ahead London | BD57WDA | Go-Ahead London | BF60VHY | First London |
| A749WEV | Arriva Original Tour | BD09ZPZ | Go-Ahead London | BD57WDC | Go-Ahead London | BF60VHZ | First London |
| A750WEV | Arriva Original Tour | BD09ZRA | Go-Ahead London | BD57WDE | Go-Ahead London | BF60VJA | First London |
| A755WEV | Arriva Original Tour | BD09ZRC | Go-Ahead London | BD57WDK | Go-Ahead London | BF60VJC | First London |
| A928SYE | Big Bus Company | BD09ZRE | Go-Ahead London | BD57WDL | Go-Ahead London | BF60VJD | First London |
| AE06HCD | Go-Ahead London | BD09ZRF | Go-Ahead London | BD57WDM | Go-Ahead London | BF60VJE | First London |
| AE06HCF | Go-Ahead London | BD09ZRG | Go-Ahead London | BD57WDN | Go-Ahead London | BF60VJG | First London |
| AE06HCG | Go-Ahead London | BD09ZRJ | Go-Ahead London | BD57WDP | Go-Ahead London | BF60VJJ | First London |
| AE06HCH | Go-Ahead London | BD09ZRK | Go-Ahead London | BD57WDR | Go-Ahead London | BF60VJK | First London |
| AE06HCJ | Go-Ahead London | BD09ZVS | Go-Ahead London | BD57WDS | Go-Ahead London | BF60VJL | First London |
| AE06HCJA | Go-Ahead London | BD09ZVT | Go-Ahead London | BD57WDT | Go-Ahead London | BF60VJM | First London |
| AE06HCK | Go-Ahead London | BD09ZVU | Go-Ahead London | BF10LSO | First London | BF60VJN | First London |
| AE06HCKC | Go-Ahead London | BD09ZVV | Go-Ahead London | BF10LSU | First London | BF60VJO | First London |
| AE09DHG | Metrobus | BD09ZVW | Go-Ahead London | BF10LSV | First London | BF60VJP | First London |
| AE09DHJ | Metrobus | BD09ZVX | Go-Ahead London | BF10LSX | First London | BF60VJU | First London |
| AE09DHK | Metrobus | BD09ZVY | Go-Ahead London | BF10LSY | First London | BF60VJV | First London |
| AE09DHL | Metrobus | BD09ZVZ | Go-Ahead London | BF10LSZ | First London | BG09JJK | Go-Ahead London |
| AE09DHM | Metrobus | BD09ZWA | Go-Ahead London | BF10LTA | First London | BG09JJL | Go-Ahead London |
| AE09DHN | Metrobus | BD09ZWB | Go-Ahead London | BF10LTE | First London | BG09JJU | Go-Ahead London |
| AE09DHO | Metrobus | BD09ZWC | Go-Ahead London | BF10LTJ | First London | BG09JJV | Go-Ahead London |
| AE09DHP | Metrobus | BD09ZWE | Go-Ahead London | BF60UTZ | First London | | |

| Reg | Operator | Reg | Operator | Reg | Operator | Reg | Operator |
|---|---|---|---|---|---|---|---|
| BG09JJX | Go-Ahead London | BJ11EAG | First London | BU05HFC | Abellio | BX04AZZ | Go-Ahead London |
| BG09JJY | Go-Ahead London | BJ11EAK | First London | BU05HFD | Abellio | BX04BAA | Go-Ahead London |
| BG09JJZ | Go-Ahead London | BJ11EAM | First London | BU05HFG | Hackney CT | BX04BAU | Go-Ahead London |
| BG09JKE | Go-Ahead London | BJ11EAO | First London | BU05HFK | Abellio | BX04BAV | Go-Ahead London |
| BG09JKF | Go-Ahead London | BJ11EAP | First London | BU05HFV | Abellio | BX04BBE | Go-Ahead London |
| BG09JKJ | Go-Ahead London | BJ11EAW | First London | BU05HFW | Abellio | BX04BBF | Go-Ahead London |
| BG59FXA | First London | BJ11EAX | First London | BU05HFX | Abellio | BX04BBJ | Go-Ahead London |
| BG59FXB | First London | BJ11EAY | First London | BU05VFD | Arriva London | BX04BKJ | Go-Ahead London |
| BG59FXC | First London | BJ11EBA | First London | BU05VFE | Arriva London | BX04BKK | Go-Ahead London |
| BG59FXD | First London | BJ11EBC | First London | BU05VFF | Arriva London | BX04BKL | Go-Ahead London |
| BG59FXE | First London | BJ11EBD | First London | BU05VFG | Arriva London | BX04BXL | Go-Ahead London |
| BG59FXF | First London | BJ11EBG | First London | BU05VFH | Arriva London | BX04BXM | Go-Ahead London |
| BG59FXH | First London | BJ11EBK | First London | BU05VFJ | Arriva London | BX04BXN | Go-Ahead London |
| BJ11DRZ | First London | BJ11EBL | First London | BV10WVD | First London | BX04BXP | Go-Ahead London |
| BJ11DSE | First London | BJ11EBM | First London | BV10WVE | First London | BX04MWW | Arriva London |
| BJ11DSO | First London | BJ11EBN | First London | BV10WVF | First London | BX04MWY | Arriva London |
| BJ11DSU | First London | BJ11EBO | First London | BV10WVG | First London | BX04MWZ | Arriva London |
| BJ11DSV | First London | BJ11EBP | First London | BV10WVH | First London | BX04MXA | Arriva London |
| BJ11DSX | First London | BJ11XGZ | Go-Ahead London | BV10WVJ | First London | BX04MXD | Arriva London |
| BJ11DSY | First London | BK10MEV | First London | BV10WVK | First London | BX04MXE | Arriva London |
| BJ11DSZ | First London | BK10MFA | First London | BV10WVL | First London | BX04MXJ | Arriva London |
| BJ11DTF | First London | BK10MFE | First London | BV10WVM | First London | BX04MXN | Arriva London |
| BJ11DTK | First London | BK10MFF | First London | BV10WVN | First London | BX04MXP | Arriva London |
| BJ11DTN | First London | BK10MFJ | First London | BV10WVO | First London | BX04MXR | Arriva London |
| BJ11DTO | First London | BK10MFN | First London | BV10WVU | First London | BX04MXS | Arriva London |
| BJ11DTU | First London | BK10MFO | First London | BV10WVW | First London | BX04MXU | Arriva London |
| BJ11DTV | First London | BK10MFZ | First London | BV10WVX | First London | BX04MXW | Arriva London |
| BJ11DTX | First London | BK10WVP | First London | BV10WWA | First London | BX04MYB | Arriva London |
| BJ11DTY | First London | BK10WVR | First London | BV10WWB | First London | BX04MYC | Arriva London |
| BJ11DTZ | First London | BK10WVS | First London | BV10WWC | First London | BX04MYD | Arriva London |
| BJ11DUA | First London | BK10WVT | First London | BV10WWD | First London | BX04MYF | Arriva London |
| BJ11DUH | First London | BL52ODK | Go-Ahead London | BV10WWE | First London | BX04MYJ | Arriva London |
| BJ11DUU | First London | BL52ODM | Go-Ahead London | BV10WWF | First London | BX04MYK | Arriva London |
| BJ11DUV | First London | BL52ODN | Go-Ahead London | BV10WWG | First London | BX04MYL | Arriva London |
| BJ11DUY | First London | BL52ODP | Go-Ahead London | BV10WWH | First London | BX04MYM | Arriva London |
| BJ11DVA | First London | BL52ODR | Go-Ahead London | BV10WWJ | First London | BX04MYN | Arriva London |
| BJ11DVB | First London | BL52ODT | Go-Ahead London | BV10WWK | First London | BX04MYR | Arriva London |
| BJ11DVC | First London | BL52ODU | Go-Ahead London | BV10WWL | First London | BX04MYS | Arriva London |
| BJ11DVF | First London | BL52ODV | Go-Ahead London | BV10WWM | First London | BX04MYT | Arriva London |
| BJ11DVG | First London | BN52GVU | Go-Ahead London | BV10WWN | First London | BX04MYU | Arriva London |
| BJ11DVH | First London | BN52GWC | Go-Ahead London | BV10WWO | First London | BX04MYV | Arriva London |
| BJ11DVK | First London | BN52GWD | Go-Ahead London | BV10WWP | First London | BX04MYW | Arriva London |
| BJ11DVL | First London | BN52GWE | Go-Ahead London | BV10WWR | First London | BX04MYY | Arriva London |
| BJ11DVM | First London | BSK157 | London Duck Tours | BV10WWS | First London | BX04MYZ | Arriva London |
| BJ11DVN | First London | BT04BUS | Go-Ahead London | BV10WWT | First London | BX04MYZ | Arriva London |
| BJ11DVO | First London | BT09GOH | Go-Ahead London | BV10WWU | First London | BX04MZE | Arriva London |
| BJ11DVP | First London | BT09GOJ | Go-Ahead London | BV10WWX | First London | BX04MZG | Arriva London |
| BJ11DVR | First London | BT09GOK | Go-Ahead London | BV10WWY | First London | BX04MZJ | Arriva London |
| BJ11DVT | First London | BT09GOP | Go-Ahead London | BV10WWZ | First London | BX04MZL | Arriva London |
| BJ11DVU | First London | BT09GOU | Go-Ahead London | BV55UCT | Go-Ahead London | BX04MZN | Arriva London |
| BJ11DVV | First London | BT09GOX | Go-Ahead London | BV55UCU | Go-Ahead London | BX04NBD | Go-Ahead London |
| BJ11DVW | First London | BT09GPE | Go-Ahead London | BV55UCW | Go-Ahead London | BX04NBK | Arriva London |
| BJ11DVX | First London | BT09GPF | Go-Ahead London | BV55UCX | Go-Ahead London | BX04NBL | Arriva London |
| BJ11DZX | First London | BT09GPJ | Go-Ahead London | BV55UCY | Go-Ahead London | BX04NCF | Arriva London |
| BJ11DZY | First London | BU04EZK | Go-Ahead London | BW03ZMZ | Quality Line | BX04NCJ | Arriva London |
| BJ11DZZ | First London | BU04UTM | Go-Ahead London | BX02YYT | Go-Ahead London | BX04NCN | Arriva London |
| BJ11EAA | First London | BU05HDY | Abellio | BX02YZE | Go-Ahead London | BX04NCU | Arriva London |
| BJ11EAC | First London | BU05HEJ | Abellio | BX04AZU | Go-Ahead London | BX04NCV | Arriva London |
| BJ11EAE | First London | BU05HFA | Abellio | BX04AZV | Go-Ahead London | BX04NCY | Arriva London |
| BJ11EAF | First London | BU05HFB | Abellio | BX04AZW | Go-Ahead London | BX04NCZ | Arriva London |

*The London Bus Handbook*

**Arriva continues to operate Route 73 using Merceded-Benz articulated buses. MA93, BX55FUM was well patronised when pictured in Park Lane.** *Mark Lyons*

| | | | | | | | |
|---|---|---|---|---|---|---|---|
| BX04NDC | Arriva London | BX54DHZ | Abellio | BX54DMZ | Abellio | BX54UDV | Go-Ahead London |
| BX04NDE | Arriva London | BX54DJD | Abellio | BX54EBC | First London | BX54UDW | Go-Ahead London |
| BX04NDF | Arriva London | BX54DJE | Abellio | BX54EFB | Go-Ahead London | BX54UDY | Go-Ahead London |
| BX04NDJ | Arriva London | BX54DJF | Abellio | BX54EFC | Go-Ahead London | BX54UDZ | Go-Ahead London |
| BX04NDK | Arriva London | BX54DJJ | Abellio | BX54EFD | Go-Ahead London | BX54UEA | Go-Ahead London |
| BX04NDL | Arriva London | BX54DJK | Abellio | BX54UCM | Go-Ahead London | BX54UEB | Go-Ahead London |
| BX04NDN | Arriva London | BX54DJO | Abellio | BX54UCN | Go-Ahead London | BX55FUH | Arriva London |
| BX04NDU | Arriva London | BX54DJU | Abellio | BX54UCO | Go-Ahead London | BX55FUJ | Arriva London |
| BX04NDV | Arriva London | BX54DJV | Abellio | BX54UCP | Go-Ahead London | BX55FUM | Arriva London |
| BX04NDY | Arriva London | BX54DJY | Abellio | BX54UCR | Go-Ahead London | BX55FUO | Arriva London |
| BX04NDZ | Arriva London | BX54DJZ | Abellio | BX54UCT | Go-Ahead London | BX55FUP | Arriva London |
| BX04NEF | Arriva London | BX54DKA | Abellio | BX54UCU | Go-Ahead London | BX55FUT | Arriva London |
| BX04NEJ | Arriva London | BX54DKD | Abellio | BX54UCV | Go-Ahead London | BX55FUU | Arriva London |
| BX04NEN | Arriva London | BX54DKE | Abellio | BX54UCW | Go-Ahead London | BX55FUV | Arriva London |
| BX05UWV | Arriva London | BX54DKF | Abellio | BX54UCZ | Go-Ahead London | BX55FUW | Arriva London |
| BX05UWW | Arriva London | BX54DKJ | Abellio | BX54UDB | Go-Ahead London | BX55FWA | Arriva London |
| BX05UWY | Arriva London | BX54DKK | Abellio | BX54UDD | Go-Ahead London | BX55FWB | Arriva London |
| BX05UWZ | Arriva London | BX54DKL | Abellio | BX54UDE | Go-Ahead London | BX55FXH | Arriva London |
| BX05UXC | Arriva London | BX54DKO | Abellio | BX54UDG | Go-Ahead London | BX55FXT | Arriva London |
| BX05UXD | Arriva London | BX54DKU | Abellio | BX54UDH | Go-Ahead London | BX55FXV | Arriva London |
| BX54DHJ | Abellio | BX54DKV | Abellio | BX54UDJ | Go-Ahead London | BX55FXW | Arriva London |
| BX54DHK | Abellio | BX54DLU | Abellio | BX54UDK | Go-Ahead London | BX55FXY | Arriva London |
| BX54DHL | Abellio | BX54DLZ | Abellio | BX54UDL | Go-Ahead London | BX55XLS | Abellio |
| BX54DHM | Abellio | BX54DME | Abellio | BX54UDM | Go-Ahead London | BX55XLT | Abellio |
| BX54DHN | Abellio | BX54DMF | Abellio | BX54UDN | Go-Ahead London | BX55XLU | Abellio |
| BX54DHO | Abellio | BX54DMO | Abellio | BX54UDO | Go-Ahead London | BX55XLV | Abellio |
| BX54DHP | Abellio | BX54DMU | Abellio | BX54UDP | Go-Ahead London | BX55XLW | Abellio |
| BX54DHV | Abellio | BX54DMV | Abellio | BX54UDT | Go-Ahead London | BX55XLY | Abellio |
| BX54DHY | Abellio | BX54DMY | Abellio | BX54UDU | Go-Ahead London | BX55XLZ | Abellio |

| | | | | | | | | |
|---|---|---|---|---|---|---|---|---|
| BX55XMA | Abellio | E359NUV | Big Bus Company | FJ54ZVB | Go-Ahead London | GN08CGU | Arriva Southern C |
| BX55XMB | Abellio | E360NUV | Big Bus Company | G32FWC | Big Bus Company | GN08CGV | Arriva Southern C |
| BX55XMC | Abellio | E764JAR | Big Bus Company | G34FWC | Big Bus Company | GN08CGX | Arriva Southern C |
| BX55XMD | Abellio | E767JAR | Arriva Original Tour | G42FWC | Big Bus Company | GN08CGY | Arriva Southern C |
| BX55XME | Abellio | E769JAR | Arriva Original Tour | G59SYE | Big Bus Company | GN08CGZ | Arriva Southern C |
| BX55XMG | Abellio | E770JAR | Arriva Original Tour | G67SYE | Big Bus Company | GN08CHC | Arriva Southern C |
| BX55XMH | Abellio | E771JAR | Arriva Original Tour | G96SGO | Big Bus Company | GN08CHD | Arriva Southern C |
| BX55XMJ | Abellio | E773JAR | Arriva Original Tour | G159FWC | Big Bus Company | GN08CHF | Arriva Southern C |
| BX55XMK | Abellio | E869JAR | Big Bus Company | G938FVX | Big Bus Company | GN08CHG | Arriva Southern C |
| BX55XML | Abellio | E881JAR | Big Bus Company | G939FVX | Big Bus Company | GN08CHH | Arriva Southern C |
| BX55XMM | Abellio | E901JAR | Big Bus Company | G943FVX | Big Bus Company | GN09AVV | Arriva Southern C |
| BX55XMP | Abellio | E949JAR | Big Bus Company | G952FVX | Big Bus Company | GN09AVW | Arriva Southern C |
| BX55XMR | Abellio | E964JAR | Arriva Original Tour | G953FVX | Big Bus Company | GN09AVX | Arriva Southern C |
| BX55XMS | Abellio | E965JAR | Arriva Original Tour | G954FVX | Big Bus Company | GN09AVY | Arriva Southern C |
| BX55XMT | Abellio | EJ52WXF | Go-Ahead London | G956FVX | Big Bus Company | GN09AVZ | Arriva Southern C |
| BX55XMU | Abellio | ESL636 | London Duck Tours | G963FVX | Big Bus Company | GN09AWA | Arriva Southern C |
| BX55XMV | Abellio | ESL660 | London Duck Tours | G969FVX | Big Bus Company | GN09AWB | Arriva Southern C |
| BX55XMW | Abellio | ESL679 | London Duck Tours | G991FVX | Big Bus Company | GN09AWC | Arriva Southern C |
| BX55XMZ | Abellio | EU04BVD | Go-Ahead London | GK53AOA | Arriva Southern C | GN10KWE | Arriva Southern C |
| BX55XNG | Abellio | EU04BVF | Go-Ahead London | GK53AOB | Arriva Southern C | GN10KWF | Arriva Southern C |
| BX55XNJ | Abellio | EU05DVW | Arriva Original Tour | GK53AOC | Arriva Southern C | GN10KWG | Arriva Southern C |
| BX55XNK | Abellio | EU05DVX | Arriva Original Tour | GK53AOD | Arriva Southern C | GN10KWH | Arriva Southern C |
| BX55XNL | Abellio | EU53PXY | Go-Ahead London | GK53AOE | Arriva Southern C | GN10KWJ | Arriva Southern C |
| BX55XNM | Abellio | EU53PXZ | Go-Ahead London | GK53AOF | Arriva Southern C | GN10KWK | Arriva Southern C |
| BX55XNN | Abellio | EU53PYA | Go-Ahead London | GK53AOG | Arriva Southern C | GN57BOU | Arriva Southern C |
| BX55XNO | Abellio | EU53PYB | Go-Ahead London | GK53AOH | Arriva Southern C | GN57BOV | Arriva Southern C |
| BX55XNP | Abellio | EU53PYD | Go-Ahead London | GK53AOJ | Arriva Southern C | GN57BPE | Arriva Southern C |
| BX55XNR | Abellio | EU53PYF | Go-Ahead London | GK53AOL | Arriva Southern C | GN57BPF | Arriva Southern C |
| BX55XNS | Abellio | EU53PYG | Go-Ahead London | GK53AON | Arriva Southern C | GN57BPK | Arriva Southern C |
| BX55XNT | Abellio | EU53PYH | Go-Ahead London | GK53AOO | Arriva Southern C | GN57BPO | Arriva Southern C |
| BX55XNU | Abellio | EU53PYJ | Go-Ahead London | GK53AOP | Arriva Southern C | GN57BPU | Arriva Southern C |
| BX55XNV | Abellio | EU53PYL | Go-Ahead London | GK53AOR | Arriva Southern C | GN57BPV | Arriva Southern C |
| BX55XNW | Abellio | EU53PYO | Go-Ahead London | GK53AOT | Arriva Southern C | GN57BPX | Arriva Southern C |
| BX55XNY | Abellio | EU53PYP | Go-Ahead London | GK53AOV | Arriva Southern C | GN57BPY | Arriva Southern C |
| BX55XNZ | Abellio | F69SYE | Big Bus Company | GK53AOW | Arriva Southern C | GN58BUP | Arriva Southern C |
| CUV217C | Arriva London | F90SYE | Big Bus Company | GK53AOX | Arriva Southern C | GN58BUU | Arriva Southern C |
| CUV305C | Go-Ahead London | F153UJN | Big Bus Company | GK53AOY | Arriva Southern C | GN58BUV | Arriva Southern C |
| CUV318C | Go-Ahead London | F326UJN | Big Bus Company | GM03TGM | Abellio | GN58LVA | Arriva Southern C |
| CUV335C | Arriva London | F418UJN | Big Bus Company | GN07AUY | Metrobus | GN58LVB | Arriva Southern C |
| D512UGT | Big Bus Company | F601XMS | First London | GN07AVR | Metrobus | HV02OZT | Hackney CT |
| D514UGT | Big Bus Company | FJ54ZDC | Go-Ahead London | GN07AVT | Metrobus | HV02PDO | Hackney CT |
| D519UGT | Big Bus Company | FJ54ZDP | Go-Ahead London | GN07AVU | Metrobus | HV52WSZ | Quality Line |
| D525UGT | Big Bus Company | FJ54ZDR | Go-Ahead London | GN07AVV | Metrobus | HX03MGJ | Hackney CT |
| D527UGT | Big Bus Company | FJ54ZDT | Go-Ahead London | GN07AVW | Metrobus | HX03MGU | Hackney CT |
| D553YNO | Arriva Original Tour | FJ54ZDU | Go-Ahead London | GN07DLE | Arriva Southern C | HX03MGV | Hackney CT |
| D675YNO | Arriva Original Tour | FJ54ZDV | Go-Ahead London | GN07DLF | Arriva Southern C | HX03MGY | Hackney CT |
| D690UGT | Big Bus Company | FJ54ZDW | Go-Ahead London | GN07DLJ | Arriva Southern C | HX03MGZ | Hackney CT |
| D692UGT | Big Bus Company | FJ54ZDX | Go-Ahead London | GN07DLK | Arriva Southern C | HX04HTP | Abellio |
| E336NUV | Big Bus Company | FJ54ZDY | Go-Ahead London | GN07DLO | Arriva Southern C | HX04HTT | Abellio |
| E337NUV | Big Bus Company | FJ54ZDZ | Go-Ahead London | GN07DLU | Arriva Southern C | HX04HTU | Abellio |
| E338NUV | Big Bus Company | FJ54ZFA | Go-Ahead London | GN07DLV | Arriva Southern C | HX04HTV | Abellio |
| E340NUV | Big Bus Company | FJ54ZTV | Go-Ahead London | GN07DLX | Arriva Southern C | HX04HTY | Abellio |
| E351NUV | Big Bus Company | FJ54ZTW | Go-Ahead London | GN07DLY | Arriva Southern C | HX04HTZ | Abellio |
| E352NUV | Big Bus Company | FJ54ZTX | Go-Ahead London | GN07DLZ | Arriva Southern C | J315BSH | Arriva Original Tour |
| E353NUV | Big Bus Company | FJ54ZTY | Go-Ahead London | GN07DME | Arriva Southern C | J316BSH | Arriva Original Tour |
| E354NUV | Big Bus Company | FJ54ZTZ | Go-Ahead London | GN07DMF | Arriva Southern C | J317BSH | Arriva Original Tour |
| E355NUV | Big Bus Company | FJ54ZUA | Go-Ahead London | GN07DMO | Arriva Southern C | J318BSH | Arriva Original Tour |
| E356NUV | Big Bus Company | FJ54ZUC | Go-Ahead London | GN07DMU | Arriva Southern C | J319BSH | Arriva Original Tour |
| E357NUV | Big Bus Company | FJ54ZUD | Go-Ahead London | GN07DMV | Arriva Southern C | J320BSH | Arriva Original Tour |
| E358NUV | Big Bus Company | FJ54ZVA | Go-Ahead London | GN08CGO | Arriva Southern C | J321BSH | Arriva Original Tour |

| Reg | Operator | Reg | Operator | Reg | Operator | Reg | Operator |
|---|---|---|---|---|---|---|---|
| J322BSH | Arriva Original Tour | KL52CXC | Arriva The Shires | KV02USE | Abellio | LF02PNE | Arriva London |
| J323BSH | Arriva Original Tour | KL52CXD | Arriva The Shires | KV02USF | Abellio | LF02PNJ | Arriva London |
| J324BSH | Arriva Original Tour | KL52CXE | Arriva The Shires | KV02USG | Abellio | LF02PNK | Arriva London |
| J325BSH | Arriva Original Tour | KL52CXF | Arriva The Shires | KV02USH | Abellio | LF02PNL | Arriva London |
| J326BSH | Arriva Original Tour | KL52CXG | Arriva The Shires | KV02USJ | Abellio | LF02PNN | Arriva London |
| J327BSH | Arriva Original Tour | KL52CXH | Arriva The Shires | KV02USL | Abellio | LF02PNO | Arriva London |
| J328BSH | Arriva Original Tour | KL52CXJ | Arriva The Shires | KV03ZFE | Hackney CT | LF02PNU | Arriva London |
| J329BSH | Arriva Original Tour | KL52CXK | Arriva The Shires | KV03ZFF | Hackney CT | LF02PNV | Arriva London |
| J330BSH | Arriva Original Tour | KL52CXM | Arriva The Shires | KV03ZFG | Hackney CT | LF02PNX | Arriva London |
| J331BSH | Arriva Original Tour | KL52CXN | Arriva The Shires | KV03ZFH | Hackney CT | LF02PNY | Arriva London |
| J332BSH | Arriva Original Tour | KL52CXO | Arriva The Shires | KV03ZFM | Abellio | LF02POA | Arriva London |
| J334BSH | Arriva Original Tour | KL52CXP | Arriva The Shires | KV03ZFN | Abellio | LF02POH | Arriva London |
| J335BSH | Arriva Original Tour | KL52CXR | Arriva The Shires | KV03ZFP | Abellio | LF02PSO | Arriva London |
| J336BSH | Arriva Original Tour | KL52CXS | Arriva The Shires | KV03ZFR | Abellio | LF02PSU | Arriva London |
| J337BSH | Arriva Original Tour | KM02HFP | Abellio | KV03ZFS | Abellio | LF02PSY | Arriva London |
| J338BSH | Arriva Original Tour | KM02HFR | Abellio | KV03ZFT | Abellio | LF02PSZ | Arriva London |
| J339BSH | Arriva Original Tour | KM02HFS | Abellio | KV03ZFU | Abellio | LF02PTO | Arriva London |
| J340BSH | Arriva Original Tour | KM02HFT | Abellio | KV03ZFW | Abellio | LF02PTU | Arriva London |
| J341BSH | Arriva Original Tour | KM02HFU | Abellio | KV03ZFX | Abellio | LF02PTX | Arriva London |
| J342BSH | Arriva Original Tour | KM02HFV | Abellio | KV03ZFY | Abellio | LF02PTY | Arriva London |
| J343BSH | Arriva Original Tour | KM02HGE | Abellio | KX54NJO | Metroline | LF02PTZ | Arriva London |
| J344BSH | Arriva Original Tour | KM02HGF | Abellio | KX59AEE | Arriva The Shires | LF02PVE | Arriva London |
| J345BSH | Arriva Original Tour | KN52NCE | Abellio | KX59AEF | Arriva The Shires | LF02PVJ | Arriva London |
| J346BSH | Arriva Original Tour | KN52NDC | Abellio | LB02YWX | Go-Ahead London | LF02PVK | Arriva London |
| J347BSH | Arriva Original Tour | KN52NDD | Abellio | LB02YWY | Go-Ahead London | LF02PVL | Arriva London |
| J348BSH | Arriva Original Tour | KN52NDE | Abellio | LB02YWZ | Go-Ahead London | LF02PVN | Arriva London |
| J349BSH | Arriva Original Tour | KN52NDF | Abellio | LB02YXA | Go-Ahead London | LF02PVO | Arriva London |
| J350BSH | Arriva Original Tour | KN52NDG | Abellio | LB02YXC | Go-Ahead London | LF06YRC | Abellio |
| J351BSH | Arriva Original Tour | KN52NDJ | Abellio | LB02YXD | Go-Ahead London | LF06YRD | Abellio |
| J352BSH | Arriva Original Tour | KN52NDY | Abellio | LB02YXE | Go-Ahead London | LF06YRE | Abellio |
| J433BSH | Arriva Original Tour | KN52NDZ | Abellio | LB02YXF | Go-Ahead London | LF06YRG | Abellio |
| JDZ2315 | First London | KN52NEJ | Abellio | LB02YXG | Go-Ahead London | LF06YRJ | Abellio |
| JJD472D | Go-Ahead London | KN52NEO | Abellio | LB02YXH | Go-Ahead London | LF06YRK | Abellio |
| JJD520D | Go-Ahead London | KN52NEU | Abellio | LB02YXJ | Go-Ahead London | LF06YRL | Abellio |
| K107SAG | London United | KN52NEY | Abellio | LB02YXK | Go-Ahead London | LF06YRM | Abellio |
| KC51NFO | Arriva Southern C | KN52NFA | Abellio | LB02YXL | Go-Ahead London | LF06YRN | Abellio |
| KC51PUX | Arriva Southern C | KP02PUJ | Abellio | LB02YXM | Go-Ahead London | LF52TGN | Go-Ahead London |
| KE51PTY | Arriva Southern C | KP02PUK | Abellio | LB02YXN | Go-Ahead London | LF52TGO | Go-Ahead London |
| KE51PTZ | Arriva Southern C | KP02PVE | Abellio | LB52URZ | Abellio | LF52TGU | Go-Ahead London |
| KE51PUA | Arriva Southern C | KP02PVU | Abellio | LF02PKA | Arriva London | LF52TGV | Go-Ahead London |
| KE51PUF | Arriva Southern C | KP02PWV | Abellio | LF02PKC | Arriva London | LF52TGX | Go-Ahead London |
| KE51PUH | Arriva Southern C | KU02YBH | Abellio | LF02PKD | Arriva London | LF52TGY | Go-Ahead London |
| KE51PUJ | Arriva Southern C | KU02YBJ | Abellio | LF02PKE | Arriva London | LF52TGZ | Go-Ahead London |
| KE51PUK | Arriva Southern C | KU02YBK | Abellio | LF02PKJ | Arriva London | LF52THG | Go-Ahead London |
| KE51PUO | Arriva Southern C | KU02YBL | Abellio | LF02PKO | Arriva London | LF52THK | Go-Ahead London |
| KE51PUU | Arriva Southern C | KU02YBM | Abellio | LF02PKU | Arriva London | LF52THN | Go-Ahead London |
| KE51PUV | Arriva Southern C | KU02YBN | Abellio | LF02PKV | Arriva London | LF52THU | Go-Ahead London |
| KE51PUY | Arriva Southern C | KU02YBO | Abellio | LF02PKX | Arriva London | LF52THV | Go-Ahead London |
| KE51PVD | Arriva Southern C | KU02YBP | Abellio | LF02PKY | Arriva London | LF52THX | Go-Ahead London |
| KL52CWN | Arriva The Shires | KU02YBR | Abellio | LF02PLJ | Arriva London | LF52THZ | Go-Ahead London |
| KL52CWO | Arriva The Shires | KU02YBS | Abellio | LF02PLN | Arriva London | LF52TJO | Go-Ahead London |
| KL52CWP | Arriva The Shires | KU52YKO | Abellio | LF02PLO | Arriva London | LF52TJU | Go-Ahead London |
| KL52CWR | Arriva The Shires | KU52YKR | Abellio | LF02PLU | Arriva London | LF52TJV | Go-Ahead London |
| KL52CWT | Arriva The Shires | KU52YKS | Abellio | LF02PLV | Arriva London | LF52TJX | Go-Ahead London |
| KL52CWU | Arriva The Shires | KV02URX | Abellio | LF02PLX | Arriva London | LF52TJY | Go-Ahead London |
| KL52CWV | Arriva The Shires | KV02URY | Abellio | LF02PLZ | Arriva London | LF52TKA | Go-Ahead London |
| KL52CWW | Arriva The Shires | KV02URZ | Abellio | LF02PMO | Arriva London | LF52TKC | Go-Ahead London |
| KL52CWZ | Arriva The Shires | KV02USB | Abellio | LF02PMV | Arriva London | LF52TKD | Go-Ahead London |
| KL52CXA | Arriva The Shires | KV02USC | Abellio | LF02PMX | Arriva London | LF52TKE | Go-Ahead London |
| KL52CXB | Arriva The Shires | KV02USD | Abellio | LF02PMY | Arriva London | LF52TKJ | Go-Ahead London |

**Heading for the Royal Albert Hall is Routemaster RM1735, 735DYE which is 39835 in the FirstBus fleet. It is one of twelve AEC Routemasters currently operated by First.** *Richard Godfrey*

| | | | | | | | |
|---|---|---|---|---|---|---|---|
| LF52TKK | Go-Ahead London | LF52UOX | Arriva London | LF52URL | Arriva London | LF52USW | Arriva London |
| LF52TKN | Go-Ahead London | LF52UOY | Arriva London | LF52URM | Arriva London | LF52USX | Arriva London |
| LF52TKO | Go-Ahead London | LF52UPA | Arriva London | LF52URN | Arriva London | LF52USY | Arriva London |
| LF52TKT | Go-Ahead London | LF52UPB | Arriva London | LF52URO | Arriva London | LF52USZ | Arriva London |
| LF52UNV | Arriva London | LF52UPC | Arriva London | LF52URP | Arriva London | LF52UTA | Arriva London |
| LF52UNW | Arriva London | LF52UPD | Arriva London | LF52URR | Arriva London | LF52UTB | Arriva London |
| LF52UNX | Arriva London | LF52UPG | Arriva London | LF52URS | Arriva London | LF52UTC | Arriva London |
| LF52UNY | Arriva London | LF52UPH | Arriva London | LF52URT | Arriva London | LF52UTE | Arriva London |
| LF52UNZ | Arriva London | LF52UPK | Arriva London | LF52URU | Arriva London | LF52UTG | Arriva London |
| LF52UOA | Arriva London | LF52UPM | Arriva London | LF52URV | Arriva London | LF52UTH | Arriva London |
| LF52UOB | Arriva London | LF52UPN | Arriva London | LF52URW | Arriva London | LF52UTL | Arriva London |
| LF52UOC | Arriva London | LF52UPO | Arriva London | LF52URX | Arriva London | LF52UTM | Arriva London |
| LF52UOD | Arriva London | LF52UPP | Arriva London | LF52URY | Arriva London | LF52ZLZ | Go-Ahead London |
| LF52UOE | Arriva London | LF52UPR | Arriva London | LF52URZ | Arriva London | LF52ZMO | Go-Ahead London |
| LF52UOG | Arriva London | LF52UPS | Arriva London | LF52USB | Arriva London | LF52ZMU | Go-Ahead London |
| LF52UOH | Arriva London | LF52UPT | Arriva London | LF52USC | Arriva London | LF52ZND | Go-Ahead London |
| LF52UOJ | Arriva London | LF52UPV | Arriva London | LF52USD | Arriva London | LF52ZNE | Go-Ahead London |
| LF52UOK | Arriva London | LF52UPW | Arriva London | LF52USE | Arriva London | LF52ZNG | Go-Ahead London |
| LF52UOL | Arriva London | LF52UPX | Arriva London | LF52USG | Arriva London | LF52ZNH | Go-Ahead London |
| LF52UOM | Arriva London | LF52UPZ | Arriva London | LF52USH | Arriva London | LF52ZNJ | Go-Ahead London |
| LF52UON | Arriva London | LF52URA | Arriva London | LF52USJ | Arriva London | LF52ZNK | Go-Ahead London |
| LF52UOO | Arriva London | LF52URB | Arriva London | LF52USL | Arriva London | LF52ZNL | Go-Ahead London |
| LF52UOP | Arriva London | LF52URC | Arriva London | LF52USM | Arriva London | LF52ZNM | Go-Ahead London |
| LF52UOR | Arriva London | LF52URD | Arriva London | LF52USN | Arriva London | LF52ZNN | Go-Ahead London |
| LF52UOS | Arriva London | LF52URE | Arriva London | LF52USO | Arriva London | LF52ZNO | Go-Ahead London |
| LF52UOT | Arriva London | LF52URG | Arriva London | LF52USS | Arriva London | LF52ZNP | Go-Ahead London |
| LF52UOU | Arriva London | LF52URH | Arriva London | LF52UST | Arriva London | LF52ZNR | Go-Ahead London |
| LF52UOV | Arriva London | LF52URJ | Arriva London | LF52USU | Arriva London | LF52ZNS | Go-Ahead London |
| LF52UOW | Arriva London | LF52URK | Arriva London | LF52USV | Arriva London | LF52ZNT | Go-Ahead London |

*The London Bus Handbook*

**Also using the Routemaster bus on service is Stagecoach. Seen passing St Paul's Churchyard is Stagecoach's 19966 (alias RM1968), ALD968B, which, follwing a recent repaint now features the white bull's eye scheme complete with small Stagecoach names.** *Mark Lyons*

| | | | | | | | |
|---|---|---|---|---|---|---|---|
| LF52ZNU | Go-Ahead London | LF52ZRE | Go-Ahead London | LF52ZTR | Go-Ahead London | LG02FBX | London United |
| LF52ZNV | Go-Ahead London | LF52ZRG | Go-Ahead London | LF55CYV | Abellio | LG02FBY | London United |
| LF52ZNW | Go-Ahead London | LF52ZRJ | Go-Ahead London | LF55CYW | Abellio | LG02FDY | London United |
| LF52ZNX | Go-Ahead London | LF52ZRK | Go-Ahead London | LF55CYX | Abellio | LG02FDZ | London United |
| LF52ZNY | Go-Ahead London | LF52ZRL | Go-Ahead London | LF55CYY | Abellio | LG02FEF | London United |
| LF52ZNZ | Go-Ahead London | LF52ZRN | Go-Ahead London | LF55CYZ | Abellio | LG02FEH | London United |
| LF52ZPB | Go-Ahead London | LF52ZRO | Go-Ahead London | LF55CZA | Abellio | LG02FEJ | London United |
| LF52ZPC | Go-Ahead London | LF52ZRP | Go-Ahead London | LF55CZB | Abellio | LG02FEK | London United |
| LF52ZPD | Go-Ahead London | LF52ZRR | Go-Ahead London | LF59XDZ | Abellio | LG02FEX | London United |
| LF52ZPE | Go-Ahead London | LF52ZRT | Go-Ahead London | LG02FAA | London United | LG02FFA | London United |
| LF52ZPG | Go-Ahead London | LF52ZRU | Go-Ahead London | LG02FAF | London United | LG02FFB | London United |
| LF52ZPH | Go-Ahead London | LF52ZRV | Go-Ahead London | LG02FAJ | London United | LG02FFK | London United |
| LF52ZPJ | Go-Ahead London | LF52ZRX | Go-Ahead London | LG02FAK | London United | LG02FFL | London United |
| LF52ZPK | Go-Ahead London | LF52ZRY | Go-Ahead London | LG02FAM | London United | LG02FFM | London United |
| LF52ZPL | Go-Ahead London | LF52ZRZ | Go-Ahead London | LG02FAO | London United | LG02FFN | London United |
| LF52ZPM | Go-Ahead London | LF52ZSD | Go-Ahead London | LG02FAU | London United | LG02FFO | London United |
| LF52ZPN | Go-Ahead London | LF52ZSO | Go-Ahead London | LG02FBA | London United | LG02FFP | London United |
| LF52ZPO | Go-Ahead London | LF52ZSP | Go-Ahead London | LG02FBB | London United | LG02FFR | London United |
| LF52ZPP | Go-Ahead London | LF52ZSR | Go-Ahead London | LG02FBC | London United | LG02FFS | London United |
| LF52ZPR | Go-Ahead London | LF52ZST | Go-Ahead London | LG02FBD | London United | LG02FFT | London United |
| LF52ZPS | Go-Ahead London | LF52ZTG | Go-Ahead London | LG02FBE | London United | LG02FFU | London United |
| LF52ZPU | Go-Ahead London | LF52ZTH | Go-Ahead London | LG02FBF | London United | LG02FFV | London United |
| LF52ZPV | Go-Ahead London | LF52ZTJ | Go-Ahead London | LG02FBJ | London United | LG02FFW | London United |
| LF52ZPW | Go-Ahead London | LF52ZTK | Go-Ahead London | LG02FBK | London United | LG02FFX | London United |
| LF52ZPY | Go-Ahead London | LF52ZTL | Go-Ahead London | LG02FBL | London United | LG02FFY | London United |
| LF52ZPZ | Go-Ahead London | LF52ZTM | Go-Ahead London | LG02FBN | London United | LG02FFZ | London United |
| LF52ZRA | Go-Ahead London | LF52ZTN | Go-Ahead London | LG02FBO | London United | LG02FGA | London United |
| LF52ZRC | Go-Ahead London | LF52ZTO | Go-Ahead London | LG02FBU | London United | LG02FGC | London United |
| LF52ZRD | Go-Ahead London | LF52ZTP | Go-Ahead London | LG02FBV | London United | LG02FGD | London United |

| | | | | | | | |
|---|---|---|---|---|---|---|---|
| LG02FGE | London United | LG52DCU | Arriva London | LJ03MHA | Arriva London | LJ03MRX | Arriva London |
| LG02FGF | London United | LG52DCV | Arriva London | LJ03MHE | Arriva London | LJ03MRY | Arriva London |
| LG02FGJ | London United | LG52DCX | Arriva London | LJ03MHF | Arriva London | LJ03MSU | Arriva London |
| LG02FGK | London United | LG52DCY | Arriva London | LJ03MHK | Arriva London | LJ03MSV | Arriva London |
| LG02FGM | London United | LG52DCZ | Arriva London | LJ03MHL | Arriva London | LJ03MSX | Arriva London |
| LG02FGN | London United | LG52DDA | Arriva London | LJ03MHM | Arriva London | LJ03MSY | Arriva London |
| LG02FGO | London United | LG52DDE | Arriva London | LJ03MHN | Arriva London | LJ03MTE | Arriva London |
| LG02FGP | London United | LG52DDF | Arriva London | LJ03MHU | Arriva London | LJ03MTF | Arriva London |
| LG02FGU | London United | LG52DDJ | Arriva London | LJ03MHV | Arriva London | LJ03MTK | Arriva London |
| LG02FGV | London United | LG52DDK | Arriva London | LJ03MHX | Arriva London | LJ03MTU | Arriva London |
| LG02FGX | London United | LG52DDL | Arriva London | LJ03MHY | Arriva London | LJ03MTV | Arriva London |
| LG02FGZ | London United | LG52XWD | Abellio | LJ03MHZ | Arriva London | LJ03MTY | Arriva London |
| LG02FHA | London United | LG52XWE | Abellio | LJ03MJE | Arriva London | LJ03MTZ | Arriva London |
| LG02FHB | London United | LG52XYJ | Abellio | LJ03MJF | Arriva London | LJ03MUA | Arriva London |
| LG02FHC | London United | LG52XYK | Abellio | LJ03MJK | Arriva London | LJ03MUB | Arriva London |
| LG02FHD | London United | LG52XYL | Abellio | LJ03MJU | Arriva London | LJ03MUW | Arriva London |
| LG02FHE | London United | LG52XYM | Abellio | LJ03MJV | Arriva London | LJ03MUY | Arriva London |
| LG02FHF | London United | LG52XYN | Abellio | LJ03MJX | Arriva London | LJ03MVC | Arriva London |
| LG02FHH | London United | LG52XYO | Abellio | LJ03MJY | Arriva London | LJ03MVD | Arriva London |
| LG02FHJ | London United | LG52XYP | Abellio | LJ03MKA | Arriva London | LJ03MVE | Arriva London |
| LG02FHK | London United | LG52XYY | Abellio | LJ03MKC | Arriva London | LJ03MVF | Arriva London |
| LG02FHL | London United | LG52XYZ | Abellio | LJ03MKD | Arriva London | LJ03MVG | Arriva London |
| LG02KGP | Go-Ahead London | LG52XZA | Abellio | LJ03MKE | Arriva London | LJ03MVT | Arriva London |
| LG02KGU | Go-Ahead London | LG52XZB | Abellio | LJ03MKF | Arriva London | LJ03MVV | Arriva London |
| LG02KGV | Go-Ahead London | LG52XZR | Abellio | LJ03MKG | Arriva London | LJ03MVW | Arriva London |
| LG02KGX | Go-Ahead London | LG52XZS | Abellio | LJ03MKK | Arriva London | LJ03MVX | Arriva London |
| LG02KGY | Go-Ahead London | LG52XZT | Abellio | LJ03MKL | Arriva London | LJ03MVY | Arriva London |
| LG02KGZ | Go-Ahead London | LJ03MBF | Arriva London | LJ03MKM | Arriva London | LJ03MVZ | Arriva London |
| LG02KHA | Go-Ahead London | LJ03MBU | Arriva London | LJ03MKN | Arriva London | LJ03MWA | Arriva London |
| LG02KHE | Go-Ahead London | LJ03MBV | Arriva London | LJ03MKU | Arriva London | LJ03MWC | Arriva London |
| LG02KHF | Go-Ahead London | LJ03MBX | Arriva London | LJ03MKV | Arriva London | LJ03MWD | Arriva London |
| LG02KHH | Go-Ahead London | LJ03MBY | Arriva London | LJ03MKX | Arriva London | LJ03MWE | Arriva London |
| LG02KHJ | Go-Ahead London | LJ03MDE | Arriva London | LJ03MKZ | Arriva London | LJ03MWF | Arriva London |
| LG02KHK | Go-Ahead London | LJ03MDF | Arriva London | LJ03MLE | Arriva London | LJ03MWG | Arriva London |
| LG02KHL | Go-Ahead London | LJ03MDK | Arriva London | LJ03MLF | Arriva London | LJ03MWK | Arriva London |
| LG02KHM | Go-Ahead London | LJ03MDN | Arriva London | LJ03MLK | Arriva London | LJ03MWL | Arriva London |
| LG02KHO | Go-Ahead London | LJ03MDU | Arriva London | LJ03MLL | Arriva London | LJ03MWN | Arriva London |
| LG02KHP | Go-Ahead London | LJ03MDV | Arriva London | LJ03MLN | Arriva London | LJ03MWP | Arriva London |
| LG02KHR | Go-Ahead London | LJ03MDX | Arriva London | LJ03MLV | Arriva London | LJ03MWU | Arriva London |
| LG02KHT | Go-Ahead London | LJ03MDY | Arriva London | LJ03MLX | Arriva London | LJ03MWV | Arriva London |
| LG02KHU | Go-Ahead London | LJ03MDZ | Arriva London | LJ03MLY | Arriva London | LJ03MWX | Arriva London |
| LG02KHV | Go-Ahead London | LJ03MEU | Arriva London | LJ03MLZ | Arriva London | LJ03MXH | Arriva London |
| LG02KHW | Go-Ahead London | LJ03MEV | Arriva London | LJ03MMA | Arriva London | LJ03MXK | Arriva London |
| LG02KHX | Go-Ahead London | LJ03MFA | Arriva London | LJ03MME | Arriva London | LJ03MXL | Arriva London |
| LG02KHY | Go-Ahead London | LJ03MFE | Arriva London | LJ03MMF | Arriva London | LJ03MXM | Arriva London |
| LG02KHZ | Go-Ahead London | LJ03MFF | Arriva London | LJ03MMK | Arriva London | LJ03MXN | Arriva London |
| LG02KJA | Go-Ahead London | LJ03MFK | Arriva London | LJ03MMU | Arriva London | LJ03MXP | Arriva London |
| LG02KJE | Go-Ahead London | LJ03MFN | Arriva London | LJ03MMV | Arriva London | LJ03MXR | Arriva London |
| LG02KJF | Go-Ahead London | LJ03MFP | Arriva London | LJ03MMX | Arriva London | LJ03MXS | Arriva London |
| LG52DAA | Arriva London | LJ03MFU | Arriva London | LJ03MOA | Arriva London | LJ03MXT | Arriva London |
| LG52DAO | Arriva London | LJ03MFV | Arriva London | LJ03MOF | Arriva London | LJ03MXU | Arriva London |
| LG52DAU | Arriva London | LJ03MFX | Arriva London | LJ03MOV | Arriva London | LJ03MXV | Arriva London |
| LG52DBO | Arriva London | LJ03MFY | Arriva London | LJ03MPF | Arriva London | LJ03MXW | Arriva London |
| LG52DBU | Arriva London | LJ03MFZ | Arriva London | LJ03MPU | Arriva London | LJ03MXX | Arriva London |
| LG52DBV | Arriva London | LJ03MGE | Arriva London | LJ03MPV | Arriva London | LJ03MXY | Arriva London |
| LG52DBY | Arriva London | LJ03MGU | Arriva London | LJ03MPX | Arriva London | LJ03MXZ | Arriva London |
| LG52DBZ | Arriva London | LJ03MGV | Arriva London | LJ03MPY | Arriva London | LJ03MYA | Arriva London |
| LG52DCE | Arriva London | LJ03MGX | Arriva London | LJ03MPZ | Arriva London | LJ03MYB | Arriva London |
| LG52DCF | Arriva London | LJ03MGY | Arriva London | LJ03MRU | Arriva London | LJ03MYC | Arriva London |
| LG52DCO | Arriva London | LJ03MGZ | Arriva London | LJ03MRV | Arriva London | LJ03MYD | Arriva London |

*The London Bus Handbook*

| | | | | | | | |
|---|---|---|---|---|---|---|---|
| LJ03MYF | Arriva London | LJ04LGL | Arriva London | LJ05GLZ | Arriva London | LJ08CTF | Arriva London |
| LJ03MYG | Arriva London | LJ04LGN | Arriva London | LJ05GME | Arriva London | LJ08CTK | Arriva London |
| LJ03MYH | Arriva London | LJ04LGV | Arriva London | LJ05GMF | Arriva London | LJ08CTO | Arriva London |
| LJ03MYK | Arriva London | LJ04LGW | Arriva London | LJ05GOP | Arriva London | LJ08CTV | Arriva London |
| LJ03MYL | Arriva London | LJ04LGX | Arriva London | LJ05GOU | Arriva London | LJ08CTX | Arriva London |
| LJ03MYM | Arriva London | LJ04LGY | Arriva London | LJ05GOX | Arriva London | LJ08CTY | Arriva London |
| LJ03MYN | Arriva London | LJ04YWE | Arriva London | LJ05GPF | Arriva London | LJ08CTZ | Arriva London |
| LJ03MYP | Arriva London | LJ04YWS | Arriva London | LJ05GPK | Arriva London | LJ08CUA | Arriva London |
| LJ03MYR | Arriva London | LJ04YWT | Arriva London | LJ05GPO | Arriva London | LJ08CUE | Arriva London |
| LJ03MYS | Arriva London | LJ04YWU | Arriva London | LJ05GPU | Arriva London | LJ08CUG | Arriva London |
| LJ03MYT | Arriva London | LJ04YWV | Arriva London | LJ05GPX | Arriva London | LJ08CUH | Arriva London |
| LJ03MYU | Arriva London | LJ04YWW | Arriva London | LJ05GPY | Arriva London | LJ08CUK | Arriva London |
| LJ03MYV | Arriva London | LJ04YWX | Arriva London | LJ05GPZ | Arriva London | LJ08CUO | Arriva London |
| LJ03MYX | Arriva London | LJ04YWY | Arriva London | LJ05GRF | Arriva London | LJ08CUU | Arriva London |
| LJ03MYY | Arriva London | LJ04YWZ | Arriva London | LJ05GRK | Arriva London | LJ08CUV | Arriva London |
| LJ03MYZ | Arriva London | LJ04YXA | Arriva London | LJ05GRU | Arriva London | LJ08CUW | Arriva London |
| LJ03MZD | Arriva London | LJ04YXB | Arriva London | LJ05GRX | Arriva London | LJ08CUY | Arriva London |
| LJ03MZE | Arriva London | LJ05BHL | Arriva London | LJ05GRZ | Arriva London | LJ08CVA | Arriva London |
| LJ03MZF | Arriva London | LJ05BHN | Arriva London | LJ05GSO | Arriva London | LJ08CVB | Arriva London |
| LJ03MZG | Arriva London | LJ05BHO | Arriva London | LJ05GSU | Arriva London | LJ08CVC | Arriva London |
| LJ03MZL | Arriva London | LJ05BHP | Arriva London | LJ07EBO | Arriva London | LJ08CVD | Arriva London |
| LJ04LDA | Arriva London | LJ05BHU | Arriva London | LJ07EBP | Arriva London | LJ08CVF | Arriva London |
| LJ04LDC | Arriva London | LJ05BHV | Arriva London | LJ07EBU | Arriva London | LJ08CVG | Arriva London |
| LJ04LDD | Arriva London | LJ05BHW | Arriva London | LJ07ECF | Arriva London | LJ08CVH | Arriva London |
| LJ04LDF | Arriva London | LJ05BHX | Arriva London | LJ07ECN | Arriva London | LJ08CVK | Arriva London |
| LJ04LDK | Arriva London | LJ05BHY | Arriva London | LJ07ECT | Arriva London | LJ08CVL | Arriva London |
| LJ04LDL | Arriva London | LJ05BHZ | Arriva London | LJ07ECU | Arriva London | LJ08CVM | Arriva London |
| LJ04LDN | Arriva London | LJ05BJV | Arriva London | LJ07ECW | Arriva London | LJ08CVO | Arriva London |
| LJ04LDU | Arriva London | LJ05BJX | Arriva London | LJ07ECX | Arriva London | LJ08CVR | Arriva London |
| LJ04LDX | Arriva London | LJ05BJY | Arriva London | LJ07ECY | Arriva London | LJ08CVS | Arriva London |
| LJ04LDY | Arriva London | LJ05BJZ | Arriva London | LJ07ECZ | Arriva London | LJ08CVT | Arriva London |
| LJ04LDZ | Arriva London | LJ05BKA | Arriva London | LJ07EDC | Arriva London | LJ08CVU | Arriva London |
| LJ04LEF | Arriva London | LJ05BKD | Arriva London | LJ07EDF | Arriva London | LJ08CVV | Arriva London |
| LJ04LEU | Arriva London | LJ05BKF | Arriva London | LJ07EDK | Arriva London | LJ08CVX | Arriva London |
| LJ04LFB | Arriva London | LJ05BKY | Arriva London | LJ07EDL | Arriva London | LJ08CVY | Arriva London |
| LJ04LFD | Arriva London | LJ05BKZ | Arriva London | LJ07EDO | Arriva London | LJ08CVZ | Arriva London |
| LJ04LFE | Arriva London | LJ05BLF | Arriva London | LJ07EDP | Arriva London | LJ08CWA | Arriva London |
| LJ04LFF | Arriva London | LJ05BLK | Arriva London | LJ07EDR | Arriva London | LJ08CWC | Arriva London |
| LJ04LFG | Arriva London | LJ05BLN | Arriva London | LJ07EDU | Arriva London | LJ08CXR | Arriva London |
| LJ04LFH | Arriva London | LJ05BLV | Arriva London | LJ07EDV | Arriva London | LJ08CXS | Arriva London |
| LJ04LFK | Arriva London | LJ05BLX | Arriva London | LJ07EDX | Arriva London | LJ08CXT | Arriva London |
| LJ04LFL | Arriva London | LJ05BLY | Arriva London | LJ07EEA | Arriva London | LJ08CXU | Arriva London |
| LJ04LFM | Arriva London | LJ05BMO | Arriva London | LJ07EEB | Arriva London | LJ08CXV | Arriva London |
| LJ04LFN | Arriva London | LJ05BMU | Arriva London | LJ07UDD | Arriva Original Tour | LJ08CYC | Arriva London |
| LJ04LFP | Arriva London | LJ05BMV | Arriva London | LJ07XEN | Arriva Original Tour | LJ08CYE | Arriva London |
| LJ04LFR | Arriva London | LJ05BMZ | Arriva London | LJ07XEO | Arriva Original Tour | LJ08CYF | Arriva London |
| LJ04LFS | Arriva London | LJ05BNA | Arriva London | LJ07XEP | Arriva Original Tour | LJ08CYG | Arriva London |
| LJ04LFT | Arriva London | LJ05BNB | Arriva London | LJ07XER | Arriva Original Tour | LJ08CYH | Arriva London |
| LJ04LFU | Arriva London | LJ05BND | Arriva London | LJ07XES | Arriva Original Tour | LJ08CYK | Arriva London |
| LJ04LFV | Arriva London | LJ05BNE | Arriva London | LJ07XET | Arriva Original Tour | LJ08CYL | Arriva London |
| LJ04LFW | Arriva London | LJ05BNF | Arriva London | LJ07XEU | Arriva Original Tour | LJ08CYO | Arriva London |
| LJ04LFX | Arriva London | LJ05BNK | Arriva London | LJ07XEV | Arriva Original Tour | LJ08CYP | Arriva London |
| LJ04LFZ | Arriva London | LJ05BNL | Arriva London | LJ07XEW | Arriva Original Tour | LJ08CYS | Arriva London |
| LJ04LGA | Arriva London | LJ05GKX | Arriva London | LJ08CSO | Arriva London | LJ08CZP | Abellio |
| LJ04LGC | Arriva London | LJ05GKY | Arriva London | LJ08CSU | Arriva London | LJ08CZR | Abellio |
| LJ04LGD | Arriva London | LJ05GKZ | Arriva London | LJ08CSV | Arriva London | LJ08CZS | Abellio |
| LJ04LGE | Arriva London | LJ05GLF | Arriva London | LJ08CSX | Arriva London | LJ08CZT | Abellio |
| LJ04LGF | Arriva London | LJ05GLK | Arriva London | LJ08CSY | Arriva London | LJ08CZU | Abellio |
| LJ04LGG | Arriva London | LJ05GLV | Arriva London | LJ08CSZ | Arriva London | LJ08CZV | Abellio |
| LJ04LGK | Arriva London | LJ05GLY | Arriva The Shires | LJ08CTE | Arriva London | LJ08CZX | Abellio |

| Reg | Operator | Reg | Operator | Reg | Operator | Reg | Operator |
|---|---|---|---|---|---|---|---|
| LJ08CZY | Abellio | LJ09KPX | Arriva London | LJ09SUV | Arriva London | LJ10HVG | Arriva London |
| LJ08CZZ | Abellio | LJ09KPY | Arriva London | LJ09SUX | Arriva London | LJ10HVH | Arriva London |
| LJ08RJY | Quality Line | LJ09KPZ | Arriva London | LJ09SUY | Arriva London | LJ10HVK | Arriva London |
| LJ09CAA | Abellio | LJ09KRD | Arriva London | LJ09SVA | Arriva London | LJ10HVL | Arriva London |
| LJ09CAE | Abellio | LJ09KRE | Arriva London | LJ09SVC | Arriva London | LJ10HVO | Arriva London |
| LJ09CAO | Abellio | LJ09KRF | Arriva London | LJ09SVD | Arriva London | LJ10HVP | Arriva London |
| LJ09CAU | Abellio | LJ09KRG | Arriva London | LJ09SVE | Arriva London | LJ10HVR | Arriva London |
| LJ09CAV | Abellio | LJ09KRK | Arriva London | LJ09SVF | Arriva London | LJ11AAE | Arriva London |
| LJ09CAX | Abellio | LJ09KRN | Arriva London | LJ10CSF | Arriva London | LJ11AAF | Arriva London |
| LJ09CBF | Abellio | LJ09KRO | Arriva London | LJ10CSO | Arriva London | LJ11AAK | Arriva London |
| LJ09CBO | Abellio | LJ09KRU | Arriva London | LJ10CSU | Arriva London | LJ11AAN | Arriva London |
| LJ09CBU | Abellio | LJ09OJZ | Abellio | LJ10CSV | Arriva London | LJ11AAO | Arriva London |
| LJ09CBV | Abellio | LJ09OKA | Abellio | LJ10CSX | Arriva London | LJ11AAU | Arriva London |
| LJ09CBX | Abellio | LJ09OKB | Abellio | LJ10CSY | Arriva London | LJ11AAX | Arriva London |
| LJ09CBY | Abellio | LJ09OKC | Abellio | LJ10CSZ | Arriva London | LJ11AAY | Arriva London |
| LJ09CCA | Abellio | LJ09OKD | Abellio | LJ10CTE | Arriva London | LJ11AAZ | Arriva London |
| LJ09CCD | Abellio | LJ09OKE | Abellio | LJ10CTF | Arriva London | LJ11ABF | Arriva London |
| LJ09CCE | Abellio | LJ09OKF | Abellio | LJ10CTK | Arriva London | LJ11ABK | Arriva London |
| LJ09CCF | Abellio | LJ09OKG | Abellio | LJ10CUH | Arriva London | LJ11ABN | Arriva London |
| LJ09CCK | Abellio | LJ09OKH | Abellio | LJ10CUK | Arriva London | LJ11ABO | Arriva London |
| LJ09CCN | Abellio | LJ09OKK | Abellio | LJ10CUO | Arriva London | LJ11ABU | Arriva London |
| LJ09CCO | Abellio | LJ09OKL | Abellio | LJ10CUU | Arriva London | LJ11ABV | Arriva London |
| LJ09CCU | Abellio | LJ09OKM | Abellio | LJ10CUV | Arriva London | LJ11ABX | Arriva London |
| LJ09CCX | Abellio | LJ09OKN | Abellio | LJ10CUW | Arriva London | LJ11ABZ | Arriva London |
| LJ09CCY | Abellio | LJ09OKO | Abellio | LJ10CUX | Arriva London | LJ11ACF | Arriva London |
| LJ09CCZ | Abellio | LJ09OKP | Abellio | LJ10CUY | Arriva London | LJ11ACO | Arriva London |
| LJ09CDE | Abellio | LJ09OKR | Abellio | LJ10CVA | Arriva London | LJ11ACU | Arriva London |
| LJ09CDF | Abellio | LJ09OKS | Abellio | LJ10CVB | Arriva London | LJ11ACV | Arriva London |
| LJ09CDK | Abellio | LJ09OKT | Abellio | LJ10CVC | Arriva London | LJ11ACX | Arriva London |
| LJ09CDN | Abellio | LJ09OKU | Abellio | LJ10CVD | Arriva London | LJ11ACY | Arriva London |
| LJ09CDO | Abellio | LJ09OKV | Abellio | LJ10CVE | Arriva London | LJ11ACZ | Arriva London |
| LJ09CDU | Abellio | LJ09OKW | Abellio | LJ10CVF | Arriva London | LJ11ADO | Arriva London |
| LJ09CDV | Abellio | LJ09OKX | Abellio | LJ10CVG | Arriva London | LJ11ADU | Arriva London |
| LJ09CDX | Abellio | LJ09OKZ | Abellio | LJ10CVH | Arriva London | LJ11ADV | Arriva London |
| LJ09CDY | Abellio | LJ09OLA | Abellio | LJ10CVK | Arriva London | LJ11ADX | Arriva London |
| LJ09CDZ | Abellio | LJ09OLB | Abellio | LJ10CVL | Arriva London | LJ11ADZ | Arriva London |
| LJ09CEA | Abellio | LJ09OLC | Abellio | LJ10CVM | Arriva London | LJ11AEA | Arriva London |
| LJ09CEF | Abellio | LJ09OLE | Abellio | LJ10CVN | Arriva London | LJ11AEB | Arriva London |
| LJ09CEK | Abellio | LJ09OLG | Abellio | LJ10CVO | Arriva London | LJ11AEC | Arriva London |
| LJ09CEN | Abellio | LJ09OLH | Abellio | LJ10CVP | Arriva London | LJ11AED | Arriva London |
| LJ09CEO | Abellio | LJ09OLK | Abellio | LJ10HTT | Arriva London | LJ11AEE | Arriva London |
| LJ09CEU | Abellio | LJ09OLM | Abellio | LJ10HTU | Arriva London | LJ11AEF | Arriva London |
| LJ09KOE | Arriva London | LJ09OLN | Abellio | LJ10HTV | Arriva London | LJ11AEG | Arriva London |
| LJ09KOH | Arriva London | LJ09OLO | Abellio | LJ10HTX | Arriva London | LJ11AEK | Arriva London |
| LJ09KOU | Arriva London | LJ09OLP | Abellio | LJ10HTZ | Arriva London | LJ11AEL | Arriva London |
| LJ09KOV | Arriva London | LJ09OLR | Abellio | LJ10HUA | Arriva London | LJ11AEM | Arriva London |
| LJ09KOW | Arriva London | LJ09OLT | Abellio | LJ10HUB | Arriva London | LJ11AEN | Arriva London |
| LJ09KOX | Arriva London | LJ09OLU | Abellio | LJ10HUK | Arriva London | LJ11AEO | Arriva London |
| LJ09KPA | Arriva London | LJ09SSO | Arriva London | LJ10HUO | Arriva London | LJ11AEP | Arriva London |
| LJ09KPE | Arriva London | LJ09SSU | Arriva London | LJ10HUP | Arriva London | LJ11AET | Arriva London |
| LJ09KPF | Arriva London | LJ09SSV | Arriva London | LJ10HUU | Arriva London | LJ11AEU | Arriva London |
| LJ09KPG | Arriva London | LJ09SSX | Arriva London | LJ10HUV | Arriva London | LJ11AEV | Arriva London |
| LJ09KPK | Arriva London | LJ09SSZ | Arriva London | LJ10HUY | Arriva London | LJ11AEW | Arriva London |
| LJ09KPL | Arriva London | LJ09STX | Arriva London | LJ10HUZ | Arriva London | LJ11AEX | Arriva London |
| LJ09KPN | Arriva London | LJ09STZ | Arriva London | LJ10HVA | Arriva London | LJ11AEY | Arriva London |
| LJ09KPO | Arriva London | LJ09SUA | Arriva London | LJ10HVB | Arriva London | LJ11AEZ | Arriva London |
| LJ09KPR | Arriva London | LJ09SUF | Arriva London | LJ10HVC | Arriva London | LJ11AFA | Arriva London |
| LJ09KPT | Arriva London | LJ09SUH | Arriva London | LJ10HVD | Arriva London | LJ11EEU | Arriva London |
| LJ09KPU | Arriva London | LJ09SUO | Arriva London | LJ10HVE | Arriva London | LJ11EFE | Arriva London |
| LJ09KPV | Arriva London | LJ09SUU | Arriva London | LJ10HVF | Arriva London | LJ11EFF | Arriva London |

**The latest livery style for hybrid buses is seen on page 21. Here, the earlier scheme is shown on HW5, LJ09KRN, an integral Wrightbus Gemini bus based on VDL DB300 units, pictured in October 2010 on route 141.** *Mark Lyons*

| | | | | | | | |
|---|---|---|---|---|---|---|---|
| LJ11EFG | Arriva London | LJ51DAO | Arriva London | LJ51DFA | Arriva London | LJ51DHO | Arriva London |
| LJ11EFK | Arriva London | LJ51DAU | Arriva London | LJ51DFC | Arriva London | LJ51DHP | Arriva London |
| LJ11EFL | Arriva London | LJ51DBO | Arriva London | LJ51DFD | Arriva London | LJ51DHV | Arriva London |
| LJ11EFM | Arriva London | LJ51DBU | Arriva London | LJ51DFE | Arriva London | LJ51DHX | Arriva London |
| LJ11EFN | Arriva London | LJ51DBV | Arriva London | LJ51DFF | Arriva London | LJ51DHY | Arriva London |
| LJ11EFO | Arriva London | LJ51DBX | Arriva London | LJ51DFG | Arriva London | LJ51DHZ | Arriva London |
| LJ11EFP | Arriva London | LJ51DBY | Arriva London | LJ51DFL | Arriva London | LJ51DJD | Arriva London |
| LJ11EFR | Arriva London | LJ51DBZ | Arriva London | LJ51DFN | Arriva London | LJ51DJE | Arriva London |
| LJ11EFS | Arriva London | LJ51DCE | Arriva London | LJ51DFO | Arriva London | LJ51DJU | Arriva London |
| LJ11EFT | Arriva London | LJ51DCF | Arriva London | LJ51DFP | Arriva London | LJ51DJV | Arriva London |
| LJ11EFU | Arriva London | LJ51DCO | Arriva London | LJ51DFU | Arriva London | LJ51DJX | Arriva London |
| LJ11EFV | Arriva London | LJ51DCU | Arriva London | LJ51DFX | Arriva London | LJ51DJY | Arriva London |
| LJ11EFW | Arriva London | LJ51DCV | Arriva London | LJ51DFY | Arriva London | LJ51DJZ | Arriva London |
| LJ11EFX | Arriva London | LJ51DCX | Arriva London | LJ51DFZ | Arriva London | LJ51DKA | Arriva London |
| LJ11EFY | Arriva London | LJ51DCY | Arriva London | LJ51DGE | Arriva London | LJ51DKD | Arriva London |
| LJ11EFZ | Arriva London | LJ51DCZ | Arriva London | LJ51DGF | Arriva London | LJ51DKE | Arriva London |
| LJ11EGC | Arriva London | LJ51DDA | Arriva London | LJ51DGO | Arriva London | LJ51DKF | Arriva London |
| LJ11EGD | Arriva London | LJ51DDE | Arriva London | LJ51DGU | Arriva London | LJ51DKK | Arriva London |
| LJ11EGE | Arriva London | LJ51DDF | Arriva London | LJ51DGV | Arriva London | LJ51DKL | Arriva London |
| LJ11EGF | Arriva London | LJ51DDK | Arriva London | LJ51DGX | Arriva London | LJ51DKN | Arriva London |
| LJ11EGK | Arriva London | LJ51DDL | Arriva London | LJ51DGY | Arriva London | LJ51DKO | Arriva London |
| LJ11EGU | Arriva London | LJ51DDN | Arriva London | LJ51DGZ | Arriva London | LJ51DKU | Arriva London |
| LJ11EGV | Arriva London | LJ51DDO | Arriva London | LJ51DHA | Arriva London | LJ51DKV | Arriva London |
| LJ11EGX | Arriva London | LJ51DDU | Arriva London | LJ51DHC | Arriva London | LJ51DKX | Arriva London |
| LJ11EGY | Arriva London | LJ51DDV | Arriva London | LJ51DHD | Arriva London | LJ51DKY | Arriva London |
| LJ11EGZ | Arriva London | LJ51DDX | Arriva London | LJ51DHF | Arriva London | LJ51DLD | Arriva London |
| LJ11EHB | Arriva London | LJ51DDY | Arriva London | LJ51DHG | Arriva London | LJ51DLF | Arriva London |
| LJ11EHC | Arriva London | LJ51DDZ | Arriva London | LJ51DHK | Arriva London | LJ51DLK | Arriva London |
| LJ51DAA | Arriva London | LJ51DEU | Arriva London | LJ51DHL | Arriva London | LJ51DLN | Arriva London |

**Aldwych is the location for this view of Arriva's VLW129, LG52DAA, a Volvo B7TL with Wrightbus Eclipse Gemini bodywork.** *Colin Lloyd*

| | | | | | | | |
|---|---|---|---|---|---|---|---|
| LJ51DLU | Arriva London | LJ53BCF | Arriva London | LJ53BFX | Arriva London | LJ53NHF | Arriva London |
| LJ51DLV | Arriva London | LJ53BCK | Arriva London | LJ53BFY | Arriva London | LJ53NHG | Arriva London |
| LJ51DLX | Arriva London | LJ53BCO | Arriva London | LJ53BGF | Arriva London | LJ53NHH | Arriva London |
| LJ51DLY | Arriva London | LJ53BCU | Arriva London | LJ53BGK | Arriva London | LJ53NHK | Arriva London |
| LJ51DLZ | Arriva London | LJ53BCV | Arriva London | LJ53BGO | Arriva London | LJ53NHL | Arriva London |
| LJ51ORA | Arriva London | LJ53BCX | Arriva London | LJ53BGU | Arriva London | LJ53NHN | Arriva London |
| LJ51ORC | Arriva London | LJ53BCY | Arriva London | LJ53NFE | Arriva London | LJ53NHO | Arriva London |
| LJ51ORF | Arriva London | LJ53BCZ | Arriva London | LJ53NFF | Arriva London | LJ53NHP | Arriva London |
| LJ51ORG | Arriva London | LJ53BDE | Arriva London | LJ53NFG | Arriva London | LJ53NHT | Arriva London |
| LJ51ORH | Arriva London | LJ53BDF | Arriva London | LJ53NFT | Arriva London | LJ53NHV | Arriva London |
| LJ51ORK | Arriva London | LJ53BDO | Arriva London | LJ53NFU | Arriva London | LJ53NHX | Arriva London |
| LJ51ORL | Arriva London | LJ53BDU | Arriva London | LJ53NFV | Arriva London | LJ53NHY | Arriva London |
| LJ51OSK | Arriva London | LJ53BDV | Arriva London | LJ53NFX | Arriva London | LJ53NHZ | Arriva London |
| LJ51OSX | Arriva London | LJ53BDX | Arriva London | LJ53NFY | Arriva London | LJ53NJF | Arriva London |
| LJ51OSY | Arriva London | LJ53BDY | Arriva London | LJ53NFZ | Arriva London | LJ53NJK | Arriva London |
| LJ51OSZ | Arriva London | LJ53BDZ | Arriva London | LJ53NGE | Arriva London | LJ53NJN | Arriva London |
| LJ53BAA | Arriva London | LJ53BEO | Arriva London | LJ53NGF | Arriva London | LJ54BAA | Arriva London |
| LJ53BAO | Arriva London | LJ53BEU | Arriva London | LJ53NGG | Arriva London | LJ54BAO | Arriva London |
| LJ53BAU | Arriva London | LJ53BEY | Arriva London | LJ53NGN | Arriva London | LJ54BAU | Arriva London |
| LJ53BAV | Arriva London | LJ53BFA | Arriva London | LJ53NGU | Arriva London | LJ54BAV | Arriva London |
| LJ53BBE | Arriva London | LJ53BFE | Arriva London | LJ53NGV | Arriva London | LJ54BBE | Arriva London |
| LJ53BBF | Arriva London | LJ53BFF | Arriva London | LJ53NGX | Arriva London | LJ54BBF | Arriva London |
| LJ53BBK | Arriva London | LJ53BFK | Arriva London | LJ53NGY | Arriva London | LJ54BBK | Arriva London |
| LJ53BBN | Arriva London | LJ53BFL | Arriva London | LJ53NGZ | Arriva London | LJ54BBN | Arriva London |
| LJ53BBO | Arriva London | LJ53BFM | Arriva London | LJ53NHA | Arriva London | LJ54BBO | Arriva London |
| LJ53BBU | Arriva London | LJ53BFN | Arriva London | LJ53NHB | Arriva London | LJ54BBU | Arriva London |
| LJ53BBV | Arriva London | LJ53BFO | Arriva London | LJ53NHC | Arriva London | LJ54BBV | Arriva London |
| LJ53BBX | Arriva London | LJ53BFP | Arriva London | LJ53NHD | Arriva London | LJ54BBX | Arriva London |
| LJ53BBZ | Arriva London | LJ53BFU | Arriva London | LJ53NHE | Arriva London | LJ54BBZ | Arriva London |

| | | | | | | | |
|---|---|---|---|---|---|---|---|
| LJ54BCE | Arriva London | LJ55BRV | Arriva London | LJ56VSP | Abellio | LJ58AVE | Arriva London |
| LJ54BCF | Arriva London | LJ55BRX | Arriva London | LJ56VST | Abellio | LJ58AVG | Arriva London |
| LJ54BCK | Arriva London | LJ55BRZ | Arriva London | LJ56VSU | Abellio | LJ58AVK | Arriva London |
| LJ54BCO | Arriva London | LJ55BSO | Arriva London | LJ56VSV | Abellio | LJ58AVT | Arriva London |
| LJ54BCU | Arriva London | LJ55BSU | Arriva London | LJ56VSX | Abellio | LJ58AVU | Arriva London |
| LJ54BCV | Arriva London | LJ55BSV | Arriva London | LJ56VSY | Abellio | LJ58AVV | Arriva London |
| LJ54BCX | Arriva London | LJ55BSX | Arriva London | LJ56VSZ | Abellio | LJ58AVX | Arriva London |
| LJ54BCY | Arriva London | LJ55BSY | Arriva London | LJ56VTA | Abellio | LJ58AVY | Arriva London |
| LJ54BCZ | Arriva London | LJ55BSZ | Arriva London | LJ56VTC | Abellio | LJ58AVZ | Arriva London |
| LJ54BDE | Arriva London | LJ55BTE | Arriva London | LJ56VTD | Abellio | LJ58AWA | Arriva London |
| LJ54BDF | Arriva London | LJ55BTF | Arriva London | LJ56VTE | Abellio | LJ58AWC | Arriva London |
| LJ54BDO | Arriva London | LJ55BTO | Arriva London | LJ56VTF | Abellio | LJ58AWF | Arriva London |
| LJ54BDU | Arriva London | LJ55BTU | Arriva London | LJ56VTG | Abellio | LJ58AWG | Arriva London |
| LJ54BDV | Arriva London | LJ55BTV | Arriva London | LJ56VTK | Abellio | LJ59AAE | Arriva London |
| LJ54BDX | Arriva London | LJ55BTX | Arriva London | LJ56VTL | Abellio | LJ59AAF | Arriva London |
| LJ54BDY | Arriva London | LJ55BTY | Arriva London | LJ56VTM | Abellio | LJ59AAK | Arriva London |
| LJ54BDZ | Arriva London | LJ55BTZ | Arriva London | LJ56VTN | Abellio | LJ59AAN | Arriva London |
| LJ54BEO | Arriva London | LJ55BUA | Arriva London | LJ56VTO | Abellio | LJ59AAO | Arriva London |
| LJ54BEU | Arriva London | LJ55BUE | Arriva London | LJ56VTP | Abellio | LJ59AAO | Arriva London |
| LJ54BFA | Arriva London | LJ55BUP | Arriva London | LJ56VTT | Abellio | LJ59AAU | Arriva London |
| LJ54BFE | Arriva London | LJ55BUR | Arriva London | LJ56VTU | Abellio | LJ59AAU | Arriva London |
| LJ54BFF | Arriva London | LJ55BUS | Arriva London | LJ56VTV | Abellio | LJ59AAV | Arriva London |
| LJ54BFK | Arriva London | LJ55BUT | Arriva London | LJ56VTW | Abellio | LJ59AAX | Arriva London |
| LJ54BFL | Arriva London | LJ55BUU | Arriva London | LJ56VTX | Abellio | LJ59AAY | Arriva London |
| LJ54BFM | Arriva London | LJ55BUV | Arriva London | LJ56VTY | Abellio | LJ59AAZ | Arriva London |
| LJ54BFN | Arriva London | LJ55BUW | Arriva London | LJ56VTZ | Abellio | LJ59ABF | Arriva London |
| LJ54BFO | Arriva London | LJ55BUX | Arriva London | LJ56VUA | Abellio | LJ59ABK | Arriva London |
| LJ54BFP | Arriva London | LJ55BUY | Arriva London | LJ56VUB | Abellio | LJ59ABN | Arriva London |
| LJ54BFV | Arriva London | LJ55BUZ | Arriva London | LJ56VUC | Abellio | LJ59ABO | Arriva London |
| LJ54BFY | Arriva London | LJ55BVD | Arriva London | LJ56VUD | Abellio | LJ59ABU | Arriva London |
| LJ54BFZ | Arriva London | LJ55BVE | Arriva London | LJ56VUE | Abellio | LJ59ABV | Arriva London |
| LJ54BGE | Arriva London | LJ55BVF | Arriva London | LJ56VUF | Abellio | LJ59ABX | Arriva London |
| LJ54BGF | Arriva London | LJ55BVG | Arriva London | LJ56VUG | Abellio | LJ59ABZ | Arriva London |
| LJ54BGK | Arriva London | LJ55BVH | Arriva London | LJ57USS | Arriva London | LJ59ACF | Arriva London |
| LJ54BGO | Arriva London | LJ55BVK | Arriva London | LJ57UST | Arriva London | LJ59ACO | Arriva London |
| LJ54BJE | Arriva London | LJ55BVL | Arriva London | LJ57USU | Arriva London | LJ59ACU | Arriva London |
| LJ54BJF | Arriva London | LJ55BVM | Arriva London | LJ57USV | Arriva London | LJ59ACV | Arriva London |
| LJ54BJK | Arriva London | LJ56AOW | Arriva London | LJ57USW | Arriva London | LJ59ACX | Arriva London |
| LJ54BJO | Arriva London | LJ56AOX | Arriva London | LJ57USX | Arriva London | LJ59ACY | Arriva London |
| LJ54BJU | Arriva London | LJ56AOY | Arriva London | LJ57USY | Arriva London | LJ59ACZ | Arriva London |
| LJ54BKG | Arriva London | LJ56APZ | Arriva London | LJ57USZ | Arriva London | LJ59ADO | Arriva London |
| LJ54BKK | Arriva London | LJ56ARF | Arriva London | LJ57UTA | Arriva London | LJ59ADV | Arriva London |
| LJ54BKL | Arriva London | LJ56ARO | Arriva London | LJ57UTB | Arriva London | LJ59ADZ | Arriva London |
| LJ54BKN | Arriva London | LJ56ARU | Arriva London | LJ57UTC | Arriva London | LJ59AEA | Arriva London |
| LJ54BKO | Arriva London | LJ56ARX | Arriva London | LJ57UTE | Arriva London | LJ59AEA | Arriva London |
| LJ54BKU | Arriva London | LJ56ARZ | Arriva London | LJ57UTF | Arriva London | LJ59AEB | Arriva London |
| LJ54BKV | Arriva London | LJ56ASO | Arriva London | LJ57YAW | Abellio | LJ59AEC | Arriva London |
| LJ54BKX | Arriva London | LJ56ASU | Arriva London | LJ57YAX | Abellio | LJ59AED | Arriva London |
| LJ54LGV | Arriva London | LJ56ASV | Arriva London | LJ57YAY | Abellio | LJ59AEE | Arriva London |
| LJ54LHF | Arriva London | LJ56ASX | Arriva London | LJ57YBA | Abellio | LJ59AEF | Arriva London |
| LJ54LHG | Arriva London | LJ56ONH | Abellio | LJ57YBB | Abellio | LJ59AEG | Arriva London |
| LJ54LHH | Arriva London | LJ56ONK | Abellio | LJ58AUC | Arriva London | LJ59AEK | Arriva London |
| LJ54LHK | Arriva London | LJ56ONL | Abellio | LJ58AUE | Arriva London | LJ59AEL | Arriva London |
| LJ54LHL | Arriva London | LJ56ONM | Abellio | LJ58AUV | Arriva London | LJ59AEM | Arriva London |
| LJ54LHM | Arriva London | LJ56ONN | Abellio | LJ58AUW | Arriva London | LJ59AEN | Arriva London |
| LJ54LHN | Arriva London | LJ56ONO | Abellio | LJ58AUX | Arriva London | LJ59AET | Arriva London |
| LJ54LHO | Arriva London | LJ56ONP | Abellio | LJ58AUY | Arriva London | LJ59AEU | Arriva London |
| LJ54LHP | Arriva London | LJ56ONR | Abellio | LJ58AVB | Arriva London | LJ59AEV | Arriva London |
| LJ54LHR | Arriva London | LJ56ONS | Abellio | LJ58AVC | Arriva London | LJ59AEW | Arriva London |
| LJ55BPZ | Arriva London | LJ56ONT | Abellio | LJ58AVD | Arriva London | LJ59AEX | Arriva London |

| | | | | | | | |
|---|---|---|---|---|---|---|---|
| LJ59AEY | Arriva London | LJ59LYT | Arriva London | LJ60AWF | Arriva London | LK03CDE | Metroline |
| LJ59AEZ | Arriva London | LJ59LYU | Arriva London | LJ60AWF | Arriva London | LK03CDF | Metroline |
| LJ59GTF | Arriva London | LJ59LYV | Arriva London | LJ60AWG | Arriva London | LK03CDG | Metroline |
| LJ59GTU | Arriva London | LJ59LYW | Arriva London | LJ60AWG | Arriva London | LK03CDJ | Metroline |
| LJ59GUA | Arriva London | LJ59LYY | Arriva London | LJ60AWH | Arriva London | LK03CDL | Metroline |
| LJ59GVC | Arriva London | LJ59LYZ | Arriva London | LJ60AWK | Arriva London | LK03CDM | Metroline |
| LJ59GVE | Arriva London | LJ59LZA | Arriva London | LJ60AWL | Arriva London | LK03CDN | Metroline |
| LJ59GVF | Arriva London | LJ59LZB | Arriva London | LJ60AWM | Arriva London | LK03CDP | Metroline |
| LJ59GVG | Arriva London | LJ59LZC | Arriva London | LJ60AWN | Arriva London | LK03CDU | Metroline |
| LJ59GVK | Arriva London | LJ59LZD | Arriva London | LJ60AWN | Arriva London | LK03CDV | Metroline |
| LJ59LVH | Arriva London | LJ59LZF | Arriva London | LJ60AWO | Arriva London | LK03CDX | Metroline |
| LJ59LVL | Arriva London | LJ59LZG | Arriva London | LJ60AWO | Arriva London | LK03CDY | Metroline |
| LJ59LVM | Arriva London | LJ59LZH | Arriva London | LJ60AWP | Arriva London | LK03CDZ | Metroline |
| LJ59LVN | Arriva London | LJ59LZK | Arriva London | LJ60AWP | Arriva London | LK03CEJ | Metroline |
| LJ59LVV | Arriva London | LJ59LZL | Arriva London | LJ60AWR | Arriva London | LK03CEN | Metroline |
| LJ59LVW | Arriva London | LJ59LZM | Arriva London | LJ60AWU | Arriva London | LK03CEU | Metroline |
| LJ59LVX | Arriva London | LJ59LZN | Arriva London | LJ60AWV | Arriva London | LK03CEV | Metroline |
| LJ59LVY | Arriva London | LJ60ASX | Arriva London | LJ60AWW | Arriva London | LK03CEX | Metroline |
| LJ59LVZ | Arriva London | LJ60ASZ | Arriva London | LJ60AWY | Arriva London | LK03CEY | Metroline |
| LJ59LWA | Arriva London | LJ60ATF | Arriva London | LJ60AWZ | Arriva London | LK03CGE | Metroline |
| LJ59LWF | Arriva London | LJ60ATK | Arriva London | LJ60AXA | Arriva London | LK03CGF | Metroline |
| LJ59LWG | Arriva London | LJ60ATN | Arriva London | LJ60AXB | Arriva London | LK03CGG | Metroline |
| LJ59LWH | Arriva London | LJ60ATO | Arriva London | LJ60AXC | Arriva London | LK03CGU | Metroline |
| LJ59LWK | Arriva London | LJ60ATU | Arriva London | LJ60AXD | Arriva London | LK03CGV | Metroline |
| LJ59LWL | Arriva London | LJ60ATV | Arriva London | LJ60AXF | Arriva London | LK03GFU | Metroline |
| LJ59LWM | Arriva London | LJ60ATX | Arriva London | LJ60AXG | Arriva London | LK03GFV | Metroline |
| LJ59LWN | Arriva London | LJ60ATY | Arriva London | LJ60AXV | Arriva London | LK03GFX | Metroline |
| LJ59LWO | Arriva London | LJ60ATZ | Arriva London | LJ60AXW | Arriva London | LK03GFY | Metroline |
| LJ59LWP | Arriva London | LJ60AUA | Arriva London | LJ60AXX | Arriva London | LK03GFZ | Metroline |
| LJ59LWR | Arriva London | LJ60AUC | Arriva London | LJ60AXY | Arriva London | LK03GGA | Metroline |
| LJ59LWS | Arriva London | LJ60AUE | Arriva London | LJ60AXZ | Arriva London | LK03GGF | Metroline |
| LJ59LWT | Arriva London | LJ60AUF | Arriva London | LJ60AYA | Arriva London | LK03GGJ | Metroline |
| LJ59LWU | Arriva London | LJ60AUH | Arriva London | LJ60AYB | Arriva London | LK03GGP | Metroline |
| LJ59LWV | Arriva London | LJ60AUK | Arriva London | LJ60AYC | Arriva London | LK03GGU | Metroline |
| LJ59LWW | Arriva London | LJ60AUL | Arriva London | LJ60AYD | Arriva London | LK03GGV | Metroline |
| LJ59LWX | Arriva London | LJ60AUM | Arriva London | LJ60AYE | Arriva London | LK03GGX | Metroline |
| LJ59LWY | Arriva London | LJ60AUN | Arriva London | LJ60AYF | Arriva London | LK03GGY | Metroline |
| LJ59LWZ | Arriva London | LJ60AUO | Arriva London | LJ60AYG | Arriva London | LK03GGZ | Metroline |
| LJ59LXA | Arriva London | LJ60AUP | Arriva London | LJ60AYH | Arriva London | LK03GHA | Metroline |
| LJ59LXB | Arriva London | LJ60AUR | Arriva London | LJ60AYH | Arriva London | LK03GHB | Metroline |
| LJ59LXP | Arriva London | LJ60AUT | Arriva London | LJ60AYK | Arriva London | LK03GHD | Metroline |
| LJ59LXR | Arriva London | LJ60AUU | Arriva London | LJ60AYK | Arriva London | LK03GHF | Metroline |
| LJ59LXS | Arriva London | LJ60AUV | Arriva London | LJ60AYL | Arriva London | LK03GHG | Metroline |
| LJ59LXT | Arriva London | LJ60AUW | Arriva London | LJ60AYM | Arriva London | LK03GHH | Metroline |
| LJ59LXU | Arriva London | LJ60AUX | Arriva London | LJ60AYM | Arriva London | LK03GHJ | Metroline |
| LJ59LXV | Arriva London | LJ60AUY | Arriva London | LJ60AYN | Arriva London | LK03GHN | Metroline |
| LJ59LXW | Arriva London | LJ60AVB | Arriva London | LJ60AYN | Arriva London | LK03GHU | Metroline |
| LJ59LXX | Arriva London | LJ60AVR | Arriva London | LJ60AYO | Arriva London | LK03GHV | Metroline |
| LJ59LXY | Arriva London | LJ60AVT | Arriva London | LJ60AYO | Arriva London | LK03GHX | Metroline |
| LJ59LXZ | Arriva London | LJ60AVU | Arriva London | LJ60AYP | Arriva London | LK03GHY | Metroline |
| LJ59LYA | Arriva London | LJ60AVV | Arriva London | LJ60AYP | Arriva London | LK03GHZ | Metroline |
| LJ59LYC | Arriva London | LJ60AVW | Arriva London | LJ60AYR | Arriva London | LK03GJF | Metroline |
| LJ59LYD | Arriva London | LJ60AVX | Arriva London | LJ60AYS | Arriva London | LK03GJG | Metroline |
| LJ59LYF | Arriva London | LJ60AVY | Arriva London | LJ60AYS | Arriva London | LK03GJU | Metroline |
| LJ59LYG | Arriva London | LJ60AVZ | Arriva London | LJ60AYT | Arriva London | LK03GJV | Metroline |
| LJ59LYH | Arriva London | LJ60AWA | Arriva London | LJ60AYU | Arriva London | LK03GJX | Metroline |
| LJ59LYK | Arriva London | LJ60AWB | Arriva London | LJ60JGY | Arriva London | LK03GJY | Metroline |
| LJ59LYO | Arriva London | LJ60AWC | Arriva London | LJ60JGZ | Arriva London | LK03GJZ | Metroline |
| LJ59LYP | Arriva London | LJ60AWD | Arriva London | LK03CDA | Metroline | LK03GKA | Metroline |
| LJ59LYS | Arriva London | LJ60AWE | Arriva London | LK03CDD | Metroline | LK03GKC | Metroline |

**Recent arrivals with Arriva include further examples of the Alexander Dennis Trident 2 with ADLs own Enviro 400 bodywork. Pictured passing the Elephant & Castle in March 2011, T175, LJ60ATZ works route 168.**
*Richard Godfrey*

| | | | | | | | |
|---|---|---|---|---|---|---|---|
| LK03GKD | Metroline | LK03GNP | Metroline | LK03NJY | First London | LK03NLM | First London |
| LK03GKE | Metroline | LK03LLX | First London | LK03NJZ | First London | LK03NLN | First London |
| LK03GKF | Metroline | LK03LLZ | First London | LK03NKA | First London | LK03NLP | First London |
| LK03GKG | Metroline | LK03LME | First London | LK03NKC | First London | LK03NLR | First London |
| LK03GKJ | Metroline | LK03LMF | First London | LK03NKD | First London | LK03NLT | First London |
| LK03GKL | Metroline | LK03LMJ | First London | LK03NKE | First London | LK03UEX | First London |
| LK03GKN | Metroline | LK03LNU | First London | LK03NKF | First London | LK03UEY | First London |
| LK03GKP | Metroline | LK03LNV | First London | LK03NKG | First London | LK03UEZ | First London |
| LK03GKU | Metroline | LK03LNW | First London | LK03NKH | First London | LK03UFA | First London |
| LK03GKV | Metroline | LK03LNX | First London | LK03NKJ | First London | LK03UFB | First London |
| LK03GKX | Metroline | LK03NFY | First London | LK03NKL | First London | LK03UFC | First London |
| LK03GKY | Metroline | LK03NFZ | First London | LK03NKM | First London | LK03UFD | First London |
| LK03GKZ | Metroline | LK03NGE | First London | LK03NKN | First London | LK03UFE | First London |
| LK03GLF | Metroline | LK03NGF | First London | LK03NKP | First London | LK03UFG | First London |
| LK03GLJ | Metroline | LK03NGG | First London | LK03NKR | First London | LK03UFJ | First London |
| LK03GLV | Metroline | LK03NHF | First London | LK03NKS | First London | LK03UFL | First London |
| LK03GLY | Metroline | LK03NHG | First London | LK03NKT | First London | LK03UFM | First London |
| LK03GLZ | Metroline | LK03NHP | First London | LK03NKU | First London | LK03UFN | First London |
| LK03GME | Metroline | LK03NHT | First London | LK03NKW | First London | LK03UFP | First London |
| LK03GMF | Metroline | LK03NHV | First London | LK03NKX | First London | LK03UFR | First London |
| LK03GMG | Metroline | LK03NHX | First London | LK03NKZ | First London | LK03UFS | First London |
| LK03GMU | Metroline | LK03NHY | First London | LK03NLA | First London | LK03UFT | First London |
| LK03GMV | Metroline | LK03NHZ | First London | LK03NLC | First London | LK03UFU | First London |
| LK03GMX | Metroline | LK03NJE | First London | LK03NLD | First London | LK03UFV | First London |
| LK03GMY | Metroline | LK03NJF | First London | LK03NLE | First London | LK03UFW | First London |
| LK03GMZ | Metroline | LK03NJJ | First London | LK03NLF | First London | LK03UFX | First London |
| LK03GNF | Metroline | LK03NJN | First London | LK03NLG | First London | LK04CPY | Metroline |
| LK03GNJ | Metroline | LK03NJV | First London | LK03NLJ | First London | LK04CPZ | Metroline |
| LK03GNN | Metroline | LK03NJX | First London | LK03NLL | First London | LK04CRF | Metroline |

| | | | | | | | |
|---|---|---|---|---|---|---|---|
| LK04CRJ | Metroline | LK04EMV | Metroline | LK04HZW | First London | LK05EZW | First London |
| LK04CRU | Metroline | LK04EMX | Metroline | LK04HZX | First London | LK05EZX | First London |
| LK04CRV | Metroline | LK04ENE | Metroline | LK04HZY | First London | LK05EZZ | First London |
| LK04CRZ | Metroline | LK04ENF | Metroline | LK04HZZ | First London | LK05FBY | First London |
| LK04CSF | Metroline | LK04ENH | Metroline | LK04JBE | First London | LK05FBZ | First London |
| LK04CSU | Metroline | LK04ENJ | Metroline | LK04JBU | First London | LK05FCA | First London |
| LK04CSV | Metroline | LK04HXA | First London | LK04JBV | First London | LK05FCB | First London |
| LK04CSX | Metroline | LK04HXB | First London | LK04JBX | First London | LK05FCC | First London |
| LK04CSY | Metroline | LK04HXC | First London | LK04JBY | First London | LK05FCM | First London |
| LK04CSZ | Metroline | LK04HXD | First London | LK04JBZ | First London | LK05FCN | First London |
| LK04CTE | Metroline | LK04HXE | First London | LK04JCJ | First London | LK05FCO | First London |
| LK04CTF | Metroline | LK04HXH | First London | LK04JCU | First London | LK05FCP | First London |
| LK04CTU | Metroline | LK04HXJ | First London | LK04JCV | First London | LK05FCU | First London |
| LK04CTV | Metroline | LK04HXL | First London | LK04JCX | First London | LK05FCV | First London |
| LK04CTX | Metroline | LK04HXM | First London | LK04JCZ | First London | LK05FCX | First London |
| LK04CTZ | Metroline | LK04HXN | First London | LK04NLZ | Metroline | LK05FCY | First London |
| LK04CUA | Metroline | LK04HXP | First London | LK04NMA | Metroline | LK05FCZ | First London |
| LK04CUC | Metroline | LK04HXR | First London | LK04NME | Metroline | LK05FDA | First London |
| LK04CUG | Metroline | LK04HXS | First London | LK04NMF | Metroline | LK05FDC | First London |
| LK04CUH | Metroline | LK04HXT | First London | LK04NMJ | Metroline | LK05FDD | First London |
| LK04CUJ | Metroline | LK04HXU | First London | LK04NMM | Metroline | LK05FDE | First London |
| LK04CUU | Metroline | LK04HXV | First London | LK04NMU | Metroline | LK05FDF | First London |
| LK04CUW | Metroline | LK04HXW | First London | LK04NMV | Metroline | LK05FDG | First London |
| LK04CUX | Metroline | LK04HXX | First London | LK04NMX | Metroline | LK05FDJ | First London |
| LK04CUY | Metroline | LK04HYA | First London | LK04NMY | Metroline | LK05FDL | First London |
| LK04CVA | Metroline | LK04HYB | First London | LK04NMZ | Metroline | LK05GFO | Metroline |
| LK04CVB | Metroline | LK04HYC | First London | LK04NNA | Metroline | LK05GFV | Metroline |
| LK04CVC | Metroline | LK04HYF | First London | LK04NNB | Metroline | LK05GFX | Metroline |
| LK04CVD | Metroline | LK04HYG | First London | LK04NNC | Metroline | LK05GFY | Metroline |
| LK04CVE | Metroline | LK04HYH | First London | LK04NND | Metroline | LK05GFZ | Metroline |
| LK04CVF | Metroline | LK04HYJ | First London | LK04NNE | Metroline | LK05GGA | Metroline |
| LK04CVG | Metroline | LK04HYL | First London | LK04NNF | Metroline | LK05GGE | Metroline |
| LK04CVH | Metroline | LK04HYM | First London | LK04NNG | Metroline | LK05GGF | Metroline |
| LK04CVJ | Metroline | LK04HYN | First London | LK04NNH | Metroline | LK05GGJ | Metroline |
| LK04CVL | Metroline | LK04HYP | First London | LK04NNJ | Metroline | LK05GGO | Metroline |
| LK04CVM | Metroline | LK04HYS | First London | LK04NNL | Metroline | LK05GGP | Metroline |
| LK04CVN | Metroline | LK04HYT | First London | LK04NNM | Metroline | LK05GGU | Metroline |
| LK04CVP | Metroline | LK04HYU | First London | LK04NNP | Metroline | LK05GGV | Metroline |
| LK04CVR | Metroline | LK04HYV | First London | LK04UWJ | Metroline | LK05GGX | Metroline |
| LK04CVS | Metroline | LK04HYW | First London | LK04UWL | Metroline | LK05GGY | Metroline |
| LK04CVT | Metroline | LK04HYX | First London | LK04UWM | Metroline | LK05GGZ | Metroline |
| LK04CVU | Metroline | LK04HYY | First London | LK04UWN | Metroline | LK05GHA | Metroline |
| LK04CVV | Metroline | LK04HYZ | First London | LK04UWP | Metroline | LK05GHB | Metroline |
| LK04CVW | Metroline | LK04HZA | First London | LK04UWR | Metroline | LK05GHD | Metroline |
| LK04CVX | Metroline | LK04HZB | First London | LK04UWS | Metroline | LK05GHF | Metroline |
| LK04EKU | Metroline | LK04HZC | First London | LK04UWT | Metroline | LK05GHG | Metroline |
| LK04EKV | Metroline | LK04HZD | First London | LK04UWU | Metroline | LK05GHH | Metroline |
| LK04EKW | Metroline | LK04HZE | First London | LK04UWV | Metroline | LK06BWC | Abellio |
| LK04EKX | Metroline | LK04HZF | First London | LK04UWW | Metroline | LK06BWD | Abellio |
| LK04EKY | Metroline | LK04HZG | First London | LK04UWX | Metroline | LK06FLA | Metroline |
| LK04EKZ | Metroline | LK04HZH | First London | LK04UWY | Metroline | LK06FLB | Metroline |
| LK04ELC | Metroline | LK04HZJ | First London | LK04UWZ | Metroline | LK06FLC | Metroline |
| LK04ELH | Metroline | LK04HZL | First London | LK04UXA | Metroline | LK07AYC | Metroline |
| LK04ELJ | Metroline | LK04HZM | First London | LK04UXB | Metroline | LK07AYD | Metroline |
| LK04ELU | Metroline | LK04HZN | First London | LK04UXC | Metroline | LK07AYE | Metroline |
| LK04ELV | Metroline | LK04HZP | First London | LK04UXD | Metroline | LK07AYF | Metroline |
| LK04ELW | Metroline | LK04HZS | First London | LK04UXE | Metroline | LK07AYG | Metroline |
| LK04ELX | Metroline | LK04HZT | First London | LK04UXF | Metroline | LK07AYH | Metroline |
| LK04EMF | Metroline | LK04HZU | First London | LK04UXG | Metroline | LK07AYJ | Metroline |
| LK04EMJ | Metroline | LK04HZV | First London | LK04UXH | Metroline | LK07AYL | Metroline |

| | | | | | | | |
|---|---|---|---|---|---|---|---|
| LK07AYM | Metroline | LK08DWA | Metroline | LK08FLZ | First London | LK09ENL | Metroline |
| LK07AYN | Metroline | LK08DWC | Metroline | LK08FNA | First London | LK09ENM | Metroline |
| LK07AYZ | Metroline | LK08DWD | Metroline | LK08FNC | First London | LK09ENN | Metroline |
| LK07AZA | Metroline | LK08DWE | Metroline | LK08FND | First London | LK09ENO | Metroline |
| LK07AZB | Metroline | LK08DWF | Metroline | LK08FNE | First London | LK09ENP | Metroline |
| LK07AZC | Metroline | LK08DWG | Metroline | LK08FNF | First London | LK09ENR | Metroline |
| LK07AZD | Metroline | LK08DWJ | Metroline | LK08FNG | First London | LK09ENT | Metroline |
| LK07AZF | Metroline | LK08DWL | Metroline | LK08FNH | First London | LK09ENU | Metroline |
| LK07AZG | Metroline | LK08DWM | Metroline | LK08LMA | First London | LK09ENV | Metroline |
| LK07AZJ | Metroline | LK08DWN | Metroline | LK08LMO | First London | LK09ENW | Metroline |
| LK07AZL | Metroline | LK08DWO | Metroline | LK08LMP | First London | LK09ENX | Metroline |
| LK07AZN | Metroline | LK08DWP | Metroline | LK08LMU | First London | LK09ENY | Metroline |
| LK07AZO | Metroline | LK08DWU | Metroline | LK08LMV | First London | LK09EOA | Metroline |
| LK07AZP | Metroline | LK08DWV | Metroline | LK08LMX | First London | LK09EOB | Metroline |
| LK07AZR | Metroline | LK08DWW | Metroline | LK08LMY | First London | LK09EOC | Metroline |
| LK07AZT | Metroline | LK08DWX | Metroline | LK08LMZ | First London | LK09EOD | Metroline |
| LK07AZU | Metroline | LK08DWY | Metroline | LK08NVD | Metroline | LK09EOE | Metroline |
| LK07AZV | Metroline | LK08DWZ | Metroline | LK08NVE | Metroline | LK10BXC | Metroline |
| LK07AZW | Metroline | LK08DXA | Metroline | LK08NVF | Metroline | LK10BXD | Metroline |
| LK07AZX | Metroline | LK08DXB | Metroline | LK08NVG | Metroline | LK10BXE | Metroline |
| LK07AZZ | Metroline | LK08DXC | Metroline | LK08NVH | Metroline | LK10BXF | Metroline |
| LK07BAA | Metroline | LK08DXD | Metroline | LK08NVJ | Metroline | LK10BXG | Metroline |
| LK07BAO | Metroline | LK08DXE | Metroline | LK08NVL | Metroline | LK10BXH | Metroline |
| LK07BAU | Metroline | LK08DXF | Metroline | LK08NVM | Metroline | LK10BXJ | Metroline |
| LK07BBE | Metroline | LK08DXG | Metroline | LK08NVN | Metroline | LK10BXL | Metroline |
| LK07BBF | Metroline | LK08DXH | Metroline | LK08NVO | Metroline | LK10BXM | Metroline |
| LK07BBJ | Metroline | LK08DXO | Metroline | LK08NVP | Metroline | LK10BXN | Metroline |
| LK07BBN | Metroline | LK08DXP | Metroline | LK09EHU | Metroline | LK10BXO | Metroline |
| LK07BBO | Metroline | LK08DXR | Metroline | LK09EKG | Metroline | LK10BXP | Metroline |
| LK07BBU | Metroline | LK08DXS | Metroline | LK09EKH | Metroline | LK10BXR | Metroline |
| LK07BBV | Metroline | LK08DXU | Metroline | LK09EKJ | Metroline | LK10BXS | Metroline |
| LK07BBX | Metroline | LK08DXV | Metroline | LK09EKL | Metroline | LK10BXU | Metroline |
| LK07BBZ | Metroline | LK08DXW | Metroline | LK09EKM | Metroline | LK10BXV | Metroline |
| LK07BCE | Metroline | LK08DXX | Metroline | LK09EKN | Metroline | LK10BXW | Metroline |
| LK07BCF | Metroline | LK08DXY | Metroline | LK09EKO | Metroline | LK10BXX | Metroline |
| LK07BCO | Metroline | LK08DXZ | Metroline | LK09EKP | Metroline | LK10BXY | Metroline |
| LK07BCU | Metroline | LK08DZA | Metroline | LK09EKR | Metroline | LK10BXZ | Metroline |
| LK07BCV | Metroline | LK08FKT | First London | LK09EKT | Metroline | LK10BYA | Metroline |
| LK07BCX | Metroline | LK08FKU | First London | LK09EKV | Metroline | LK10BYB | Metroline |
| LK07BCY | Metroline | LK08FKV | First London | LK09EKW | Metroline | LK10BYC | Metroline |
| LK07BCZ | Metroline | LK08FKW | First London | LK09EKX | Metroline | LK10BYD | Metroline |
| LK07BDE | Metroline | LK08FKX | First London | LK09EKY | Metroline | LK10BYG | Metroline |
| LK07BDO | Metroline | LK08FKY | First London | LK09EKZ | Metroline | LK10BYJ | Metroline |
| LK07BDU | Metroline | LK08FKZ | First London | LK09ELC | Metroline | LK10BYL | Metroline |
| LK07BDV | Metroline | LK08FLA | First London | LK09ELH | Metroline | LK10BYM | Metroline |
| LK07BDX | Metroline | LK08FLC | First London | LK09ELJ | Metroline | LK10BYN | Metroline |
| LK07BDY | Metroline | LK08FLD | First London | LK09ELO | Metroline | LK10BYO | Metroline |
| LK07BDZ | Metroline | LK08FLE | First London | LK09ELU | Metroline | LK10BYP | Metroline |
| LK07BEJ | Metroline | LK08FLF | First London | LK09ELV | Metroline | LK10BYR | Metroline |
| LK07BEO | Metroline | LK08FLG | First London | LK09ELW | Metroline | LK10BYS | Metroline |
| LK07BEU | Metroline | LK08FLH | First London | LK09ELX | Metroline | LK10BYT | Metroline |
| LK07BEY | Metroline | LK08FLJ | First London | LK09EMF | Metroline | LK10BYU | Metroline |
| LK07CBF | Abellio | LK08FLL | First London | LK09EMJ | Metroline | LK10BYV | Metroline |
| LK07CBV | Abellio | LK08FLM | First London | LK09EMV | Metroline | LK10BYW | Metroline |
| LK07CBX | Abellio | LK08FLN | First London | LK09EMX | Metroline | LK10BYX | Metroline |
| LK07ELH | Metroline | LK08FLP | First London | LK09ENC | Metroline | LK10BYY | Metroline |
| LK07ELJ | Metroline | LK08FLR | First London | LK09ENE | Metroline | LK10BYZ | Metroline |
| LK07ELO | Metroline | LK08FLV | First London | LK09ENF | Metroline | LK10BZA | Metroline |
| LK08DVY | Metroline | LK08FLW | First London | LK09ENH | Metroline | LK10BZB | Metroline |
| LK08DVZ | Metroline | LK08FLX | First London | LK09ENJ | Metroline | LK10BZC | Metroline |

*The London Bus Handbook*

Metroline DEL849, LK08DWA, is seen in Station Road, New Barnet while heading for St Albans on route 84. The Enviro 200-bodied Dart is the most numerous single-deck model currently being supplied to TfL operators. *Mark Lyons*

| | | | | | | | | |
|---|---|---|---|---|---|---|---|---|
| LK10BZD | Metroline | LK11CWV | Metroline | LK11CYF | Metroline | LK51XGS | Metroline |
| LK10BZE | Metroline | LK11CWW | Metroline | LK51JYL | Metrobus | LK51XGT | Metroline |
| LK10BZF | Metroline | LK11CWX | Metroline | LK51JYL | Metrobus | LK51XGU | Metroline |
| LK10BZG | Metroline | LK11CWY | Metroline | LK51JYN | Metrobus | LK51XGV | Metroline |
| LK10BZH | Metroline | LK11CWZ | Metroline | LK51JYO | First London | LK51XGW | Metroline |
| LK10BZJ | Metroline | LK11CXA | Metroline | LK51UYD | First London | LK51XGX | Metroline |
| LK10BZL | Metroline | LK11CXB | Metroline | LK51UYE | First London | LK51XGY | Metroline |
| LK10BZM | Metroline | LK11CXC | Metroline | LK51UYF | First London | LK51XGZ | Metroline |
| LK10BZN | Metroline | LK11CXD | Metroline | LK51UYG | First London | LK51XHA | Metroline |
| LK10BZO | Metroline | LK11CXE | Metroline | LK51UYH | First London | LK51XHB | Metroline |
| LK10BZP | Metroline | LK11CXF | Metroline | LK51UYJ | First London | LK53EXT | First London |
| LK10BZR | Metroline | LK11CXG | Metroline | LK51UYP | First London | LK53EXU | First London |
| LK10BZS | Metroline | LK11CXJ | Metroline | LK51UYR | First London | LK53EXV | First London |
| LK10BZT | Metroline | LK11CXK | Metroline | LK51UYX | First London | LK53EXW | First London |
| LK10BZU | Metroline | LK11CXL | Metroline | LK51UYY | First London | LK53EXX | First London |
| LK10BZV | Metroline | LK11CXN | Metroline | LK51UYZ | First London | LK53EXZ | First London |
| LK10BZX | Metroline | LK11CXO | Metroline | LK51UZA | First London | LK53EYA | First London |
| LK10BZY | Metroline | LK11CXP | Metroline | LK51UZB | First London | LK53EYB | First London |
| LK11CWF | Metroline | LK11CXR | Metroline | LK51XGD | Metroline | LK53EYC | First London |
| LK11CWG | Metroline | LK11CXS | Metroline | LK51XGE | Metroline | LK53EYD | First London |
| LK11CWJ | Metroline | LK11CXT | Metroline | LK51XGG | Metroline | LK53EYF | First London |
| LK11CWL | Metroline | LK11CXU | Metroline | LK51XGH | Metroline | LK53EYG | First London |
| LK11CWM | Metroline | LK11CXV | Metroline | LK51XGJ | Metroline | LK53EYH | First London |
| LK11CWN | Metroline | LK11CXW | Metroline | LK51XGL | Metroline | LK53EYJ | First London |
| LK11CWO | Metroline | LK11CXX | Metroline | LK51XGM | Metroline | LK53EYL | First London |
| LK11CWP | Metroline | LK11CXY | Metroline | LK51XGN | Metroline | LK53EYM | First London |
| LK11CWR | Metroline | LK11CXZ | Metroline | LK51XGO | Metroline | LK53EYO | First London |
| LK11CWT | Metroline | LK11CYA | Metroline | LK51XGP | Metroline | LK53EYP | First London |
| LK11CWU | Metroline | LK11CYE | Metroline | LK51XGR | Metroline | LK53EYR | First London |

*The London Bus Handbook*

| Reg | Operator | Reg | Operator | Reg | Operator | Reg | Operator |
|---|---|---|---|---|---|---|---|
| LK53EYT | First London | LK53LYD | Metroline | LK55AAJ | First London | LK56FHJ | Metroline |
| LK53EYU | First London | LK53LYF | Metroline | LK55AAN | First London | LK56FHM | Metroline |
| LK53EYV | First London | LK53LYG | Metroline | LK55AAU | First London | LK56FHN | Metroline |
| LK53EYW | First London | LK53LYH | First London | LK55AAV | First London | LK56FHO | Metroline |
| LK53EYX | First London | LK53LYJ | First London | LK55AAX | First London | LK56FHP | Metroline |
| LK53EYY | First London | LK53LYO | First London | LK55AAY | First London | LK56FHR | Metroline |
| LK53EYZ | First London | LK53LYP | First London | LK55AAZ | First London | LK56FHS | Metroline |
| LK53EZA | First London | LK53LYR | First London | LK55ABF | First London | LK56FHT | Metroline |
| LK53EZB | First London | LK53LYT | First London | LK55ACU | First London | LK56JKE | Abellio |
| LK53EZC | First London | LK53LYU | First London | LK55ACX | Abellio | LK56JKF | Abellio |
| LK53EZD | First London | LK53LYV | First London | LK55ADU | Abellio | LK56JKJ | Abellio |
| LK53EZE | First London | LK53LYW | First London | LK55ADV | Abellio | LK56JKN | Abellio |
| LK53EZF | First London | LK53LYX | First London | LK55KJV | Metroline | LK56JKO | Abellio |
| LK53EZV | First London | LK53LYY | First London | LK55KJX | Metroline | LK56JKV | Abellio |
| LK53EZW | First London | LK53LYZ | First London | LK55KJY | Metroline | LK57AXF | Metroline |
| LK53EZX | First London | LK53LZA | First London | LK55KJZ | Metroline | LK57AXG | Metroline |
| LK53EZZ | First London | LK53LZB | First London | LK55KKA | Metroline | LK57AXH | Metroline |
| LK53FAO | First London | LK53LZC | First London | LK55KKB | Metroline | LK57AXJ | Metroline |
| LK53FBC | First London | LK53LZD | First London | LK55KKC | Metroline | LK57AXM | Metroline |
| LK53FCF | First London | LK53LZE | First London | LK55KKD | Metroline | LK57AXN | Metroline |
| LK53FCG | First London | LK53LZF | First London | LK55KKE | Metroline | LK57AXO | Metroline |
| LK53FCJ | First London | LK53LZG | First London | LK55KKF | Metroline | LK57AXP | Metroline |
| LK53FCL | First London | LK53LZH | First London | LK55KKG | Metroline | LK57AXR | Metroline |
| LK53FCX | First London | LK53LZM | First London | LK55KKH | Metroline | LK57AXS | Metroline |
| LK53FCY | First London | LK53LZN | First London | LK55KKJ | Metroline | LK57AXT | Metroline |
| LK53FCZ | First London | LK53LZO | First London | LK55KKL | Metroline | LK57AXU | Metroline |
| LK53FDA | First London | LK53LZP | First London | LK55KKM | Metroline | LK57AXV | Metroline |
| LK53FDC | First London | LK53LZR | First London | LK55KKO | Metroline | LK57AXW | Metroline |
| LK53FDD | First London | LK53LZT | First London | LK55KKP | Metroline | LK57AXX | Metroline |
| LK53FDE | First London | LK53LZU | First London | LK55KKR | Metroline | LK57AXY | Metroline |
| LK53FDF | First London | LK53LZV | First London | LK55KKS | Metroline | LK57AXZ | Metroline |
| LK53FDG | First London | LK53LZW | First London | LK55KKT | Metroline | LK57AYA | Metroline |
| LK53FDJ | First London | LK53LZX | First London | LK55KKU | Metroline | LK57AYB | Metroline |
| LK53FDM | First London | LK53MBF | First London | LK55KKV | Metroline | LK57AYC | Metroline |
| LK53FDN | First London | LK54FKW | First London | LK55KKY | Metroline | LK57AYD | Metroline |
| LK53FDO | First London | LK54FKX | First London | LK55KKZ | Metroline | LK57AYE | Metroline |
| LK53FDP | First London | LK54FLA | First London | LK55KLA | Metroline | LK57AYF | Metroline |
| LK53FDU | First London | LK54FLB | First London | LK55KLE | Metroline | LK57AYG | Metroline |
| LK53FDV | First London | LK54FLC | First London | LK55KLF | Metroline | LK57AYH | Metroline |
| LK53FDX | First London | LK54FLD | First London | LK55KLJ | Metroline | LK57AYJ | Metroline |
| LK53FDY | First London | LK54FLE | First London | LK55KLL | Metroline | LK57AYL | Metroline |
| LK53FDZ | First London | LK54FLF | First London | LK55KLM | Metroline | LK57AYM | Metroline |
| LK53FEF | First London | LK54FLG | First London | LK55KLO | Metroline | LK57AYN | Metroline |
| LK53FEG | First London | LK54FLH | First London | LK55KLP | Metroline | LK57AYO | Metroline |
| LK53FEH | First London | LK54FNO | First London | LK55KLS | Metroline | LK57AYP | Metroline |
| LK53FEJ | First London | LK54FNP | First London | LK55KLU | Metroline | LK57AYS | Metroline |
| LK53LXM | Metroline | LK54FWE | Metroline | LK55KLV | Metroline | LK57AYT | Metroline |
| LK53LXN | Metroline | LK54FWF | Metroline | LK55KLX | Metroline | LK57AYU | Metroline |
| LK53LXO | Metroline | LK54FWG | Metroline | LK55KLZ | Metroline | LK57AYV | Metroline |
| LK53LXP | Metroline | LK54FWH | Metroline | LK55KMA | Metroline | LK57AYW | Metroline |
| LK53LXR | Metroline | LK54FWJ | Metroline | LK55KME | Metroline | LK57AYX | Metroline |
| LK53LXT | Metroline | LK54FWK | Metroline | LK55KMF | Metroline | LK57AYY | Metroline |
| LK53LXU | Metroline | LK54FWM | Metroline | LK55KMG | Metroline | LK57EHS | Metroline |
| LK53LXV | Metroline | LK54FWN | Metroline | LK55KMJ | Metroline | LK57EHT | Metroline |
| LK53LXW | Metroline | LK54FWO | Metroline | LK55KMM | Metroline | LK57EHU | Metroline |
| LK53LXX | Metroline | LK54FWP | Metroline | LK55KMO | Metroline | LK57EHV | Metroline |
| LK53LXY | Metroline | LK54FWR | Metroline | LK56FHE | Metroline | LK57EHW | Metroline |
| LK53LXZ | Metroline | LK54FWT | Metroline | LK56FHF | Metroline | LK57EHX | Metroline |
| LK53LYA | Metroline | LK55AAE | First London | LK56FHG | Metroline | LK57EHY | Metroline |
| LK53LYC | Metroline | LK55AAF | First London | LK56FHH | Metroline | LK57EHZ | Metroline |

*The London Bus Handbook*

| | | | | | | | |
|---|---|---|---|---|---|---|---|
| LK57EJA | Metroline | LK58ECY | First London | LK59CWY | First London | LK60AEU | Metroline |
| LK57EJD | First London | LK58ECZ | First London | LK59CWZ | First London | LK60AEV | Metroline |
| LK57EJE | First London | LK58EDO | First London | LK59CXA | First London | LK60AEW | Metroline |
| LK57EJF | First London | LK58EDP | First London | LK59CXB | First London | LK60AEX | Metroline |
| LK57EJG | First London | LK58EDR | First London | LK59CXC | First London | LK60AEY | Metroline |
| LK57EJJ | First London | LK58KFW | Metroline | LK59CXD | First London | LK60AEZ | Metroline |
| LK57EJL | First London | LK58KFX | Metroline | LK59CXE | First London | LK60AFA | Metroline |
| LK57EJN | First London | LK58KFY | Metroline | LK59CXF | First London | LK60AFE | Metroline |
| LK57EJO | First London | LK58KFZ | Metroline | LK59CXG | First London | LK60AFF | Metroline |
| LK57KAU | Metroline | LK58KGA | Metroline | LK59CXH | First London | LK60AFN | Metroline |
| LK57KAX | Metroline | LK58KGE | Metroline | LK59CXJ | First London | LK60AFO | Metroline |
| LK57KBE | Metroline | LK58KGF | Metroline | LK59CXL | First London | LK60AFU | Metroline |
| LK57KBF | Metroline | LK58KGG | Metroline | LK59CXM | First London | LK60AFV | Metroline |
| LK57KBJ | Metroline | LK58KGJ | Metroline | LK59CXN | First London | LK60AFX | Metroline |
| LK57KBN | Metroline | LK58KGN | Metroline | LK59CXO | First London | LK60AFY | Metroline |
| LK57KBO | Metroline | LK58KGO | Metroline | LK59CXP | First London | LK60AFZ | Metroline |
| LK58CMZ | Metroline | LK58KGU | Metroline | LK59FCO | First London | LK60AGO | Metroline |
| LK58CNA | Metroline | LK58KGV | Metroline | LK59FCP | First London | LK60AGU | Metroline |
| LK58CNC | Metroline | LK58KGW | Metroline | LK59FCU | First London | LK60AGV | Metroline |
| LK58CNE | Metroline | LK58KHC | Metroline | LK59FCV | First London | LK60AGY | Metroline |
| LK58CNF | Metroline | LK58KHD | Metroline | LK59FCX | First London | LK60AGZ | Metroline |
| LK58CNN | Metroline | LK58KHE | Metroline | LK59FCY | First London | LK60AHA | Metroline |
| LK58CNO | Metroline | LK58KHF | Metroline | LK59FDE | First London | LK60AHC | Metroline |
| LK58CNU | Metroline | LK58KHG | Metroline | LK59FDF | First London | LK60AHD | Metroline |
| LK58CNV | Metroline | LK58KHH | Metroline | LK59FDG | First London | LK60AHE | Metroline |
| LK58CNX | Metroline | LK58KHL | Metroline | LK59FDJ | First London | LK60AHG | Metroline |
| LK58CNY | Metroline | LK58KHM | Metroline | LK59FDL | First London | LK60AHJ | Metroline |
| LK58CNZ | Metroline | LK58KHO | Metroline | LK59FDM | First London | LK60AHL | Metroline |
| LK58COA | Metroline | LK58KHP | Metroline | LK59FDN | First London | LK60AHN | Metroline |
| LK58COH | Metroline | LK58KHR | Metroline | LK59FDO | First London | LK60AHO | Metroline |
| LK58COJ | Metroline | LK58KHT | Metroline | LK59FDP | First London | LK60AHP | Metroline |
| LK58COU | Metroline | LK58KHU | Metroline | LK59FDU | First London | LK60AHU | Metroline |
| LK58CPE | Metroline | LK59AUW | Metroline | LK59FDV | First London | LK60AHV | Metroline |
| LK58CPF | Metroline | LK59AUY | Metroline | LK59FDX | First London | LK60AHX | Metroline |
| LK58CPN | Metroline | LK59AVB | Metroline | LK59FDY | First London | LK60AHY | Metroline |
| LK58CPO | Metroline | LK59AVC | Metroline | LK59FDZ | First London | LK60AHZ | Metroline |
| LK58CPU | Metroline | LK59AVD | Metroline | LK59FEF | First London | LK60AJO | Metroline |
| LK58CPV | Metroline | LK59AVF | Metroline | LK59FEG | First London | LK60AJU | Metroline |
| LK58CRF | Metroline | LK59AVG | Metroline | LK59FEH | First London | LK60AJV | Metroline |
| LK58CRV | Metroline | LK59AVJ | Metroline | LK59FEJ | First London | LK60AJX | Metroline |
| LK58CRX | Metroline | LK59AVL | Metroline | LK59FEM | First London | LK60AJY | Metroline |
| LK58CRZ | Metroline | LK59AVM | Metroline | LK59FEO | First London | LK60AKF | Metroline |
| LK58CSF | Metroline | LK59AVN | Metroline | LK59FEP | First London | LK60HPE | First London |
| LK58CSU | Metroline | LK59AVO | Metroline | LK59FET | First London | LK60HPF | First London |
| LK58CSX | Metroline | LK59AVP | Metroline | LK59FEU | First London | LK60HPJ | First London |
| LK58CSY | Metroline | LK59AVR | Metroline | LK59JJU | Metroline | LK60HPL | First London |
| LK58CSZ | Metroline | LK59AVT | Metroline | LK60AEA | Metroline | LK60HPN | First London |
| LK58CTE | Metroline | LK59AVU | Metroline | LK60AEB | Metroline | LN51DUA | First London |
| LK58CTF | Metroline | LK59AVV | Metroline | LK60AEC | Metroline | LN51DUH | First London |
| LK58CTO | Metroline | LK59AVW | Metroline | LK60AED | Metroline | LN51DUJ | First London |
| LK58CTU | Metroline | LK59AVX | Metroline | LK60AEE | Metroline | LN51DUU | First London |
| LK58CTV | Metroline | LK59CWN | First London | LK60AEF | Metroline | LN51DUV | First London |
| LK58CTX | Metroline | LK59CWO | First London | LK60AEG | Metroline | LN51DUY | First London |
| LK58CTY | Metroline | LK59CWP | First London | LK60AEJ | Metroline | LN51DVG | First London |
| LK58CTZ | Metroline | LK59CWR | First London | LK60AEL | Metroline | LN51DVH | First London |
| LK58CUA | Metroline | LK59CWT | First London | LK60AEM | Metroline | LN51DVK | First London |
| LK58CZS | First London | LK59CWU | First London | LK60AEN | Metroline | LN51DVM | First London |
| LK58ECV | First London | LK59CWV | First London | LK60AEO | Metroline | LN51DVO | First London |
| LK58ECW | First London | LK59CWW | First London | LK60AEP | Metroline | LN51DVP | First London |
| LK58ECX | First London | LK59CWX | First London | LK60AET | Metroline | LN51DVR | First London |

*The London Bus Handbook*

**Eight VDL SB200 LF fuelcell buses with Wrightbus Pulsar 2 bodywork are currently being supplied to First for roure RV1. Pictured shortly after it entered service, 62995, LK60HPN, is seen at Upper Ground. The batch carry the WSH local type prefix letters.** *Mark Lyons*

| | | | | | | | |
|---|---|---|---|---|---|---|---|
| LN51DVT | First London | LN51GJV | First London | LN51GNP | First London | LN51KXY | Metroline |
| LN51DVV | First London | LN51GJX | First London | LN51GNU | First London | LN51KXZ | Metroline |
| LN51DVW | First London | LN51GJY | First London | LN51GNY | First London | LN51KYA | Metroline |
| LN51DVX | First London | LN51GJZ | First London | LN51GNZ | First London | LN51KYB | Metroline |
| LN51DVY | First London | LN51GKA | First London | LN51GOA | First London | LN51KYC | Metroline |
| LN51DVZ | First London | LN51GKD | First London | LN51GOC | First London | LN51KYE | Metroline |
| LN51DWA | First London | LN51GKE | First London | LN51GOE | First London | LN51KYF | Metroline |
| LN51DWD | First London | LN51GKF | First London | LN51GOH | First London | LN51KYG | Metroline |
| LN51DWG | First London | LN51GKG | First London | LN51GOJ | First London | LN51KYH | Metroline |
| LN51DWJ | First London | LN51GKJ | First London | LN51GOK | First London | LN51KYJ | Metroline |
| LN51DWK | First London | LN51GKU | First London | LN51GOP | First London | LN51KYK | Metroline |
| LN51DWL | First London | LN51GKV | First London | LN51GOU | First London | LN51KYO | Metroline |
| LN51DWM | First London | LN51GKX | First London | LN51KXD | Metroline | LN51KYP | Metroline |
| LN51DWO | First London | LN51GKY | First London | LN51KXE | Metroline | LN51KYR | Metroline |
| LN51DWP | First London | LN51GKZ | First London | LN51KXF | Metroline | LN51KYS | Metroline |
| LN51DWU | First London | LN51GLF | First London | LN51KXG | Metroline | LN51KYT | Metroline |
| LN51DWW | First London | LN51GLJ | First London | LN51KXH | Metroline | LN51KYU | Metroline |
| LN51DWX | First London | LN51GLK | First London | LN51KXJ | Metroline | LN51KYV | Metroline |
| LN51DWY | First London | LN51GLV | First London | LN51KXK | Metroline | LN51KYW | Metroline |
| LN51DWZ | First London | LN51GLY | First London | LN51KXL | Metroline | LN51KYX | Metroline |
| LN51DXA | First London | LN51GMF | First London | LN51KXM | Metroline | LN51KYY | Metroline |
| LN51DXB | First London | LN51GMG | First London | LN51KXO | Metroline | LN51KYZ | Metroline |
| LN51DXC | First London | LN51GMO | First London | LN51KXP | Metroline | LN51KZA | Metroline |
| LN51DXD | First London | LN51GMU | First London | LN51KXR | Metroline | LN51KZB | Metroline |
| LN51DXE | First London | LN51GMX | First London | LN51KXS | Metroline | LN51KZC | Metroline |
| LN51DXF | First London | LN51GMY | First London | LN51KXT | Metroline | LN51KZD | Metroline |
| LN51DXG | First London | LN51GMZ | First London | LN51KXU | Metroline | LN51NRJ | First London |
| LN51DXH | First London | LN51GNF | First London | LN51KXV | Metroline | LN51NRK | First London |
| LN51GJO | First London | LN51GNJ | First London | LN51KXW | Metroline | LN51NRL | First London |

| | | | | | | | |
|---|---|---|---|---|---|---|---|
| LR02BAA | Metroline | LR52BNJ | Metroline | LT02ZDU | Metrobus | LV52HFP | Stagecoach |
| LR02BAO | Metroline | LR52BNK | Metroline | LT02ZDV | Metrobus | LV52HFR | Stagecoach |
| LR02BAU | Metroline | LR52BNL | Metroline | LT02ZDW | Metrobus | LV52HFS | Stagecoach |
| LR02BAV | Metroline | LR52BNN | Metroline | LT02ZDX | Metrobus | LV52HFT | Stagecoach |
| LR02BBE | Metroline | LR52BNO | Metroline | LT02ZFJ | First London | LV52HFU | Stagecoach |
| LR02BBF | Metroline | LR52BNU | Metroline | LT02ZFK | First London | LV52HFU | Stagecoach |
| LR02BBJ | Metroline | LR52BNV | Metroline | LT02ZFL | First London | LV52HFW | Stagecoach |
| LR02BBK | Metroline | LR52BNX | Metroline | LT02ZFM | First London | LV52HFX | Stagecoach |
| LR02BBN | Metroline | LR52BNY | Metroline | LT52WUM | First London | LV52HFY | Stagecoach |
| LR02BBO | Metroline | LR52BNZ | Metroline | LT52WUO | First London | LV52HFZ | Stagecoach |
| LR02BBU | Metroline | LR52BOF | Metroline | LT52WUP | First London | LV52HGA | Stagecoach |
| LR02BBV | Metroline | LR52BOH | Metroline | LT52WUR | First London | LV52HGC | Stagecoach |
| LR02BBX | Metroline | LR52BOJ | Metroline | LT52WVB | First London | LV52HGD | Stagecoach |
| LR02BBZ | Metroline | LR52BOU | Metroline | LT52WVC | First London | LV52HGE | Stagecoach |
| LR02BCE | Metroline | LR52BOV | Metroline | LT52WVD | First London | LV52HGF | Stagecoach |
| LR02BCF | Metroline | LR52BPE | Metroline | LT52WVE | First London | LV52HGG | Stagecoach |
| LR02BCK | Metroline | LR52LTF | Hackney CT | LT52WXG | First London | LV52HGJ | Stagecoach |
| LR02BCO | Metroline | LR52LTJ | Hackney CT | LT52WXJ | First London | LV52HGK | Stagecoach |
| LR02BCU | Metroline | LR52LTK | Hackney CT | LT52WXK | First London | LV52HGL | Stagecoach |
| LR02BCV | Metroline | LR52LTN | Hackney CT | LT52XAA | First London | LV52HGM | Stagecoach |
| LR02BCX | Metroline | LR52LTO | Hackney CT | LT52XAB | First London | LV52HGN | Stagecoach |
| LR02BCY | Metroline | LR52LWE | Hackney CT | LT52XAC | First London | LV52HGO | Stagecoach |
| LR02BCZ | Metroline | LR52LWF | Hackney CT | LT52XAD | First London | LV52HJY | Stagecoach |
| LR02BDE | Metroline | LR52LWH | Hackney CT | LT52XAE | First London | LV52HJZ | Stagecoach |
| LR02BDF | Metroline | LR52LWJ | Hackney CT | LT52XAF | First London | LV52HKA | Stagecoach |
| LR02BDO | Metroline | LR52LYC | Hackney CT | LT52XAG | First London | LV52HKB | Stagecoach |
| LR02BDU | Metroline | LR52LYJ | Hackney CT | LT52XAH | First London | LV52HKC | Stagecoach |
| LR02BDV | Metroline | LT02NUK | First London | LT52XAJ | First London | LV52HKD | Stagecoach |
| LR02BDX | Metroline | LT02NUM | First London | LT52XAK | First London | LV52HKE | Stagecoach |
| LR02BDY | Metroline | LT02NUO | First London | LV51YCC | Big Bus Company | LV52HKF | Stagecoach |
| LR02BDZ | Metroline | LT02NUP | First London | LV51YCD | Big Bus Company | LV52HKG | Stagecoach |
| LR02BEJ | Metroline | LT02NUU | First London | LV51YCE | Big Bus Company | LV52HKH | Stagecoach |
| LR02BEO | Metroline | LT02NUV | First London | LV51YCF | Big Bus Company | LV52HKJ | Stagecoach |
| LR02BEU | Metroline | LT02NVE | First London | LV51YCG | Big Bus Company | LV52HKK | Stagecoach |
| LR02BEY | Metroline | LT02NVH | First London | LV51YCH | Big Bus Company | LV52HKL | Stagecoach |
| LR02BFA | Metroline | LT02NVJ | First London | LV51YCJ | Big Bus Company | LV52HKM | Stagecoach |
| LR02BFE | Metroline | LT02NVK | First London | LV51YCK | Big Bus Company | LV52HKN | Stagecoach |
| LR02LYX | First London | LT02NVM | First London | LV51YCL | Big Bus Company | LV52HKO | Stagecoach |
| LR02LYY | First London | LT02NVN | First London | LV51YCM | Big Bus Company | LV52HKP | Stagecoach |
| LR02LYZ | First London | LT02NVO | First London | LV51YCN | Big Bus Company | LV52HKT | Stagecoach |
| LR02LZA | First London | LT02NVP | First London | LV51YCO | Big Bus Company | LV52HKU | Stagecoach |
| LR02LZB | First London | LT02NVR | First London | LV52HDO | Stagecoach | LV52USV | Stagecoach |
| LR02LZC | First London | LT02NVS | First London | LV52HDU | Stagecoach | LX03BTE | Stagecoach |
| LR02LZD | First London | LT02ZBX | First London | LV52HDX | Stagecoach | LX03BTF | Stagecoach |
| LR02LZE | First London | LT02ZBY | First London | LV52HDY | Stagecoach | LX03BTU | Stagecoach |
| LR52BLK | Metroline | LT02ZBZ | First London | LV52HDZ | Stagecoach | LX03BTV | Stagecoach |
| LR52BLN | Metroline | LT02ZCA | First London | LV52HEJ | Stagecoach | LX03BTY | Stagecoach |
| LR52BLV | Metroline | LT02ZCE | First London | LV52HFA | Stagecoach | LX03BTZ | Stagecoach |
| LR52BLX | Metroline | LT02ZCF | First London | LV52HFB | Stagecoach | LX03BUA | Stagecoach |
| LR52BLZ | Metroline | LT02ZDC | Metrobus | LV52HFC | Stagecoach | LX03BUE | Stagecoach |
| LR52BMO | Metroline | LT02ZDD | Metrobus | LV52HFD | Stagecoach | LX03BUH | Stagecoach |
| LR52BMU | Metroline | LT02ZDE | Metrobus | LV52HFE | Stagecoach | LX03BUJ | Stagecoach |
| LR52BMV | Metroline | LT02ZDF | Metrobus | LV52HFF | Stagecoach | LX03BUP | Stagecoach |
| LR52BMY | Metroline | LT02ZDG | Metrobus | LV52HFH | Stagecoach | LX03BUU | Stagecoach |
| LR52BMZ | Metroline | LT02ZDM | Metrobus | LV52HFJ | Stagecoach | LX03BUV | Stagecoach |
| LR52BNA | Metroline | LT02ZDN | Metrobus | LV52HFK | Stagecoach | LX03BUW | Stagecoach |
| LR52BNB | Metroline | LT02ZDO | Metrobus | LV52HFL | Stagecoach | LX03BVA | Stagecoach |
| LR52BND | Metroline | LT02ZDP | Metrobus | LV52HFM | Stagecoach | LX03BVB | Stagecoach |
| LR52BNE | Metroline | LT02ZDR | Metrobus | LV52HFN | Stagecoach | LX03BVC | Stagecoach |
| LR52BNF | Metroline | LT02ZDS | Metrobus | LV52HFO | Stagecoach | LX03BVD | Stagecoach |

| | | | | | | | |
|---|---|---|---|---|---|---|---|
| LX03BVE | Stagecoach | LX03BYC | Stagecoach | LX03EXU | Go-Ahead London | LX03ORS | Stagecoach |
| LX03BVF | Stagecoach | LX03BYD | Stagecoach | LX03EXV | Go-Ahead London | LX03ORT | Stagecoach |
| LX03BVG | Stagecoach | LX03BYF | Stagecoach | LX03EXW | Go-Ahead London | LX03ORU | Stagecoach |
| LX03BVH | Stagecoach | LX03BYG | Stagecoach | LX03EXZ | Go-Ahead London | LX03ORV | Stagecoach |
| LX03BVJ | Stagecoach | LX03BYH | Stagecoach | LX03HDC | Stagecoach | LX03ORW | Stagecoach |
| LX03BVK | Stagecoach | LX03BYJ | Stagecoach | LX03HDH | First London | LX03ORY | Stagecoach |
| LX03BVL | Stagecoach | LX03BYL | Stagecoach | LX03HDL | Stagecoach | LX03ORZ | Stagecoach |
| LX03BVM | Stagecoach | LX03BYM | Stagecoach | LX03HDN | Stagecoach | LX03OSA | Stagecoach |
| LX03BVN | Stagecoach | LX03BYN | Stagecoach | LX03HDU | Stagecoach | LX03OSB | Stagecoach |
| LX03BVP | Stagecoach | LX03BYP | Stagecoach | LX03HDV | Go-Ahead London | LX03OSC | Stagecoach |
| LX03BVR | Stagecoach | LX03BYR | Stagecoach | LX03HDY | Stagecoach | LX03OSD | Stagecoach |
| LX03BVS | Stagecoach | LX03BYS | Stagecoach | LX03HDZ | Stagecoach | LX03OSE | Stagecoach |
| LX03BVT | Stagecoach | LX03BYT | Stagecoach | LX03HEJ | Stagecoach | LX03OSG | Stagecoach |
| LX03BVU | Stagecoach | LX03BYU | Stagecoach | LX03HEU | Stagecoach | LX03OSJ | Stagecoach |
| LX03BVV | Stagecoach | LX03BYV | Stagecoach | LX03HEV | Stagecoach | LX03OSK | Stagecoach |
| LX03BVW | Stagecoach | LX03BYW | Stagecoach | LX03NEU | Stagecoach | LX03OSL | Stagecoach |
| LX03BVY | Stagecoach | LX03BYY | Stagecoach | LX03NEY | Stagecoach | LX03OSM | Stagecoach |
| LX03BVZ | Stagecoach | LX03BYZ | Stagecoach | LX03NFA | Stagecoach | LX03OSN | Stagecoach |
| LX03BWA | Stagecoach | LX03BZA | Stagecoach | LX03NFC | Stagecoach | LX03OSP | Stagecoach |
| LX03BWB | Stagecoach | LX03BZB | Stagecoach | LX03NFD | Stagecoach | LX03OSR | Stagecoach |
| LX03BWC | Stagecoach | LX03BZC | Stagecoach | LX03NFE | Stagecoach | LX03OSU | Stagecoach |
| LX03BWD | Stagecoach | LX03BZD | Stagecoach | LX03NFF | Stagecoach | LX03OSV | Stagecoach |
| LX03BWE | Stagecoach | LX03BZE | Stagecoach | LX03NFG | Stagecoach | LX03OSW | Stagecoach |
| LX03BWF | Stagecoach | LX03BZF | Stagecoach | LX03NFH | Stagecoach | LX03OSY | Stagecoach |
| LX03BWG | Stagecoach | LX03BZG | Stagecoach | LX03NFJ | Stagecoach | LX03OSZ | Stagecoach |
| LX03BWH | Stagecoach | LX03BZH | Stagecoach | LX03NFK | Stagecoach | LX03OTA | Stagecoach |
| LX03BWJ | Stagecoach | LX03BZJ | Stagecoach | LX03NFL | Stagecoach | LX03OTB | Stagecoach |
| LX03BWK | Stagecoach | LX03BZK | Stagecoach | LX03NFM | Stagecoach | LX03OTC | Stagecoach |
| LX03BWL | Stagecoach | LX03BZL | Stagecoach | LX03NFN | Stagecoach | LX03OTD | Stagecoach |
| LX03BWM | Stagecoach | LX03BZM | Stagecoach | LX03NFP | Stagecoach | LX03OTE | Stagecoach |
| LX03BWN | Stagecoach | LX03BZN | Stagecoach | LX03NFR | Stagecoach | LX03OTF | Stagecoach |
| LX03BWP | Stagecoach | LX03BZP | Stagecoach | LX03NFT | Stagecoach | LX03OTG | Stagecoach |
| LX03BWU | Stagecoach | LX03BZR | Stagecoach | LX03NFV | Stagecoach | LX03OTH | Stagecoach |
| LX03BWV | Stagecoach | LX03BZS | Stagecoach | LX03NFY | Stagecoach | LX03OTJ | Stagecoach |
| LX03BWW | Stagecoach | LX03BZT | Stagecoach | LX03NFZ | Stagecoach | LX04FWL | Stagecoach |
| LX03BWY | Stagecoach | LX03BZU | Stagecoach | LX03NGE | Stagecoach | LX04FWM | Stagecoach |
| LX03BWZ | Stagecoach | LX03BZV | Stagecoach | LX03NGF | Stagecoach | LX04FWN | Stagecoach |
| LX03BXA | Stagecoach | LX03BZW | Stagecoach | LX03NGJ | Stagecoach | LX04FWP | Stagecoach |
| LX03BXB | Stagecoach | LX03BZY | Stagecoach | LX03NGU | Stagecoach | LX04FWR | Stagecoach |
| LX03BXC | Stagecoach | LX03CAA | Stagecoach | LX03NGV | Stagecoach | LX04FWS | Stagecoach |
| LX03BXD | Stagecoach | LX03CAE | Stagecoach | LX03NGY | Stagecoach | LX04FWT | Stagecoach |
| LX03BXE | Stagecoach | LX03CAU | Stagecoach | LX03NGZ | Stagecoach | LX04FWU | Stagecoach |
| LX03BXF | Stagecoach | LX03CAV | Stagecoach | LX03NHA | Stagecoach | LX04FWV | Stagecoach |
| LX03BXG | Stagecoach | LX03CBF | Stagecoach | LX03OJN | Metrobus | LX04FWW | Stagecoach |
| LX03BXH | Stagecoach | LX03CBU | Stagecoach | LX03OJP | Metrobus | LX04FWY | Stagecoach |
| LX03BXJ | Stagecoach | LX03CBV | Stagecoach | LX03OPT | Stagecoach | LX04FWZ | Stagecoach |
| LX03BXK | Stagecoach | LX03CBY | Stagecoach | LX03OPU | Stagecoach | LX04FXA | Stagecoach |
| LX03BXL | Stagecoach | LX03ECV | Go-Ahead London | LX03OPV | Stagecoach | LX04FXB | Stagecoach |
| LX03BXM | Stagecoach | LX03ECW | Go-Ahead London | LX03OPW | Stagecoach | LX04FXC | Stagecoach |
| LX03BXN | Stagecoach | LX03ECY | Go-Ahead London | LX03OPY | Stagecoach | LX04FXD | Stagecoach |
| LX03BXP | Stagecoach | LX03EDR | Go-Ahead London | LX03OPZ | Stagecoach | LX04FXE | Stagecoach |
| LX03BXR | Stagecoach | LX03EDU | Go-Ahead London | LX03ORA | Stagecoach | LX04FXF | Stagecoach |
| LX03BXS | Stagecoach | LX03EDV | Go-Ahead London | LX03ORC | Stagecoach | LX04FXG | Stagecoach |
| LX03BXU | Stagecoach | LX03EEA | Go-Ahead London | LX03ORF | Stagecoach | LX04FXH | Stagecoach |
| LX03BXV | Stagecoach | LX03EEB | Go-Ahead London | LX03ORG | Stagecoach | LX04FXJ | Stagecoach |
| LX03BXW | Stagecoach | LX03EEF | Go-Ahead London | LX03ORH | Stagecoach | LX04FXK | Stagecoach |
| LX03BXY | Stagecoach | LX03EEG | Go-Ahead London | LX03ORJ | Stagecoach | LX04FXL | Stagecoach |
| LX03BXZ | Stagecoach | LX03EEH | Go-Ahead London | LX03ORK | Stagecoach | LX04FXM | Stagecoach |
| LX03BYA | Stagecoach | LX03EEJ | Go-Ahead London | LX03ORN | Stagecoach | LX04FXP | Stagecoach |
| LX03BYB | Stagecoach | LX03EEM | Go-Ahead London | LX03ORP | Stagecoach | LX04FXR | Stagecoach |

| Reg | Operator | Reg | Operator | Reg | Operator | Reg | Operator |
|---|---|---|---|---|---|---|---|
| LX04FXS | Stagecoach | LX04LBL | Stagecoach | LX05EZS | Go-Ahead London | LX06AHC | Stagecoach |
| LX04FXT | Stagecoach | LX04LBN | Stagecoach | LX05EZT | Go-Ahead London | LX06AHD | Stagecoach |
| LX04FXU | Stagecoach | LX04LBP | Stagecoach | LX05EZU | Go-Ahead London | LX06AHE | Stagecoach |
| LX04FXV | Stagecoach | LX04LBU | Stagecoach | LX05EZV | Go-Ahead London | LX06AHF | Stagecoach |
| LX04FXW | Stagecoach | LX04LBV | Stagecoach | LX05EZW | Go-Ahead London | LX06DYS | Go-Ahead London |
| LX04FXY | Stagecoach | LX04LBY | Stagecoach | LX05EZZ | Go-Ahead London | LX06DYT | Go-Ahead London |
| LX04FXZ | Stagecoach | LX04LCA | Stagecoach | LX05FAA | Go-Ahead London | LX06DYU | Go-Ahead London |
| LX04FYA | Stagecoach | LX04LCC | Stagecoach | LX05FAF | Go-Ahead London | LX06DYV | Go-Ahead London |
| LX04FYB | Stagecoach | LX04LCE | Stagecoach | LX05FAJ | Go-Ahead London | LX06DYW | Go-Ahead London |
| LX04FYC | Stagecoach | LX04LCF | Stagecoach | LX05FAK | Go-Ahead London | LX06DYY | Go-Ahead London |
| LX04FYD | Stagecoach | LX04LCG | Stagecoach | LX05FAM | Go-Ahead London | LX06DZA | Go-Ahead London |
| LX04FYE | Stagecoach | LX04LCJ | Stagecoach | LX05FAO | Go-Ahead London | LX06DZB | Go-Ahead London |
| LX04FYF | Stagecoach | LX04LCK | Stagecoach | LX05FAU | Go-Ahead London | LX06DZC | Go-Ahead London |
| LX04FYG | Stagecoach | LX04LCM | Stagecoach | LX05FBA | Go-Ahead London | LX06DZE | Go-Ahead London |
| LX04FYH | Stagecoach | LX04LCN | Stagecoach | LX05FBB | Go-Ahead London | LX06DZF | Go-Ahead London |
| LX04FYK | Stagecoach | LX04LCP | Stagecoach | LX05FBC | Go-Ahead London | LX06DZG | Go-Ahead London |
| LX04FYL | Stagecoach | LX04LCT | Stagecoach | LX05FBD | Go-Ahead London | LX06DZH | Go-Ahead London |
| LX04FYM | Stagecoach | LX04LCU | Stagecoach | LX05FBE | Go-Ahead London | LX06DZJ | Go-Ahead London |
| LX04FYN | Stagecoach | LX04LCV | Stagecoach | LX05FBF | Go-Ahead London | LX06DZK | Go-Ahead London |
| LX04FYP | Stagecoach | LX05BVY | Stagecoach | LX05FBJ | Go-Ahead London | LX06DZL | Go-Ahead London |
| LX04FYR | Stagecoach | LX05BVZ | Stagecoach | LX05FBK | Go-Ahead London | LX06DZM | Go-Ahead London |
| LX04FYS | Stagecoach | LX05BWA | Stagecoach | LX05FBL | Go-Ahead London | LX06DZN | Go-Ahead London |
| LX04FYT | Stagecoach | LX05BWB | Stagecoach | LX05FBN | Go-Ahead London | LX06DZO | Go-Ahead London |
| LX04FYT | Stagecoach | LX05BWC | Stagecoach | LX05FBO | Go-Ahead London | LX06DZP | Go-Ahead London |
| LX04FYU | Stagecoach | LX05BWD | Stagecoach | LX05FBU | Go-Ahead London | LX06DZR | Go-Ahead London |
| LX04FYV | Stagecoach | LX05BWE | Stagecoach | LX05FBV | Go-Ahead London | LX06DZS | Go-Ahead London |
| LX04FYW | Stagecoach | LX05BWF | Stagecoach | LX05FBY | Go-Ahead London | LX06DZT | Go-Ahead London |
| LX04FYY | Stagecoach | LX05BWG | Stagecoach | LX05FBZ | Go-Ahead London | LX06DZU | Go-Ahead London |
| LX04FYZ | Stagecoach | LX05BWH | Stagecoach | LX05FCA | Go-Ahead London | LX06DZV | Go-Ahead London |
| LX04FZA | Stagecoach | LX05BWJ | Stagecoach | LX05FCC | Go-Ahead London | LX06DZW | Go-Ahead London |
| LX04FZB | Stagecoach | LX05BWK | Stagecoach | LX05FCD | Go-Ahead London | LX06DZY | Go-Ahead London |
| LX04FZC | Stagecoach | LX05EXZ | Go-Ahead London | LX05FCE | Go-Ahead London | LX06DZZ | Go-Ahead London |
| LX04FZD | Stagecoach | LX05EYA | Go-Ahead London | LX05FCF | Go-Ahead London | LX06EAA | Go-Ahead London |
| LX04FZE | Stagecoach | LX05EYM | Go-Ahead London | LX05GDV | Arriva Original Tour | LX06EAC | Go-Ahead London |
| LX04FZF | Stagecoach | LX05EYO | Go-Ahead London | LX05GDY | Arriva Original Tour | LX06EAF | Go-Ahead London |
| LX04FZG | Stagecoach | LX05EYP | Go-Ahead London | LX05GDZ | Arriva Original Tour | LX06EAG | Go-Ahead London |
| LX04FZH | Stagecoach | LX05EYR | Go-Ahead London | LX05GEJ | Arriva Original Tour | LX06EAJ | Go-Ahead London |
| LX04FZJ | Stagecoach | LX05EYS | Go-Ahead London | LX05HRO | Arriva Original Tour | LX06EAK | Go-Ahead London |
| LX04FZK | Stagecoach | LX05EYT | Go-Ahead London | LX05HSC | Arriva Original Tour | LX06EAL | Go-Ahead London |
| LX04KZG | Stagecoach | LX05EYU | Go-Ahead London | LX05KNZ | Arriva Original Tour | LX06EAM | Go-Ahead London |
| LX04KZJ | Stagecoach | LX05EYV | Go-Ahead London | LX05KOA | Arriva Original Tour | LX06EAO | Go-Ahead London |
| LX04KZK | Stagecoach | LX05EYW | Go-Ahead London | LX05LLM | Stagecoach | LX06EAP | Go-Ahead London |
| LX04KZL | Stagecoach | LX05EYY | Go-Ahead London | LX05LLN | Stagecoach | LX06EAW | Go-Ahead London |
| LX04KZM | Stagecoach | LX05EYZ | Go-Ahead London | LX05LLO | Stagecoach | LX06EAY | Go-Ahead London |
| LX04KZN | Stagecoach | LX05EZA | Go-Ahead London | LX05LLP | Stagecoach | LX06EBA | Go-Ahead London |
| LX04KZP | Stagecoach | LX05EZB | Go-Ahead London | LX06AFF | Stagecoach | LX06EBC | Go-Ahead London |
| LX04KZR | Stagecoach | LX05EZC | Go-Ahead London | LX06AFJ | Stagecoach | LX06EBD | Go-Ahead London |
| LX04KZS | Stagecoach | LX05EZD | Go-Ahead London | LX06AFK | Stagecoach | LX06EBE | Go-Ahead London |
| LX04KZT | Stagecoach | LX05EZE | Go-Ahead London | LX06AFN | Stagecoach | LX06EBG | Go-Ahead London |
| LX04KZU | Stagecoach | LX05EZF | Go-Ahead London | LX06AFO | Stagecoach | LX06EBJ | Go-Ahead London |
| LX04KZV | Stagecoach | LX05EZG | Go-Ahead London | LX06AFU | Stagecoach | LX06EBK | Go-Ahead London |
| LX04KZW | Stagecoach | LX05EZH | Go-Ahead London | LX06AFV | Stagecoach | LX06EBL | Go-Ahead London |
| LX04KZY | Stagecoach | LX05EZJ | Go-Ahead London | LX06AFY | Stagecoach | LX06EBM | Go-Ahead London |
| LX04KZZ | Stagecoach | LX05EZK | Go-Ahead London | LX06AFZ | Stagecoach | LX06EBN | Go-Ahead London |
| LX04LBA | Stagecoach | LX05EZL | Go-Ahead London | LX06AGO | Stagecoach | LX06EBO | Go-Ahead London |
| LX04LBE | Stagecoach | LX05EZM | Go-Ahead London | LX06AGU | Stagecoach | LX06EBP | Go-Ahead London |
| LX04LBF | Stagecoach | LX05EZN | Go-Ahead London | LX06AGV | Stagecoach | LX06EBU | Go-Ahead London |
| LX04LBG | Stagecoach | LX05EZO | Go-Ahead London | LX06AGY | Stagecoach | LX06EBV | Go-Ahead London |
| LX04LBJ | Stagecoach | LX05EZP | Go-Ahead London | LX06AGZ | Stagecoach | LX06EBZ | Go-Ahead London |
| LX04LBK | Stagecoach | LX05EZR | Go-Ahead London | LX06AHA | Stagecoach | LX06ECA | Go-Ahead London |

| Reg | Operator | Reg | Operator | Reg | Operator | Reg | Operator |
|---|---|---|---|---|---|---|---|
| LX06ECC | Go-Ahead London | LX07BXR | Go-Ahead London | LX09ACU | Stagecoach | LX09AYF | Go-Ahead London |
| LX06ECD | Go-Ahead London | LX07BXS | Go-Ahead London | LX09ACV | Stagecoach | LX09AYG | Go-Ahead London |
| LX06ECE | Go-Ahead London | LX07BXU | Go-Ahead London | LX09ACY | Stagecoach | LX09AYH | Go-Ahead London |
| LX06ECF | Go-Ahead London | LX07BXV | Go-Ahead London | LX09ACZ | Stagecoach | LX09AYJ | Go-Ahead London |
| LX06ECJ | Go-Ahead London | LX07BXW | Go-Ahead London | LX09ADO | Stagecoach | LX09AYK | Go-Ahead London |
| LX06ECN | Go-Ahead London | LX07BXY | Go-Ahead London | LX09ADU | Stagecoach | LX09AYL | Go-Ahead London |
| LX06ECT | Go-Ahead London | LX07BYA | Go-Ahead London | LX09ADV | Stagecoach | LX09AYM | Go-Ahead London |
| LX06ECV | Go-Ahead London | LX07BYB | Go-Ahead London | LX09ADZ | Stagecoach | LX09AYN | Go-Ahead London |
| LX06EYT | Go-Ahead London | LX07BYC | Go-Ahead London | LX09AEA | Stagecoach | LX09AYO | Go-Ahead London |
| LX06EYU | Go-Ahead London | LX07BYD | Go-Ahead London | LX09AEB | Stagecoach | LX09AYP | Go-Ahead London |
| LX06EYV | Go-Ahead London | LX07BYF | Go-Ahead London | LX09AEC | Stagecoach | LX09AYS | Go-Ahead London |
| LX06EYW | Go-Ahead London | LX07BYG | Go-Ahead London | LX09AED | Stagecoach | LX09AYT | Go-Ahead London |
| LX06EYY | Go-Ahead London | LX07BYH | Go-Ahead London | LX09AEE | Stagecoach | LX09AYU | Go-Ahead London |
| LX06EYZ | Go-Ahead London | LX07BYJ | Go-Ahead London | LX09AEF | Stagecoach | LX09AYV | Go-Ahead London |
| LX06EZA | Go-Ahead London | LX07BYK | Go-Ahead London | LX09AEG | Stagecoach | LX09AYW | Go-Ahead London |
| LX06EZB | Go-Ahead London | LX07BYL | Go-Ahead London | LX09AEJ | Stagecoach | LX09AYY | Go-Ahead London |
| LX06EZC | Go-Ahead London | LX07BYM | Go-Ahead London | LX09AEK | Stagecoach | LX09AYZ | Go-Ahead London |
| LX06EZD | Go-Ahead London | LX07BYN | Go-Ahead London | LX09AEL | Stagecoach | LX09AZA | Go-Ahead London |
| LX06EZE | Go-Ahead London | LX07BYO | Go-Ahead London | LX09AEM | Stagecoach | LX09AZB | Go-Ahead London |
| LX06EZF | Go-Ahead London | LX07BYP | Go-Ahead London | LX09AEN | Stagecoach | LX09AZD | Go-Ahead London |
| LX06EZG | Go-Ahead London | LX07BYR | Go-Ahead London | LX09AEO | Stagecoach | LX09AZF | Go-Ahead London |
| LX06EZH | Go-Ahead London | LX07BYS | Go-Ahead London | LX09AEP | Stagecoach | LX09AZG | Go-Ahead London |
| LX06EZJ | Go-Ahead London | LX07BYT | Go-Ahead London | LX09AET | Stagecoach | LX09AZJ | Go-Ahead London |
| LX06EZK | Go-Ahead London | LX07BYU | Go-Ahead London | LX09AEU | Stagecoach | LX09AZL | Go-Ahead London |
| LX06EZL | Go-Ahead London | LX07BZH | Go-Ahead London | LX09AEV | Stagecoach | LX09AZN | Go-Ahead London |
| LX06EZM | Go-Ahead London | LX08EBP | Go-Ahead London | LX09AEW | Stagecoach | LX09AZO | Go-Ahead London |
| LX06EZN | Go-Ahead London | LX08EBU | Go-Ahead London | LX09AEY | Stagecoach | LX09AZP | Go-Ahead London |
| LX06EZO | Go-Ahead London | LX08EBV | Go-Ahead London | LX09AEZ | Stagecoach | LX09AZR | Go-Ahead London |
| LX06EZP | Go-Ahead London | LX08EBZ | Go-Ahead London | LX09AFA | Stagecoach | LX09AZT | Go-Ahead London |
| LX06EZR | Go-Ahead London | LX08ECA | Go-Ahead London | LX09AFE | Stagecoach | LX09BGK | Stagecoach |
| LX06EZS | Go-Ahead London | LX08ECC | Go-Ahead London | LX09AFF | Stagecoach | LX09BGU | Stagecoach |
| LX06EZT | Go-Ahead London | LX08ECD | Go-Ahead London | LX09AFJ | Stagecoach | LX09BGV | Stagecoach |
| LX06EZU | Go-Ahead London | LX08ECE | Go-Ahead London | LX09AFK | Stagecoach | LX09BXG | Go-Ahead London |
| LX06EZV | Go-Ahead London | LX08ECF | Go-Ahead London | LX09AFN | Stagecoach | LX09BXH | Go-Ahead London |
| LX06EZW | Go-Ahead London | LX08ECJ | Go-Ahead London | LX09AFO | Stagecoach | LX09BXJ | Go-Ahead London |
| LX06EZZ | Go-Ahead London | LX08ECN | Go-Ahead London | LX09AFU | Stagecoach | LX09BXK | Go-Ahead London |
| LX06FAA | Go-Ahead London | LX08ECT | Go-Ahead London | LX09AFV | Stagecoach | LX09BXL | Go-Ahead London |
| LX06FAF | Go-Ahead London | LX08ECV | Go-Ahead London | LX09AFY | Stagecoach | LX09BXM | Go-Ahead London |
| LX06FAJ | Go-Ahead London | LX08ECW | Go-Ahead London | LX09AFZ | Stagecoach | LX09BXO | Go-Ahead London |
| LX06FAK | Go-Ahead London | LX08ECY | Go-Ahead London | LX09AGO | Stagecoach | LX09BXP | Go-Ahead London |
| LX06FAM | Go-Ahead London | LX09AAE | Stagecoach | LX09AGU | Stagecoach | LX09BXR | Go-Ahead London |
| LX06FAO | Go-Ahead London | LX09AAF | Stagecoach | LX09AGV | Stagecoach | LX09BXS | Go-Ahead London |
| LX06FAU | Go-Ahead London | LX09AAJ | Stagecoach | LX09AGY | Stagecoach | LX09EVB | Go-Ahead London |
| LX06FBA | Go-Ahead London | LX09AAK | Stagecoach | LX09AGZ | Stagecoach | LX09EVC | Go-Ahead London |
| LX06FBB | Go-Ahead London | LX09AAN | Stagecoach | LX09AHA | Stagecoach | LX09EVD | Go-Ahead London |
| LX06FBC | Go-Ahead London | LX09AAO | Stagecoach | LX09AHC | Stagecoach | LX09EVF | Go-Ahead London |
| LX06FBD | Go-Ahead London | LX09AAU | Stagecoach | LX09AHD | Stagecoach | LX09EVG | Go-Ahead London |
| LX06FBE | Go-Ahead London | LX09AAV | Stagecoach | LX09AHE | Stagecoach | LX09EVH | Go-Ahead London |
| LX06FKL | Go-Ahead London | LX09AAY | Stagecoach | LX09AHF | Stagecoach | LX09EVJ | Go-Ahead London |
| LX06FKM | Go-Ahead London | LX09AAZ | Stagecoach | LX09AXC | Go-Ahead London | LX09EZU | Go-Ahead London |
| LX06FKN | Go-Ahead London | LX09ABF | Stagecoach | LX09AXU | Go-Ahead London | LX09EZV | Go-Ahead London |
| LX06FKO | Go-Ahead London | LX09ABK | Stagecoach | LX09AXV | Go-Ahead London | LX09EZW | Go-Ahead London |
| LX07BXH | Go-Ahead London | LX09ABN | Stagecoach | LX09AXW | Go-Ahead London | LX09EZZ | Go-Ahead London |
| LX07BXJ | Go-Ahead London | LX09ABO | Stagecoach | LX09AXY | Go-Ahead London | LX09FAF | Go-Ahead London |
| LX07BXK | Go-Ahead London | LX09ABU | Stagecoach | LX09AXZ | Go-Ahead London | LX09FAJ | Go-Ahead London |
| LX07BXL | Go-Ahead London | LX09ABV | Stagecoach | LX09AYA | Go-Ahead London | LX09FAK | Go-Ahead London |
| LX07BXM | Go-Ahead London | LX09ABZ | Stagecoach | LX09AYB | Go-Ahead London | LX09FAM | Go-Ahead London |
| LX07BXN | Go-Ahead London | LX09ACF | Stagecoach | LX09AYC | Go-Ahead London | LX09FAO | Go-Ahead London |
| LX07BXO | Go-Ahead London | LX09ACJ | Stagecoach | LX09AYD | Go-Ahead London | LX09FAU | Go-Ahead London |
| LX07BXP | Go-Ahead London | LX09ACO | Stagecoach | LX09AYE | Go-Ahead London | LX09FBA | Go-Ahead London |

*The London Bus Handbook*

| Reg | Operator | Reg | Operator | Reg | Operator | Reg | Operator |
|---|---|---|---|---|---|---|---|
| LX09FBB | Go-Ahead London | LX10AVD | Go-Ahead London | LX11AZU | Stagecoach | LX11BHJ | Stagecoach |
| LX09FBC | Go-Ahead London | LX11AVP | Stagecoach | LX11AZV | Stagecoach | LX11BHK | Stagecoach |
| LX09FBD | Go-Ahead London | LX11AVR | Stagecoach | LX11AZW | Stagecoach | LX11BHL | Stagecoach |
| LX09FBE | Go-Ahead London | LX11AVT | Stagecoach | LX11AZZ | Stagecoach | LX11BHN | Stagecoach |
| LX09FBF | Go-Ahead London | LX11AVU | Stagecoach | LX11BAA | Stagecoach | LX11BHO | Stagecoach |
| LX09FBG | Go-Ahead London | LX11AVV | Stagecoach | LX11BAO | Stagecoach | LX11BHP | Stagecoach |
| LX09FBJ | Go-Ahead London | LX11AVW | Stagecoach | LX11BAU | Stagecoach | LX11BHU | Stagecoach |
| LX09FBK | Go-Ahead London | LX11AVY | Stagecoach | LX11BAV | Stagecoach | LX11BHV | Stagecoach |
| LX09FBN | Go-Ahead London | LX11AVZ | Stagecoach | LX11BBE | Stagecoach | LX11BHW | Stagecoach |
| LX09FBO | Go-Ahead London | LX11AWC | Stagecoach | LX11BBF | Stagecoach | LX11BHY | Stagecoach |
| LX09FBU | Go-Ahead London | LX11AWF | Stagecoach | LX11BBJ | Stagecoach | LX11BHZ | Stagecoach |
| LX09FBV | Go-Ahead London | LX11AWG | Stagecoach | LX11BBK | Stagecoach | LX11BJE | Stagecoach |
| LX09FBY | Go-Ahead London | LX11AWH | Stagecoach | LX11BBN | Stagecoach | LX11BJF | Stagecoach |
| LX09FBZ | Go-Ahead London | LX11AWJ | Stagecoach | LX11BBO | Stagecoach | LX11BJJ | Stagecoach |
| LX09FCA | Go-Ahead London | LX11AWM | Stagecoach | LX11BBV | Stagecoach | LX11BJK | Stagecoach |
| LX09FCC | Go-Ahead London | LX11AWN | Stagecoach | LX11BBZ | Stagecoach | LX11BJO | Stagecoach |
| LX09FCD | Go-Ahead London | LX11AWO | Stagecoach | LX11BCE | Stagecoach | LX11BJU | Stagecoach |
| LX09FCE | Go-Ahead London | LX11AWP | Stagecoach | LX11BCF | Stagecoach | LX11BJV | Stagecoach |
| LX09FYS | Stagecoach | LX11AWR | Stagecoach | LX11BCK | Stagecoach | LX11BJY | Stagecoach |
| LX09FYT | Stagecoach | LX11AWU | Stagecoach | LX11BCO | Stagecoach | LX11BJZ | Stagecoach |
| LX09FYU | Stagecoach | LX11AWV | Stagecoach | LX11BCU | Stagecoach | LX11BKA | Stagecoach |
| LX09FYV | Stagecoach | LX11AWW | Stagecoach | LX11BCV | Stagecoach | LX11BKD | Stagecoach |
| LX09FYW | Stagecoach | LX11AWY | Stagecoach | LX11BCY | Stagecoach | LX11BKE | Stagecoach |
| LX09FYY | Stagecoach | LX11AWZ | Stagecoach | LX11BCZ | Stagecoach | LX11BKF | Stagecoach |
| LX09FYZ | Stagecoach | LX11AXA | Stagecoach | LX11BDE | Stagecoach | LX11BKG | Stagecoach |
| LX09FZA | Stagecoach | LX11AXB | Stagecoach | LX11BDF | Stagecoach | LX11BKJ | Stagecoach |
| LX09FZB | Stagecoach | LX11AXC | Stagecoach | LX11BDO | Stagecoach | LX11BKK | Stagecoach |
| LX09FZC | Stagecoach | LX11AXD | Stagecoach | LX11BDU | Stagecoach | LX11BKL | Stagecoach |
| LX09FZD | Stagecoach | LX11AXF | Stagecoach | LX11BDV | Stagecoach | LX11BKN | Stagecoach |
| LX09FZE | Stagecoach | LX11AXG | Stagecoach | LX11BDY | Stagecoach | LX11BKO | Stagecoach |
| LX09FZF | Stagecoach | LX11AXH | Stagecoach | LX11BDZ | Stagecoach | LX11BKU | Stagecoach |
| LX09FZG | Stagecoach | LX11AXJ | Stagecoach | LX11BEJ | Stagecoach | LX11BKV | Stagecoach |
| LX09FZH | Stagecoach | LX11AXK | Stagecoach | LX11BEO | Stagecoach | LX11BKY | Stagecoach |
| LX09FZJ | Stagecoach | LX11AXM | Stagecoach | LX11BEU | Stagecoach | LX11BKZ | Stagecoach |
| LX09FZK | Stagecoach | LX11AXN | Stagecoach | LX11BEY | Stagecoach | LX11BLF | Stagecoach |
| LX09FZL | Stagecoach | LX11AXO | Stagecoach | LX11BFA | Stagecoach | LX11BLJ | Stagecoach |
| LX09FZM | Stagecoach | LX11AXP | Stagecoach | LX11BFF | Stagecoach | LX11BLK | Stagecoach |
| LX09FZN | Stagecoach | LX11AXR | Stagecoach | LX11BFJ | Stagecoach | LX11BLN | Stagecoach |
| LX09FZO | Stagecoach | LX11AXS | Stagecoach | LX11BFK | Stagecoach | LX11BLV | Stagecoach |
| LX09FZP | Stagecoach | LX11AXT | Stagecoach | LX11BFL | Stagecoach | LX11BLZ | Stagecoach |
| LX09FZR | Stagecoach | LX11AYS | Stagecoach | LX11BFM | Stagecoach | LX11BMO | Stagecoach |
| LX09FZS | Stagecoach | LX11AYT | Stagecoach | LX11BFN | Stagecoach | LX11BMU | Stagecoach |
| LX09FZT | Stagecoach | LX11AYU | Stagecoach | LX11BFO | Stagecoach | LX11BMV | Stagecoach |
| LX09FZU | Stagecoach | LX11AYV | Stagecoach | LX11BFP | Stagecoach | LX11BMY | Stagecoach |
| LX09FZV | Stagecoach | LX11AYW | Stagecoach | LX11BFU | Stagecoach | LX11CVL | Go-Ahead London |
| LX09FZW | Stagecoach | LX11AYY | Stagecoach | LX11BFV | Stagecoach | LX11CVM | Go-Ahead London |
| LX10AUC | Stagecoach | LX11AYZ | Stagecoach | LX11BFY | Stagecoach | LX11CVN | Go-Ahead London |
| LX10AUE | Stagecoach | LX11AZA | Stagecoach | LX11BFZ | Stagecoach | LX11CVO | Go-Ahead London |
| LX10AUF | Stagecoach | LX11AZB | Stagecoach | LX11BGE | Stagecoach | LX11CVP | Go-Ahead London |
| LX10AUH | Stagecoach | LX11AZC | Stagecoach | LX11BGF | Stagecoach | LX11CVR | Go-Ahead London |
| LX10AUJ | Stagecoach | LX11AZD | Stagecoach | LX11BGK | Stagecoach | LX11CVS | Go-Ahead London |
| LX10AUP | Go-Ahead London | LX11AZF | Stagecoach | LX11BGO | Stagecoach | LX11CVT | Go-Ahead London |
| LX10AUR | Go-Ahead London | LX11AZG | Stagecoach | LX11BGU | Stagecoach | LX11CVU | Go-Ahead London |
| LX10AUT | Go-Ahead London | LX11AZJ | Stagecoach | LX11BGV | Stagecoach | LX11CVV | Go-Ahead London |
| LX10AUU | Go-Ahead London | LX11AZL | Stagecoach | LX11BGY | Stagecoach | LX11CVW | Go-Ahead London |
| LX10AUV | Go-Ahead London | LX11AZN | Stagecoach | LX11BGZ | Stagecoach | LX11CVY | Go-Ahead London |
| LX10AUW | Go-Ahead London | LX11AZO | Stagecoach | LX11BHA | Stagecoach | LX11CVZ | Go-Ahead London |
| LX10AUY | Go-Ahead London | LX11AZP | Stagecoach | LX11BHD | Stagecoach | LX11CWA | Go-Ahead London |
| LX10AVB | Go-Ahead London | LX11AZR | Stagecoach | LX11BHE | Stagecoach | LX11CWC | Go-Ahead London |
| LX10AVC | Go-Ahead London | LX11AZT | Stagecoach | LX11BHF | Stagecoach | LX11CWD | Go-Ahead London |

*The London Bus Handbook*

April 2010 and Go-Ahead's SE38, LX10AUR, is seen in Stansfield Road while working route 300. The Enviro 200 has been supplied in various sizes. Here is a 10.2 metre version. *Richard Godfrey*

| | | | | | | | |
|---|---|---|---|---|---|---|---|
| LX11CWE | Go-Ahead London | LX51FGN | Stagecoach | LX51FJN | Stagecoach | LX51FLL | Stagecoach |
| LX11CWG | Go-Ahead London | LX51FGO | Stagecoach | LX51FJO | Stagecoach | LX51FLM | Stagecoach |
| LX11CWJ | Go-Ahead London | LX51FGU | Stagecoach | LX51FJP | Stagecoach | LX51FLN | Stagecoach |
| LX11CWK | Go-Ahead London | LX51FGV | Stagecoach | LX51FJV | Stagecoach | LX51FLP | Stagecoach |
| LX11CWL | Go-Ahead London | LX51FHA | Stagecoach | LX51FJY | Stagecoach | LX51FLR | Stagecoach |
| LX11CWM | Go-Ahead London | LX51FHB | Stagecoach | LX51FJZ | Stagecoach | LX51FLV | Stagecoach |
| LX11CWN | Go-Ahead London | LX51FHF | Stagecoach | LX51FKA | Stagecoach | LX51FLW | Stagecoach |
| LX11CWO | Go-Ahead London | LX51FHG | Stagecoach | LX51FKB | Stagecoach | LX51FLZ | Stagecoach |
| LX11CWP | Go-Ahead London | LX51FHH | Stagecoach | LX51FKD | Stagecoach | LX51FMA | Stagecoach |
| LX11CWR | Go-Ahead London | LX51FHJ | Stagecoach | LX51FKE | Stagecoach | LX51FMC | Stagecoach |
| LX11CWT | Go-Ahead London | LX51FHK | Stagecoach | LX51FKF | Stagecoach | LX51FMD | Stagecoach |
| LX11CWU | Go-Ahead London | LX51FHL | Stagecoach | LX51FKG | Stagecoach | LX51FME | Stagecoach |
| LX11CWV | Go-Ahead London | LX51FHN | Stagecoach | LX51FKJ | Stagecoach | LX51FMF | Stagecoach |
| LX11CWW | Go-Ahead London | LX51FHO | Stagecoach | LX51FKL | Stagecoach | LX51FMG | Stagecoach |
| LX11CWY | Go-Ahead London | LX51FHP | Stagecoach | LX51FKO | Stagecoach | LX51FMJ | Stagecoach |
| LX11CWZ | Go-Ahead London | LX51FHS | Stagecoach | LX51FKR | Stagecoach | LX51FMK | Stagecoach |
| LX11CXA | Go-Ahead London | LX51FHT | Stagecoach | LX51FKT | Stagecoach | LX51FML | Stagecoach |
| LX11CXB | Go-Ahead London | LX51FHU | Stagecoach | LX51FKU | Stagecoach | LX51FMO | Stagecoach |
| LX11CXC | Go-Ahead London | LX51FHV | Stagecoach | LX51FKW | Stagecoach | LX51FMP | Stagecoach |
| LX11CXD | Go-Ahead London | LX51FHW | Stagecoach | LX51FKZ | Stagecoach | LX51FMU | Stagecoach |
| LX11DVA | Go-Ahead London | LX51FHY | Stagecoach | LX51FLB | Stagecoach | LX51FMV | Stagecoach |
| LX11DVB | Go-Ahead London | LX51FHZ | Stagecoach | LX51FLC | Stagecoach | LX51FMY | Stagecoach |
| LX11DVC | Go-Ahead London | LX51FJA | Stagecoach | LX51FLD | Stagecoach | LX51FMZ | Stagecoach |
| LX11DVF | Go-Ahead London | LX51FJC | Stagecoach | LX51FLE | Stagecoach | LX51FNA | Stagecoach |
| LX11DVG | Go-Ahead London | LX51FJD | Stagecoach | LX51FLF | Stagecoach | LX51FNC | Stagecoach |
| LX11DVH | Go-Ahead London | LX51FJE | Stagecoach | LX51FLG | Stagecoach | LX51FND | Stagecoach |
| LX51FFO | Stagecoach | LX51FJF | Stagecoach | LX51FLH | Stagecoach | LX51FNE | Stagecoach |
| LX51FFW | Stagecoach | LX51FJJ | Stagecoach | LX51FLJ | Stagecoach | LX51FNF | Stagecoach |
| LX51FGJ | Stagecoach | LX51FJK | Stagecoach | LX51FLK | Stagecoach | LX51FNG | Stagecoach |

*The London Bus Handbook*

| | | | | | | | |
|---|---|---|---|---|---|---|---|
| LX51FNH | Stagecoach | LX53BAA | Go-Ahead London | LX53KBE | Stagecoach | LX55EAG | Go-Ahead London |
| LX51FNJ | Stagecoach | LX53BAO | Go-Ahead London | LX53KBF | Stagecoach | LX55EAJ | Go-Ahead London |
| LX51FNK | Stagecoach | LX53BBZ | Go-Ahead London | LX53KBJ | Stagecoach | LX55EPA | Stagecoach |
| LX51FNL | Stagecoach | LX53BDO | Go-Ahead London | LX53KBK | Stagecoach | LX55EPC | Stagecoach |
| LX51FNM | Stagecoach | LX53BDY | Go-Ahead London | LX53KBN | Stagecoach | LX55EPD | Stagecoach |
| LX51FNN | Stagecoach | LX53BEY | Go-Ahead London | LX53KBO | Stagecoach | LX55EPE | Stagecoach |
| LX51FNO | Stagecoach | LX53BFK | Go-Ahead London | LX53KBP | Stagecoach | LX55EPF | Stagecoach |
| LX51FNP | Stagecoach | LX53BGE | Go-Ahead London | LX53KBV | Stagecoach | LX55EPJ | Stagecoach |
| LX51FNR | Stagecoach | LX53BJK | Go-Ahead London | LX53KBW | Stagecoach | LX55EPK | Stagecoach |
| LX51FNS | Stagecoach | LX53BJO | Go-Ahead London | LX53KBZ | Stagecoach | LX55EPL | Stagecoach |
| LX51FNT | Stagecoach | LX53BJU | Go-Ahead London | LX53KCA | Stagecoach | LX55EPN | Stagecoach |
| LX51FNU | Stagecoach | LX53JXU | Stagecoach | LX53KCC | Stagecoach | LX55EPO | Stagecoach |
| LX51FNV | Stagecoach | LX53JXV | Stagecoach | LX53KCE | Stagecoach | LX55EPP | Stagecoach |
| LX51FNW | Stagecoach | LX53JXW | Stagecoach | LX53KCF | Stagecoach | LX55EPU | Stagecoach |
| LX51FNY | Stagecoach | LX53JXY | Stagecoach | LX53KCG | Stagecoach | LX55EPV | Stagecoach |
| LX51FNZ | Stagecoach | LX53JYA | Stagecoach | LX53KCJ | Stagecoach | LX55EPY | Stagecoach |
| LX51FOA | Stagecoach | LX53JYB | Stagecoach | LX53KCK | Stagecoach | LX55EPZ | Stagecoach |
| LX51FOC | Stagecoach | LX53JYC | Stagecoach | LX53LGF | Stagecoach | LX55ERJ | Stagecoach |
| LX51FOD | Stagecoach | LX53JYD | Stagecoach | LX53LGG | Stagecoach | LX55ERK | Stagecoach |
| LX51FOF | Stagecoach | LX53JYE | Stagecoach | LX53LGJ | Stagecoach | LX55ERO | Stagecoach |
| LX51FOH | Stagecoach | LX53JYF | Stagecoach | LX53LGK | Stagecoach | LX55ERU | Stagecoach |
| LX51FOJ | Stagecoach | LX53JYG | Stagecoach | LX53LGL | Stagecoach | LX55ERV | Stagecoach |
| LX51FOK | Stagecoach | LX53JYH | Stagecoach | LX53LGN | Stagecoach | LX55ERY | Stagecoach |
| LX51FOM | Stagecoach | LX53JYJ | Stagecoach | LX53LGO | Stagecoach | LX55ERZ | Stagecoach |
| LX51FON | Stagecoach | LX53JYK | Stagecoach | LX53LGU | Stagecoach | LX55ESF | Stagecoach |
| LX51FOP | Stagecoach | LX53JYL | Stagecoach | LX53LGV | Stagecoach | LX55ESG | Stagecoach |
| LX51FOT | Stagecoach | LX53JYN | Stagecoach | LX53LGW | Stagecoach | LX55ESN | Stagecoach |
| LX51FOV | Stagecoach | LX53JYO | Stagecoach | LX54GYV | Go-Ahead London | LX55ESO | Stagecoach |
| LX51FPA | Stagecoach | LX53JYP | Stagecoach | LX54GYW | Go-Ahead London | LX55HGC | Stagecoach |
| LX51FPC | Stagecoach | LX53JYR | Stagecoach | LX54GYY | Go-Ahead London | LX56DZU | Stagecoach |
| LX51FPD | Stagecoach | LX53JYT | Stagecoach | LX54GYZ | Go-Ahead London | LX56DZV | Stagecoach |
| LX51FPE | Stagecoach | LX53JYU | Stagecoach | LX54GZB | Go-Ahead London | LX56DZW | Stagecoach |
| LX51FPF | Stagecoach | LX53JYV | Stagecoach | LX54GZC | Go-Ahead London | LX56DZY | Stagecoach |
| LX53AYM | Go-Ahead London | LX53JYW | Stagecoach | LX54GZD | Go-Ahead London | LX56DZZ | Stagecoach |
| LX53AYN | Go-Ahead London | LX53JYY | Stagecoach | LX54GZE | Go-Ahead London | LX56EAA | Stagecoach |
| LX53AYO | Go-Ahead London | LX53JYZ | Stagecoach | LX54GZF | Go-Ahead London | LX56EAC | Stagecoach |
| LX53AYP | Go-Ahead London | LX53JZA | Stagecoach | LX54GZG | Go-Ahead London | LX56EAE | Stagecoach |
| LX53AYT | Go-Ahead London | LX53JZC | Stagecoach | LX54GZH | Go-Ahead London | LX56EAF | Stagecoach |
| LX53AYU | Go-Ahead London | LX53JZD | Stagecoach | LX54GZK | Go-Ahead London | LX56EAG | Stagecoach |
| LX53AYV | Go-Ahead London | LX53JZE | Stagecoach | LX54GZL | Go-Ahead London | LX56EAJ | Stagecoach |
| LX53AYW | Go-Ahead London | LX53JZF | Stagecoach | LX54GZM | Go-Ahead London | LX56EAK | Stagecoach |
| LX53AYY | Go-Ahead London | LX53JZG | Stagecoach | LX54GZN | Go-Ahead London | LX56EAM | Stagecoach |
| LX53AYZ | Go-Ahead London | LX53JZH | Stagecoach | LX54GZO | Go-Ahead London | LX56EAO | Stagecoach |
| LX53AZA | Go-Ahead London | LX53JZJ | Stagecoach | LX54GZP | Go-Ahead London | LX56EAP | Stagecoach |
| LX53AZB | Go-Ahead London | LX53JZK | Stagecoach | LX54GZR | Go-Ahead London | LX56EAW | Stagecoach |
| LX53AZC | Go-Ahead London | LX53JZL | Stagecoach | LX54GZT | Go-Ahead London | LX56EAY | Stagecoach |
| LX53AZD | Go-Ahead London | LX53JZM | Stagecoach | LX54GZU | Go-Ahead London | LX56EBA | Stagecoach |
| LX53AZF | Go-Ahead London | LX53JZN | Stagecoach | LX54GZV | Go-Ahead London | LX56ETD | Go-Ahead London |
| LX53AZG | Go-Ahead London | LX53JZO | Stagecoach | LX54GZW | Go-Ahead London | LX56ETE | Go-Ahead London |
| LX53AZJ | Go-Ahead London | LX53JZP | Stagecoach | LX54GZY | Go-Ahead London | LX56ETF | Go-Ahead London |
| LX53AZL | Go-Ahead London | LX53JZR | Stagecoach | LX54GZZ | Go-Ahead London | LX56ETJ | Go-Ahead London |
| LX53AZN | Go-Ahead London | LX53JZT | Stagecoach | LX54HAA | Go-Ahead London | LX56ETK | Go-Ahead London |
| LX53AZO | Go-Ahead London | LX53JZU | Stagecoach | LX54HAE | Go-Ahead London | LX56ETL | Go-Ahead London |
| LX53AZP | Go-Ahead London | LX53JZV | Stagecoach | LX54HAO | Go-Ahead London | LX56ETO | Go-Ahead London |
| LX53AZR | Go-Ahead London | LX53JZW | Stagecoach | LX54HAU | Go-Ahead London | LX56ETR | Go-Ahead London |
| LX53AZT | Go-Ahead London | LX53KAE | Stagecoach | LX54HBA | Go-Ahead London | LX56ETT | Go-Ahead London |
| LX53AZU | Go-Ahead London | LX53KAJ | Stagecoach | LX54HBB | Go-Ahead London | LX56ETU | Go-Ahead London |
| LX53AZV | Go-Ahead London | LX53KAK | Stagecoach | LX55EAC | Go-Ahead London | LX56ETV | Go-Ahead London |
| LX53AZW | Go-Ahead London | LX53KAO | Stagecoach | LX55EAE | Go-Ahead London | LX56ETY | Go-Ahead London |
| LX53AZZ | Go-Ahead London | LX53KAU | Stagecoach | LX55EAF | Go-Ahead London | LX56ETZ | Go-Ahead London |

*The London Bus Handbook*

**Go-Ahead have been working on hybrid single-deck buses since 2005. Here one of seven VDL hybrid SB120s with Wrightbus Electrocity bodywork is WHY3, LX55EAE. Six more of the model are expected to arrive in 2011.** *Mark Lyons*

| | | | | | | | |
|---|---|---|---|---|---|---|---|
| LX56EUA | Go-Ahead London | LX57CKY | Go-Ahead London | LX58CCV | Stagecoach | LX58CFN | Stagecoach |
| LX56EUB | Go-Ahead London | LX57CLF | Go-Ahead London | LX58CCY | Stagecoach | LX58CFO | Stagecoach |
| LX56EUC | Go-Ahead London | LX57CLJ | Go-Ahead London | LX58CDE | Stagecoach | LX58CFP | Stagecoach |
| LX56EUD | Go-Ahead London | LX57CLN | Go-Ahead London | LX58CDF | Stagecoach | LX58CFU | Stagecoach |
| LX57CHV | Go-Ahead London | LX57CLO | Go-Ahead London | LX58CDK | Stagecoach | LX58CFV | Stagecoach |
| LX57CHY | Go-Ahead London | LX57CLV | Go-Ahead London | LX58CDN | Stagecoach | LX58CFY | Stagecoach |
| LX57CHZ | Go-Ahead London | LX57CLY | Go-Ahead London | LX58CDO | Stagecoach | LX58CFZ | Stagecoach |
| LX57CJE | Go-Ahead London | LX57CLZ | Go-Ahead London | LX58CDU | Stagecoach | LX58CGE | Stagecoach |
| LX57CJF | Go-Ahead London | LX58BZW | Stagecoach | LX58CDV | Stagecoach | LX58CGF | Stagecoach |
| LX57CJJ | Go-Ahead London | LX58BZY | Stagecoach | LX58CDY | Stagecoach | LX58CGG | Stagecoach |
| LX57CJO | Go-Ahead London | LX58CAA | Stagecoach | LX58CDZ | Stagecoach | LX58CGK | Stagecoach |
| LX57CJU | Go-Ahead London | LX58CAE | Stagecoach | LX58CEA | Stagecoach | LX58CGO | Stagecoach |
| LX57CJV | Go-Ahead London | LX58CAO | Stagecoach | LX58CEF | Stagecoach | LX58CGU | Stagecoach |
| LX57CJY | Go-Ahead London | LX58CAU | Stagecoach | LX58CEJ | Stagecoach | LX58CGV | Stagecoach |
| LX57CJZ | Go-Ahead London | LX58CAV | Stagecoach | LX58CEK | Stagecoach | LX58CGY | Stagecoach |
| LX57CKA | Go-Ahead London | LX58CBF | Stagecoach | LX58CEN | Stagecoach | LX58CGZ | Stagecoach |
| LX57CKC | Go-Ahead London | LX58CBO | Stagecoach | LX58CEO | Stagecoach | LX58CHC | Stagecoach |
| LX57CKD | Go-Ahead London | LX58CBU | Stagecoach | LX58CEU | Stagecoach | LX58CHD | Stagecoach |
| LX57CKE | Go-Ahead London | LX58CBV | Stagecoach | LX58CEV | Stagecoach | LX58CHF | Stagecoach |
| LX57CKF | Go-Ahead London | LX58CBY | Stagecoach | LX58CEY | Stagecoach | LX58CHG | Stagecoach |
| LX57CKG | Go-Ahead London | LX58CCA | Stagecoach | LX58CFA | Stagecoach | LX58CHH | Stagecoach |
| LX57CKJ | Go-Ahead London | LX58CCD | Stagecoach | LX58CFD | Stagecoach | LX58CHJ | Stagecoach |
| LX57CKK | Go-Ahead London | LX58CCE | Stagecoach | LX58CFE | Stagecoach | LX58CHK | Stagecoach |
| LX57CKL | Go-Ahead London | LX58CCF | Stagecoach | LX58CFF | Stagecoach | LX58CHL | Stagecoach |
| LX57CKN | Go-Ahead London | LX58CCJ | Stagecoach | LX58CFG | Stagecoach | LX58CHN | Stagecoach |
| LX57CKO | Go-Ahead London | LX58CCK | Stagecoach | LX58CFJ | Stagecoach | LX58CHO | Stagecoach |
| LX57CKP | Go-Ahead London | LX58CCN | Stagecoach | LX58CFK | Stagecoach | LX58CHV | Stagecoach |
| LX57CKU | Go-Ahead London | LX58CCO | Stagecoach | LX58CFL | Stagecoach | LX58CWG | Go-Ahead London |
| LX57CKV | Go-Ahead London | LX58CCU | Stagecoach | LX58CFM | Stagecoach | LX58CWJ | Go-Ahead London |

| Reg | Operator | Reg | Operator | Reg | Operator | Reg | Operator |
| --- | --- | --- | --- | --- | --- | --- | --- |
| LX58CWK | Go-Ahead London | LX59AOL | Stagecoach | LX59CYU | Go-Ahead London | LX59DFG | Go-Ahead London |
| LX58CWL | Go-Ahead London | LX59AOM | Stagecoach | LX59CYV | Go-Ahead London | LX59DFJ | Go-Ahead London |
| LX58CWM | Go-Ahead London | LX59CLU | Stagecoach | LX59CYW | Go-Ahead London | LX59DFK | Go-Ahead London |
| LX58CWN | Go-Ahead London | LX59CLV | Stagecoach | LX59CYY | Go-Ahead London | LX59ECF | Stagecoach |
| LX58CWO | Go-Ahead London | LX59CLY | Stagecoach | LX59CYZ | Go-Ahead London | LX59ECJ | Stagecoach |
| LX58CWP | Go-Ahead London | LX59CLZ | Stagecoach | LX59CZA | Go-Ahead London | LX59ECN | Stagecoach |
| LX58CWR | Go-Ahead London | LX59CME | Stagecoach | LX59CZB | Go-Ahead London | LX59ECT | Stagecoach |
| LX58CWT | Go-Ahead London | LX59CMF | Stagecoach | LX59CZC | Go-Ahead London | LX59ECV | Stagecoach |
| LX58CWU | Go-Ahead London | LX59CMK | Stagecoach | LX59CZD | Go-Ahead London | LX59ECW | Stagecoach |
| LX58CWV | Go-Ahead London | LX59CMO | Stagecoach | LX59CZF | Go-Ahead London | LX59ECY | Stagecoach |
| LX58CWW | Go-Ahead London | LX59CMU | Stagecoach | LX59CZG | Go-Ahead London | LX59ECZ | Stagecoach |
| LX58CWY | Go-Ahead London | LX59CMV | Stagecoach | LX59CZH | Go-Ahead London | LX59EDC | Stagecoach |
| LX58CWZ | Go-Ahead London | LX59CMY | Stagecoach | LX59CZJ | Go-Ahead London | LX59EDF | Stagecoach |
| LX58CXA | Go-Ahead London | LX59CMZ | Stagecoach | LX59CZK | Go-Ahead London | LX59EDJ | Stagecoach |
| LX58CXB | Go-Ahead London | LX59CNA | Stagecoach | LX59CZL | Go-Ahead London | LX59EDK | Stagecoach |
| LX58CXC | Go-Ahead London | LX59CNC | Stagecoach | LX59CZM | Go-Ahead London | LX59EDL | Stagecoach |
| LX58CXD | Go-Ahead London | LX59CNE | Stagecoach | LX59CZN | Go-Ahead London | LX59EDO | Stagecoach |
| LX58CXE | Go-Ahead London | LX59CNF | Stagecoach | LX59CZO | Go-Ahead London | LX60DVY | Go-Ahead London |
| LX58CXF | Go-Ahead London | LX59CNJ | Stagecoach | LX59CZP | Go-Ahead London | LX60DVZ | Go-Ahead London |
| LX58CXG | Go-Ahead London | LX59CNK | Stagecoach | LX59CZR | Go-Ahead London | LX60DWA | Go-Ahead London |
| LX58CXH | Go-Ahead London | LX59CNN | Stagecoach | LX59CZS | Go-Ahead London | LX60DWC | Go-Ahead London |
| LX58CXJ | Go-Ahead London | LX59CNO | Stagecoach | LX59CZT | Go-Ahead London | LX60DWD | Go-Ahead London |
| LX58CXK | Go-Ahead London | LX59CNU | Stagecoach | LX59CZU | Go-Ahead London | LX60DWE | Go-Ahead London |
| LX58CXL | Go-Ahead London | LX59CNV | Stagecoach | LX59CZV | Go-Ahead London | LX60DWF | Go-Ahead London |
| LX58CXN | Go-Ahead London | LX59CNY | Stagecoach | LX59CZW | Go-Ahead London | LX60DWG | Go-Ahead London |
| LX58CXO | Go-Ahead London | LX59CNZ | Stagecoach | LX59CZY | Go-Ahead London | LX60DWJ | Go-Ahead London |
| LX58CXP | Go-Ahead London | LX59COA | Stagecoach | LX59CZZ | Go-Ahead London | LX60DWK | Go-Ahead London |
| LX58CXR | Go-Ahead London | LX59COH | Stagecoach | LX59DAA | Go-Ahead London | LX60DWL | Go-Ahead London |
| LX58CXS | Go-Ahead London | LX59COJ | Stagecoach | LX59DAO | Go-Ahead London | LX60DWM | Go-Ahead London |
| LX58CXT | Go-Ahead London | LX59COU | Stagecoach | LX59DAU | Go-Ahead London | LX60DWN | Go-Ahead London |
| LX58CXU | Go-Ahead London | LX59CPE | Stagecoach | LX59DBO | Go-Ahead London | LX60DWO | Go-Ahead London |
| LX58CXV | Go-Ahead London | LX59CPF | Stagecoach | LX59DBU | Go-Ahead London | LX60DWP | Go-Ahead London |
| LX58CXW | Go-Ahead London | LX59CPK | Stagecoach | LX59DBV | Go-Ahead London | LX60DWU | Go-Ahead London |
| LX58CXY | Go-Ahead London | LX59CPN | Stagecoach | LX59DBY | Go-Ahead London | LX60DWV | Go-Ahead London |
| LX58CXZ | Go-Ahead London | LX59CPO | Stagecoach | LX59DBZ | Go-Ahead London | LX60DWW | Go-Ahead London |
| LX58CYA | Go-Ahead London | LX59CPU | Stagecoach | LX59DCE | Go-Ahead London | LX60DWY | Go-Ahead London |
| LX58CYC | Go-Ahead London | LX59CPV | Stagecoach | LX59DCF | Go-Ahead London | LX60DWZ | Go-Ahead London |
| LX58CYE | Go-Ahead London | LX59CPY | Stagecoach | LX59DCO | Go-Ahead London | LX60DXA | Go-Ahead London |
| LX58CYF | Go-Ahead London | LX59CPZ | Stagecoach | LX59DCU | Go-Ahead London | LX60DXB | Go-Ahead London |
| LX58CYG | Go-Ahead London | LX59CRF | Stagecoach | LX59DCV | Go-Ahead London | LX60DXC | Go-Ahead London |
| LX58DDJ | Go-Ahead London | LX59CRJ | Stagecoach | LX59DCY | Go-Ahead London | LX60DXD | Go-Ahead London |
| LX58DDK | Go-Ahead London | LX59CRK | Stagecoach | LX59DCZ | Go-Ahead London | LX60DXE | Go-Ahead London |
| LX58DDL | Go-Ahead London | LX59CRU | Stagecoach | LX59DDA | Go-Ahead London | LX60DXF | Go-Ahead London |
| LX58DDN | Go-Ahead London | LX59CRV | Stagecoach | LX59DDE | Go-Ahead London | LX60DXG | Go-Ahead London |
| LX58DDO | Go-Ahead London | LX59CRZ | Stagecoach | LX59DDF | Go-Ahead London | LX60DXH | Go-Ahead London |
| LX59ANF | Stagecoach | LX59CSF | Stagecoach | LX59DDJ | Go-Ahead London | LX60DXJ | Go-Ahead London |
| LX59ANP | Stagecoach | LX59CSO | Stagecoach | LX59DDK | Go-Ahead London | LX60DXK | Go-Ahead London |
| LX59ANR | Stagecoach | LX59CYA | Go-Ahead London | LX59DDL | Go-Ahead London | LX60DXM | Go-Ahead London |
| LX59ANU | Stagecoach | LX59CYC | Go-Ahead London | LX59DDN | Go-Ahead London | LX60DXO | Go-Ahead London |
| LX59ANV | Stagecoach | LX59CYE | Go-Ahead London | LX59DDO | Go-Ahead London | LX60DXP | Go-Ahead London |
| LX59AOA | Stagecoach | LX59CYF | Go-Ahead London | LX59DDU | Go-Ahead London | LX60DXR | Go-Ahead London |
| LX59AOB | Stagecoach | LX59CYG | Go-Ahead London | LX59DDV | Go-Ahead London | LX60DXS | Go-Ahead London |
| LX59AOC | Stagecoach | LX59CYH | Go-Ahead London | LX59DDY | Go-Ahead London | LX60DXT | Go-Ahead London |
| LX59AOD | Stagecoach | LX59CYJ | Go-Ahead London | LX59DDZ | Go-Ahead London | LY02OAA | Stagecoach |
| LX59AOE | Stagecoach | LX59CYK | Go-Ahead London | LX59DEU | Go-Ahead London | LY02OAB | Stagecoach |
| LX59AOF | Stagecoach | LX59CYL | Go-Ahead London | LX59DFA | Go-Ahead London | LY02OAC | Stagecoach |
| LX59AOG | Stagecoach | LX59CYO | Go-Ahead London | LX59DFC | Go-Ahead London | LY02OAD | Stagecoach |
| LX59AOH | Stagecoach | LX59CYP | Go-Ahead London | LX59DFD | Go-Ahead London | LY02OAE | Stagecoach |
| LX59AOJ | Stagecoach | LX59CYS | Go-Ahead London | LX59DFE | Go-Ahead London | LY02OAG | Stagecoach |
| LX59AOK | Stagecoach | LX59CYT | Go-Ahead London | LX59DFF | Go-Ahead London | LY02OAN | Stagecoach |

*The London Bus Handbook*

**In this February view intrepid passengers see the London sites from the top deck of Big Bus DA209, PF08USB as it approaches London Bridge. The Preston-based index marks reflect its build by East Lancs (now Optare) at its facility in Blackburn.** *Richard Godfrey*

| | | | | | | | |
|---|---|---|---|---|---|---|---|
| LY02OAP | Stagecoach | M507VJO | Metrobus | P502RYM | Go-Ahead London | PF08URP | Big Bus Company |
| LY02OAS | Stagecoach | M508VJO | Metrobus | P503RYM | Go-Ahead London | PF08URR | Big Bus Company |
| LY02OAU | Stagecoach | M516VJO | Metrobus | P504RYM | Go-Ahead London | PF08URS | Big Bus Company |
| LY02OAV | Stagecoach | M520VJO | Metrobus | P507RYM | Go-Ahead London | PF08URU | Big Bus Company |
| LY02OAW | Stagecoach | MX09HHW | Go-Ahead London | P508RYM | Hackney CT | PF08URV | Big Bus Company |
| LY02OAX | Stagecoach | MX10DXR | Hackney CT | P514RYM | Go-Ahead London | PF08URW | Big Bus Company |
| LY02OAZ | Stagecoach | MXT179 | Arriva Original Tour | P674MLE | Metroline | PF08URX | Big Bus Company |
| LY02OBB | Stagecoach | N136YRW | London United | P675MLE | Metroline | PF08URZ | Big Bus Company |
| LY02OBC | Stagecoach | N137YRW | London United | P737RYL | Go-Ahead London | PF08USB | Big Bus Company |
| LY02OBD | Stagecoach | N138YRW | London United | PA04CYC | London United | PF08USC | Big Bus Company |
| LY02OBE | Stagecoach | N139YRW | London United | PA04CYE | London United | PF52TFX | Hackney CT |
| LY02OBF | Stagecoach | N140YRW | London United | PA04CYF | London United | PF52TGZ | Hackney CT |
| LY02OBG | Stagecoach | N232TPK | Metrobus | PA04CYG | London United | PF52WPT | Go-Ahead London |
| LY02OBH | Stagecoach | N281DWY | London United | PA04CYH | London United | PF52WPU | Go-Ahead London |
| LY02OBJ | Stagecoach | N282DWY | London United | PA04CYJ | London United | PF52WPV | Go-Ahead London |
| LY02OBK | Stagecoach | N283DWY | London United | PA04CYK | London Sovereign | PF52WPW | Go-Ahead London |
| LY02OBL | Stagecoach | N284DWY | London United | PA04CYL | London Sovereign | PF52WPX | Go-Ahead London |
| LY02OBM | Stagecoach | N285DWY | London United | PA04CYP | London Sovereign | PF52WPY | Go-Ahead London |
| LY52ZDX | Stagecoach | N286DWY | London United | PA04CYS | London Sovereign | PF52WPZ | Go-Ahead London |
| LY52ZDZ | Stagecoach | N288DWY | London United | PA04CYT | London Sovereign | PF52WRA | Go-Ahead London |
| LY52ZFA | Stagecoach | NKJ785 | Arriva Original Tour | PE56UFH | Quality Line | PF52WRC | Go-Ahead London |
| LY52ZFB | Stagecoach | NML604E | Go-Ahead London | PE56UFJ | Quality Line | PF52WRD | Go-Ahead London |
| LY52ZFC | Stagecoach | OAY770P | London Duck Tours | PE56UFK | Quality Line | PF52WRE | Go-Ahead London |
| LY52ZFD | Stagecoach | OHV739Y | Big Bus Company | PE56UFL | Quality Line | PF52WRG | Go-Ahead London |
| LY52ZFE | Stagecoach | P274FPK | Metrobus | PE56UFM | Quality Line | PG04WGN | London United |
| LY52ZFF | Stagecoach | P278FPK | Metrobus | PE56UFN | Quality Line | PG04WGP | London United |
| LY52ZFG | Stagecoach | P283FPK | Metrobus | PE56UFP | Quality Line | PG04WGU | London United |
| LY52ZFH | Stagecoach | P285FPK | Metrobus | PE56UFR | Quality Line | PG04WGV | London United |
| M506VJO | Metrobus | P380FPK | Metrobus | PE56UFS | Quality Line | PG04WGW | London United |

| Reg | Operator | Reg | Operator | Reg | Operator | Reg | Operator |
|---|---|---|---|---|---|---|---|
| PG04WGX | London United | PJ02TVN | Go-Ahead London | PJ53OUX | London Sovereign | PN07KRO | Metrobus |
| PG04WGY | London United | PJ02TVO | Go-Ahead London | PJ53OUY | London Sovereign | PN07KRU | Metrobus |
| PG04WGZ | London United | PJ02TVP | Go-Ahead London | PJ53OVA | London Sovereign | PN07KRV | Metrobus |
| PG04WHA | London United | PJ02TVT | Go-Ahead London | PJ53OVB | London Sovereign | PN07KRX | Metrobus |
| PG04WHB | London United | PJ02TVU | Go-Ahead London | PJ53SOF | Go-Ahead London | PN07KRZ | Quality Line |
| PG04WHC | London United | PJ52LVP | Go-Ahead London | PJ53SOH | Go-Ahead London | PN07KSE | Quality Line |
| PG04WHD | London United | PJ52LVR | Go-Ahead London | PJ53SOU | Go-Ahead London | PN08SWJ | Hackney CT |
| PG04WHE | London United | PJ52LVS | Go-Ahead London | PJ53SPU | Go-Ahead London | PN09EKR | Metrobus |
| PG04WHF | London United | PJ52LVT | Go-Ahead London | PJ53SPV | Go-Ahead London | PN09EKT | Metrobus |
| PG04WHH | London United | PJ52LVU | Go-Ahead London | PJ53SPX | Go-Ahead London | PN09EKU | Metrobus |
| PG04WHJ | London United | PJ52LVV | Go-Ahead London | PJ53SPZ | Go-Ahead London | PN09EKV | Metrobus |
| PG04WHK | London United | PJ52LVW | Go-Ahead London | PJ53SRO | Go-Ahead London | PN09EKW | Metrobus |
| PG04WHL | London United | PJ52LVX | Go-Ahead London | PJ53SRU | Go-Ahead London | PN09EKX | Metrobus |
| PG04WHM | London United | PJ52LVY | Go-Ahead London | PL03AGZ | Go-Ahead London | PN09EKY | Metrobus |
| PG04WHN | London United | PJ52LVZ | Go-Ahead London | PL05PLN | Quality Line | PN09ELO | Metrobus |
| PG04WHP | London United | PJ52LWA | Go-Ahead London | PL05PLO | Quality Line | PN09ELU | Metrobus |
| PG04WHR | London United | PJ52LWC | Go-Ahead London | PL05PLU | Quality Line | PN09ELV | Metrobus |
| PG04WHS | London United | PJ52LWD | Go-Ahead London | PL05PLV | Quality Line | PN09ELW | Metrobus |
| PG04WHT | London United | PJ52LWE | Go-Ahead London | PL05PLX | Quality Line | PN09ELX | Metrobus |
| PG04WHU | London United | PJ52LWF | Go-Ahead London | PL51LDJ | Go-Ahead London | PN09EMF | Metrobus |
| PG04WHV | London United | PJ52LWG | Go-Ahead London | PL51LDK | Go-Ahead London | PN09EMK | Metrobus |
| PG04WHW | London United | PJ52LWH | Go-Ahead London | PL51LDN | Go-Ahead London | PN09EMV | Metrobus |
| PG04WHX | London United | PJ52LWK | Go-Ahead London | PL51LDO | Go-Ahead London | PN09EMX | Metrobus |
| PG04WHY | London United | PJ52LWL | Go-Ahead London | PL51LDU | Go-Ahead London | PN09ENC | Metrobus |
| PG04WJA | London United | PJ52LWM | Go-Ahead London | PL51LDY | Go-Ahead London | PN09ENE | Metrobus |
| PJ02RAU | Go-Ahead London | PJ52LWN | Go-Ahead London | PL51LDZ | Go-Ahead London | PN09ENF | Metrobus |
| PJ02RAX | Go-Ahead London | PJ52LWO | Go-Ahead London | PL51LEF | Go-Ahead London | PN09ENH | Metrobus |
| PJ02RBF | Go-Ahead London | PJ52LWP | Go-Ahead London | PN02XBH | Go-Ahead London | PN09ENK | Metrobus |
| PJ02RBO | Go-Ahead London | PJ52LWR | Go-Ahead London | PN02XBJ | Go-Ahead London | PN09ENL | Metrobus |
| PJ02RBU | Go-Ahead London | PJ52LWS | Go-Ahead London | PN02XBK | Go-Ahead London | PN09ENM | Metrobus |
| PJ02RBV | Go-Ahead London | PJ52LWT | Go-Ahead London | PN02XBL | Go-Ahead London | PN09ENO | Metrobus |
| PJ02RBX | Go-Ahead London | PJ52LWU | Go-Ahead London | PN02XBM | Go-Ahead London | PN09ENP | Metrobus |
| PJ02RBY | Go-Ahead London | PJ52LWV | Go-Ahead London | PN02XBO | Go-Ahead London | PN09ENR | Metrobus |
| PJ02RBZ | Go-Ahead London | PJ52LWW | Go-Ahead London | PN02XBP | Go-Ahead London | PN09ENT | Metrobus |
| PJ02RCF | Go-Ahead London | PJ52LWX | Go-Ahead London | PN02XBR | Go-Ahead London | PN09ENU | Metrobus |
| PJ02RCO | Go-Ahead London | PJ53NKG | Go-Ahead London | PN02XBU | Go-Ahead London | PN09ENV | Metrobus |
| PJ02RCU | Go-Ahead London | PJ53NKH | Go-Ahead London | PN02XBV | Go-Ahead London | PN09ENW | Metrobus |
| PJ02RCV | Go-Ahead London | PJ53NKK | Go-Ahead London | PN02XBW | Go-Ahead London | PN09ENY | Big Bus Company |
| PJ02RCX | Go-Ahead London | PJ53NKL | Go-Ahead London | PN03ULY | Hackney CT | PN09EOA | Big Bus Company |
| PJ02RCY | Go-Ahead London | PJ53NKM | Go-Ahead London | PN03UMB | Hackney CT | PN09EOB | Big Bus Company |
| PJ02RCZ | Go-Ahead London | PJ53NKN | Go-Ahead London | PN03UMK | Hackney CT | PN09EOC | Big Bus Company |
| PJ02RDO | Go-Ahead London | PJ53NKO | Go-Ahead London | PN06UYL | Metrobus | PN09EOD | Big Bus Company |
| PJ02RDU | Go-Ahead London | PJ53NKP | Go-Ahead London | PN06UYM | Metrobus | PN09EOE | Big Bus Company |
| PJ02RDV | Go-Ahead London | PJ53NKR | Go-Ahead London | PN06UYO | Metrobus | PN09EOF | Big Bus Company |
| PJ02RDX | Go-Ahead London | PJ53NKS | Go-Ahead London | PN06UYP | Metrobus | PN09EOH | Big Bus Company |
| PJ02RDY | Go-Ahead London | PJ53NKT | Go-Ahead London | PN06UYR | Metrobus | PN09EOJ | Big Bus Company |
| PJ02RDZ | Go-Ahead London | PJ53NKW | Go-Ahead London | PN06UYS | Metrobus | PN09EOK | Big Bus Company |
| PJ02REU | Go-Ahead London | PJ53NKX | Go-Ahead London | PN06UYT | Metrobus | PN10FOC | Big Bus Company |
| PJ02RFE | Go-Ahead London | PJ53NKZ | Go-Ahead London | PN06UYU | Metrobus | PN10FOD | Big Bus Company |
| PJ02RFF | Go-Ahead London | PJ53NLA | Go-Ahead London | PN06UYV | Metrobus | PN10FOF | Big Bus Company |
| PJ02RFK | Go-Ahead London | PJ53NLC | Go-Ahead London | PN06UYW | Metrobus | PN10FOH | Big Bus Company |
| PJ02RFL | Go-Ahead London | PJ53NLD | Go-Ahead London | PN06UYX | Metrobus | PN10FOJ | Big Bus Company |
| PJ02RFN | Go-Ahead London | PJ53NLE | Go-Ahead London | PN06UYY | Metrobus | PN10FOK | Big Bus Company |
| PJ02RFO | Go-Ahead London | PJ53NLF | Go-Ahead London | PN07KPY | Hackney CT | PO54ABZ | London Sovereign |
| PJ02RFX | Go-Ahead London | PJ53OUN | London Sovereign | PN07KPZ | Hackney CT | PO54ACF | London Sovereign |
| PJ02RFY | Go-Ahead London | PJ53OUO | London Sovereign | PN07KRD | Hackney CT | PO54ACJ | London Sovereign |
| PJ02RFZ | Go-Ahead London | PJ53OUP | London Sovereign | PN07KRE | Hackney CT | PO54ACU | London Sovereign |
| PJ02RGO | Go-Ahead London | PJ53OUU | London Sovereign | PN07KRF | Hackney CT | PO54ACV | London Sovereign |
| PJ02RGU | Go-Ahead London | PJ53OUV | London Sovereign | PN07KRG | Hackney CT | PO54ACX | London Sovereign |
| PJ02RGV | Go-Ahead London | PJ53OUW | London Sovereign | PN07KRK | Metrobus | PO54ACY | London Sovereign |

| | | | | | | | |
|---|---|---|---|---|---|---|---|
| PO54ACZ | London Sovereign | RD02BJU | Abellio | S107EGK | Go-Ahead London | S256JUA | Arriva London |
| PO54ADU | London United | RD02BJV | Abellio | S108EGK | Go-Ahead London | S257JUA | Arriva London |
| PO54ADV | London United | RD02BJX | Abellio | S109EGK | Go-Ahead London | S258JUA | Arriva London |
| PO54OOD | London United | RD02BJZ | Abellio | S110EGK | Go-Ahead London | S262JUA | Arriva London |
| PO54OOE | London United | RG51FWX | First London | S112EGK | Go-Ahead London | S263JUA | Arriva London |
| PO54OOF | London United | RG51FXA | First London | S112EGK | Metrobus | S264JUA | Arriva London |
| PO54OOG | London United | RG51FXB | First London | S113EGK | Go-Ahead London | S272JUA | Arriva Southern C |
| PO56JEU | Metrobus | RG51FXC | First London | S114EGK | Go-Ahead London | S284JUA | Arriva Southern C |
| PO56JFA | Metrobus | RG51FXD | First London | S115EGK | Go-Ahead London | S284JUA | Arriva The Shires |
| PO56JFE | Metrobus | RG51FXE | First London | S116EGK | Go-Ahead London | S285JUA | Arriva Southern C |
| PO56JFF | Metrobus | RG51FXF | First London | S117EGK | Go-Ahead London | S285JUA | Arriva The Shires |
| PO56JFG | Metrobus | RG51FXH | First London | S169JUA | Arriva London | S286JLP | Metroline |
| PO56JFJ | Metrobus | RL02FOT | Abellio | S170JUA | Arriva London | S287JLP | Metroline |
| PO56JFK | Metrobus | RL02FOU | Abellio | S171JUA | Arriva London | S288JLP | Metroline |
| PO56JFN | Metrobus | RL02FVM | Abellio | S172JUA | Arriva London | S289JLP | Metroline |
| PO56JFU | Metrobus | RL02FVN | Abellio | S173JUA | Arriva London | S290JLP | Metroline |
| R101GNW | Arriva London | RL02ZTB | Abellio | S174JUA | Arriva London | S291JUA | Arriva Southern C |
| R124RLY | Go-Ahead London | RL02ZTC | Abellio | S175JUA | Arriva London | S291JUA | Arriva The Shires |
| R125RLY | Go-Ahead London | RL51DNU | Metroline | S176JUA | Arriva London | S292JLP | Metroline |
| R140RLY | Go-Ahead London | RL51DNV | Metroline | S177JUA | Arriva London | S293JLP | Metroline |
| R142RLY | Go-Ahead London | RL51DNX | Metroline | S178JUA | Arriva London | S294JLP | Metroline |
| R146RLY | Go-Ahead London | RL51DNY | Metroline | S179JUA | Arriva London | S297JLP | Metroline |
| R147RLY | Go-Ahead London | RL51DOA | Metroline | S180JUA | Arriva London | S298JLP | Metroline |
| R151RLY | Go-Ahead London | RL51DOH | Metroline | S181JUA | Arriva London | S301MKH | London United |
| R153RLY | Go-Ahead London | RL51DOJ | Metroline | S182JUA | Arriva London | S306MKH | London United |
| R370LGH | Go-Ahead London | RL51DOU | Metroline | S183JUA | Arriva London | S307MKH | London United |
| R371LGH | Go-Ahead London | RN52EOV | Abellio | S211JUA | Arriva London | S310MKH | London United |
| R376LGH | Go-Ahead London | RN52EYK | Abellio | S212JUA | Arriva London | S311MKH | London United |
| R447LGH | Go-Ahead London | RN52EYL | Abellio | S213JUA | Arriva London | S322JUA | Arriva London |
| R456LGH | Go-Ahead London | RN52FPA | Abellio | S214JUA | Arriva London | S518TCF | Abellio |
| R464LGH | Go-Ahead London | RN52FPC | Abellio | S215JUA | Arriva London | S519TCF | Abellio |
| R487LGH | Go-Ahead London | RN52FRD | Abellio | S215LLO | First London | S638JGP | Go-Ahead London |
| R508SJM | Abellio | RN52FRF | Abellio | S216JUA | Arriva London | S638JGP | Metrobus |
| R649TLM | First London | RN52FVR | Abellio | S216LLO | First London | S801BWC | Stagecoach |
| R741BMY | Metrobus | RN52FVS | Abellio | S217JUA | Arriva London | S954JGX | Go-Ahead London |
| R742BMY | Metrobus | RN52FXD | Abellio | S218JUA | Arriva London | SK02TZN | Abellio |
| R743BMY | Metrobus | RN52FYO | Abellio | S218LLO | First London | SK02TZO | Abellio |
| R744BMY | Metrobus | RN52FZA | Abellio | S219JUA | Arriva London | SK02TZP | Abellio |
| R745BMY | Metrobus | RSL602 | London Duck Tours | S220JUA | Arriva London | SK02TZR | Abellio |
| R746FGX | Metrobus | RX51FGG | Abellio | S221JUA | Arriva London | SK02TZS | Abellio |
| R747FGX | Metrobus | RX51FGJ | Abellio | S223JUA | Arriva London | SK02TZT | Abellio |
| R945YOV | London United | RX51FGK | Abellio | S224JUA | Arriva London | SK02TZU | Abellio |
| R946YOV | London United | RX51FGM | Abellio | S225JUA | Arriva London | SK02TZV | Abellio |
| R948YOV | London United | RX51FGN | Abellio | S226JUA | Arriva London | SK02TZW | Abellio |
| R949YOV | London United | RX51FGO | Abellio | S227JUA | Arriva London | SK02TZX | Abellio |
| R950YOV | London United | RX51FGP | Abellio | S228JUA | Arriva London | SK02XGT | London United |
| R951YOV | London United | RX51FNP | Metroline | S229JUA | Arriva London | SK02XGU | London United |
| R952YOV | London United | RX51FNS | Metroline | S230JUA | Arriva London | SK02XGV | London United |
| R953YOV | London United | RX51FNT | Metroline | S231JUA | Arriva London | SK02XGW | London Sovereign |
| R954YOV | London United | RX51FNU | Metroline | S232JUA | Arriva London | SK02XGX | London Sovereign |
| RA51KGE | Abellio | RX51FNV | Metroline | S233JUA | Arriva London | SK02XHD | London Sovereign |
| RA51KKD | Abellio | RX51FNW | Metroline | S234JUA | Arriva London | SK02XHE | London Sovereign |
| RA51KKE | Abellio | RX51FNY | Metroline | S235JUA | Arriva London | SK02XHG | London Sovereign |
| RA51KKF | Abellio | S91EGK | Go-Ahead London | S236JUA | Arriva The Shires | SK02XHH | London Sovereign |
| RA51KKG | Abellio | S101EGK | Go-Ahead London | S237JUA | Arriva London | SK02XHJ | London Sovereign |
| RA51KKH | Abellio | S102EGK | Go-Ahead London | S239JUA | Arriva London | SK02XHL | London Sovereign |
| RA51KLE | Abellio | S103EGK | Go-Ahead London | S245JUA | Arriva London | SK02XHM | London Sovereign |
| RA51KVS | Abellio | S104EGK | Go-Ahead London | S247JUA | Arriva London | SK02XHN | London Sovereign |
| RD02BJK | Abellio | S105EGK | Go-Ahead London | S254JUA | Arriva London | SK02XHO | London Sovereign |
| RD02BJO | Abellio | S106EGK | Go-Ahead London | S255JUA | Arriva London | SK02XHP | London Sovereign |

*The London Bus Handbook*

| Reg | Operator | Reg | Operator | Reg | Operator | Reg | Operator |
|---|---|---|---|---|---|---|---|
| SK02XHR | London Sovereign | SK07DZL | Quality Line | SN03EAC | London United | SN03YBG | Metrobus |
| SK07DWG | Go-Ahead London | SK07DZM | Go-Ahead London | SN03EAE | London United | SN03YBH | Metrobus |
| SK07DWJ | Go-Ahead London | SK07DZN | Go-Ahead London | SN03EAF | London United | SN03YBK | Metrobus |
| SK07DWK | Go-Ahead London | SK07DZO | Go-Ahead London | SN03EAG | London United | SN03YBR | Metrobus |
| SK07DWL | Go-Ahead London | SK07HLM | London United | SN03EAJ | London United | SN03YBS | Metrobus |
| SK07DWM | Go-Ahead London | SK07HLN | London United | SN03EAM | London United | SN03YBT | Metrobus |
| SK07DWO | Go-Ahead London | SK07HLO | London United | SN03EAP | London United | SN03YBX | Metrobus |
| SK07DWP | Go-Ahead London | SK07HLP | London United | SN03EAW | London United | SN03YBY | Metrobus |
| SK07DWU | Go-Ahead London | SK07HLR | London United | SN03EAX | London United | SN03YBZ | Metrobus |
| SK07DWV | Go-Ahead London | SK07HLU | London United | SN03EBA | London United | SN03YCD | Metrobus |
| SK07DWW | Go-Ahead London | SK07HLV | London United | SN03EBC | London United | SN03YCE | Metrobus |
| SK07DWX | Go-Ahead London | SK52MKV | London United | SN03EBD | London United | SN03YCF | Metrobus |
| SK07DWY | Go-Ahead London | SK52MLU | Go-Ahead London | SN03EBF | London United | SN03YCK | Metrobus |
| SK07DWZ | Go-Ahead London | SK52MLV | Go-Ahead London | SN03EBG | London United | SN03YCL | Metrobus |
| SK07DXA | Go-Ahead London | SK52MLX | Go-Ahead London | SN03EBJ | London United | SN03YCM | Metrobus |
| SK07DXB | Go-Ahead London | SK52MLY | Go-Ahead London | SN03EBK | London United | SN03YCT | Metrobus |
| SK07DXE | London United | SK52MLZ | Go-Ahead London | SN03EBL | London United | SN06BNA | Go-Ahead London |
| SK07DXF | London United | SK52MMA | Go-Ahead London | SN03EBM | London United | SN06BNB | Go-Ahead London |
| SK07DXG | London United | SK52MME | Go-Ahead London | SN03LDY | London United | SN06BND | Go-Ahead London |
| SK07DXH | London United | SK52MMU | Go-Ahead London | SN03LDZ | London United | SN06BNE | Go-Ahead London |
| SK07DXJ | London United | SK52MMV | Go-Ahead London | SN03LEF | London United | SN06BNF | Go-Ahead London |
| SK07DXL | London United | SK52MMX | Go-Ahead London | SN03LEJ | London United | SN06BNJ | Go-Ahead London |
| SK07DXM | London United | SK52MOA | Go-Ahead London | SN03LEV | London United | SN06BNK | Go-Ahead London |
| SK07DXO | London United | SK52MOF | Go-Ahead London | SN03LFA | London United | SN06BNL | Go-Ahead London |
| SK07DXP | London United | SK52MOU | Go-Ahead London | SN03LFB | London United | SN06BNO | Go-Ahead London |
| SK07DXR | London United | SK52MOV | Go-Ahead London | SN03LFD | London United | SN06BNU | Go-Ahead London |
| SK07DXS | London United | SK52MPE | Go-Ahead London | SN03LFE | London United | SN06BNV | Go-Ahead London |
| SK07DXT | London United | SK52MPF | Go-Ahead London | SN03LFF | London United | SN06BNX | Go-Ahead London |
| SK07DXU | London United | SK52MPO | Go-Ahead London | SN03LFG | London United | SN06BNY | Go-Ahead London |
| SK07DXV | London United | SK52MPU | London United | SN03LFH | London United | SN06BNZ | Go-Ahead London |
| SK07DXW | London United | SK52MPV | London United | SN03LFJ | London United | SN06BOF | Go-Ahead London |
| SK07DXX | London United | SK52MPX | London United | SN03LFK | London United | SN06BPE | Arriva London |
| SK07DXY | London United | SK52MPY | London United | SN03LFL | London United | SN06BPF | Arriva London |
| SK07DXZ | London United | SK52MSO | London United | SN03LFM | London United | SN06BPK | Arriva London |
| SK07DYC | London United | SK52URV | London United | SN03LFP | London United | SN06BPU | Arriva London |
| SK07DYD | London United | SK52URW | London United | SN03LFR | London United | SN06BPV | Arriva London |
| SK07DYF | London United | SK52URX | London United | SN03LFS | London United | SN06BPX | Arriva London |
| SK07DYG | London United | SK52URY | London United | SN03LFT | London United | SN06BPY | Arriva London |
| SK07DYH | London United | SK52URZ | London United | SN03WKU | Metrobus | SN06BPZ | Arriva London |
| SK07DYJ | London United | SK52USB | London United | SN03WKY | Metrobus | SN06BRF | Arriva London |
| SK07DYM | London United | SK52USC | London United | SN03WLA | Metrobus | SN06JPV | London United |
| SK07DYN | London United | SK52USD | London United | SN03WLE | Metrobus | SN06JPX | London United |
| SK07DYO | London United | SK52USF | London United | SN03WLF | Metrobus | SN08AAO | Metroline |
| SK07DYP | London United | SK52USG | London United | SN03WLH | Metrobus | SN09CDU | First London |
| SK07DYS | London United | SK52USH | London United | SN03WLL | Metrobus | SN09CDV | First London |
| SK07DYT | London United | SK52USJ | London United | SN03WLP | Metrobus | SN09CDX | First London |
| SK07DYU | London United | SK52USL | London United | SN03WLU | Metrobus | SN09CDY | First London |
| SK07DYV | London United | SMK735F | First London | SN03WLX | Metrobus | SN09CDZ | First London |
| SK07DYW | London United | SMK760F | Stagecoach | SN03WLZ | Metrobus | SN09CEA | First London |
| SK07DYX | London United | SN03DZJ | London United | SN03WMC | Metrobus | SN09CEF | First London |
| SK07DYY | London United | SN03DZK | London United | SN03WMF | Metrobus | SN09CEJ | First London |
| SK07DZA | Quality Line | SN03DZM | London United | SN03WMG | Metrobus | SN09CEK | First London |
| SK07DZB | Quality Line | SN03DZP | London United | SN03WMK | Metrobus | SN09CEO | First London |
| SK07DZC | Quality Line | SN03DZR | London United | SN03WMP | Metrobus | SN09CEU | First London |
| SK07DZD | Quality Line | SN03DZS | London United | SN03WMT | Metrobus | SN09CEV | First London |
| SK07DZE | Quality Line | SN03DZT | London United | SN03WMV | Metrobus | SN09CEX | First London |
| SK07DZF | Quality Line | SN03DZV | London United | SN03WMY | Metrobus | SN09CEY | First London |
| SK07DZG | Quality Line | SN03DZW | London United | SN03YBA | Metrobus | SN09CFA | First London |
| SK07DZH | Quality Line | SN03DZX | London United | SN03YBB | Metrobus | SN09CFD | First London |
| SK07DZJ | Quality Line | SN03EAA | London United | SN03YBC | Metrobus | SN09CFE | First London |

*The London Bus Handbook*

| | | | | | | | |
|---|---|---|---|---|---|---|---|
| SN09CFF | First London | SN11BOH | First London | SN51SZE | London United | SN53EUV | London United |
| SN09CFG | First London | SN11BOJ | First London | SN51SZF | Abellio | SN53EUW | London United |
| SN09CFJ | First London | SN11BOU | First London | SN51SZT | London United | SN53EUX | London United |
| SN09CFK | First London | SN11BOV | First London | SN51SZU | London United | SN53EUY | London United |
| SN09CFL | First London | SN11BPE | First London | SN51TAU | London United | SN53EUZ | London United |
| SN09CFM | First London | SN11BPF | First London | SN51TAV | London United | SN53KHR | London United |
| SN09CFO | First London | SN11BPK | First London | SN51TBO | London United | SN53KHT | London United |
| SN09CFP | First London | SN11BPO | First London | SN51TBU | London United | SN53KHU | London United |
| SN09CFU | First London | SN11BPU | First London | SN51TBV | London United | SN53KHV | London United |
| SN09CFV | First London | SN11BPV | First London | SN51TBX | London Sovereign | SN53KHW | London United |
| SN09CFX | First London | SN11BPX | First London | SN51TBY | London United | SN53KHX | London United |
| SN09CFY | First London | SN11BPY | First London | SN51TBZ | London United | SN53KHY | London United |
| SN09CFZ | First London | SN11BPZ | First London | SN51TCJ | London United | SN53KHZ | London United |
| SN09CGE | First London | SN11BRF | First London | SN51TCK | London United | SN53KJA | London United |
| SN09CGF | First London | SN11BRV | First London | SN51TCO | London United | SN53KJE | London United |
| SN09CGG | First London | SN11BRZ | First London | SN51TCU | London United | SN53KJF | London United |
| SN09CGK | First London | SN11BSO | First London | SN51TCV | London United | SN53KJJ | London United |
| SN09CGO | First London | SN11BSU | First London | SN51TCX | London United | SN53KJK | London United |
| SN09CGU | First London | SN11BSV | First London | SN51TCY | London United | SN53KJO | London United |
| SN09CGV | First London | SN11BSX | First London | SN51TCZ | London United | SN53KJU | London United |
| SN09CHC | London United | SN11BSY | First London | SN51TDO | London United | SN53KJV | London United |
| SN09CHD | London United | SN11BSZ | First London | SN51TDU | London United | SN53KKF | Go-Ahead London |
| SN09CHF | London United | SN11BTE | First London | SN51TDV | London United | SN53KKG | Go-Ahead London |
| SN09CHG | London United | SN11BTO | First London | SN51TDX | London United | SN53KKH | Go-Ahead London |
| SN09CHH | London United | SN11BTU | First London | SN51TDZ | London United | SN53KKJ | Go-Ahead London |
| SN10CAV | London United | SN11BTY | Go-Ahead London | SN51TEJ | London United | SN53KKL | Go-Ahead London |
| SN10CAX | London United | SN11BTZ | Go-Ahead London | SN51TEO | London United | SN53KKM | Go-Ahead London |
| SN10CBF | London United | SN11BVA | Go-Ahead London | SN51TEU | London United | SN53KKO | Go-Ahead London |
| SN10CBO | London United | SN11BVE | Go-Ahead London | SN51UAD | Go-Ahead London | SN53KKP | Go-Ahead London |
| SN10CBU | London United | SN11BVF | Go-Ahead London | SN51UAE | Go-Ahead London | SN53KKR | Go-Ahead London |
| SN10CBV | London United | SN11BVH | Go-Ahead London | SN51UAF | Go-Ahead London | SN53KKT | Go-Ahead London |
| SN10CBX | London United | SN11BVJ | Go-Ahead London | SN51UAG | Go-Ahead London | SN53KKU | Go-Ahead London |
| SN10CBY | London United | SN11BVO | Go-Ahead London | SN51UAH | Go-Ahead London | SN53KKV | Go-Ahead London |
| SN10CCA | London United | SN11BVP | Go-Ahead London | SN51UAJ | Go-Ahead London | SN53KKW | Go-Ahead London |
| SN10CCD | London United | SN11BVU | Go-Ahead London | SN51UAK | Go-Ahead London | SN53KKX | Go-Ahead London |
| SN10CCE | London United | SN11BVV | Go-Ahead London | SN51UAL | Go-Ahead London | SN54GPV | Metrobus |
| SN10CCF | London United | SN11BVW | Go-Ahead London | SN51UAM | Go-Ahead London | SN54GPX | Metrobus |
| SN10CCJ | London United | SN51SXG | London United | SN51UAO | Go-Ahead London | SN54GPY | Metrobus |
| SN10CCK | London United | SN51SXH | London United | SN51UAP | Go-Ahead London | SN54GPZ | Metrobus |
| SN10CCO | London United | SN51SXJ | London United | SN51UAR | Go-Ahead London | SN54GRF | Metrobus |
| SN10CCU | London United | SN51SXK | Abellio | SN51UAS | Go-Ahead London | SN54GRK | Metrobus |
| SN11BMU | First London | SN51SYA | London United | SN51UAT | Go-Ahead London | SN55DVR | London United |
| SN11BMV | First London | SN51SYC | London United | SN51UAU | Go-Ahead London | SN55DVT | London United |
| SN11BMY | First London | SN51SYE | London United | SN51UAV | Go-Ahead London | SN55DVU | London United |
| SN11BMZ | First London | SN51SYF | London United | SN51UAW | Go-Ahead London | SN55DVV | London United |
| SN11BNA | First London | SN51SYG | London United | SN51UAX | Go-Ahead London | SN55DVW | London United |
| SN11BNB | First London | SN51SYH | London United | SN51UAY | Go-Ahead London | SN55HKD | London United |
| SN11BND | First London | SN51SYJ | London United | SN51UAZ | Go-Ahead London | SN55HKE | London United |
| SN11BNE | First London | SN51SYO | London United | SN51UCO | Quality Line | SN55HKF | London United |
| SN11BNF | First London | SN51SYR | London United | SN53EUF | London United | SN55HKG | London United |
| SN11BNJ | First London | SN51SYS | London United | SN53EUH | London United | SN55HKH | London United |
| SN11BNK | First London | SN51SYT | London United | SN53EUJ | London United | SN55HKJ | London United |
| SN11BNL | First London | SN51SYU | London United | SN53EUK | London United | SN55HKK | London United |
| SN11BNO | First London | SN51SYV | London United | SN53EUL | London United | SN55HKL | London United |
| SN11BNU | First London | SN51SYW | London United | SN53EUM | London United | SN55HKM | London United |
| SN11BNV | First London | SN51SYX | London United | SN53EUO | London United | SN55HKO | London United |
| SN11BNX | First London | SN51SYY | London United | SN53EUP | London United | SN55HKP | London United |
| SN11BNY | First London | SN51SYZ | London United | SN53EUR | London United | SN55HKU | London United |
| SN11BNZ | First London | SN51SZC | London United | SN53EUT | London United | SN55HKV | London United |
| SN11BOF | First London | SN51SZD | London United | SN53EUU | London United | SN55HKW | London United |

The Enviro 400 bodywork is assembled at Falkirk in Scotland where many of the vehicles are first registered. Carrying 'SN' plates is London United's hybrid ADH14, SN60BYK, one of twenty-two of the hybrid model to enter service recently. *Mark Lyons*

| | | | | | | | |
|---|---|---|---|---|---|---|---|
| SN55HKX | London United | SN58CFK | First London | SN58CHR | First London | SN60BYD | London United |
| SN55HKY | London United | SN58CFL | First London | SN58CHT | First London | SN60BYF | London United |
| SN55HKY | London United | SN58CFM | First London | SN58EOR | London United | SN60BYG | London United |
| SN55HKZ | London United | SN58CFO | First London | SN58EOS | London United | SN60BYH | London United |
| SN55HLA | London United | SN58CFP | First London | SN59AVR | Abellio | SN60BYJ | London United |
| SN55HLC | London United | SN58CFU | First London | SN59AVT | Abellio | SN60BYK | London United |
| SN55HSD | London United | SN58CFV | First London | SN59AVU | Abellio | SN60BYL | London United |
| SN55HSE | London United | SN58CFX | First London | SN59AVV | Abellio | SN60BYM | London United |
| SN56AYC | Go-Ahead London | SN58CFY | First London | SN59AVW | Abellio | SN60BYO | London United |
| SN56AYD | Go-Ahead London | SN58CFZ | First London | SN59AVX | Abellio | SN60BYP | London United |
| SN57DWE | Hackney CT | SN58CGE | First London | SN59AVY | Abellio | SN60BYR | London United |
| SN57DWF | Hackney CT | SN58CGF | First London | SN59AVZ | Abellio | SN60BYS | London United |
| SN58CDY | First London | SN58CGG | First London | SN59AWA | Abellio | SN60BYT | London United |
| SN58CDZ | First London | SN58CGK | First London | SN59AWC | Abellio | SN60BYU | London United |
| SN58CEA | First London | SN58CGO | First London | SN59AWF | Abellio | SN60BZA | Go-Ahead London |
| SN58CEF | First London | SN58CGU | First London | SN59AWG | Abellio | SN60BZB | Go-Ahead London |
| SN58CEJ | First London | SN58CGV | First London | SN59AWH | Abellio | SN60BZC | Go-Ahead London |
| SN58CEK | First London | SN58CGX | First London | SN59AWJ | Abellio | SN60BZD | Go-Ahead London |
| SN58CEO | First London | SN58CGY | First London | SN59AWM | Abellio | SN60BZE | Go-Ahead London |
| SN58CEU | First London | SN58CGZ | First London | SN59AWO | Abellio | SN60BZF | Go-Ahead London |
| SN58CEV | First London | SN58CHC | First London | SN59AWP | Abellio | SN60BZG | Go-Ahead London |
| SN58CEX | First London | SN58CHD | First London | SN59AWR | Abellio | SN60BZH | Go-Ahead London |
| SN58CEY | First London | SN58CHF | First London | SN59AWU | Abellio | SN60BZJ | Go-Ahead London |
| SN58CFA | First London | SN58CHG | First London | SN60BXX | London United | SN60BZK | Go-Ahead London |
| SN58CFD | First London | SN58CHH | First London | SN60BXY | London United | SN60BZL | Go-Ahead London |
| SN58CFE | First London | SN58CHJ | First London | SN60BXZ | London United | SN60BZM | Go-Ahead London |
| SN58CFF | First London | SN58CHK | First London | SN60BYA | London United | SN60BZO | Go-Ahead London |
| SN58CFG | First London | SN58CHL | First London | SN60BYB | London United | SN60BZP | Go-Ahead London |
| SN58CFJ | First London | SN58CHO | First London | SN60BYC | London United | SN60BZR | Go-Ahead London |

*The London Bus Handbook*

| Reg | Operator | Reg | Operator | Reg | Operator | Reg | Operator |
|---|---|---|---|---|---|---|---|
| SN60BZS | Go-Ahead London | T109KLD | Metroline | T218XBV | Arriva London | T360PRH | London United |
| SN60BZT | Go-Ahead London | T110KLD | Metroline | T219XBV | Arriva London | T361PRH | London United |
| SN60BZU | Go-Ahead London | T112KLD | Metroline | T220XBV | Arriva London | T362PRH | London United |
| SN60BZV | Go-Ahead London | T113KLD | Metroline | T259JLD | First London | T363PRH | London United |
| SN60BZW | Go-Ahead London | T114KLD | Metroline | T291JLD | First London | T364PRH | London United |
| SN60BZX | Go-Ahead London | T115KLD | Metroline | T292JLD | First London | T365PRH | London United |
| SN60BZY | Go-Ahead London | T116KLD | Metroline | T293JLD | First London | T366PRH | London United |
| SN60EAX | London United | T117KLD | Metroline | T294FGN | Arriva London | T367PRH | London United |
| SN60EAY | London United | T118KLD | Metroline | T294JLD | First London | T368PRH | London United |
| SN60EBA | London United | T119KLD | Metroline | T295FGN | Arriva London | T369PRH | London United |
| SN60EBC | London United | T120KLD | Metroline | T295JLD | First London | T370PRH | London United |
| SN60EBD | London United | T122KLD | Metroline | T297JLD | First London | T371PRH | London United |
| SN60EBF | London United | T124KLD | Metroline | T298JLD | First London | T372PRH | London United |
| SN60EBG | London United | T125KLD | Metroline | T306FGN | Arriva London | T373PRH | London United |
| SN60EBJ | London United | T126KLD | Metroline | T307FGN | Arriva London | T374PRH | London United |
| SN60EBK | London United | T127KLD | Metroline | T308FGN | Arriva London | T375PRH | London United |
| SN60EBL | London United | T128KLD | Metroline | T309FGN | Arriva London | T421GGO | Arriva London |
| SN60EBM | London United | T129KLD | Metroline | T309SMV | Metrobus | T433LGP | Hackney CT |
| SN60EBO | London United | T132CLO | Metroline | T310FGN | Arriva London | T455PRH | London United |
| SN60EBP | London United | T133CLO | Metroline | T310SMV | Metrobus | T701JLD | First London |
| SN60EBU | London United | T134CLO | Metroline | T311FGN | Arriva London | T702JLD | First London |
| SN60EBV | London United | T135CLO | Metroline | T311SMV | Metrobus | T703JLD | First London |
| SN60EBX | London United | T136CLO | Metroline | T312FGN | Arriva London | T806LLC | First London |
| SN60EBZ | London United | T137CLO | Metroline | T313FGN | Arriva London | T807LLC | First London |
| SN60ECA | London United | T138CLO | Metroline | T314FGN | Arriva London | T822LLC | First London |
| SN60ECC | London United | T139CLO | Metroline | T315FGN | Arriva London | T976SRH | London United |
| SN60ECD | London United | T140CLO | Metroline | T316FGN | Arriva London | T977SRH | London United |
| SN60ECE | London United | T141CLO | Metroline | T317FGN | Arriva London | T978SRH | London United |
| SN60ECF | London United | T142CLO | Metroline | T318FGN | Arriva London | T979SRH | London United |
| SN60ECJ | London United | T143CLO | Metroline | T319FGN | Arriva London | T980SRH | London United |
| SN60ECT | London United | T144CLO | Metroline | T320FGN | Arriva London | UAR247Y | Arriva Original Tour |
| SN60ECV | London United | T145CLO | Metroline | T322FGN | Arriva London | UAR250Y | Arriva Original Tour |
| T35KLD | Metroline | T146CLO | Metroline | T323FGN | Arriva London | UAR776Y | Arriva Original Tour |
| T37KLD | Metroline | T148CLO | Metroline | T324FGN | Arriva London | V102MEV | Stagecoach |
| T39KLD | Metroline | T182CLO | Metroline | T325FGN | Arriva London | V103MEV | Stagecoach |
| T41KLD | Metroline | T191CLO | Metroline | T334PRH | London United | V104MEV | Stagecoach |
| T43KLD | Metroline | T192CLO | Metroline | T335PRH | London United | V105MEV | Stagecoach |
| T48KLD | Metroline | T193CLO | Metroline | T336PRH | London United | V109MEV | Stagecoach |
| T49KLD | Metroline | T199CLO | Metroline | T337PRH | London United | V112MEV | Stagecoach |
| T53KLD | Metroline | T202CLO | Metroline | T338PRH | London United | V113MEV | Stagecoach |
| T67KLD | Metroline | T202XBV | Arriva Original Tour | T339PRH | London United | V118GBY | Metroline |
| T68KLD | Metroline | T203XBV | Arriva Original Tour | T340PRH | London United | V119GBY | Metroline |
| T69KLD | Metroline | T204XBV | Arriva Original Tour | T341PRH | London United | V120GBY | Metroline |
| T71KLD | Metroline | T205CLO | Metroline | T342PRH | London United | V122GBY | Metroline |
| T72KLD | Metroline | T205XBV | Arriva Original Tour | T343PRH | London United | V124GBY | Metroline |
| T73KLD | Metroline | T206XBV | Arriva Original Tour | T344PRH | London United | V125GBY | Metroline |
| T74KLD | Metroline | T207XBV | Arriva Original Tour | T345PRH | London United | V126GBY | Metroline |
| T76KLD | Metroline | T208CLO | Metroline | T346PRH | London United | V126MEV | Stagecoach |
| T78KLD | Metroline | T208XBV | Arriva Original Tour | T347PRH | London United | V127GBY | Metroline |
| T79KLD | Metroline | T209CLO | Metroline | T348PRH | London United | V127MEV | Stagecoach |
| T81KLD | Metroline | T209XBV | Arriva Original Tour | T349PRH | London United | V128GBY | Metroline |
| T97KLD | Metroline | T210XBV | Arriva Original Tour | T350PRH | London United | V128MEV | Stagecoach |
| T98KLD | Metroline | T211XBV | Arriva Original Tour | T351PRH | London United | V129GBY | Metroline |
| T101KLD | Metroline | T212XBV | Arriva Original Tour | T352PRH | London United | V129MEV | Stagecoach |
| T103KLD | Metroline | T213XBV | Arriva Original Tour | T353PRH | London United | V130GBY | Metroline |
| T104KLD | Metroline | T214XBV | Arriva Original Tour | T354PRH | London United | V130MEV | Stagecoach |
| T105KLD | Metroline | T215XBV | Arriva London | T356PRH | London United | V131GBY | Metroline |
| T106KLD | Metroline | T216XBV | Arriva London | T357PRH | London United | V132GBY | Metroline |
| T107KLD | Metroline | T217XBV | Arriva London | T358PRH | London United | V133GBY | Metroline |
| T108KLD | Metroline | T218CLO | Metroline | T359PRH | London United | V134GBY | Metroline |

| Reg | Operator | Reg | Operator | Reg | Operator | Reg | Operator | Reg | Operator |
|---|---|---|---|---|---|---|---|---|---|
| V134MEV | Stagecoach | V203OOE | London United | V330KMY | Metrobus | V765HBY | Metroline |
| V136MEV | Stagecoach | V204MEV | Stagecoach | V331DGT | Arriva London | V781FKH | London United |
| V140MEV | Stagecoach | V204OOE | London United | V331KMY | Metrobus | V782FKH | London United |
| V141MEV | Stagecoach | V205MEV | Stagecoach | V332DGT | Arriva London | V783FKH | London United |
| V143MEV | Stagecoach | V205OOE | London United | V334DGT | Arriva London | V784FKH | London United |
| V144MEV | Stagecoach | V206MEV | Stagecoach | V335DGT | Arriva London | V785FKH | London United |
| V149MEV | Stagecoach | V206OOE | London United | V336DGT | Arriva London | V787FKH | London United |
| V151MEV | Stagecoach | V207MEV | Stagecoach | V337DGT | Arriva London | V788FKH | London United |
| V152MEV | Stagecoach | V207OOE | London United | V338DGT | Arriva London | V789FKH | London United |
| V153MEV | Stagecoach | V208MEV | Stagecoach | V339DGT | Arriva London | V790FKH | London United |
| V157MEV | Stagecoach | V208OOE | London United | V341DGT | Arriva London | V791FKH | London United |
| V159MEV | Stagecoach | V209MEV | Stagecoach | V342DGT | Arriva London | V792FKH | London United |
| V161MEV | Stagecoach | V211MEV | Stagecoach | V343DGT | Arriva London | V793FKH | London United |
| V162MEV | Stagecoach | V212MEV | Stagecoach | V344DGT | Arriva London | V794FKH | London United |
| V162MXV | Stagecoach | V214MEV | Stagecoach | V345DGT | Arriva London | V795FKH | London United |
| V163MXV | Stagecoach | V215MEV | Stagecoach | V346DGT | Arriva London | V796FKH | London United |
| V164MEV | Stagecoach | V216MEV | Stagecoach | V347DGT | Arriva London | V797FKH | London United |
| V165MEV | Stagecoach | V217MEV | Stagecoach | V348DGT | Arriva London | V798FKH | London United |
| V166MEV | Stagecoach | V218MEV | Stagecoach | V349DGT | Arriva London | V799FKH | London United |
| V167MEV | Stagecoach | V219MEV | Stagecoach | V351DGT | Arriva London | V801KAG | London Sovereign |
| V170MEV | Stagecoach | V220MEV | Stagecoach | V352DGT | Arriva London | V802KAG | London Sovereign |
| V171MEV | Stagecoach | V221MEV | Stagecoach | V353DGT | Arriva London | V803KAG | London United |
| V172MEV | Stagecoach | V301MDP | Abellio | V354DGT | Arriva London | V805KAG | London United |
| V174MEV | Stagecoach | V302MDP | Abellio | V355DGT | Arriva London | V806KAG | London United |
| V175MEV | Stagecoach | V303MDP | Abellio | V356DGT | Arriva London | V807KAG | London United |
| V176OOE | London United | V304MDP | Abellio | V356DLH | First London | V808KAG | London United |
| V177MEV | Stagecoach | V305MDP | Abellio | V357DGT | Arriva London | V809KAG | London United |
| V177OOE | London United | V306MDP | Abellio | V358DGT | Arriva London | V810KAG | London United |
| V178MEV | Stagecoach | V307GLB | Metroline | V359DGT | Arriva London | V811KAG | London United |
| V178OOE | London United | V307MDP | Abellio | V361DGT | Arriva London | V812KAG | London United |
| V179OOE | London United | V308MDP | Abellio | V362DGT | Arriva London | V813KAG | London United |
| V180OOE | London United | V309MDP | Abellio | V363DGT | Arriva London | V814KAG | London United |
| V181MEV | Stagecoach | V314GLB | Metroline | V363OWC | Stagecoach | V815KAG | London United |
| V181OOE | London United | V315KGW | Abellio | V364DGT | Arriva London | V816KAG | London United |
| V182MEV | Stagecoach | V316KGW | Abellio | V364OWC | Stagecoach | V886FKH | London United |
| V182OOE | London United | V317KGW | Abellio | V365DGT | Arriva London | V893HLH | First London |
| V183MEV | Stagecoach | V318KGW | Abellio | V474KJN | Stagecoach | V895HLH | First London |
| V184MEV | Stagecoach | V322KGW | Abellio | V475KJN | Stagecoach | V896HLH | First London |
| V185MEV | Stagecoach | V322KMY | Metrobus | V477KJN | Stagecoach | V904KAG | London United |
| V186MEV | Stagecoach | V323KGW | Abellio | V628LGC | Arriva London | VLT5 | Arriva London |
| V187OOE | London United | V323KMY | Metrobus | V633LGC | Arriva London | VLT6 | Arriva London |
| V188OOE | London United | V324GBY | First London | V640LGC | Arriva London | VLT9 | Go-Ahead London |
| V189OOE | London United | V324KMY | Metrobus | V650LGC | Arriva London | VLT12 | Arriva London |
| V190MEV | Stagecoach | V325GBY | First London | V660LGC | Arriva London | VLT14 | Stagecoach |
| V190OOE | London United | V325KGW | Abellio | V749HBY | Metroline | VLT27 | Arriva London |
| V191OOE | London United | V325KMY | Metrobus | V750HBY | Metroline | VLT32 | Arriva London |
| V192MEV | Stagecoach | V326DGT | Arriva London | V751HBY | Metroline | VLT47 | Arriva London |
| V192OOE | London United | V326GBY | First London | V752HBY | Metroline | VLT60 | Go-Ahead London |
| V193MEV | Stagecoach | V326KMY | Metrobus | V753HBY | Metroline | VLT173 | Arriva London |
| V193OOE | London United | V327DGT | Arriva London | V754HBY | Metroline | VLT240 | Stagecoach |
| V194MEV | Stagecoach | V327GBY | First London | V755HBY | Metroline | VLT244 | Arriva London |
| V194OOE | London United | V327KGW | Abellio | V756HBY | Metroline | VLT295 | Arriva London |
| V195MEV | Stagecoach | V327KMY | Metrobus | V757HBY | Metroline | VSL143 | London Duck Tours |
| V196MEV | Stagecoach | V328KGW | Abellio | V758HBY | Metroline | VX10EBN | Arriva Southern C |
| V197MEV | Stagecoach | V328KMY | Metrobus | V759HBY | Metroline | VX10EBO | Arriva Southern C |
| V198MEV | Stagecoach | V329DGT | Arriva London | V760HBY | Metroline | VX10EBP | Arriva Southern C |
| V199MEV | Stagecoach | V329KGW | Abellio | V761HBY | Metroline | VX10EBU | Arriva Southern C |
| V202MEV | Stagecoach | V329KMY | Metrobus | V762HBY | Metroline | VX10EBV | Arriva Southern C |
| V202OOE | London United | V330DGT | Arriva London | V763HBY | Metroline | VX10EBX | Arriva Southern C |
| V203MEV | Stagecoach | V330KGW | Abellio | V764HBY | Metroline | VX58DXA | London United |

| | | | | | | | |
|---|---|---|---|---|---|---|---|
| VYJ806 | Arriva London | W367VGJ | Arriva London | W435WGH | Go-Ahead London | W489WGH | Go-Ahead London |
| W112WGT | Metroline | W368VGJ | Arriva London | W435WGJ | Arriva London | W491WGH | Go-Ahead London |
| W114WGT | Metroline | W368VLN | First London | W436CRN | Abellio | W492WGH | Go-Ahead London |
| W116EON | London United | W369VGJ | Arriva London | W436WGJ | Arriva London | W493WGH | Go-Ahead London |
| W116WGT | Metroline | W369VLN | First London | W437CRN | Abellio | W494WGH | Go-Ahead London |
| W117EON | London United | W371VGJ | Arriva London | W437WGJ | Arriva London | W495WGH | Go-Ahead London |
| W117WGT | Metroline | W372VGJ | Arriva London | W438CRN | Abellio | W496WGH | Go-Ahead London |
| W118EON | London United | W373VGJ | Arriva London | W438WGJ | Arriva London | W497WGH | Go-Ahead London |
| W118WGT | Metroline | W374VGJ | Arriva London | W448BCW | London United | W501WGH | Go-Ahead London |
| W119EON | London United | W376VGJ | Arriva London | W449BCW | London United | W502WGH | Go-Ahead London |
| W119WGT | Metroline | W376VLN | First London | W451BCW | London United | W503WGH | Go-Ahead London |
| W122EON | London United | W377VGJ | Arriva London | W452BCW | London United | W504WGH | Go-Ahead London |
| W122WGT | Metroline | W377VLN | First London | W453BCW | London United | W506WGH | Go-Ahead London |
| W124EON | London United | W378VGJ | Arriva London | W454BCW | London United | W507WGH | Go-Ahead London |
| W124WGT | Metroline | W378VLN | First London | W457BCW | London United | W508WGH | Go-Ahead London |
| W126EON | London United | W379VGJ | Arriva London | W457WGH | Go-Ahead London | W509WGH | Go-Ahead London |
| W126WGT | Metroline | W379VLN | First London | W458BCW | London United | W511WGH | Go-Ahead London |
| W127EON | London United | W381VGJ | Arriva London | W458WGH | Go-Ahead London | W512WGH | Go-Ahead London |
| W127WGT | Metroline | W382VGJ | Arriva London | W459WGH | Go-Ahead London | W513WGH | Go-Ahead London |
| W128EON | London United | W383VGJ | Arriva London | W461WGH | Go-Ahead London | W514WGH | Go-Ahead London |
| W128WGT | Metroline | W384VGJ | Arriva London | W461XKX | Arriva London | W516WGH | Go-Ahead London |
| W129EON | London United | W385VGJ | Arriva London | W462WGH | Go-Ahead London | W517WGH | Go-Ahead London |
| W131EON | London United | W386VGJ | Arriva London | W462XKX | Arriva London | W518WGH | Go-Ahead London |
| W132EON | London United | W387VGJ | Arriva London | W463WGH | Go-Ahead London | W519WGH | Go-Ahead London |
| W132WGT | Metroline | W388VGJ | Arriva London | W463XKX | Arriva London | W521WGH | Go-Ahead London |
| W133EON | London United | W389VGJ | Arriva London | W464WGH | Go-Ahead London | W522WGH | Go-Ahead London |
| W133ULR | Metroline | W391VGJ | Arriva London | W464XKX | Arriva London | W523WGH | Go-Ahead London |
| W133WGT | Metroline | W392VGJ | Arriva London | W465WGH | Go-Ahead London | W524WGH | Go-Ahead London |
| W134EON | London United | W393VGJ | Arriva London | W465XKX | Arriva London | W526WGH | Go-Ahead London |
| W134ULR | Metroline | W394VGJ | Arriva London | W466WGH | Go-Ahead London | W527WGH | Go-Ahead London |
| W134WGT | Metroline | W395VGJ | Arriva London | W466XKX | Arriva London | W529WGH | Go-Ahead London |
| W136ULR | Metroline | W396VGJ | Arriva London | W467WGH | Go-Ahead London | W531WGH | Go-Ahead London |
| W136WGT | Metroline | W397VGJ | Arriva London | W467XKX | Arriva London | W532WGH | Go-Ahead London |
| W137EON | London United | W398VGJ | Arriva London | W468WGH | Go-Ahead London | W533WGH | Go-Ahead London |
| W137ULR | Metroline | W399VGJ | Arriva London | W468XKX | Arriva London | W534WGH | Go-Ahead London |
| W137WGT | Metroline | W401VGJ | Arriva London | W469WGH | Go-Ahead London | W536WGH | Go-Ahead London |
| W138EON | London United | W401WGH | Go-Ahead London | W469XKX | Arriva London | W537WGH | Go-Ahead London |
| W138ULR | Metroline | W402VGJ | Arriva London | W471WGH | Go-Ahead London | W538WGH | Go-Ahead London |
| W138WGT | Metroline | W402WGH | Go-Ahead London | W471XKX | Arriva London | W539WGH | Go-Ahead London |
| W139EON | London United | W403VGJ | Arriva London | W472WGH | Go-Ahead London | W541WGH | Go-Ahead London |
| W139ULR | Metroline | W403WGH | Go-Ahead London | W472XKX | Arriva London | W542WGH | Go-Ahead London |
| W141EON | London United | W404VGJ | Arriva London | W473WGH | Go-Ahead London | W543WGH | Go-Ahead London |
| W141ULR | Metroline | W404WGH | Go-Ahead London | W473XKX | Arriva London | W578DGU | Go-Ahead London |
| W142ULR | Metroline | W407VGJ | Arriva London | W474XKX | Arriva London | W874VGT | Quality Line |
| W143ULR | Metroline | W408VGJ | Arriva London | W475WGH | Go-Ahead London | W875VGT | Quality Line |
| W143WGT | Metroline | W408WGH | Go-Ahead London | W475XKX | Arriva London | W876VGT | Quality Line |
| W144ULR | Metroline | W409VGJ | Arriva London | W476WGH | Go-Ahead London | W905WGH | Go-Ahead London |
| W146ULR | Metroline | W409WGH | Go-Ahead London | W476XKX | Arriva London | W907VLN | First London |
| W147ULR | Metroline | W411VGJ | Arriva London | W477XKX | Arriva London | W929VLN | First London |
| W148ULR | Metroline | W412VGJ | Arriva London | W478XKX | Arriva London | W956WGH | Go-Ahead London |
| W149ULR | Metroline | W413VGJ | Arriva London | W479WGH | Go-Ahead London | W996WGH | Go-Ahead London |
| W149WGT | Metroline | W414VGJ | Arriva London | W479XKX | Arriva London | W997WGH | Go-Ahead London |
| W151ULR | Metroline | W415WGH | Go-Ahead London | W481XKX | Arriva London | WLT324 | Stagecoach |
| W152ULR | Metroline | W425WGH | Go-Ahead London | W482WGH | Go-Ahead London | WLT348 | Arriva London |
| W153ULR | Metroline | W428WGH | Go-Ahead London | W483WGH | Go-Ahead London | WLT372 | Arriva London |
| W187CNO | Stagecoach | W431WGJ | Arriva London | W484WGH | Go-Ahead London | WLT385 | Arriva London |
| W332VGX | Metrobus | W432WGJ | Arriva London | W485WGH | Go-Ahead London | WLT461 | Stagecoach |
| W334VGX | Metrobus | W433WGJ | Arriva London | W486WGH | Go-Ahead London | WLT516 | Go-Ahead London |
| W362VLN | First London | W434WGJ | Arriva London | W487WGH | Go-Ahead London | WLT554 | Arriva London |
| W366VGJ | Arriva London | W435CRN | Abellio | W488WGH | Go-Ahead London | WLT575 | Stagecoach |

*The London Bus Handbook*

| Reg | Operator | Reg | Operator | Reg | Operator | Reg | Operator |
|---|---|---|---|---|---|---|---|
| WLT644 | Metroline | X241NNO | Stagecoach | X317NNO | Stagecoach | X385NNO | Stagecoach |
| WLT652 | Stagecoach | X242NNO | Stagecoach | X319HLL | Metroline | X386NNO | Stagecoach |
| WLT664 | Arriva London | X243NNO | Stagecoach | X319KRX | Abellio | X388NNO | Stagecoach |
| WLT676 | Arriva London | X246NNO | Stagecoach | X319NNO | Stagecoach | X389NNO | Stagecoach |
| WLT719 | Arriva London | X246PGT | Arriva London | X322HLL | Metroline | X392NNO | Stagecoach |
| WLT751 | Arriva London | X247NNO | Stagecoach | X322KRX | Abellio | X395NNO | Stagecoach |
| WLT807 | Arriva London | X247PGT | Arriva London | X322NNO | Stagecoach | X396NNO | Stagecoach |
| WLT826 | Metroline | X248NNO | Stagecoach | X324HLL | Metroline | X397NNO | Stagecoach |
| WLT871 | Stagecoach | X248PGT | Arriva London | X324NNO | Stagecoach | X398NNO | Stagecoach |
| WLT880 | London United | X249NNO | Stagecoach | X326HLL | Metroline | X401HLR | First London |
| WLT888 | Arriva London | X249PGT | Arriva London | X326NNO | Stagecoach | X415FGP | Arriva London |
| WLT892 | Arriva London | X251NNO | Stagecoach | X327HLL | Metroline | X416FGP | Arriva London |
| WLT895 | Arriva London | X252NNO | Stagecoach | X329HLL | Metroline | X417FGP | Arriva London |
| WLT897 | Arriva London | X253NNO | Stagecoach | X331HLL | Metroline | X418FGP | Arriva London |
| WLT901 | Arriva London | X254NNO | Stagecoach | X332HLL | Metroline | X419FGP | Arriva London |
| WLT903 | Metroline | X256NNO | Stagecoach | X334HLL | Metroline | X421FGP | Arriva London |
| WLT970 | Arriva London | X257NNO | Stagecoach | X335HLL | Metroline | X422FGP | Arriva London |
| WLT997 | Arriva London | X258NNO | Stagecoach | X336HLL | Metroline | X423FGP | Arriva London |
| X149FBB | Go-Ahead London | X259NNO | Stagecoach | X336NNO | Stagecoach | X424FGP | Arriva London |
| X151FBB | Go-Ahead London | X261NNO | Stagecoach | X337HLL | Metroline | X425FGP | Arriva London |
| X152FBB | Go-Ahead London | X262NNO | Stagecoach | X338HLL | Metroline | X426FGP | Arriva London |
| X153FBB | Go-Ahead London | X263NNO | Stagecoach | X338NNO | Stagecoach | X427FGP | Arriva London |
| X154FBB | Go-Ahead London | X267NNO | Stagecoach | X339HLL | Metroline | X428FGP | Arriva London |
| X157FBB | Go-Ahead London | X268NNO | Stagecoach | X339NNO | Stagecoach | X429FGP | Arriva London |
| X158FBB | Go-Ahead London | X277NNO | Stagecoach | X341HLL | Metroline | X431FGP | Arriva London |
| X159FBB | Go-Ahead London | X278NNO | Stagecoach | X341NNO | Stagecoach | X432FGP | Arriva London |
| X161FBB | Go-Ahead London | X279NNO | Stagecoach | X342HLL | Metroline | X433FGP | Arriva London |
| X162FBB | Go-Ahead London | X281NNO | Stagecoach | X342NNO | Stagecoach | X434FGP | Arriva London |
| X163FBB | Go-Ahead London | X282NNO | Stagecoach | X343HLL | Metroline | X435FGP | Arriva London |
| X164FBB | Go-Ahead London | X285NNO | Stagecoach | X343NNO | Stagecoach | X436FGP | Arriva London |
| X165FBB | Go-Ahead London | X286NNO | Stagecoach | X344NNO | Stagecoach | X437FGP | Arriva London |
| X166FBB | Go-Ahead London | X288NNO | Stagecoach | X344YGU | Metrobus | X438FGP | Arriva London |
| X167FBB | Go-Ahead London | X289NNO | Stagecoach | X346NNO | Stagecoach | X439FGP | Arriva London |
| X168FBB | Go-Ahead London | X291NNO | Stagecoach | X347NNO | Stagecoach | X441FGP | Arriva London |
| X169FBB | Go-Ahead London | X292NNO | Stagecoach | X348NNO | Stagecoach | X442FGP | Arriva London |
| X171FBB | Go-Ahead London | X293NNO | Stagecoach | X349NNO | Stagecoach | X443FGP | Arriva London |
| X172FBB | Go-Ahead London | X294NNO | Stagecoach | X351NNO | Stagecoach | X445FGP | Arriva London |
| X201UMS | London United | X295NNO | Stagecoach | X352NNO | Stagecoach | X446FGP | Arriva London |
| X202UMS | London United | X296NNO | Stagecoach | X353NNO | Stagecoach | X447FGP | Arriva London |
| X203UMS | London United | X297NNO | Stagecoach | X354NNO | Stagecoach | X448FGP | Arriva London |
| X224WNO | Stagecoach | X298NNO | Stagecoach | X356NNO | Stagecoach | X449FGP | Arriva London |
| X226WNO | Stagecoach | X299NNO | Stagecoach | X357NNO | Stagecoach | X451FGP | Arriva London |
| X227WNO | Stagecoach | X301NNO | Stagecoach | X358NNO | Stagecoach | X452FGP | Arriva London |
| X228WNO | Stagecoach | X302NNO | Stagecoach | X362NNO | Stagecoach | X453FGP | Arriva London |
| X229NNO | Stagecoach | X303NNO | Stagecoach | X364NNO | Stagecoach | X454FGP | Arriva London |
| X229WNO | Stagecoach | X304NNO | Stagecoach | X365NNO | Stagecoach | X457FGP | Arriva Southern C |
| X231NNO | Stagecoach | X307NNO | Stagecoach | X366NNO | Stagecoach | X458FGP | Arriva Southern C |
| X231WNO | Stagecoach | X308NNO | Stagecoach | X367NNO | Stagecoach | X459FGP | Arriva Southern C |
| X232NNO | Stagecoach | X309NNO | Stagecoach | X368NNO | Stagecoach | X471GGO | Arriva London |
| X232WNO | Stagecoach | X311KRX | Abellio | X369NNO | Stagecoach | X475GGO | Arriva London |
| X233NNO | Stagecoach | X311NNO | Stagecoach | X371NNO | Stagecoach | X478GGO | Arriva London |
| X233WNO | Stagecoach | X312KRX | Abellio | X372NNO | Stagecoach | X481GGO | Arriva London |
| X234NNO | Stagecoach | X312NNO | Stagecoach | X373NNO | Stagecoach | X485GGO | Arriva London |
| X234WNO | Stagecoach | X313KRX | Abellio | X376NNO | Stagecoach | X501EGK | Go-Ahead London |
| X235WNO | Stagecoach | X313NNO | Stagecoach | X378NNO | Stagecoach | X501GGO | Arriva London |
| X236WNO | Stagecoach | X314KRX | Abellio | X379NNO | Stagecoach | X501JLO | First London |
| X237WNO | Stagecoach | X314NNO | Stagecoach | X381NNO | Stagecoach | X502EGK | Go-Ahead London |
| X238NNO | Stagecoach | X315KRX | Abellio | X382NNO | Stagecoach | X502GGO | Arriva London |
| X238WNO | Stagecoach | X315NNO | Stagecoach | X383NNO | Stagecoach | X502JLO | First London |
| X239NNO | Stagecoach | X317KRX | Abellio | X384NNO | Stagecoach | X503EGK | Go-Ahead London |

**Odd man out in the batch of Pointer-bodied Dennis Darts is DE1004, Y63LTF. Operating from Metroline's Brentford depot it is seen on route 117 in June 2011 shortly after having been repainted.** *Mark Lyons*

| | | | | | | | |
|---|---|---|---|---|---|---|---|
| X503GGO | Arriva London | X523GGO | Arriva London | X553EGK | Go-Ahead London | X587EGK | Go-Ahead London |
| X504EGK | Go-Ahead London | X523UAT | London Sovereign | X554EGK | Go-Ahead London | X587ORV | Hackney CT |
| X504GGO | Arriva London | X524GGO | Arriva London | X556EGK | Go-Ahead London | X588EGK | Go-Ahead London |
| X504JLO | First London | X524UAT | London Sovereign | X557EGK | Go-Ahead London | X588ORV | Hackney CT |
| X506EGK | Go-Ahead London | X526GGO | Arriva London | X558EGK | Go-Ahead London | X589EGK | Go-Ahead London |
| X506GGO | Arriva London | X526UAT | London Sovereign | X559EGK | Go-Ahead London | X589ORV | Hackney CT |
| X507EGK | Go-Ahead London | X527GGO | Arriva London | X561EGK | Go-Ahead London | X591EGK | Go-Ahead London |
| X507GGO | Arriva London | X527UAT | London Sovereign | X562EGK | Go-Ahead London | X591ORV | Hackney CT |
| X508EGK | Go-Ahead London | X529GGO | Arriva London | X563EGK | Go-Ahead London | X592EGK | Go-Ahead London |
| X508GGO | Arriva London | X529UAT | London Sovereign | X564EGK | Go-Ahead London | X592ORV | Hackney CT |
| X508HLR | First London | X531GGO | Arriva London | X566EGK | Go-Ahead London | X593EGK | Go-Ahead London |
| X509EGK | Go-Ahead London | X531UAT | London Sovereign | X567EGK | Go-Ahead London | X593ORV | Hackney CT |
| X511HLR | First London | X532GGO | Arriva London | X568EGK | Go-Ahead London | X594EGK | Go-Ahead London |
| X511UAT | London Sovereign | X532UAT | London Sovereign | X569EGK | Go-Ahead London | X594ORV | Hackney CT |
| X512HLR | First London | X533GGO | Arriva London | X571EGK | Go-Ahead London | X595EGK | Go-Ahead London |
| X512UAT | London Sovereign | X533UAT | London Sovereign | X575EGK | Go-Ahead London | X595ORV | Hackney CT |
| X513HLR | First London | X534GGO | Arriva London | X576EGK | Go-Ahead London | X596EGK | Go-Ahead London |
| X513UAT | London Sovereign | X536GGO | Arriva London | X578EGK | Go-Ahead London | X597EGK | Go-Ahead London |
| X514UAT | London Sovereign | X537GGO | Arriva London | X579EGK | Go-Ahead London | X598EGK | Go-Ahead London |
| X516UAT | London Sovereign | X538GGO | Arriva London | X581EGK | Go-Ahead London | X599EGK | Go-Ahead London |
| X517UAT | London Sovereign | X544EGK | Go-Ahead London | X582EGK | Go-Ahead London | X615EGK | Go-Ahead London |
| X518UAT | London Sovereign | X546EGK | Go-Ahead London | X583EGK | Go-Ahead London | X616EGK | Go-Ahead London |
| X519GGO | Arriva London | X546GGO | Arriva London | X584EGK | Go-Ahead London | X635LLX | Metroline |
| X519UAT | London Sovereign | X547EGK | Go-Ahead London | X584ORV | Hackney CT | X636LLX | Metroline |
| X521GGO | Arriva London | X548EGK | Go-Ahead London | X585EGK | Go-Ahead London | X637LLX | Metroline |
| X521UAT | London Sovereign | X549EGK | Go-Ahead London | X585ORV | Hackney CT | X638LLX | Metroline |
| X522GGO | Arriva London | X551EGK | Go-Ahead London | X586EGK | Go-Ahead London | X639LLX | Metroline |
| X522UAT | London Sovereign | X552EGK | Go-Ahead London | X586ORV | Hackney CT | X641LLX | Metroline |

| Reg | Operator | Reg | Operator | Reg | Operator | Reg | Operator |
|---|---|---|---|---|---|---|---|
| X642LLX | Metroline | Y37HWB | Abellio | Y208NLK | Metroline | Y294TKJ | Arriva Southern C |
| X643LLX | Metroline | Y38HWB | Abellio | Y209NLK | Metroline | Y295FJN | Stagecoach |
| X644LLX | Metroline | Y38YVV | Abellio | Y232NLK | Metroline | Y295TKJ | Arriva Southern C |
| X645LLX | Metroline | Y63LTF | Metroline | Y233NLK | Metroline | Y296FJN | Stagecoach |
| X646LLX | Metroline | Y116HWB | Abellio | Y234NLK | Metroline | Y296TKJ | Arriva Southern C |
| X647LLX | Metroline | Y118HWB | Abellio | Y235HWB | Abellio | Y297TKJ | Arriva Southern C |
| X648LLX | Metroline | Y133HWB | Abellio | Y235NLK | Metroline | Y298TKJ | Arriva Southern C |
| X649LLX | Metroline | Y134HWB | Abellio | Y236NLK | Metroline | Y299TKJ | Arriva Southern C |
| X651LLX | Metroline | Y143NLK | Metroline | Y237FJN | Stagecoach | Y301TKJ | Arriva Southern C |
| X652LLX | Metroline | Y144NLK | Metroline | Y237NLK | Metroline | Y302TKJ | Arriva Southern C |
| X653LLX | Metroline | Y146NLK | Metroline | Y238FJN | Stagecoach | Y303TKJ | Arriva Southern C |
| X654LLX | Metroline | Y147NLK | Metroline | Y238NLK | Metroline | Y329FJN | Stagecoach |
| X656EGK | Go-Ahead London | Y148NLK | Metroline | Y239FJN | Stagecoach | Y32HWB | Abellio |
| X656LLX | Metroline | Y149NLK | Metroline | Y239NLK | Metroline | Y331FJN | Stagecoach |
| X657LLX | Metroline | Y152NLK | Metroline | Y241FJN | Stagecoach | Y332FJN | Stagecoach |
| X658LLX | Metroline | Y153NLK | Metroline | Y242FJN | Stagecoach | Y334FJN | Stagecoach |
| X659LLX | Metroline | Y154NLK | Metroline | Y243FJN | Stagecoach | Y335FJN | Stagecoach |
| X661LLX | Metroline | Y157NLK | Metroline | Y244FJN | Stagecoach | Y336FJN | Stagecoach |
| X662LLX | Metroline | Y158NLK | Metroline | Y246FJN | Stagecoach | Y337FJN | Stagecoach |
| X663LLX | Metroline | Y159NLK | Metroline | Y246NLK | Metroline | Y338FJN | Stagecoach |
| X664LLX | Metroline | Y161NLK | Metroline | Y247FJN | Stagecoach | Y339FJN | Stagecoach |
| X665LLX | Metroline | Y162NLK | Metroline | Y248FJN | Stagecoach | Y342FJN | Stagecoach |
| X688HLF | First London | Y163NLK | Metroline | Y248NLK | Metroline | Y343FJN | Stagecoach |
| X689HLF | First London | Y164NLK | Metroline | Y249FJN | Stagecoach | Y344FJN | Stagecoach |
| X697HLF | First London | Y165NLK | Metroline | Y249NLK | Metroline | Y346FJN | Stagecoach |
| X698HLF | First London | Y166NLK | Metroline | Y251FJN | Stagecoach | Y347FJN | Stagecoach |
| X699EGK | Go-Ahead London | Y167NLK | Metroline | Y252FJN | Stagecoach | Y348FJN | Stagecoach |
| X699HLF | First London | Y168NLK | Metroline | Y252NLK | Metroline | Y348HMY | Metrobus |
| X702EGK | Go-Ahead London | Y169NLK | Metroline | Y253FJN | Stagecoach | Y349FJN | Stagecoach |
| X705EGK | Go-Ahead London | Y171NLK | Metroline | Y258NLK | Metroline | Y351FJN | Stagecoach |
| X707EGK | Go-Ahead London | Y172NLK | Metroline | Y261NLK | Metroline | Y351HMY | Metrobus |
| X731HLF | First London | Y173NLK | Metroline | Y262FJN | Stagecoach | Y352HMY | Metrobus |
| X733HLF | First London | Y174NLK | Metroline | Y262NLK | Metroline | Y353FJN | Stagecoach |
| X734HLF | First London | Y176NLK | Metroline | Y263NLK | Metroline | Y356FJN | Stagecoach |
| X738HLF | First London | Y177NLK | Metroline | Y264NLK | Metroline | Y356HMY | Metrobus |
| X742HLF | First London | Y178NLK | Metroline | Y265FJN | Stagecoach | Y359HMY | Metrobus |
| X743HLF | First London | Y179NLK | Metroline | Y265NLK | Metroline | Y359NHK | Stagecoach |
| X744HLF | First London | Y181NLK | Metroline | Y267FJN | Stagecoach | Y361HMY | Metrobus |
| X745EGK | Go-Ahead London | Y182NLK | Metroline | Y268FJN | Stagecoach | Y361NHK | Stagecoach |
| X745HLF | First London | Y183NLK | Metroline | Y269FJN | Stagecoach | Y362HMY | Metrobus |
| X746JLO | First London | Y184NLK | Metroline | Y271FJN | Stagecoach | Y362NHK | Stagecoach |
| X747JLO | First London | Y185NLK | Metroline | Y272FJN | Stagecoach | Y363HMY | Metrobus |
| X748JLO | First London | Y186NLK | Metroline | Y273FJN | Stagecoach | Y363NHK | Stagecoach |
| X763HLR | First London | Y187NLK | Metroline | Y277FJN | Stagecoach | Y364HMY | Metrobus |
| X764HLR | First London | Y188NLK | Metroline | Y279FJN | Stagecoach | Y364NHK | Stagecoach |
| X766HLR | First London | Y189NLK | Metroline | Y281FJN | Stagecoach | Y365HMY | Metrobus |
| X767HLR | First London | Y191NLK | Metroline | Y282FJN | Stagecoach | Y366HMY | Metrobus |
| X768HLR | First London | Y192NLK | Metroline | Y283FJN | Stagecoach | Y366NHK | Stagecoach |
| X769HLR | First London | Y193NLK | Metroline | Y284FJN | Stagecoach | Y367HMY | Metrobus |
| X771HLR | First London | Y194NLK | Metroline | Y285FJN | Stagecoach | Y367NHK | Stagecoach |
| X772HLR | First London | Y195NLK | Metroline | Y286FJN | Stagecoach | Y367NHK | Stagecoach |
| X773HLR | First London | Y196NLK | Metroline | Y287FJN | Stagecoach | Y368HMY | Metrobus |
| X774HLR | First London | Y197NLK | Metroline | Y289FJN | Stagecoach | Y368NHK | Stagecoach |
| X776HLR | First London | Y198NLK | Metroline | Y291FJN | Stagecoach | Y368NHK | Stagecoach |
| X778HLR | First London | Y199NLK | Metroline | Y291TKJ | Arriva Southern C | Y369HMY | Metrobus |
| X779HLR | First London | Y201NLK | Metroline | Y292FJN | Stagecoach | Y371HMY | Metrobus |
| X785HLR | First London | Y202NLK | Metroline | Y292TKJ | Arriva Southern C | Y371NHK | Stagecoach |
| X967HLT | First London | Y203NLK | Metroline | Y293FJN | Stagecoach | Y372FJN | Stagecoach |
| X968HLT | First London | Y204NLK | Metroline | Y293TKJ | Arriva Southern C | Y372HMY | Metrobus |
| XDZ5917 | London Sovereign | Y207NLK | Metroline | Y294FJN | Stagecoach | Y372NHK | Stagecoach |

Richmond Bridge is the location for this view of Abellio 8535, YX10FEO, one of twenty-three Enviro 200-bodied Darts from the 2010 intake allocated to Twickenham. *Mark Lyons*

| | | | | | | | |
|---|---|---|---|---|---|---|---|
| Y373FJN | Stagecoach | Y409NHK | Stagecoach | Y468UGC | Arriva Southern C | Y502UGC | Arriva London |
| Y373HMY | Metrobus | Y429NHK | Stagecoach | Y469UGC | Arriva Southern C | Y503UGC | Arriva London |
| Y373NHK | Stagecoach | Y434NHK | Stagecoach | Y471UGC | Arriva London | Y504UGC | Arriva London |
| Y374FJN | Stagecoach | Y436NHK | Stagecoach | Y473UGC | Arriva London | Y506UGC | Arriva London |
| Y374HMY | Metrobus | Y437NHK | Stagecoach | Y474UGC | Arriva London | Y507UGC | Arriva London |
| Y374NHK | Stagecoach | Y438NHK | Stagecoach | Y475UGC | Arriva London | Y508NHK | Stagecoach |
| Y376FJN | Stagecoach | Y441NHK | Stagecoach | Y476UGC | Arriva London | Y508UGC | Arriva London |
| Y376HMY | Metrobus | Y442NHK | Stagecoach | Y477UGC | Arriva London | Y509NHK | Stagecoach |
| Y376NHK | Stagecoach | Y443NHK | Stagecoach | Y478UGC | Arriva London | Y509UGC | Arriva London |
| Y377HMY | Metrobus | Y445NHK | Stagecoach | Y479UGC | Arriva London | Y511NHK | Stagecoach |
| Y377NHK | Stagecoach | Y446NHK | Stagecoach | Y481UGC | Arriva London | Y511UGC | Arriva London |
| Y378HMY | Metrobus | Y447NHK | Stagecoach | Y482UGC | Arriva London | Y512NHK | Stagecoach |
| Y378NHK | Stagecoach | Y448NHK | Stagecoach | Y483UGC | Arriva London | Y512UGC | Arriva London |
| Y379HMY | Metrobus | Y449NHK | Stagecoach | Y484UGC | Arriva London | Y513UGC | Arriva London |
| Y379NHK | Stagecoach | Y451UGC | Arriva Southern C | Y485UGC | Arriva London | Y514NHK | Stagecoach |
| Y381NHK | Stagecoach | Y452NHK | Stagecoach | Y486UGC | Arriva London | Y514UGC | Arriva London |
| Y382NHK | Stagecoach | Y452UGC | Arriva London | Y487UGC | Arriva London | Y516UGC | Arriva London |
| Y384NHK | Stagecoach | Y453NHK | Stagecoach | Y488UGC | Arriva London | Y517NHK | Stagecoach |
| Y385NHK | Stagecoach | Y454NHK | Stagecoach | Y489UGC | Arriva London | Y517UGC | Arriva London |
| Y386NHK | Stagecoach | Y458NHK | Stagecoach | Y491UGC | Arriva London | Y518UGC | Arriva London |
| Y388NHK | Stagecoach | Y461UGC | Arriva Southern C | Y492UGC | Arriva London | Y519UGC | Arriva London |
| Y389NHK | Stagecoach | Y462NHK | Stagecoach | Y493UGC | Arriva London | Y521UGC | Arriva The Shires |
| Y391NHK | Stagecoach | Y462UGC | Arriva Southern C | Y494UGC | Arriva London | Y522NHK | Stagecoach |
| Y392NHK | Stagecoach | Y463UGC | Arriva Southern C | Y495UGC | Arriva London | Y522UGC | Arriva London |
| Y393NHK | Stagecoach | Y464NHK | Stagecoach | Y496UGC | Arriva London | Y523UGC | Arriva London |
| Y395NHK | Stagecoach | Y464UGC | Arriva Southern C | Y497UGC | Arriva London | Y524NHK | Stagecoach |
| Y401NHK | Stagecoach | Y465UGC | Arriva Southern C | Y498UGC | Arriva London | Y524UGC | Arriva London |
| Y404NHK | Stagecoach | Y466UGC | Arriva Southern C | Y499UGC | Arriva London | Y526NHK | Stagecoach |
| Y407NHK | Stagecoach | Y467UGC | Arriva Southern C | Y501UGC | Arriva London | Y526UGC | Arriva London |

| Reg | Operator | Reg | Operator | Reg | Operator | Reg | Operator |
|---|---|---|---|---|---|---|---|
| Y527NHK | Stagecoach | Y732TGH | Go-Ahead London | Y907TGH | Go-Ahead London | YJ06LFK | Arriva The Shires |
| Y527UGC | Arriva London | Y733TGH | Go-Ahead London | Y908TGH | Go-Ahead London | YJ06LFL | Arriva The Shires |
| Y529NHK | Stagecoach | Y734TGH | Go-Ahead London | Y909TGH | Go-Ahead London | YJ06YRP | Arriva The Shires |
| Y529UGC | Arriva London | Y735TGH | Go-Ahead London | Y967TGH | Go-Ahead London | YJ06YRR | Arriva The Shires |
| Y531NHK | Stagecoach | Y736TGH | Go-Ahead London | Y968TGH | Go-Ahead London | YJ06YRS | Arriva The Shires |
| Y531UGC | Arriva The Shires | Y737TGH | Go-Ahead London | Y969TGH | Go-Ahead London | YJ06YRT | Arriva The Shires |
| Y532UGC | Arriva London | Y738TGH | Go-Ahead London | Y971TGH | Go-Ahead London | YJ06YRU | Arriva The Shires |
| Y533UGC | Arriva London | Y739TGH | Go-Ahead London | Y972TGH | Go-Ahead London | YJ08XDH | Hackney CT |
| Y534XAG | London Sovereign | Y741TGH | Go-Ahead London | Y973TGH | Go-Ahead London | YJ09EYT | London United |
| Y536XAG | London Sovereign | Y742TGH | Go-Ahead London | Y974TGH | Go-Ahead London | YJ09EYU | London United |
| Y537XAG | London United | Y743TGH | Go-Ahead London | Y975TGH | Go-Ahead London | YJ09EYV | London United |
| Y538XAG | London United | Y744TGH | Go-Ahead London | Y976TGH | Go-Ahead London | YJ09EYW | London United |
| Y539XAG | London United | Y745TGH | Go-Ahead London | Y978TGH | Go-Ahead London | YJ09EYX | London United |
| Y541UGC | Arriva London | Y746TGH | Go-Ahead London | Y979TGH | Go-Ahead London | YJ09EYY | London United |
| Y541XAG | London United | Y747TGH | Go-Ahead London | Y981TGH | Go-Ahead London | YJ09EYZ | London United |
| Y542UGC | Arriva London | Y748TGH | Go-Ahead London | Y982TGH | Go-Ahead London | YJ09EZA | London United |
| Y542XAG | London United | Y749TGH | Go-Ahead London | Y983TGH | Go-Ahead London | YJ09EZB | London United |
| Y543UGC | Arriva London | Y801DGT | Arriva London | Y984TGH | Go-Ahead London | YJ09EZC | London United |
| Y543XAG | London Sovereign | Y801TGH | Go-Ahead London | Y985TGH | Go-Ahead London | YJ09EZD | London United |
| Y544UGC | Arriva London | Y802DGT | Arriva London | Y986TGH | Go-Ahead London | YJ09EZE | London United |
| Y544XAG | London Sovereign | Y802TGH | Go-Ahead London | Y987TGH | Go-Ahead London | YJ09EZF | London United |
| Y546UGC | Arriva London | Y803DGT | Arriva London | Y988TGH | Go-Ahead London | YJ09MHK | Quality Line |
| Y546XAG | London Sovereign | Y803TGH | Go-Ahead London | Y989TGH | Go-Ahead London | YJ09MHL | Quality Line |
| Y547UGC | Arriva London | Y804DGT | Arriva London | YE06HNT | Arriva The Shires | YJ09MHM | Quality Line |
| Y547XAG | London Sovereign | Y805DGT | Arriva London | YE06HNU | Arriva The Shires | YJ09MHN | Quality Line |
| Y548UGC | Arriva London | Y805TGH | Go-Ahead London | YE06HPA | Arriva The Shires | YJ09MHO | Quality Line |
| Y548XAG | London Sovereign | Y806DGT | Arriva London | YE06HPC | Arriva The Shires | YJ09MHU | Quality Line |
| Y549UGC | Arriva London | Y808TGH | Go-Ahead London | YE06HPF | Arriva The Shires | YJ09MHV | Quality Line |
| Y549XAG | London United | Y809TGH | Go-Ahead London | YE06HPJ | Arriva The Shires | YJ09MHX | Quality Line |
| Y551XAG | London United | Y811TGH | Go-Ahead London | YE06HPK | Arriva The Shires | YJ10EYF | Hackney CT |
| Y552XAG | London United | Y812TGH | Go-Ahead London | YE06HPL | Arriva The Shires | YJ10EYG | Hackney CT |
| Y553XAG | London United | Y813TGH | Go-Ahead London | YE06HPN | Arriva The Shires | YJ10EYH | Hackney CT |
| Y554XAG | London United | Y814TGH | Go-Ahead London | YE06HPO | Arriva The Shires | YJ10EYK | Hackney CT |
| Y556XAG | London United | Y815TGH | Go-Ahead London | YE06HPP | Arriva The Shires | YJ10EYL | Hackney CT |
| Y557XAG | London United | Y816TGH | Go-Ahead London | YE06HPU | Arriva The Shires | YJ11EHG | London United |
| Y652NLO | Metroline | Y817TGH | Go-Ahead London | YE06HPX | Arriva Southern C | YJ11EHH | London United |
| Y653NLO | Metroline | Y818TGH | Go-Ahead London | YE06HPY | Arriva Southern C | YJ11EHK | London United |
| Y654NLO | Metroline | Y819TGH | Go-Ahead London | YE06HPZ | Arriva Southern C | YJ11EHL | London United |
| Y656NLO | Metroline | Y821TGH | Go-Ahead London | YE06HRA | Arriva The Shires | YJ11EHM | London United |
| Y657NLO | Metroline | Y822TGH | Go-Ahead London | YE06HRC | Arriva The Shires | YJ11EHN | London United |
| Y658NLO | Metroline | Y823TGH | Go-Ahead London | YE06HRD | Arriva The Shires | YJ11EHO | London United |
| Y659NLO | Metroline | Y824TGH | Go-Ahead London | YE06HRF | Arriva The Shires | YJ11EHP | London United |
| Y661NLO | Metroline | Y825TGH | Go-Ahead London | YE06HRG | Arriva The Shires | YJ11EHR | London United |
| Y662NLO | Metroline | Y826TGH | Go-Ahead London | YE06HRJ | Arriva The Shires | YJ11EHS | London United |
| Y663NLO | Metroline | Y827TGH | Go-Ahead London | YE52FGU | Quality Line | YJ11EHT | London United |
| Y664NLO | Metroline | Y828TGH | Go-Ahead London | YE52FHH | Quality Line | YJ11EHU | London United |
| Y665NLO | Metroline | Y829TGH | Go-Ahead London | YE52FHJ | Quality Line | YJ11EHV | London United |
| Y667NLO | Metroline | Y831TGH | Go-Ahead London | YE52FHK | Quality Line | YJ11EHW | London United |
| Y668NLO | Metroline | Y832TGH | Go-Ahead London | YE52FHL | Quality Line | YJ11EHX | London United |
| Y669NLO | Metroline | Y833TGH | Go-Ahead London | YE52FHM | Quality Line | YJ11EHZ | London United |
| Y671JSG | Stagecoach | Y842TGH | Go-Ahead London | YE52FHN | Quality Line | YJ11PFA | Hackney CT |
| Y671NLO | Metroline | Y843TGH | Go-Ahead London | YE52FHO | Quality Line | YJ11PFD | Hackney CT |
| Y672NLO | Metroline | Y844TGH | Go-Ahead London | YE52FHP | Quality Line | YJ11PFE | Hackney CT |
| Y673NLO | Metroline | Y845TGH | Go-Ahead London | YE52FHR | Quality Line | YJ11PFF | Hackney CT |
| Y674NLO | Metroline | Y846TGH | Go-Ahead London | YE52FHS | Quality Line | YJ11PFG | Hackney CT |
| Y675NLO | Metroline | Y847TGH | Go-Ahead London | YJ06LDK | Arriva The Shires | YJ11PFK | Hackney CT |
| Y703TGH | Go-Ahead London | Y848TGH | Go-Ahead London | YJ06LFE | Arriva The Shires | YJ11PFN | Hackney CT |
| Y704TGH | Go-Ahead London | Y849TGH | Go-Ahead London | YJ06LFF | Arriva The Shires | YJ11PFO | Hackney CT |
| Y729TGH | Go-Ahead London | Y851TGH | Go-Ahead London | YJ06LFG | Arriva The Shires | YJ54CFG | Arriva The Shires |
| Y731TGH | Go-Ahead London | Y864KTF | Abellio | YJ06LFH | Arriva The Shires | YJ55WOA | Arriva The Shires |

*The London Bus Handbook*

**Starting to enter service as we go to press are the first of sixteen Optare Tempo buses for London United. Seen on route H37 is OT5, YJ11EHM. All are allocated to Hounslow.** *Mark Lyons*

| | | | | | | | |
|---|---|---|---|---|---|---|---|
| YJ55WOB | Arriva The Shires | YJ58VBT | London United | YM55SXH | Metrobus | YN05HCC | Metrobus |
| YJ55WOC | Arriva The Shires | YJ58VBU | London United | YM55SXO | Metrobus | YN05HCD | Metrobus |
| YJ55WOD | Arriva The Shires | YJ58VBV | London United | YM55SXP | Metrobus | YN05HCE | Metrobus |
| YJ55WOH | Arriva The Shires | YJ58VBX | London United | YM55SXR | Metrobus | YN05HCF | Metrobus |
| YJ55WOM | Arriva The Shires | YJ58VBY | London United | YN03DFA | Metrobus | YN05HCG | Metrobus |
| YJ55WOR | Arriva The Shires | YJ58VBZ | London United | YN03DFC | Metrobus | YN05HFE | Metrobus |
| YJ55WOU | Arriva The Shires | YJ59NRN | Hackney CT | YN03DFD | Metrobus | YN05HFF | Metrobus |
| YJ55WOV | Arriva The Shires | YJ59NRO | Hackney CT | YN03DFE | Metrobus | YN05HFG | Metrobus |
| YJ55WOX | Arriva The Shires | YJ60GGE | Arriva Southern C | YN03DFG | Metrobus | YN05HFH | Metrobus |
| YJ55WPO | Arriva The Shires | YJ60KGA | Quality Line | YN03DFJ | Metrobus | YN05HFJ | Metrobus |
| YJ56WVF | Metrobus | YJ60KGE | Quality Line | YN03DFK | Metrobus | YN06JXR | Metrobus |
| YJ56WVG | Metrobus | YJ60KGF | Quality Line | YN03DFL | Metrobus | YN06JXS | Metrobus |
| YJ58PHY | London United | YJ60KGG | Quality Line | YN03DFP | Metrobus | YN06JXT | Metrobus |
| YJ58PHZ | London United | YJ60KGK | Quality Line | YN03DFU | Metrobus | YN06JXU | Metrobus |
| YJ58PJO | London United | YJ60KGN | Quality Line | YN03DFV | Metrobus | YN06JXV | Metrobus |
| YJ58PJU | London United | YJ60KGO | Quality Line | YN03DFX | Metrobus | YN06JXW | Metrobus |
| YJ58VBA | London United | YJ60KGP | Quality Line | YN03DFY | Metrobus | YN06JXX | Metrobus |
| YJ58VBB | London United | YJ60LRX | Hackney CT | YN03UPM | Metrobus | YN06JXY | Metrobus |
| YJ58VBC | London United | YJ60LRY | Hackney CT | YN03UWU | Metrobus | YN06JXZ | Metrobus |
| YJ58VBD | London United | YM55SWU | Metrobus | YN03UWY | Metrobus | YN06JYB | Metrobus |
| YJ58VBE | London United | YM55SWV | Metrobus | YN03WPP | Metrobus | YN06JYC | Metrobus |
| YJ58VBF | London United | YM55SWX | Metrobus | YN03WPR | Metrobus | YN06JYD | Metrobus |
| YJ58VBG | London United | YM55SWY | Metrobus | YN03WRF | Metrobus | YN06JYE | Metrobus |
| YJ58VBK | London United | YM55SXA | Metrobus | YN03WRG | Metrobus | YN06JYF | Metrobus |
| YJ58VBL | London United | YM55SXB | Metrobus | YN03WRJ | Metrobus | YN06JYG | Metrobus |
| YJ58VBM | London United | YM55SXC | Metrobus | YN03WRL | Metrobus | YN06JYH | Metrobus |
| YJ58VBN | London United | YM55SXD | Metrobus | YN03WRP | Metrobus | YN06JYJ | Metrobus |
| YJ58VBO | London United | YM55SXE | Metrobus | YN03ZXF | Quality Line | YN06JYK | Metrobus |
| YJ58VBP | London United | YM55SXF | Metrobus | YN05HCA | Metrobus | YN06JYL | Metrobus |

| Reg | Operator | Reg | Operator | Reg | Operator | Reg | Operator |
|---|---|---|---|---|---|---|---|
| YN06JYO | Metrobus | YN51KVF | Abellio | YN53RYZ | Metrobus | YN55NKG | London Sovereign |
| YN07EXF | Metrobus | YN51KVG | Abellio | YN53RZA | Metrobus | YN55NKH | London Sovereign |
| YN07EXG | Metrobus | YN51KVH | Abellio | YN53RZB | Metrobus | YN55NKJ | London Sovereign |
| YN07EXH | Metrobus | YN51KVJ | Abellio | YN53RZC | Metrobus | YN55NKK | London Sovereign |
| YN07EXK | Metrobus | YN51KVK | Abellio | YN53RZD | Metrobus | YN55NKL | London Sovereign |
| YN07EXM | Metrobus | YN51KVL | Abellio | YN53RZE | Metrobus | YN55NKM | London United |
| YN07EXO | Metrobus | YN51KVM | Abellio | YN53RZF | Metrobus | YN55NKO | London United |
| YN07LKF | Metrobus | YN51KVO | Abellio | YN53SUF | Quality Line | YN55NKP | London United |
| YN07LKG | Metrobus | YN51KVP | Abellio | YN53SVK | Quality Line | YN55NKR | London United |
| YN08DEU | London United | YN51KVR | Abellio | YN53SVL | Quality Line | YN55NKS | London United |
| YN08DFJ | Metrobus | YN51KVS | Abellio | YN53SVO | Quality Line | YN55NKT | London United |
| YN08DFK | Metrobus | YN51KVT | Abellio | YN53SVP | Quality Line | YN55NKU | London United |
| YN08DFL | Metrobus | YN51KVU | Abellio | YN53SVR | Quality Line | YN55NKW | London United |
| YN08DFO | Metrobus | YN51KVV | Abellio | YN53SWF | Quality Line | YN55NKX | London United |
| YN08DFP | Metrobus | YN51KVW | Abellio | YN53USG | Metrobus | YN55NKZ | London United |
| YN08DFU | Metrobus | YN51KVX | Abellio | YN53ZXA | Quality Line | YN55NLA | London United |
| YN08DFV | Metrobus | YN51KVZ | Abellio | YN53ZXB | Quality Line | YN55NLC | London United |
| YN08DFX | Metrobus | YN51KWA | Abellio | YN54AJU | Metrobus | YN55NLD | London United |
| YN08DFY | Metrobus | YN51KWB | Abellio | YN54AJV | Metrobus | YN55NLE | London United |
| YN08DFZ | Metrobus | YN51KWC | Abellio | YN54AJX | Metrobus | YN55NLG | London United |
| YN08DHA | London United | YN51KWD | Abellio | YN54AJY | Metrobus | YN55NLJ | London United |
| YN08DHC | London United | YN51KWE | Abellio | YN54LKU | Hackney CT | YN55NLK | London United |
| YN08DHD | London United | YN51KWF | Abellio | YN54LLA | Hackney CT | YN55NLL | London United |
| YN08DHE | London United | YN51KWG | Abellio | YN54OAA | London Sovereign | YN55NLM | London United |
| YN08DHF | London United | YN53ENE | Hackney CT | YN54OAB | London Sovereign | YN55NLO | London United |
| YN08DHG | London United | YN53ENF | Hackney CT | YN54OAC | London Sovereign | YN55NLP | London United |
| YN08DHJ | London United | YN53ENH | Hackney CT | YN54OAE | London Sovereign | YN55NLR | London United |
| YN08DHK | London United | YN53ENM | Hackney CT | YN54OAG | London Sovereign | YN55PWJ | Metrobus |
| YN08DHL | London United | YN53RXF | Metrobus | YN54OAH | London Sovereign | YN55PWK | Metrobus |
| YN08DHM | London United | YN53RXG | Metrobus | YN55NHA | London United | YN55PWL | Metrobus |
| YN08DHO | London United | YN53RXH | Metrobus | YN55NHB | London United | YN55PWO | Metrobus |
| YN08DHP | London United | YN53RXJ | Metrobus | YN55NHC | London United | YN55PWU | Metrobus |
| YN08DHU | London United | YN53RXK | Metrobus | YN55NHD | London United | YN55PWV | Metrobus |
| YN08DHV | London United | YN53RXL | Metrobus | YN55NHE | London United | YN55PWX | Metrobus |
| YN08DHX | London United | YN53RXM | Metrobus | YN55NHF | London United | YN55PZC | Metrobus |
| YN08DHY | London United | YN53RXO | Metrobus | YN55NHG | London United | YN55PZD | Metrobus |
| YN08DHZ | London United | YN53RXP | Metrobus | YN55NHH | London United | YN55PZE | Metrobus |
| YN08DMY | Go-Ahead London | YN53RXR | Metrobus | YN55NHJ | London United | YN55PZF | Metrobus |
| YN08MRU | London United | YN53RXT | Metrobus | YN55NHK | London United | YN55PZG | Metrobus |
| YN08MRV | London United | YN53RXU | Metrobus | YN55NHL | London United | YN55PZH | Metrobus |
| YN08MRX | London United | YN53RXV | Metrobus | YN55NHM | London United | YN55PZJ | Metrobus |
| YN08MRY | London United | YN53RXW | Metrobus | YN55NHO | London United | YN55PZL | Metrobus |
| YN08OAS | Metrobus | YN53RXX | Metrobus | YN55NHP | London United | YN55PZM | Metrobus |
| YN08OAU | Metrobus | YN53RXY | Metrobus | YN55NHT | London Sovereign | YN55PZO | Metrobus |
| YN08OAV | Metrobus | YN53RXZ | Metrobus | YN55NHU | London Sovereign | YN55PZP | Metrobus |
| YN08OAW | Metrobus | YN53RYA | Metrobus | YN55NHV | London Sovereign | YN55PZR | Metrobus |
| YN08OAX | Metrobus | YN53RYB | Metrobus | YN55NHX | London Sovereign | YN55PZU | Metrobus |
| YN08OAY | Metrobus | YN53RYC | Metrobus | YN55NHY | London Sovereign | YN55PZV | Metrobus |
| YN08OAZ | Metrobus | YN53RYD | Metrobus | YN55NHZ | London Sovereign | YN55PZW | Metrobus |
| YN08OBP | Metrobus | YN53RYF | Metrobus | YN55NJE | London Sovereign | YN55PZX | Metrobus |
| YN08OBR | Metrobus | YN53RYH | Metrobus | YN55NJF | London Sovereign | YN56FBA | London United |
| YN51KUU | Abellio | YN53RYK | Metrobus | YN55NJJ | London Sovereign | YN56FBB | London United |
| YN51KUV | Abellio | YN53RYM | Metrobus | YN55NJK | London Sovereign | YN56FBO | London United |
| YN51KUW | Abellio | YN53RYP | Metrobus | YN55NJU | London Sovereign | YN56FBU | London United |
| YN51KUX | Abellio | YN53RYR | Metrobus | YN55NJV | London Sovereign | YN56FBV | London United |
| YN51KUY | Abellio | YN53RYT | Metrobus | YN55NKA | London Sovereign | YN56FBX | London United |
| YN51KVA | Abellio | YN53RYV | Metrobus | YN55NKC | London Sovereign | YN56FBY | London United |
| YN51KVC | Abellio | YN53RYW | Metrobus | YN55NKD | London Sovereign | YN56FBZ | London United |
| YN51KVD | Abellio | YN53RYX | Metrobus | YN55NKE | London Sovereign | YN56FCA | London United |
| YN51KVE | Abellio | YN53RYY | Metrobus | YN55NKF | London Sovereign | YN56FCC | London United |

| Reg | Operator | Reg | Operator | Reg | Operator | Reg | Operator |
|---|---|---|---|---|---|---|---|
| YN56FCD | London United | YR10BCE | Metrobus | YT09BKA | London United | YT10XCM | London United |
| YN56FCE | London United | YR10BCF | Metrobus | YT09BKD | Metrobus | YT10XCN | London United |
| YN56FCF | London United | YR10BCK | Metrobus | YT09BKE | Metrobus | YT10XCO | London United |
| YN56FCG | London United | YR10BCO | Metrobus | YT09BKF | Metrobus | YT51EAX | Abellio |
| YN56FCJ | London United | YR10BCU | Metrobus | YT09BKG | Metrobus | YT51EBA | Abellio |
| YN56FDA | Metrobus | YR10FFW | London United | YT09BKJ | Metrobus | YT51EBG | Abellio |
| YN56FDC | Metrobus | YR10FFX | London United | YT09BKK | Metrobus | YT59BPU | London United |
| YN56FDD | Metrobus | YR10FFY | London United | YT09BKL | Metrobus | YT59DXY | London United |
| YN56FDE | Metrobus | YR10FFZ | London United | YT09BKN | Metrobus | YT59DXZ | London United |
| YN56FDF | Metrobus | YR10FGA | London United | YT09BKO | Metrobus | YT59DYA | Metrobus |
| YN56FDG | Metrobus | YR10FGC | London United | YT09BKU | Metrobus | YT59DYB | Metrobus |
| YN56FDJ | Metrobus | YR10FGD | London United | YT09BKV | Metrobus | YT59DYC | Metrobus |
| YN56FDK | Metrobus | YR10FGE | London United | YT09BKX | Metrobus | YT59DYD | Metrobus |
| YN56FDL | Metrobus | YR10FGF | London United | YT09BKY | Metrobus | YT59DYF | Metrobus |
| YN56FDM | Metrobus | YR10FGG | London United | YT09BKZ | Metrobus | YT59DYG | Metrobus |
| YN56FDO | Metrobus | YR10FGJ | London United | YT09BMO | London United | YT59DYH | Metrobus |
| YN56FDP | Metrobus | YR10FGK | London United | YT09BMU | London United | YT59DYJ | Metrobus |
| YN56FDU | Metrobus | YR10FGM | London United | YT09BMY | London United | YT59DYM | Metrobus |
| YN56FDV | Metrobus | YR10FGN | London United | YT09BMZ | London United | YT59DYN | Metrobus |
| YN56FDX | Metrobus | YR10FGO | London United | YT09BNA | London United | YT59DYO | Metrobus |
| YN56FDY | Metrobus | YR10FGP | London United | YT09BNB | London United | YT59DYP | Metrobus |
| YN56FDZ | Metrobus | YR52VFH | Go-Ahead London | YT09BND | London United | YT59DYS | Metrobus |
| YN56FEF | Metrobus | YR52VFJ | Go-Ahead London | YT09BNE | London United | YT59DYU | Metrobus |
| YN56FEG | Metrobus | YR52VFK | Go-Ahead London | YT09BNF | London United | YT59DYV | Metrobus |
| YP02LCC | Abellio | YR52VFL | Go-Ahead London | YT09BNJ | London United | YT59DYW | Metrobus |
| YP02LCF | Abellio | YR52VFM | Go-Ahead London | YT09BNK | London United | YT59DYX | London United |
| YP52CTO | Metrobus | YR52VFN | Go-Ahead London | YT09BNL | London United | YT59DYY | London United |
| YP58ACF | London United | YR58SNY | Metrobus | YT09BNN | London United | YT59PBF | London United |
| YP58ACJ | London United | YR58SNZ | Metrobus | YT09ZCA | London United | YT59PBO | London United |
| YP58ACO | London United | YR59FYO | London United | YT09ZCE | London United | YT59PBV | London United |
| YP58UFV | Metrobus | YR59FYP | London United | YT09ZCF | London United | YT59PBX | London United |
| YP59ODS | London United | YR59FYS | London United | YT09ZCJ | London United | YT59PBY | London United |
| YP59ODT | London United | YR59FYT | London United | YT09ZCK | London United | YT59PBZ | London United |
| YP59ODU | London United | YR59FYU | London United | YT09ZCL | London United | YT59PCF | London United |
| YP59ODV | London United | YR59FYV | London United | YT09ZCN | London United | YT59PCO | London United |
| YP59ODW | London United | YR59FYW | London United | YT09ZCO | London United | YT59PCU | London United |
| YP59ODX | London United | YR59FYX | London United | YT09ZCU | London United | YT59RXR | London Sovereign |
| YP59OEA | London United | YR59FYY | London United | YT10UWA | London United | YT59RXS | London Sovereign |
| YP59OEB | London United | YR59FYZ | London United | YT10UWB | London United | YT59RXU | London Sovereign |
| YP59OEC | London United | YR59FZA | London United | YT10UWD | London United | YT59RXV | London Sovereign |
| YP59OED | London United | YR59FZB | London United | YT10UWF | London United | YT59RXW | London Sovereign |
| YP59OEE | London United | YR59FZC | London United | YT10UWG | London United | YT59RXX | London Sovereign |
| YP59OEF | London United | YR59FZD | London United | YT10UWH | London United | YT59RXY | London Sovereign |
| YP59OEG | London United | YR59FZE | London United | YT10XBU | London United | YT59RXZ | London Sovereign |
| YP59OEH | London United | YR59FZF | London United | YT10XBV | London United | YT59RYA | London Sovereign |
| YP59OEJ | London United | YR59FZG | London United | YT10XBW | London United | YT59RYB | London Sovereign |
| YP59OEK | London United | YR59NPA | Hackney CT | YT10XBX | London United | YT59RYC | London Sovereign |
| YP59OEL | London United | YR59NPC | Hackney CT | YT10XBY | London United | YT59RYD | London Sovereign |
| YP59OEM | London United | YR59NPD | Hackney CT | YT10XBZ | London United | YT59RYF | London Sovereign |
| YP59OEN | London United | YR59NPE | Hackney CT | YT10XCA | London United | YT59RYG | London Sovereign |
| YP59OEO | London United | YR59NPF | Hackney CT | YT10XCB | London United | YT59RYH | London Sovereign |
| YP59OER | London United | YR59NPG | Hackney CT | YT10XCC | London United | YT59RYJ | London Sovereign |
| YP59OES | London United | YR59NPJ | Hackney CT | YT10XCD | London United | YT59RYK | London Sovereign |
| YP59OET | London United | YR59NPK | Hackney CT | YT10XCE | London United | YT59RYM | London Sovereign |
| YP59OEU | London United | YR59NPN | Hackney CT | YT10XCF | London United | YT59RYN | London Sovereign |
| YP59OEV | London United | YR59NPO | Hackney CT | YT10XCG | London United | YT59RYO | London Sovereign |
| YP59OEW | London United | YT09BJU | London United | YT10XCH | London United | YT59SFF | London United |
| YP59OEX | London United | YT09BJV | London United | YT10XCJ | London United | YT59SFK | London United |
| YP59OEY | London United | YT09BJX | London United | YT10XCK | London United | YT59SFN | London United |
| YP59OEZ | London United | YT09BJY | London United | YT10XCL | London United | YT59SFO | London United |

| Reg | Operator | Reg | Operator | Reg | Operator | Reg | Operator |
|---|---|---|---|---|---|---|---|
| YT59SFU | London United | YX08GVV | Dial-a-Ride | YX09ETO | Dial-a-Ride | YX09FMU | First London |
| YT59SFV | London United | YX08GVW | Dial-a-Ride | YX09ETR | Dial-a-Ride | YX09FMV | First London |
| YT59SFX | London United | YX08GVY | Dial-a-Ride | YX09ETU | Dial-a-Ride | YX09FNJ | First London |
| YT59SFY | London United | YX08GVZ | Dial-a-Ride | YX09ETV | Dial-a-Ride | YX09FNK | First London |
| YT59SFZ | London United | YX08GWA | Dial-a-Ride | YX09ETY | Dial-a-Ride | YX09HJJ | London United |
| YT59SG0 | London United | YX08GWC | Dial-a-Ride | YX09ETZ | Dial-a-Ride | YX09HJK | London United |
| YT59SGU | London United | YX08GWF | Dial-a-Ride | YX09EUA | Dial-a-Ride | YX09HJN | London United |
| YT59SGV | London United | YX08GWG | Dial-a-Ride | YX09EUB | Dial-a-Ride | YX09HJO | London United |
| YT59SGX | London United | YX08KXJ | Dial-a-Ride | YX09EUC | Dial-a-Ride | YX09HJU | London United |
| YT59SGY | London United | YX08KXK | Dial-a-Ride | YX09EUF | Dial-a-Ride | YX09HJV | London United |
| YT59SGZ | London United | YX08KXL | Dial-a-Ride | YX09EUH | Dial-a-Ride | YX09HJY | London United |
| YT59SHJ | London United | YX08KXM | Dial-a-Ride | YX09EUJ | Dial-a-Ride | YX09HJZ | London United |
| YT59SHV | London United | YX08KXN | Dial-a-Ride | YX09EUK | Dial-a-Ride | YX09HKA | London United |
| YU02GHA | Go-Ahead London | YX08KXP | Dial-a-Ride | YX09EUL | Dial-a-Ride | YX09HKB | London United |
| YU02GHD | Go-Ahead London | YX08KXR | Dial-a-Ride | YX09EUP | Dial-a-Ride | YX09HKC | London United |
| YU02GHG | Go-Ahead London | YX08KXT | Dial-a-Ride | YX09EUR | Dial-a-Ride | YX09HKD | London United |
| YU02GHH | Go-Ahead London | YX08KXW | Dial-a-Ride | YX09EUT | Dial-a-Ride | YX09HKE | London United |
| YU02GHJ | Go-Ahead London | YX08MDV | London United | YX09EUW | Dial-a-Ride | YX09HKH | London United |
| YU02GHK | Go-Ahead London | YX08MDY | London United | YX09EUY | Dial-a-Ride | YX09HKJ | London United |
| YU02GHN | Go-Ahead London | YX08MDZ | London United | YX09EUZ | Dial-a-Ride | YX09HKK | London United |
| YU02GHO | Go-Ahead London | YX08MEU | London United | YX09EVB | Dial-a-Ride | YX09HKL | London United |
| YU52XVK | Metrobus | YX08MEV | London United | YX09EVC | Dial-a-Ride | YX09HKM | London United |
| YU52XVR | Metrobus | YX08MFA | London United | YX09EVF | Dial-a-Ride | YX09HKN | London United |
| YV03PZE | Metrobus | YX08MFK | London United | YX09EVK | Dial-a-Ride | YX09HKO | London United |
| YV03PZF | Metrobus | YX08MFN | London United | YX09FKS | First London | YX09HKP | London United |
| YV03PZG | Metrobus | YX08MFO | London United | YX09FKT | First London | YX09HKR | London United |
| YV03PZH | Metrobus | YX08MHM | London United | YX09FKU | First London | YX09HKT | London United |
| YV03PZJ | Metrobus | YX09AEA | First London | YX09FKV | First London | YX09HKT | London United |
| YV03PZK | Metrobus | YX09AEB | First London | YX09FKW | First London | YX09HKU | London United |
| YV03PZL | Metrobus | YX09AEC | First London | YX09FKY | First London | YX09HKV | London United |
| YV03PZM | Metrobus | YX09AED | First London | YX09FLA | First London | YX09HKZ | London United |
| YV03PZW | Metrobus | YX09AEE | First London | YX09FLB | First London | YX09HLA | London United |
| YV03PZX | Metrobus | YX09AEF | First London | YX09FLC | First London | YX09HRL | Dial-a-Ride |
| YV03PZY | Metrobus | YX09AEG | First London | YX09FLD | First London | YX09HRM | Dial-a-Ride |
| YV03PZZ | Metrobus | YX09AEJ | First London | YX09FLE | First London | YX09HRN | Dial-a-Ride |
| YV03RAU | Metrobus | YX09AEK | First London | YX09FLF | First London | YX09HRO | Dial-a-Ride |
| YV03RAX | Metrobus | YX09AEL | First London | YX09FLG | First London | YX10AYD | Hackney CT |
| YV03RBF | Metrobus | YX09AEM | First London | YX09FLH | First London | YX10AYF | Hackney CT |
| YV03RBU | Metrobus | YX09AEO | First London | YX09FLJ | First London | YX10BCU | First London |
| YV03RBX | Metrobus | YX09AEP | First London | YX09FLK | First London | YX10BCV | First London |
| YV03RCY | Metrobus | YX09AET | First London | YX09FLL | First London | YX10BCY | First London |
| YV03RCZ | Metrobus | YX09AEU | First London | YX09FLM | First London | YX10BCZ | First London |
| YX08FKE | Dial-a-Ride | YX09AEU | First London | YX09FLN | First London | YX10BDE | First London |
| YX08FKF | Dial-a-Ride | YX09AEV | First London | YX09FLP | First London | YX10BDF | First London |
| YX08FKG | Dial-a-Ride | YX09AEW | First London | YX09FLR | First London | YX10BDO | First London |
| YX08FKJ | Dial-a-Ride | YX09AEY | First London | YX09FLV | First London | YX10BDU | First London |
| YX08FKK | Dial-a-Ride | YX09AEZ | First London | YX09FLW | First London | YX10BDV | First London |
| YX08FKL | Dial-a-Ride | YX09AFA | First London | YX09FLZ | First London | YX10BDY | First London |
| YX08FKM | Dial-a-Ride | YX09AFE | First London | YX09FMA | First London | YX10BDZ | First London |
| YX08FKO | Dial-a-Ride | YX09AFF | First London | YX09FMC | First London | YX10BEJ | First London |
| YX08FKP | Dial-a-Ride | YX09AFJ | First London | YX09FMD | First London | YX10BEO | First London |
| YX08FKR | Dial-a-Ride | YX09AFK | First London | YX09FME | First London | YX10BEU | First London |
| YX08FKS | Dial-a-Ride | YX09ESY | Dial-a-Ride | YX09FMF | First London | YX10BEY | First London |
| YX08FKT | Dial-a-Ride | YX09ETA | Dial-a-Ride | YX09FMG | First London | YX10BFA | First London |
| YX08FKU | Dial-a-Ride | YX09ETD | Dial-a-Ride | YX09FMJ | First London | YX10BFE | First London |
| YX08FKV | Dial-a-Ride | YX09ETE | Dial-a-Ride | YX09FMK | First London | YX10BFF | First London |
| YX08FKW | Dial-a-Ride | YX09ETF | Dial-a-Ride | YX09FML | First London | YX10BFJ | First London |
| YX08FKZ | Dial-a-Ride | YX09ETJ | Dial-a-Ride | YX09FMM | First London | YX10BFK | First London |
| YX08GVT | Dial-a-Ride | YX09ETK | Dial-a-Ride | YX09FMO | First London | YX10BFK | First London |
| YX08GVU | Dial-a-Ride | YX09ETL | Dial-a-Ride | YX09FMP | First London | YX10BFM | First London |

*The London Bus Handbook*

| | | | | | | | |
|---|---|---|---|---|---|---|---|
| YX10BFN | First London | YX11AEF | Abellio | YX58DTV | Abellio | YX58EFN | Dial-a-Ride |
| YX10BFO | First London | YX11AEG | Abellio | YX58DTY | Abellio | YX58EFO | Dial-a-Ride |
| YX10BFP | First London | YX11AEJ | Abellio | YX58DTZ | Abellio | YX58EGD | Dial-a-Ride |
| YX10BFU | First London | YX11AEK | Abellio | YX58DUA | First London | YX58EGE | Dial-a-Ride |
| YX10BFV | First London | YX11AEL | Abellio | YX58DUH | First London | YX58EGF | Dial-a-Ride |
| YX10BFY | First London | YX11AEM | Abellio | YX58DUJ | First London | YX58EGJ | Dial-a-Ride |
| YX10BFZ | First London | YX11AEN | Abellio | YX58DUU | First London | YX58EGZ | Dial-a-Ride |
| YX10BGE | First London | YX11AEO | Abellio | YX58DUV | London United | YX58EHB | Dial-a-Ride |
| YX10BGF | First London | YX11AEP | Abellio | YX58DUY | London United | YX58EHG | Dial-a-Ride |
| YX10BGK | First London | YX11AET | Abellio | YX58DVA | London United | YX58EHH | Dial-a-Ride |
| YX10BGO | First London | YX11AEU | First London | YX58DVB | London United | YX58EHJ | Dial-a-Ride |
| YX10BGU | First London | YX11AEV | First London | YX58DVC | London United | YX58EHK | Dial-a-Ride |
| YX10BGV | First London | YX11AEW | First London | YX58DVF | London United | YX58EHL | Dial-a-Ride |
| YX10BGY | First London | YX11AEY | First London | YX58DVG | London United | YX58EHR | Dial-a-Ride |
| YX10EBA | Abellio | YX11AEZ | First London | YX58DVH | London United | YX58FOF | First London |
| YX10EBC | Abellio | YX11AFA | First London | YX58DVJ | London United | YX58FOH | First London |
| YX10EBD | Abellio | YX11AFE | First London | YX58DVK | London United | YX58FOJ | First London |
| YX10EBF | Abellio | YX11AFF | First London | YX58DVL | London United | YX58FOK | First London |
| YX10EBG | Abellio | YX11AFJ | First London | YX58DVM | London United | YX58FOM | First London |
| YX10EBJ | Abellio | YX11AFK | First London | YX58DVN | London United | YX58FON | First London |
| YX10EBK | Abellio | YX11AFN | First London | YX58DVO | London United | YX58FOP | First London |
| YX10EBL | Abellio | YX11AFO | First London | YX58DVP | London United | YX58FOT | First London |
| YX10EBM | Abellio | YX11AFU | First London | YX58DVR | London United | YX58FOU | First London |
| YX10FEF | Abellio | YX11AFV | First London | YX58DVT | London United | YX58FOV | First London |
| YX10FEG | Abellio | YX11AFY | First London | YX58DVU | London United | YX58FPA | First London |
| YX10FEH | Abellio | YX11AFZ | First London | YX58DVV | London United | YX58FPC | First London |
| YX10FEJ | Abellio | YX11AGO | First London | YX58DVW | London United | YX58FPD | First London |
| YX10FEK | Abellio | YX11AHA | Abellio | YX58DVY | First London | YX58FPE | First London |
| YX10FEM | Abellio | YX11AHC | Abellio | YX58DVZ | First London | YX58FPF | First London |
| YX10FEO | Abellio | YX11AHD | Abellio | YX58DWA | First London | YX58FPG | First London |
| YX10FEP | Abellio | YX11AHE | Abellio | YX58DWD | First London | YX58FPJ | First London |
| YX10FET | Abellio | YX11AHF | Abellio | YX58DWE | First London | YX58FPK | First London |
| YX10FEU | Abellio | YX11AHG | Abellio | YX58DWF | First London | YX58FPL | First London |
| YX10FEV | Abellio | YX11AHJ | Abellio | YX58DWG | First London | YX58FPN | First London |
| YX10FFA | Abellio | YX11AHK | Abellio | YX58DWJ | First London | YX58FPO | First London |
| YX10FFB | Abellio | YX11AHL | Abellio | YX58DWK | London United | YX58FPT | First London |
| YX10FFC | Abellio | YX11AHN | Abellio | YX58DWL | First London | YX58FPU | First London |
| YX10FFD | Abellio | YX11AHO | Abellio | YX58DWM | First London | YX58FPV | First London |
| YX10FFE | Abellio | YX11AHP | Abellio | YX58DWN | First London | YX58FPY | First London |
| YX10FFG | Abellio | YX11AHU | Abellio | YX58DWO | First London | YX58FRC | First London |
| YX10FFH | Abellio | YX11CNK | First London | YX58DWP | First London | YX58FRD | First London |
| YX10FFJ | Abellio | YX11CNN | First London | YX58DWU | First London | YX58GSO | Dial-a-Ride |
| YX10FFK | Abellio | YX11CNO | First London | YX58DWV | First London | YX58GSY | Dial-a-Ride |
| YX10FFL | Abellio | YX11CNU | First London | YX58DWY | First London | YX58GSZ | Dial-a-Ride |
| YX10FFM | Abellio | YX11CNV | First London | YX58DWZ | First London | YX58GTF | Dial-a-Ride |
| YX10FFN | Abellio | YX11CNY | First London | YX58DXB | Metrobus | YX58GTU | Dial-a-Ride |
| YX10FFW | Hackney CT | YX11CPE | Go-Ahead London | YX58DXC | Metrobus | YX58GTY | Dial-a-Ride |
| YX10FFY | Dial-a-Ride | YX11CPF | Go-Ahead London | YX58DXD | Metrobus | YX58GTZ | Dial-a-Ride |
| YX10FFZ | Dial-a-Ride | YX11CPK | Go-Ahead London | YX58EET | Dial-a-Ride | YX58HVA | First London |
| YX10FGA | Dial-a-Ride | YX11CPN | Go-Ahead London | YX58EEU | Dial-a-Ride | YX58HVB | First London |
| YX10FGC | Dial-a-Ride | YX11CPO | Go-Ahead London | YX58EEV | Dial-a-Ride | YX58HVC | First London |
| YX10FGD | Dial-a-Ride | YX11CPU | Go-Ahead London | YX58EEW | Dial-a-Ride | YX58HVD | First London |
| YX10FGE | Dial-a-Ride | YX11CPV | Go-Ahead London | YX58EEY | Dial-a-Ride | YX58HVE | First London |
| YX10FGF | Dial-a-Ride | YX11CPY | Go-Ahead London | YX58EEZ | Dial-a-Ride | YX58HVF | First London |
| YX10FGG | Dial-a-Ride | YX11CPZ | Go-Ahead London | YX58EFA | Dial-a-Ride | YX58HVG | First London |
| YX11AEA | Abellio | YX11CVV | Dial-a-Ride | YX58EFC | Dial-a-Ride | YX58HVH | First London |
| YX11AEB | Abellio | YX11CVW | Dial-a-Ride | YX58EFD | Dial-a-Ride | YX58HVJ | First London |
| YX11AEC | Abellio | YX11CVY | Dial-a-Ride | YX58EFE | Dial-a-Ride | YX58HVK | First London |
| YX11AED | Abellio | YX11EVG | Dial-a-Ride | YX58EFE | Dial-a-Ride | YX58HVL | First London |
| YX11AEE | Abellio | YX57HBZ | Dial-a-Ride | YX58EFF | Dial-a-Ride | YX58HVM | First London |

*The London Bus Handbook*

| Reg | Operator | Reg | Operator | Reg | Operator | Reg | Operator |
| --- | --- | --- | --- | --- | --- | --- | --- |
| YX59AAO | Dial-a-Ride | YX60BZE | London Sovereign | YX60DXO | First London | | |
| YX59ABN | Dial-a-Ride | YX60BZF | London Sovereign | YX60DXP | First London | YX60FCO | Go-Ahead London |
| YX59ABU | Dial-a-Ride | YX60BZG | London Sovereign | YX60DXT | Go-Ahead London | YX60FCP | Go-Ahead London |
| YX59ABV | Dial-a-Ride | YX60BZH | London United | YX60DXU | Go-Ahead London | YX60FCU | Go-Ahead London |
| YX59ABZ | Dial-a-Ride | YX60BZJ | London United | YX60DXW | Go-Ahead London | YX60FCV | Go-Ahead London |
| YX59ACF | Dial-a-Ride | YX60BZN | First London | YX60DYN | Dial-a-Ride | YX60FCY | Go-Ahead London |
| YX59ACJ | Dial-a-Ride | YX60BZO | First London | YX60DYO | Dial-a-Ride | YX60FCZ | Go-Ahead London |
| YX59ACO | Dial-a-Ride | YX60CAA | London United | YX60DYP | Dial-a-Ride | YX60FDA | Go-Ahead London |
| YX59ACU | Dial-a-Ride | YX60CAE | London United | YX60DYS | Dial-a-Ride | YX60FSN | Go-Ahead London |
| YX59ACV | Dial-a-Ride | YX60CAO | London United | YX60DYT | Dial-a-Ride | YX60FSO | Go-Ahead London |
| YX59ACY | Dial-a-Ride | YX60CAU | London United | YX60DYU | Dial-a-Ride | YX60FSP | Go-Ahead London |
| YX59ADO | Dial-a-Ride | YX60CAV | London United | YX60DYY | Dial-a-Ride | YX60FSS | Go-Ahead London |
| YX59ADU | Dial-a-Ride | YX60CBF | London United | YX60DZA | Dial-a-Ride | YX60FSU | Go-Ahead London |
| YX59ADV | Dial-a-Ride | YX60CBO | London United | YX60DZF | Dial-a-Ride | YX60FTO | Metrobus |
| YX59ADZ | Dial-a-Ride | YX60CBU | London United | YX60DZG | Dial-a-Ride | YX60FTP | Metrobus |
| YX59AEA | Dial-a-Ride | YX60CBV | London United | YX60DZJ | Dial-a-Ride | YX60FTT | Metrobus |
| YX59AEB | Dial-a-Ride | YX60CBY | London United | YX60DZL | Dial-a-Ride | YX60FTU | Metrobus |
| YX59BYA | London Sovereign | YX60CCA | London United | YX60EOE | Go-Ahead London | YX60FTV | Metrobus |
| YX59BYB | London Sovereign | YX60CCD | London United | YX60EOF | Go-Ahead London | YX60FTY | Metrobus |
| YX59BYC | London Sovereign | YX60CCE | London United | YX60EOG | Go-Ahead London | YX60FTZ | Metrobus |
| YX59BYD | London Sovereign | YX60CCF | London United | YX60EOH | Go-Ahead London | YX60FUA | First London |
| YX59BYF | London Sovereign | YX60CCJ | London United | YX60EOJ | Go-Ahead London | YX60FUB | First London |
| YX59BYG | London Sovereign | YX60CCK | London United | YX60EOK | Go-Ahead London | YX60FUD | First London |
| YX59BYH | London Sovereign | YX60CCN | London United | YX60EOL | Go-Ahead London | YX60FUE | First London |
| YX59BYJ | Abellio | YX60CCO | London United | YX60EOO | Go-Ahead London | YX60FUF | First London |
| YX59BYK | Abellio | YX60CJE | Dial-a-Ride | YX60EOP | Go-Ahead London | YX60FUG | First London |
| YX59BYL | Abellio | YX60CJF | Dial-a-Ride | YX60EPO | Go-Ahead London | YX60FUH | First London |
| YX59BYM | Abellio | YX60CJJ | Dial-a-Ride | YX60EPP | Go-Ahead London | YX60FUJ | First London |
| YX59BYN | Abellio | YX60CJO | Dial-a-Ride | YX60EPU | Go-Ahead London | YX60FUM | First London |
| YX59BYO | Abellio | YX60CJU | Dial-a-Ride | YX60EVR | Dial-a-Ride | YX60FUO | First London |
| YX59BYP | Abellio | YX60CJV | Dial-a-Ride | YX60FBU | Go-Ahead London | YX60FUP | First London |
| YX59BYR | Abellio | YX60CJY | Dial-a-Ride | YX60FBY | Go-Ahead London | YX60FUT | First London |
| YX59BYS | Abellio | YX60CKG | Dial-a-Ride | YX60FBZ | Go-Ahead London | YX60FUV | Metrobus |
| YX59BYT | Abellio | YX60CKJ | Dial-a-Ride | YX60FCA | Go-Ahead London | YX60FUW | Metrobus |
| YX59BYU | Abellio | YX60CKK | Dial-a-Ride | YX60FCC | Go-Ahead London | YX60FUY | Metrobus |
| YX59BYV | Abellio | YX60CKU | Dial-a-Ride | YX60FCD | Go-Ahead London | YX60FVA | Metrobus |
| YX59BYW | Abellio | YX60CKV | Dial-a-Ride | YX60FCE | Go-Ahead London | YX60FVB | Metrobus |
| YX60BZA | London Sovereign | YX60CLV | Dial-a-Ride | YX60FCF | Go-Ahead London | YX60FVC | Metrobus |
| YX60BZB | London Sovereign | YX60CLY | Dial-a-Ride | YX60FCG | Go-Ahead London | YX60FVD | Metrobus |
| YX60BZC | London Sovereign | YX60DXL | First London | YX60FCL | Go-Ahead London | YX60FVE | Metrobus |
| YX60BZD | London Sovereign | YX60DXM | First London | YX60FCM | Go-Ahead London | | |

ISBN 9781904875550   © Published by *British Bus Publishing Ltd*, June 2011

**British Bus Publishing Ltd, 16 St Margaret's Drive, Telford, TF1 3PH
Telephone: 01952 255669**

web; www.britishbuspublishing.co.uk - e-mail: sales@britishbuspublishing.co.uk